SO 2 $41.55

3-6503

FUNDAMENTALS
OF TRANSPORTATION
ENGINEERING

C.S. PAPACOSTAS

University of Hawaii at Manoa

PRENTICE-HALL, INC., Englewood Cliffs, New Jersey 07632

Library of Congress Cataloging-in-Publication

PAPACOSTAS, C. S.
Fundamentals of transportation engineering.

Includes bibliographies and index.
1. Transportation engineering. I. Title.
TA1145.P33 1987 629.04 86-22524
ISBN 0-13-344870-3

Editorial/production supervision and
interior design: *Joan McCulley*
Cover design: *George Cornell*
Manufacturing buyer: *Rhett Conklin*

© 1987 by Prentice-Hall, Inc.
A Division of Simon & Schuster
Englewood Cliffs, New Jersey 07632

All rights reserved. No part of this book may be reproduced, in any form or by any means, without permission in writing from the publisher.

Printed in the United States of America

10 9 8 7 6 5 4 3 2 1

ISBN 0-13-344870-3 025

PRENTICE-HALL INTERNATIONAL (UK) LIMITED, *London*
PRENTICE-HALL OF AUSTRALIA PTY. LIMITED, *Sydney*
PRENTICE-HALL CANADA INC., *Toronto*
PRENTICE-HALL HISPANOAMERICANA, S.A., *Mexico*
PRENTICE-HALL OF INDIA PRIVATE LIMITED, *New Delhi*
PRENTICE-HALL OF JAPAN, INC., *Tokyo*
PRENTICE-HALL OF SOUTHEAST ASIA PTE. LTD., *Singapore*
EDITORA PRENTICE-HALL DO BRASIL, LTDA., *Rio de Janeiro*

To My Parents
Symeon and Loulla

CONTENTS

PREFACE

The scope of transportation engineering is enormous. Clearly, the tremendous impact that transportation-related decisions have on society cannot be addressed in a single textbook or in a single course of study. This textbook provides a solid introduction to the field by covering its major topical areas in a well-organized manner. It is intended to be a learning tool for the novice civil engineering student. Hence, its pedagogical strategy emphasizes subject continuity and smooth transition. The textbook begins with what is most familiar to the student and gradually introduces new concepts. These are clearly developed and illustrated by carefully chosen examples, most of which are accompanied by discussions and interpretations of the results. Although not totally ignored, policy issues, questions relating to management, and the theoretical treatment of methodological subtleties remain in the background.

Chapter 1 introduces the reader to basic definitions and classifications of transportation systems, to the role that government plays in transportation decisions, and to the fundamental concepts of mathematical modeling. Several of these topics are treated in greater detail at appropriate points throughout the textbook.

Chapter 2 begins with a review of the equations of rectilinear and curvilinear motion of a single vehicle, introduces the influence of driver perception-reaction times on the vehicle's motion, and illustrates their combined effect on the design, control, and operation of transportation facilities. The geometric design formulas that are based on the equations of motion and on human factors are then developed and applied to the alignment design of highways and railways and to the channelization of intersections and interchanges.

Chapter 3 is concerned with uninterrupted vehicular stream flow. The single-vehicle equations and human-factor models of Chapter 2 are extended to formulate a general model of vehicular flow for the case of uniformly scheduled rapid-transit operations. The fundamental variables of flow are defined, and the basic trade-off between speed and safety is clarified. The relationships between the stream variables that arise from this trade-off and their respective diagrams are explained and illustrated. The traffic flow model is then extended to the case of highways, the statistical nature of traffic measurements is explained, and the method of least square regression is developed and applied to speed-concentration relationships. The moving-observer method of measurement is presented to illustrate one way by which the data used in model calibration can be obtained, and the application of calibrated flow-concentration relationships to explain shock-wave phenomena in traffic is also presented.

Chapter 4 introduces the concept of highway level of service and presents practical methods of highway-capacity analysis and the relationship of these concepts to the theoretical models of Chapter 3. The capacity of rapid transit lines is also examined.

Chapter 5 is concerned with flow interruptions and their effect on system capacity. Models of transit-station capacity are presented first. Highway signal systems and signal coordination are examined next, and the basic concepts of the critical movement method of signalized intersection analysis are presented and applied.

Chapter 6 introduces the fundamentals of probability theory, queuing systems, and digital computer simulation and illustrates their application to traffic situations.

Chapter 7 includes a treatment of the evolution of transportation-planning processes by tracing the history of land transportation systems in the United States and by placing an emphasis on the confluence of three factors: technological change, private interests, and changing governmental policy.

The sequential process of forecasting the direct (user) impacts of urban-transportation systems is presented in Chapter 8. The most prevalent travel-behavior models of trip generation, trip distribution, modal choice, and network analysis are examined and illustrated, and their method of calibration is explained.

Chapter 9 is essentially an inventory of alternative transportation-demand forecasting models. Chapter 10 discusses three important externalities of transportation systems and includes several quantitative models of air quality, noise generation, and energy consumption. Appendix A contains a technical memorandum issued in 1982 by the U. S. Federal Highway Administration to guide the conduct and documentation of environmental assessments of transportation proposals and, by its nature, conveys the breadth and depth of transportation engineering.

Chapter 11 is concerned with system evaluation. It discusses the traditional benefit-cost analysis of alternative proposals and various techniques of effectiveness evaluation including rating, ranking, and scoring methods. Appendix B presents the basic character of money, its time value, and the most important interest and discount formulas.

The choice of topics, the order and manner of presentation, and the inclusion of numerous example problems and exercises form a solid introduction to transportation engineering for both undergraduate students whose program of study includes only one course in the area and for students that plan to pursue advanced study in this field.

Many people contributed to the development of this textbook either directly or indirectly. I would be remiss if I were to neglect acknowledging the influence that Joseph S. Drake, my unofficial mentor at Carnegie-Mellon University, has had on my professional development. I am also grateful to my good friend Michael J. Demetsky, professor of civil engineering at the University of Virginia, for reviewing the entire manuscript. Special thanks go to two colleagues at the University of Hawaii: N. Norby Nielsen, who commented on the contents of Appendix B, and Robert A. Grace, who shared with me his valuable experience about writing a textbook; to Gordon G. W. Lum, Executive Director of the Oahu Metropolitan Planning Organization, who has given me several planning and policy documents; and to Ken Myers of the Hawaii Office of the Federal Highway Administration, who promptly responded to my request for official information. Joseph F. Murray of Prentice-Hall was the catalyst during the early stages of this undertaking. Finally, "mahalo" to the hundreds of students through whom the manuscript was tested and refined over the years.

Honolulu, Hawaii C. S. Papacostas

CHAPTER 1

INTRODUCTION

1.1 THE TRANSPORTATION SYSTEM

1.1.1 Definition and Scope

A transportation system may be defined as consisting of the *fixed facilities,* the *flow entities,* and the *control system* that permit *people and goods* to overcome the friction of geographical space *efficiently* in order to *participate* in a *timely* manner in some *desired activity*.

At first glance, this definition may appear to be either trivial or pretentious. After all, "overcoming the friction of geographical space" is a very awkward way of saying "to move from point *A* to point *B*"! However, this definition helps you to appreciate the breadth of transportation engineering and to delineate the purpose and scope of this introductory text. It identifies the functional components of a transportation system (the fixed facilities, the flow entities, and the control system) and encapsulates the fact that transportation provides the connectivity that facilitates other societal interactions.

1.1.2 Fixed Facilities

Fixed facilities are the physical components of the system that are fixed in space and constitute the *network* of *links* (e.g., roadway segments, railway track, pipes) and *nodes* (e.g., intersections, interchanges, transit terminals, harbors, and airports) of the transportation system. Their design, which has traditionally been within the realm of civil engineering, includes soil and foundation engineering, structural design, the design of drainage systems, and *geometric design,* which is concerned with the physical proportioning of the elements of fixed facilities. Although related, geometric design is different from other aspects of design (e.g., structural design, which is concerned with the strength of structures to withstand efficiently the expected forces or loads), which are covered elsewhere in the typical civil engineering curriculum.

1.1.3 Flow Entities and Technology

Flow entities are the units that traverse the fixed facilities. They include vehicles, container units, railroad cars, etc. In the case of the highway system, the fixed facilities are expected to accommodate a wide variety of vehicle types ranging from bicycles to large tractor-trailer combinations. For the purposes of geometric design, the American Association of State Highway and Transportation Officials (AASHTO) has specified a set of *design vehicles,* each describing a typical class of highway vehicles [1.1].

In this textbook, flow entities are considered only in terms of their generic characteristics (such as size, weight, and acceleration and deceleration capabilities) rather than in terms of their specific technological design, which is normally undertaken by mechanical and electrical engineers. Thus vehicular motion and vehicle flow equations are expressed as general relationships between the generic variables and can be applied to many vehicle technologies once their specific attributes are determined.

1.1.4 Control System

The *control system* consists of *vehicular control* and *flow control*. Vehicular control refers to the technological way in which individual vehicles are guided on the fixed facilities. Such control can be manual or automated. The proper geometric design of the fixed facilities must incorporate, in addition to the characteristics of the vehicle, the characteristics of the vehicular control system. In the case of highway facilities, where the vehicles are manually controlled, these include driver characteristics, such as the time a driver takes to perceive and react to various stimuli; examples of such *human factors* are included in this textbook. In the case of automated systems, similar but more precisely definable response times exist as well.

The flow control system consists of the means that permit the efficient and smooth operation of streams of vehicles and the reduction of conflicts between vehicles. This system includes various types of signing, marking, and signal systems and the concomitant rules of operation. Some discussion of traffic signal systems is included in Chapter 5.

1.1.5 Transportation Demand

The definition of a transportation system given at the beginning of this chapter addresses another consideration that is of concern to transportation specialists: Transportation systems are constructed neither as pure expressions of engineering ingenuity nor as monuments of purely aesthetic quality. They are built in order to serve people in undertaking their economic, social, and cultural activities. In the jargon of the economist, the demand for transportation is *derived,* or *indirect,* meaning that people do not normally travel or move their possessions for the sake of movement but in order to accomplish something else, for example, to go to school, to work, to shop, or to visit with friends. By the same token, workers do not place themselves in the middle of the morning and evening rush hours because they enjoy traffic congestion but because their work schedules require it. Transportation engineers are among the professionals that are concerned with accommodating these societal activities by providing efficient ways to satisfy the population's needs for mobility. As used in the above definition of a transportation system, the word *efficient* stands for the balancing a variety of often conflicting requirements that society in general considers to be important. These requirements include, but are not limited to, cost considerations, convenience, protection of environmental quality, and protection of individual rights. In order to be responsive to these needs, transportation engineers often cooperate with other professionals, including economists, planners, and social scientists.

1.1.6 Quantification versus Valuation

Suppose that the following question was posed to a classical physicist and to an Aristotelian philosopher:

> An object is let go from a height of 20 feet directly above the head of a person. What will the value of the object's velocity be at the instant when it comes in contact with the person's head?

It should not be surprising if the classical physicist, after mentally applying the appropriate equation, were to reply: "Well . . . the object's velocity will be about 36 feet per second." However, an engineering student may be somewhat surprised at the philosopher's response along this line: "I believe that, to the person, the object's velocity at that instant will be of no value whatsoever."

The difference between the two answers lies in the meaning that each of the respondents attached to the term "value." The philosopher's use of the word is related to the quality of a thing being useful or desirable to someone or perhaps how much desirable or undesirable. Clearly, the assignment of such value is subjective: It depends on the *value system* of the person making the assessment. On the other hand, the physicist's reponse involved an attempt to objectively *quantify* the state of the object's velocity, which is independent of the person who attempts to assess it. Of course, the physicist could have given the wrong answer either by using the wrong equation (i.e., not understanding how gravity works) or by making a calculation error when using the right equation.

Engineers often encounter both meanings of value in their work. For example, suppose that an engineer is asked to estimate the reduction in carbon monoxide emissions that would result from a public policy that aims to encourage people to form car pools.

Using the best available mathematical formulation of the problem, the engineer would produce an estimate in essentially the same way as the physicist.

Now, consider that the implementation of the public policy requires the expenditure of a certain level of funding and that an estimate of this level has been obtained as objectively as the current understanding of the subject allows. Having quantified these estimates does not in itself reveal whether the implementation of the policy is desirable or not. Before such a decision can be made, it is necessary to place relative values on the costs associated with the implementation of the policy and on the benefits that will be derived from it. Simply stated, to make this "apples-and-oranges" decision, someone or some group must assess whether reducing pollutant emissions (by x parts per million) is worth the expenditure of y dollars.

In the private sector of the economy, individuals frequently make such judgments based on their own value systems. By contrast, decisions made in the public sector generally involve compromises between the often-conflicting values of the groups that constitute the community (e.g., those in the construction industry versus environmentalists vis-à-vis the construction of a freeway).

This textbook emphasizes the basic methods and techniques that are presently available to the practitioner for the purpose of *quantifying* the impacts or consequences of transportation-related proposals. The chapter on *evaluation* includes some techniques that are often used to aid the selection of the most suitable course of action from a set of alternatives. The real-world application of these evaluative techniques, however, *presupposes* the existence of a value system. Certain analysts tend to valuate the consequences of transportation proposals based on their analyses of the economic choices of consumers, whereas others base their valuations on other philosophical perspectives. One of the fundamental purposes of government is to provide the mechanism for the resolution of such differences.

1.2 TRANSPORTATION SYSTEM CLASSIFICATION

1.2.1 Classification Schemes

Transportation systems can be categorized in several ways. For example, they may be classified according to the types of technology they employ, according to the function or type of service they provide, according to who owns or is responsible for their implementation and operation, and so forth. Each of these diverse typologies views transportation systems from a different perspective and is useful in making distinctions that are relevant to different types of transportation-related decisions.

The definition of the transportation system given in Subsection 1.1.1 makes a distinction between *passenger* and *freight* transportation. Both are needed to satisfy human needs and both constitute a significant portion of the U.S. gross national product (GNP). During the past few decades, the total U.S. expenditures for personal and freight transportation have fluctuated, respectively, around 12% and 8% of the GNP [1.2].

1.2.2 Major Transportation Subsystems

The transportation system is further categorized into four major subsystems according to the medium on which the flow elements are supported. These subsystems are commonly referred to as *modes,* but it should be understood that this term is also used to make finer distinctions between the various means of travel. For example, driving alone and forming car pools are sometimes considered to be different modes. The four major subsystems are

1. Land transportation
   a. Highway
   b. Rail
2. Air transportation
   a. Domestic
   b. International
3. Water transportation
   a. Inland
   b. Coastal
   c. Ocean
4. Pipelines
   a. Oil
   b. Gas
   c. Other

Pipelines differ from the other three subsystems in that they are suited only for freight transportation and they do not employ vehicles. The flow element is simply the material that moves through the pipeline conduits. Pipelines are usually classified according to the product they transport, for example, crude oil and oil products, natural gas, or coal slurry. Since the design of pipelines and their support facilities, such as pumping stations, is covered in detail in hydraulic engineering courses of study, further concentration on this subject in the main chapters of this textbook is not warranted.

The water transportation subsystem consists of inland, coastal, and ocean transportation. The inland portion uses rivers, lakes, and artificial canals and typically employs platform-supported flow elements such as barges. The main portion of the inland water transportation of the United States lies in the eastern part of the nation. It is predominantly devoted to the transportation of bulky freight over long distances. The coastal and ocean components employ hull-supported vessels of various weights and sizes and are also predominantly used for the movement of freight. Although not visible to the eye, ocean lanes joining harbor facilities have been established by international conventions.

The air transportation system uses aircraft that are supported by stationary or rotary air foils. This subsystem may be conveniently divided into domestic and international services. It is predominantly used for passenger transportation and carries only a miniscule amount of freight, usually confined to specialized items such as mail and valuable commodities. The major structural components of this subsystem are airports of various classes, that is, the network nodes. As in the case of ocean transportation, network links (i.e., air lanes) connecting these nodes have been established, and a sophisticated guidance and control system has evolved over the years.

The land transportation subsystem is further subdivided into its highway and railway components because of their fundamental technological differences and because of the fact that their networks are spatially separated. As a passenger-carrying mode, the railway component had its heyday in the nineteenth century and has shown a general decline in recent decades, particularly in the United States as compared to other developed countries. As a result of historical and economic factors, the United States possesses one of the most comprehensive highway networks in the world. It would not be an overstatement to say that highway mobility is an intrinsic characteristic of modern America.

Tables 1.2.1 and 1.2.2 illustrate the 1983 share of the major national subsystems in the intercity transportation of people and goods. Table 1.2.1 presents the modal shares for both the total tonnage carried and the total ton-mileage. The two columns illustrate an important difference between subsystems. For example, highway freight transportation accounted for 36.3% of the total tonnage but only 18.1% of the ton-mileage. This means that, on the average, the distances over which freight is carried by this subsystem are relatively short. The water transportation subsystem shows a reverse pattern, that is, it carries its bulky freight for longer average distances. Not shown on the table are characteristics such as cost, speed of travel, and quality of service, which affect the suitability of the transportation modes to the carriage of various types of commodities. Table 1.2.2 summarizes the 1983 distribution of *intercity* passenger-miles of travel among the major modes. It is clear that the highway network constitutes the predominant passenger mode of travel, with 84.9% of the total. This percentage was mainly attributable to the automobile; only 1.6% of the intercity passenger mileage involved intercity buses.

1.2.3 Private and Public Transportation

Transportation services are also classified as either *for-hire* or *not-for-hire* services. These categories are also known, respectively, as *public* and *private* transportation, but these terms refer to their availability to the general public and to private parties, respectively,

TABLE 1.2.1 1982 MODAL SHARES OF UNITED STATES INTERCITY FREIGHT

Mode		Tons	Ton-miles (%)
Land	Highway	36.3	18.1
	Rail	27.4	28.0
Oil pipeline		18.2	19.7
Water		18.0	34.0
Air		0.1	0.2

SOURCE: Based on data from Transportation Policy Associates [1.2].

TABLE 1.2.2 1983 SHARES OF UNITED STATES INTERCITY PASSENGER-MILES

Mode		Percent
Highway	Automobile	83.3
	Bus	1.6
Rail		0.6
Air		14.5
Water		0.0

SOURCE: Based on data from Transportation Policy Associates [1.2].

and not to their ownership. For example, a city bus system may be owned either privately or publicly. In either case, the service provided is public transportation because the system is available for use by the general public. For-hire systems are further classified into *contract carriers* and *common carriers*. The former stand ready to provide service to the public under individual contractual arrangements. Common carriers, on the other hand, generally offer scheduled service and are open to all members of the public willing to pay the posted fare. The terms *mass transportation* or *mass transit* usually refer to the common carriage of passengers. Taxis, car rentals, and certain other individually arranged services belong to the category of contract public transportation.

1.2.4 Urban Transportation Systems

The *intracity* or *urban* distribution of freight is predominantly accomplished by the highway subsystem using vans and trucks of various sizes. The major movements within urban areas are related to the travel undertaken by people. Water-based urban transportation is found in only a few cities, and air transportation is unsuited for urban travel. Thus the means of travel available for urban passenger transportation are in the main land-based and include private transportation (walking and private motor vehicles) and various public transportation services, of which some are highway-based (i.e., regular city buses), others are not (e.g., urban rail transit systems). The latter operate on an *exclusive right of way* unrestricted from the interference caused by highway vehicles; however, systems that are commonly thought to use *shared right of ways,* such as buses, can also operate on exclusive facilities, thus improving their service quality to levels that rival those of certain other exclusive pathway systems. The following brief history of urban transportation is presented to aid the understanding of contemporary terminology.

Initially, modern-era cities were pedestrian-oriented. Even after the development of mechanized long-distance transportation systems such as railroads, the size of most cities was sufficiently small for people to walk to most places. Private transportation in the form of horseback and animal-drawn carriages was sufficient for longer distances. Public transportation in the form of *sedan chairs* in European cities and *jinrikisha* (rickshaw) in Japan was the exception rather than the rule. The first public transportation service per se has been attributed to the French mathematician Pascal, who in 1662 began to offer a horse-drawn service in Paris. However, horse- and mule-drawn *omnibuses* (derived from "omnis," meaning "all," i.e., offering services to the general public) did not come into their own until the midnineteenth century. These services spread widely in Europe and America and remained a major mode of urban public transportation into the early 1900s. In 1832, the first horse-drawn rail streetcar began service in Harlem, New York, and portended the eventual replacement of the omnibus (which was driven on cobblestone pavements) by rail-supported *horse-drawn streetcars* that offered a much more comfortable ride. They operated along designated routes in mixed traffic at relatively low speeds and made frequent stops to take on and discharge passengers. Since propulsive power was the greatest limitation of horse-drawn streetcars, alternate power sources were sought. An early contender was the *cable car,* in which the vehicle is propelled by attaching it to a continuously moving cable. The cable is kept in motion by a stationary source of power. One of the most famous cable car systems opened in San Francisco in

1873, and a few cable car systems are extant to this day, mostly at special locations such as steep inclines and ore mines. Experimentation with the steam engine also occurred, but the major power-supply breakthrough came in the late 1800s in the form of rail-supported *electric streetcars,* which received their power from overhead wires. At about the same time, intercity railroads began to extend their lines into a few major central cities like London and Boston. These urban extensions are known as *commuter railroads,* since their urban service is confined to moving commuters between suburban areas and the city during the morning and evening peak hours. Unlike the typical streetcar lines, these heavy-rail systems offered limited express service without many intermediate stops and operated on their own rights of way. The superior service of these exclusive pathway lines encouraged the development of heavy-rail *rapid-transit systems* that were capable of moving large numbers of passengers quickly within the elsewhere congested city. The first underground steam engine rapid-transit line opened in London in 1863, and the first elevated urban railroad line, also using steam, was inaugurated in New York City 5 years later. Both cities subsequently converted their systems to electricity. Many large, high-density cities followed suit. Most other cities relied exclusively on electric streetcar lines.

The next chapter in the evolution of transportation in general and public transportation in particular belongs to the adaptation of the internal combustion engine to motorized transportation. In the area of urban public transportation, the *motor bus* began to make inroads into the electric-streetcar market around 1920. Coupled with an increasing willingness of government to support the construction of streets and highways and with comparatively low fuel costs, the city bus emerged victorious over the electric streetcar, in some instances after a transition to the hybrid *trolley bus,* which operated on rubber tires but gathered its power from overhead wires. The conversion to city buses occurred despite a courageous attempt by the Electric Railways Presidents Conference Committee (PCC) in the 1930s to systematically develop a superior streetcar, the marvelous PCC car. The same technology that replaced the electric streetcar also marked the beginning of the demise of its successor, the city bus, and public transportation in general. The source of this demise was the private automobile, which attracted patronage from public-transportation systems. To add insult to injury, a few entrepreneurs even began to use their automobiles to offer competing for-hire services by seeking customers at transit stops. These *jitney* services are undoubtly the precursors of the modern *taxi,* which now operates in a regulated environment.

During the 1960s, several societal changes encouraged a reevaluation of the automobile-based urban system and led to a revision of the hencetofore highway-oriented federal transportation policy to include support for the improvement, research, and development of public-transportation systems. The following are terms found in this technical literature in this connection.*

> *Rapid transit* refers to all exclusive right-of-way systems. To clarify other technological differences, modifiers such as heavy rail, light rail, fixed guideway,

*Further discussion of specific technologies that belong to these overlapping categories may be found in the technical literature (e.g., [1.3–1.12]).

personal, and bus are prefixed to "rapid transit." Light-rail transit and buses can be operated in mixed traffic and as rapid-transit modes. *Personal rapid transit* (PRT) refers to systems that operate on exclusive pathways employing small vehicles to allow for frequent service and scheduling flexibility; they may be described as "horizontal elevators."

Fixed-guideway transit refers to systems in which the vehicles are affixed to a guideway and include *dual-rail* systems, *monorail* systems of various types, rubber-tired systems that are attached to the guideway either on the side of the vehicle or on a third rail, and so forth. *Automated guideway transit* (AGT) refers to fixed-guideway systems that operate without the intervention of an on-board operator; they may or may not be PRT systems.

Articulated systems are systems in which flow units can be connected to form trains. An *articulated bus* is a long bus that consists of two sections connected by a flexible joint, also known as a *bandy bus* from the German word for tapeworm (bandwurm).

Dual-mode systems are systems in which vehicles can operate on the street under manual control and on automated guideways. Two types of automated operation have been proposed. The first employs a guideway consisting of moving pallets on which vehicles of various types may be carried, and the second uses vehicles with a secondary electric motor that may be attached to the power source of the automated guideway. *Automated highways* have also been proposed.

Demand-responsive systems are systems that enjoy flexibility in route or time scheduling or both to respond to the actual demand placed on them. These systems represent an attempt to rival the flexibility of the private automobile, in contrast to the traditional *fixed route–fixed schedule* transit systems. Taxis are naturally demand responsive but other systems have also been developed, including *dial-a-ride* and prescheduled systems that allow for the dispatching and rerouting of common carriers to serve temporally changing demands. These types of *paratransit* systems have found applicability as specialized services for elderly and handicapped persons.

1.3 THE ROLE OF GOVERNMENT

1.3.1 Governmental Participation

A characteristic of human social organizations is the establishment of a "government," which—in an impartial sense—may be defined as consisting of the rules of conduct, the collective decision-making processes, and the means of enforcing the rules that attempt to impart social and economic order and to maintain the cohesiveness of a society.

A transportation system provides the necessary connectivity that enhances the interaction between people. It is a historical fact that, by facilitating the movement of peoples and the spreading of ideas, advances in transportation technology have been closely related to the evolution of civilization as we know it. Since ancient times, cities have developed in locations that took advantage of the availability of transportation connections such as rivers and protected harbors. The Roman Empire was held together by a very elaborate system of roadways, some of which (e.g., the Appian Way) remain to the present day. Catanese and Snyder [1.13] state that, in eighteenth-century England,

> transportation was the key to industrialization. Unless raw materials could be brought to the factories and finished products distributed to market areas, the industrial revolution could not happen.

Similarly, the westward expansion in nineteenth-century America would not have been possible without the construction of the transcontinental railroads; many modern American cities have had their origins at the junctures of railroad lines. Because of the profound role that transportation plays in society, governments have always become involved in the provision, operation, and regulation of transportation systems through the enactment of laws and through the establishment of public planning processes.

The specific actions that a government takes at any given time as well as the method by which it chooses to implement those actions reflect the contemporary value system of the society it represents. Conceptually, there exists a continuum of governmental forms ranging from anarchy (i.e., complete lack of governmental intervention in the affairs of people) to totalitarianism (i.e., complete control by government). Actual governmental structures lie somewhere between the two extremes.

The United States governmental structure places a high value on individual freedom and civil rights. Individuals and groups are permitted to pursue what they consider to be in their best interests. They are also afforded relatively greater opportunities to vie with others in persuading the government to take actions favoring what they value. Citizen participation is, in fact, a requirement of public planning law [1.14]. Dissent and difference of opinion are tolerated and permitted to find expression in the political arena.

1.3.2 Instruments of Governmental Involvement

In rough outline, the typical ways by which the government intervenes in the market place to accomplish objectives that, in its representational role, it finds to be in the public interest include *soft promotion, regulation,* and *investment*. Incidentally, at any given time, the meaning of the term *public interest* is largely implicit in the specific actions that the government takes and, thus, is itself in a state of flux. Also, differences of opinion as to what is in the public interest frequently arise.

Soft promotion refers to attempts by the government to encourage or to discourage certain situations without legally requiring them. An advertising campaign favoring car-pooling aimed at reducing rush-hour congestion and obviating the need for costly highway construction or as a strategy to reduce energy consumption is an example of soft promotion.

Regulation refers to those government actions that place legal requirements on individuals and firms to satisfy the public interest. Transportation-related examples of regulation include the establishment of automobile bumper standards to reduce fatalities, automobile air-pollution-emission standards to improve environmental quality, and engine-efficiency standards to conserve energy. Other examples include the regulation of airline route structures to ensure the availability of service to all and the regulation of the rates that trucking companies can charge their customers.

Investment involves the financial support, public financing, or even public ownership of various systems or services. Subsidies to privately owned bus companies to ensure service to mobility-disadvantaged groups, public ownership of highways to maintain a comprehensive level of accessibility, and participation in the construction of airports and harbors are but a few examples of investment actions.

1.4 TOOLS AND APPLICATIONS

1.4.1 Background

The typical program of study leading to the first course in transportation engineering includes the basic sciences, mathematics, and computer programming. The subject matter of those courses of study stresses the basic tools needed for work in the field of engineering. The latter differs from the pure sciences in that it is more concerned with the *application* of scientific knowledge. When seeking solutions to real-world problems, attendant questions of economy and other considerations prescribe a need to employ appropriate simplifying assumptions. In order to be useful, such simplifications must render a problem amenable to efficient solution while retaining the essential aspects of the postulated situation. The importance of making judicious assumptions that are based on a clear understanding of the problem at hand cannot be overemphasized. The engineering courses in the student's curriculum usually identify the generally accepted assumptions that apply to specific situations. In turn, these assumptions are based on the current state of the art and are themselves subject to change as our understanding of engineering systems is enhanced through additional experience and research. The student should always be attentive to the fundamental assumptions that are involved in a particular situation and the extent to which these assumptions can affect the results.

1.4.2 Mathematical Models

Transportation engineers employ models to study and analyze the systems of concern. A *model* may be defined as the representation of a part of reality. Figure 1.4.1 shows that models may be classified as *physical* or *mathematical* on one hand and as *static* or *dynamic* on the other [1.15]. Static models represent the structure of a system, whereas dynamic models also incorporate a representation of the system's process, that is, the way in which it changes over time. The familiar models of molecular structures are examples of physical static models. Physical dynamic models include wind tunnels, where facsimiles of systems based on the laws of similitude are tested before implementation. Such models also include models relying on analogy, such as those representing the vibration of a mechanism via

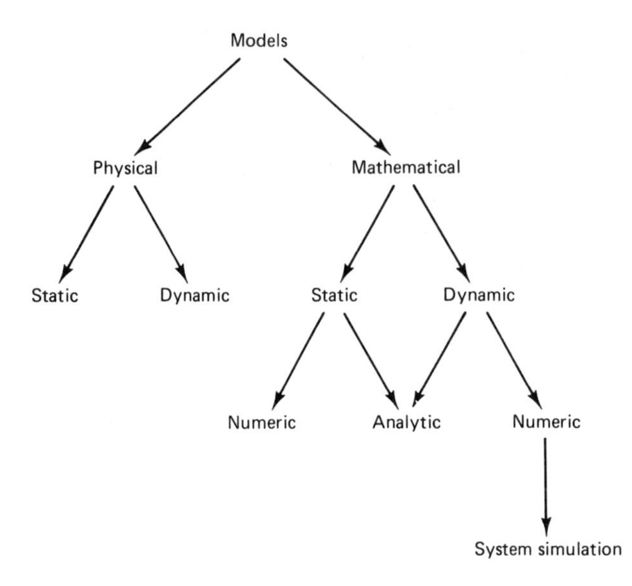

Figure 1.4.1 Types of models. (*SOURCE*: Gordon [1.15], Fig. 1-5, p. 11.)

an equivalent electrical circuit; see Fig. 1.4.2. *Analog computers* are well suited for this type of modeling. It is interesting to recognize that the two diagrams shown in Fig. 1.4.2 are, in fact, static representations of a mechanical and an electrical system. When constructed, the electrical circuit can be used as a physical dynamic model of the mechanical system.

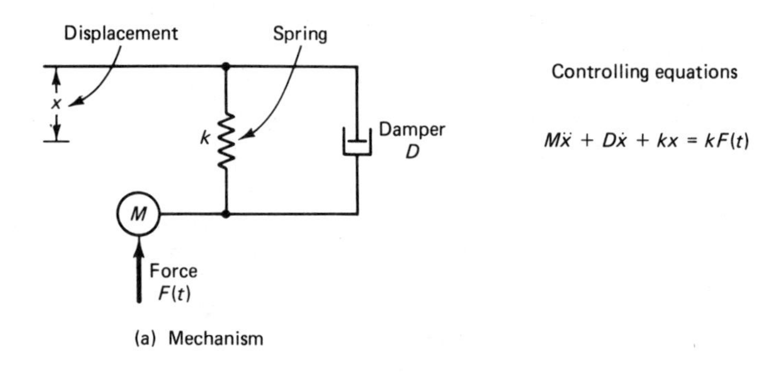

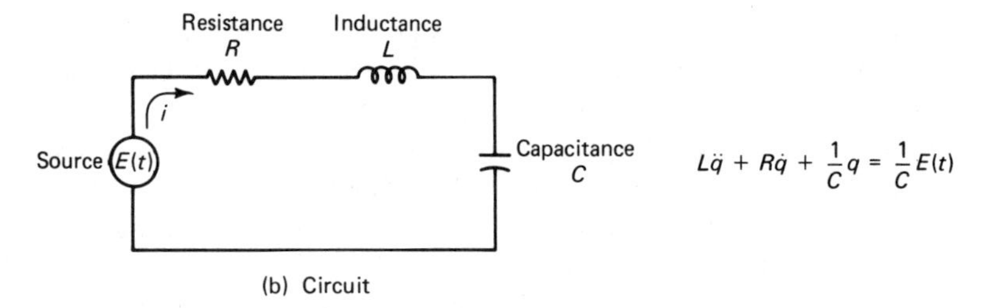

Figure 1.4.2 Model analogy. (*SOURCE*: Gordon [1.15], Fig. 1-6, p. 11.)

A mathematical model employs one or more equations to represent a system and its behavior. Thus Newton's second law and Bernoulli's equation are examples of mathematical models. In addition to being either static or dynamic, mathematical models may be classified according to the method of solution employed, for example, analytical or numerical. Numerical models have proliferated in recent years because they are amenable to solution by *digital computers*.

All models are abstractions of the systems they represent. In other words, a system and its model are not identical in all respects: The model is a simplified representation of the system. Consequently, a number of different models can be used to describe the same system. The appropriate model to a particular endeavor should be selected in such a way as to strike a balance between ease of application on one hand and realistic representation of the subject system on the other. For example, Newton's theory is sufficiently accurate for the cases examined in engineering mechanics to be given preference over the more complicated Theory of Relativity. The same is not true, however, for the study of interplanetary motion.

1.4.3 Components of Mathematical Models

A mathematical model can have one of an infinite number of mathematical forms. It can be linear, nonlinear, exponential, differential and so forth. Most of the mathematical models with which the student is conversant have been simply presented to the student and, therefore, the fact that someone (usually the person whose name is associated with the model) had to *postulate* its mathematical form possibly remains obtuse. Researchers are constantly faced with the problem of model postulation, and in many situations, including certain areas of transportation engineering, analysts are also required to select the mathematical forms of their models.

Selecting a mathematical form, however, is not the same as having a useful model. Consider, for example, the following mathematical form relating four variables, X, Y, Z, and W:

$$Y = a\,X^b Z^c W^d \tag{1.4.1}$$

In this equation, variable Y is a function of the other three. In other words, Y can be computed if the numerical values of X, Z, and W are known. For this reason Y is called the *dependent*, or *explained*, variable and the other three are called the *independent*, or *explanatory*, variables. The model also contains four constants, a, b, c, and d, that must also be known. These constants are referred to as the *parameters* of the model. Viewed from the purely mathematical perspective, this equation has certain characteristics, including a range, which can be examined by investigating its behavior as its components are varied. But from the applied perspective, the dependent and independent variables must represent specific items of interest to the analyst, the mathematical form must in fact describe the relationship between these variables, and the parameters must be assigned realistic numerical values.

Model calibration is the process by which the numerical values of the parameters of a postulated model are determined. It is usually accomplished through the use of statistical methods and is based on *experimental* knowledge of the dependent and independent variables. This means that, once the nature of the variables is identified, a series of experiments are conducted to obtain a set of N simultaneous observations on the dependent and independent variables, in our case, Y_i, X_i, Z_i, W_i, with i varying from 1 to N. These observations are then employed to estimate (usually by statistical methods) the numerical values of the model parameters that render the postulated model capable of reproducing the experimental data. To avoid misspecification of the mathematical form that relates the variables, alternative functions may be postulated and calibrated. The one that best describes the experimental data can then be selected. In this manner, it is ensured that the selected calibrated model is realistic.

Model validation refers to the testing of a calibrated model using empirical data other than those used to calibrate the model in the first place. This is how scientific theories (models) are tested, modified, or replaced. An improved model must be able to explain everything that the old model can plus something that the old model cannot. As mentioned earlier, the old model may still be a useful tool as long as the scope of its applicability is understood.

To comprehend the importance of the above modeling steps, consider that X and Z in Eq. 1.4.1 stand for the masses M_1 and M_2 of two bodies, W stands for the distance R separating them, and the dependent variable Y represents their mutual attraction force F. Moreover, assume that the calibration of this postulate vis-à-vis experimental observations has resulted in the following numerical values of the model's parameters:

$$a = K = 3.442(10^{-8})\,\frac{\text{ft}^4}{\text{lb-s}^4}$$

$$b = c = 1 \quad \text{and} \quad d = -2$$

Equation 1.4.1 becomes:

$$F = \frac{KM_1M_2}{R^2} \tag{1.4.2}$$

which is Newton's law of gravitation.

1.4.4 Transportation Models

The study of many engineering subjects, most appropriately, tends to concentrate on systems of physical objects under the influence of forces. Stripped to its essentials, the transportation system involves a physical phenomenon, the motion of flow entities on the fixed facilities. Hence, mathematical *models of the physical system* are required, including the equations of motion.

Additionally, transportation engineering must explicitly incorporate the human dimension, which consists of *human factors* and *human behavior*. As used in this textbook, the term "human factors" refers to those measurable characteristics of human beings that are relatively difficult to modify, such as sensory, perceptual, and kinesthetic characteristics. A driver's perception-reaction time that elapses between the instant when a stimulus is first displayed (e.g., the onset of the amber phase of a traffic signal) and the instant when a driver reacts to the stimulus (e.g., applying the brakes) is a specific example of a human factor that can be measured either in the field or in the laboratory. *Human-factor models* are needed in addition to models of the physical transportation system.

The line of demarcation between human factors and human behavior is not very clear. Nevertheless, the use of the term human behavior in this textbook will generally refer to the way in which people act, the types of choices they make, and so forth. Specifically, this textbook will be concerned with *travel behavior,* which includes the way people decide whether and when to travel, where to go, how to get there, and the like. The transportation engineer's arsenal of mathematical models includes *models of human behavior*. Human behavior is in a continuous state of flux and is affected by technological changes: The behavioral patterns of the ancient Greeks were very different from those of modern Americans, but the range of visual perception of the two populations has remained about the same. In fact, no universally applicable calibrated model of travel behavior exists. Even when using the same mathematical form, transportation studies for different cities must calibrate the forms to conform to local conditions.

1.5 SUMMARY

This chapter defined a transportation system in terms of its fixed facilities, flow entities, and control system and identified its general function as that of providing the necessary connectivity that facilitates other societal activities. A brief outline of several transportation classification schemes for intercity and urban systems followed. The means by which government participates in the transportation sector (i.e., promotion, regulation, and investment) were presented in order to place transportation engineering within its larger societal context. The fundamental concepts of mathematical modeling (i.e., model postulation, calibration, and validation) were presented and the three categories of quantitative models used by transportation engineers (i.e., models of the physical system, human factor models, and travel behavior models) were explained. A distinction between quantification and valuation was also drawn.

1.6 EXERCISES

1. Prepare a list of the various modes of travel that are available in your community and discuss each one in terms of the transportation system categories presented in Chapter 1.
2. Identify all modes of travel that are available to you for your daily commute to school and explain the reasons underlying your usual choice of mode.
3. Conduct a survey of at least 30 of your classmates, inquiring about their choices of travel mode for their school trips; based on the results of your survey, calculate the relative utilization of each mode by students.
4. Based on a 1-week study of a local newspaper, prepare a report outlining several examples of government participation in the transportation sector. For each case, identify the specific arguments for and against government involvement.

5. The following relationship is known to exist between stress and strain below the yield point of steel:

$$(\text{stress}) = (\text{modulus of elasticity})(\text{strain})$$

Discuss this mathematical model in terms of the modeling considerations highlighted in Chapter 1. How would you estimate the modulus of elasticity of a new type of steel?

1.7 REFERENCES

1.1 American Association of State Highway and Transportation Officials, *A Policy on Geometric Design of Highways and Streets,* Washington, D.C., 1984.

1.2 Transportation Policy Associates, *Transportation in America, A Statistical Analysis of Transportation in the United States,* 2nd ed., Washington, D.C., 1984.

1.3 VUCHIC, VUKAN R., *Urban Public Transportation Systems and Technology,* Prentice-Hall, Inc., Englewood Cliffs, N.J., 1981.

1.4 WATKINS, R. A., et al., *Urban Transportation Planning System Lexicon,* prepared by Rock Creek Associates for the U.S. Department of Transportation: Urban Mass Transportation Administration, Report UMTA-UPM20-81-1.

1.5 Highway Research Board, *Demand-Actuated Transportation Systems,* Special Report 124, National Research Council, Washington, D.C., 1971.

1.6 IRVING, JACK H. (ed. and principal author), *Fundamentals of Personal Rapid Transit,* Lexington Books, Heath, Lexington, Mass., 1978.

1.7 Transportation Research Board, *Dual Mode Transportation,* Special Report 170, National Research Council, Washington, D.C., 1976.

1.8 ———, *Light Rail Transit,* Special Report 161, National Research Council, Washington, D.C., 1975.

1.9 ———, *Light Rail Transit: Planning and Technology,* Special Report 182, National Research Council, Washington, D.C., 1978.

1.10 ———, *Light Rail Transit: Policy, Design, and Implementation,* Special Report 195, National Research Council, Washington, D.C., 1982.

1.11 ———, *Paratransit,* Special Report 164, National Research Council, Washington, D.C., 1976.

1.12 ———, *Better Use of Existing Transportation Facilities,* Special Report 153, National Research Council, Washington, D.C., 1975.

1.13 CATANESE, A. J., AND J. C. SNYDER (eds.), *Introduction to Urban Planning,* McGraw-Hill Book Company, New York, 1979.

1.14 Transportation Research Board, *Citizen Participation in Transportation Planning,* Special Report 142, National Research Council, Washington, D.C., 1973.

1.15 GORDON, G., *System Simulation,* 2nd ed., Prentice-Hall, Inc., Englewood Cliffs, N.J., 1978.

CHAPTER 2

VEHICLE MOTION, HUMAN FACTORS, AND GEOMETRIC DESIGN

2.1 INTRODUCTION

Stripped to its barest essentials, a transportation system involves the motion of vehicles. It is, therefore, essential to review the basic *kinematic* and *kinetic* equations of motion. These two branches of dynamics are related: *Kinematics* is the study of motion irrespective of the forces that cause it, whereas *kinetics* accounts for these forces. The motion of a body can be *rectilinear* or *curvilinear* and can be investigated in relation to a fixed coordinate system (i.e., *absolute* motion) or in relation to a moving coordinate system (i.e., *relative* motion). In this chapter, the basic equations of motion of a single vehicle are cast in the form in which they are used for the purposes of design. Three examples of human-factor models are then introduced to illustrate how human characteristics can be incorporated in design. The important difference between the *maximum* technological capabilities of vehicles on one hand and the *practical* design levels necessitated by considerations of passenger *safety* and *comfort* is explained. Finally, the methods of *geometric design* are presented for the horizontal and vertical alignment of highways and railways and for the channelization of intersections and interchanges. Geometric design is concerned only with the size, shape, and geometry of transportation facilities. Other aspects of engineering design are also needed for the successful implementation of these facilities, including the proper selection of pavement and structural materials, geotechnical design, and the structural design of various components such as bridges. In addition, complex decisions related to whether a new facility is needed, or whether an existing facility should be improved must necessarily precede the design phase.

2.2 EQUATIONS OF MOTION

2.2.1 Rectilinear Motion

The rectilinear *position* x of a particle is measured from a reference point and has units of length. The displacement of the particle is the difference in its position between two instants.

Velocity v is the displacement of the particle divided by the time over which the displacement occurs. In the limit, the instantaneous value of velocity is given by the first derivative of displacement with respect to time:

$$v = \frac{dx}{dt} \tag{2.2.1}$$

Speed is a scalar quantity and is equal to the magnitude of velocity, which is a vector. However, the two terms are used interchangeably in this textbook when the meaning is clear from the context.

Acceleration a is the rate of change of velocity with respect to time:

$$a = \frac{dv}{dt} \tag{2.2.2}$$

It can be positive, zero, or negative. Negative acceleration (i.e., *deceleration*) is often denoted by d, and its magnitude is given in the positive. Thus a deceleration of 16 ft/s^2 is the same as an acceleration of -16 ft/s^2.

Applying the chain rule,

$$a = \left(\frac{dv}{dx}\right)\left(\frac{dx}{dt}\right)$$

or

$$a = \left(\frac{dv}{dx}\right)v$$

which leads to:

$$v\,dv = a\,dx \tag{2.2.3}$$

Often, the given variables are expressed as functions of time or of each other [e.g., $a = f(v)$], and the specific relationships between pairs of variables are derived through the application of the calculus. These relationships are often plotted to aid the visualization of the particle's motion.

The simplest case of rectilinear motion is the case of *constant acceleration,* where

$$\frac{dv}{dt} = a = \text{constant}$$

Separating variables and integrating over the limits $t = 0$ to t,

$$\int_{v_0}^{v} dv = \int_0^t a\, dt$$

$$v = at + v_0 \tag{2.2.4}$$

The velocity of the particle can also be expressed as a function of distance by integrating Eq. 2.2.3 over the appropriate limits of integration to yield:

$$\tfrac{1}{2}(v^2 - v_0^2) = a(x - x_0)$$

which, upon the rearrangement of terms, becomes

$$x - x_0 = \frac{v^2 - v_0^2}{2a} \tag{2.2.6}$$

This expression is useful for computing the distance traveled by a vehicle at constant acceleration (or deceleration) from an initial velocity v_0 to a final velocity v.

In view of Eq. 2.2.1, Eq. 2.2.4 may be integrated to express x as a function of time:

$$x = \tfrac{1}{2}at^2 + v_0t + x_0 \tag{2.2.7}$$

Example 2.1: Constant Acceleration

A vehicle approaches an intersection at 30 mi/h. At time $t = 0$ it begins to decelerate at $d = 16$ ft/s^2. Calculate the time it would take the vehicle to stop. Given that, at the beginning of deceleration, the vehicle was located 55 ft away from the stopping line, determine whether it was able to stop legally (i.e., behind the stopping line). Plot the relationships of acceleration, velocity, and position as functions of time and the relationship between velocity and position.

Solution Set the positive x-axis in the direction of motion, with the origin at the initial position of the vehicle. Thus at $t = 0$, $x = 0$, $v = 44$ ft/s, and $a = -16$ ft/s^2. This is the case of constant acceleration. The time it took the vehicle to stop from an initial velocity of 44 ft/s is given by Eq. 2.2.4:

$$0 = -16t + 44 \quad \text{or} \quad t = 2.75 \text{ s}$$

The distance covered during deceleration may be computed either from Eq. 2.2.6 or from Eq. 2.2.7:

$$x = 60.5 \text{ ft}$$

Since this is greater than the available distance of 55 ft, the vehicle was not able to stop before reaching the stopping line.

The required plots are shown in the accompanying figure.

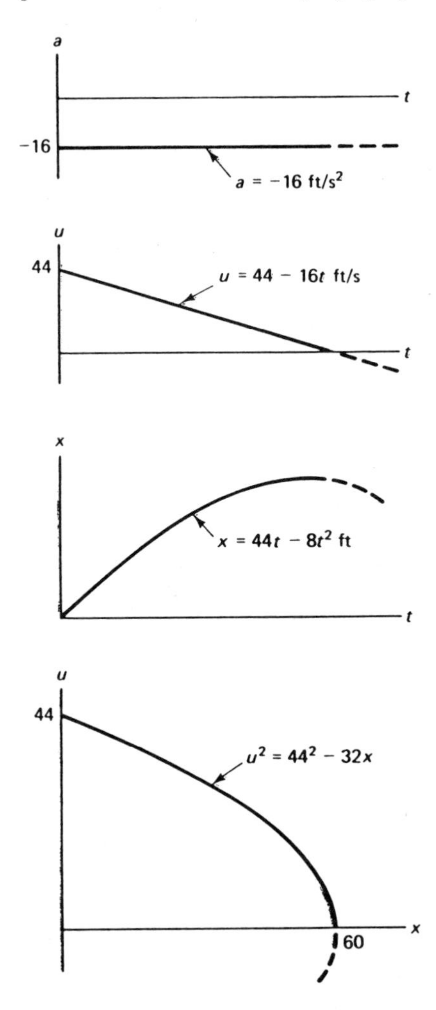

Figure P.2.1

Discussion Since acceleration is the derivative of velocity with respect to time, the slope of the $v - t$ diagram is equal to the acceleration at time t. In this example, the slope of the $v - t$ diagram is negative, constant, and equal to -16 ft/s^2. Similarly, the particle's velocity is equal to the slope of the $x - t$ diagram. Thus, when velocity is equal to zero, the $x - t$ diagram attains a critical point, in this case, a maximum. The plots of the mathematical functions derived earlier extend beyond the instant when the vehicle comes to a complete stop (see dotted lines). This range is not applicable in this situation because the subject vehicle will not continue to decelerate at 16 ft/s^2 beyond that instant—that is, reverse its direction by backing up! The assumption of an "average" constant deceleration is an idealized but often acceptable approximation.

Example 2.2: Acceleration as a Function of Velocity

The acceleration of a vehicle from an initial speed v_0 is given by the relationship [2.1]:

$$a = \frac{dv}{dt} = A - Bv \tag{2.2.8}$$

where A and B are constant. Derive and plot the $x - t$, $a - t$ and $v - t$ relationships assuming that, at $t = 0$, $x = 0$.

Solution This is a case of variable acceleration. Consequently, the equations employed in Example 2.1 do not apply. Separating the variables of Eq. 2.2.8 and integrating over the appropriate limits:

$$\int_{v_0}^{v} \frac{dv}{A - Bv} = \int_0^t dt$$

or

$$\left(\frac{-1}{B}\right) \ln(A - Bv) \Bigg|_{v_0}^{v} = t$$

and

$$\frac{A - Bv}{A - Bv_0} = e^{-Bt}$$

Solving for v as a function of t:

$$v = \left(\frac{A}{B}\right)(1 - e^{-Bt}) + v_0 e^{-Bt}$$

Substitution of this expression into Eq. 2.2.8 results in the needed relationship of acceleration as a function of time:

$$a = (A - Bv_0)\, e^{-Bt}$$

Finally, substituting $v = dx/dt$ into the $v - t$ equation and integrating leads to the following $x - t$ relationship:

$$x = \left(\frac{A}{B}\right)t - \left(\frac{A}{B^2}\right)(1 - e^{-Bt}) + \left(\frac{v_0}{B}\right)(1 - e^{-Bt})$$

The required plots are shown in the accompanying figure.

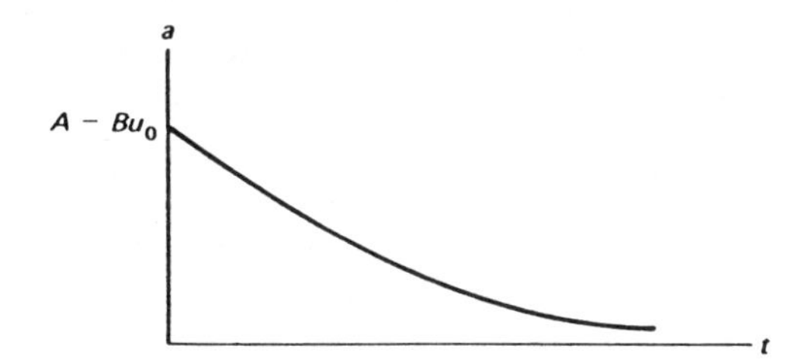

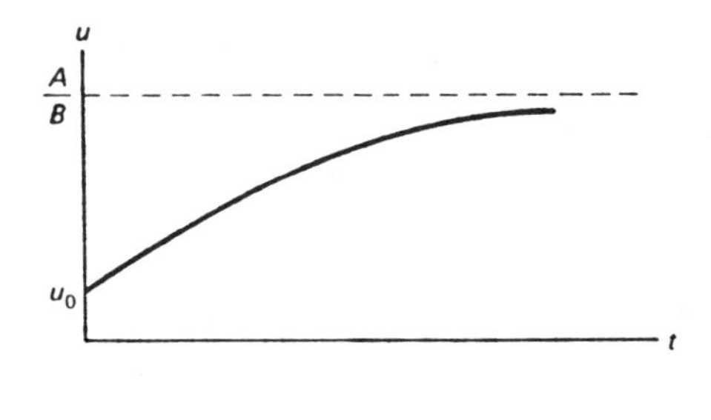

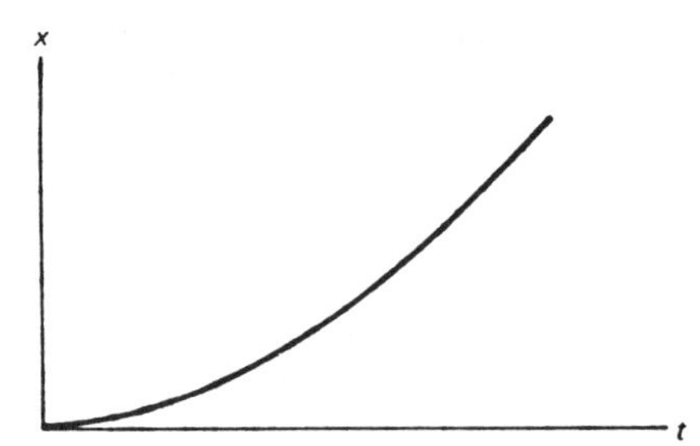

Figure P.2.2

Discussion Equation 2.2.8 closely approximates the situation where a vehicle traveling at an initial speed v_0 attempts to accelerate as quickly as possible to its maximum speed ("pressing the accelerator to the floor"). Examination of the value of acceleration at $t = 0$ shows that the initial value of acceleration depends on the initial speed. Moreover, A has the dimensions of acceleration and is the maximum acceleration that the vehicle can attain starting from rest (i.e., $v_0 = 0$). Theoretically, the maximum speed attainable by the vehicle is A/B. This can be verified by examining the $v - t$ curve in the limit. The values of the constants A and B depend on the technological design of the subject vehicle and can be measured experimentally. Dimensional consistency requires B to have the units of 1/time. The equations developed so far are based on kinematics. They are used in the study of kinetics where the relationship between force, mass, and acceleration is of prime concern. Newton's second law provides the fundamental equation relating the three variables:

$$F = ma \tag{2.2.9}$$

2.2.2 Braking Distance

A very common case of rectilinear motion is the case of a vehicle braking on a grade, that is, while moving either uphill or downhill. Figure 2.2.1 shows the major forces acting on a vehicle as it climbs uphill. Ignoring all resistances except friction and grade resistance, the free-body diagram of the vehicle becomes as shown in Fig. 2.2.2.

It is customary to designate the *braking distance* D_b in the horizontal direction rather than along the incline, which is taken as the x-axis. For small incline angles α, the difference between the two distances is very small as their relationship verifies:

$$D_b = x \cos \alpha \tag{2.2.10}$$

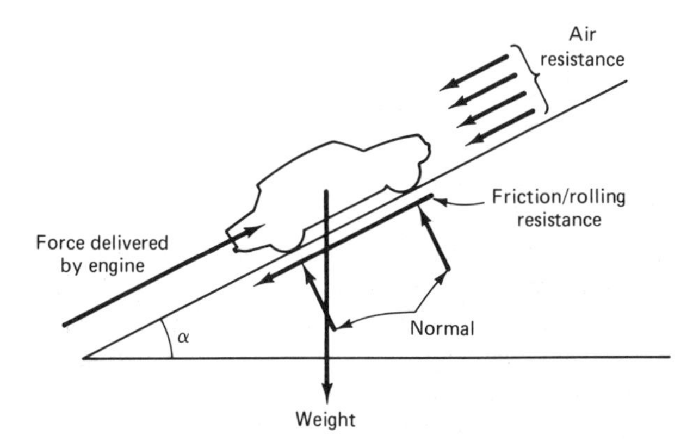

Figure 2.2.1 Forces acting on a moving vehicle.

where both x and D_b are measured from the point at which braking commences.

The condition of static equilibrium is satisfied in the y-direction with the y-component of the vehicle's weight counteracted by the normal force $N = W \cos \alpha$. Equation 2.2.9 in the x-direction yields:

$$\left(\frac{W}{g}\right)a + Wf \cos \alpha + W \sin \alpha = 0 \tag{2.2.11}$$

Substituting Eq. 2.2.10 into Eq. 2.2.6 and solving for acceleration,

$$a = (v^2 - v_0^2)\frac{\cos \alpha}{2D_b} \tag{2.2.12}$$

Substituting Eq. 2.2.12 in Eq. 2.2.11, dividing by $W \cos \alpha$, and solving for D_b gives

$$D_b = \frac{v_0^2 - v^2}{2g(f + G)} \tag{2.2.13}$$

where $G = \tan \alpha$, or the *percent grade* divided by 100.

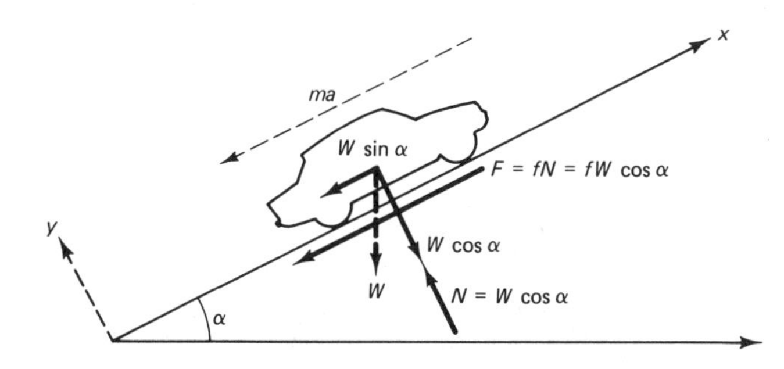

Figure 2.2.2 Vehicle braking.

Repeating the above solution for the case when a vehicle is braking while traveling downhill yields an equation identical to Eq. 2.2.13 except for a reversal of the sign of G in the denominator. Equation 2.2.13 is often expressed to cover both situations as:

$$D_b = \frac{v_0^2 - v^2}{2g(f \pm G)} \tag{2.2.14}$$

where the plus and minus signs correspond to *uphill* and *downhill* braking, respectively. It is easy to remember the proper sign by remembering that the uphill braking distance is shorter than the downhill braking distance because of the effect of gravity.

To compute the total braking distance from an initial speed v_0 to a complete stop, simply substitute $v = 0$. For level paths, the gradient G is equal to zero. The fact that Eq. 2.2.6 was used in the development of the above model implies that the acceleration rate is assumed to be constant. This assumption is reflected in the value of the coefficient of friction f, which is considered to represent the average effect of friction during the entire braking maneuver. The coefficient of friction, of course, depends on the characteristics of the contacting surfaces, that is, the vehicle's tires and the pavement. Because of a wide range of possible pavement-tire combinations and conditions, the coefficient of friction is often calculated experimentally as follows: At the location of interest where G is known, the braking distance needed to stop a vehicle from a known speed is measured. These values are then substituted in Eq. 2.2.13 to obtain the value of f. For the purposes of statistical reliability, the test is repeated a number of times. As a rule of thumb, f is approximately equal to 0.6 when the pavement is dry and about 0.3 when the pavement is wet. On ice, of course, f is much lower. The coefficient of friction has also been found to decrease somewhat with increasing initial speed [2.2]. Engineering design is normally based on wet rather than dry conditions.

Equation 2.2.14 can also aid in the estimation of initial speed v_0 at which a vehicle was traveling prior to a collision based on the length of the skid marks left on the pavement. However, the speed at impact v must also be estimated. This is accomplished by considering the kinetic energy dissipated for the damage or deformation sustained by the vehicle(s) involved in the collision.

Example 2.3: Braking Distance

A driver of a car applied the brakes and barely avoided hitting an obstacle on the roadway. The vehicle left skid marks of 88 ft. Assuming that $f = 0.6$, determine whether the driver was in violation of the 45-mi/h speed limit at that location if she was traveling

(a) Uphill on a 3° incline
(b) Downhill on a 2.3° incline
(c) On a level roadway

Also compute the average deceleration developed in each case.

Solution The stopping distance D_b is computed from the length of the skid marks using Eq. 2.2.10, and the initial velocity is calculated by Eq. 2.2.14, since the final velocity is zero in all three cases. The kinematic relationship of Eq. 2.2.6 can then be solved to compute the corresponding deceleration.

Case	G	D_b (ft)	v_0 (ft/s)	d (ft/s^2)
(a)	0.05	87.88	60.65	20.90
(b)	0.04	87.93	56.30	18.03
(c)	0.00	88.00	58.31	19.32

Since the speed limit was 45 mi/h, or 66 ft/s, the driver was not speeding in any of the three cases.

Discussion The kinematic Eq. 2.2.6 and the kinetic Eq. 2.2.14 describe the same phenomenon. Comparison of these equations shows that the deceleration of the braking vehicle can be expressed in terms of two components: The first is due to the friction developed between the tires and the pavement and the second is due to the effect of grade. The difference between D_b and the distance traveled along the incline x is very small for typical highway grades. Finally, the coefficient of friction given in this problem implies a dry pavement.

2.2.3 Curvilinear Motion

Vehicles do not traverse straight paths exclusively but must also negotiate curved paths, as illustrated by Fig. 2.2.3(a). The figure shows the direction of velocity is always tangent to the path. The vehicle's acceleration may be resolved into two components in the tangential and normal directions, respectively. The magnitude of the tangential component is

$$a_t = \frac{dv}{dt} \tag{2.2.15}$$

The normal component of the acceleration acts toward the center of curvature and has a magnitude of

$$a_n = \frac{v^2}{\rho} \tag{2.2.16}$$

where ρ is the radius of curvature of the path. For a constant velocity v, the tangential component of the acceleration vanishes, but the normal component remains. For circular paths, the radius of curvature is constant and equal to the radius of the circular path R.

Figure 2.2.3(b) shows the tangential and normal components of the forces acting on a vehicle as it traverses a curved path. Applying Newton's second law to the two directions:

$$\Sigma F_t = m\left(\frac{dv}{dt}\right) \tag{2.2.17}$$

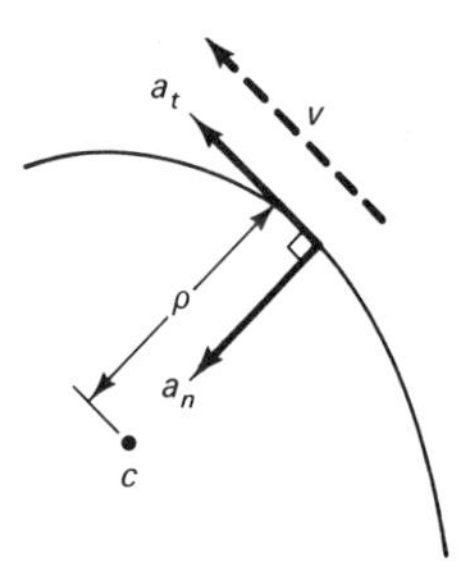

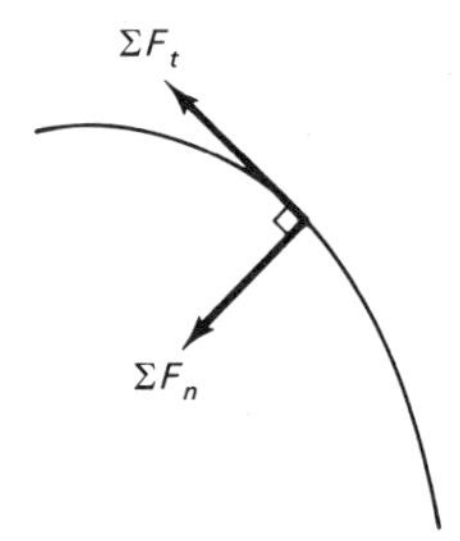

Figure 2.2.3 Curvilinear motion.

and

$$\Sigma F_n = \frac{mv^2}{\rho} \tag{2.2.18}$$

For a horizontal roadway cross section *AA*, as shown in Fig. 2.2.4(b), the only force in the normal direction is due to the *side friction* between the vehicle's tires and the pavement, which resists the tendency of the vehicle to slide. To minimize this tendency, highway design provides for the banking, or *superelevation*, of the cross section of the roadway, as shown in Fig. 2.2.4(c): The cross section is tilted by an angle β so that the component of the vehicle's weight along the tilted pavement surface also resists the sliding tendency of the vehicle. This effect is extremely pronounced in the design of car-racing tracks because of the large normal accelerations developed at racing speeds. The slope to which a highway cross section is tilted is known as the *rate of superelevation*. It is denoted by the letter e and equals the tangent of the angle β. The banking angle β should not be confused with the grade angle α discussed in Subsection 2.2.2.

Figure 2.2.5 shows the free-body diagram of the vehicle as it travels along a circular path at the verge of sliding. In the y-direction perpendicular to the surface of the pavement,

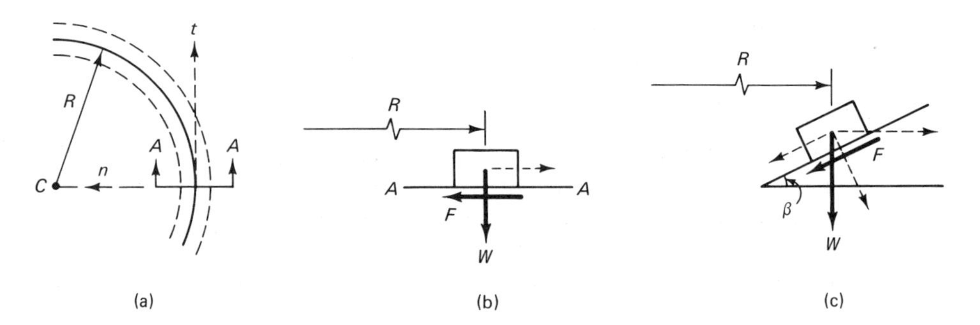

Figure 2.2.4 Lateral effect.

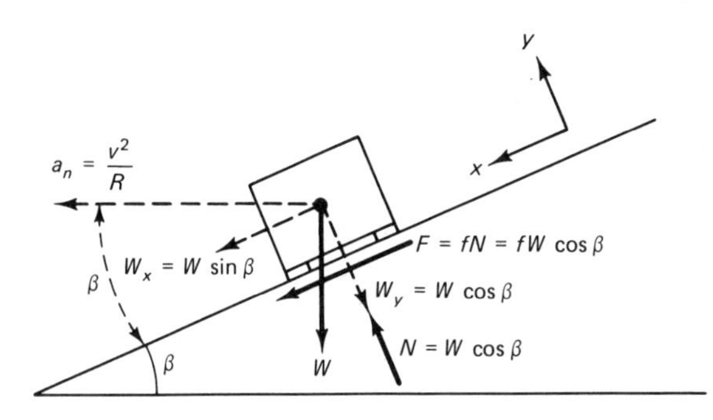

Figure 2.2.5 Free-body diagram of turning vehicle.

static equilibrium is satisfied, as the y-component of the vehicle's weight is counteracted by the normal force. Writing Newton's second law for the x-direction:

$$W \sin \beta + fW \cos \beta = ma_n \cos \beta$$

$$= \left(\frac{W}{g}\right)\left(\frac{v^2}{R}\right) \cos \beta$$

Dividing both sides by $W \cos \beta$,

$$e + f = \frac{v^2}{gR} \qquad (2.2.19)$$

where $e = \tan \beta$ and f is the *coefficient of side friction*.

Example 2.4: Curvilinear Motion

A 2000-lb vehicle is traveling along a horizontal circular path of radius $R = 500$ ft. At the instant of interest, the vehicle is traveling at 88 ft/s while decelerating at 8 ft/s^2. Determine the total horizontal force acting on the vehicle.

Solution As Fig. 2.2.3(b) illustrates, the total force can be resolved into a tangential and a normal component as follows:

$$F_t = ma_t = \left(\frac{2000}{32.2}\right)(-8) = -497 \text{ lb}$$

and

$$F_n = ma_n = m\left(\frac{v^2}{R}\right) = \left(\frac{2000}{32.2}\right)\left(\frac{88^2}{500}\right) = 962 \text{ lb}$$

The total horizontal force F is 1083 lb, as shown in the accompanying figure.

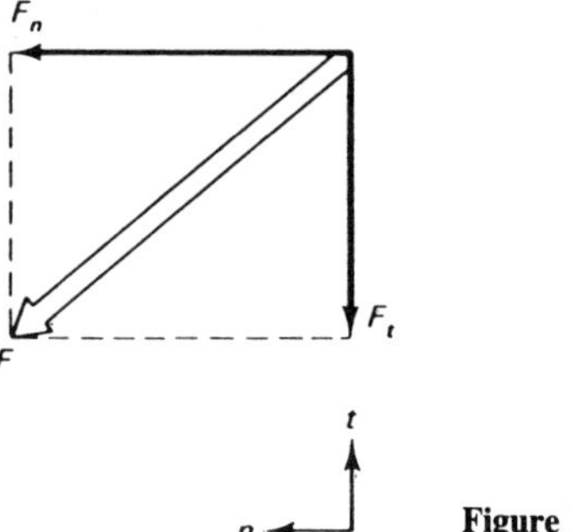

Figure P.2.4

Discussion The direction of the tangential force in this case is in the negative direction, because the vehicle is decelerating. The normal force, however, is still in the direction toward the center of curvature. The total force, of course, is given by the vector addition of the two components.

Example 2.5: Superelevation

A vehicle is traveling along a horizontal circular curve of radius $R = 1000$ ft at the legal speed limit of 60 mi/h. Given that the coefficient of side friction is 0.2, determine the angle β at which the pavement should be banked in order to avoid outward sliding.

Solution From Eq. 2.2.19,

$$e = \left(\frac{v^2}{gR}\right) - f = 0.04 \text{ ft/ft}$$

Hence, $\tan \beta = e = 0.04$ and $\beta = 2.3°$.

Discussion The friction developed between the tires and the pavement is aided by gravity so that the curve can be safely negotiated at 60 mi/h, or 88 ft/s. Solving Eq. 2.2.19 for v with $e = 0$ shows that, without superelevating the pavement cross section, the maximum safe speed would be 80 ft/s, or about 55 mi/h.

When the center of gravity of the vehicle is high above the pavement, there exists the danger of overturning; Fig. 2.2.6 is used to examine this situation. Note that at the instant when overturning or tipping is imminent, the normal force is acting on the outside wheel idealized by point A. The location of the center of gravity of the vehicle is given by X and Y in relation to point A. Taking moments about point A gives:

$$XW \cos \beta + YW \sin \beta = \left(\frac{Y}{e} - X\right) (\sin \beta)\, ma_n$$

Dividing both sides by $W \cos \beta$ and rearranging terms,

$$\frac{v^2}{gR} = \frac{X + Ye}{Y - Xe} \tag{2.2.20}$$

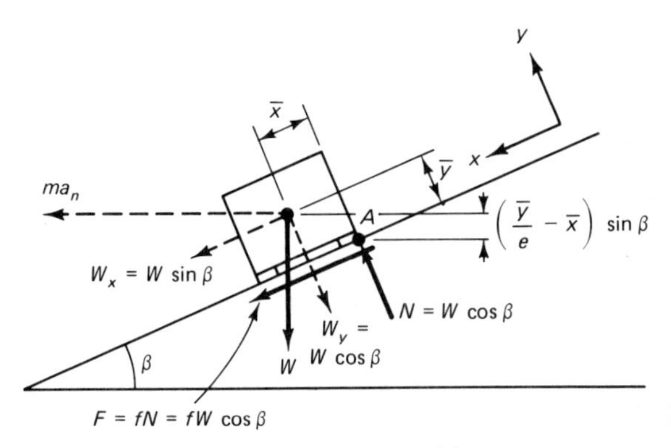

Figure 2.2.6 The case of overturning.

Example 2.6: Slipping and Overturning

A truck with a center of gravity at $X = 4$ ft and $Y = 5$ ft is traveling on a circular path of radius $R = 600$ ft and superelevation $e = 0.05$. Determine the maximum safe speed to avoid both slipping and overturning, assuming that the coefficient of side friction is 0.2.

Solution Equation 2.2.19 applies to slipping. The maximum speed to avoid slipping is:

$$v^2 = gR(e + f) \quad \text{or} \quad v = 69.5 \text{ ft/s}$$

The maximum speed to avoid overturning is given by Eq. 2.2.20:

$$v = 130.8 \text{ ft/s}$$

The maximum safe speed is 69.5 ft/s, the smaller of the two.

Discussion The proper design of highways involves the selection of a design speed, the radius of curvature, and the superelevation rate. Determining the chance of overturning requires knowledge of the dimensions of the vehicles using the roadway. If the dimensions of vehicles change subsequent to the construction of the roadway, the highway engineer is left with a number of choices, including roadway reconstruction, changing the speed limit, or prohibiting certain vehicles from using the roadway.

2.2.4 Relative Motion

It is often practical to examine the motion of one particle in relation to another. For example, the motion of vehicles on a highway may be studied from the point of view of the driver of a moving vehicle. The simplest case of *relative motion* involves the motion of one particle B relative to a coordinate system (x, y, z) that is *translating* but not rotating with respect to a fixed coordinate system (X, Y, Z), as shown by Fig. 2.2.7.

The relationship between the position vectors of the two particles in relation to the

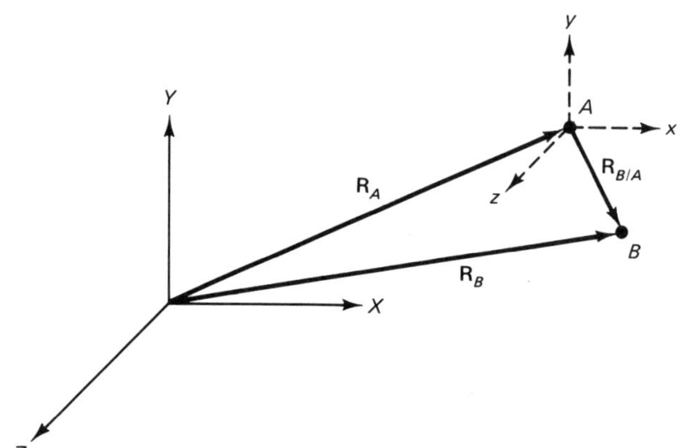

Figure 2.2.7 Relative position of two particles.

fixed system, $\mathbf{r}_A$ and $\mathbf{r}_B$, and the position vector $\mathbf{r}_{B/A}$ of B with respect to the moving particle A is:

$$\mathbf{r}_B = \mathbf{r}_A + \mathbf{r}_{B/A} \tag{2.2.21a}$$

Differentiating with respect to time,

$$\mathbf{v}_B = \mathbf{v}_A + \mathbf{v}_{B/A} \tag{2.2.21b}$$

and

$$\mathbf{a}_B = \mathbf{a}_A + \mathbf{a}_{B/A} \tag{2.2.21c}$$

Example 2.7: Relative Motion

A police car, A, equipped with a radar capable of measuring the relative speed and the relative acceleration between it and another vehicle, B, is following a suspected speeding vehicle in a 40-mi/h straight roadway. At the instant of interest, the police car is accelerating at 8 ft/s^2 from a speed of 50 mi/h. The radar reads $v_{B/A} = -5$ mi/h and $a_{B/A} = -16$ ft/s^2. Determine the absolute speed and acceleration of the vehicle B.

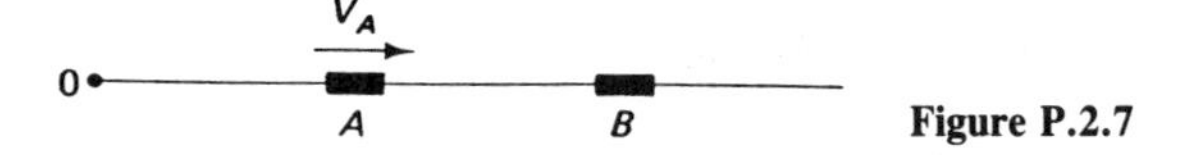

Figure P.2.7

Solution

$$v_{B/A} = v_B - v_A$$

or

$$-5 = v_B - 50 \quad \text{and} \quad v_B = 45 \text{ mi/h}$$

Similarly,

$$a_{B/A} = a_B - a_A$$

or

$$-16 = a_B - 8 \quad \text{and} \quad a_B = -8 \text{ ft/s}^2$$

Discussion The driver, B, was going 5 mi/h above the speed limit and was decelerating at 8 ft/s², perhaps to minimize the consequences of the transgression.

Example 2.8: Polar Coordinates

Car A is traveling at $v = 88$ ft/s. At the instant shown, $d\mathbf{r}/dt = -25.4\mathbf{n}_r$ and $d\boldsymbol{\theta}/dt = 1.47\mathbf{n}_\theta$ rad/s, where $\mathbf{n}_r$ and $\mathbf{n}_\theta$ are unit vectors in the r- and θ-directions, respectively. Determine the absolute velocity of car B.

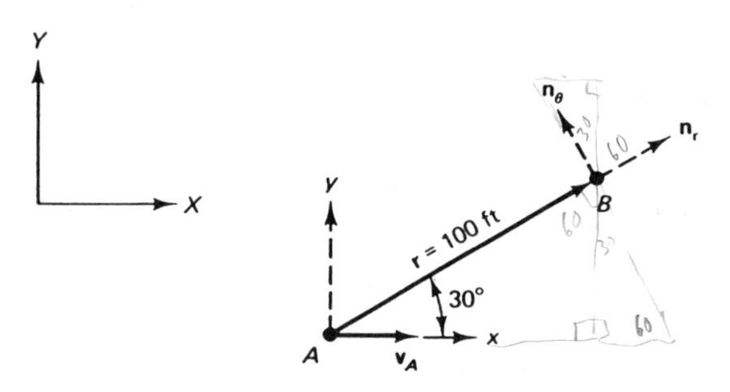

Figure P.2.8

Solution 1: The relative velocity expressed in the r- and θ-directions is

$$\mathbf{v}_{B/A} = \left(\frac{dr}{dt}\right)\mathbf{n}_r + \left(\frac{r\,d\theta}{dt}\right)\mathbf{n}_\theta$$

or

$$\mathbf{v}_{B/A} = -25.4\mathbf{n}_r + (100)(0.147)\mathbf{n}_\theta$$

Since

$$\mathbf{n}_r = \cos 30°\mathbf{i} + \sin 30°\mathbf{j} = 0.866\mathbf{i} + 0.500\mathbf{j}$$

and

$$\mathbf{n}_\theta = -\sin 30°\mathbf{i} + \cos 30°\mathbf{j} = -0.500\mathbf{i} + 0.866\mathbf{j}$$

where $\mathbf{i}$ and $\mathbf{j}$ are unit vectors in the x- and y-directions,

$$\begin{aligned}\mathbf{v}_{B/A} &= -25.4(0.866\mathbf{i} + 0.500\mathbf{j}) + 14.7(0.500\mathbf{i} + 0.866\mathbf{j})\\ &= -29.3\mathbf{i}\end{aligned}$$

Hence

$$\mathbf{v}_B = \mathbf{v}_A + \mathbf{v}_{B/A} = 88\mathbf{i} - 29.3\mathbf{i} = 58.7\mathbf{i}$$

Solution 2:

$$\mathbf{r}_{B/A} = r(\cos\theta)\mathbf{i} + r(\sin\theta)\mathbf{j}$$

Recalling that for a purely translating frame, $d\mathbf{i}/dt = d\mathbf{j}/dt = 0$,

$$\begin{aligned}\mathbf{v}_{B/A} &= \frac{d\mathbf{r}_{B/A}}{dt} \\ &= (-r\sin\theta\theta' + r'\cos\theta)\mathbf{i} + (-r\cos\theta\theta' + r'\sin\theta)\mathbf{j} \\ &= 29.3\mathbf{i}\end{aligned}$$

as before.

2.3 HUMAN FACTORS

2.3.1. Perception-Reaction

The equations developed so far are based purely on the equations of motion without taking into account the effect of driver performance on the motion described. For example, Eq. 2.2.14 gives the braking distance for a vehicle from the moment when the brakes take effect to the moment when the vehicle reaches its final speed. Normally, a driver undertakes such a maneuver in response to a stimulus such as avoiding an object on the roadway. When a stimulus appears, a driver requires a certain amount of time to perceive and comprehend it, to decide on the appropriate response, and to react accordingly. The vehicle *braking* distance or time constitute only a portion of the overall *stopping* distance or time. In many applications the overall maneuver may be divided into two parts: *perception-reaction,* which includes the occurrences up to the beginning of the vehicular response, and braking, which is described by the equations of motion developed in the previous section. If a driver takes 1.5 s to perceive and react to a hazard in the vehicle's path, at a speed of 60 mi/h (88 ft/s) the vehicle would cover 132 ft before the braking phase begins.

Figure 2.3.1. presents the findings of a study conducted by Johannson and Rumar [2.3] regarding driver response times to anticipated braking. The continuous curve at the low end of the histogram represents the reaction time of the person who took the measurements and which was accounted for in computing the driver data shown. Johannson and Rumar also found that the response times were longer than those shown when the drivers were surprised. The figure illustrates the presence of a great deal of variability between individuals. In order to enhance safety, engineering designs that incorporate driver characteristics are typically based on values in the 85th to the 95th percentile range.

Driver response is related to driver characteristics and conditions such as age,

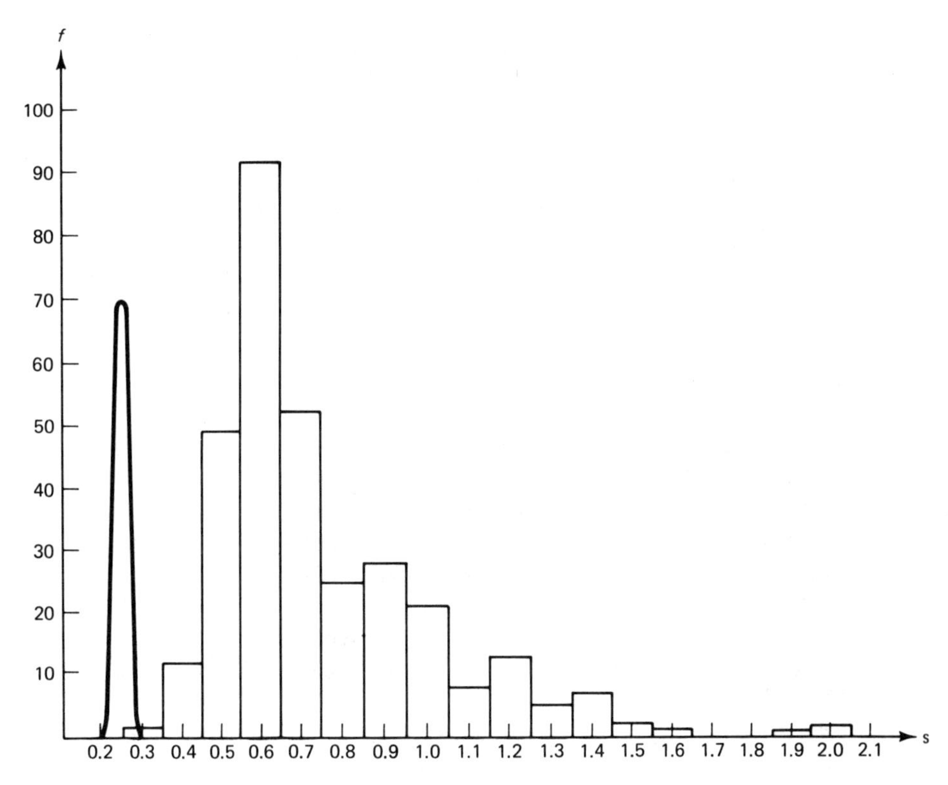

Figure 2.3.1 Distribution of brake reaction times. (*SOURCE*: Johannson and Rumar [2.3], Fig. 1, p. 26.)

medical condition, alcohol and drug use, fatigue, and sleep deprivation. It also depends on the complexity of the stimulus and the complexity of the required response. Good traffic engineering designs attempt to minimize the stimuli and driving tasks to which the driver must attend at the same time. This is the "one task at a time" rule, which, due to the complexity of the driving environment, is not always possible.

Example 2.9

Using the data of Example 2.3, determine the stopping distances horizontally (D_s) and along the pavement (X_s) in each of the three cases, given that the driver's perception-reaction time was $\delta = 1.5$ s.

Solution The distance traveled during the perception-reaction time must be added to the

Case	D_s (ft)	X_s
(a)	178.73	178.98
(b)	172.31	172.45
(c)	175.47	175.47

braking distance to compute the total stopping distance. *Assuming* that the vehicle was not accelerating during the time interval δ, the distances traveled during δ were $X_r = \delta\, v_0$ along the pavement and $D_r = X_r \cos \alpha$ horizontally.

Discussion The difference between the two distances D_s and X_s is insignificant considering typical highway grades. The reason computed stopping distances are longer for steeper grades is because of differences in the initial speeds required to stop within the 88 ft specified *in this case*. The assumption of constant speed prior to the stopping maneuver has an effect on the results.

2.3.2. Dilemma Zones

Most probably, the reader has encountered the situation of approaching a signalized intersection just when the traffic signal turned amber (yellow) and has faced the decision of whether to apply the brakes in order to stop for the red signal or to attempt to clear the intersection on yellow. On occasion, the reader may have felt that it was impossible to safely execute either maneuver. The duration of the amber phase of the traffice signal, τ, is related to this situation. A properly selected amber duration that incorporates the motion of the vehicle during the driver's perception-reaction time can eliminate this problem, and a design formula has been developed by Gazis, Herman, and Maradudin [2.4] as follows.

Figure 2.3.2 shows a vehicle approaching a signalized intersection at a speed v_0. When the signal turns yellow, the vehicle is located at a distance x from the stopping line. The driver must then decide whether to stop or go. The stopping maneuver requires that the vehicle can travel no more than the distance x to the stopping line. Clearing the intersection, on the other hand, requires that the vehicle must travel a distance of at least $(x + w + L)$, where w is the width of the intersection and L is the length of the vehicle. Moreover, this distance must be covered prior to the onset of red (i.e., during yellow). Employing the subscripts 1 and 2 to represent the clearing and the stopping maneuvers, respectively,

$$(x - v_0\delta_2) \geqslant \frac{v_0^2}{2a_2} \qquad (2.3.1)$$

is necessary for a successful stopping maneuver.

The left side of this inequality is the difference between the total distance to the stopping line minus the distance traveled during perception-reaction at the approach speed v_0, and it therefore specifies the maximum braking distance available to the vehicle. For a successful stopping maneuver, this distance should be equal to or greater than the braking distance required by the vehicle at a deceleration a_2. The smallest deceleration rate to accomplish the task is given by the solution of Eq. 2.3.1 as:

$$a_2 = \frac{v_0^2}{2(x - v_0\delta_2)} \qquad (2.3.2)$$

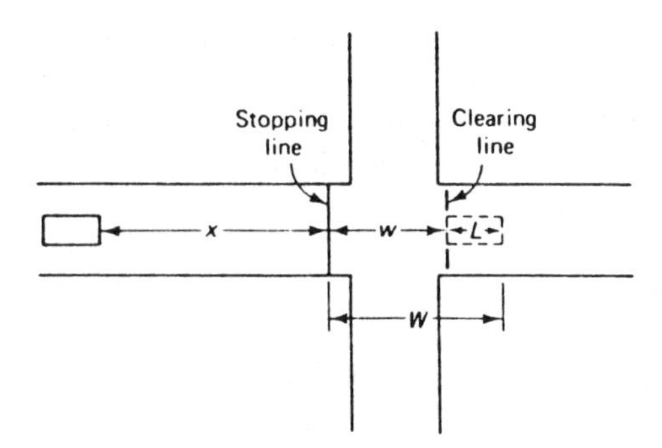

Figure 2.3.2 Vehicle approaching a signalized intersection. (*SOURCE*: Gazis, Herman, and Maradudin [2.4], Fig. 1, p. 114.)

Considering v_0 and δ_2 to be known, the relationship between x and a_2 is plotted on Fig. 2.3.3. It is a rectangular parabola with an asymptote at $x = v_0\delta_2$, or the perception-reaction distance. This is reasonable because, if the vehicle were closer to the stopping line at the onset of amber, it would enter the intersection before the commencement of braking. The mathematical relationship shows the deceleration a_2 to be unbounded. However, there exists a practical upper limit $a_2(\max)$ to the deceleration that a real vehicle can develop. Furthermore, this limit is often higher than the deceleration rate that the driver and passengers of the vehicle would consider comfortable. The comfortable deceleration rate a_2^* is normally in the vicinity of 8 to 10 ft/s^2 when passengers are seated

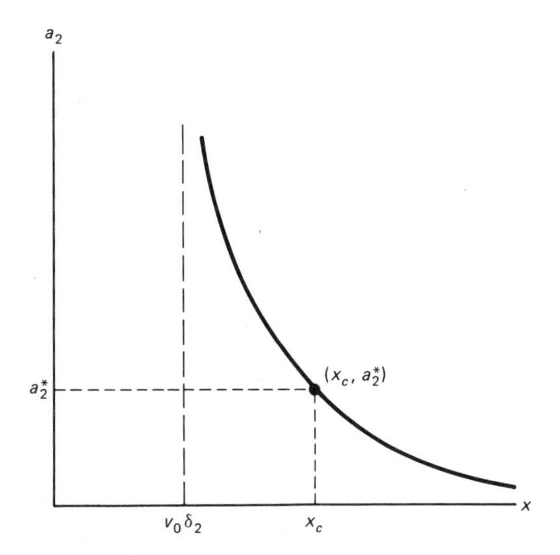

Figure 2.3.3 Acceleration requirements for stopping. (*SOURCE*: Gazis, Herman, and Maradudin [2.4], Fig. 2, p. 115.)

and around 4 or 5 ft/s^2 when passengers are standing, as in a transit vehicle. The distinction between the *maximum attainable level* and a *desired lower level* must always be kept in mind. The corresponding distance x_c represents the minimum distance for which the vehicle can be stopped comfortably. For shorter distances it would be uncomfortable, unsafe, or impossible to stop. This critical distance is

$$x_c = v_0\delta_2 + \frac{v_0^2}{2\, a_2^*} \tag{2.3.3}$$

A successful clearing maneuver is represented by

$$(x + w + L - v_0\delta_1) \leq v_0(\tau - \delta_1) + \tfrac{1}{2}a_1(\tau - \delta_1)^2 \tag{2.3.4}$$

The right side of Eq., 2.3.4 represents the distance traveled from an initial speed v_0 at constant acceleration a_1 during the time interval $(\tau - \delta_1)$, that is, subsequent to the perception-reaction time and before the onset of the red. The left side of Eq. 2.3.4 represents the distance available for the clearing maneuver. The acceleration needed just to clear the intersection is

$$a_1 = \frac{2x}{(\tau - \delta_1)^2} + \frac{2(w + L - v_0\,\tau)}{(\tau - \delta_1)^2} \tag{2.3.5}$$

which, for known values of W, L, v_0, and δ_1, represents a straight line, as shown in Figure 2.3.4. The distance x_a corresponds to the maximum comfortable acceleration rate a_1^*, and the x-intercept specifies the maximum distance between the vehicle and the stopping line from which the vehicle can clear the intersection without accelerating.

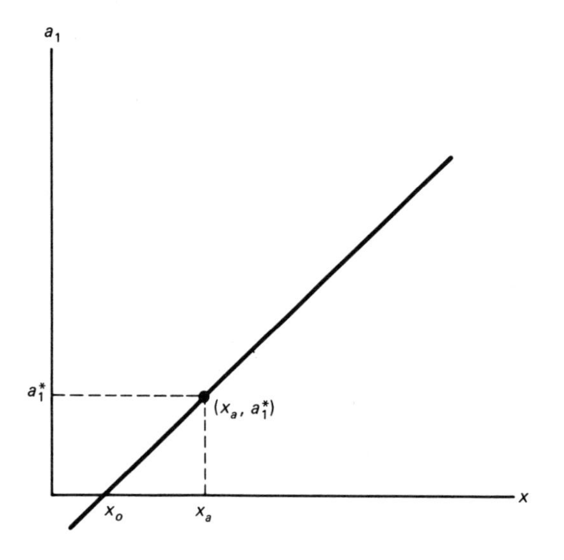

Figure 2.3.4 Acceleration requirements for clearing. (*SOURCE*: Gazis, Herman, and Maradudin [2.4], Fig. 2, p. 115.)

The distance

$$x_o = v_0 \tau - (w + L) \tag{2.3.6}$$

is relevant to this analysis because a vehicle that approaches the intersection at the speed limit should not be required to accelerate in order to clear the intersection and thus break the law. The distance x_o defines a point beyond which a vehicle traveling at the speed limit would not be able to safely or legally clear the intersection on yellow.

For a particular site, the relative magnitudes of the two critical distances x_o and x_c determine whether a vehicle can or cannot safely execute either or both maneuvers, as illustrated by Figure 2.3.5. In part (a), $x_c < x_o$ and the driver can execute either maneuver no matter where the vehicle is located at the onset of amber. The limiting case is represented by part (b). A problem becomes apparent when $x_c > x_o$, when a *dilemma zone* of length $x_c - x_o$ exists: A vehicle approaching the intersection at the legal speed limit can execute neither of the two maneuvers safely, legally, and comfortably if it happens to be located within the dilemma zone at the onset of amber.

The dilemma zone may be eliminated either by changing the speed limit which in certain locations may be undesirable or by selecting an appropriate minimum duration for the amber signal phase that results in $x_c = x_o$. In this case Eq. 2.3.3 and Eq. 2.3.6 yield:

$$\tau_{\min} = \delta_2 + \frac{v_0}{2\, a_2^*} + \frac{w + L}{v_0} \tag{2.3.7}$$

Thus properly selected values of a vehicle length, human factors (i.e., comfortable deceleration and sufficient perception-reaction time), and speed limit v_0 specify the *minimum* amber duration which, barring *driver error,* ensures that if the vehicle cannot stop, it can clear the intersection.

Example 2.10

A driver traveling at the speed limit of 30 mi/h was cited for crossing an intersection on red. He claimed he was innocent because the duration of the amber display was improper and, consequently, a dilemma zone existed at that location. Using the following data, determine whether the driver's claim was correct.

amber duration = 4.5 s

perception-reaction time = 1.5 s

comfortable deceleration = 10 ft/s^2

car length = 15 ft

intersection width = 50 ft

Solution The required minimum duration of the amber phase is

$$\tau_{\min} = 1.5 + \tfrac{44}{20} + \tfrac{65}{44} = 5.18 \text{ s}$$

Since the actual duration was 4.5 s, the driver's claim cannot be dismissed. There was a dilemma zone, the length of which was

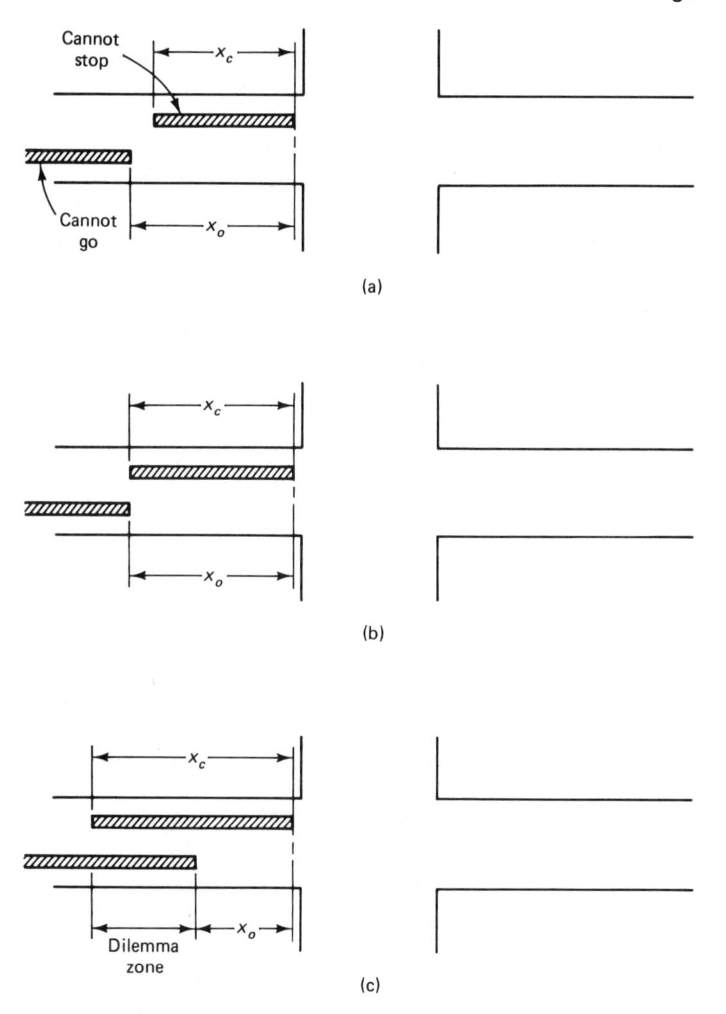

Figure 2.3.5 Dilemma zone. (*SOURCE*: Gazis, Herman, and Maradudin [2.4], Fig. 7, p. 121.)

$$x_c - x_o = v_0\,\delta_2 - v_0\,\tau + \left(\frac{v_0^2}{2a_2^*}\right) + w + L$$

$$= 29.8 \text{ ft}$$

Whether the vehicle was within the dilemma zone at the onset of amber and whether the driver was not speeding cannot be proven.

Example 2.11

A car stalled 50 ft from the stopping line at an approach to a signalized intersection of $w = 40$ ft. The driver managed to start it again at the moment the traffic signal turned yellow and decided to clear the intersection. Given that the car accelerated according to

$$a = 4.8 - 0.06v \text{ ft/s}^2$$

and that $\tau = 4.5$ s and $\delta_1 = 1.0$ s, determine whether the driver was able to clear the intersection on yellow.

Solution Of the available 4.5 s of yellow, 1 s elapsed during perception-reaction. According to Example 2.2, during the remaining 3.5 s, the vehicle covered a distance of

$$x = \frac{4.8}{0.06}(3.5) - \frac{4.8}{0.06^2}[1 - e^{-(0.06)(3.5)}] + 0 = 27.45 \text{ ft}$$

Since $27.45 < (50 + L)$, the driver was unable to clear the intersection on yellow.

Discussion In this case, the given acceleration was a function of speed and implicitly of time. Therefore, the distance traveled had to be computed accordingly. The design in Eq. 2.3.7 is based on a vehicle approaching at the speed limit and either decelerating at an average rate or clearing the intersection without having to accelerate.

2.3.3 Visual Acuity

A driver visually perceives the actions of other vehicles, the location of objects, traffic-control devices, and the general traffic environment. *Visual acuity* refers to the sharpness with which a person can see an object [2.1, 2.5, 2.13]. One measurement of visual acuity is the *recognition acuity* obtained by the use of the standard Snellen chart familiar to anyone who has visited an ophthalmologist for an eye examination: The subject is asked to read letters of different heights from a specified distance. The result of the test is specified in relation to a subject of normal vision. Normal vision is taken to mean that, in a well-lit environment, a person can recognize a letter of about $\frac{1}{3}$ in. in height at a distance of 20 ft; the visual acuity of this person is given as 20/20. A person with worse vision must be closer to the display in order to recognize the same letter. This relative visual acuity is designated by a ratio such as 20/40, meaning that the subject can clearly see an object at a distance of 20 ft when a distance of 40 ft is sufficient for a person with normal vision. Alternatively, the person with 20/40 vision requires an object twice as large as the one that a person with normal vision can clearly discern from the same distance.

Visual acuity is affected by factors such as the contrast and brightness of the object, the level of illumination, and the relative motion between the observer and the object. Visual acuity is termed *static* in the absence of relative motion and *dynamic* when relative motion exists. Night driving requires artificial illumination of signs either by permanent fixtures or by reliance on the vehicle's headlights. In addition, acuity decreases with increasing visual angles, as illustrated by Figure 2.3.6. The most clear vision occurs within a cone of vision in the vicinity of 3°. The clarity of vision is fairly good up to approximately 10°, beyond which lies the region of peripheral vision, which may extend up to 160°. For practical design, traffic signs should be placed within the 10° cone and at locations permitting ample distance for perception-reaction and maneuver execution.

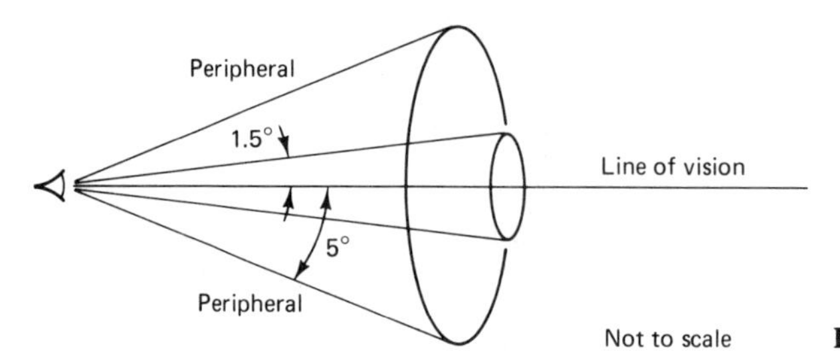

Figure 2.3.6 Cones of vision.

Example 2.12

A driver with 20/20 vision can read a sign from a distance of 90 ft. If the letter size is 2 in., how close would a person with 20/50 vision have to be in order to be able to read the same sign?

For the given definition of normal vision, calculate the height of the lettering that a driver with 20/60 vision can read from a distance of (a) 90 ft and (b) 36 ft.

Solution The distance x from the location of the sign can be computed by simple proportions as follows:

$$x = (90 \text{ ft})(20/50) = 36 \text{ ft}$$

Similarly, the required letter heights can be obtained by proportioning as:

(a) $h = (2 \text{ in.})\frac{60}{20} = 6$ in.
(b) $h = (2 \text{ in.})\frac{60}{50} = 2.4$ in.

Example 2.13

Assume that a driver with normal vision can read a sign from a distance of 50 ft. for each inch of letter height and that the "design driver" has a 20/40 vision. Determine how far away from an exit ramp a directional sign should be located to allow a safe reduction of speed from 60 mi/h to 30 mi/h, given a perception-reaction time of 2.5 s, a coefficient of friction of 0.30, a letter size of 8 in., and a level freeway.

Solution As specified, a driver with normal vision can recognize the sign from a distance of $50 \times 8 = 400$ ft. A driver with 20/40 vision must be no more than 200 ft away. Including perception-reaction, the distance traveled to decelerate from 60 mi/h to 30 mi/h is

$$x = v_0 t + \frac{v_0^2 - v^2}{2g\,(f + G)} = (88)(1.5) + \frac{88^2 - 44^2}{2(32.2)(0.30)} = 433 \text{ ft}$$

Hence the sign must be located at least $433 - 200 = 233$ ft, or about 250 ft, in advance of the exit ramp.

Discussion The solution to this problem brings to bear the perception-reaction phenomenon discussed in Subsection 2.3.1 and the braking distance covered in Subsection 2.2.2. More-

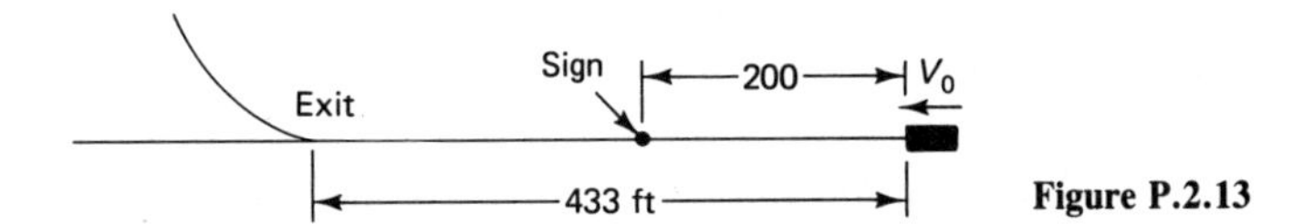

Figure P.2.13

over, the "design driver" does not represent the best performer, and the design conditions assume a wet pavement (i.e., $f = 0.30$).

2.3.4 Lateral Displacement

When approaching an object located near their paths, as shown by Figure 2.3.7, drivers show a tendency to displace laterally away from the object even though it may not be on their direct path. Taragin [2.6] reported a set of experiments, which measured this tendency: Various objects were placed at different lateral distances on two-lane and multilane highways of various pavement widths, and the effects of these objects were compared to cases where no object was present. The measured effects consisted of speed adjustments, the longitudinal distance l at which vehicles were seen to displace laterally, and the magnitude of the observed lateral displacement.

The major results of the experiments included the following: The narrower the pavement and the closer the object to the pavement edge, the greater the magnitude of lateral displacement. When the object was placed at the edge of pavement, the lateral

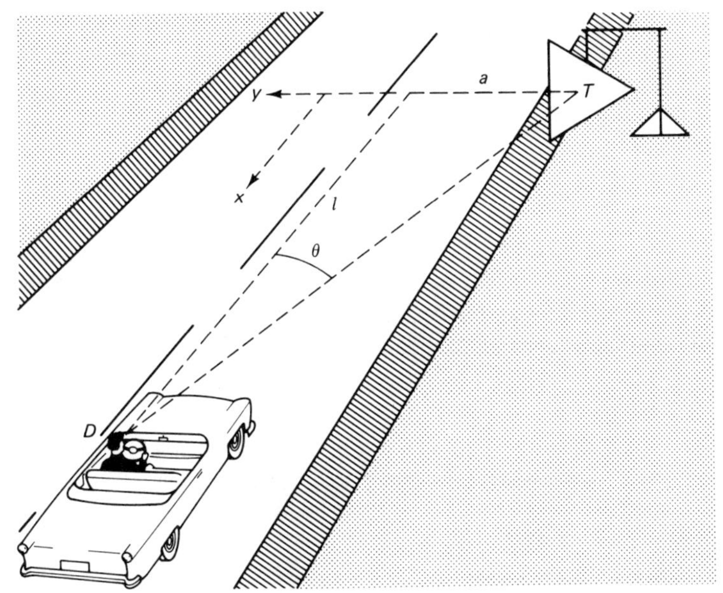

Figure 2.3.7 Geometry of lateral clearance. (*SOURCE*: Michaels and Gozan [2.7], Fig. 1, p. 2, with slight modification.)

displacement was found to be 3.3 ft in the case of two-lane highways with 8-ft lanes and 1.8 ft for 12-ft lanes. In certain cases, speed reductions became apparent.

Subsequent research by Michaels and Gozan [2.7] compared two mathematical models of this phenomenon and concluded that "a model of lateral displacement based on the rate of change of visual angle accounts best for the obtained results." Mathematically, this model can be derived as follows.

The relationship between the longitudinal distance l, the lateral placement of the object a, and the visual angle θ is:

$$l = a \cot \theta \tag{2.3.7}$$

$$\frac{dl}{dt} = -a \csc^2\theta \frac{d\theta}{dt} \tag{2.3.8}$$

Since $dl/dt = -v$, the vehicle's velocity and $\csc^2\theta = (a^2 + l^2)/a^2$,

$$\frac{d\theta}{dt} = \frac{va}{a^2 + l^2} \tag{2.3.9}$$

Thus given the vehicle's speed, the longitudinal distance l, and the rate of change of the visual angle, the driver can estimate the lateral placement of the object to judge whether it lies in the vehicle's path or not. If the object lies directly in the vehicle's path (i.e., $a = 0$), the driver cannot detect any angular change. According to this human factor model, each driver has a subjective *critical rate of change in visual angle*, below which the driver presumes that the vehicle is in a collision path and displaces away from the object in the lateral direction.

Michaels and Gozan pointed out that this model explains Taragin's findings with regard to speed adjustments, and they provide additional information regarding other factors affecting both the magnitude of lateral displacement, including the size, shape, and brightness of the object.

This model can be extended to situations where the object is another moving vehicle on the roadway, in which case the equations of relative motion must be employed [2.1].

The understanding of the driver characteristic described in this section can aid in controlling vehicular speeds in highway construction zones through the proper placement of cones or barricades and in design decisions relating to the placement of objects (signs, bridge abutments, and raised medians) along highways.

Example 2.14

A vehicle traveling at 40 mi/h was observed to displace laterally when it was located 300 ft away from a bridge abutment placed 6 ft to the right of its path. At what longitudinal distance from the same abutment would you expect the same driver to displace laterally when traveling at 60 mi/h?

Solution By Eq. 2.3.9, the critical rate of change in visual angle for this driver is:

$$\left(\frac{d\theta}{dt}\right)_{cr} = 0.0039 \text{ rad/s}$$

For the case of $v = 60$ mi/h $= 88$ ft/s,

$$0.0039 = \frac{(88)(6)}{6^2 + l^2}$$

and

$$l = 368 \text{ ft}$$

2.4 GEOMETRIC DESIGN OF HIGHWAYS

2.4.1 Introduction

Geometric design refers to the physical proportioning of facilities, as distinguished from other aspects of design, such as structural design. This section addresses the basic components of geometric design, with the emphasis placed on highway facilities. The five elements examined are the cross section, horizontal alignment, superelevation, vertical alignment, and channelization.

2.4.2 Functional Classification of Highways

In the United States, highways are classified according to the function they serve (*functional classification*) and with respect to the entity (private, municipal, state, or federal) responsible for their construction, maintenance, and operation (*jurisdictional classification*). Of the two, the functional classification is more relevant to geometric design. Table 2.4.1 lists the major functional categories of highways in the United States [2.2, 2.5, 2.8]. Figure 2.4.1 is a conceptual description of the relative emphasis that each highway category places on the functions of providing "mobility" (i.e., continuous travel) on one hand and "accessibility" (i.e., direct access to abutting property) on the other: Local streets are predominantly designed for accessibility rather than mobility, whereas high-level facilities such as expressways and freeways are predominantly designed for high-

TABLE 2.4.1 HIGHWAY FUNCTIONAL CLASSIFICATION

Rural		Urban	
Principal arterials	Freeways	Principal arterials	Interstate freeways
			Other freeways/expressways
	Other		Other
Minor arterials		Minor arterials	
Collectors	Major	Collector streets	
	Minor		
Local roads		Local streets	

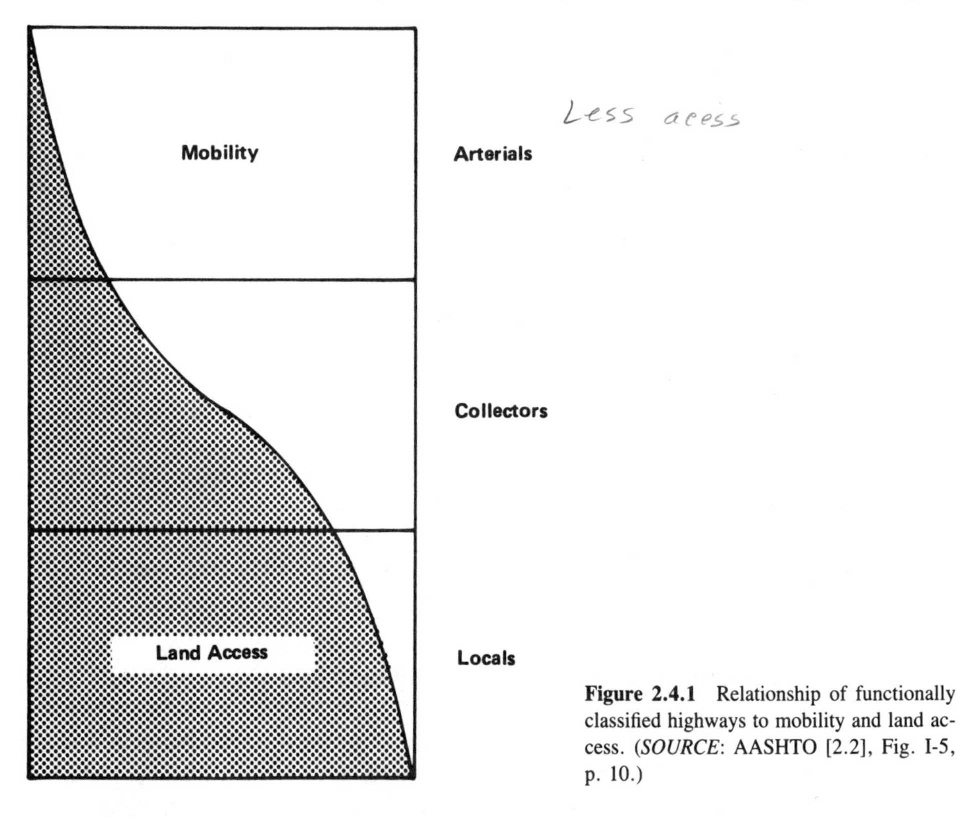

Figure 2.4.1 Relationship of functionally classified highways to mobility and land access. (*SOURCE*: AASHTO [2.2], Fig. I-5, p. 10.)

speed continuous movement. The technical difference between freeways and expressways is that the former are characterized by *full control of access,* meaning that access to and egress from these facilities are permitted only at controlled locations such as entrance and exit ramps, whereas the latter have *partial control of access,* meaning that access or egress may also be permitted directly from or to abutting property or via a limited number of at-grade intersections. The functional hierarchies of rural and urban highways are schematically illustrated by Fig. 2.4.2.

Generally, the design requirements for the various highway types follow the functions served. At one extreme, local roads and streets are designed primarily for light, low-speed traffic to gain access to residences and other land uses; they are closely spaced and are often designed to discourage through traffic. At the other extreme, freeways are designed for high traffic levels at high speeds; they are sparsely spaced and are designed to facilitate continuous travel between major activity centers. Urban and rural principal arterials are interconnected to serve continuous intercity and interstate movements.

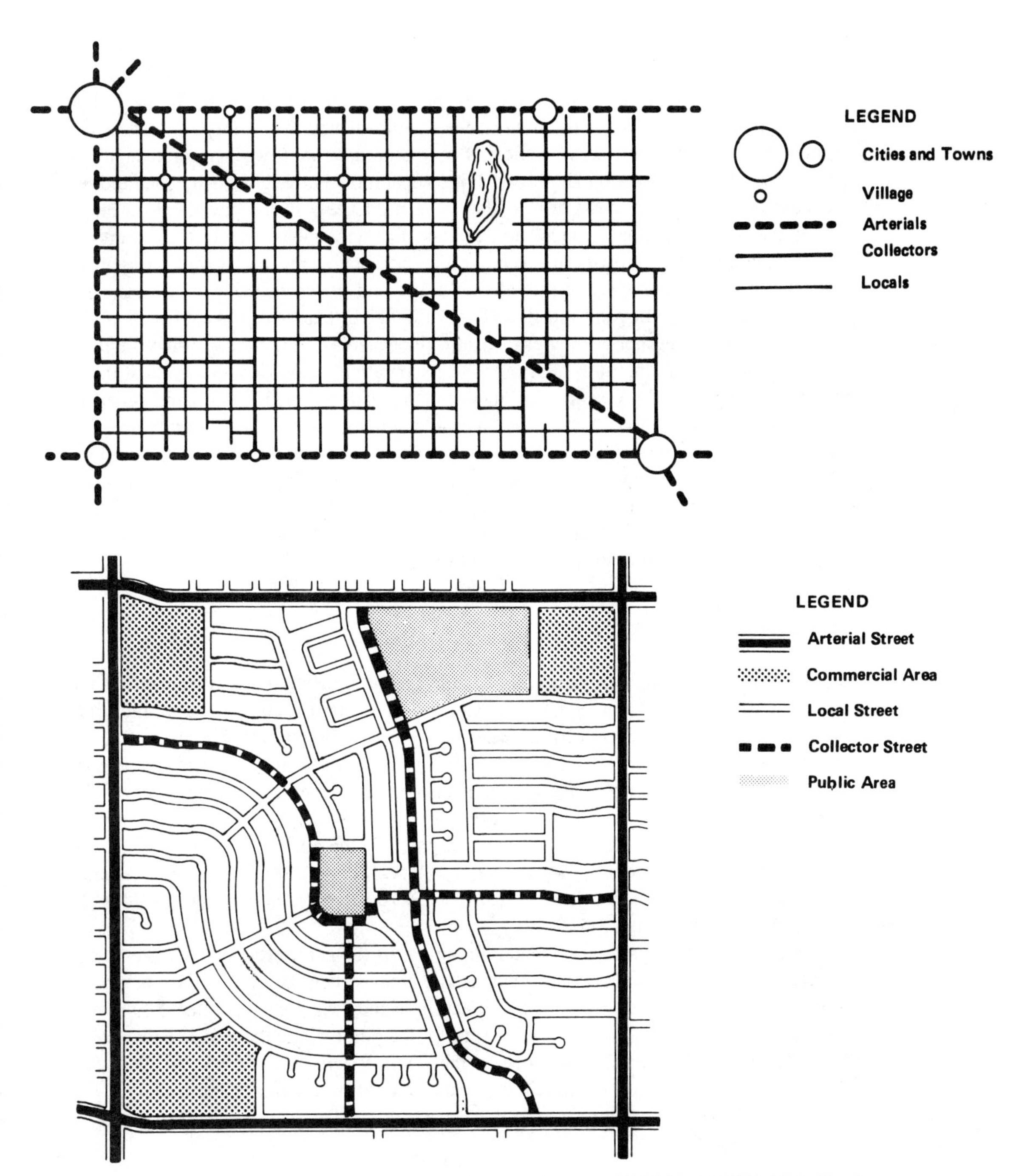

Figure 2.4.2 Illustration of functionally classified highways. (*SOURCE*: AASHTO [2.2], Figs. I-3 and I-4, pp. 7–8.)

2.4.3 Cross-Section Design

Cross-section design refers to the profile of the facility perpendicular to the centerline and extending to the limits of the right of way within which the facility is constructed. Figure 2.4.3 illustrates the cross section of a typical *undivided* two-lane rural highway with a lane in each direction of travel. Lane separation is designated by longitudinal *pavement markings*. A *normal crown,* that is, a mild slope in the pavement on either side of the center line, is provided to facilitate the removal of water. Depending on drainage requirements, crowns in the range of $\frac{1}{8}$ to about $\frac{1}{4}$ in./ft of width are typical. Paved or unpaved *shoulders* are provided at either end of the *travel-way* pavement for emergency situations. Beyond the shoulders, drainage ditches are provided with cut or filled side slopes at appropriate angles to ensure slope stability. Figure 2.4.4 shows typical types of *divided* multilane rural highways. The separation of the two directions of travel may be accomplished by constructing independent roadways and by utilizing raised or depressed *medians*. Various types of *barriers* (including guardrails and concrete barriers) may be used along the median and at the end of the *clear zone* beyond the shoulders. Depending on their function, urban facilities may also be either undivided or divided. Urban roadways often incorporate drainage ditches or gutters and raised curbs. Urban arterials can be at ground level (i.e., *at grade*), *elevated,* or *depressed;* they may also contain special bus lanes and rail transitways within their rights of way.

2.4.4 Horizontal Alignment

The *horizontal alignment* of a highway, railway, or transit guideway represents the projection of the facility on a horizontal plane. It generally consists of straight-line segments (*tangents*) connected by *circular curves* either directly (*simple curves*) or via intermediate *transition curves*. Figure 2.4.5 illustrates these two common geometric arrangements. The length of the facility is measured along the horizontal alignment of a control line (such as the center line of a highway) and is usually expressed in terms of 100-ft *stations* from a reference point. Thus a point on the alignment designated as *sta. 14* is located at a distance of 14 stations (i.e., 14 × 100 = 1400 ft) from the reference point. Similarly, a point identified as *sta. 14 + 56.70* is located at a distance of 1456.70 ft from the reference point.

Figure 2.4.6 shows the horizontal alignment of the center line of a simple curve. A simple circular curve connects two tangents, which—when projected—meet at a *point of intersection,* or PI. Proceeding in the direction of increasing station values, point A is designated as the *point of curvature* (PC), that is, the point where the curve begins. Point B, or the end of the curve, is denoted as the *point of tangency,* or PT. At these two points, of course, the radii of the circular curve are perpendicular to the tangents. The length of the curve AB equals

$$L = 2\pi R\left(\frac{\Delta}{360}\right) \tag{2.4.1}$$

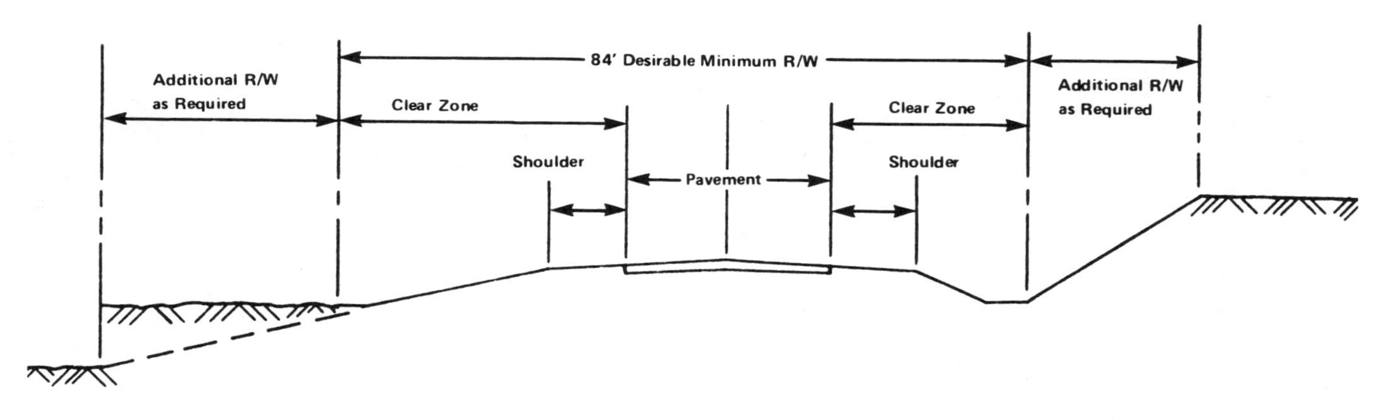

Figure 2.4.3 Cross section of a two-lane rural highway. (*SOURCE*: AASHTO [2.2], Fig. VII-1, p. 541.)

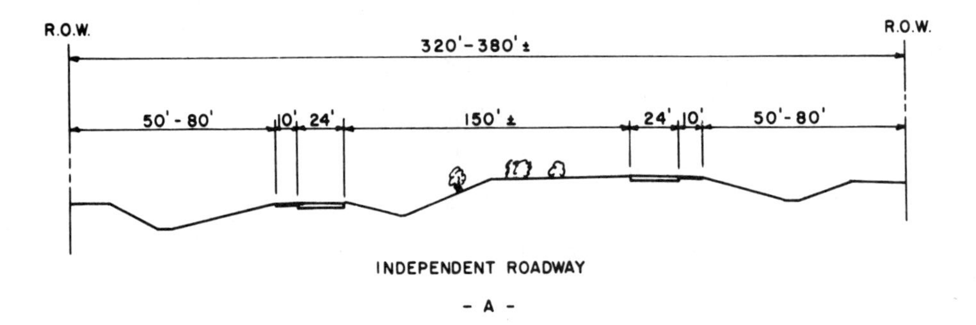

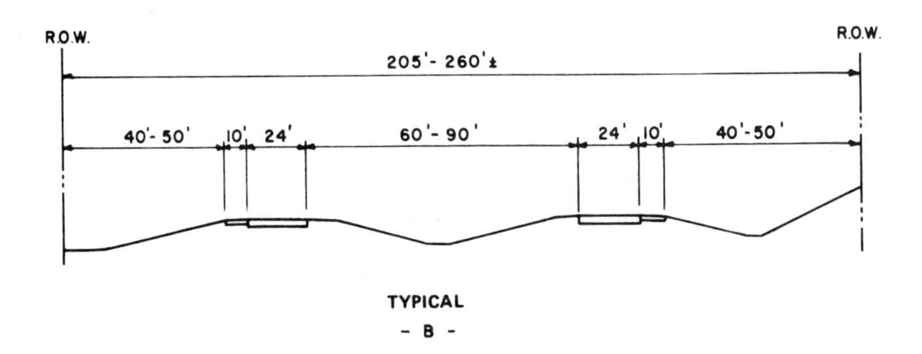

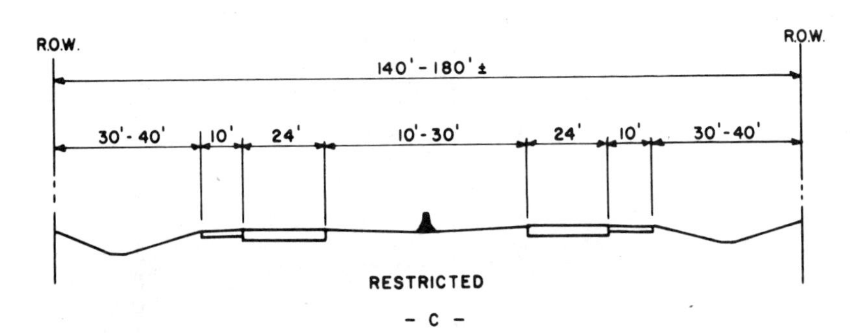

Figure 2.4.4 Cross sections of four-lane rural highways. (*SOURCE*: AASHTO [2.2], Fig. VIII-48, p. 713.)

where R is the curve radius. Other important distances and equations are shown in Fig. 2.4.6.

Two straight lines intersecting at the PI can be connected by an infinite number of circular curves. Each of these curves may be defined by its radius R or by its *degree of curve D*, for which two alternative definitions are encountered in practice. The *arc*

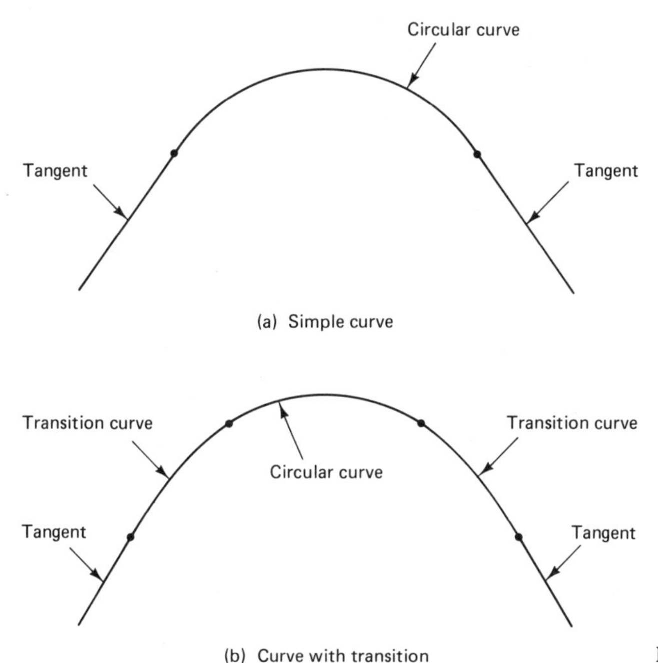

Figure 2.4.5 Typical horizontal curves.

definition is preferred by highway engineers and is equal to the central angle (in degrees) subtended by an arc of 100 ft. In this case, the radius of the curve and the degree of curve are related by the following proportion:

$$\frac{100}{2\pi R} = \frac{D}{360}$$

or

$$D = \left(\frac{5729.58}{R}\right)^{\circ} \tag{2.4.2}$$

Railway design, on the other hand, uses the *chord definition* for the degree of curve, which is equal to the angle subtended by a chord of 100 ft, in which case the relationship between the radius and the degree of curve is

$$\sin\left(\frac{D}{2}\right) = \frac{50}{R} \tag{2.4.3}$$

Figure 2.4.7 illustrates the two definitions of the degree of curve. In either case, specifying the degree of curve is equivalent to specifying the radius. The degree of curve D must not be confused with the *external angle* of deflection (Δ) between the tangents, which is equal to the total *central angle* subtended by the entire length of the curve AB.

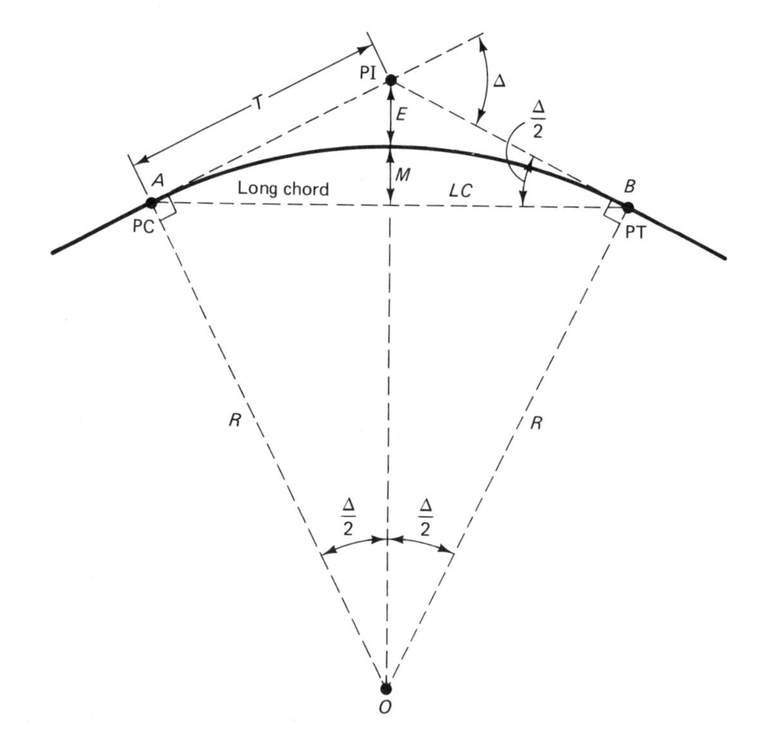

D: Degree of curve (see text)

E: External distance $= R\left(\sec \frac{\Delta}{2} - 1\right)$

M: Middle ordinate distance $= R\left(1 - \cos \frac{\Delta}{2}\right)$

T: Length of tangent $= R \tan \frac{\Delta}{2}$

L: Length of curve $= 100 \frac{\Delta}{D}$

LC: Long chord $= 2R \sin \frac{\Delta}{2}$

Figure 2.4.6 Simple circular curve.

Using the arc definition for the degree of curve, the following relationship between the length of the curve L, the degree of curve D, and the external angle Δ becomes apparent:

$$L = \frac{100\Delta}{D} \tag{2.4.4}$$

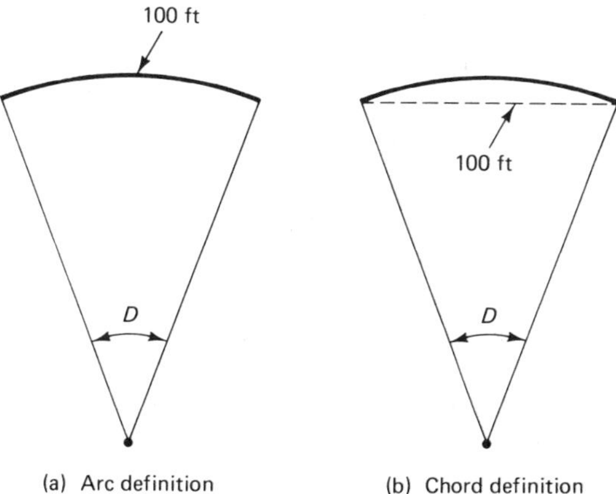

Figure 2.4.7 Degree of curve.

2.4.5 Determination of Design Radius

The requirement for lateral banking or *superelevating* of the cross section of curved paths (discussed in Subsection 2.2.3) imposes a constraint on the *minimum radius* that the curve may have. Equation 2.2.19 (reproduced as Eq. 2.4.5) expresses the relationship between the superelevation rate e, the design speed v, the coefficient of side friction f, and the curve radius R:

$$e + f = \frac{v^2}{gR} \tag{2.4.5}$$

An alternate specification of this formula found in United States design manuals is the following mixed-unit equation:

$$e + f = \frac{v^2}{15R} \tag{2.4.6}$$

where the design speed has units of miles per hour and the radius is specified in feet.

The maximum allowable design value for e (AASHTO, [2.2]) is 0.12 ft/ft and the suggested maximum is set at 0.10, but special conditions may override these values. For example, a maximum superelevation rate of 0.08 ft/ft may be more appropriate at localities where snow and ice conditions occur. The maximum design values for the coefficient of side friction depend on speed and range from about 0.17 at 20 mi/h to 0.11 at 80 mi/h. According to Eq. 2.4.5, the *minimum radius* for the selected design speed is

$$R_{\text{min}} = \frac{v^2}{g(e_{\text{max}} + f_{\text{max}})} \tag{2.4.7}$$

and the corresponding *maximum degree of curve* is given by Eq. 2.4.2.

From the perspective of the driver, the longer the radius the better. Thus the minimum radius does not represent the desired design radius. Where conditions permit the selection of a design radius that is longer than the minimum, the design value of e can be computed by:

$$e_{\text{des}} = \frac{v^2}{gR} - f \qquad \text{for } R > R_{\text{min}} \tag{2.4.8}$$

Example 2.15

Calculate the maximum degree of curve and the minimum radius of a simple circular curve with an external angle of 100°. The design speed is 50 mi/h, the corresponding value of f_{max} is 0.14, and the maximum design value for e is 0.10. Also calculate the design value for e for a curve that has a radius of 800 ft.

Solution By either Eq. 2.4.5 or Eq. 2.4.6,

$$R = 695 \text{ ft}$$

and by Eq. 2.4.2,

$$D = \frac{5729.58}{695} = 8.24°$$

The external angle does not enter these calculations.

For a radius of 800 ft, Eq. 2.4.8 yields

$$e_{\text{des}} = 0.21 - 0.14 = 0.07 \text{ ft/ft}$$

2.4.6 Superelevation Design

Banking of the cross section is needed on the curved portion of the facility but is not necessary along the tangent segments of the horizontal alignment. Consequently, a transition of the cross section from the normal crown on the tangent to a fully superelevated pavement on the curve must be developed.

As an illustration of superelevation design, consider a simple circular curve for the two-lane highway of Fig. 2.4.8. The cross section is at the normal crown at point A and fully superelevated at point E. Point B represents the intermediate condition, where the outside edge of the travel way has been rotated to the level of the center line; point C represents the condition where the outside edge, the center line, and the inside edge are aligned at a slope equal to the normal crown. Since the normal crown is milder than the design superelevation rate, the cross section must be further rotated until it reaches full superelevation at point E with an intermediate slope at the PC (i.e., point D). The distances AB and BE along the horizontal alignment are called the *tangent runout* and the *superelevation runoff,* respectively. The length of the superelevation runoff depends on the rate at which the cross section is rotated.

The selection of the length of superelevation runoff is not an exact science. Table 2.4.2 presents minimum lengths for *two-lane* rural highways having either 10- or 12-ft

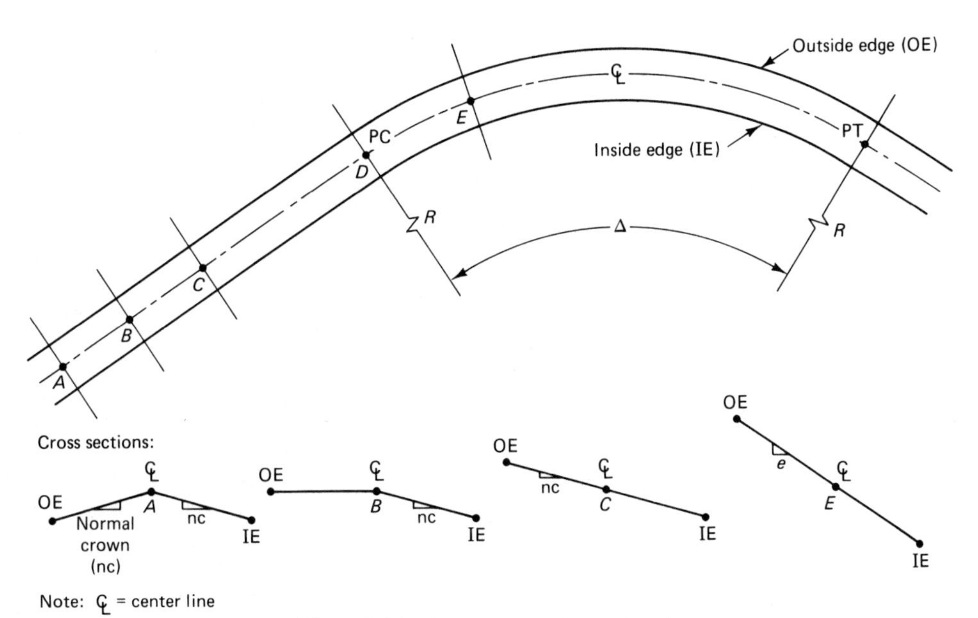

Figure 2.4.8 Development of superelevation.

TABLE 2.4.2 REQUIRED LENGTH OF SUPERELEVATION RUNOFF FOR TWO-LANE ROADS

Superelevation rate, e	L-Length of runoff (ft) for design speed (mi/h) of: 20	30	40	50	60	65	70
			12-ft lanes				
0.02	30	35	40	50	55	60	60
0.04	60	70	85	95	110	115	120
0.06	95	110	125	145	160	170	180
0.08	125	145	170	190	215	230	240
0.10	160	180	210	240	270	290	300
			10-ft lanes				
0.02	25	30	35	40	45	50	50
0.04	50	60	70	80	90	95	100
0.06	80	90	105	120	135	145	150
0.08	105	120	140	160	180	190	200
0.10	130	150	175	200	225	240	250
Design minimum length regardless of superelevation	50	100	125	150	175	190	200

SOURCE: AASHTO [2.2]; Table III-14, p. 200.

lanes. However, the same source [2.2] also suggests that for several practical and aesthetic reasons lengths between 100 and 250 ft may be more appropriate. The superelevation runoff lengths for three-, four-, and six-lane highways should be 1.2, 1.5, and 2.0 times those calculated for two-lane highways.

On simple curves, about two-thirds of the superelevation runoff is placed on the tangent and the rest on the curve. When transition curves are used, the superelevation runoff is developed on them. Transition curves (see Fig. 2.4.5) are usually introduced on high-speed curves. Most often, they are appropriate lengths of spirals with end radii of curvature that are consistent with those of the tangent (i.e., infinite at the TS and the ST) and the circular curve (i.e, R at the SC and the CS).

Figure 2.4.9 illustrates four common methods of developing the transition to full superelevation. For ease of presentation, the curved alignment is shown to be stretched out into a straight line. The first method rotates the pavement about the center line, the second about the inside edge, and the third about the outside edge. The fourth method applies to pavements that begin with a straight cross-section slope and are revolved about the outside edge. This type of cross slope may be found on the separate roadways that make up a divided multilane facility (see Fig. 2.4.4). The longitudinal profile of the pavement along the length of the highway corresponding to each of the four methods of obtaining full superelevation is shown in Fig. 2.4.9. In (a), the location of the inside edge, the center line, and the outside edge are shown relative to the elevation of the center line. In (b) and (c), the edge and center line profiles are shown relative to the unrotated centerline, that is, the "theoretical center line profile." At point A of the first three diagrams, the outside edge is as far below the center line as the inside edge, the difference in elevation being equal to the normal crown times the pavement width in each travel direction. At point B, the outside edge has reached the level of the center line, and at point C the outside edge is located as far above as the inside edge is below the center line. Finally, at point E the cross section is fully superelevated. The reverse of these profiles is found at the other end of the circular curve. As the note at the bottom of Fig. 2.4.9 suggests, the angular breaks should be rounded by smooth curves.

Example 2.16

Draw the longitudinal profile of the curve of Example 2.15 using the minimum radius for a two-lane rural highway given a normal crown of $\frac{1}{4}$ in./ft and a lane width $W = 12$ ft.

Solution With the calculated radius of 695 ft and an external angle of 100°, Eq. 2.4.1 gives a curve length of

$$L = 1213 \text{ ft}$$

For $e = 0.10$, a design speed $v = 50$ mi/h, and 12-ft lanes, the suggested minimum length of superelevation runoff (Table 2.4.2) is 240 ft. Place two-thirds (or 160 ft) of the runoff on each tangent at either end and the rest (80 ft) on the curve. This leaves $1213 - 2 \times 80 = 1053$ ft of the curve's length at full superelevation. Rotation about the center lines means that, at full superelevation, the inside and outside edges are offset by $W \times e = 12 \times 0.10 = 1.2$ ft from the center line. At the normal cross section, the two edges are $12 \times 0.25 = 3$ in. or 0.25 ft, below the center line. Simple calculations lead to a longitudinal profile, as shown in the accompanying figure.

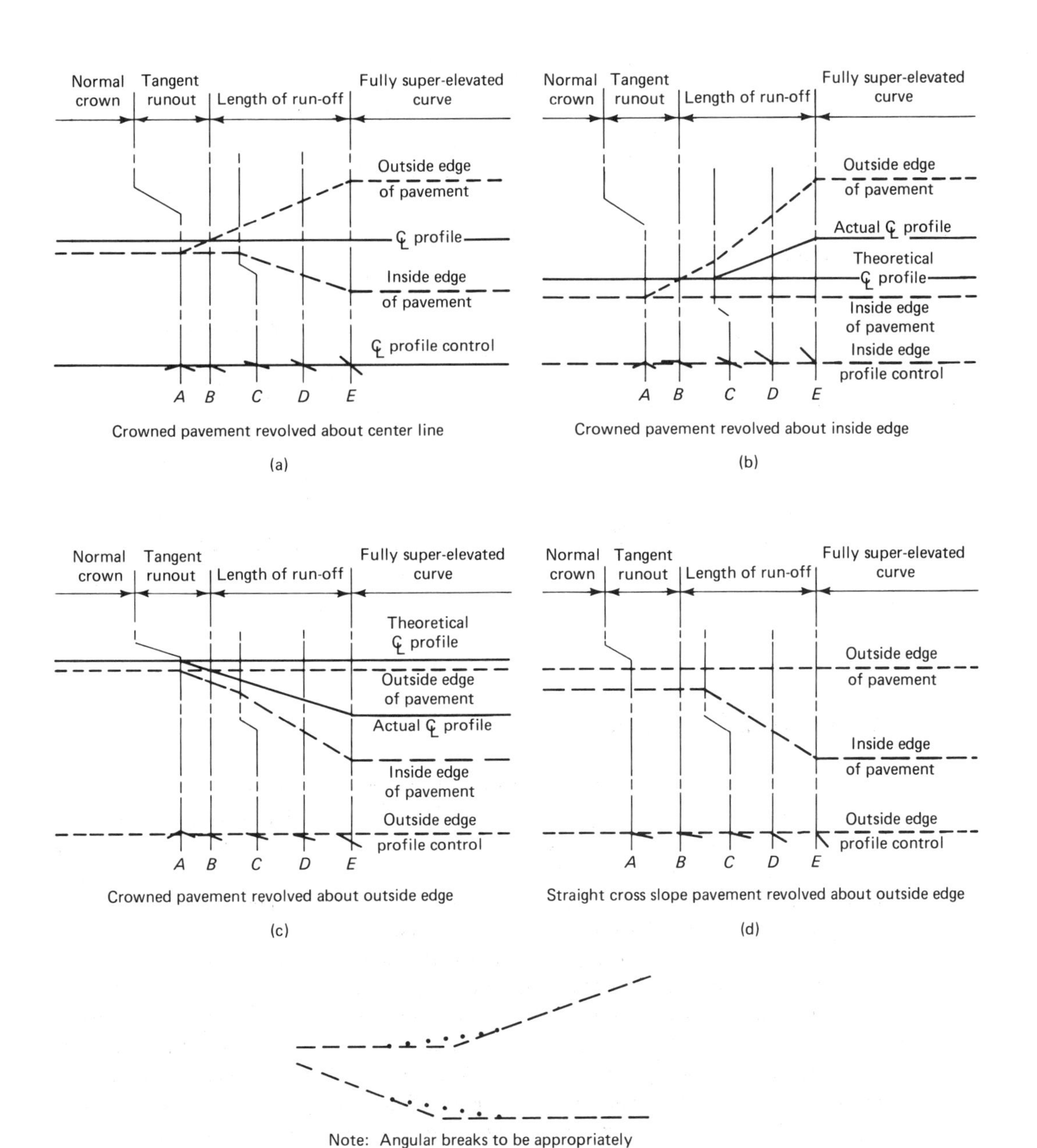

Figure 2.4.9 Methods of attaining full superelevation. (*SOURCE*: AASHTO [2.2], Fig. III-15, p. 205.)

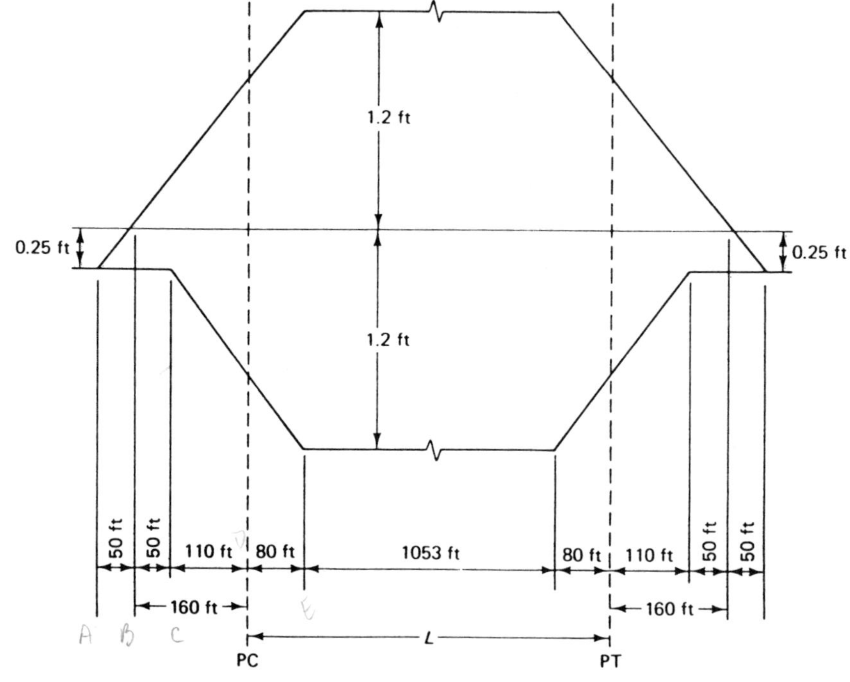

Figure P. 2.16

2.4.7 Vertical Alignment

The vertical alignment of highways and railways consists of *grade tangents* connected with *parabolic vertical curves*. The desirable maximum design grades and gradient change depend on facility type and on vehicular characteristics. For highways, the desirable maximum grades range from about 2% for freeways to about 6% for local streets. Higher grades may be unavoidable at locations of difficult topography, and the combined effect of gradient and the length over which it is sustained (i.e., the *length of grade*) must also be considered, especially at locations frequently used by heavy vehicles with limited climbing capability. Railroad design tolerates much smaller maximum grades, with about 4% representing the limit corresponding to the worst topography. The maximum grades for fixed-guideway transit systems are a function of the tract and wheel combinations employed. Rail-on-rail systems are similar to railroads, whereas rubber-tire systems approach the highway case. Some systems are specifically designed for very steep inclines.

The *length of a vertical curve is measured along the horizontal alignment,* and a point on the curve is specified by its station location on the horizontal alignment and its elevation from a datum. The beginning and end of a vertical curve are denoted, respectively, as the *vertical point of curvature* (VPC) and the *vertical point of tangency* (VPT), and the point where the grade lines intersect is known as the *vertical point of intersection* (VPI). Figure 2.4.10 describes a *symmetrical* vertical curve for which the grade tangents

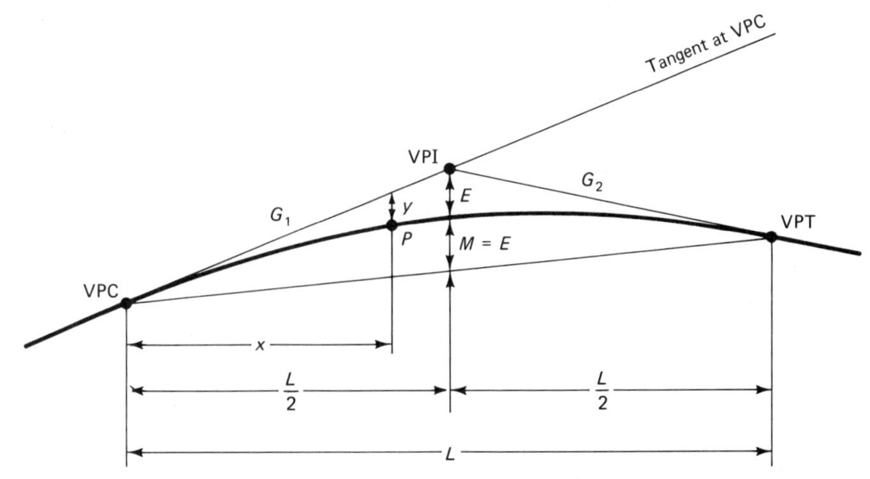

Figure 2.4.10 Symmetric vertical curve.

are equal; asymmetrical vertical curves are used only in places of unusual constraints. The figure applies to both *crest* curves, as shown, and *sag* curves, the latter being merely a reflection of the former with the curve lying above the VPI. In the case of symmetrical curves, a vertical line passing through the VPI bisects the length of the curve, but the high (or low) point of the curve does not necessarily lie directly below (or above) the VPI. For convenience, the horizontal alignment is shown as a straight line, but in reality it may be prescribing a curved path. Moreover, there is no necessary coincidence between the VPC, the VPI, and the VPT on one hand and the PC, the PI, and the PT on the other.

Denoting the *percent grade* at the VPC as G_1 and the percent grade at the VPT as G_2, the total change in grade

$$A = G_2 - G_1 \text{ percent} \tag{2.4.9}$$

is negative in the case of crest curves and positive in the case of sag curves. The ratio of the curve's length to the absolute value of the change in grade

$$K = \frac{L}{|A|} \tag{2.4.10}$$

specifies the *vertical curvature* of the curve. The *external distance* E from the VPI to the middle of the curve is

$$E = \frac{AL}{800} \text{ ft} \tag{2.4.11}$$

where L is the length of the curve in feet. Note that E is positive in the case of sag curves and negative in the case of crest curves, indicating that the midpoint of the curve lies above and below the VPI, respectively.

Other vertical *offsets* y between the grade tangent passing through the VPC and the vertical curve are calculated by

$$y = 4E\left(\frac{x}{L}\right)^2 \tag{2.4.12}$$

where x distance along the horizontal alignment from the VPC to the point of interest. The high (or low) point is located at a distance

$$X = \frac{LG_1}{G_1 - G_2} \qquad X \geqslant 0 \tag{2.4.13}$$

from the VPC. The *curve elevation* of any point P is computed by

$$\text{elevation of } P = \left[\text{elevation of VPC} + \left(\frac{G_1}{100}\right)x\right] + y \tag{2.4.14}$$

where the term in brackets represents the *tangent elevation* on the vertical tangent passing throught the VPC. In practice, curve elevations are computed at 25- or 50-ft intervals. In addition, the elevations of critical points such as the high or low point and points where necessary clearances below the pavement (e.g., drainage facilities such as culverts) or above the pavement (e.g., overpasses) are calculated.

Example 2.17

A 600-ft vertical curve connects a +4% grade to a −2% grade at station 25 + 60.55 and elevation 648.64 ft. Calculate the location and elevation of the VPC, the middle of the curve, the VPT, and the curve elevation at stations 24 + 00 and 27 + 00.

Solution The curve is a crest with $A = -2 - (+4) = -6\%$ and $K = \frac{600}{6} = 100$. The middle distance is $E = -4.5$ ft. The middle point of the curve is 4.5 ft below the VPI at sta. 25 + 60.55. The VPC and the VPT are located at either side of the VPI at distances of $L/2 = 300$ ft, or 3 stations. Hence, the VPC is $3 \times 4 = 12$ ft below the VPI at sta. 22 + 60.55, and the VPT is $3 \times 2 = 6$ ft below the VPI at sta. 28 + 60.55. The high point is located at a distance $X = 400$ ft, or 4 stations from the VPC (i.e., at sta. 26 + 60.55). The following table illustrates the use of Eqs. 2.4.12 and 2.4.14 to calculate the required curve elevations.

Point P (sta.)	x (ft)	Tangent elevation	Offset y (ft)	Curve elevation
22 + 60.55 (VPC)	000.00	636.64	0.00	636.64
24 + 00.00	139.45	642.22	−0.97	641.25
25 + 60.55	300.00	648.64	−4.50	644.14
26 + 60.55 (high)	400.00	652.64	−8.00	644.64
27 + 00.00	439.45	654.22	−9.66	644.56
28 + 60.55 (VPT)	600.00	660.64	−18.00	642.64

Discussion The accompanying figure shows the vertical curve. Offsets are measured in relation to the tangent at the VPC irrespective of whether the subject point P is to the right or to the left of the VPI. The negative sign of the offsets indicates that the curve elevations are below the tangent elevations. The application of Eq. 2.4.12 in the given table resulted in the same curve elevations for the middle point and for the VPT as those obtained by the calculations preceding the table. All the tabulated results could have been obtained by viewing the curve from the VPT. In that case, G_1 and G_2 would be $+2\%$ and -4%, respectively, the distance x would be measured to the left of the VPT, and the offsets would be measured from the tangent at the VPT.

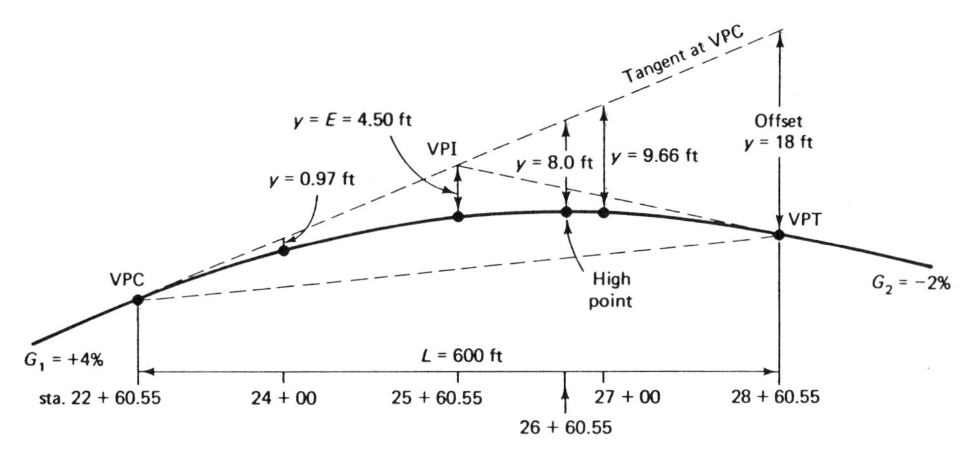

Figure P.2.17

2.4.8 Stopping and Passing Sight Distance

The design of a facility must ensure that drivers are provided with adequate *sight distances* to perceive dangerous situations ahead and to take preventive action. If an object is present in the vehicle's path, warranting that the vehicle be stopped to avoid a mishap, the object must be visible to the driver from a distance at least equal to a minimum *stopping sight distance*, S_s. Table 2.4.3 presents the design values suggested by AASHTO [2.2], which incorporate several practical approximations.

To overtake another vehicle safely on two-lane highways (i.e., one lane in each direction), a driver must consider the relative speeds and positions of the driver's own vehicle, the vehicle to be overtaken, and an oncoming vehicle in the opposite direction. A successful passing maneuver involves the elements shown in Fig. 2.4.11. The minimum *passing sight distances* suggested by AASHTO for various design speeds are also shown. Safe stopping sight distances must be adhered to at all points along the alignment and where adequate passing distances are not possible, no-passing zones must be established. Reducing the speed limit to assure adequate sight distances is also a possibility, but frequent speed limit changes should be avoided.

TABLE 2.4.3 STOPPING SIGHT DISTANCE

		Brake reaction				Stopping sight distance	
Design speed (mi/h)	Assumed speed for condition (mi/h)	Time (s)	Distance (ft)	Coefficient of friction f	Braking distance on level[a] (ft)	Computed[a] (ft)	Rounded for design (ft)
20	20–20	2.5	73.3– 73.3	0.40	33.3– 33.3	106.7–106.7	125–125
25	24–25	2.5	88.0– 91.7	0.38	50.5– 54.8	138.5–146.5	150–150
30	28–30	2.5	102.7–110.0	0.35	74.7– 85.7	177.3–195.7	200–200
35	32–35	2.5	117.3–128.3	0.34	100.4–120.1	217.7–248.4	225–250
40	36–40	2.5	132.0–146.7	0.32	135.0–166.7	267.0–313.3	275–325
45	40–45	2.5	146.7–165.0	0.31	172.0–217.7	318.7–382.7	325–400
50	44–50	2.5	161.3–183.3	0.30	215.1–277.8	376.4–461.1	400–475
55	48–55	2.5	176.0–201.7	0.30	256.0–336.1	432.0–537.8	450–550
60	52–60	2.5	190.7–220.0	0.29	310.8–413.8	501.5–633.8	525–650
65	55–65	2.5	201.7–238.3	0.29	347.7–485.6	549.4–724.0	550–725
70	58–70	2.5	212.7–256.7	0.28	400.5–583.3	613.1–840.0	625–850

[a]Different values for the same speed result from using unequal coefficients of friction.
SOURCE: AASHTO [2.2]; Table III-1, p. 138.

2.4.9 Geometrics of Sight Distance

On the horizontal plane, the available sight distance is affected by the presence of objects, embankments, and other restrictions, as shown by Fig. 2.4.12. The effect of curvature (i.e., either R or D) is captured by the inserted equations.

On crests, the vertical curvature of the facility itself causes sight restrictions, as illustrated by Fig. 2.4.13(a), which shows the line of sight between the driver's eyes (located at a distance h_1 above the pavement) and the top of an object of height h_2. For many years, the design specifications promulgated by AASHTO [2.9] provided for an eye height of 3.75 ft, an object height of 6 in. for the computation of stopping sight distance, and an object height of 4.5 ft for the computation of passing sight distance. The rationale for these values was that an object of less than 6 in. in height is lower than the undercarriage height of the vast majority of vehicles on the roadway, and a height of 4.5 ft represents the height of oncoming vehicles that are relevant to the passing maneuver. Because of changing vehicular dimensions, subsequent research has recommended a modification of these values. In 1984, AASHTO [2.2] lowered the values for the driver's eye height and the height of oncoming vehicles to 3.50 and 4.25 ft, respectively. The 6-in. object height involved in the calculation of stopping sight distances has been retained.

On sag curves the worst situation occurs at night when the line of sight is limited within the area of headlight illumination [Fig.2.4.13(b)].

In either case, the sight distance may be shorter, equal to, or longer than the length

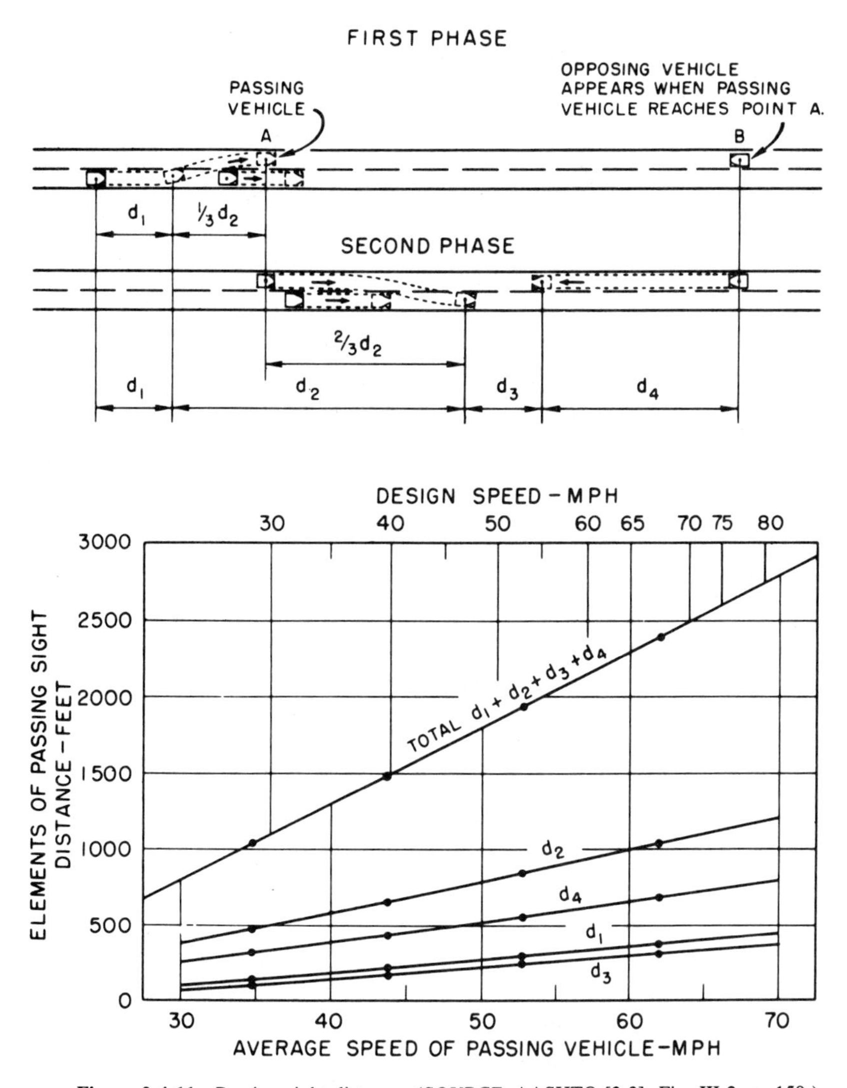

Figure 2.4.11 Passing sight distance. (*SOURCE*: AASHTO [2.2], Fig. III-2, p. 150.)

of the curve. The following equations can be used to calculate the minimum length of curve that satisfies a given sight-distance requirement:

Crest vertical curves:

$$L = \frac{|A|S^2}{200\left(\sqrt{h_1} + \sqrt{h_2}\right)^2} \qquad \text{for } S \leq L \qquad (2.4.15a)$$

S is defined (from speed)
L is calculated

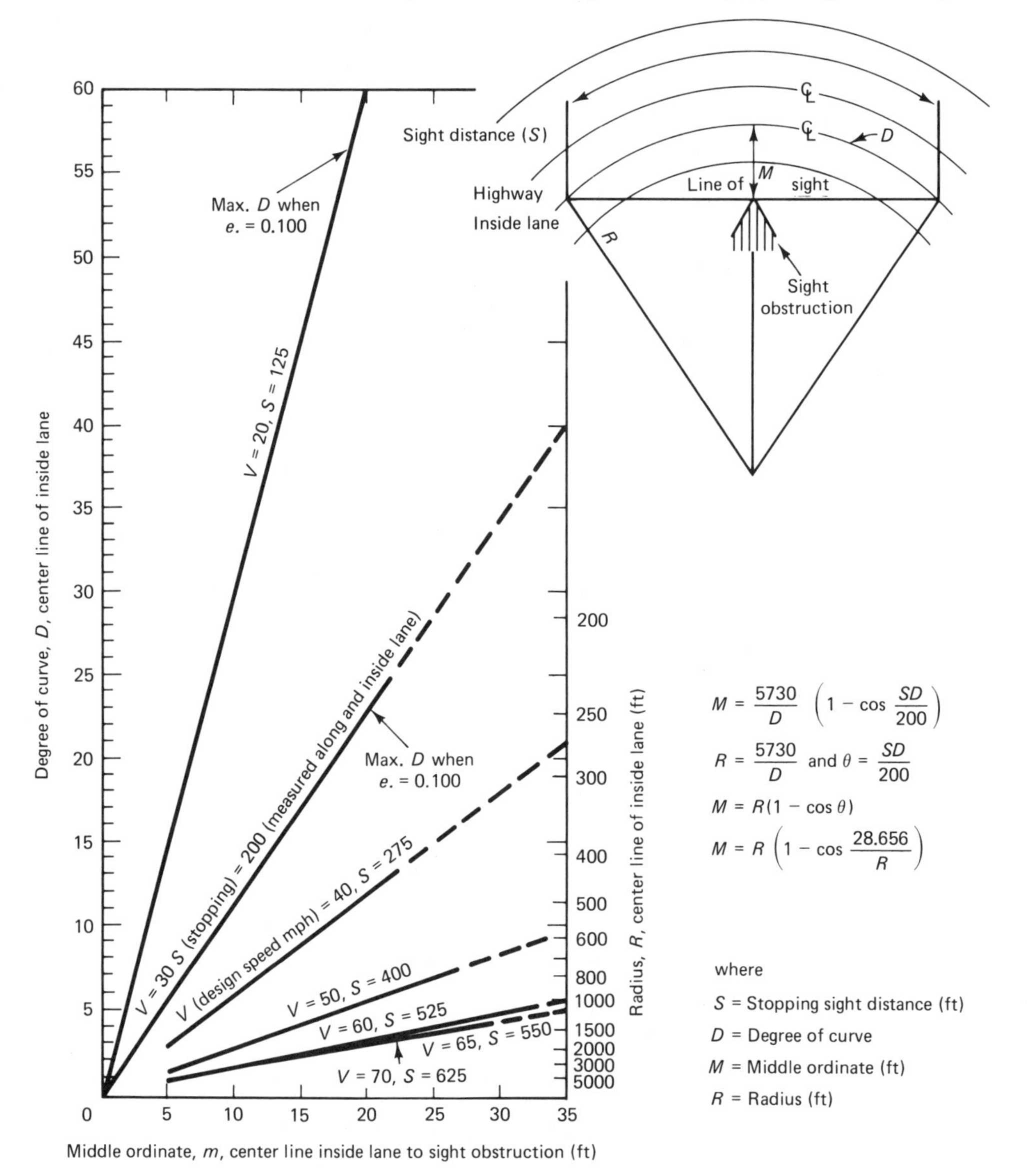

Figure 2.4.12 Geometry of horizontal sight distance. (*SOURCE*: AASHTO [2.2], Fig. III-25, p. 244.)

$$L = 2S - \frac{200\left(\sqrt{h_1} + \sqrt{h_2}\right)^2}{|A|} \qquad \text{for } S \geq L \tag{2.4.15b}$$

Sag vertical curves:

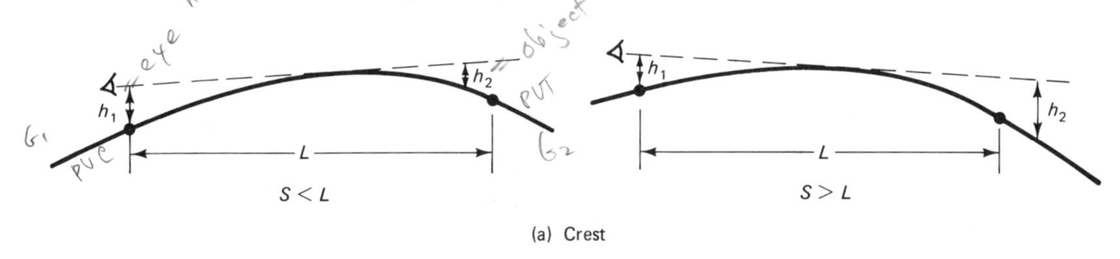

(a) Crest

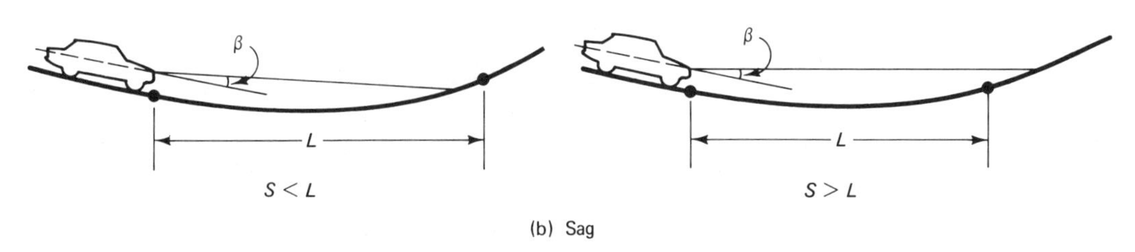

(b) Sag

Figure 2.4.13 Geometry of vertical sight distance.

$$L = \frac{|A|S^2}{200(h + S \tan \beta)} \qquad \text{for } S \leq L \qquad (2.4.16a)$$

$$L = 2S - \frac{200(h + S \tan \beta)}{|A|} \qquad \text{for } S \geq L \qquad (2.4.16b)$$

where L = length of curve (ft)

S = sight distance (ft)

$|A| = |G_2 - G_1|$ (%)

h_1 = height of driver's eyes (ft)

h_2 = height of object (ft)

h = headlight height (ft); approximately 2 ft

and

β = beam angle; approximately 1°

Figure 2.4.14 illustrates that stopping and passing distances may be measured directly on scaled horizontal and vertical profiles.

Example 2.18

For a design speed of 50 mi/h, determine the minimum length of a crest vertical curve with $A = -4\%$ that meets the 1984 AASHTO criteria for (a) stopping and (b) passing.

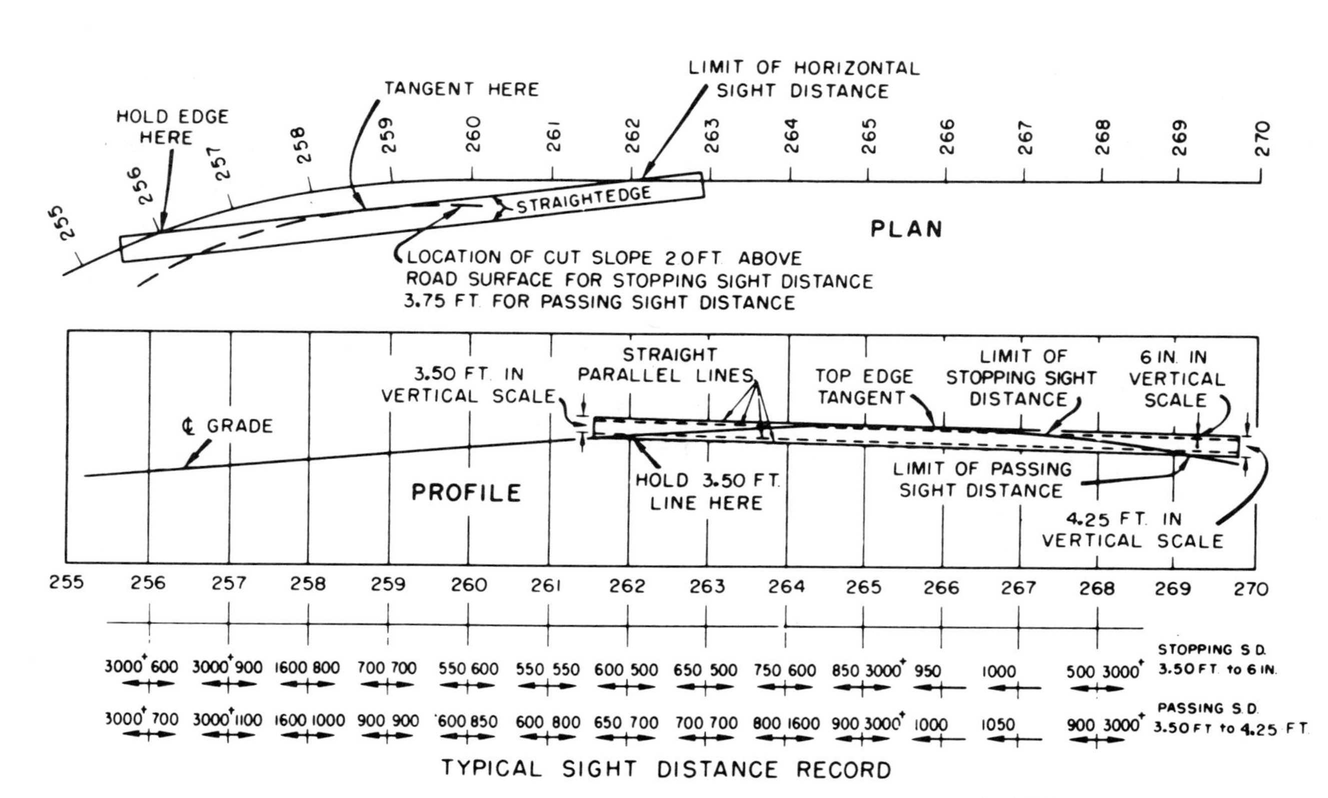

Figure 2.4.14 Scaling and recording sight distances. (*SOURCE*: AASHTO [2.2], Fig. III-3, p. 161.)

Solution

(a) Since A is negative, the curve is a crest. Conservatively, a minimum stopping sight distance of 475 ft is obtained from Table 2.4.3 and substituted in Eqs. 2.4.15 along with the AASHTO recommended heights of $h_1 = 3.50$ and $h_2 = 0.5$ ft:

$$\text{for } S \leqslant L: \quad L = 679 \text{ ft}$$

$$\text{for } S \geqslant L: \quad L = 618 \text{ ft}$$

The first answer is selected because it satisfies the contraint, that is, $475 < 679$.

(b) The minimum recommended passing sight distance of about 1700 ft is obtained from Fig. 2.4.11 for a design speed of 50 mi/h. With $h_1 = 3.50$ and $h_2 = 4.25$ ft, the crest equations yield:

$$\text{for } S \leqslant L: \quad L = 3738 \text{ ft}$$

$$\text{for } S \geqslant L: \quad L = 2627 \text{ ft}$$

Since the first satisfies the condition $S \leqslant L$, it gives the proper answer.

2.4.10 Discussion of Alignment Design

So far, the basic elements of the horizontal and vertical design have been discussed separately. These two aspects of the three-dimensional control line must be integrated and drawn to a suitable scale to aid in the eventual layout and construction of the facility. Figure 2.4.15 illustrates the standard plan and profile drawings of the center line of a two-lane highway.

On the horizontal plane, the highway segment prescribes a circular curve to which 400-ft transition spirals have been introduced. The station locations of important points are clearly marked, and the characteristics of the curves are specified. The location of the PI is fixed and referenced to local monuments, and other surveying benchmarks are included. The property lines that are crossed by the highway and existing structures are also identified.

The "stretched-out" vertical profile of the center line is shown on the lower portion of the figure: It consists of a crest curve connecting a +4% grade and a −4% grade, followed by a sag curve between the −4% grade and a +5.02% grade. The irregular solid line represents the existing ground elevation to which the vertical alignment or grade line conforms as much as possible. Fitting the grade line to the existing ground, however, must meet maximum grade and adequate sight-distance criteria as explained earlier. Another major consideration in grade control is related to the amounts of earthwork required. Economic considerations warrant that *cut* and *fill* should be balanced within the limits of the construction area as much as possible to avoid the cost of bringing extra material (*borrow*) to the site and the cost of removing excess excavated quantities to locations that lie outside the site (*overhaul*).

The process of selecting, designing, and locating the final alignment of a facility connecting two points is a highly complex undertaking. It begins with a determination

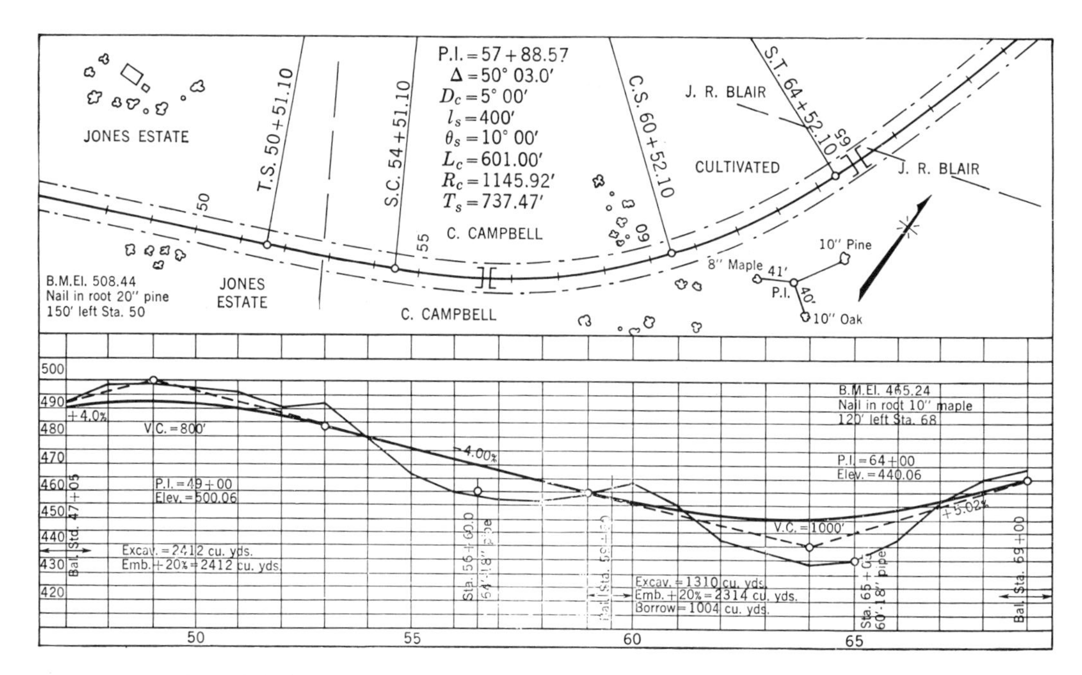

Figure 2.4.15 Typical plan and profile of a highway. (*SOURCE*: T. F. Hickerson [2.12], *Route Surveys and Design*, 4th ed., McGraw-Hill, 1959, Fig. 8, p. 55. Reproduced with permission of the publisher.)

that such a facility is, in fact, needed. Given that the need for a facility has been established, a sequence of interrelated steps follows. These entail the collection and study of the necessary information, including topographic maps, the conducting of photogrammetric reconnaissance surveys, the identification of alternative alignments, the preliminary selection of the preferred alignment, the surveying and mapping of the corridor through which the preferred alignment passes, and the design of the final alignment. These activities take place within a variety of economic, legal, and environmental constraints. For example, federal legislation requires that proposed facilities should have a minimum impact on environmentally sensitive areas, natural habitats of endangered species, and sites of historical and archaeological significance. Only after these and other socioeconomic requirements have been met in a satisfactory manner would the phases of detailed surveying and route layout and, finally, construction proceed.

2.4.11 Delineation of Vehicular Paths

In addition to the design of the horizontal and vertical alignment of a highway, geometric design includes the delineation of vehicular paths within the travel way to conform to the physical (space) requirements of vehicles and to the steering tendencies of drivers. Figure 2.4.16 illustrates the practice of *curve widening* that is recommended for sharp

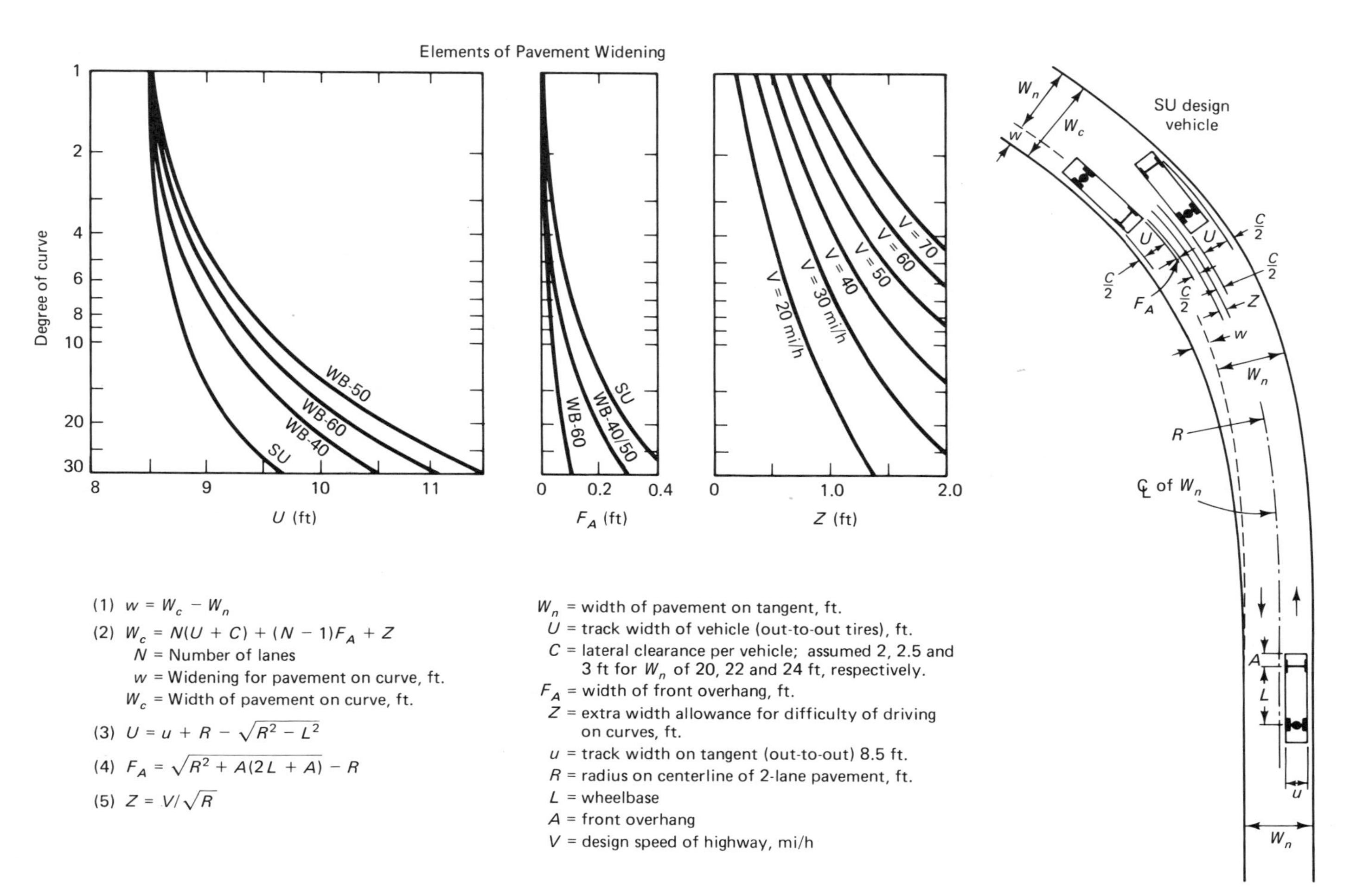

Figure 2.4.16 Curve widening. (*SOURCE*: AASHTO [2.2], Fig. III-24, p. 239.)

curves to allow for the fact that the vehicle's front and rear wheels do not track exactly the same trajectories and in response to a tendency on the part of drivers to steer away from the pavement's edge.

The proper delineation of vehicular paths is accomplished by a number of devices, including longitudinal and transverse pavement markings, raised medians and islands, curbing, guardrails, and the like. These devices are accompanied by appropriate directional signs and other pavement markings, such as painted turning arrows [2.10].

The most common pavement markings in the direction of travel are *yellow* and *white lines,* the former separating paths in opposing directions and the latter delineating paths in the same direction. In either cease, *solid lines* designate segments where path changes for the purpose of either passing or lane changing are prohibited. *Broken lines* permit the execution of such maneuvers.

At intersection and interchange areas where conflicting paths are found, special design efforts are necessary either to minimize the number of conflicting movements or to reduce their severity. Figure 2.4.17 shows the major types of freeway interchanges, where, by introducing special directional roadways, the more severe *crossing conflicts* are eliminated in favor of the less severe *merging* and *diverging conflicts*. This practice often necessitates the construction of *grade-separated* facilities, i.e., underpasses and overpasses. Additionally, *auxiliary lanes,* such as acceleration and deceleration lanes, permit safe speed changes and reduce the speed differences between conflicting vehicles.

The conflicts in the area of *at-grade* intersections are typically reduced by the spatial separation of paths (*channelization*) and by the temporal separation of conflicting movements (e.g., by *signal control*).

2.4.12 Design Vehicles

Whether designing special roadways at an interchange or channelizing an at-grade intersection, it is important to consider the turning characteristics of the vehicles that are expected to use the facility. For purposes of design consistency, the weights, dimensions, and operating characteristics of ten types of vehicles have been selected to represent the wide variety of vehicular types that normally use the highway system. Table 2.4.4 summarizes the dimensions of these design vehicles, and Fig. 2.4.18 shows the space requirements for a W-60 design vehicle when executing a 90° and a 180° turn at the minimum turning radius for that vehicle that correspond to low speeds. The selection of the proper design vehicle for a particular application must allow for the great majority of the vehicles that are expected to use the facility. For example, while the BUS design vehicle may be adequate for downtown streets, the largest WB-60 vehicle is appropriate for the design of truck routes.

2.4.13 Channelization of At-Grade Intersections

Channelization has been defined as "the separation or regulation of conflicting traffic movements into definite paths by means of traffic islands or pavement markings to facilitate the safe and orderly movements of both vehicles and pedestrians" [2.11].

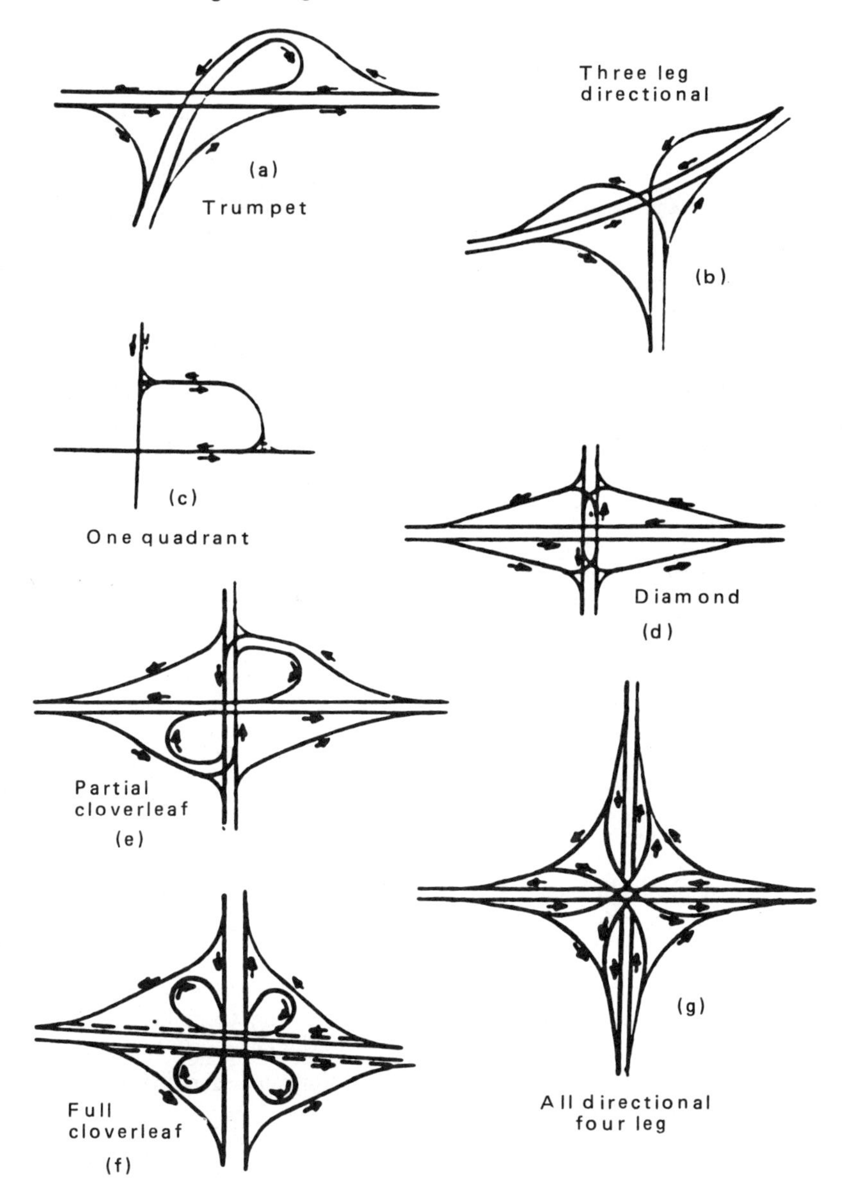

Figure 2.4.17 Interchange types. (*SOURCE*: AASHTO [2.2], Fig. X-1, p. 898.)

At-grade intersections are classified into Y-, T-, four-leg, multileg, and rotary intersections. Within each category, a very large number of variations is possible and, in fact, no two intersections are exactly the same. Consequently, each intersection must be treated individually as a separate design problem. Each design consists of the placement of combinations of triangular and elongated islands, the latter including medians and median treatments, edge-of-pavement treatments, pavement markings, and associated signing and traffic controls.

TABLE 2.4.4 DESIGN VEHICLES

		Dimension (ft)									
		Overall			Overhang						
Design vehicle type	Symbol	Height	Width	Length	Front	Rear	WB_1	WB_2	S	T	WB_3
Passenger car	P	4.25	7	19	3	5	11				
Single unit truck	SU	13.5	8.5	30	4	6	20				
Single unit bus	BUS	13.5	8.5	40	7	8	25				
Articulated bus	A-BUS	10.5	8.5	60	8.5	9.5	18		4[a]	20[a]	
Combination trucks											
Intermediate semitrailer	WB-40	13.5	8.5	50	4	6	13	27			
Large semitrailer	WB-50	13.5	8.5	55	3	2	20	30			
"Double bottom" semi-trailer—full-trailer	WB-60	13.5	8.5	65	2	3	9.7	20	4[b]	5.4[b]	20.9
Recreation vehicles											
Motor home	MH		8	30	4	6	20				
Car and camper trailer	P/T		8	49	3	10	11	5	18		
Car and boat trailer	P/B		8	42	3	8	11	5	15		

[a]Combined dimension 24, split is estimated.

[b]Combined dimension 9, 4, split is estimated.

WB_1, WB_2, WB_3 are effective vehicle wheelbases.

S is the distance from the rear effective axle to the hitch point.

T is the distance from the hitch point to the lead effective axle of the following unit.

SOURCE: AASHTO [2.2]; Table II-1, p. 21.

The channelization devices must be of sufficient number and size to command the attention of motorists, but cluttered designs containing too many small islands and signs must be avoided. The design should provide natural and well-defined paths to minimize vehicle wander. It must enhance the confidence and convenience of drivers by affording them adequate sight distances, by clearly guiding them into the proper channels of movements, and by preventing the choice of prohibited paths. The possibility of multiple paths between the same two points must be eliminated, and drivers should not be required to make many decisions at the same time.

Whenever possible, especially at high-speed locations, auxiliary storage lanes should be provided for turning vehicles that are required either to slow down or to stop. Moreover, the angles and areas of conflict must be controlled. The length over which merging and diverging movements are accommodated must be of adequate length, and these movements must be confined to low angles. Crossing paths should minimize the area of conflict and, hence, be as close to right angles as possible.

Among the channelization concepts illustrated by Fig. 2.4.19 are the rounded or bullet-shaped median openings and the corner curb radii that are designed to fit the paths of vehicles as closely as possible. The corners of islands are also rounded, and the island edges on the approach side are slightly offset to guide, or "catch," the vehicle into the proper channel.

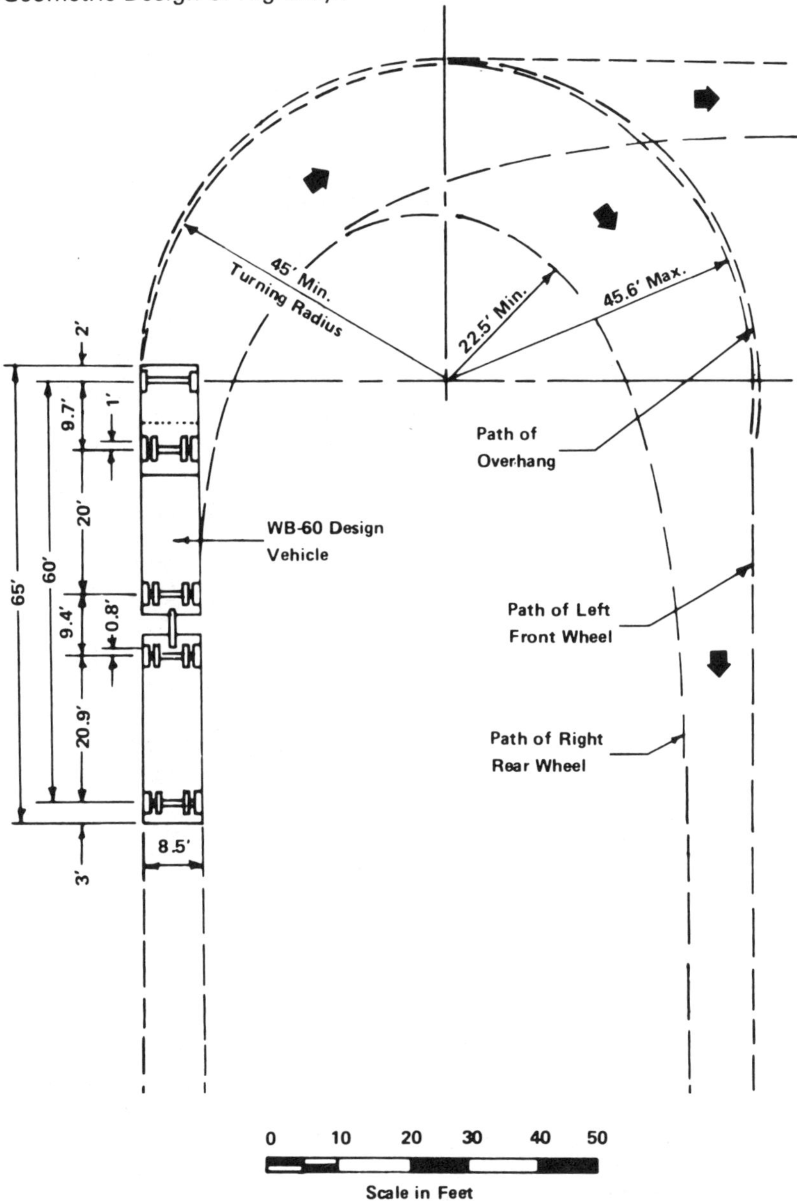

Figure 2.4.18 Minimum turning path for W-60 design vehicle. (*SOURCE*: AASHTO [2.2], Fig. II-7, p. 31.)

2.4.14 Three-Centered Curves

The pavement edge along turning roadways must also be consistent with the path of the design vehicle. Simple circular curves are sufficient for the smaller vehicles and for small angles of turn. Compound curves are more appropriate for larger vehicles and for angles

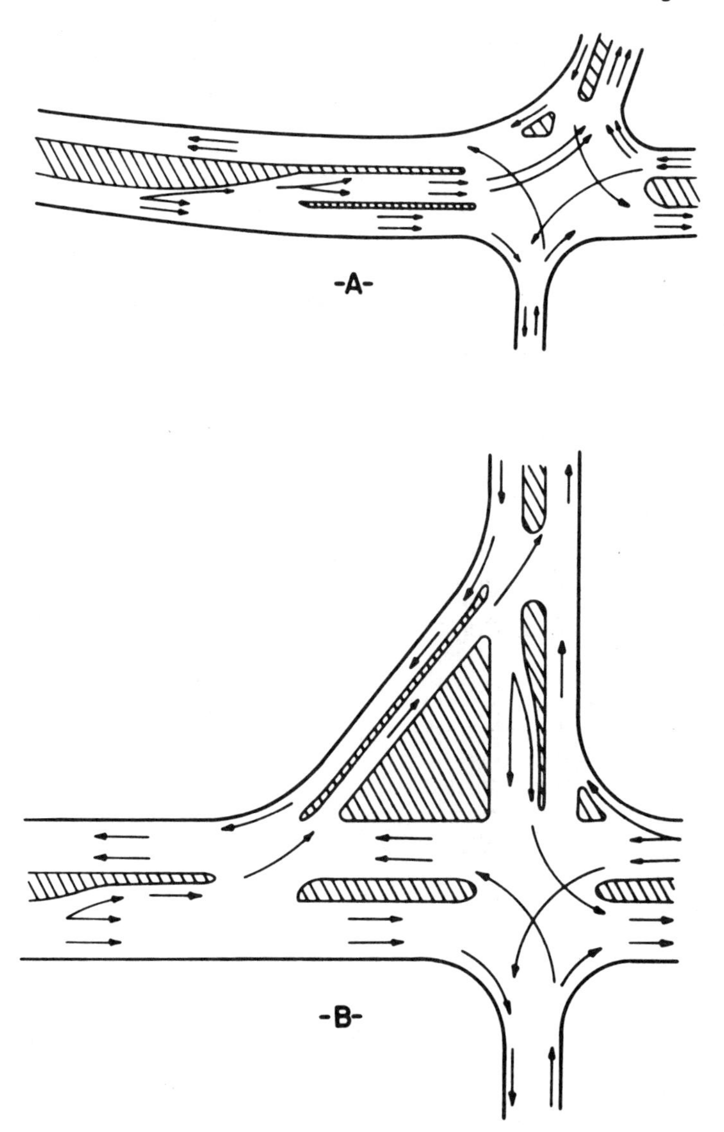

Figure 2.4.19 Example of channelization. (*SOURCE*: AASHTO [2.2], Fig. IX-50, p. 839.)

of turn greater than 90°. The three-centered compound curve is widely used under these conditions. It consists of three smoothy connected simple curves of different radii lying on the same side of the two tangents that intersect at an external angle Δ (Fig. 2.4.20). It can be *symmetrical* or *asymmetrical* depending on whether the first and third curves are the same or different.

Figure 2.4.21 is a more detailed drawing of the curve's geometry. The middle curve is shown to fit two tangents intersecting at point I and parallel to the original at

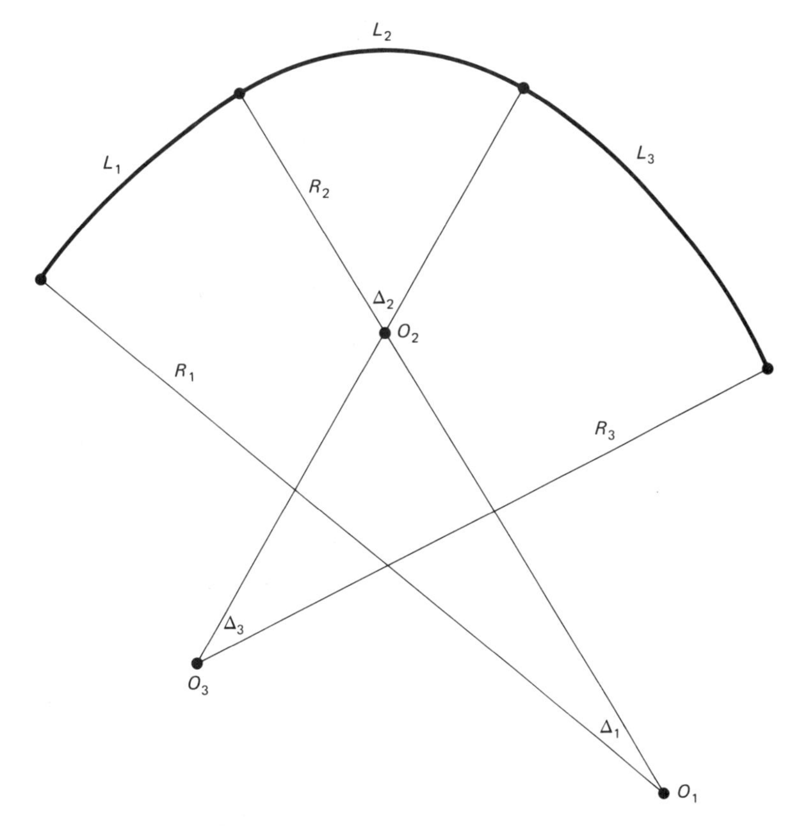

Figure 2.4.20 Three-centered curve.

offset distances of P_1 and P_2. Thus the central angle of arc AB is equal to the total external angle. The first simple curve begins at point E and shares the same tangent with the second simple curve at point C. Similarly, the third curve is tangent to the middle curve at point D. The central angle subtended by arcs AC and DB are equal to the respective central angles of the outlying simple curves and

$$\Delta_1 + \Delta_2 + \Delta_3 = \Delta \tag{2.4.17}$$

Each of the simple curves may be described in terms of the variables discussed in relation to Fig. 2.4.6. Thus the external distances T_1, T_2, and T_3 of each component curve segment can be computed by:

$$T_i = R_i \tan\left(\frac{\Delta_i}{2}\right) \tag{2.4.18}$$

and the external angles for each curve are as shown.

The expression for the offset $P_1 = EL$ may be derived as follows:

$$LJ = KE = R_2$$

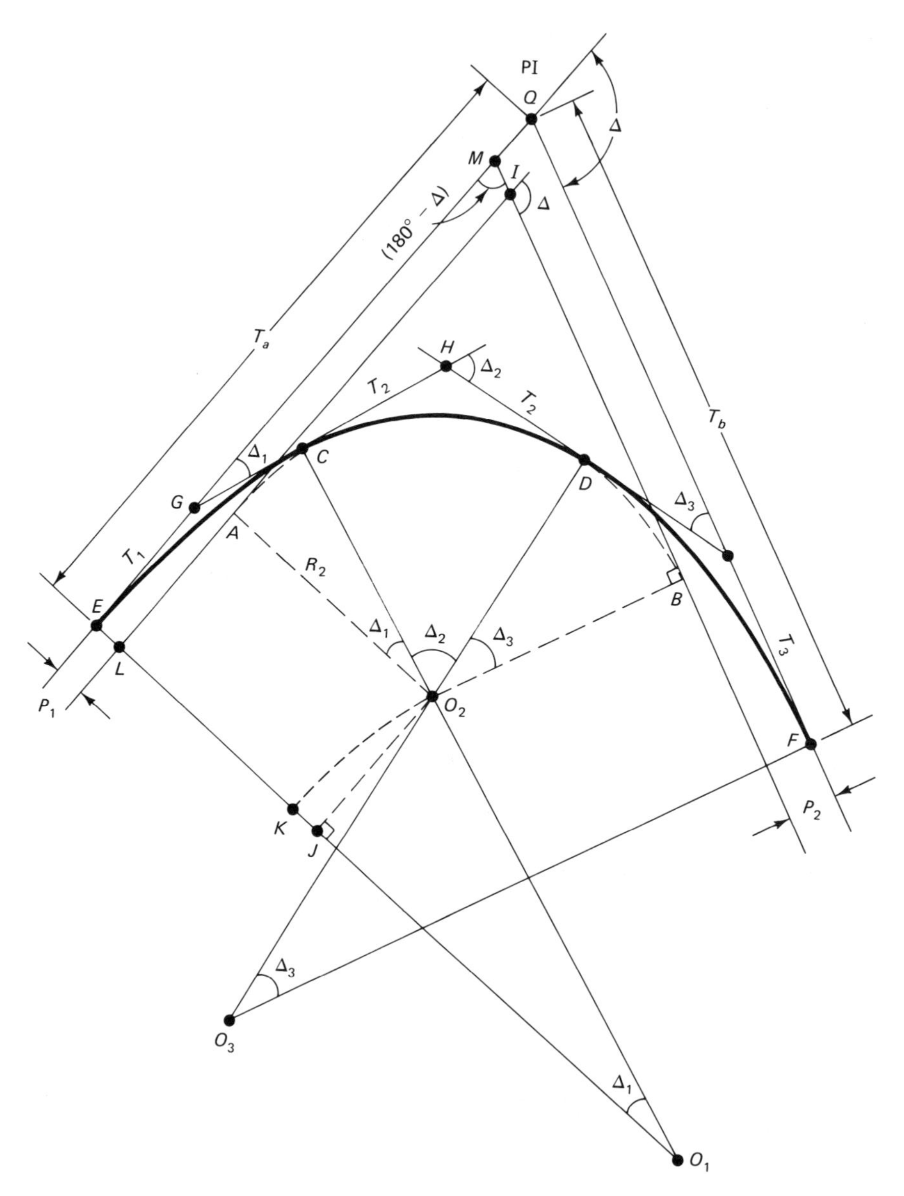

Figure 2.4.21 Geometry of three-centered curves.

Hence

$$P_1 = EL = KJ$$

or

$$P_1 = KO_1 - O_1O_2 \cos\Delta_2$$
$$= (R_1 - R_2) - (R_1 - R_2)\cos\Delta_2$$

and (2.4.19a)

$$P_1 = (R_1 - R_2)(1 - \cos\Delta_2)$$

Similarly,

$$P_2 = (R_3 - R_2)(1 - \cos\Delta_3) \tag{2.4.19b}$$

Finally, it can be shown that the total external distances T_a and T_b are

$$T_a = \frac{R_3 - R_1\cos\Delta - (R_3 - R_2)\cos\Delta_3 - (R_2 - R_1)\cos(\Delta_3 + \Delta_2)}{\sin\Delta} \tag{2.4.20a}$$

$$T_b = \frac{R_1 - R_3\cos\Delta - (R_1 - R_2)\cos\Delta_1 - (R_2 - R_3)\cos(\Delta_1 + \Delta_2)}{\sin\Delta} \tag{2.4.20b}$$

For symmetrical curves,

$$T_a = T_b = \frac{R_1 \sin\frac{\Delta}{2} - (R_1 - R_2)\sin\frac{\Delta_2}{2}}{\cos\frac{\Delta}{2}} \tag{2.4.21}$$

Table 2.4.5 lists the edge-of-pavement curve designs corresponding to combinations of design vehicle and degree of curve for vehicle speeds of 10 mi/h or less.

2.5 SUMMARY

This chapter reviewed the fundamental kinematic and kinetic equations of particle motion and developed the formulas that govern the rectilinear and curvilinear motion of single vehicles. Basic models of human factors were then introduced to illustrate how driver responses to stimuli in the driving environment can be incorporated in highway design. The factors examined included driver perception-reaction, visual acuity, and responses

TABLE 2.4.5 MINIMUM EDGE-OF-PAVEMENT DESIGN CURVES
Simple Curves

Angle of turn (degrees)	Design vehicle	Simple curve radius	Simple curve radius with taper		
			Radius (ft)	Offset (ft)	Taper (ft:ft)
30	P	60	—	—	—
	SU	100	—	—	—
	WB-40	150	—	—	—
	WB-50	200	—	—	—
	WB-55	275	—	—	—
45	P	50	—	—	—
	SU	75	—	—	—
	WB-40	120	—	—	—
	WB-50	—	120	2.0	15:1
	WB-55	—	140	2.0	15:1
60	P	40	—	—	—
	SU	60	—	—	—
	WB-40	90	—	—	—
	WB-50	—	95	3.0	15:1
	WB-55	—	110	3.0	15:1
75	P	35	25	2.0	10:1
	SU	55	45	2.0	10:1
	WB-40	—	60	2.0	15:1
	WB-50	—	65	3.0	15:1
	WB-55	—	90	3.0	15:1
90	P	30	20	2.5	10:1
	SU	50	40	2.0	10:1
	WB-40	—	45	4.0	10:1
	WB-50	—	60	4.0	15:1
	WB-55	—	75	4.0	15:1
105	P	—	20	2.5	8:1
	SU	—	35	3.0	10:1
	WB-40	—	40	4.0	10:1
	WB-50	—	55	4.0	15:1
	WB-55	—	65	5.0	15:1
120	P	—	20	2.0	10:1
	SU	—	30	3.0	10:1
	WB-40	—	35	5.0	8:1
	WB-50	—	45	4.0	15:1
	WB-55	—	50	6.0	15:1
135	P	—	20	1.5	15:1
	SU	—	30	4.0	8:1
	WB-40	—	30	8.0	6:1
	WB-50	—	40	6.0	10:1
	WB-55	—	45	7.0	10:1
150	P	—	18	2.0	10:1
	SU	—	30	4.0	8:1
	WB-40	—	30	6.0	8:1
	WB-50	—	35	7.0	6:1
	WB-55	—	40	7.0	8:1

TABLE 2.4.5 *(continued)*

Angle of turn (degrees)	Design vehicle	Simple curve radius	Simple curve radius with taper		
			Radius (ft)	Offset (ft)	Taper (ft:ft)
180	P	—	15	0.5	20:1
	SU	—	30	1.5	10:1
	WB-40	—	20	9.5	5:1
	WB-50	—	25	9.5	5:1
	WB-55	—	25	14.5	5:1

Three-Centered Curves

Angle of turn (degrees)	Design vehicle	3-centered compound		3-centered compound	
		Curve radii (ft)	Symmetric offset (ft)	Curve radii (ft)	Asymmetric offset (ft)
30	P	—	—	—	—
	SU	—	—	—	—
	WB-40	—	—	—	—
	WB-50	—	—	—	—
	WB-55	—	—	—	—
45	P	—	—	—	—
	SU	—	—	—	—
	WB-40	—	—	—	—
	WB-50	200–100–200	3.0	—	—
	WB-55	200–120–200	3.0	140–100–300	1.0–1.5
60	P	—	—	—	—
	SU	—	—	—	—
	WB-40	—	—	—	—
	WB-50	200–75–200	5.5	200–75–275	2.0–6.0
	WB-55	200–85–200	5.0	120–80–240	1.0–7.5
75	P	100–25–100	2.0	—	—
	SU	120–45–120	2.0	—	—
	WB-40	120–45–120	5.0	120–45–200	2.0–6.5
	WB-50	150–50–150	6.0	150–50–225	2.0–10.0
	WB-55	200–70–200	7.0	120–60–200	2.0–10.0
90	P	100–20–100	2.5	—	—
	SU	120–40–120	2.0	—	—
	WB-40	120–40–120	5.0	120–40–200	2.0–6.0
	WB-50	180–40–180	6.0	120–40–200	2.0–10.0
	WB-55	200–65–200	7.0	100–55–260	2.0–10.0
105	P	100–20–100	2.5	—	—
	WU	100–35–100	3.0	—	—
	WB-40	100–35–100	5.0	100–55–200	2.0–8.0
	WB-50	180–45–180	8.0	150–40–210	2.0–10.0
	WB-55	240–50–240	8.0	100–45–500	4.0–10.0
120	P	100–20–100	2.0	—	—
	SU	100–30–100	3.0	—	—
	WB-40	120–30–120	6.0	100–30–180	2.0–9.0

TABLE 2.4.5 *(continued)*

Three-Centered Curves

		3-centered compound		3-centered compound	
Angle of turn (degrees)	Design vehicle	Curve radii (ft)	Symmetric offset (ft)	Curve radii (ft)	Asymmetric offset (ft)
	WB-50	180–40–180	8.5	150–35–220	2.0–12.0
	WB-55	400–40–400	10.0	100–35–500	6.0–15.0
135	P	100–20–100	1.5	—	—
	SU	100–30–100	4.0	—	—
	WB-40	120–30–120	6.5	100–25–180	3.0–13.0
	WB-50	160–35–160	9.0	130–30–185	3.0–14.0
	WB-55	300–35–300	10.0	100–35–400	3.0–15.0
150	P	75–85–75	2.0	—	—
	SU	100–30–100	4.0	—	—
	WB-40	100–30–100	6.0	90–25–160	1.0–12.0
	WB-50	160–35–160	7.0	120–30–180	3.0–14.0
	WB-55	300–40–300	9.5	120–30–400	7.0–16.0
180	P	50–15–50	0.5	—	—
	SU	100–30–100	1.5	—	—
	WB-40	100–20–100	9.5	85–20–150	6.0–13.0
	WB-50	130–25–130	9.5	100–25–180	6.0–13.0
	WB-55	300–25–300	14.6	180–35–200	10.0–12.0

SOURCE: AASHTO [2.2]; Tables IX-1 and IX-2, pp. 735–737.

to laterally placed objects. Perception-reaction was shown to affect the total distance covered by a stopping vehicle and the presence of "dilemma zones" at signalized intersections; laterally located objects create a tendency for the driver to slow down and to steer the vehicle away from them even when the vehicle is not on a collision course with the objects.

The basic aspects of geometric design, that is, the proportioning of the visible elements of fixed facilities, were covered next. The elements described included cross-section design, horizontal alignment, superelevation, vertical alignment, and channelization. To ensure safe operation, driver needs were shown to be met through the provision of adequate stopping and passing sight distances, and by the proper selection and placement of channelization treatments, including pavement markings, elongated and triangular islands, and medians. Vehicle characteristics are reflected in the selection of appropriate design vehicles.

2.6 EXERCISES

1. Given the acceleration pattern shown, (a) derive and plot the relationship between speed and time and (b) calculate the total distance traveled during the 20-s interval. At $t = 0$ the vehicle was traveling at 12 mi/h.

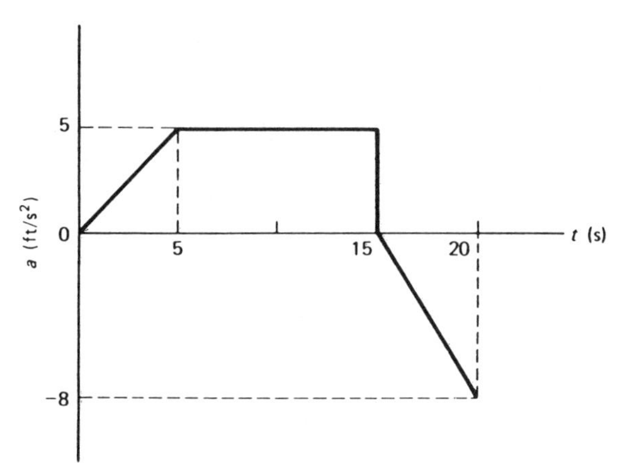

Figure E.2.1

2. The driver of a car traveling up a 2% grade at an initial speed V_0 applied the brakes abruptly and the vehicle slid to a complete stop at an average deceleration of 8 ft/s^2. Was the pavement wet or dry?

3. At time $t = 0$ two persons entered the elevator of the tower shown in the accompanying figure. The first person rode to the restaurant level. The second person went to the observation deck. Plot the time-elevation and the velocity-elevation diagrams for each of the two persons considering that the elevator started up 3 s after they entered, made no intermediate stops between the ground and the restaurant levels, and stayed for 6 s at the restaurant level. The elevator manufacturer's brochure provides the following technological specifications: acceleration = 5 ft/s^2; deceleration = 4 ft/s^2; and maximum cruising velocity = 20 ft/s.

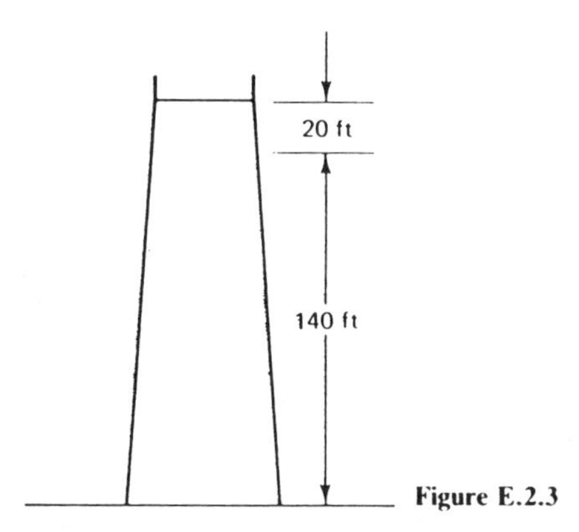

Figure E.2.3

4. A rapid-transit system uses a tubular guideway in which a close-fitting vehicle is propelled by a pressure difference between the front and rear cross-sectional areas. At departure time t_0,

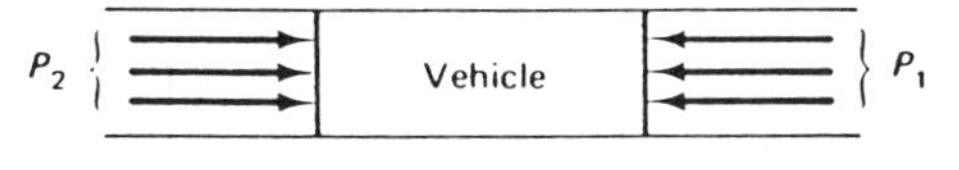

(a)

Figure E.2.4a

the pressure difference $P_2 - P_1$ is instantaneously raised from zero to some initial level and the vehicle accelerates forward. The pressure difference is then decreased until it reaches zero and the vehicle attains its cruising velocity, which is sustained until the vehicle begins its deceleration toward the next station. Neglecting friction, (a) express acceleration, velocity,

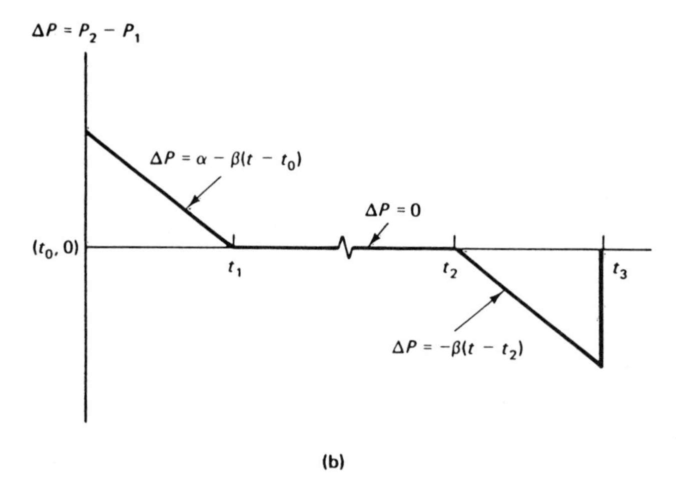

Figure E.2.4b

and distance traveled as functions of time, and (b) sketch the relationship between velocity and time for the movement between two stations 1 mi apart. Use the following data.

$$
\begin{aligned}
A &= \text{cross-sectional area of the vehicle} = 100 \text{ ft}^2 \\
W &= \text{vehicle weight} = 40{,}000 \text{ lb} \\
\alpha &= 100 \text{ lb/ft}^2 \\
\beta &= 3.33 \text{ lb/ft}^2\text{-s}
\end{aligned}
$$

5. A car collided with a telephone pole and left 20-ft skid marks on the dry pavement. Based on the damages sustained, an engineer estimated that the speed at collision was 15 mi/h. If the roadway had a +3% grade, calculate the speed of the car at the onset of skidding.

6. A large rock became visible to a driver at a distance of 175 ft. Assuming a perception-reaction time of 0.8 s, an initial speed of 42 mi/h, a coefficient of friction equal to 0.5, and a level roadway, calculate the speed at impact.

7. Plot the relationship between the approach speed v and the length of the dilemma zone for the following data: $a_2 = 0.5\ g$, $\delta_2 = 1.0$ s, $w = 65$ ft, $L = 15$ ft, and $\tau = 4.5$ s. To help you interpret this plot, draw another diagram in which the v versus x_c and the v versus x_o relationships are superposed.

8. Assuming a comfortable deceleration of 8 ft/s^2, an intersection width of 42 ft, a perception-reaction time of 0.9 s, and a vehicle length of 18 ft, plot $\tau_{\min}$ versus approach speed v_0. At what speed does $\tau_{\min}$ attain a minimum? What is that minimum?

9. Prepare a computer program for the general case of Exercise 2.8. Run your program several times and plot the results.

10. A driver with 20/40 vision and a sixth-grade education needs 2 s to read a directional sign. The letter size is such that the sign can be read by a person with 20/20 vision from a distance of 200 ft. Does the subject driver have enough time to read the sign at a speed of 30 mi/h?

11. The street name signs at a certain location can be discerned by a person with 20/40 vision from a distance of 300 ft. How much larger should they be in order to be legible to a person with 20/50 vision from a distance of 450 ft?
12. A witness with 20/60 vision supplied to the investigating officer the license plate number of a vehicle involved in a hit-and-run accident. If, under the conditions that prevailed at the time of the accident, a license plate can be read by a person with 20/20 vision from a distance of 180 ft, what is the maximum distance for which the witness's testimony can be relied upon?
13. Vehicles A and B are traveling toward each other in the opposing lanes on a straight segment of a two-lane highway at 35 and 40 mi/h, respectively. If the critical rates of angular change of the two drivers are 0.0065 and 0.0055 rad/s, determine (a) which driver will be the first to displace laterally and (b) the longitudinal distance between vehicles when the displacement will occur. Assume that the lateral separation between the two vehicles is 6 ft.
14. Inside a tunnel, the distance between the drivers and the curb is 10 ft. Assuming that the drivers fix their eyes on the curb at an angle of 2°, calculate the appropriate speed limit for a critical angular rate of change of 0.005 rad/s.
15. How far to the side of the drivers of Exercise 2.14 should the curb be to allow a speed of 45 mi/h?
16. What is the maximum allowable degree of curve (arc definition) for a two-lane highway if $e_{max} = 0.08$, $f_{max} = 0.12$, and the design speed is 50 mi/h?
17. A simple highway curve is planned to connect two horizontal tangents that intersect at sta. 2500 + 00.0 at an external angle of 52°. For a design speed of 60 mi/h and a curve radius of about 1.25 times the minimum allowable, calculate (a) the design rate of superelevation and (b) the required length of superelevation runoff. Assume a four-lane undivided highway and 10-ft lanes. Clearly state any other assumptions you think are needed.
18. Sketch the plan view and the longitudinal profile of your curve design (Exercise 2.17) assuming a normal crown of 0.02 ft/ft and pavement rotation about the center line.
19. A sight obstruction is located at a distance of 20 ft from the center of the inside lane of a highway that prescribes a circular curve (Fig. 2.4.12). If the degree of curve for the centerline of the inside lane is 15°, calculate (a) the curve's radius and (b) the available horizontal sight distance. Does the computed sight distance meet the AASHTO stopping criterion for a speed of 35 mi/h?
20. A 2000-ft vertical curve connects a +3% grade to a −5% grade. If the vertical tangents intersect at sta. 52 + 60.55 and elevation 877.62 ft, calculate the elevations at the VPC, VPT, high point, and sta. 54 + 00.
21. A −4% grade and a 0% grade meeting at sta. 24 + 40 and elevation 2421.54 ft are joined by an 800-ft vertical curve. The curve passes under an overpass at sta. 25 + 00. If the lowest elevation of the overpass is 2439.93 ft, calculate the available clearance.
22. A +2% grade meets a +6% grade at sta. 10 + 30 and elevation 168.21 ft. For a design speed of 55 mi/h, find the minimum length of vertical curve that satisfies the 1984 AASHTO stopping sight-distance criterion. Also calculate the elevation of the middle point of this curve.
23. Calculate the available passing sight distance on a 2000-ft vertical curve with $G_1 = +5\%$ and $G_2 = -2\%$ for (a) the pre-1984 and (b) the post-1984 oncoming vehicle and driver eye heights.
24. Show that Eq. 2.4.20a is correct.
25. Prove that Eq. 2.4.21 applies to three-centered symmetrical curves.

26. Sketch and compare a simple curve and a simple curve with taper for an SU design vehicle (see Table 2.4.5) and a 75° angle of turn.
27. Sketch and compare a three-centered symmetrical, a three-centered asymmetrical, and a simple curve with taper for the WB-40 design vehicle and an angle of turn of 135°.
28. Prepare a computer program that, given the station location and elevation of the intersection of two vertical grades and the required sight distance, calculates (a) the minimum length of vertical curve, (b) the station location and elevation of the VPC and the VPT, and (c) the curve elevation of any specified intermediate point.

2.7 REFERENCES

2.1 DREW, DONALD R., *Traffic Flow Theory and Control,* McGraw-Hill, New York, 1968.

2.2 American Association of State Highway and Transportation Officials, *A Policy on Geometric Design of Highways and Streets,* Washington, D.C., copyright 1984. Used by permission.

2.3 JOHANNSON, GUNNAR, AND KÄRE RUMAR, "Drivers' Brake Reaction Times," *Human Factors,* 13, 1 (1971): 23–27. Copyright 1971 by the Human Factors Society, Inc. Fig. (1), p. 26, reproduced by permission.

2.4 GAZIS, DENOS, ROBERT HERMAN, AND ALEXEI MARADUDIN, "The Problem of the Amber Signal in Traffic Flow," *Operations Research,* 8 (1960): 112–132.

2.5 Institute of Transportation Engineers, *Transportation and Traffic Engineering Handbook,* Prentice-Hall, Inc., Englewood Cliffs, N.J., 1976.

2.6 TARAGIN, A., "Driver Behavior as Affected by Objects on Highway Shoulders," *Highway Research Board Proceedings,* National Research Council, 34 (1955): 453–472.

2.7 MICHAELS, R. M., AND L. W. GOZAN, "Perceptual and Field Factors Causing Lateral Displacement," *Highway Research Record* No. 25, Highway Research Board, National Research Council, Washington, D.C., 1963.

2.8 Federal Highway Administration, *Highway Functional Classification: Concepts, Criteria and Procedures,* U.S. Department of Transportation, Washington, D.C., 1974.

2.9 American Association of State Highway Officials, *A Policy on Geometric Design of Rural Highways,* Washington, D.C., 1965.

2.10 Federal Highway Administration, *Manual on Uniform Traffic Control Devices for Streets and Highways,* U.S. Department of Transportation, Washington, D.C., 1971.

2.11 American Association of State Highway and Transportation Officials, *A Policy on Design of Urban Highways and Arterial Streets,* Washington, D.C., 1973.

2.12 HICKERSON, THOMAS F., *Route Surveys and Design,* McGraw-Hill, New York, 1959.

2.13 KANTOWITZ, BARRY H. AND ROBERT D. SORKIN, *Human Factors: Understanding People-System Relationships,* John Wiley, New York, 1983.

CHAPTER 3

VEHICULAR FLOW MODELS

3.1 INTRODUCTION

Chapter 2 was primarily concerned with the motion of a single vehicle. From the resulting equations of motion, the basic geometric design formulas for highways were derived and their application was illustrated. Occasionally, single vehicles traverse the transportation facilities without significant interference from other vehicles. But the same facilities also experience simultaneous usage by streams of vehicles. The resulting traffic conditions range from almost free flow when only a few relatively unconstrained vehicles occupy a roadway to highly congested conditions when the roadway is jammed with slow-moving vehicles. This chapter examines the consequences of vehicular interactions. The equations developed in Chapter 2 are used to formulate a general model of a vehicular stream for the simple case of identically scheduled vehicles on an exclusive right of way. This model is then extended to the case of highway traffic, where a great amount of variability prevails. The determinant of these traffic flow models is the car-following rule adopted by drivers in an attempt to maximize their speeds while maintaining an acceptable level of safety. They accomplish this by adjusting the distance between vehicles, depending on their speed. The basic variables that describe the prevailing conditions within a vehicular stream (flow, concentration, and mean speed) are introduced and the fundamental relationship between the three stream variables is postulated and applied to several traffic phenomena, including the propagation of shock waves in traffic. A useful statistical method of curve fitting, least squares regression, is also introduced for use in this and subsequent chapters.

3.2 VEHICULAR STREAM MODELS

3.2.1 Vehicular Following

Consider the case of vehicles following each other on a long stretch of roadway or guideway. Furthermore, assume that these vehicles are not required to interrupt their motion for reasons that are external to the traffic stream, such as traffic lights, transit stations, and the like. In this case of *uninterrupted flow,* the only interference that a single vehicle experiences is caused by other vehicles on the roadway. Figure 3.2.1 shows two typical stream vehicles traveling at a speed v and a *spacing* s between the front of the leading vehicle to the front of the following vehicle. As a general rule, the spacing between vehicles should be such that if a sudden deceleration becomes necessary for a leading vehicle, the following vehicle has ample time and distance to perceive the situation, react to it, and be able to decelerate safely without colliding with the stopping, leading vehicle. A similar rule was applied in Chapter 2 to compute the necessary safe stopping distance that served as a criterion for the proper geometric design of roadways.

Figure 3.2.1(a) shows the locations of the leading and following vehicles described above at the moment when the leading vehicle begins to decelerate, and Fig. 3.2.1(b) shows the limiting acceptable conditions at the end of the stopping maneuver of the following vehicle. Parenthetically, the term *vehicle* may be taken to mean a vehicular train consisting of a number of articulated vehicles rather than a single vehicle. Using the following notation, a relationship between spacing, speed, and deceleration (assumed constant) can be developed:

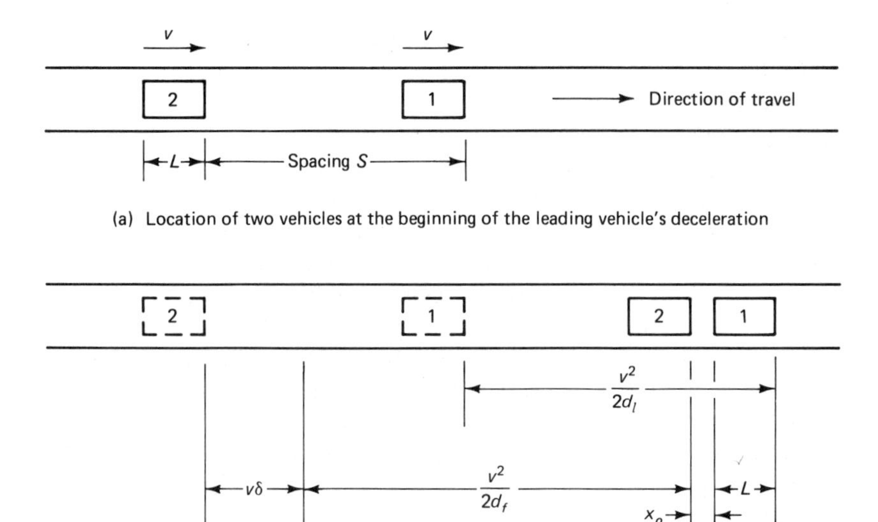

Figure 3.2.1 Vehicle following.

v = initial speed of the two vehicles

d_l = deceleration rate of the leading vehicle

d_f = deceleration rate of the following vehicle

δ = perception-reaction time of the following vehicle

x_o = safety margin after stop

L = length of vehicle

N = number of vehicles in a train (if applicable)

Under constant deceleration, the braking distance of the leading vehicle is

$$x_l = \frac{v^2}{2d_l} \tag{3.2.1}$$

Including perception-reaction, the total distance that would be covered by the responding following vehicle is:

$$x_f = v\delta + \frac{v^2}{2d_f} \tag{3.2.2}$$

In terms of the initial spacing s, the length of the vehicular unit (NL), and the safety margin x_o,

$$x_f = s + x_l - NL - x_o \tag{3.2.3}$$

Substituting Eqs. 3.2.1 and 3.2.2 in Eq. 3.2.3 and solving for s,

$$s = v\delta + \frac{v^2}{2d_f} - \frac{v^2}{2d_l} + NL + x_o \tag{3.2.4}$$

Thus, given the speed of normal operation of the system and the other performance parameters, it is possible to compute the necessary spacing so that the following vehicle will just be able to avoid a collision by anticipating a potential stopping maneuver by the vehicle ahead. The application of this equation to a specific system requires the specification of the *anticipated* deceleration of the leading vehicle and the *desired* deceleration of the following vehicle. The combined choice of particular values for these variables has some important implications with respect to the level of safety provided by the system's operation.

3.2.2 Safety Considerations

Three particular values of deceleration are relevant to the operation's safety level [3.1]:

d_n = normal or comfortable deceleration

d_e = emergency deceleration

TABLE 3.2.1 SAFETY REGIME DEFINITIONS

Regime	Deceleration of leading vehicle	Deceleration of following vehicle
a	∞	d_n
b	d_e	d_n
c	∞	d_e
d	$d_l = d_f$	
e	(no braking)	

Note: For $d_e < 2d_n$, regime c is safer than regime b.
SOURCE: Vuchic [3.1]; From Table 7.3, p. 538.

∞ = "instantaneous" or "stonewall" stop

Normal deceleration is related to passenger comfort as discussed in Chapter 2. The instantaneous stop condition may arise when an accident or a stalled vehicle or other obstruction suddenly comes within the perception field of the subject vehicle.

The safest level of operation occurs when the spacing between vehicles is such that the following vehicle can safely stop by applying *normal* deceleration even when the leading vehicle comes to a stonewall stop. A lower level of safety results when the spacing is selected so that the following vehicle would have to apply the *emergency* brake rather

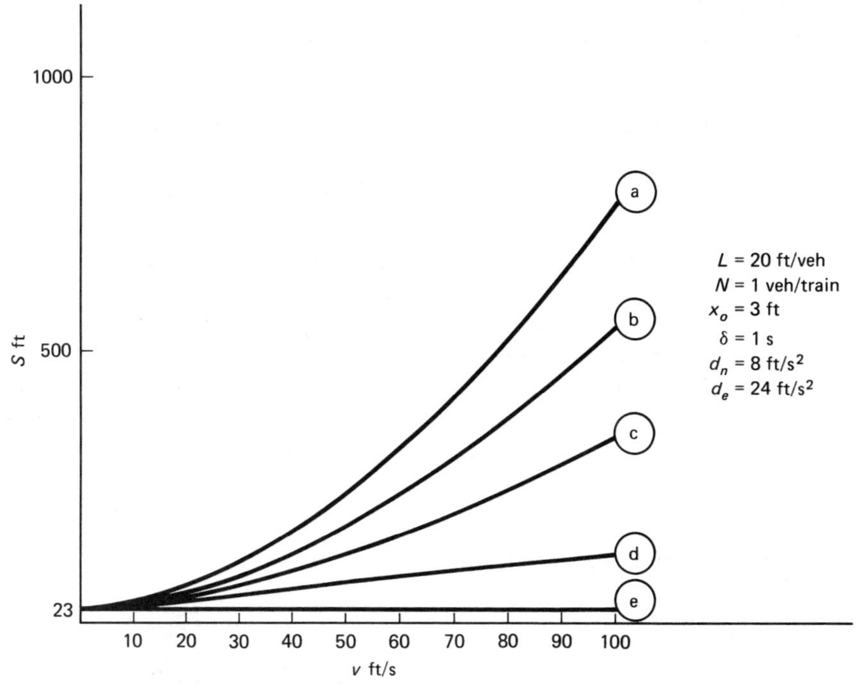

Figure 3.2.2 Spacing versus speed.

than normal deceleration in order to avoid a collision. The combinations of leading and following vehicle decelerations that designate various *safety regimes* are shown in Table 3.2.1.

Figure 3.2.2 plots spacing versus speed (Eq. 3.2.4) for the four safety regimes corresponding to the values inserted in the figure. Also included in Fig. 3.2.2 is the limiting case of a hypothetical continuous train, which is assumed to operate at any constant speed without ever having to decelerate [3.1]. The figure clearly shows that the higher the level of safety, the higher the required spacing just to avoid a collision. On this basis alone it would seem reasonable to choose the safest level of operation. However, by increasing the level of safety, the capacity of the system (i.e., the maximum number of vehicles or passengers that can be accommodated during a given period of time) suffers. Consequently, a *trade-off* between safety and capacity exists.

3.3 STREAM VARIABLES

3.3.1 Spacing and Concentration

Consider the uniform operation described in the preceding section and assume that a single photograph of a roadway segment is taken at an instant of time. The photograph would show a number of equally spaced vehicles along the roadway segment. The ratio of the number of vehicles appearing on the photograph to the length of the roadway segment is defined as the *concentration* k of the vehicular stream. This is an instantaneous measurement taken at the instant when the photograph was taken. Since the operation of the system described here is uniform (i.e., constant spacing and operating speed), the numerical value of concentration obtained at any instant of time on any segment of roadway will be the same. However, if the spacings and speeds of the vehicles that make up the stream are not equal, as is the case with the typical operation of highways, the value of concentration can vary with time and can also differ from one location to another at the same time. The dimensions of concentration (which is sometimes referred to as *density*) are given in terms of vehicles per length of roadway, for example, vehicles per mile (or veh/mi). The relationship between spacing (or average spacing when not constant) and concentration is:

$$s = \frac{1}{k} \tag{3.3.1}$$

3.3.2. Headway and Flow

Consider a stationary observer next to the roadway. Vehicles pass the observer's location one after another at intervals of time defined as the *headways* between vehicles and denoted by the letter h. In the simple example described above, the headway between vehicles is constant and can be computed by dividing the constant spacing by the constant speed of system operation. It is not too difficult, however, to imagine a situation, such as highway traffic, where the measured headway between subsequent vehicles varies. In either case, during a period of observation T, the observer would count a number of headways, each corresponding to an individual vehicle in relation to its leader, the sum of which equals the total time of observation T. The number of vehicles counted at the point of observation divided by the total observation time is defined as the stream *flow* q—sometimes referred to as *volume* V—and measured in vehicles per unit time, for example, vehicles per hour (veh/h). Flow is a *measurement at a point* on the roadway over time. The relationship between headway (or average headway when variable) and flow is

$$h = \frac{1}{q} \tag{3.3.2}$$

3.3.3 Average or Mean Speed

The third basic measurement of traffic is that of *average,* or *mean, speed*. In the case of the uniform vehicular stream described above, all vehicles were assumed to operate at the same speed v. Therefore the average speed of any group of vehicles in the stream is also equal to v. This is not always the case, however. In a typical highway situation, for example, vehicles are traveling at different speeds, which they adjust as they traverse the highway. The problem of when, where, and how to take speed measurements that are representative of the traffic stream is not trivial [3.2]. For example, the speeds of successive vehicles may be taken at a single point of the roadway over a long period of time. These speeds are also known as *spot speeds*. Alternatively, the speeds of all the vehicles occupying a length of highway may be taken at the same instant. Also, by taking two aerial photographs of the highway separated by a small interval of time, the speed of each vehicle may be calculated by dividing the distance traveled by that time interval. The method by which the speed measurements are taken and the way in which their average is computed affect the results and interpretation of this quantity. Two common ways of computing the average, or mean, speed are the *time mean speed* and the *space mean speed*. The time mean speed U_t is the *arithmetic average* of the spot speeds just defined, that is,

$$U_t = \frac{1}{N} \sum_{1}^{N} U_i \tag{3.3.3}$$

where N is the number of observed vehicles and U_i is the spot speed of the ith vehicle.

The space mean speed is calculated on the basis of the average travel time it takes N vehicles to traverse a length of roadway D. The ith vehicle traveling at speed U_i will take

$$t_i = \frac{D}{U_i} \tag{3.3.4}$$

seconds to cover the distance D. Thus the average travel time for N vehicles will be

$$t_{\text{ave}} = \frac{1}{N} \sum_{1}^{N} \frac{D}{U_i} \tag{3.3.5}$$

and the average speed based on the average travel time (i.e., the space mean speed) is the *harmonic average* of the spot speeds, or

$$U_s = \frac{1}{\frac{1}{N} \sum_{1}^{N} \frac{1}{U_i}} \tag{3.3.6}$$

The two average speeds may be calculated alternatively by

$$U_t = \frac{\sum_{1}^{N} \Delta x_i}{N \, \Delta t} \tag{3.3.7}$$

and

$$U_s = \frac{N \, \Delta x}{\sum_{1}^{N} \Delta t_i} \tag{3.3.8}$$

where Δx_i is the distance traveled by the ith vehicle during a fixed time interval Δt and Δt_i is the time taken by the ith vehicle to cover a fixed distance Δx [3.3, 3.4].

There are, of course, many other ways to take speed measurements and averages. However, for the purposes of this textbook, it suffices to state that the space mean speed (and not the time mean speed) is the proper stream speed average needed in this chapter's mathematical models.

Example 3.1

The spot speeds of four vehicles were observed to be 30, 40, 50, and 60 ft/s, respectively. Compute the time mean speed and the space mean speed.

Solution The time mean speed is the arithmetic average of the spot speeds, or

$$\frac{30 + 40 + 50 + 60}{4} = 45 \text{ ft/s}$$

On the other hand, the space mean speed is the harmonic average. Equation 3.3.6 yields:

$$U_s = 42.1 \text{ ft/s}$$

Discussion The same results may be obtained by applying Eq. 3.3.7 (with, say, $\Delta t = 1$ s) and Eq. 3.3.8 (with $\Delta x = 1$ ft). The time mean speed is greater than the space mean speed. This is always the case because of the relative contribution to each average of slow- and fast-moving vehicles.

3.3.4 Time-Distance Diagrams of Flow

The vehicular variables (spacing, headway, vehicle speed) and stream variables (flow, concentration, mean speed) just described can be clearly illustrated via a *time-distance diagram* of the trajectories of the vehicles constituting a traffic stream. Figure 3.3.1 is such a diagram for the simple case of uniformly operated vehicles represented as particles. Since in this case the speed of the vehicles is constant, the time-distance plot for each vehicle is simply a straight line, the slope of which, dx/dt, equals the speed, v. A point on a plot represents the location of the subject vehicle at the corresponding instant of time. A horizontal line (line AA, for example) intersects a number of time-distance lines and the (time) difference between pairs of vehicles along the horizontal line is the headway between those vehicles. Also, this horizontal line represents a stationary observer whose location does not change with time. The number of vehicles that the observer would be able to count over a period of observation T is equal to the number of times the horizontal line AA intersects a vehicle time-distance line: The higher the number of vehicles counted during time T, the higher the stream flow.

A vertical line (BB) represents the conditions prevailing at a given instant. The difference between subsequent vehicles is the spacing between vehicles. Also, line BB represents an aerial photograph of the stream at that instant: The number of time-distance

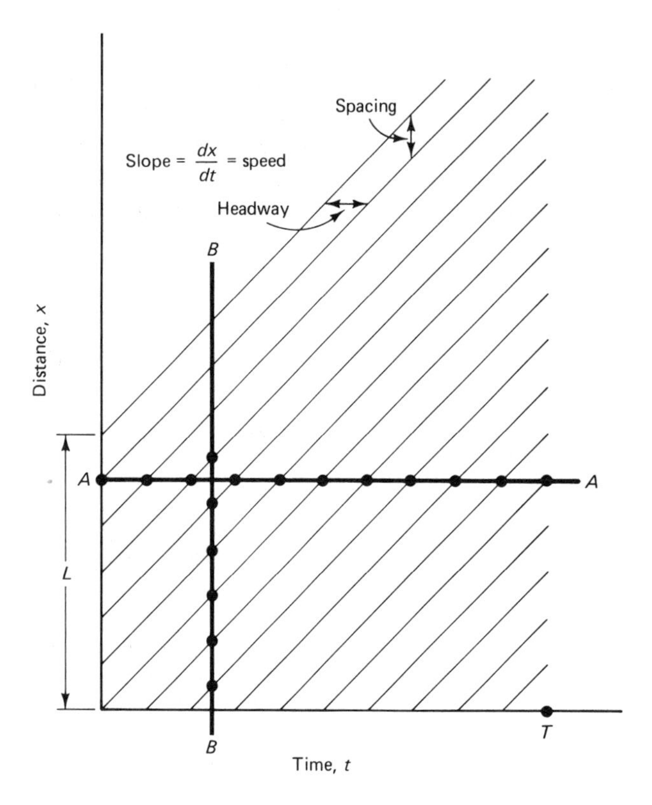

Figure 3.3.1 Time-distance diagram: uniform flow.

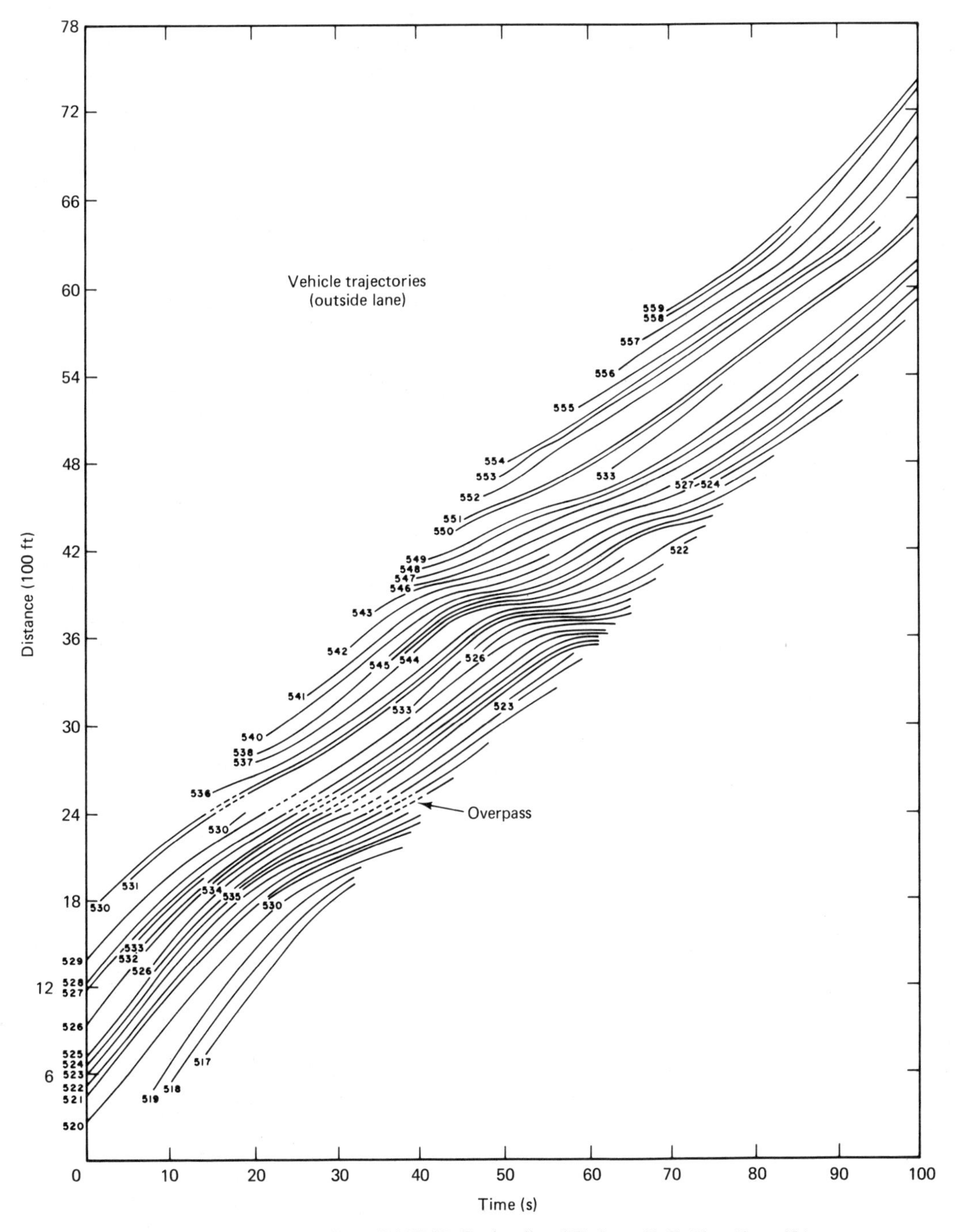

Figure 3.3.2 Highway flow. (*SOURCE*: Rockwell and Treiterer [3.5], Fig. 46, p. 65.)

lines that are intersected by line BB corresponds to the number of vehicles that would appear on a photograph of the roadway segment shown. The smaller the number of such vehicles, the lower the stream concentration.

The problem of determining a representative measure of mean speed becomes clearer when viewing the time-distance diagram of the stream. One way to average the speeds of vehicles in the stream is to measure their speeds as they pass a given location (i.e., the slopes of the time-distance lines as they cross line AA), the speeds of all vehicles in the stream at an instant (i.e. the slopes of time-distance lines as they cross line BB), the speeds computed for a small interval of time (Δt) over the length of the highway, the speeds computed for a small interval of distance (Δx) over a long period of time, or even by computing the average speed for each vehicle over the entire length of roadway and averaging that. This may seem irrelevant in the case of uniformly scheduled vehicles shown on Fig. 3.3.1, since all the vehicles are assumed to maintain the same speed throughout their movement. But in cases of nonuniform operations, the problem becomes clear. The reader is encouraged to consider the differences obtained by computing the alternate speed averages just described for the typical highway traffic time-distance diagram illustrated by Fig. 3.3.2, which represents a stream of vehicles on the curb lane of a highway in Columbus, Ohio [3.5]. The data shown were collected by aerial photogrammetry from a helicopter flying above the highway. The extent of any vertical line BB on the diagram is the range within the view of the camera at the corresponding instant. Any such line shows a great amount of variability in spacings at and between instants and at various locations. The slopes of the vehicle time-distance diagrams change, indicating speed changes, and the concentration of vehicles is seen to exhibit great variability, higher when and where the lines are densely packed and lower when and where they are sparsely packed. It is interesting to note that concentration is highest at points where the speeds are lowest. This phenomenon is eminently reasonable: When the speeds are low, the safe spacing selected by individual drivers is shorter leading to higher concentrations. The effect of this relationship on stream flow is not as obvious.

3.4 VEHICULAR STREAM EQUATIONS AND DIAGRAMS

3.4.1 The Fundamental Equation of a Vehicular Stream

If two vehicles are traveling at a spacing s and speed u, the headway between them is simply $h = s/u$. Substituting Eqs. 3.3.1 and 3.3.2 in this relationship leads to the fundamental equation describing a traffic stream:

$$q = uk \tag{3.4.1}$$

Note that the units balance to vehicles per hour on both sides of this equation, which represents a three-dimensional relationship between the basic vehicular stream variables: flow, mean speed, and concentration. It is of the utmost importance to realize that the three variables vary simultaneously. Consequently, it would be generally incorrect to attempt to compute the value of one of the three variables by varying another while holding the third constant. As it was shown earlier, when speed is increased, the safe spacing between vehicles also increases, causing the concentration to decrease. According to Eq. 3.4.1, the resulting flow is given by the product of a *higher speed* times a *lower concentration*. Hence, the flow may increase, decrease, or remain the same, depending on the relative magnitudes of these two opposing effects.

To gain a clearer understanding of this phenomenon, consider the two-dimensional *projections* of Eq. 3.4.1 on the *u-k, u-q,* and *q-k* planes, first for the simple case of uniform flow and then for the more complex case of highway traffic.

3.4.2 The Case of Uniform Flow

Substituting Eq. 3.3.1 into Eq. 3.2.4, solving for k in terms of u, and adjusting the units of concentration to vehicles per mile leads to:

$$k = f(u) = \frac{1}{u\delta + \dfrac{u^2}{2d_f} - \dfrac{u^2}{2d_l} + NL + x_o} \qquad (3.4.2)$$

This equation is plotted in Fig. 3.4.1 with k on the abscissa and u on the ordinate for the values that are inserted in the figure and for four of the five safety regimens discussed

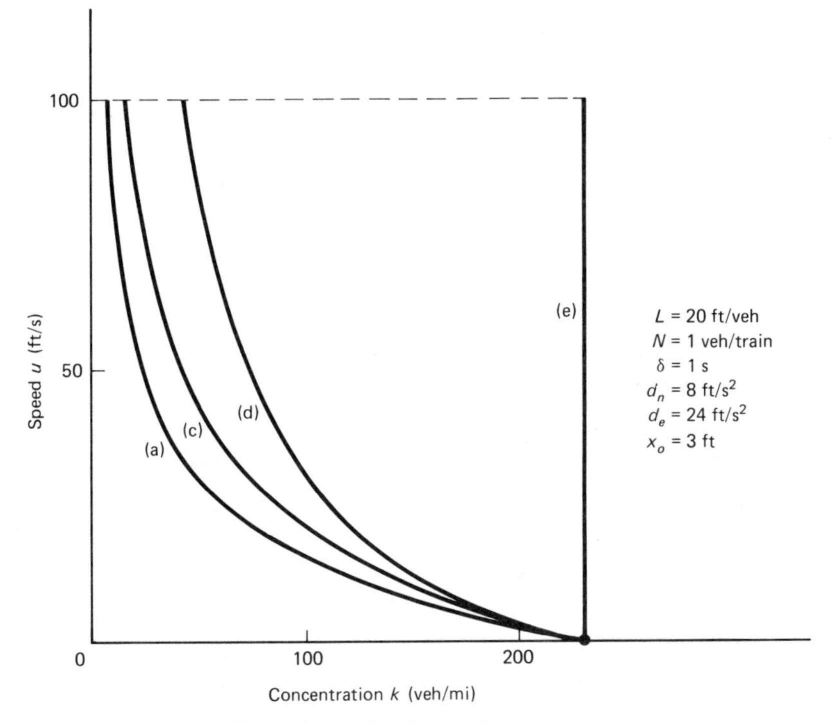

Figure 3.4.1 Speed-concentration curves.

earlier, including the limiting case of the hypothetical continuous train. Excepting the hypothetical case, the relationship between speed and concentration is seen to be monotonically decreasing as should be expected: the higher the speed, the longer the required spacing and, consequently, the lower the concentration. The conditions around very low concentration and very high speed are referred to as the *free-flow conditions* and the maximum speed at zero concentration is known as the *free-flow speed* u_f. Although Eq. 3.4.2 shows speed to approach infinity asymptotically as concentration approaches zero, for all practical purposes there exists a maximum speed (see dotted line), which depends on the technological characteristics of the system.

In view of Eq. 3.4.1, multiplication of both sides of Eq. 3.4.2 by the mean speed u leads to:

$$q = \frac{u}{u\delta + \dfrac{u^2}{2d_f} - \dfrac{u^2}{2d_l} + NL + x_o} \tag{3.4.3}$$

Figure 3.4.2 shows the plots of this relationship for each of the four safety regimes. The units of q have been converted to vehicles per hour. For each value of u, each of the curves shown represents the flow that is attainable if the spacing is kept *just long enough* to avoid a collision in accordance with the corresponding safety regime. Stream operations between the curves, that is, at safety levels along the continuum from one safety regime cutoff point to another, are quite possible. In other words, if viewed alone, each of the

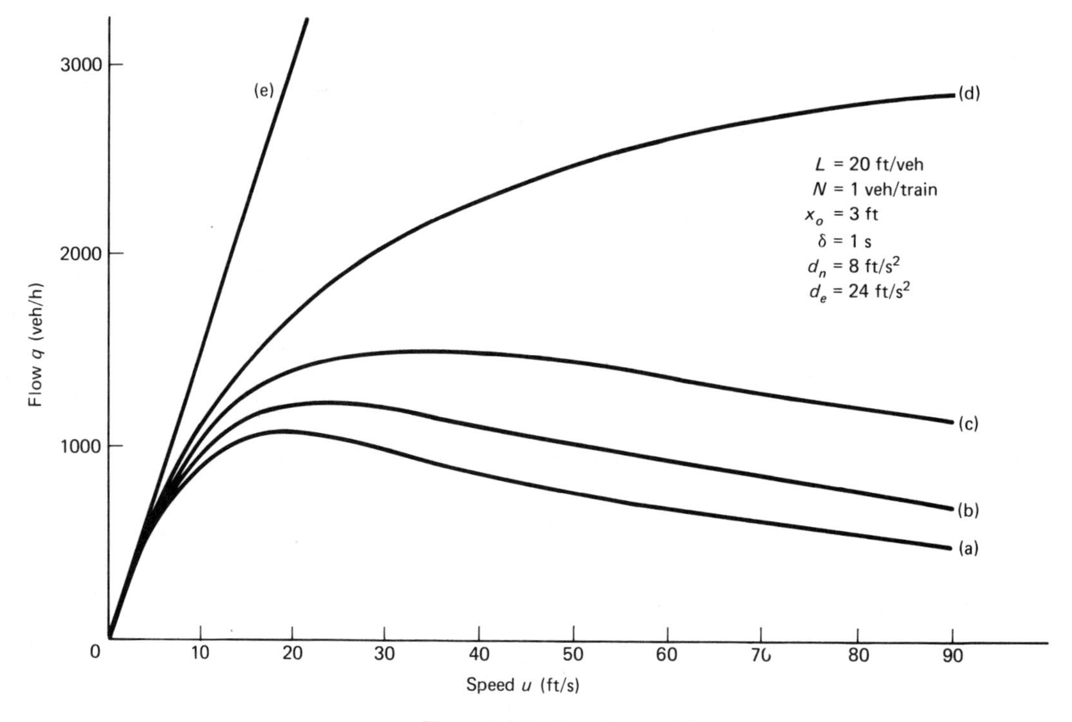

Figure 3.4.2 Speed-flow relationships.

four curves outlines an area of operation in terms of q and u that offers a level of safety *equal to or better* than the safety regime represented.

Each curve indicates zero flow at zero speed, meaning that, since no vehicle is moving, zero vehicles *per unit time* flow by a point on the facility. At the high-speed end, the flow exhibits a decline because of the increasingly longer spacing requirements for safe operation. The *maximum flow* (q_{max}) shown on each curve is the *capacity* of the roadway or guideway at the specified safety regime. The units of capacity are the same as the units of flow, that is, vehicles per unit time and *not* simply vehicles. Capacity occurs at an intermediate speed u_m and not at maximum (i.e., free) flow: Up to u_m, increasing speed corresponds to increasing flow; beyond u_m, increasing speed is associated with decreasing flow. Hence, in this range, a trade-off exists between speed and flow: Higher speeds can be attained only by sacrificing the throughput capability of the highway or guideway.

Finally, the relationship between flow and concentration can be examined by solving Eq. 3.4.2 for u in terms of k and multiplying both sides by k to obtain:

$$q = ku(k) \tag{3.4.4}$$

Figure 3.4.3 shows a typical plot of this relationship for safety regime b as described before and, for the sake of discussion, the hypothetical train as well. The free-flow end

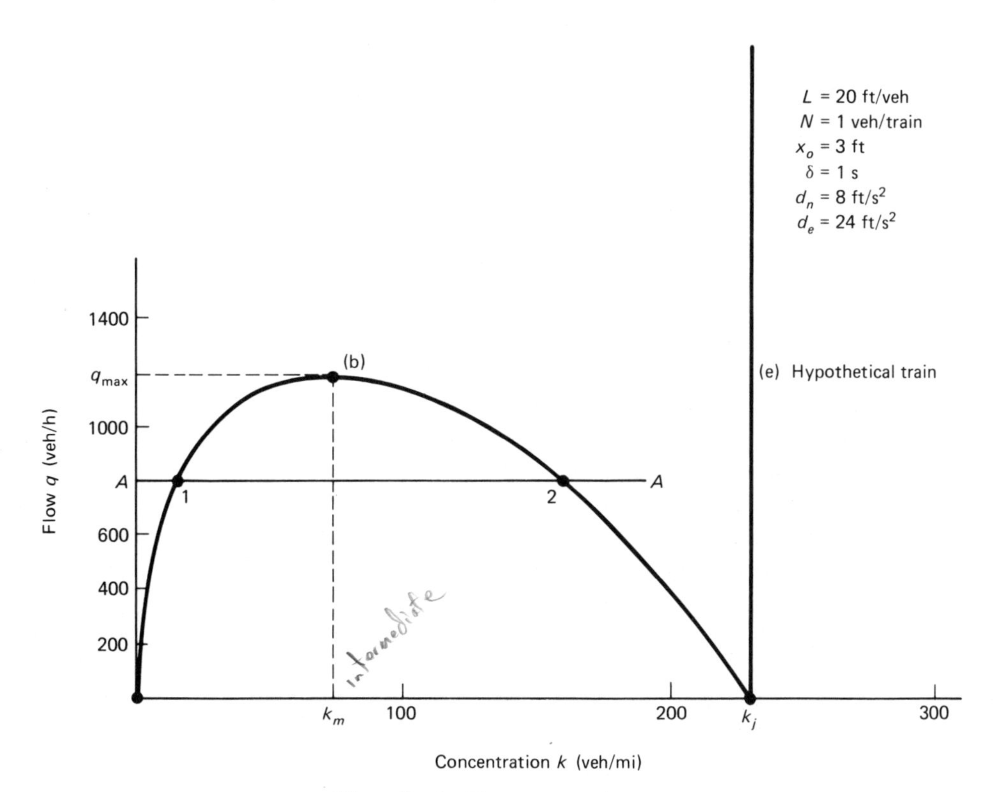

Figure 3.4.3 Flow-concentration curve.

of Fig. 3.4.3 (i.e., low flow and low concentration) corresponds to the high-speed end of Figs. 3.4.1 and 3.4.2. At the other end of the diagram, concentration attains its maximum value, flow is zero, and speed is also zero. In other words, the roadway or guideway is occupied by as many vehicles as it can hold, but no vehicle is moving. Hence, no flow is developed. These conditions correspond to a traffic jam, where maximum "packing" of stationary vehicles occurs. The value of concentration at that end is denoted by the *jam concentration* k_j. Again, maximum flow or capacity occurs at intermediate values of speed u_m and concentration k_m.

The horizontal line *AA* in Fig. 3.4.3 intersects the *q-k* curve at *two* points. Although the flow is the same at these points, the concentration is different. Also, the speeds corresponding to these two points are different (see Figs. 3.4.1 and 3.4.2). Point 1 represents conditions that are closer to free-flow, whereas point 2 represents conditions that are more congested. If a straight line is drawn from the origin to a point on the *q-k* curve, the *slope* of this line is simply equal to q/k, which—according to Eq. 3.4.1—is equal to the mean speed u. Therefore it is possible to specify the numerical values of the three basic stream variables (q, k, and u) by using only one of the three diagrams. It is customary (especially in highway traffic analysis) to use the *q-k* diagram for this purpose.

Figure 3.4.4 shows a *q-k* curve for some safety regime, say *b*. As discussed earlier, operating conditions that do not lie exactly on the curve are quite possible. For example, all points associated with safety regime *d* lie above the regime *b* curve shown. Thus, it is the desired level of safety that fixes the q, k, and u points on a particular curve and not the physical capabilities of the system. Consider, for example, the limiting hypothetical case of a continuous train that operates on a closed loop at a constant speed u and that is never required to decelerate [3.1]. In this case, considerations of safe stopping are not relevant. Theoretically, the concentration of the continuous train can be kept at jammed conditions on the track. Point *C* represents a stationary train at jam concentration, zero flow, and zero speed. If the train is operated at some constant speed u, its concentration remains at jam concentration, but the flow becomes finite (see point *D*, Fig. 3.4.4). If the operating speed is higher, as exemplified by the slope of line *BE*, the conditions associated with point *E* result. Thus the vertical line at jam concentration represents this hypothetical case. Clearly, it is physically impossible to operate the system at any of the conditions shown to the right of this line.

Now consider line *AB*. The slope of this line represents a high speed. This line would represent situations where the same high speed can be maintained at all values of concentration, a situation that is approached in the case of car racing: Irrespective of concentration, the speeds that race-track drivers sustain are very high. Of course, in the case of car racing the predominant consideration is not safety but speed.

Points below this race-track line are also attainable. Thus, for a given transportation technology, triangle *ABC* encloses the area on the *q-k* plane within which it is physically possible to operate the system. Within this triangle, the conditions described by points below as well as above the *q-k* curve shown are physically possible. Even points lying on the *k*-axis may be given a physical interpretation. For example, point *H* may represent a sparsely occupied parking lane at concentration below jammed conditions, zero speed,

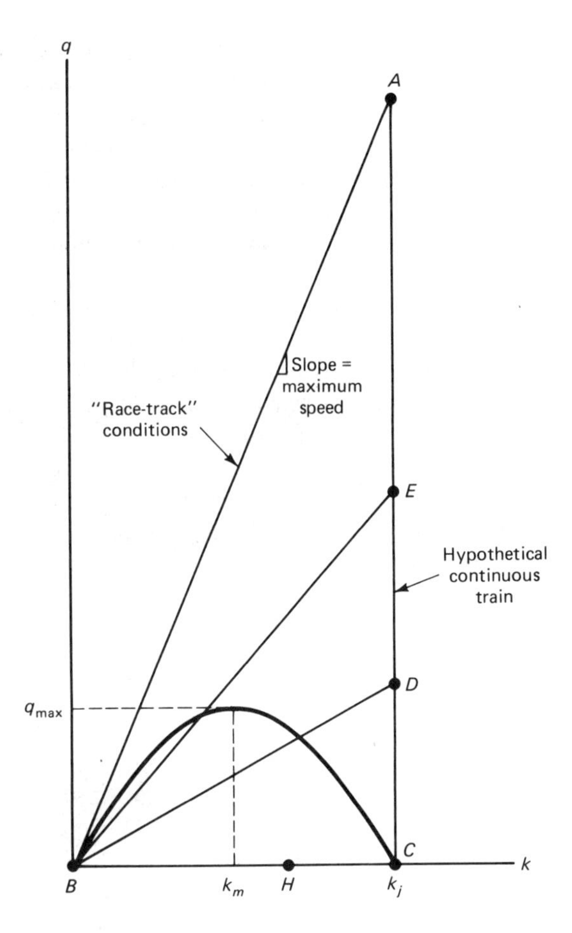

Figure 3.4.4 Flow interpretations.

and zero flow. But in this case, speed (that is, getting to a destination as quickly as possible) is not important!

What gives rise to the q-k curve shown within the region ABC in a typical travel situation is the trade-off between a desire to get to one's destination as quickly as possible (i.e., maximize speed) on one hand and getting there safely (as reflected by the preferred safety regime) on the other.

3.4.3 The Case of Highway Traffic Flow

The case of uniform flow considered above approximates the operation of a uniformly scheduled transit service on an exclusive right of way, where the decisions relating to the trade-off between safety and speed that give rise to the typical q-k diagram (see Fig. 3.4.3) are made explicitly by the operator of the system. In the case of highway traffic, drivers make their own decisions regarding this trade-off. Some drivers keep close to the car in front of them and try to increase their speeds when possible, whereas others keep unusually long spacings by stressing safety more than speed [3.6]. In addition, highway vehicles are not identical but exhibit a great amount of variability in size and technological attributes. The upshot of all these individual differences is a statistical *clustering* of points representing the stream conditions around a curve similar in shape to that shown on Fig. 3.4.3, and the stream diagrams and equations are typically estimated by statistical methods. This difference not withstanding, the flow diagrams of highway traffic exhibit the same general form and are subject to the same kind of interpretation as those developed for the simple case of uniformly scheduled rapid transit.

Figure 3.4.5 illustrates the general form of the *u-k, u-q,* and *q-k* diagrams corresponding to highway flow. The *u-k* relationship is monotonically decreasing, reflecting the rule that drivers follow on the average as they follow one another. The rule of the road suggested by many city traffic ordinances of keeping a distance of one car-length for each 10-mi/h increment of speed is but one such *car-following rule*. The *q-u* and *q-k* relationships are "backward bending" as before, with maximum flow occurring at an intermediate speed u_m and concentration k_m. Typically, given the *u-k* relationship, it is possible to estimate the other two relationships by following the procedure that was applied earlier for the case of uniformly scheduled transit.

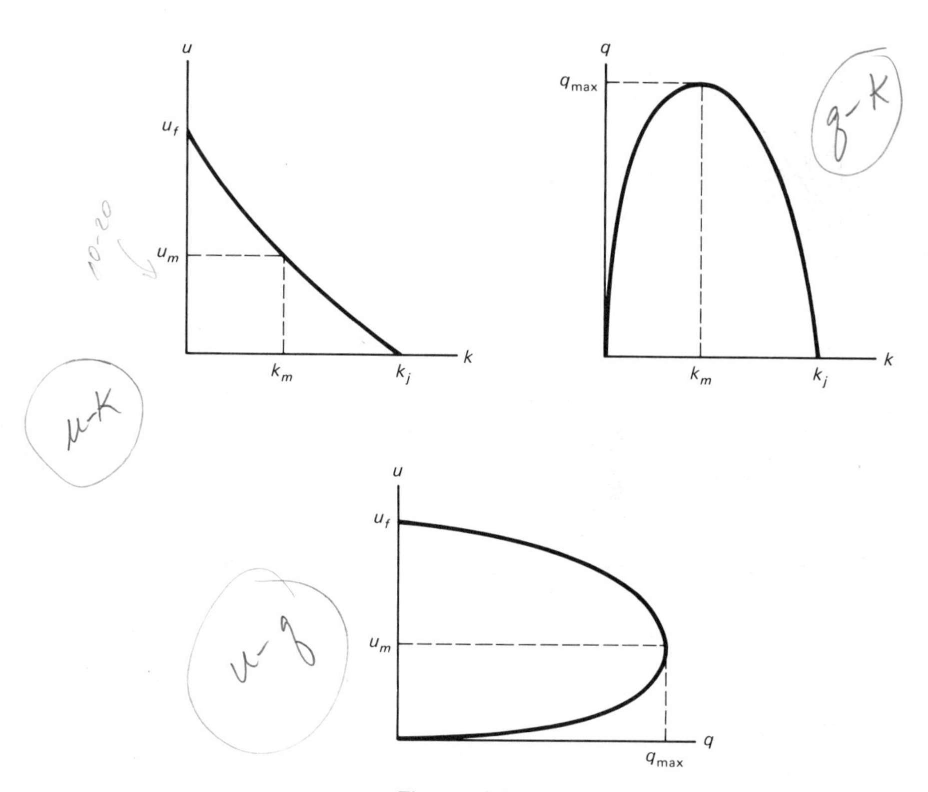

Figure 3.4.5 Flow curves.

Example 3.2

Assume that drivers in fact follow the rule of the road of keeping a gap of one car-length (L) for each 10-mi/h increment of speed. Assuming a car-length of 20 ft, develop the equations of stream flow and draw the u-k, q-u and q-k diagrams.

Solution According to the rule of the road, the safe spacing is a function of speed, or

$$s = L + \left(\frac{u}{10}\right)L = \frac{20 + 2u}{5280} \text{ mi/veh}$$

Applying Eq. 3.3.1 to find the implied k-u relationship,

$$k = \frac{1}{s} = \frac{2640}{10 + u} \text{ veh/mi}$$

or

$$10k + uk = 2640$$

But according to Eq. 3.4.1, $q = uk$. Thus the relationship between q and k becomes

$$q = 2640 - 10k \text{ veh/h}$$

Finally, expressing this equation in terms of u rather than k,

$$q = 2640 - \frac{26{,}400}{10 + u}$$

The three diagrams of flow are shown in the accompanying figures.

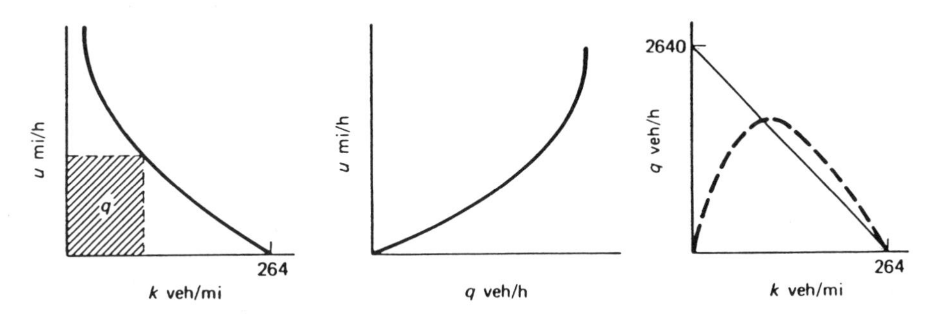

Figure P.3.2

Discussion The u-k diagram has the expected general shape, showing a monotonically decreasing function. Note that the shaded area equals the product $q = uk$. The q-u and q-k diagrams, however, seem to deviate from the expected "backward bending" shape illustrated by the dotted line on the q-k diagram. In view of the observed conditions on actual facilities, this implies that the rule of the road becomes unrealistic for low concentrations and high speeds. In fact, the equations just developed allow vehicles to travel at very high speeds, which is unrealistic. In other words, if the dotted line represents realistic conditions, it may be said that the rule of the road is a linear approximation of the stream conditions at the upper range of concentration. Moreover, the capacity of the roadway is not to be found at zero concentration, as the extrapolating of the straight line beyond its proper range would indicate.

Example 3.3

Given that the relationship between speed and concentration obtained from actual data is $u = 54.5 - 0.24k$, repeat the steps of Example 3.2 to estimate q_{max}, u_m, and k_j.

Solution To find the relationship between q and k, multiply both sides of the given u-k relationship by k and substitute the fundamental Eq. 3.4.1 in the result:

$$q = uk = 54.5k - 0.24k^2$$

To find the q-u relationship, solve the given equation for k and multiply both sides of the result by u:

$$k = 227 - 4.17u$$

and

$$q = uk = 227u - 4.17u^2$$

The plots of the three flow relationships are shown in the accompanying figure.

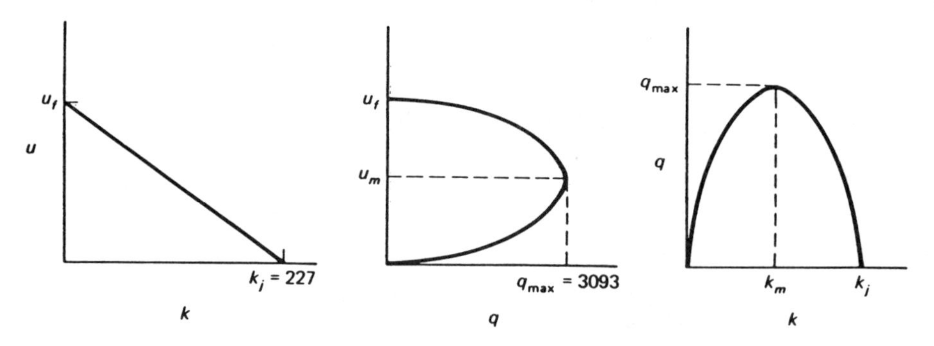

Figure P.3.3

To find k_j, the given equation is evaluated at $u = 0$. Thus $k_j = 227$ veh/mi. The free-flow speed u_f occurs at $k = 0$ and equals 54.5 mi/h.

The capacity of the highway is $q_{max} = u_m k_m = 3093$ veh/h. The reader is asked to verify these results by applying the calculus to maximize q using either the q-k or the q-u relationship.

Discussion The above results indicate that the general mathematical form of a *linear* u-k relationship is:

$$u = u_f\left(1 - \frac{k}{k_j}\right)$$

This relationship was first postulated by Greenshields [3.7]. If the u-k relationship is linear, the q-u and q-k relationships are both parabolic. In that case, capacity, or q_{max}, occurs at $u_m = u_f/2$ and $k_m = k_j/2$.

omit

3.5 MODEL CALIBRATION: THE METHOD OF LEAST SQUARES

3.5.1 Experimental Data and Model Parameters

In many engineering and scientific applications, relationships between variables are established by conducting experimental studies either in the laboratory or in the field. The data collected in this manner may be plotted and the relationship between them discerned. Figure 3.5.1 represents a plot (known as a *scatter diagram*) of such observations, each described in terms of a pair of values X and Y that resulted from an experiment. The two variables may represent the stress and strain of steel samples, the speed and concentration of a traffic stream, or city population and volume of long-distance telephone calls. Because of experimental and other errors of measurement, the points shown on the scatter diagram will not fall precisely on a smooth curve. For this reason, the task of the analyst becomes threefold: To hypothesize the mathematical form of the relationship between the two variables (*model postulation*), to estimate the parameters of the model based on the experimental data (*model calibration*), and to determine how well the calibrated relationship explains the observed data (*goodness of fit*).

One method of deriving the relationship between the two variables X and Y plotted in Fig. 3.5.1 is freehand approximation. However, the resulting relationship between the variables as well as the assessment of the goodness of fit will be highly subjective. For this reason, a well-defined and rigorous technique of curve fitting is usually preferred. The *method of least squares* is a technique that yields the best-fitting line of a postulated form to a set of data. For example, the following are two possible mathematical forms that may be postulated in the case of a relationship involving two variables Y and X:

$$Y = a + bX \tag{3.5.1a}$$

$$Y = c + dX + eX^2 \tag{3.5.1b}$$

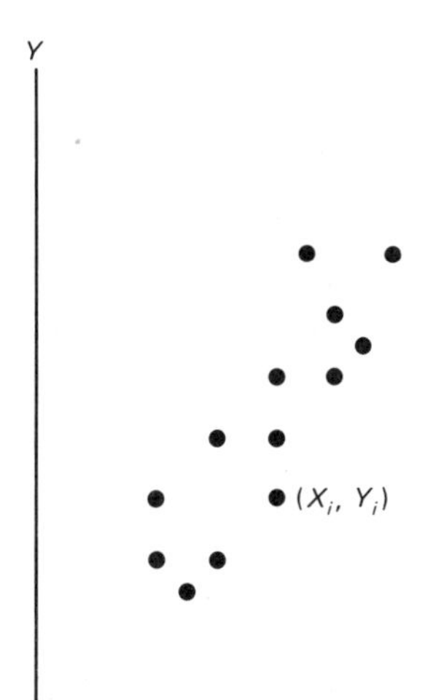

Figure 3.5.1 A scatter diagram.

where X is the independent, or explanatory, variable, Y is the dependent, or explained, variable, and the constant coefficients are the model parameters. Since a set of paired values of (X_i, Y_i) are the known results of an experiment, *calibrating the model means determining the unknown values of the parameters that fix the postulated equation to the one that best fits the data*. The method of least squares determines the numerical values of the coefficients that minimize the sum of square deviations between the observed values of the dependent variable Y_i and the estimated values $\hat{Y}_i$ that would be obtained by applying the calibrated relationship.

3.5.2 Simple Linear Regression

Consider the scatter diagram of Fig. 3.5.2. If it can be assumed that the relationship between X and Y is linear, then the method of least squares linear regression can be used to find the one straight line that best fits the data shown. An infinite number of straight lines can be drawn through the scatter diagram, each having its unique pair of parameters, that is, the Y-intercept a and the slope b. Hence, the problem reduces to finding those values of a and b that define the best-fitting straight line. This line will then be used to describe the relationship between X and Y as

$$Y = a + bX \tag{3.5.2}$$

Considering the ith observation shown on Fig. 3.5.2, a difference exists between the observed value of Y_i corresponding to X_i and the estimated value of Y that would be obtained by substituting X_i in Eq. 3.5.2. The estimated value of Y is denoted by $\hat{Y}_i$ to distinguish it from the observed value Y_i. The difference between the two is known as

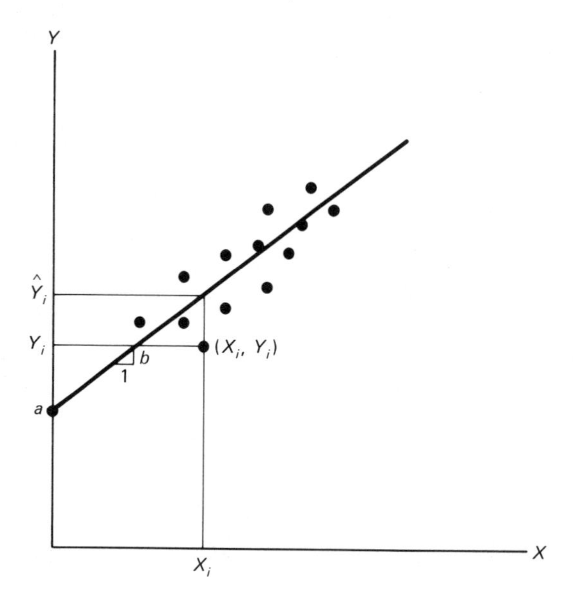

Figure 3.5.2 Linear regression.

the *error, deviation,* or *residual.* The straight line that minimizes some measure of the sum of all such deviations would appear to be the best-fitting straight line. In order to weigh equally the positive and negative deviations (in other words, in order to ensure that the straight line passes *through* the scatter diagram), the deviations are squared and their sum is minimized, that is to say, the specific values of a and b are selected in such a way as to minimize the sum of square deviations.

In mathematical terms, find the values of a and b that minimize the sum:

$$S = \sum_{i=1}^{N} (Y_i - \hat{Y}_i)^2 \tag{3.5.3}$$

To minimize S with respect to a and b, Eq. 3.5.3 must be expressed in terms of these two parameters. This is accomplished by substituting Eq. 3.5.2 in Eq. 3.5.3:

$$S = \sum_{i=1}^{N} (Y_i - a - bX_i)^2 \tag{3.5.4}$$

Setting the partial derivatives of S with respect to a and b equal to zero,

$$\frac{\partial S}{\partial a} = \sum_{i=1}^{N} [2\,(Y_i - a - bX_i)(-1)] = 0 \tag{3.5.5a}$$

$$\frac{\partial S}{\partial b} = \sum_{i=1}^{N} [2\,(Y_i - a - bX_i)(-X_i)] = 0 \tag{3.5.5b}$$

Dividing by 2 and rearranging terms gives

$$Na + \left(\sum_{i=1}^{N} X_i\right)b = \sum_{i=1}^{N} Y_i \tag{3.5.6a}$$

$$\left(\sum_{i=1}^{N} X_i\right)a + \left(\sum_{i=1}^{N} X_i^2\right)b = \left(\sum_{i=1}^{N} X_iY_i\right) \tag{3.5.6b}$$

These two equations, known as the *characteristic equations,* are linear with two unknowns a and b, since the coefficients of the two unknowns and the constant terms on the right-hand side can be computed using the known data of the original experiment.

Application of *Cramer's rule* leads to:

$$b = \frac{\begin{vmatrix} N & \Sigma Y_i \\ \Sigma X_i & \Sigma X_iY_i \end{vmatrix}}{\begin{vmatrix} N & \Sigma X_i \\ \Sigma X_i & \Sigma X_i^2 \end{vmatrix}} = \frac{N(\Sigma X_iY_i) - (\Sigma X_i)(\Sigma Y_i)}{N(\Sigma X_i^2) - (\Sigma X_i)^2} \tag{3.5.7}$$

Substituting the mean values of the observations $\overline{X}$ and $\overline{Y}$ defined as

$$\overline{X} = \frac{\sum_{i=1}^{N} X_i}{N} \quad \text{and} \quad \overline{Y} = \frac{\sum_{i=1}^{N} Y_i}{N} \tag{3.5.8}$$

where N is the total number of experimental data, Eq. 3.5.7 can be rewritten as

$$b = \frac{\Sigma(X_i - \overline{X})(Y_i - \overline{Y})}{\Sigma(X_i - \overline{X})^2} \tag{3.5.9}$$

Dividing Eq. 3.5.6a by the number of observations N and substituting Eqs. 3.5.8,

$$\overline{Y} = a + b\overline{X} \tag{3.5.10}$$

In other words, the point $(\overline{X}, \overline{Y})$ satisfies the equation of the best-fitting line. This means that *the best-fitting straight line always passes through the mean of the observations.*

By substituting the value of b obtained from either Eq. 3.5.7 or Eq. 3.5.9 into Eq. 3.5.10, the Y-intercept a becomes:

$$a = \overline{Y} - b\overline{X} \tag{3.5.11}$$

Thus, given a set of N observations (X_i, Y_i), the parameters of the best-fitting straight line are given by Eq. 3.5.9 and Eq. 3.5.11.

Example 3.4

Given the following measurements of traffic speed u and concentration k, apply the method of least squares to find the best-fitting straight line $u = a + bk$.

u	50	45	40	30	25
k	10	20	36	39	70

Solution Speed is the dependent variable, concentration is the independent variable, and a and b are the desired parameters of the postulated linear model. These parameters are calibrated by using Eqs. 3.5.9 and 3.5.11 arranged in tabular form below:

u	k	$u - \overline{u}$	$k - \overline{k}$	$(u - \overline{u})(k - \overline{k})$	$(k - \overline{k})^2$
50	10	12	−25	−300	625
45	20	7	−15	−105	225
40	36	2	1	2	1
30	39	−8	4	−32	16
25	70	−13	35	−455	1225
190	175	0	0	−890	2092

where:
$\overline{u} = 190/5 = 38$
$\overline{k} = 175/5 = 35$

Hence

$$b = \frac{-890}{2092} = -0.43$$

$$a = \bar{u} - b\bar{k} = 38 + (0.43)(35) = 53.05$$

and

$$u = 53.05 - 0.43k$$

The scatter diagram and the best-fitting straight line are shown in the accompanying figure.

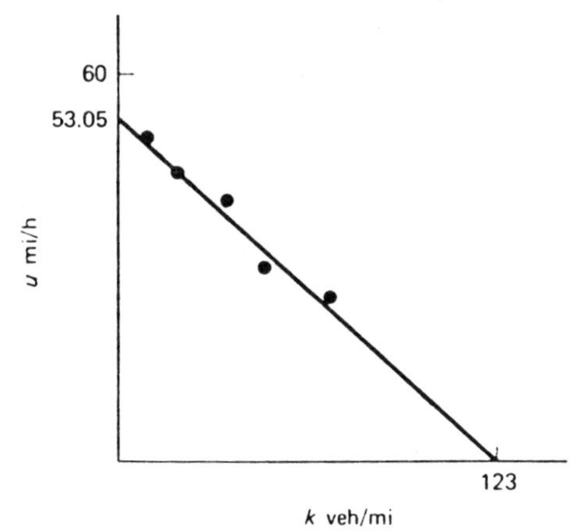

Figure P.3.4

Discussion The coefficient b turned out to be negative, as one would expect from the discussion of the general speed-concentration relationship. Also, it should be noted that the technique did not determine the mathematical form of the relationship: A linear form was postulated and the best straight line according to the regression criterion was the result.

Example 3.5

Repeat the procedure of Example 3.4 using the following set of observations:

u	70	20	15	50	35
k	10	23	39	38	65

Solution Proceeding as before,

u	k	$u - \bar{u}$	$k - \bar{k}$	$(u - \bar{u})(k - \bar{k})$	$(k - \bar{k})^2$
70	10	32	−25	−800	625
20	23	−18	−12	216	144
15	39	−23	4	−92	16
50	38	12	3	36	16
35	65	−3	30	−90	1225
190	175	0	0	−730	1694

where:
$\bar{u} = 190/5 = 38$
$\bar{k} = 175/5 = 35$

Hence,

$$b = \frac{-730}{1694} = -0.43$$

$$a = \bar{u} - b\bar{k} = 38 + (0.43)(35) = 53.05$$

and

$$u = 53.05 - 0.43k$$

The best-fitting straight line through the given data is shown in the accompanying figure.

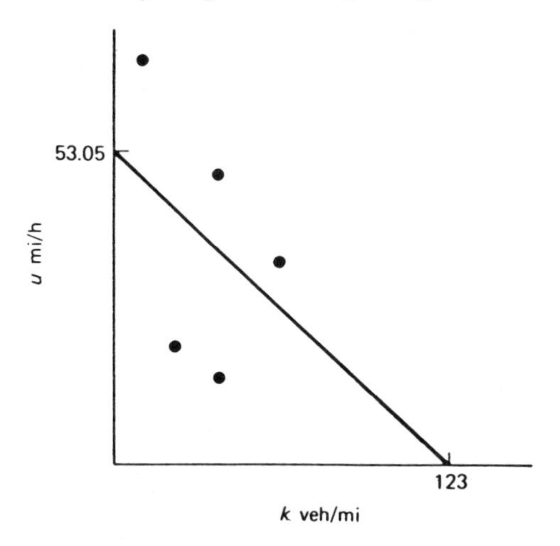

Figure P.3.5

Discussion As far as the calculation of the model's parameters is concerned, this problem is identical to the preceding problem. In both cases, the best straight lines passing through the respective scatter diagrams were found. Note, however, that both problems led to identical regression equations. But a comparison of the two diagrams reveals that the first represents a tighter fit to the data than the second. Although the two sets of data led to the same relationship, the analyst would have more confidence in using the equation in the case represented by the first than the second set of experimental observations. A quantitative way of quantifying the "goodness of fit" is needed. The next section addresses this question.

3.5.3 Correlation

The sum

$$\text{TSS} = \sum (Y_i - \bar{Y})^2 \tag{3.5.12}$$

called the *total sum of square deviations from the mean,* or the *total variation,* is a measure of the degree to which the Y-observations are spread around their average value. It can be shown (see the exercises) that:

$$\sum(Y_i - \bar{Y})^2 = \sum(Y_i - \hat{Y}_i)^2 + \sum(\hat{Y}_i - \bar{Y})^2 \tag{3.5.13}$$

The first term on the right side of Eq. 3.5.13 is the *error sum of squares* (ESS) that the regression technique minimizes. It is also known as the *unexplained variation*. The second term represents the sum of squares of the difference between the estimated values of $\hat{Y}$ that lie on the regression line and the average value of $\overline{Y}$, which, as proven in the previous section, also lies on the regression line. Thus these differences are explained by the presence of the line. The sum of the squares of these quantities is known as the *explained variation*. The goodness of fit of a regression line increases with the proportion of the total variation that is explained by the line. The *coefficient of determination*

$$r^2 = \frac{\text{TSS} - \text{ESS}}{\text{TSS}} = \frac{\Sigma(\hat{Y}_i - \overline{Y})^2}{\Sigma(Y_i - \overline{Y})^2} \tag{3.5.14}$$

quantifies this fact. It ranges from zero when none of the total variation is explained by the regression line to unity when all the variation is explained by the line. It is denoted as a squared quantity to capture the fact that it is always nonnegative. The square root of the coefficient of determination is called the *coefficient of correlation*. Its value can range from -1 to $+1$. In the case of linear regression, the sign of r is the same as the sign of the slope b of the regression line. Figure 3.5.3 illustrates that if r is near $+1$, there exists a high positive correlation; if it is near -1, there exists a high negative correlation; and if it is around zero, there exists no correlation between X and Y. The following formula gives the proper magnitude *and* sign of r:

$$r = \frac{N(\Sigma X_i Y_i) - (\Sigma X_i)(\Sigma Y_i)}{\{[N(\Sigma X_i^2) - (\Sigma X_i)^2]\,[N(\Sigma Y_i^2) - (\Sigma Y_i)^2]\}^{1/2}} \tag{3.5.15}$$

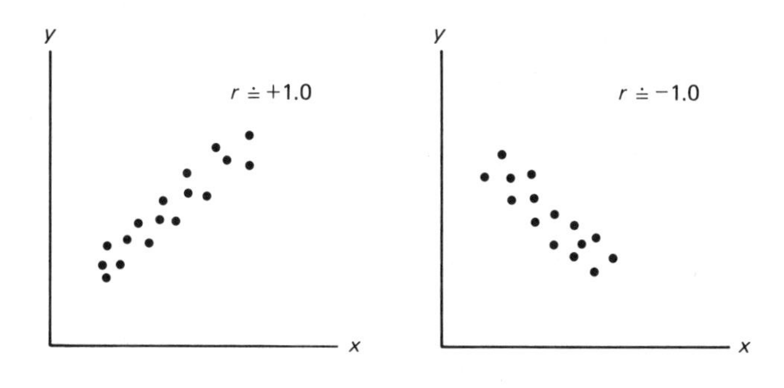

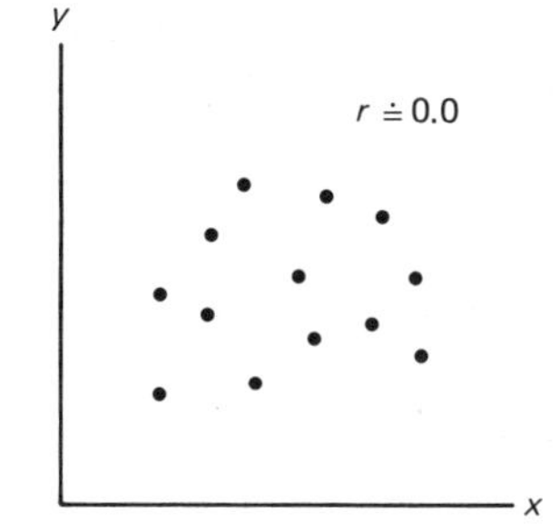

Figure 3.5.3 Correlation.

Example 3.6

Compute the coefficient of correlation between X and Y using the data of Examples 3.4 and 3.5.

Solution Using Eq. 3.5.15,

$$r = -0.95 \quad \text{for the data of Example 3.4}$$

and

$$r = -0.39 \quad \text{for the data of Example 3.5}$$

Discussion As expected, both correlations are negative and the first case represents a better fit than the second.

3.5.4 Multiple Linear Regression

Simple linear regression involves only *two* variables. But often, it is appropriate to postulate relationships that include two or more independent variables, each of which partially explains the value of the dependent variable Y. A relationship between the dependent and the independent variables of the form:

$$Y = a_0 + a_1 X_1 + a_2 X_2 + \cdots + a_p X_p \tag{3.5.16}$$

calibrated by the method of least squares is known as a *multiple linear regression* model.

Although a detailed treatment of the method of multiple regression is beyond the scope of this textbook, it is of some value to point out certain characteristics of the model. First, it should be understood that every experimental observation used in the calibration process must consist of $(p + 1)$ observations $(Y_i, X_{1i}, X_{2i}, \ldots, X_{pi})$. Calibration of the relationship means, as before, the estimation of the numerical values of the parameters of the model (i.e., the constant a_0 and the coefficients $a_1, \ldots, a_p$ in order to minimize the sum of squared deviations).

Second, the independent variables to be included in the relationship must be chosen so that they are not highly correlated among themselves. The simple correlation coefficient between pairs of potential independent variables may be computed via Eq. 3.5.15. When this criterion is satisfied, each of the terms on the right side of Eq. 3.5.16 would be independent of the rest, capturing the effect of that specific variable X on the value of the dependent variable Y. If, on the other hand, two X's included in the equation were highly correlated, then it would be very difficult to examine the effect of each on the dependent variable, since varying one of the two X's necessarily involves a change in the other.

Third, each of the selected independent variables must be highly correlated with the dependent variable Y; otherwise it would have no explanatory power.

Several calibration procedures are available for multiple-regression relationships. One technique adds the independent variables one at a time and assesses the degree to which the addition of the last variable improves the relationship. On this basis, a final relationship emerges, which includes the set of independent variables that provide the best fit. A *coefficient of multiple correlation* and various statistical tests can aid in assessing the goodness of fit.

3.5.5 Direct Nonlinear Regression

Linear regression (whether simple or multiple) assumes that the relationship between dependent and independent variables is, in fact, linear. Thus, when linear regression is applied to the observations illustrated by the scatter diagram of Fig. 3.5.4, the result will be the best-fitting straight line (see broken line), even though the underlying relationship is clearly not linear.

To calibrate nonlinear relationships, one of two methods is frequently used. The first method involves specifying a nonlinear model and proceeding through the minimization of the sum of squared deviations, as in the case of simple linear regression, except that the postulated nonlinear form is substituted in Eq. 3.5.3 prior to the minimization step. This is illustrated next for the best-fitting parabola to a set of experimental data.

Example 3.7: Least Squares Parabola

Fit an equation of the form $Y = a + bX + cX^2$ to the following data:

Y	30	40	65	85
X	2	3	4	5

Solution The unknown parameters a, b, and c are computed by minimizing the sum of squared deviations, or

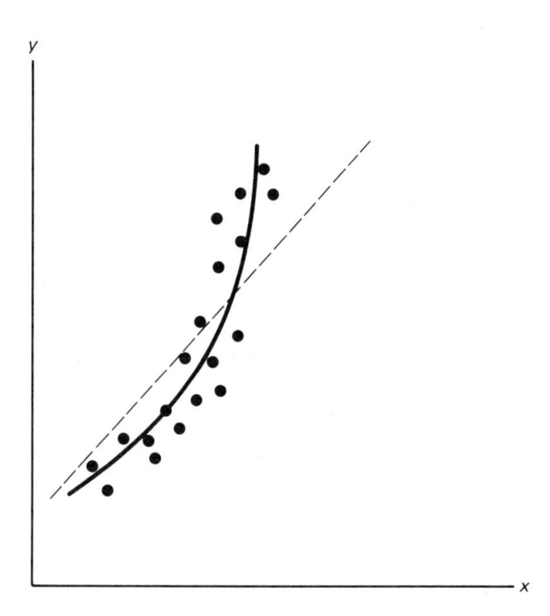

Figure 3.5.4. Nonlinearity.

$$\min S = \sum (Y_i - \hat{Y}_i)^2$$
$$= \sum (Y_i - a - bX_i - cX_i^2)^2$$

The following characteristic equations result from setting the partial derivatives of S with respect to a, b, and c equal to zero and separating variables:

$$\sum Y_i = aN + b\left(\sum X_i\right) + c\left(\sum X_i^2\right)$$
$$\sum\left(X_iY_i\right) = a\left(\sum X_i\right) + b\left(\sum X_i^2\right) + c\left(\sum X_i^3\right)$$
$$\sum\left(X_i^2Y_i\right) = a\left(\sum X_i^2\right) + b\left(\sum X_i^3\right) + c\left(\sum X_i^4\right)$$

Substituting the given data in the characteristic equations,

$$220 = 4a + 14b + 54c$$
$$865 = 14a + 54b + 224c$$
$$3645 = 54a + 224b + 978c$$

which, when solved simultaneously, yield the following values:

$$a = 16, \quad b = 1.5, \quad \text{and} \quad c = 2.5$$

Thus the best-fitting parabola of the postulated type becomes:

$$Y = 16 + 1.5X + 2.5X^2$$

Discussion Again, it must be emphasized that the technique did not select the functional form but merely determined the best line of the form supplied by the analyst. Care must be taken to express the sum of squared deviations to be minimized in terms of the postulated form. The reader is encouraged to find the least squares equations of the forms $Y = aX + bX^2$, $Y = a + bX^2$, and $Y = bX^2$ using the same data and to compare the results of the three regression lines. The first and last of these equations "force" the line to pass through the origin.

3.5.6 Linear Regression with Transformed Variables

The second method of calibrating nonlinear relationships applies when a nonlinear relationship can be transformed to a linear relationship, as Fig. 3.5.5 illustrates. In this case, *linear regression is applied to the transformed relationship* to determine the values of *its* parameters, which are then transformed back to the parameters of the original model.

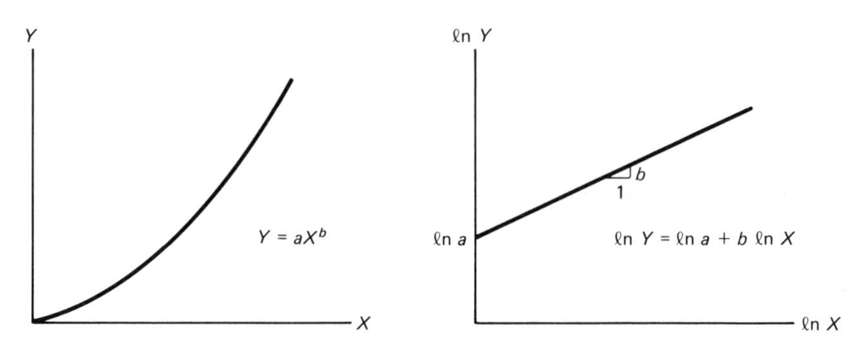

Figure 3.5.5 Variable transformation.

Example 3.8

The following speed and concentration measurements were taken on a highway:

u	50	35	35	25	20
k	10	40	50	80	100

It is desired to calibrate a speed-concentration equation of the form proposed by Underwood, that is, $u = u_f \exp(-k/k_m)$. Determine the parameters of this model using simple linear regression.

Solution The postulated relationship is not linear. However, taking the natural logarithm of both sides,

$$\ln u = \ln u_f - \left(\frac{k}{k_m}\right)$$

The following substitutions render this equation in the proper linear regression form:

$$Y = \ln u \qquad X = k \qquad a = \ln u_f \quad \text{and} \quad b = \frac{-1}{k_m}$$

Performing simple linear regression of X on Y as before leads to

$$a = 4.01, \qquad b = -0.01, \quad \text{and} \quad Y = 4.01 - 0.01X$$

To find the values of the parameters of the original model, make the inverse transformation:

$$u_f = e^a = 55 \text{ mi/h} \quad \text{and} \quad k_m = \frac{-1}{b} = 100 \text{ veh/mi}$$

and

$$u = 55\, e^{-k/100}$$

Discussion The free-flow speed of 55 mi/h and the concentration at capacity of 100 veh/mi represent the best-fitting Underwood relationship to the given data. This equation may be applied as in Section 3.4 to find the implied $q - k$ and $u - k$ curves and to estimate the capacity of the roadway, which (the student should verify) happens to be 2023 veh/h.

3.6 STREAM MEASUREMENTS: THE MOVING-OBSERVER METHOD

3.6.1 Introduction

The preceding section developed the method of least squares, which can be used to determine the relationship between two or more variables based on a set of experimental observations. Examples of calibrating $u-k$ relationships were also presented. The data used in curve fitting were assumed to be obtained from an appropriate experiment or experimental observation session. Many vehicular stream-measurement techniques are available for collecting the necessary data [3.2]. Because flow, speed, and concentration are interrelated, a proper measurement technique must take simultaneous measurements on two of the three variables; the third variable can be computed by applying Eq. 3.4.1. Taking measurements of only one of the three variables cannot describe the prevailing vehicular stream conditions. For example, the stream flow can be measured as the ratio of the number of vehicles crossing a pneumatic tube recorder that is stretched across a highway at a given location divided by the total time of measurement. Recall, however, that the same value of q is found at two points on the $q-k$ diagram (Fig. 3.4.3), one closer to free-flow and the other toward the jammed-flow end of the diagram. This means that, in order to distinguish between these two conditions, the values of k and u must also be known.

3.6.2 The Moving-Observer Method

The moving-observer method of traffic stream measurement has been developed to provide simultaneous measurements of stream variables. It involves an observer, who is taking certain measurements while moving in relation to the traffic stream being measured.

Referring to the two-way street operation illustrated by Fig. 3.6.1, consider the problem of measuring the stream conditions prevailing in the northbound direction. To develop the appropriate equation of the moving-observer method, consider two cases, corresponding to the *relative motion* between the observer and the vehicular stream being measured.

The first case considers the traffic stream relative to the observer, that is, it assumes a stationary observer and a moving vehicular stream. If N_o vehicles overtake the observer during a period of observation T, the observed flow is simply equal to:

$$q = \frac{N_o}{T} \quad \text{or} \quad N_o = qT \tag{3.6.1}$$

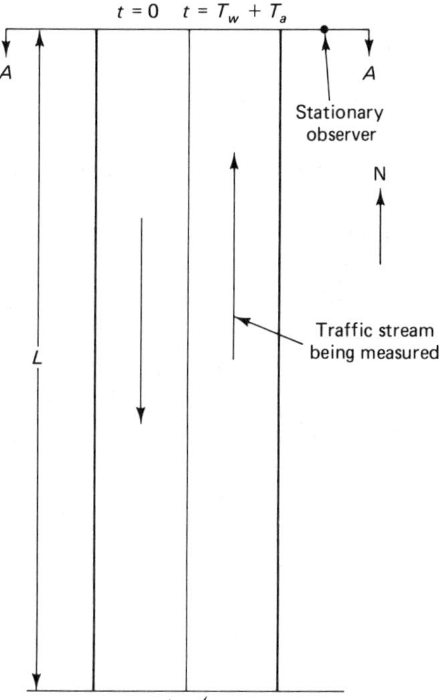

Figure 3.6.1 The moving observer method.

The second case (i.e., the movement of the observer relative to the stream) assumes that only the observer is moving and the rest of the traffic is stationary. By traveling a distance L, the observer would overtake a number of vehicles N_p. Thus the concentration of the stream being measured may be computed as:

$$k = \frac{N_p}{L} \quad \text{or} \quad N_p = kVT \tag{3.6.2}$$

where V is the observer's speed and T is the time it takes the observer to traverse the distance L.

Now, consider that the observer is actually moving within the traffic stream being measured. In that case, some vehicles M_o will overtake the observer, and some vehicles M_p will be overtaken by the observer in a test vehicle. The magnitudes of the two counts will depend on the relative speeds between the test vehicle and the rest of the traffic: If the test vehicle is traveling faster than average, it will overtake more vehicles than will overtake it, and vice versa. This case is the combined effect of the "relative" counts described for the two cases of the previous paragraph. Denoting the difference between the two counts as M,

$$M = M_o - M_p = qT - kVT \tag{3.6.3}$$

and dividing both sides of Eq. 3.6.3 by T,

$$\frac{M}{T} = q - kV \tag{3.6.4}$$

This is the basic equation of the moving-observer method, which relates the stream variables q and k to the counts M, T, and V that can be obtained by the test vehicle. The test vehicle's speed V should not be confused with the unknown mean speed u of the stream.

The values of M, T, and V taken on any particular test run are substituted in Eq. 3.6.4, leaving the two unknown stream variables q and k. To solve for these unknowns, two independent equations are needed, and a second test run, at a different test vehicle speed to ensure independence, can provide the second equation. Normally, one test run is performed *with traffic* (i.e., moving in the direction of the stream being measured) and the other is performed *against traffic* (i.e., moving in the opposite direction). In both cases, however, the test vehicle counts the M_o and M_p vehicles in the vehicular stream whose conditions are being measured.

When the test vehicle is moving against traffic, it will only be overtaken (in a relative sense) by vehicles in the stream; it will overtake no vehicles. In this case, then, M is simply equal to the number of vehicles in the northbound stream that the test vehicle encounters while traveling south.

Substituting the measurements taken during the two test runs into Eq. 3.6.4 and using subscripts w and a to refer to the test runs "with" and "against" traffic, respectively:

$$\frac{M_w}{T_w} = q - kV_w \tag{3.6.5a}$$

$$\frac{M_a}{T_a} = q + kV_a \tag{3.6.5b}$$

The plus sign in the second equation reflects the fact that the test vehicle travels in the negative direction.

The simultaneous solution of these equations yields

$$q = \frac{M_w + M_a}{T_w + T_a} \tag{3.6.6}$$

The units of q are vehicles per unit time, which is consistent with the definition of stream flow. However, whether this value is in fact the unknown stream flow is a legitimate question. Recalling that flow is a point measurement, the answer to this question would be affirmative if a point along the roadway length L can be found where a flow measurement during the total observation time $(T_w + T_a)$ yields the stream flow obtained by Eq. 3.6.6. Point A on Fig. 3.6.1 is such a point.

To prove this claim, consider the following situation: Assume that the test vehicle begins its run against traffic at time zero. At the same time, an independent observer located at point A begins to count the vehicles passing that point and continues to do so until the test vehicle crosses the same point going north. The test vehicle reaches the end of the run against traffic T_a units of time after the start of the test. It then turns around instantaneously and begins the test run with traffic, which takes T_w units of time. The total number of vehicles that would cross line A during the total time $(T_a + T_w)$ is equal to the number of vehicles M_a that the test vehicle encounters during its run against traffic *plus* the number of vehicles that overtake the test vehicle during its run with traffic *minus* any vehicles that the test vehicle overtakes during its run with traffic. The difference between the latter two counts taken during the run in the direction of the stream is simply equal to M_w, as defined before. The sum of M_a and M_w is exactly the number of vehicles that the independent observer at point A will be able to count during the time $(T_w + T_a)$. Consequently, the computation of Eq. 3.6.6 yields the required stream flow q.

To calculate the space mean speed u for the vehicular stream, Eq. 3.6.5a is rewritten as:

$$\frac{M_w}{T_w} = q - \left(\frac{q}{u}\right)\left(\frac{L}{T_w}\right) \tag{3.6.7}$$

The quantity (L/u) is the time T it takes the average vehicle in the stream to traverse the length L. This average time can be computed from Eq. 3.6.7:

$$T = T_w - \frac{M_w}{q} \tag{3.6.8}$$

where T_w is the travel time of the test vehicle in the direction of the stream being measured, M_w is the count taken during that run, and q is the flow computed by Eq. 3.6.6.

Equation 3.6.8 relates the travel time of the test vehicle to the average travel time of the vehicles in the stream. If the test vehicle is traveling faster than average, it will overtake more vehicles than will overtake it, and M_w will be negative. Consequently, the average stream travel time will be greater than the test vehicle's travel time. If the test vehicle is slower than the rest of the traffic, M_w will be positive, and the average stream travel time (Eq. 3.6.8) will be less than the test vehicle's. Finally, if the test vehicle is traveling at the average stream speed, it will (on the average) overtake as many vehicles as will overtake it, and Eq. 3.6.8 will reflect this fact. Once the average stream travel time is computed from Eq. 3.6.8, the average stream speed can be obtained from

$$u = \frac{L}{T} \tag{3.6.9}$$

This speed is the *space mean speed* because it is computed on the basis of travel time as described in Section 3.3. The calculation of the stream concentration is a matter of substitution of the flow computed from Eq. 3.6.6 and the mean speed computed from Eq. 3.6.9 into Eq. 3.4.1.

To ensure statistical reliability, the test is run a number of times (usually five or six) and the average results are employed in the final calculations.

Example 3.9

A bicycle racer practices every day at different times. Her route includes a ride along a 0.5-mi bikeway and back, as shown in the accompanying figure.

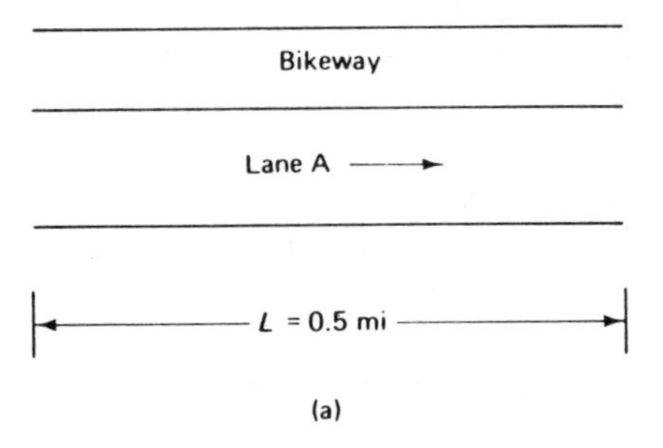

Figure P.3.9a

Since she is a traffic engineer, she has made it a habit to count the number of cars in lane A that she meets while riding southward (M_s), the number of cars in lane that overtake her while riding northward (M_o), and the number of cars in lane A that she overtakes while riding northward (M_p). The given table summarizes the average measurements that she obtained for each period of the day.

Time of day	M_s	M_o	M_p
9:00–9:00 A.M.	107	10	74
9:00–10:00	113	25	41
10:00–11:00	30	15	5
11:00–12:00	79	18	9

Given that the bicyclist travels at a constant speed of 20 mi/h, (a) find the traffic stream conditions for each period of the day, (b) calibrate $u = a + bk$ and plot the q-k relationship, and (c) estimate the capacity of lane A.

Solution (a) It takes the bicyclist (0.5 mi/20 mi/h = 0.025 h to traverse the half-mile distance. Hence, $T_a = T_w = 0.025$ h. For each period of the day, the flow, average travel time, mean speed, and concentration of lane A are computed as illustrated for the 8:00–9:00 A.M. period:

$$q_1 = \frac{107 + 10 - 74}{0.025 + 0.025} = 860 \text{ veh/h}$$

$$u_1 = \frac{0.5}{0.025 - \dfrac{(10 - 75)}{860}} = 5 \text{ mi/h}$$

$$k_1 = q_1/u_1 = 172 \text{ veh/mi}$$

The results for the other periods of the day are:

$$q_2 = 1940 \qquad q_3 = 800 \qquad q_4 = 1760$$

$$u_2 = 15 \qquad u_3 = 40 \qquad u_4 = 25$$

$$k_2 = 129 \qquad k_3 = 20 \qquad k_4 = 70$$

(b) To find the speed-concentration relationship of the form $u = a + bk$, apply simple linear regression to the pairs (k,u), with u as the dependent variable. The result is

$$u = 42.76 - 0.22k$$

Multiply both sides of this equation by k and substitute $q = uk$:

$$q = 42.76k - 0.22k^2$$

which is a parabola similar to that of Example 3.3 The plots of the last two equations are shown in the accompanying figure, along with the original data points.

(c) As in Example 3.3, q_{max} occurs at $u_m = u_f/2$ and $k_m = k_j/2$. Moreover, $u_f = 42.76$ mi/h at $k = 0$, and $k_j = 194$ veh/mi at $u = 0$. Hence,

$$q_{max} = 2074 \text{ veh/h}$$

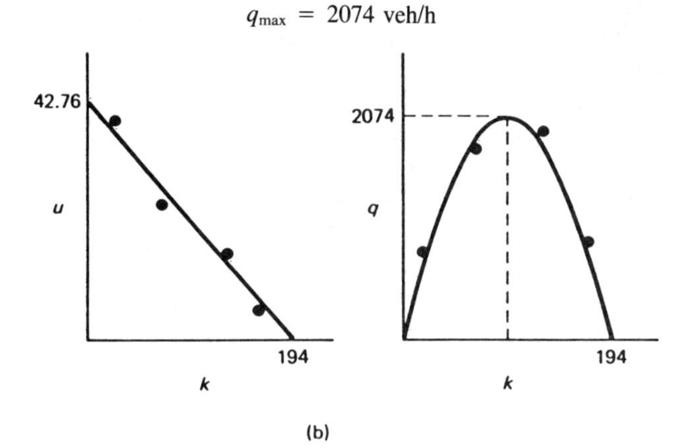

Figure P.3.9b

Discussion This example summarizes three important parts of this chapter: It illustrates the use of the moving-observer method to take traffic stream measurements, it applies the method of least squares to calibrate the relationship between u and k, and it applies the fundamental characteristics of traffic streams to find the q-k curve.

The first step assumed that the traffic conditions prevailing during each period of the day remain relatively stable from day to day, since the observations were averaged by time of day. The results show that during the morning peak hour between 8:00 and 9:00 A.M. lane A is very congested with very low speed ($u = 5$ mi/h) and high concentration ($k = 172$ veh/mi). Between 9:00 and 10:00 A.M., the traffic eases and the prevailing conditions move closer to free flow. Finally, between 11:00 A.M. and 12:00 noon, concentration increases and speed decreases once more, perhaps due to the lunchtime crowd.

With regard to the regression step in the solution, it is important once more to note that the form of the relationship had to be specified by the analyst. Alternative model forms could also have been tried and the best among these selected based on the correlation coefficient and other statistical tests.

The last part of the solution (i.e., finding the capacity of the lane) is identical to Example 3.3.

3.7 SHOCK WAVES IN TRAFFIC

3.7.1 Introduction

Suppose that a traffic stream is moving on a roadway at a given flow, speed, and concentration as illustrated by point 1 on the q-k diagram of Figure 3.7.1. Based on the calibrated diagram shown, point 1 corresponds to a flow of 1000 veh/h, a concentration of 25 veh/mi, and a mean speed (i.e., the slope of chord 0-1) of 40 mi/h. The spacing between vehicles may be computed by Eq. 3.3.1 to be about 212 ft. Now, assume that a truck in the stream decides to slow down to 10 mi/h. If passing is not permitted, the following vehicles will also have to slow down to match the truck's speed. With time, a moving platoon of vehicles traveling at 10 mi/h will grow behind the truck. At any instant, the last vehicle to join the platoon will be traveling at 10 mi/h, but farther upstream vehicles would continue to approach the platoon at the original conditions. Since the vehicles within the platoon are traveling slower than before they joined, they will tend to adjust their spacing to a shorter safe spacing than before. The resulting stream conditions for vehicles within the platoon are represented by point 2 on Figure 3.7.1, where the slope of chord 0-2 is the platoon speed. In this example, the values of platoon flow and concentration are shown to be 1200 veh/h and 120 veh/mi, respectively.

Thus at any time after the truck slowed down, a stationary observer will see a platoon defined by the truck at its front and the last vehicle to join at its rear. The platoon, consisting of slow-moving vehicles at relatively high concentrations, is moving with a speed of 10 mi/h and grows in length as more vehicles join it. After some time, the traffic

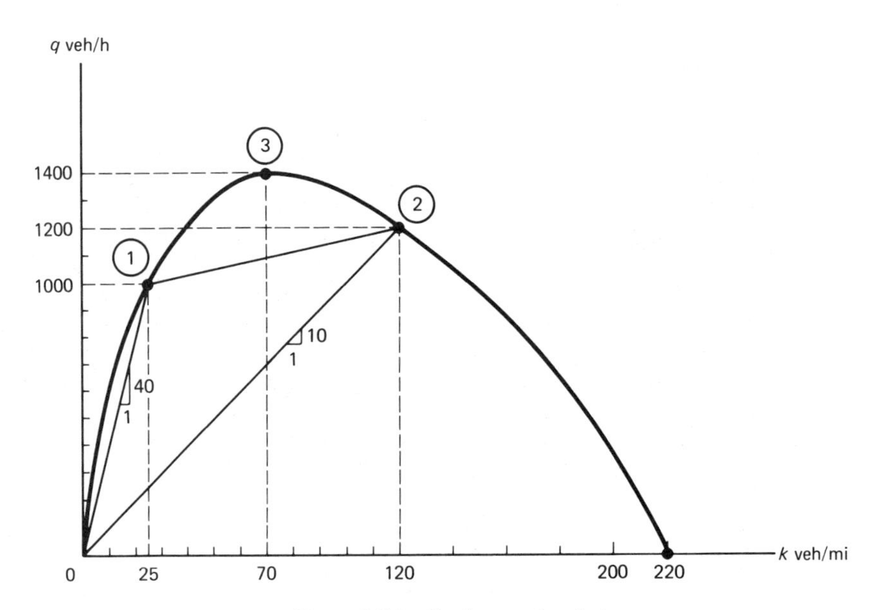

Figure 3.7.1 Shock wave description.

conditions in front of the truck are at free flow (i.e., zero concentration). Behind the last vehicle to join the platoon the stream conditions are at 40 mi/h and a concentration of 25 veh/mi. Figure 3.7.2 illustrates the dynamics of platoon formation described above: At time $t = 0$, the vehicles in the stream are shown to travel at the average stream conditions corresponding to point 1 of Figure 3.7.1. The truck slows down to 10 mi/h at this instant. A short time later, the truck has displaced somewhat and a following vehicle is shown to have matched its speed. The platoon now contains two vehicles [Figure 3.7.2(b)]. Later on, additional vehicles join the moving platoon, as illustrated. Figure 3.7.2(d) shows a clear roadway in front of the truck, the high-concentration platoon behind the truck, and approaching vehicles at the original stream conditions farther upstream. The same situation is described by the time-distance diagram of Figure 3.7.3.

Using a hydrodynamic analogy [3.8], a *shock wave* is said to exist whenever traffic streams of varying stream conditions meet. In the above example, there are two such lines of demarcation, or shock waves. One is seen between the platoon conditions and the free-flow conditions in front of the platoon (line *AA*, Figure 3.7.2). The other is seen between the approach conditions and the platoon conditions (line *BB*, Figure 3.7.2). The shock wave at the front of the platoon is defined by the truck, whereas the shock wave at the rear of the platoon is defined by the last vehicle to join the platoon. Figures 3.7.2 and 3.7.3 show that the shock waves *AA* and *BB* displace with time in relation to the

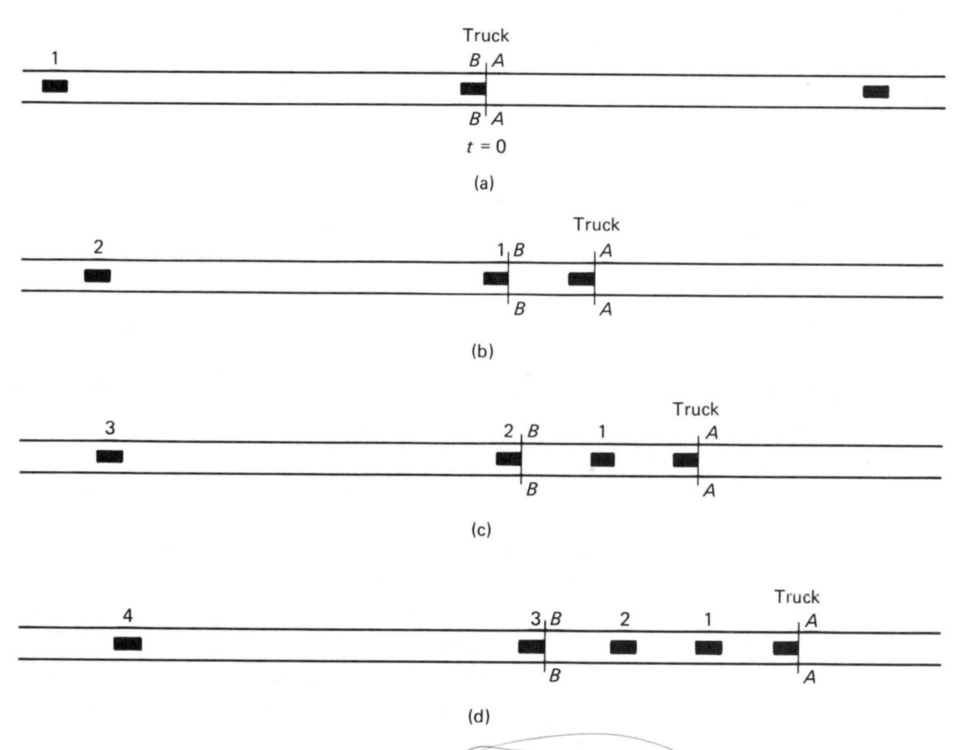

Figure 3.7.2 Platoon formation.

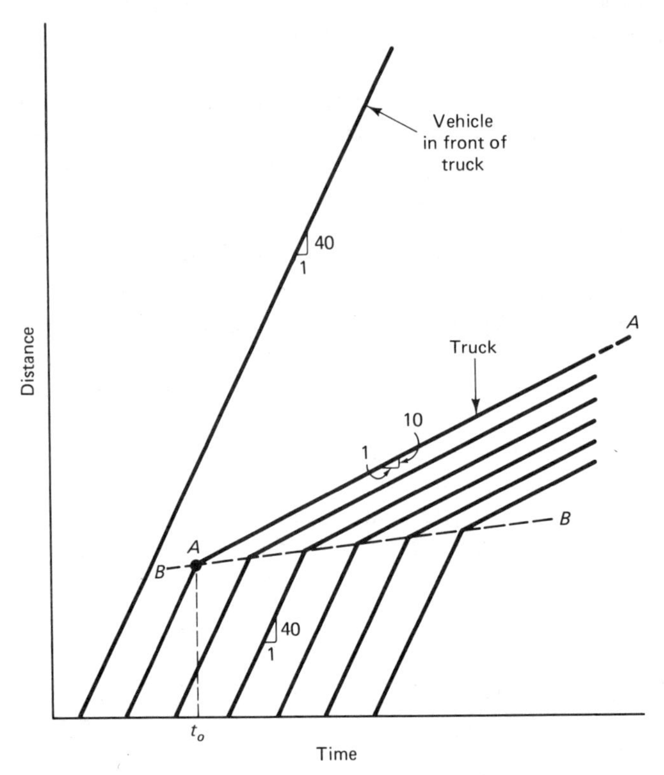

Figure 3.7.3 Time-distance diagram of platoon formation.

roadway. The rate at which the platoon grows is related to the relative speeds of the two shock waves *AA* and *BB*. Moreover, given the platoon concentration (120 veh/mi in this case) and the length of the platoon, the number of vehicles within the platoon can easily be computed.

If, after a time, the truck driver decides either to accelerate or to exit the highway, the vehicles stuck behind the truck will be free to increase their speeds, and another shock wave will begin between the release conditions and the platoon conditions. The next section shows that the fundamental diagram of stream flow can be used to explain the shock wave phenomenon.

3.7.2 The Shock Wave Equation

It has been shown [3.8] that the speed of a traffic stream shock wave is given by the slope of the chord connecting the two stream conditions that define the shock wave (e.g., points 1 and 2, Figure 3.7.1). Labeling the two conditions as *a* and *b in the direction of traffic movement,* the *magnitude and direction* of the speed of the shock wave between the two conditions are given by

$$U_{sw} = \frac{q_b - q_a}{k_b - k_a} \tag{3.7.1}$$

If the sign of the shock wave speed is positive, the shock wave is traveling in the direction of stream flow; if it is zero, the shock wave is stationary with respect to the roadway; if it is negative, the shock wave moves in the upstream direction. The example illustrated by Figs. 3.7.2 and 3.7.3 shows two shock waves both traveling in the direction of the stream of vehicles. Situations arise where the shock wave travels in the opposite direction. For example, consider the case where a vehicular stream is interrupted by a traffic signal. Vehicles stopped by the red light are packed at jam concentration (i.e., zero speed and flow). Upstream of the stationary platoon, vehicles approach the platoon at the approach conditions. The shock wave between the approaching vehicles and the jammed vehicles defined by the last vehicle to be stopped is, in fact, moving in the negative (i.e., upstream) direction.

Example 3.10

For the illustration of Fig. 3.7.1, determine the magnitude and direction of the speeds of the two shock waves *AA* and *BB* and determine the rate at which the platoon is growing behind the truck.

Solution The conditions that define the shock wave at the front of the platoon are (1) the platoon conditions (i.e., $q_a = 1200$ veh/h and $k_a = 120$ veh/mi) and (2) the free-flow conditions in front of the truck (i.e., $q_b = 0$ and $k_b = 0$). Equation 3.7.1 yields the speed of the shock wave *AA*:

$$U_{sw}(AA) = \frac{0 - 1200}{0 - 120} = +10 \text{ mi/h}$$

which happens to be the speed of the truck, as expected in this situation. The speed of the shock wave at the rear of the platoon defined by (1) the approach conditions (i.e., $q_a = 1000$ veh/h and $k_a = 25$ veh/mi) and (2) the platoon conditions is

$$U_{sw}(BB) = \frac{1200 - 1000}{120 - 25} = +2.1 \text{ mi/h}$$

The front of the platoon moves at 10 mi/h forward relative to the roadway and the rear of the platoon travels at 2.1 mi/h in the same direction. The rate of growth of the platoon is given by the relative speed between the two, or 10.0 − 2.1 = 7.9 mi/h. The platoon grows at this rate as it travels forward.

Discussion The speed of the front of the platoon is the same as the speed of the truck only because the conditions in front of the truck are at free flow (see Fig. 3.7.3). In the general case, however, the speed of the shock wave should not be confused with the speed of any of the vehicles in the stream, as the speed of shock wave *BB* in this example clarifies. Platoon vehicles are traveling at 10 mi/h, approaching vehicles are traveling at 40 mi/h (see slope of line 0-1, Fig. 3.7.1), but the shock wave between the two travels at 2.1 mi/h. It is of interest to note that although the truck forced the traffic to slow down, the flow increased from 1000 to 1200 veh/h, a situation of which the frustrated drivers would be unaware. In certain cases, slowing the traffic via the traffic-control system may be a good way of increasing the flow. But this consequence goes totally unnoticed by the drivers.

Example 3.11

For Example 3.10, assume that the truck exited the traffic stream 10 min after slowing down. Vehicles at the front of the platoon were then released to a speed of 20 mi/h and a concentration of 70 veh/mi. Compute the amount of time it took the 10-mi/h platoon to disappear.

Solution The release conditions imply a flow of (20 mi/h)(70 veh/mi) = 1400 veh/h (i.e., point 3 on Fig. 3.7.1). At the end of 10 min (or $\frac{1}{6}$ h) the platoon had grown to a length of

$$L = (7.9 \text{ mi/h})(\tfrac{1}{6} \text{ h}) = 1.3 \text{ mi}$$

Incidentally, at that instant the 120-veh/mi platoon contained (1.3)(120) = 156 vehicles. After the truck exited the traffic stream, a shock wave between (1) the platoon conditions and (2) the release conditions developed. The speed of this shock wave is

$$U_{sw} = \frac{1400 - 1200}{70 - 120} = -4.0 \text{ mi/h}$$

relative to the roadway. Thus the shock wave at the front of the platoon moved upstream at 4.0 mi/h, whereas the shock wave at the rear of the platoon continued to move downstream at 2.1 mi/h. The relative speed of the two waves was 4.0 + 2.1 = 6.1 mi/h. Since the platoon was 1.3 mi long to begin with, it took (1.3)/(6.1) = 0.21 h after the truck's departure for the platoon to dissipate totally.

Discussion The accompanying time-distance diagram plots the location of the front and the rear of the platoon from the moment the truck slowed down to the moments when

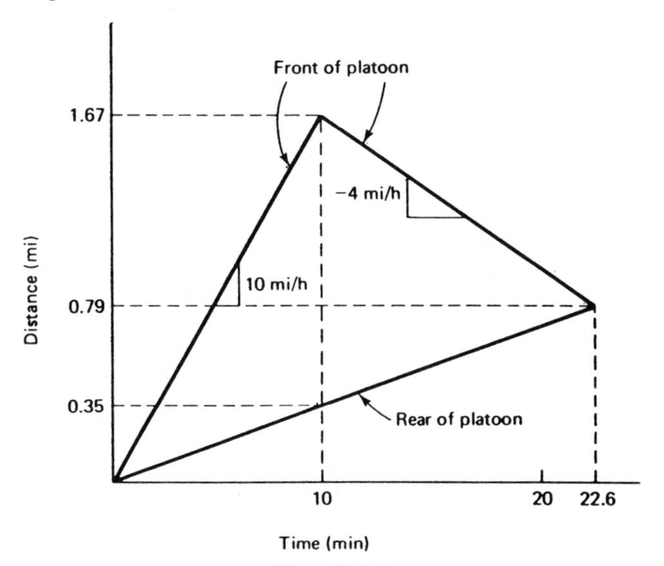

Figure P.3.11

the last vehicle caught in the platoon was released. At any instant, the difference between the two represents the length of the platoon, which is seen to grow from 0 to 1.3 mi during the first 10 min and then to shrink back to 0 approximately 12.6 min after the truck's exit. During this second phase, the front and rear of the platoon were defined by different vehicles at different times as vehicles at the front were sequentially released and additional vehicles joined at the rear.

The point where the platoon disappeared was 0.79 mi from the initial point, even though the front of the platoon had been as far as 1.67 mi ahead of the location where the truck slowed down.

Example 3.12

For Example 3.11, determine the speed of the shock wave that commenced at the instant when the 10-mi/h platoon was totally eliminated.

Solution After the last platoon vehicle was released, a shock wave commenced between (1) the approach conditions behind this last vehicle and (2) the release conditions in front of it. The speed of this new shock wave was

$$U_{sw} = \frac{1400 - 1000}{70 - 25} = +8.9 \text{ mi/h forward}$$

Discussion The appearance of this, perhaps unexpected, shock wave illustrates the complexity of the dynamics of traffic flow. These accordionlike movements occur back and forth as vehicles slow down and accelerate in response to various stimuli, including other vehicles, traffic controls, sight-distance restrictions, sharp horizontal curves, and so forth. The 8.9 mi/h shock wave presumably continued as long as the approach and release conditions were sustained. In reality, these conditions change over time, as a comparison between the traffic at midnight vis-à-vis the morning rush hour would attest. Moreover, even under identical *average* conditions, there is enough variability in individual vehicle conditions to cause the continuous commencement and dissipation of such shock waves.

3.8 SUMMARY

This chapter extended the equations of single-vehicle motion to vehicular interactions. A general relationship between safe spacing and speed was developed and shown to affect the capacity of highways and transitways. Based on the single-vehicle variables of speed, spacing, and headway, the fundamental variables of vehicular streams (average speed, concentration, and flow) were defined, and the fundamental relationship between the stream variables was examined. A method of measuring stream conditions (the moving-observer method) and a method of calibrating the relationships between them (least squares regression) were also presented. Finally, the phenomenon of shock waves in traffic streams was illustrated.

3.9 EXERCISES

1. A rapid-transit system employing single vehicles is scheduled at constant headways. For safety regime b, plot the relationship between spacing in feet and speed in feet per second using the following data: perception-reaction time = 1.5 s, normal deceleration = 8 ft/s^2, emergency deceleration = 32 ft/s^2, vehicle length = 40 ft, and safety clearance x_o = 4 ft.
2. Repeat the solution to Exercise 1 for safety regime a.
3. For Exercises 1 and 2, calculate the maximum flows in vehicles per hour and the corresponding speeds.
4. Given $s = 0.30/(60 - u)$, where s is the spacing in miles and u is the speed in miles per hour, derive the relationships u-k, u-q, and q-k. Also estimate the capacity (i.e., q_{max}) of the roadway.
5. For the data of Exercise 4, plot spacing in feet versus headway in seconds.
6. Prepare a computer program, which, given the necessary inputs and a particular safety regime, calculates the spacing for increasing values of speed.
7. A study of the traffic using a tunnel showed that the following speed-concentration relationship applies:

$$u = 17.2 \ln(228/k) \text{ mi/h}$$

Find (a) the capacity of the tunnel, (b) the values of speed and concentration at capacity, and (c) the jam concentration.

8. The u-k relationship for a particular freeway lane was found to be

$$u + 2.6 = 0.001(k - 240)^2$$

Given that the speed is in miles per hour and the concentration is in vehicles per mile, find (a) the free-flow speed, (b) the jam concentration, (c) the lane capacity, and (d) the speed at capacity.

9. The following relationship applies to a particular urban highway:

$$q = 273u - 70u \ln u$$

Calculate q_{max}, u_m, k_m, and u_f.

10. Show that Eqs. 3.5.7 and 3.5.9 are equivalent.
11. Use the data of Example 3.7 to fit a curve of the form $Y = aX^2$ by direct nonlinear regression.
12. Repeat Exercise 11 assuming that $Y = aX^b$ by linear regression with transformed variables.
13. Plot and compare the results of Example 3.7 and Exercises 11 and 12.
14. The following data were obtained from an experiment:

X	1	3	4	6	8	9	11	14
Y	9	8	7	5	4	4	2	1

Fit a line of the form $Y = a + bX$, and calculate and interpret the coefficient of correlation.

15. According to the General Motors Research Laboratory, the fuel consumption rate of passenger cars is of the form

$$F = K_1 + \frac{K_2}{V}$$

where F is the fuel consumption in gallons per mile, V is the space mean speed, and K_1 and K_2 are calibration parameters. The following data were obtained by an experiment using a typical mix of passenger cars.

F	0.40	0.10	0.12	0.07	0.06
V	2.50	10.20	14.08	25.12	52.00

Calibrate, sketch, and interpret this model.

16. The following data were taken on a highway:

u	52	34	36	22	21	mi/h
k	8	41	48	70	105	veh/mi

(a) Estimate the free-flow speed assuming that $q = AkB^k$. (b) Calculate the capacity of the highway. (c) Find u_m and k_m.

17. A moving observer conducted two test runs on a 5-mi stretch of roadway. Both tests were in the direction of traffic. Given the following measurements, calculate the flow, concentration, space mean speed, average spacing, and average headway of the traffic stream.

Test run	Test vehicle speed (mi/h)	$M_o - M_p$ vehicles
1	10	100
2	20	−150

18. While taking measurements by the moving-observer method, a test vehicle covered a 1-mi section in 1.5 min going against traffic and 2.5 min going with traffic. Given that the traffic flow was 800 veh/h and that the test vehicle passed 10 more vehicles than passed it when going with traffic, find (a) the number of vehicles encountered by the test vehicle while moving against traffic, (b) the speed of the traffic being measured, (c) the concentration of the traffic stream, and (d) whether on its run with traffic, the test vehicle was traveling faster or slower than the traffic stream.

19. Given the following u-k relationship,

$$u = 30 \ln \left(\frac{300}{k}\right) \text{ mi/h}$$

find the jam concentration, the capacity of the roadway, and the speed of the shock wave between conditions $u_a = 60$ mi/h and $u_b = 40$ mi/h.

20. A line of traffic moving at a speed of 30 mi/h and a concentration of 50 veh/mi is stopped for 30 s at a red light. Calculate (a) the velocity and direction of the stopping wave, (b) the length of the line of cars stopped during the 30 s of red, and (c) the number of cars stopped during the 30 s of red. Assume a jam concentration of 250 veh/mi.

21. A vehicular stream at $q_a = 1200$ veh/h and $k_a = 100$ veh/mi is interrupted by a flagperson for 5 min beginning at time $t = t_o$. At time $t = t_o + 5$ minutes, vehicles at the front of the stationary platoon begin to be released at $q_b = 1600$ veh/h and $u_b = 20$ mi/h. Assuming that $k_j = 240$ veh/mi, (a) plot the location of the front of the platoon versus time and the location of the rear of the platoon versus time and (b) plot the length of the growing platoon versus time.

22. A 15-mi/h school zone is in effect from 7:30 to 9:00 A.M. Traffic measurements taken on October 10, 1985, showed that at precisely 9:00 A.M., the conditions presented in the accompanying figure prevailed. How long did it take for the 3-mi platoon to disappear, and what was the speed of the shock wave that commenced at the moment when the platoon dissipated completely?

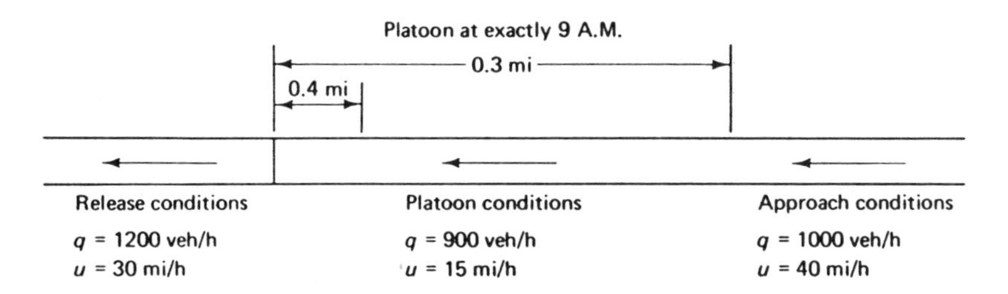

23. You were the driver of the *sixth* car to be stopped by a red light. *Ten* seconds elapsed after the onset of the following green before you were able to get going again. Given that the release flow was 1200 veh/h, calculate the release concentration and the release mean speed. Assume an average car length $L = 18$ ft and a safety margin $x_o = 2$ ft.

24. Prepare a computer program that calculates the speed of the shock wave between two conditions specified by input values for k_a and k_b. Assume that $u = C - Dk$, where C and D are parametric values to be specified by the user of your program. Your program should be constrained by

$$40 \leq u_f \leq 70 \text{ mi/h}$$
$$200 \leq k_j \leq 300 \text{ veh/mi}$$

Run your program several times and interpret the results.

3.10 REFERENCES

3.1 VUCHIC, VUKAN R., *Urban Public Transportation Systems and Technology,* Prentice-Hall, Inc., Englewood Cliffs, N.J., © 1981. Table 7.3, p. 538, used by permission.

3.2 GERLOUGH, DANIEL L., and MATTHEW J. HUBER, *Traffic Flow Theory, A Monograph,* Special Report 165, Transportation Research Board, National Research Council, Washington, D.C., 1975.

3.3. DICKEY, JOHN W., *Metropolitan Transportation Planning,* Scripta Book Company (McGraw-Hill), New York, 1975.

3.4 Institute of Transportation Engineers, *Transportation and Traffic Engineering Handbook,* Prentice-Hall, Inc., Englewood Cliffs, N.J., 1976.

3.5 ROCKWELL, THOMAS H., and JOSEPH TREITERER, *Sensing and Communication Between Vehicles,* National Cooperative Highway Research Program Report 51, Highway Research Board, National Research Council, Washington, D.C., 1968.

3.6 SYNODINOS, N. E., and C. S. PAPACOSTAS, "Driving Habits and Behaviour Patterns of University Students," *International Review of Applied Psychology,* 34 (1985): 241–57.

3.7 GREENSHIELDS, B. D., "A Study of Traffic Capacity," *Highway Research Board Proceedings,* National Research Council, 14 (1935): 448–77.

3.8 LIGHTHILL, M. J., and G. B. WHITMAN, "On Kinematic Waves: II. A Theory of Traffic Flow on Long Crowded Roads," *Proceedings of the Royal Society* (London), Series A, 229, no. 1178 (1955): 317–345.

CHAPTER 4

CAPACITY ANALYSIS OF ACTUAL SYSTEMS

4.1 INTRODUCTION

The mathematical models of vehicular streams that were developed in Chapter 3 are valid representations of the general phenomena they describe because they are based on valid principles. For example, Eq. 3.2.4 relates the spacing between a leading and a following vehicle to operating speed via a number of technological parameters, including the normal and emergency deceleration rates, the length of the vehicles, the response time of the following vehicle to a sudden deceleration by the leading vehicle, and a desired safety level. As a mathematical tool, the equation can be applied to any combination of parametric values. However, to be representative of a particular system, the equation must be evaluated using the specific attributes of the system under study.

This chapter is concerned with the stream characteristics of actual transportation systems. The flow relationships and the capacities of selected urban mass-transportation systems operating on exclusive pathways and a model that can be used to estimate the fleet size required to provide a desired flow are followed by a practical method of examining the capacity and level of service of high-level highway facilities (i.e., freeways and expressways). The described highway capacity method can be used either in order to determine the number of highway lanes required to satisfy a desired level of service, or to estimate the level of service prevailing on a highway given its geometric design and the actual flow conditions. Finally, calibrated pedestrian flow models are presented and discussed, and the fundamental similarity between vehicular and pedestrian flow models is illustrated.

4.2 URBAN MASS-TRANSPORTATION SYSTEMS

4.2.1 Background

In Chapter 1, a historical note about the evolution of public transportation systems was presented in order to clarify the nomenclature associated with these systems. Among the categories discussed were the following:

Light rail transit (LRT) is essentially a modernized electric streetcar with possibilities of articulation and capable of being operated both in mixed traffic and on exclusive rights of way. The PCC car is a very successful electric streetcar design that resulted from the cooperative efforts of the Electric Railway Presidents' Conference Committee during the 1930s.

Personal rapid transit (PRT) refers to system designs that generally employ small vehicles operating on a network of exclusive pathways and characterized by route and scheduling flexibility.

Automated guideway transit (AGT) is designed to operate on exclusive guideways without intervention from an onboard driver in an attempt to minimize labor costs and to increase productivity; it may or may not be a PRT system.

Rail rapid transit (RRT) generally refers to high-performance, electrically-propelled, multicar systems that operate on grade-separated rail facilities with few stops.

Regional rail (RGR) [4.1] or commuter rail (CR) [4.2] denotes multicar diesel or electric trains with very few stops that had its origins as an extension of intercity railroads.

An articulated bus is a long urban motor bus consisting of two sections, which are connected by a flexible joint to allow for short turning radii and increased passenger-holding capacity vis-à-vis the standard 40-ft urban bus.

Table 4.2.1 taken from Vuchic [4.1] lists the attributes of the typical designs listed in the last row from each of these categories.

4.2.2 Uninterrupted Speed-Flow Relationships

Figures 4.2.1 and 4.2.2 present the $q-u$ relationships derived by Vuchic [4.1] and specify the typical operational safety regimes of the technological systems listed in Table 4.2.1. Vuchic uses the term *way capacity* to refer to the flow on the curve corresponding to a specific safety regime. This is to capture the fact that each $q - u$ curve represents the maximum flow possible for a given speed and a specific safety regime. Note, however, that for each curve, there exists a speed for which the flow (or way capacity) is maximum. This is what, in this textbook, is referred to as the capacity of the system, q_{max}.

Figure 4.2.1 presents flow in terms of *vehicles per hour*. Also note that certain of the systems plotted permit *transit units* (TU) or trains, each consisting of a number of such vehicles. Each train may be thought of as a series of vehicles having a jam spacing in contrast to the much longer spacing between transit units. Thus, the coupling of vehicles into transit units in effect organizes the stream into a series of small spacings (and

TABLE 4.2.1 CHARACTERISTICS OF TYPICAL TRANSIT SYSTEMS

Item	Unit (Mode →)	Standard bus	Articulated bus	Single 4-axle LRT vehicle	Personal rapid transit	2-car AGT	2-car articulated LRT	8-car AGT	6-car RRT	10-car RRT/RGR
n	veh/TU	1	1	1	1	2	2	8	6	10
l'	m	12.0	17.0	14.0	2.3	6.5	24.0	10.7	18.0	21.0
C_v	sps/veh	53[b]	73[b]	110	4[b]	40	189	70	145	175
S_0	m	1	1	2	1	1	2	1	2	2
t_r	s	1	1	1	0	0	1	0	0	0
b_n	m/s^2	1.4	1.4	1.2	1.6	1.4	1.2	1.4	1.1	1.1
b_e	m/s^2	4.0	4.0	3.0	5.0	4.0	3.0	4.0	1.8	1.8
V_{max}	km/h	90	80	80	70	50	90	80	100	120
v_{max}	m/s	25.0	22.2	22.2	19.4	13.9	25.0	22.2	27.7	33.3
Operating safety regime		c	c	b	a	a	a	a	a	a
Typical model		GMC's "New Look"	M.A.N.	PCC	Aramis	Airtrans	DÜWAG U-2	Skybus	Munich U-Bahn	San Francisco BART

[a]Data given are typical for the selected models. They are taken from the models given, with the exception of a few rounded or modified values to eliminate nontypical features (e.g., BART's A and C cars have different lengths; Airtrans' V_{max} = 27 km/h). Acceleration rate a = 0.8 m/s^2 and station standing time t_s = 20 s are assumed for all modes.

[b]Assumes seating only.

SOURCE: Vuchic [4.1]; Table 7.4, p. 550.

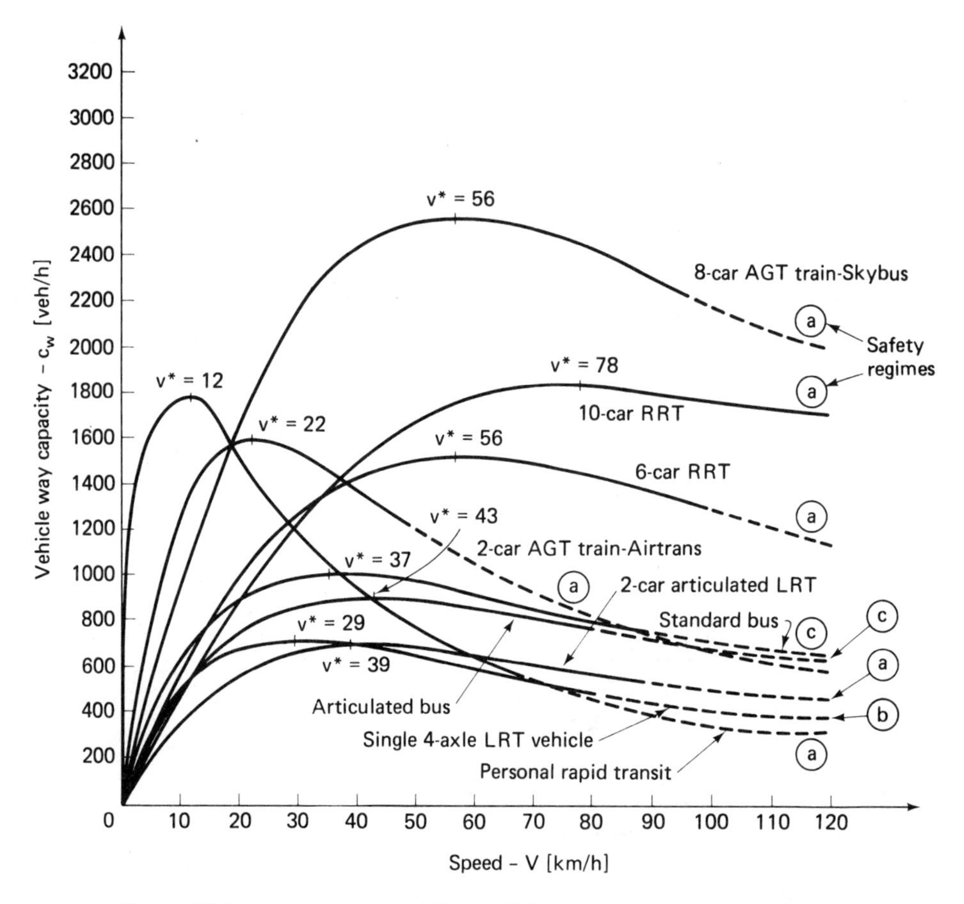

Figure 4.2.1 Actual system speed flow: vehicles per hour. (*SOURCE*: Vuchic [4.1], Fig. 7.10, p. 551.)

headways) followed by a larger spacing (and headway). This arrangement results in a higher vehicular flow than if single vehicles were scheduled individually at the constant spacing required by the same safety regime.

Figure 4.2.2 presents the flow characteristics of the same technological systems, not in terms of vehicles per hour but in terms of what Vuchic calls *spaces per hour*. Consequently, these curves represent the passenger-carrying capability of each system.

Two important points relating to Figs. 4.2.1 and 4.2.2 must be stressed here. First, system comparisons of passenger flow on one hand and vehicular flow and capacity on the other do not lead to the same conclusion with respect to dominance of one system over another. It should also be noted that just because a system is capable of carrying a certain flow of passengers, it does not necessarily mean that it actually carries that maximum. To illustrate this point consider the private automobile: The passenger-holding capacity of a typical automobile is about five to six passengers. But actual usage shows

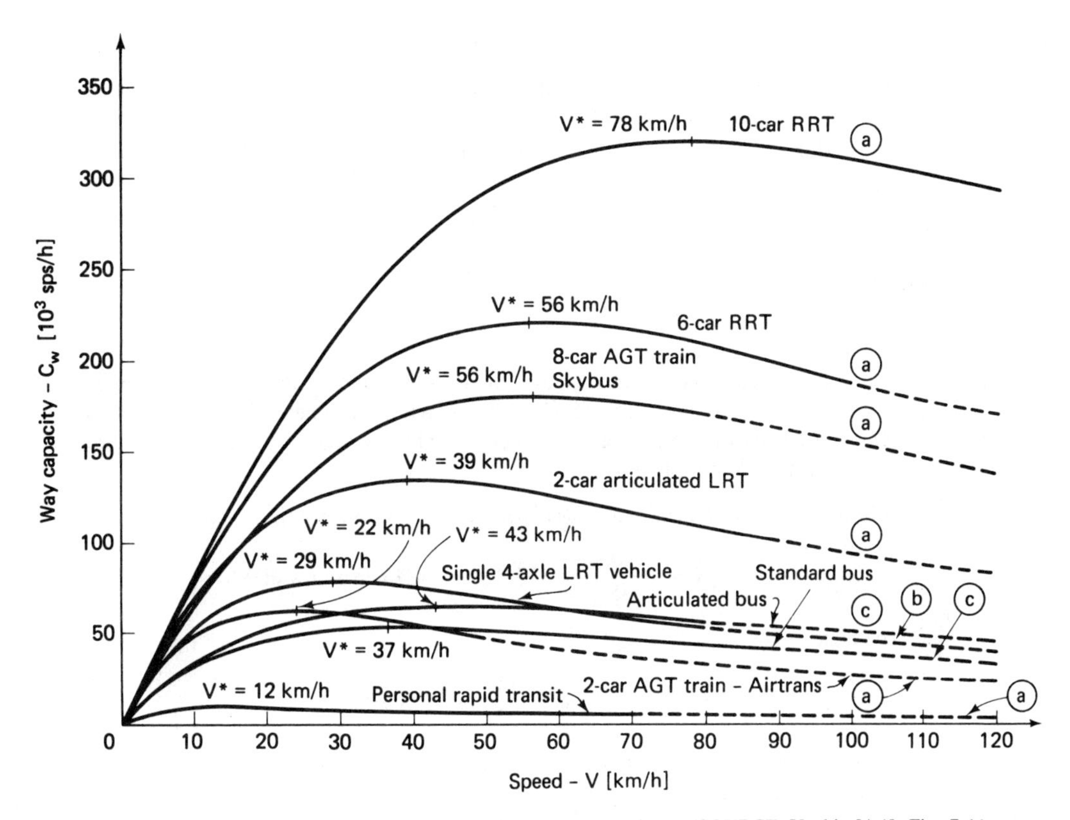

Figure 4.2.2 Actual system speed flow: spaces per hour. (*SOURCE*: Vuchic [4.1], Fig. 7.11, p. 552.)

an average loading of 1.5 to 2.0 passengers per automobile, depending on the time of day, the trip purpose, and other factors.

The second point worthy of mention in connection with Figs. 4.2.1 and 4.2.2 is the fact that, irrespective of how flow is considered (i.e., passenger or vehicular), there are ranges where one system dominates another, but there are also ranges where the reverse is true. Thus, in many cases, it is not possible to state unequivocably that one system is always superior to another. Differences in safety regime, capital and operating costs, and system flexibility are among the variables that enter the calculus of choosing between systems.

Know well

4.2.3 Fleet Size

The *number* of vehicles needed to sustain a transit line *flow* of q vehicles per hour for a time period T is affected by the fact that some vehicles may be able to traverse the line more than one time during T. A vehicular count over the time period T will yield

$$N = qT \text{ vehicles} \tag{4.2.1}$$

some of which will be counted more than one time. Assuming that the round-trip time of a single vehicle is T_{rt}, this vehicle will, on the average, traverse the line approximately T/T_{rt} times. Hence, to provide N vehicle departures during T, a fleet F of

$$F = N\left(\frac{T_{rt}}{T}\right) = qT_{rt} \tag{4.2.2}$$

is needed.

Example 4.1

A transit line employing nonarticulated vehicles is expected to carry 10,000 passengers during the 2-hr morning peak period. Given a round-trip time of 30 min and an average vehicle occupancy of 75 passengers, calculate the hourly flow q and the number of vehicles F required to provide this flow.

Solution The number of vehicular departures needed to carry the given demand is

$$N = \frac{10{,}000}{75} = 133.3 \quad \text{or} \quad 134 \text{ departures in 2 h}$$

The hourly flow is

$$q = \frac{134}{2} = 67 \text{ veh/h}$$

Assuming that this flow is attainable, the number of vehicles needed is

$$F = (67 \text{ veh/h})\,(0.5 \text{ h}) = 33.5, \quad \text{or} \quad 34 \text{ vehicles}$$

4.2.4 Transit Network Fleet Size

The preceding subsection developed a simple formula that can be used to estimate the number of vehicles needed to accommodate a known passenger demand on a single line. The calculation of the fleet size needed to provide services on a large transit network consisting of many transit lines is complicated by the fact that the travel desires of people vary by time of day and by spatial orientation. Moreover, the selection of appropriate transit lines is a difficult task, which frequently results in overlapping lines and transferring between lines. As a simple illustration of line overlapping, consider the two-line network of Fig. 4.2.3.

The vehicle flow requirements for each link of the network are shown in parentheses for the inbound movement (i.e., toward node 3) and in brackets for the outbound movement (i.e., away from node 3). The two transit lines shown overlap on the link 2-3; hence passengers on this link can choose either line. In order to accommodate the known demand, the line requirements must satisfy the following conditions:

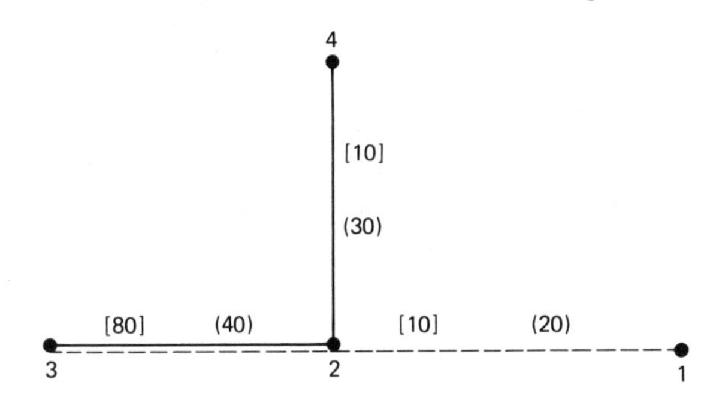

Line	Service
1	1:1, 2, 3 2:3, 2, 1
2	3:4, 2, 3 4:3, 2, 4

Figure 4.2.3 Transit line overlap. (*SOURCE*: Papacostas [4.3], Fig. 2.10, p. 38.)

$$N_{\text{I}} \geqslant 30 \text{ departures} \tag{4.2.3a}$$

$$N_{\text{II}} \geqslant 20 \tag{4.2.3b}$$

and

$$N_{\text{I}} + N_{\text{II}} \geqslant 80 \tag{4.2.3c}$$

The problem then is to distribute the extra flow on link 2-3 (i.e., $80 - 30 - 20 = 30$) between the two lines. This may be accomplished by minimizing the fleet size, for example,

$$\min F = \sum \left(\frac{N_i T_{rt,\ i}}{T} \right) \tag{4.2.4}$$

or, since the above minimization would generally favor shorter lines, by some other rule, such as distributing the extra flow to the overlapping lines in proportion to the minimum needs according to constraints 4.2.3a and 4.2.3b [4.3]. Another option involves the introduction of a shuttle line between points 2 and 3. Computer-based methods of transit network analysis are available in the technical literature [4.4].

4.3. HIGHWAY CAPACITY AND LEVEL OF SERVICE

4.3.1 Background

The general relationships among highway flow, concentration, and speed were derived and interpreted in Chapter 3, which also illustrated the moving-observer method of measuring these variables, and discussed the least squares regression method of calibrating flow relationships based on actual measurements.

From the practical point of view, it is often difficult to devote the resources needed for data collection and curve fitting for each specific highway segment under investigation. Moreover, it is impossible to take measurements on a facility that is under design, that is, before it is actually built. Yet the designer must anticipate the operational characteristics of the facility in order to make prudent geometric design decisions. Such estimates are based on observations of existing facilities of similar types, and practical methods of analysis and design that utilize these estimates have evolved and been codified over the years [4.5–4.9]. This section summarizes the basic method by which the capacity of long segments of highway facilities that are removed from the influence of external interruptions (i.e., at-grade intersections or entrance and exit ramps) can be assessed. The concept of *level of service* is first introduced, and a method of estimating the capacity and operating conditions of freeway segments is presented.

4.3.2 Level of Service

The earlier discussion of the fundamental diagrams of vehicular streams pointed out that each diagram, $q-k$ or $u-q$, encloses a region that subtends the stream conditions meeting a certain safety level. It was also shown that the counteracting incentives of safety versus speed tend to cause actual stream conditions to cluster around the curve. Moreover, since the $q-k$ and $u-q$ curves were "backward bending," each level of flow q was shown to correspond to two distinct stream conditions on either side of capacity: one closer to free-flow and the other toward traffic jam conditions. To capture this difference, the 1965 *Highway Capacity Manual* [4.6] uses the concept of *level of service,* as illustrated by Fig. 4.3.1. The overall shape of this conceptualized relationship is the familiar $u-q$

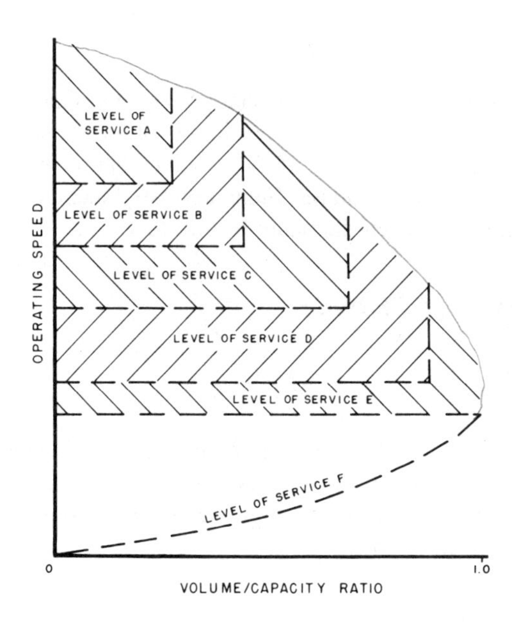

Figure 4.3.1 Levels of service. (*SOURCE*: Highway Research Board [4.6], Fig. 4.1, p. 81.)

curve, except that the abscissa plots the normalized flow (or volume), that is, flow divided by the capacity of the roadway. The resulting volume-to-capacity (V/C) ratio ranges from 0 to 1. The area encompassed by the normalized $u-q$ curve is divided into six subareas denoted by the letters *A* to *F*, each designating a specific level of service.

The qualitative description of the conditions that correspond to each level of service found in the 1965 *Highway Capacity Manual* [4.6] have been superseded by new definitions, which appear in the 1985 *Highway Capacity Manual* as follows:

> *Level-of-service A* represents free flow. Individual users are virtually unaffected by the presence of others in the traffic stream. Freedom to select desired speeds and to maneuver within the traffic stream is extremely high. The general level of comfort and convenience provided to the motorist, passenger, or pedestrian is excellent.
>
> *Level-of-service B* is in the range of stable flow, but the presence of other users in the traffic stream begins to be noticeable. Freedom to select desired speeds is relatively unaffected, but there is a slight decline in the freedom to maneuver within the traffic stream from LOS A. The level of comfort and convenience provided is somewhat less than LOS A, because the presence of others in the traffic stream begins to affect individual behavior.
>
> *Level-of-service C* is in the range of stable flow, but marks the beginning of the range of flow in which the operation of individual users becomes significantly affected by the presence of others, and maneuvering within the traffic stream requires substantial vigilance on the part of the user. The general level of comfort and convenience declines noticeably at this level.
>
> *Level-of-service D* represents high-density, but stable, flow. Speed and freedom to maneuver are severely restricted, and the driver or pedestrian experiences a generally poor level of comfort and convenience. Small increases in traffic flow will generally cause operational problems at this level.
>
> *Level-of-service E* represents operating conditions at or near the capacity level. All speeds are reduced to a low, but relatively uniform value. Freedom to maneuver within the traffic stream is extremely difficult, and it is generally accomplished by forcing a vehicle or pedestrian to "give way" to accommodate such maneuvers. Comfort and convenience levels are extremely poor, and driver or pedestrian frustration is generally high. Operations at this level are usually unstable, because small increases in flow or minor perturbations within the traffic stream will cause breakdowns.
>
> *Level-of-service F* is used to define forced or breakdown flow. This condition exists whenever the amount of traffic approaching a point exceeds the amount which can traverse the point. Queues form behind such locations. Operations within the queue are characterized by stop-and-go waves, and they are extremely unstable. Vehicles may progress at reasonable speeds for several hundred feet or more, then be required to stop in a cyclic fashion. Level-of-service F is used to describe the operating conditions within the queue, as well as at the point of breakdown. It should be noted, however, that in many cases operating conditions of vehicles or pedestrians discharged from the queue may be quite good. Nevertheless, it is the point at which arrival flow exceeds discharge flow which causes the queue to form, and level of service F is an appropriate designation for such points ([4.7], pp. 1–3 and 1–4).

The foregoing description of the six levels of service reveals several interesting facts. First, level-of-service E around maximum flow or capacity does not correspond to acceptably comfortable and convenient conditions from the point of view of the driver.

Second, as the description of level-of-service A implies, the specific $u-q$ curve and the actual capacity of a roadway depend on its physical and operating characteristics. The former include items such as grades and sight distances, as described in Chapter 2, and the latter include factors such as posted speed limits and vehicle mix. Third, along the $u-q$ curve, each level of service constitutes a range of speeds and flows demarcated by upper and lower limits in the values of concentration, as illustrated by Fig. 4.3.2.

4.3.3 "Ideal" Freeway Conditions

This subsection introduces the procedure recommended by the *1985 Highway Capacity Manual* [4.7] for the calculation of the capacity and level of service of a geometrically uniform section of a freeway that is removed from the vicinity of external interruptions. The procedure estimates the capacity of a freeway in terms of passenger-car equivalents under the following "ideal conditions," and then modifies this estimate to capture the effect of any deviations from the ideal conditions that are present at the freeway section under study.

Lane width and lateral clearance. Ideal conditions require that lanes be at least 12 ft wide and that obstructions such as bridge abutments be located at a lateral distance of at least 6 ft from the edge of pavement. The typical driver responses to lateral restrictions were presented in Section 2.3.

Trucks, buses, and grades. Ideal conditions represent level roadways and a vehicular stream that consists entirely of passenger cars. Larger and slower vehicles such as buses and trucks tend to have an adverse effect on the vehicular flow that the freeway can accommodate, especially at locations characterized by long stretches of vertical grades.

Uniformity of demand. Within statistically acceptable limits, the flow conditions are assumed to be uniform throughout the period of analysis. Peaking of the demand within the period of analysis would cause disruptions and shock waves, which,

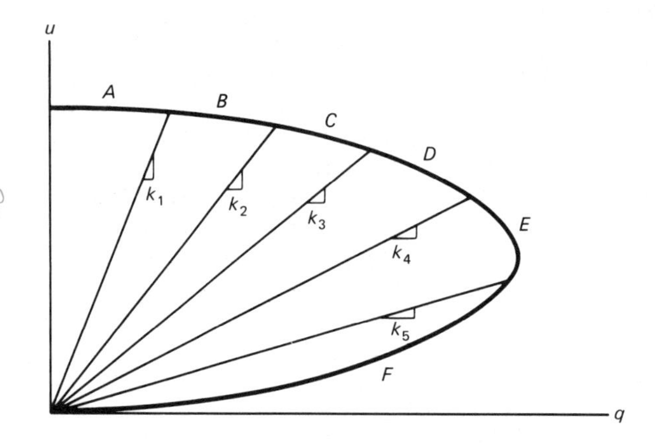

Figure 4.3.2 Level of service, speed, flow, and concentration.

as Chapter 3 explained, would take some time to dissipate completely. The typical period of analysis is 1 h. In order to quantify the degree to which the demand is peaked, a very important distinction is made between the term *volume V*, on one hand, and *rate of flow q* on the other. Volume is defined as

> the number of vehicles passing a point on a highway or highway lane during one hour, expressed as vehicles per hour [4.8].

whereas rate of flow is defined as

> the number of vehicles passing a point on a highway or highway lane during some period of time *less* than one hour, expressed as *an equivalent rate* in vehicles per hour [4.8] (emphasis added by the author).

Thus if 100 vehicles were counted during a 5-min period, the rate of flow would be 100 vehicles per 5-min period *times* twelve 5-min periods per hour *equals* 1200 veh/h. The actual volume V counted during the entire hour to which the above 5-min period belongs may or may not equal 1200 veh/h. The consecutive 60 min (1-hr period) of the day when a highway experiences the highest volume as just defined is known as the *peak hour*. The ratio of the peak-hour volume to the *maximum* rate of flow computed on the basis of an interval t within the peak hour is known as the *peak-hour factor* (PHF). Thus, given a volume V and a maximum rate of flow q based on a set interval t less than 1 hr (e.g., 5 min), the peak-hour factor is:

$$\text{PHF} = \frac{V}{q} = \frac{V}{N_t(60/t)} \tag{4.3.1}$$

where N_t is the maximum number of vehicles counted during any interval t within the hour. For the purpose of highway capacity analysis, t is taken to be around 5 min. The analysis of intersections (see Chapter 5) uses a t of 15 min. In either case, the PHF is a measure of demand uniformity or demand peaking, as the following examples illustrate.

Example 4.2: Uniform Demand

Assume that 50 vehicles were counted during each of all possible 5-min intervals during the peak hour. Compute the PHF.

Solution The total number of vehicles that were counted during the entire hour was 600 vehicles. Thus

$$V = 600 \text{ veh/h}$$

The rate of flow based on the maximum number of vehicles observed during *any* 5-min period was, according to the denominator of Eq. 4.3.1:

$$q = 50(\tfrac{60}{5}) = 600 \text{ veh/h}$$

Hence the PHF is

$$\text{PHF} = \frac{600}{600} = 1.00$$

Example 4.3: Extremely Peaked Demand

Consider the extreme case where 150 vehicles were counted during a 5-min interval and no vehicles were observed during the rest of the hour.

Solution The counted volume was 150 veh/h. On the other hand, the rate of flow based on the 5-min interval was:

$$q = 150(\tfrac{60}{5}) = 1800 \text{ veh/h}$$

Hence the PHF is

$$\text{PHF} = \frac{150}{1800} = 0.083$$

Discussion The two examples calculated the PHF for two (unrealistically) extreme conditions and found that, for an absolutely uniform demand, the PHF is equal to unity, whereas for an absolutely peaked demand (i.e., the entire hourly volume observed during a 5-min period), it was 0.083. In realistic conditions, the PHF would lie between these limits: The closer it is to unity, the more uniform the demand and, conversely, the closer the PHF is to 0, the more peaked the demand. It can easily be shown that the theoretical lower bound of the PHF is 0.25 when t is taken to be 15 min. In the discussion that follows, the term *flow* denotes the rate of flow. Consequently, when hourly volumes are given, they must be converted to flows by:

$$q = \frac{V}{\text{PHF}}$$

4.3.4 Freeway Capacity and Level of Service

The technical literature contains highly refined procedures for incorporating the above (and other) factors in the study of freeway segments. Only a rough outline of these procedures is included here to familiarize the reader with the rationale of the method. For the sake of clarity, the notation used in the following paragraphs is partly the author's.

Figure 4.3.3 presents the speed-flow relationship per freeway lane for several freeway designs, defined by the design speed and the number of lanes available, under ideal conditions. The design speed is designated as the *average highway speed* (AHS) to allow for the computation of a single value for the entire highway segment under investigation when it consists of subsections that have different design speeds: The AHS is the average of these design speeds weighted by the length of each subsection. Moreover, the design speed is the speed used to design the facility (see Chapter 3) and not the posted speed limit. The figure shows that, under ideal conditions, the capacity of a freeway lane is about 2000 passenger cars per hour (pc/h) for designs speeds of 60 and 70 mi/h and about 1900 pc/h for design speeds of 50 mi/h.

Table 4.3.1 summarizes the speed, flow, and concentration ranges corresponding to the six levels of service for the same freeway designs. In each case, capacity corresponds to the limiting flow for level-of-service E. The table shows that, for a 70-mi/h design

BASIC FREEWAY SEGMENTS

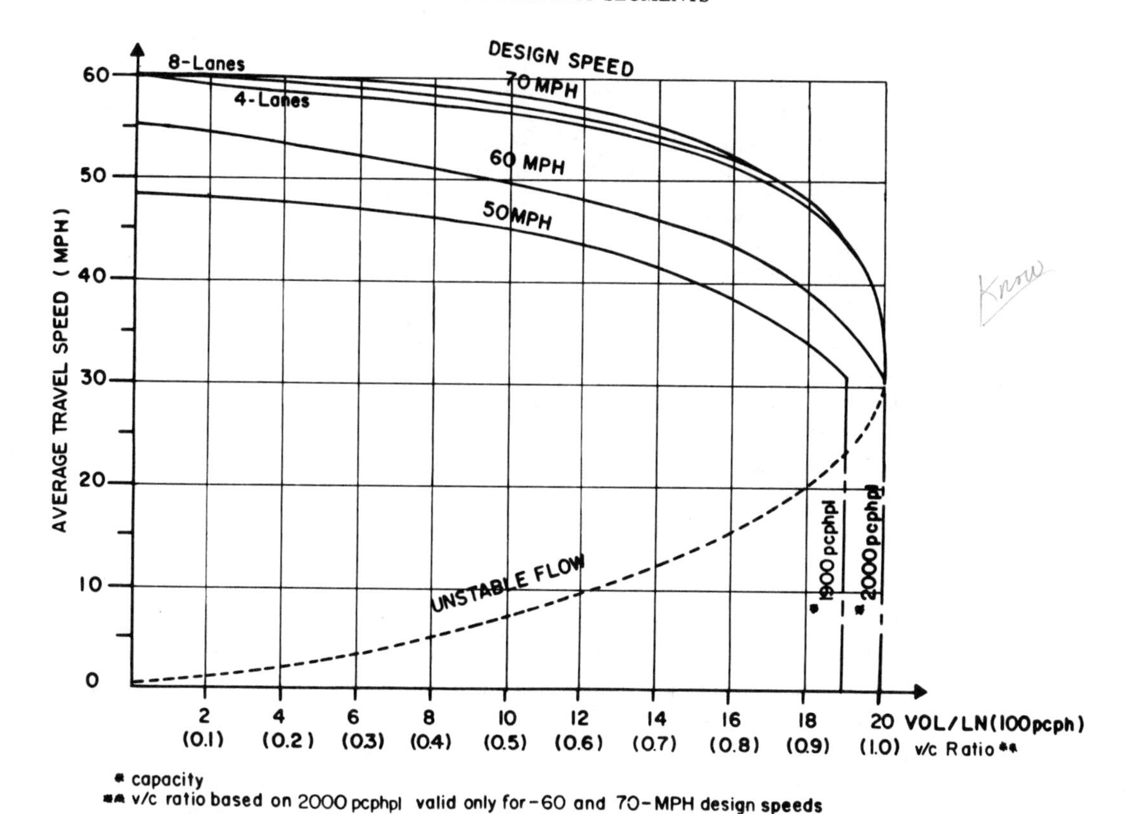

Figure 4.3.3 Speed-flow relationship under ideal conditions. (*SOURCE*: Transportation Research Board [4.7], Fig. 3-4, p. 3.5.)

speed, level-of-service C corresponds to speeds between 54 and 57 mi/h, concentrations (i.e., densities) between 20 and 30 passenger cars per mile (pc/mi) per lane, a single-lane flow between 1100 and 1550 pc/h/lane, and a v/c ratio between 0.54 and 0.77. With appropriate adjustments, the values found in the table can be used either to analyze the conditions prevailing on a particular facility—that is, to determine the operating level of service when the number of lanes and the actual freeway volume are known—or to design a facility—that is, to determine the number of lanes needed to accommodate a given volume under a desired level of service.

The column of Table 4.3.1 that is labeled *maximum service flow* (MSF) was derived by the following equation:

$$\text{MSF}_i = q_{\max} \left(\frac{v}{c}\right)_i \text{ pc/h} \quad \text{and} \quad \text{ideal conditions} \tag{4.3.2}$$

TABLE 4.3.1 LEVEL OF SERVICE FOR BASIC FREEWAY SECTIONS

		70 mi/h design speed			60 mi/h design speed			50 mi/h design speed		
LOS	Density (pc/mi/l)	Speed[b] (mi/h)	v/c	MSF[a] (pc/h/l)	Speed[b] (mi/h)	v/c	MSF[a] (pc/h/l)	Speed[b] (mi/h)	v/c	MSF[a] (pc/h/l)
A	≤12	≥60	0.35	700	—	—	—	—	—	—
B	≤20	≥57	0.54	1100	≥50	0.49	1000	—	—	—
C	≤30	≥54	0.77	1550	≥47	0.69	1400	≥43	0.67	1300
D	≤42	≥46	0.93	1850	≥42	0.84	1700	≥40	0.83	1600
E	≤67	≥30	1.00	2000	≥30	1.00	2000	≥28	1.00	1900
F	>67	<30	c	c	<30	c	c	<28	c	c

[a]Maximum service flow rate per lane under ideal conditions.

[b]Average travel speed.

[c]Highly variable, unstable.

Note: All values of *MSF* rounded to the nearest 50 pc/h.

SOURCE: Transportation Research Board [4.7]; Table 3-1, p. 3.8.

where MSF_i is the maximum service volume corresponding to level-of-service i that can be accommodated by a freeway lane under ideal conditions, $q_{\max}$ is the capacity of a freeway lane (i.e., the MSF at level-of-service E), and $(v/c)_i$ is the maximum volume-to-capacity ratio corresponding to level-of-service i. The table entries for the MSF have been rounded to the nearest 50 pc/h/lane.

The following equation converts an *ideal lane flow* q^*, expressed in passenger cars per hour per lane, to the *service flow* q, expressed in vehicles per hour, for a freeway consisting of N lanes, under the prevailing conditions:

$$q = q^* N f_w f_{hv} \tag{4.3.3}$$

where

q = prevailing (service) flow in veh/h

q^* = ideal flow in pc/h/lane

N = number of freeway lanes

f_w = adjustment for the combined effect of lane widths other than 12 ft and for lateral obstructions closer to 6 ft

f_{hv} = adjustment factor for the presence of heavy vehicles

The adjustment factor f_w, obtained from Table 4.3.2, depends on the number of lanes provided by the freeway, the lane width, the lateral distance from the traveled way know

TABLE 4.3.2 ADJUSTMENT FACTORS FOR RESTRICTED LANE WIDTH AND LATERAL CLEARANCE

Distance from traveled pavement[a] (ft)	Adjustment factor, f_w							
	Obstructions on one side of the roadway				Obstructions on both sides of the roadway			
	Lane width (ft)							
	12	11	10	9	12	11	10	9
	4-Lane freeway (2 lanes each direction)							
≥6	1.00	0.97	0.91	0.81	1.00	0.97	0.91	0.81
5	0.99	0.96	0.90	0.80	0.99	0.96	0.90	0.80
4	0.99	0.96	0.90	0.80	0.98	0.95	0.89	0.79
3	0.98	0.95	0.89	0.79	0.96	0.93	0.87	0.77
2	0.97	0.94	0.88	0.79	0.94	0.91	0.86	0.76
1	0.93	0.90	0.85	0.76	0.87	0.85	0.80	0.71
0	0.90	0.87	0.82	0.73	0.81	0.79	0.74	0.66
	6- or 8-Lane freeway (3 or 4 lanes each direction)							
≥6	1.00	0.96	0.89	0.78	1.00	0.96	0.89	0.78
5	0.99	0.95	0.88	0.77	0.99	0.95	0.88	0.77
4	0.99	0.95	0.88	0.77	0.98	0.94	0.87	0.77
3	0.98	0.94	0.87	0.76	0.97	0.93	0.86	0.76
2	0.97	0.93	0.87	0.76	0.96	0.92	0.85	0.75
1	0.95	0.92	0.86	0.75	0.93	0.89	0.83	0.72
0	0.94	0.91	0.85	0.74	0.91	0.87	0.81	0.70

[a]Certain types of obstruction, high-type median barriers in particular, do not cause any deleterious effect on traffic flow. Judgment should be exercised in applying these factors.

SOURCE: Transportation Research Board [4.7]; Table 3-2, p. 3.13.

to objects such as bridge abutments, and on whether the laterally placed objects are found on one or on both sides of the roadway. When objects are present on both sides but are located at different distances, the average distance is used in the table.

The following equation represents an approximation of the adjustment for heavy vehicles:

$$f_{hv} = \frac{1}{1 + P_T(E_T - 1) + P_R(E_R - 1) + P_B(E_B - 1)} \tag{4.3.4}$$

where P_T, P_R, and P_B correspond to the proportions of trucks, recreational vehicles, and buses, respectively, in the traffic stream, and E_T, E_R, and E_B are the passenger car equivalents for trucks, recreational vehicles, and buses. The latter depend on the general terrain of the highway and are given in Table 4.3.3.

Know

TABLE 4.3.3 PASSENGER-CAR EQUIVALENTS ON EXTENDED GENERAL FREEWAY SEGMENTS

Factor	Type of terrain		
	Level	Rolling	Mountainous
E_T for trucks	1.7	4.0	8.0
E_B for buses	1.5	3.0	5.0
E_R for RV's	1.6	3.0	4.0

SOURCE: Transportation Research Board [4.7]; Table 3-3, p. 3.13.

Example 4.4: Design

A freeway that is being designed is expected to carry a volume of 3000 veh/h. Trucks and buses are estimated to constitute 12% and 5% of the traffic, respectively, and no recreational vehicles are anticipated. Determine the minimum number of lanes required to provide level-of-service C, given a peak hour factor of 0.80, a rolling terrain, a design speed of 70 mi/h, 12-ft lanes, and adequate lateral clearances.

Solution The service flow is:

$$SF = q = \frac{V}{PHF} = \frac{3000}{0.80} = 3750 \text{ veh/h}$$

From Table 4.3.1 the ideal lane flow for level-of service C is:

$$MSF_C = 1550 \text{ pc/h/lane}$$

From Table 4.3.2, the adjustment factor f_w is equal to 1.00, and from Eq. 4.3.4

$$f_{hv} = \frac{1}{1 + 0.12\,(4 - 1) + 0.05\,(3 - 1)} = 0.68$$

Solving Eq. 4.3.3 for the number of lanes, N,

$$N = \frac{3750}{(1550)\,(1.00)\,(0.68)} = 3.56, \quad \text{or} \quad 4 \text{ lanes}$$

Example 4.5: Analysis

A freeway on a level terrain carries a volume $V = 4500$ veh/h on four 11-foot lanes in one direction. The vehicle mix consists of 75% passenger cars, 10% trucks, 10% buses, and 5% recreational vehicles. Lateral obstructions are located at a distance of 5 ft on the right side and 3 ft on the left side of the roadway. Given that the design speed is 60 mi/h and the peak hour factor is 0.75, calculate the level of service provided and the v/c ratio.

Solution The service flow is:

$$SF = q = \frac{V}{PHF} = \frac{4500}{0.75} = 6000 \text{ veh/h}$$

For rolling terrain and the given percentages of heavy vehicles, Eq. 4.3.4 yields:

$$f_{hv} = \frac{1}{1 + (0.10)(0.7) + (0.05)(0.6) + (0.10)(0.5)}$$
$$= 0.87$$

With an average lateral clearance on both sides of $(5 + 3)/2 = 4$ ft, a lane width of 11 ft, and an 8-lane freeway (4 lanes in each direction), Table 4.3.2 yields:

$$f_w = 0.94$$

Solving Eq. 4.3.3 for q^*,

$$q^* = \frac{6000}{(4)(0.94)(0.87)} = 1834 \text{ pc/h/lane}$$

Consulting Table 4.3.1 for a design speed of 60 mi/h, the computed ideal lane flow falls within the range of level-of-service E. The corresponding v/c ratio is:

$$\frac{v}{c} = \frac{1834}{2000} = 0.92$$

4.3.5 Capacity Restrictions

The previous subsection dealt with the uninterrupted flow of vehicles on long freeway sections. Under these circumstances, variations in flow conditions and stoppages are possible as a result of *nonrecurring* random events or incidents such as accidents, spilled loads, disabled and slow-moving vehicles, and other extraordinary events. In addition, geometric restrictions give rise to high concentrations, or congestion, along the stream channel. These include reductions of capacity at lane drops (i.e., at points where the number of lanes decreases), at points of abrupt alignment changes, and at locations where two streams come together, such as merging areas. When the approaching volume (i.e., the demand) exceeds the capacity of these locations, conditions of high concentration begin to appear upstream, and shock waves develop between these conditions and the approaching flow farther upstream. The duration and the severity of the congested flow depend on the degree of capacity reduction and on the pattern of demand over time. The high-concentration platoon may spill into similar conditions at adjacent capacity restrictions. Because such restrictions are permanent in space and the demand for travel exhibits a daily regularity, these effects are *recurring* events that take place during the regular periods of high demand [4.10].

4.4 PEDESTRIAN FLOW

4.4.1 Background

Pedestrian-flow models have been developed that bear a close resemblance to the concepts discussed in connection with vehicular streams. The speed of a pedestrian regime is, naturally, measured in units of distance divided by time, for example, feet per second.

Flow is given in terms of pedestrians per unit width of a walkway per unit time. It is thus a point measurement in the same way as highway flow, where the point at which flow is observed stretches across a number of lanes. Pedestrians, of course, are not normally obliged to follow strictly any type of lane assignment, but pedestrian flow per linear foot of walkway width is a tangible measure. Concentration or density is specified as the number of pedestrians per unit area, for example, pedestrians per square foot. The reciprocal of pedestrian concentration is called *space* and has units of surface area per pedestrian (e.g., square feet per pedestrian). Its vehicular stream equivalent is spacing. It is easy to conceive of the above definitions in the usual manner and to extend the model to incorporate a concept of pedestrian level of service. In fact, the fundamental relationship $q = uk$ has been found to apply in the case of pedestrians under generally uninterrupted conditions.

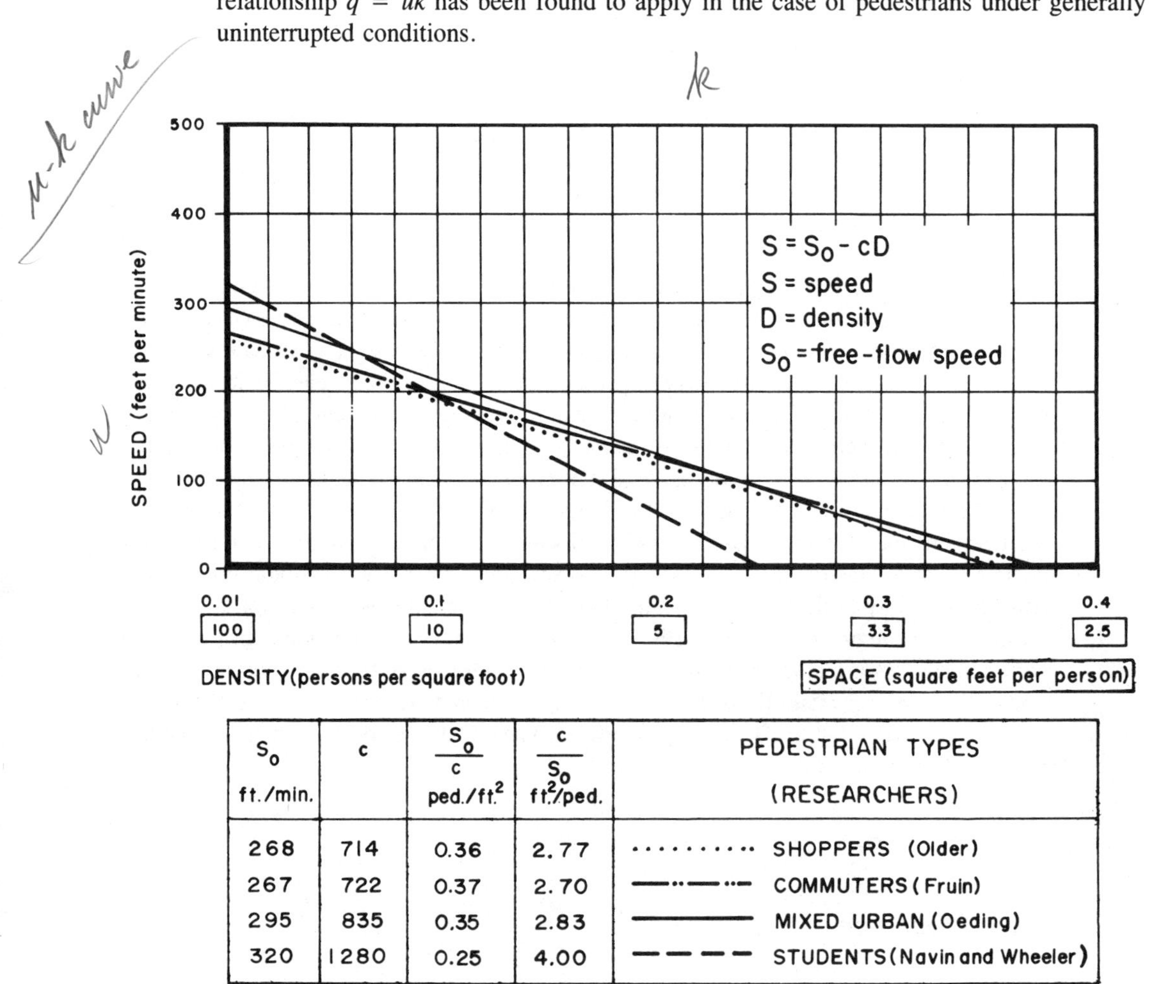

S_0 ft./min.	c	$\frac{S_0}{c}$ ped./ft.^{2}	$\frac{c}{S_0}$ ft.^{2}/ped.	PEDESTRIAN TYPES (RESEARCHERS)
268	714	0.36	2.77	·········· SHOPPERS (Older)
267	722	0.37	2.70	—··—·· COMMUTERS (Fruin)
295	835	0.35	2.83	——— MIXED URBAN (Oeding)
320	1280	0.25	4.00	— — — STUDENTS (Navin and Wheeler)

Figure 4.4.1 Pedestrian speed—density/space relationship. (*SOURCE*: Transportation Research Board [4.8], Fig. 1, p. 116.)

4.4.2 Pedestrian-Flow Models

Figure 4.4.1 presents the calibrated pedestrian speed-concentration relationships obtained by several researchers. These diagrams conform to the general shape observed in the case of vehicular flow, that is, they are monotonically decreasing from free-flow speed at zero concentration to zero speed at jammed concentration. Figure 4.4.2 presents the speed-flow relationships corresponding to the aforementioned calibrated *u-k* curves. Obviously, the vehicular stream parallel extends to this diagram as well: The maximum pedestrian flow (i.e., capacity) occurs at an intermediate point between free-flow and jammed conditions. Figure 4.4.3 plots the v/c ratio versus space, that is, the reciprocal of concentration. It is of interest to note the point identified by a cross at a very low value of space (i.e., at high concentration) and high speed corresponding to "close order military formation": This point represents the race-track conditions discussed in connection with vehicular flow in Chapter 3. The parallel between vehicular and pedestrian flow does not end here. The concept of level of service is also meaningful in the case of pedestrian flow.

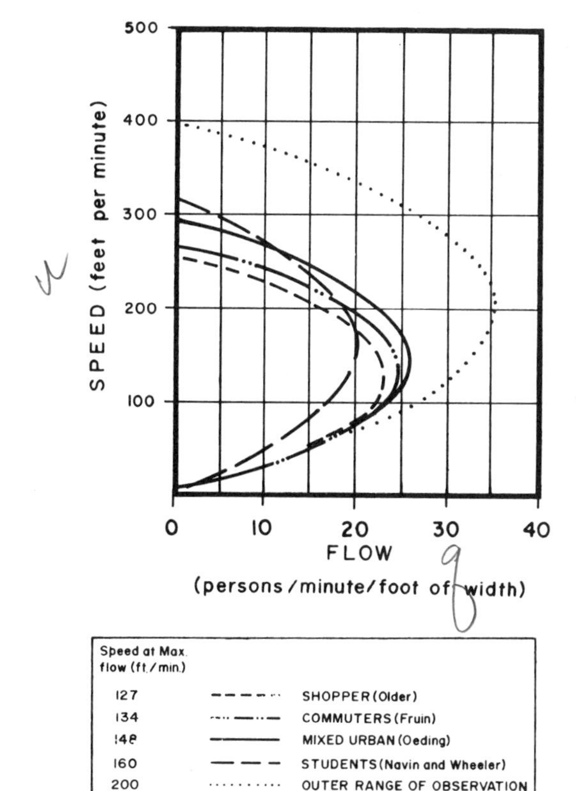

Figure 4.4.2 Pedestrian speed—flow relationship. (*SOURCE*: Transportation Research Board [4.8], Fig. 3, p. 118.)

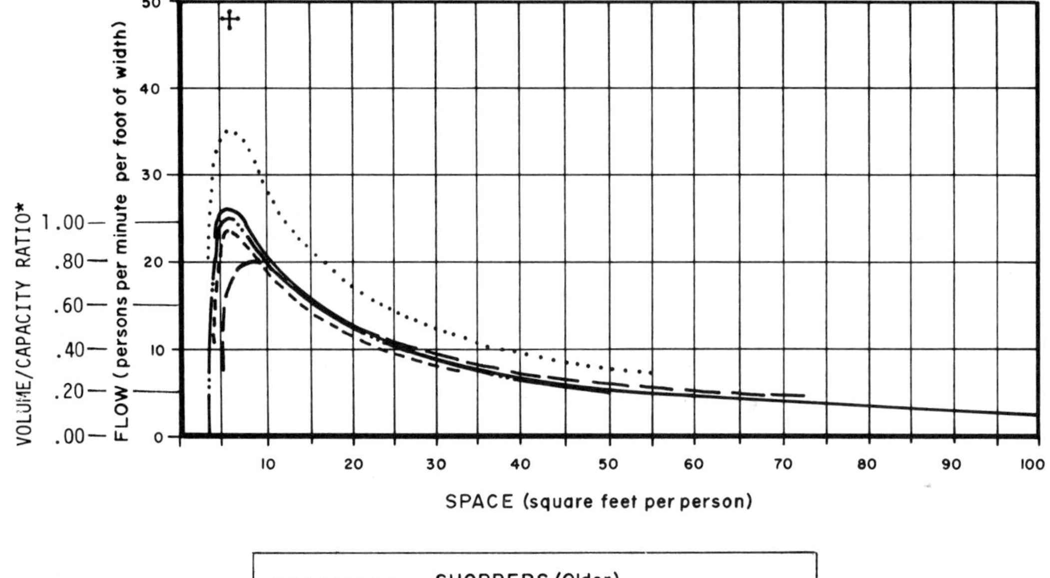

Figure 4.4.3 Pedestrian flow—space relationship. (*SOURCE*: Transportation Research Board [4.8], Fig. 2, p. 117.)

TABLE 4.4.1 PEDESTRIAN LEVELS OF SERVICE ON WALKWAYS

Level of service	Space (ft^2/ped)	Expected flows and speeds: Ave. speed, S (ft/min)	Flow rate, v (ped/min/ft)	Vol/cap ratio, v/c
A	≥130	≥260	≤ 2	≤0.08
B	≥ 40	≥250	≤ 7	≤0.28
C	≥ 24	≥240	≤10	≤0.40
D	≥ 15	≥225	≤15	≤0.60
E	≥ 6	≥150	≤25	≤1.00
F	< 6	<150	Variable	

*Average conditions for 15 min.

SOURCE: Transportation Research Board [4.7]; Table 13-3, p. 13.8.

LEVEL OF SERVICE A

Pedestrian Space: ≥ 130 sq ft/ped   Flow Rate: ≤ 2 ped/min/ft

At walkway LOS A, pedestrians basically move in desired paths without altering their movements in response to other pedestrians. Walking speeds are freely selected, and conflicts between pedestrians are unlikely.

LEVEL OF SERVICE B

Pedestrian Space: ≥ 40 sq ft/ped   Flow Rate: ≤ 7 ped/min/ft

At LOS B, sufficient area is provided to allow pedestrians to freely select walking speeds, to bypass other pedestrians, and to avoid crossing conflicts with others. At this level, pedestrians begin to be aware of other pedestrians, and to respond to their presence in the selection of walking path.

LEVEL OF SERVICE C

Pedestrian Space: ≥ 24 sq ft/ped   Flow Rate: ≤ 10 ped/min/ft

At LOS C, sufficient space is available to select normal walking speeds, and to bypass other pedestrians in primarily unidirectional streams. Where reverse-direction or crossing movements exist, minor conflicts will occur, and speeds and volume will be somewhat lower.

LEVEL OF SERVICE D

Pedestrian Space: ≥ 15 sq ft/ped   Flow Rate: ≤ 15 ped/min/ft

At LOS D, freedom to select individual walking speed and to bypass other pedestrians is restricted. Where crossing or reverse-flow movements exist, the probability of conflict is high, and its avoidance requires frequent changes in speed and position. The LOS provides reasonably fluid flow; however, considerable friction and interaction between pedestrians is likely to occur.

LEVEL OF SERVICE E

Pedestrian Space: ≥ 6 sq ft/ped   Flow Rate: ≤ 25 ped/min/ft

At LOS E, virtually all pedestrians would have their normal walking speed restricted, requiring frequent adjustment of gait. At the lower range of this LOS, forward movement is possible only by "shuffling." Insufficient space is provided for passing of slower pedestrians. Cross- or reverse-flow movements are possible only with extreme difficulties. Design volumes approach the limit of walkway capacity, with resulting stoppages and interruptions to flow.

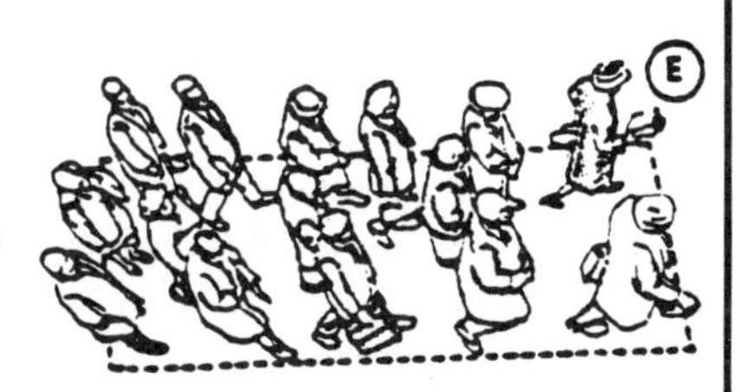

LEVEL OF SERVICE F

Pedestrian Space: ≤ 6 sq ft/ped   Flow Rate: variable

At LOS F, all walking speeds are severely restricted, and forward progress is made only by "shuffling." There is frequent, unavoidable contact with other pedestrians. Cross- and reverse-flow movements are virtually impossible. Flow is sporadic and unstable. Space is more characteristic of queued pedestrians than of moving pedestrian streams.

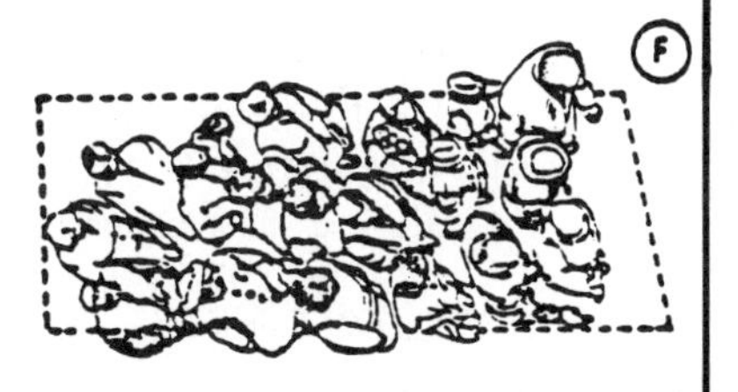

Figure 4.4.4 Levels of service on walkways. (*SOURCE*: Transportation Research Board [4.7], Fig. 13-8, 13.9.)

4.4.3 Pedestrian Level of Service

Table 4.4.1 presents the recommended ranges of pedestrian levels of service in terms of the space (and, implicitly, concentration), speed, and flow. The delimiting values of the v/c ratio are also shown. Figure 4.4.4 illustrates the typical levels of concentration that are encountered within each level of service. Pedestrian capacity is found to be the "maximum service flow" for level-of-service E. It corresponds to about 25 pedestrians per minute per foot of walkway width. Forced flow (i.e., level-of-service F) includes the "backward bending" portion of the *u-k* and *q-k* diagrams.

4.5 SUMMARY

This chapter presented the flow and capacity characteristics of selected transportation systems. The flow-speed relationships of typical urban mass transportation systems that have been derived by Vuchic [4.1] were presented and discussed, and a brief discussion of the fleet size required to provide a desirable transit vehicle flow followed. The concept of highway level of service was introduced next, and the 1985 *Highway Capacity Manual* [4.7] method for analyzing and designing freeway sections that are removed from external interruptions was presented. Finally, the applicability of the flow relationships of Chapter 3 to pedestrian flow was illustrated.

4.6 EXERCISES

1. A rapid-transit system employs vehicles that can be connected into transit units. To investigate the effect of vehicular articulation, calculate the capacity (veh/h) and the speed at capacity (ft/s) by varying the number of vehicles per train from $N = 1$ to $N = 5$. Assume a perception-reaction time of 1.5 s, a vehicular length of 40 ft, a normal deceleration of 5 ft/s^2, a clearance length x_o of 4 ft, and a safety regime *a*.
2. Repeat Exercise 1 for safety regime *b*, assuming an emergency deceleration of 15 ft/s^2.
3. Computerize your solution procedure to Exercises 1 and 2.
4. For the system of Example 4.1, calculate the effect of a 5-min decrease in the round-trip time on the fleet size. Also calculate the before and after headways between vehicles.
5. For the system of Exercise 4, calculate the average headway that would result if the original 34 vehicles were still used.
6. The peak-hour volumes at two locations were counted and found to be equal. However, the PHFs were 0.85 at the first location and 0.60 at the second. Describe the difference between the two locations.
7. The following twelve consecutive 5-min vehicle counts were taken on a highway:

60 50 40 60 90 80 100 120 140 95 60 30

70

(a) Plot the histogram of these counts and the histogram of the flow rates computed on the basis of the above counts, and (b) calculate the hourly volume and the PHF.

8. Show that for $t = 15$ min, the PHF can theoretically range from 0.25 to 1.00.

9. Obstructions are located at the edge of the pavement on one side of a six-lane highway. Estimate the percent increase in the highway's capacity that may result from relocating the obstructions to a distance of 6 ft. Assume 10-ft lanes.

10. A six-lane freeway accommodates 3500 veh/h in the peak direction. This volume includes 10% trucks, no buses and no recreational vehicles. The freeway is in rolling terrain, is designed for 60 mi/h, and otherwise conforms to the ideal conditions. Given that the peak 5-min traffic count is 350 vehicles, estimate (a) the capacity of the freeway in one direction, (b) the prevailing level of service, and (c) the prevailing speed.

11. For the freeway of Exercise 10, calculate the range of volumes at the same PHF for which the prevailing level of service would be C.

12. For the freeway of Exercise 10, find the number of lanes needed in one direction to ensure a level-of-service C or better.

13. Estimate the one-way capacity of a highway section that is removed from any major interruptions given four 11-ft lanes in each direction, a uniform demand, obstructions at both sides at 3 ft from the edge of pavement, 5% buses, 20% trucks, mountainous terrain, and a 50 mi/h design speed.

14. Derive Eq. 4.3.4.

15. An airport corridor is 50 ft wide. Given a peak demand of 600 pedestrians per minute, calculate (a) the prevailing level of service, (b) the approximate concentration, and (c) the approximate average speed.

4.7 REFERENCES

4.1 VUCHIC, VUKAN R., *Urban Public Transportation Systems and Technology,* Prentice-Hall, Inc., Englewood Cliffs, N.J., © 1981, pp. 550–52. Table 7.4 and Figures 4.2.1 and 4.2.2 reprinted by permission.

4.2 WATKINS, R. A., et al., *Urban Transportation Planning System Lexicon,* prepared by Rock Creek Associates for the U.S. Department of Transportation: Urban Mass Transportation Administration, Report UMTA-UPM20-81-1, 1981.

4.3 PAPACOSTAS, C. S., *Energy and Pollution Implications of Bus-Automobile Alternatives,* Ph. D. Dissertation, Carnegie-Mellon University, Pittsburgh, Pennsylvania, 1974.

4.4 DIAL, ROBERT B., SCOTT G. RUTHERFORD, AND LAWRENCE QUILLIAN, *Transit Network Analysis: INET,* U.S. Department of Transportation, Urban Mass Transportation Administration, Report No. UMTA-UPM-20-79-3, 1979.

4.5 Bureau of Public Roads, *Highway Capacity Manual,* U.S. Government Printing Office, Washington, D.C., 1950.

4.6 Highway Research Board, *Highway Capacity Manual,* Special Report 87, National Research Council, Washington, D.C., 1965.

4.7 Transportation Research Board, *Highway Capacity Manual,* Special Report 209, National Research Council, Washington, D.C., 1985.

4.8 ———, *Interim Materials on Highway Capacity,* Circular 212, Transportation Research Board, National Research Council, Washington, D.C., 1980.

4.9 ———, *Proposed Chapters for the 1985 Highway Capacity Manual,* Circulars 281 and 284, Transportation Research Board, National Research Council, Washington, D.C., 1984.

4.10 CAPELLE, DONALD G., *Freeway Traffic Management,* National Cooperative Highway Research Program, Project 20-3D, Final Report, Sept. 1979.

CHAPTER 5

FLOW INTERRUPTIONS

5.1 INTRODUCTION

Traffic streams are often subject to intended interruptions: Transit vehicles are stopped at transit stations to discharge and take on passengers; highway traffic is interrupted at street intersections to permit the use of the same space by several vehicular streams. With regard to at-grade street intersections, the *1965 Highway Capacity Manual* [5.1] states that:

> Intersections not only control, to a large extent, the capability of major and secondary arterial streets to accommodate the flow of vehicles and pedestrians, but they also may seriously affect or limit the ability of nearby freeways to perform at maximum efficiency.

With respect to transit stations, Vuchic [5.2] states that:

> . . . station capacity governs the capacity of a transit line in a vast majority of cases.

This chapter is concerned with stream-flow interruptions. The case of scheduled rapid-transit vehicles is examined first, and a model of transit station capacity is developed. The operation of signalized street intersections is covered next. Following some basic definitions, the technique of coordinating signal systems in order to minimize the effect of interruptions is described, and a simplified method for assessing the capacity and level of service of at-grade signalized intersections is presented.

5.2 TRANSIT INTERRUPTIONS

5.2.1 Background

The movement of a transit vehicle *between* stations can be described by the equations of motion covered in Chapter 2. A typical vehicle or train leaving a station will accelerate to a *cruising speed* and maintain that speed until the point when it must begin to decelerate to a complete stop at the next station. The distance and time over which the cruising speed is maintained depend on the distance between the two stations, that is, the *station spacing*. Following a *dwelling time* at a station, the vehicle again enters its acceleration phase.

Figure 5.2.1 illustrates the time-distance diagram of uniformly scheduled arrivals and departures at a typical station. For simplicity, individual transit units are shown as points. The identical decelerating, dwelling, and accelerating phases of two consecutive units are shown in Fig. 5.2.1(a) for the situation where only one unit is permitted to occupy the station at any time. The headway between two units, measured horizontally, is constant as long as it is measured between points when the two vehicles are, respectively, in the same state (e.g., entering the station, leaving the station, half-way in their dwelling phase). On the other hand, the spacing between units, measured vertically, varies with time. Figure 5.2.1(b) shows two consecutive units that are permitted to dwell at the station simultaneously. The time period shown begins during the dwelling phase of unit 1 and ends with the departure of unit 3. Unit 4 is shown to have arrived prior to the departure of unit 3. The way in which headway and spacing are measured in this situation is identical to that of Fig. 5.2.1(a).

The minimum headway at which units enter and exit a station is affected by the combined effect of the dwelling time and the number of units that can be accommodated at the station simultaneously. This minimum station-headway is most often longer than the minimum headway that is technologically attainable under uninterrupted conditions.

5.2.2 Transit Stations

The basic element of a transit station is the *platform,* where vehicles or trains stop to take on and drop off passengers. Although differing in geometric design and also in the terminology employed, all passenger-serving stations, including simple bus stops, rapid-transit stations, harbors, and airport terminals, share this basic element. A *terminal* is a large station that accommodates high volumes of entering, leaving, and transferring passengers or freight. The physical facilities preceding and following the platform, on which vehicles decelerate and accelerate, respectively, can be considered to be a part of the station. In addition, some station designs include vehicle holding areas on either side of the platform to be occupied by vehicles awaiting clearance to enter or exit the station.

The maximum number of vehicles (and passengers) that a station can process in a given period of time, that is, the station's capacity, depends on the number and type of

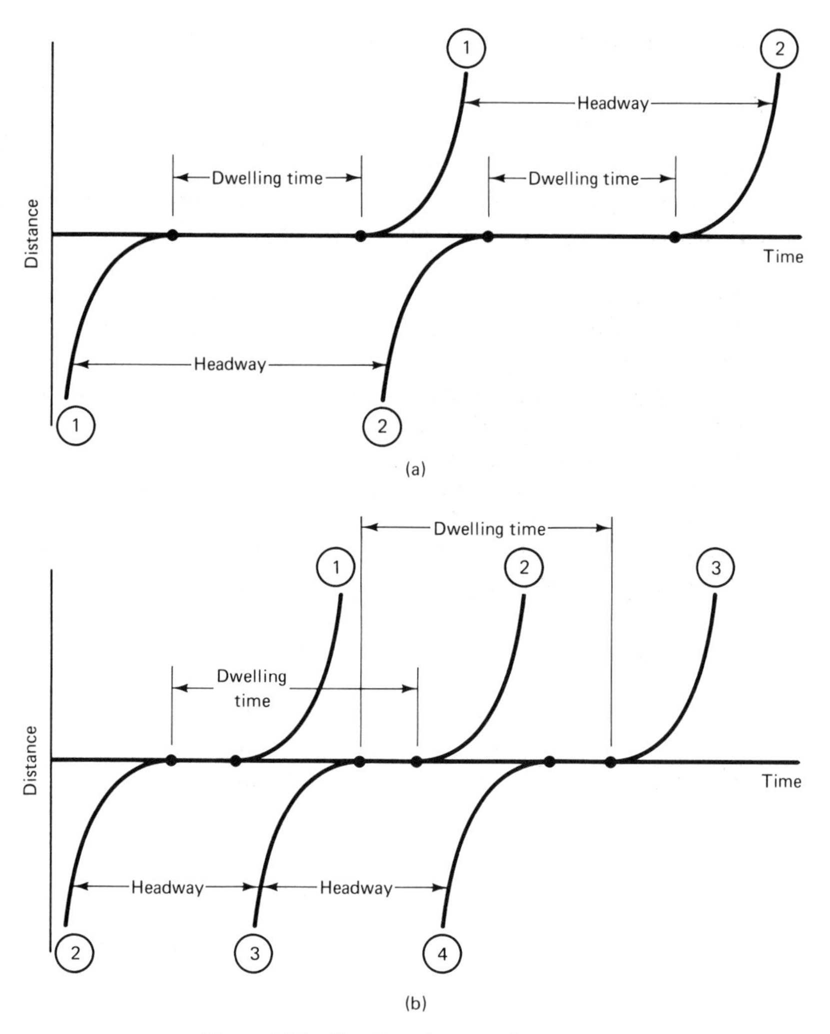

Figure 5.2.1 Transit station operations.

platforms available, the desired level of safety, and related rules of operation. The length of each platform limits the maximum number of vehicles that can be accommodated simultaneously either singly or in trains.

Station platforms can be either *off-line* or *on-line*. Off-line platforms branch out of the main line so that when a local vehicle or train is at the station, another unit not scheduled to serve that station can proceed on the main line. Because overtaking is not possible at on-line platform locations, vehicles that are not scheduled to serve a station may be delayed behind local vehicles serving the station.

5.2.3 Single-Platform Capacity

The simplest type of transit station consists of a single on-line platform capable of accommodating a train of N vehicles of length L and allowing only one train to occupy the platform at any given time. Figure 5.2.2 shows the operation of two consecutive trains of length (NL) from the moment when the first begins its deceleration into the station to the moment when the second comes to a complete stop at the station, the location of which is shown on the distance axis. Each train is represented by the two parallel trajectories of its front and rear. The headway between the two trains consists of three parts: the dwelling time, the time it takes the first train to clear the platform, and a "safety" clearance interval. A clearance interval of zero represents the limiting situation when the second train reaches the front of the platform at the moment when the first vehicle clears it. The length of the clearance interval is related to the level of safety associated with the operation. The technical literature (e.g., [5.2] and [5.3]) discusses the details of safety-regime analysis of station operations for various technologies. For the purposes of this textbook, the minimum headway under uninterrupted conditions for a desired safety regime (given by the reciprocal of Eq. 3.4.3) is used as an approximation for the length of the clearance interval. The minimum station headway then becomes:

$$h_s(\min) = T_{\text{dwell}} + \left(\frac{2NL}{a_n}\right)^{\frac{1}{2}} + \left(\delta + \frac{u}{2d_f} - \frac{u}{2d_1} + \frac{NL + x_o}{u}\right) \tag{5.2.1}$$

where the second term represents the time it takes a train of N vehicles to clear the platform while accelerating at normal acceleration a_n and the third to last terms give the minimum headway under uninterrupted conditions.

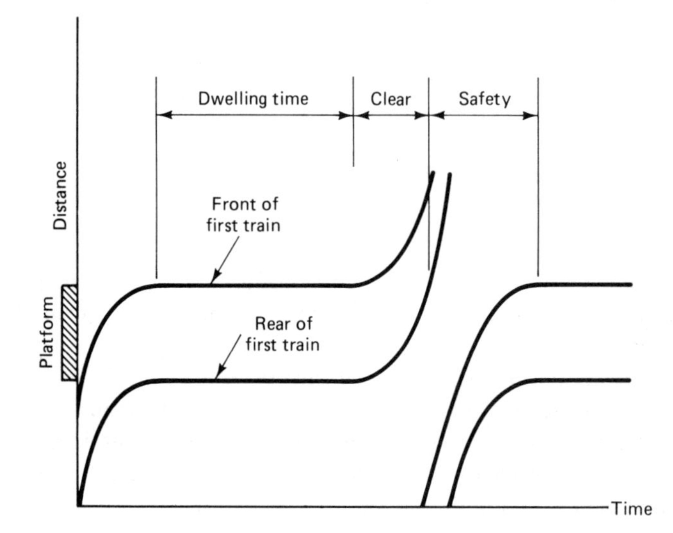

Figure 5.2.2 Transit station times.

Example 5.1

Plot the relationship between cruising speed and station vehicle flow for the system described in connection with Fig. 3.4.2 for safety regime *a*. Assume a dwelling time of 10 s and a normal acceleration of 8 ft/s^2.

Solution For safety regime *a*, the following vehicle maintains a spacing such that it can stop at normal deceleration in the eventuality that the leading vehicles stops "instantaneously."

Substituting in Eq. 5.2.1:

$$h_s(\text{min}) = 10 + (5.0)^{\frac{1}{2}} + 1 + \frac{u}{16} - 0 + \frac{20 + 3}{u}$$

$$= 13.24 + \frac{u}{16} + \frac{23}{u}$$

$$\text{and } q = (3600)\left(13.24 + \frac{u}{16} + \frac{23}{u}\right)^{-1} \text{ veh/h}$$

This equation is plotted in the accompanying figure.

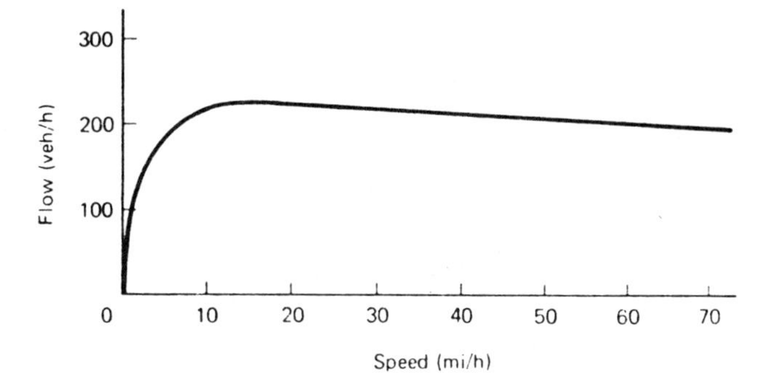

Figure P.5.1

Discussion The maximum flow for safety regime *a* occurs at $u = 19.18$ ft/s and equals 230 veh/h, which is significantly below the capacity corresponding to uninterrupted conditions (see Fig. 3.4.2).

5.2.4 Other Designs

The capacity of a station can be enhanced by providing multiple parallel platforms, simultaneous dwelling, off-line platforms, and possible combinations of the three. Figure 5.2.3 illustrates two possibilities. The first involves on-line simultaneous dwelling by platoons of three units, whereas the second shows the case of *n* parallel platforms. It is noteworthy that the pattern of headways becomes more complex; in the case depicted by

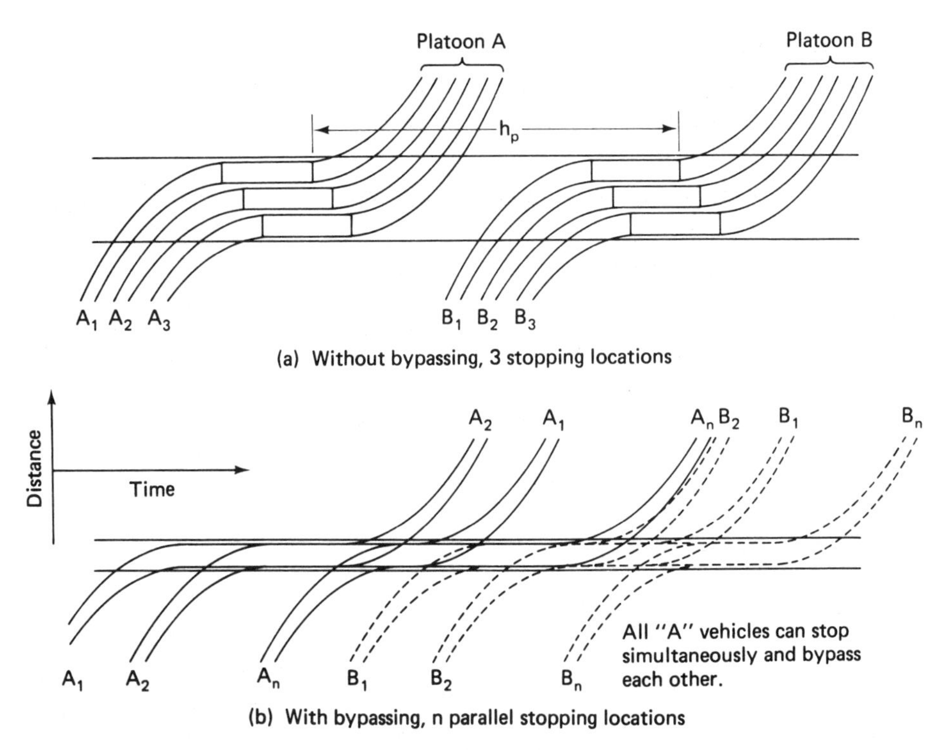

Figure 5.2.3 Operation of stations with simultaneous standing. (*SOURCE*: Vuchic [5.2], Fig. 7.18, p. 566.)

Fig. 5.2.3(a), the headways within platoons are much shorter than the headways between platoons.

5.3 HIGHWAY INTERRUPTIONS

5.3.1 Background

The most common interruption of highway flow, especially in urban areas, is the at-grade intersection where a common space is shared by several traffic streams. The conflicts between streams may be reduced either by separating them in space (i.e., by constructing overpasses), or by separating them in time (i.e., by interrupting each stream via signal controls). To maintain a smooth progression of traffic through intersectional areas, the geometric design of intersections frequently includes the addition of regular and special turning lanes.

5.3.2. Types of Signals

The typical traffic signal controlling an intersection provides a sequential display of the green, amber, red, and special indications, such as single or combined turning arrows, to each approach. One complete sequence of the signal displays constitutes the signal cycle, the duration, or *length,* of which is equal to the sum of the durations of its components.

Traffic signals can be *pretimed* or *demand-actuated* [5.3, 5.4]. Pretimed signals repeat a preset constant cycle. Demand-actuated signals have the capability to respond to the presence of vehicles or pedestrians at the intersection. They are augmented by detectors and the necessary control logic to respond to the demands placed on them. Ensuring a proper clearance interval between the green and the red phases (see Subsection 2.3.2) is part of this logic. *Semiactuated* signals are implemented at intersections of a major and a minor street, with the detectors placed only on the minor-street approaches to the intersection. The heavily used major street is given a green display, which is interrupted only when either vehicles are detected on the lightly used minor street or when a predetermined maximum green duration for the major street is reached. A maximum length of green is specified in order to rectify problems arising from a failure of the minor-street detectors to recognize the presence of vehicles. *Fully actuated* signals employ detectors on all legs of the intersection and are applicable to intersections of streets that carry about equal but fluctuating flows. *Volume-density* or *flow-concentration* controllers are capable of sensing detailed demand information and of responding to it by revising the cycle lengths and the phasing pattern of the signal. A complex extension of this is a signal-control system that employs a central computer to control the flows on large highway networks. Special types of demand-actuated signals recognize and give priority to particular classes of vehicles, such as city buses or emergency vehicles.

5.3.3 Time-Distance Diagram of Interrupted Flow

Figure 5.3.1 shows an idealized time-distance diagram for an interrupted traffic stream. The signal is stationary and its display changes over time. A total of 12 vehicles are shown. At time $t = 0$ vehicle 1 is already stopped by the red light. Vehicles 2 to 8 consecutively join the stopped platoon. Line *AB* represents the shock wave between the approach conditions and the stationary-platoon conditions (see Section 3.7). After an *initial* (or *start-up*) *delay* due mostly to the first driver's perception-reaction following the onset of green, the platoon leader moves through the intersection. Subsequent vehicles follow at a shorter release headway. Line *CB* represents the shock wave at the front of the platoon between the jam and the release conditions. When the two shock waves meet, the stationary platoon is totally dissipated. In the case shown, this event occurs before the onset of the following red, so that vehicles 9, 10, and 11 are able to clear the intersection without interruption. Finally, vehicle 12 is obliged to stop for the next red display. As explained in Chapter 3, a third shock wave between the approach and the

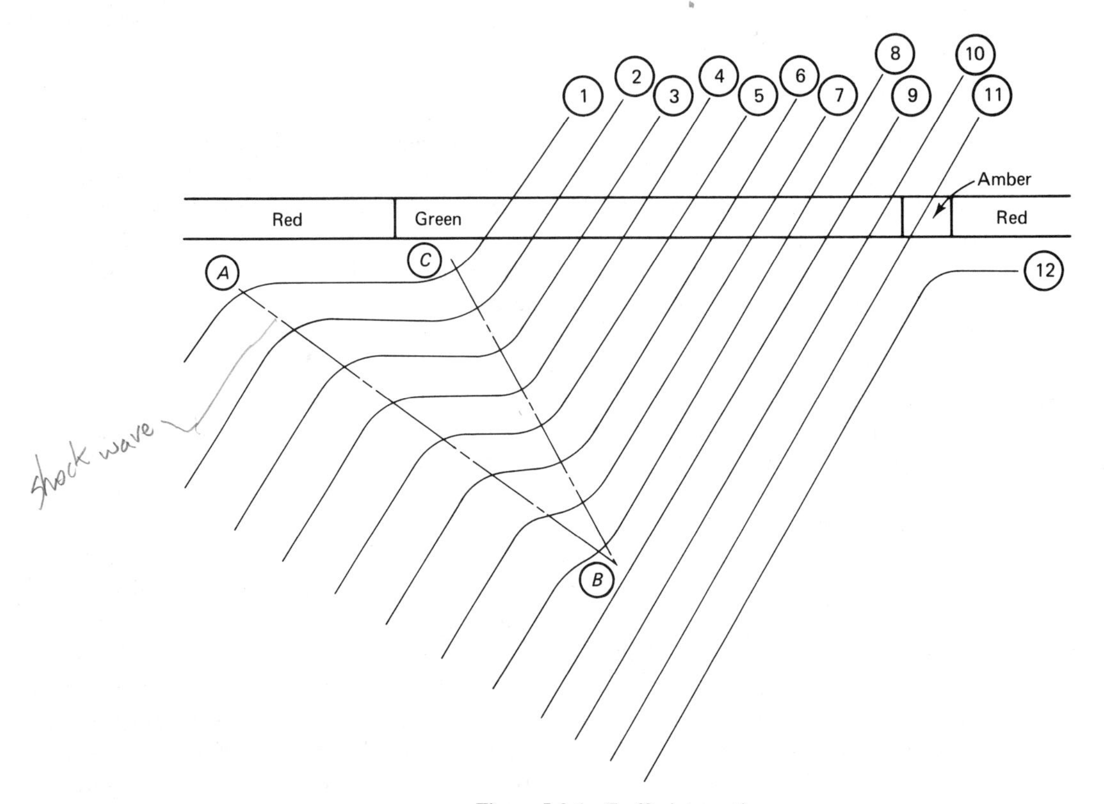

Figure 5.3.1 Traffic interruption.

release conditions may commence when the stationary platoon disappears, but, for simplicity, this shock wave is not shown in Fig. 5.3.1.

5.3.4 Pretimed Signal Coordination

The fact that certain vehicles can avoid stopping at an intersection presents the opportunity to coordinate a series of pretimed signals to allow platoons of vehicles to clear all the signals without interruption [5.4]. This scheme works when the signals being coordinated have the same cycle length but not necessarily the same distribution of green, amber, and red within the common cycle. Figure 5.3.2 shows a system of four intersections, three of which are signalized. The relative timing of each signal is specified by its *offset,* which is the time difference between a reference time and the beginning of the *first complete* green phase thereafter. The two pairs of parallel lines drawn on the figure represent the constant-speed trajectories of the first and last vehicles in each direction that can clear all intersections without stopping. The time difference between the parallel trajectories in each direction of movement is known as the *through band* for the direction.

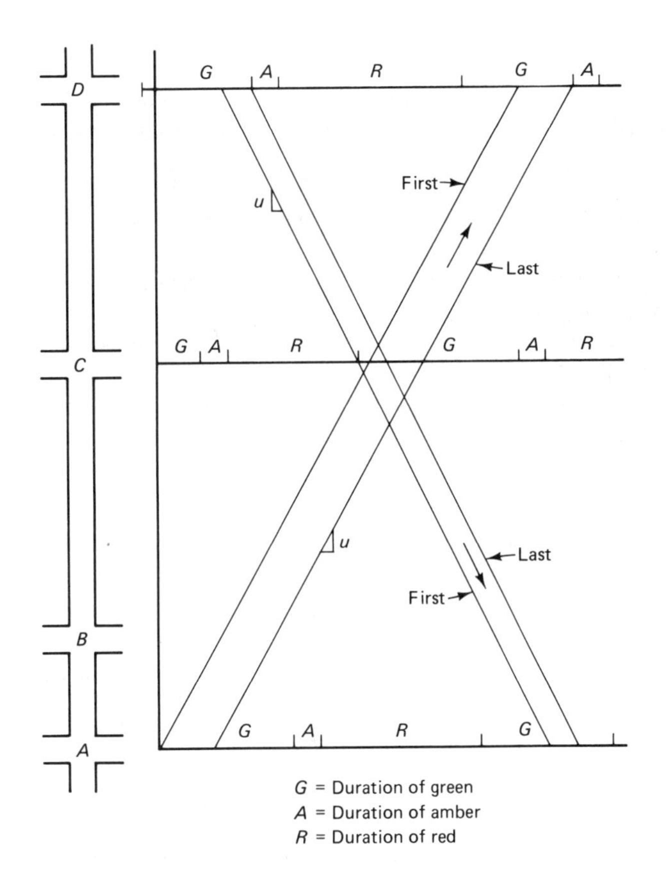

Figure 5.3.2 Pretimed signal coordination.

Dividing the through band by the average vehicular headway gives the number of vehicles constituting the uninterrupted platoon. The *width of the through band,* measured in seconds, may be adjusted by "sliding" each signal diagram horizontally. A *balanced design* refers to the case when the through bands in the two directions of travel are equal. A balanced design, however, does not always represent the best design. For instance, a *preferential design* may be more appropriate during the morning or evening peak periods on streets with unbalanced directional flows.

The solution to a signal-coordination problem may be accomplished graphically, analytically, or by computer, using several simple equations. For example, the time it takes a vehicle to travel between intersections at a constant speed equals the distance traveled divided by the speed. Also, the following equation may be used to discern the status of a signal at any time $t = T$ after the reference time $t = 0$:

$$\text{time into cycle} = \{T - \text{offset}\} \text{ modulo } C \tag{5.3.1}$$

Knowledge of the duration of the green, amber, and red displays can pinpoint the exact status of the signal at $t = T$.

Example 5.2

A signal has an offset of 10 s, a green, $G = 50$ s, an amber, $Y = 5$ s, and a red, $R = 65$ s. Find the status of the signal at times (a) $t = 45$ s, (b) 150 s, (c) 720 s, and (d) 782 s.

Solution: The signal cycle $C = (G + Y + R) = 120$ s. Apply Eq. 5.3.1.

(a) For $t = 45$: $(45 - 10)/120 = 0$ remainder 35; 35 s into the (0 + 1) (i.e., first) cycle. Since $35 < G$, the display is green.
(b) For $t = 150$: $(150 - 10)/120 = 1$ remainder 20; 20 s into the second cycle. Since $20 < G$, the display is also green.
(c) For $t = 720$: $(720 - 10)/120 = 5$ remainder 110: 110 s into sixth cycle. Since $(G + Y) < 110 < C$, the display is red.
(d) For $t = 782$: $(782 - 10)/120 = 6$ remainder 52; 52 s into the seventh cycle. Since $G < 52 < (G + Y)$, the display is amber.

Example 5.3

The signals at the intersections of the one-way street have been pretimed and coordinated as follows:

Intersection	Green	Amber	Red	Offset	Distance from A
A	40 s	5 s	35 s	0 s	—
B	50 s	5 s	25 s	40 s	2000 ft
C	35 s	5 s	40 s	10 s	5000 ft

Given a design speed of 30 mi/h, determine the width of the resulting through band.

Solution The three signals have equal cycles of 80 s. Therefore signal coordination is possible. A vehicle clearing intersection A at time $t = 0$ will arrive at B (2000 ft)/(44 ft/s) = 45.5 s later. At this instant, the display at B is 5.5 s into the first green display. Hence the vehicle can proceed toward C without interruption. It will reach C at $t = 45.5 + (3000/44) = 113.7$ s. At this time, the signal at C is 23.7 s into the second cycle and is green. Therefore, this vehicle can clear all three intersections.

To find the last vehicle that can do the same, the remaining green duration after the passage of the first vehicle is calculated (see the accompanying figure):

$$\text{at A: } 40 - 0 = 40 \text{ s}$$

$$\text{at B: } 90 - 45.5 = 44.5 \text{ s}, \quad \text{or} \quad 50 - 5.5 = 44.5 \text{ s}$$

and

$$\text{at C: } 125 - 113.7 = 11.3 \text{ s}, \quad \text{or} \quad 35 - 23.7 = 11.3 \text{ s}$$

The minimum of these values defines the width of the through band (i.e., 11.3 s) and fixes the trajectory of the last vehicle as shown on the diagram.

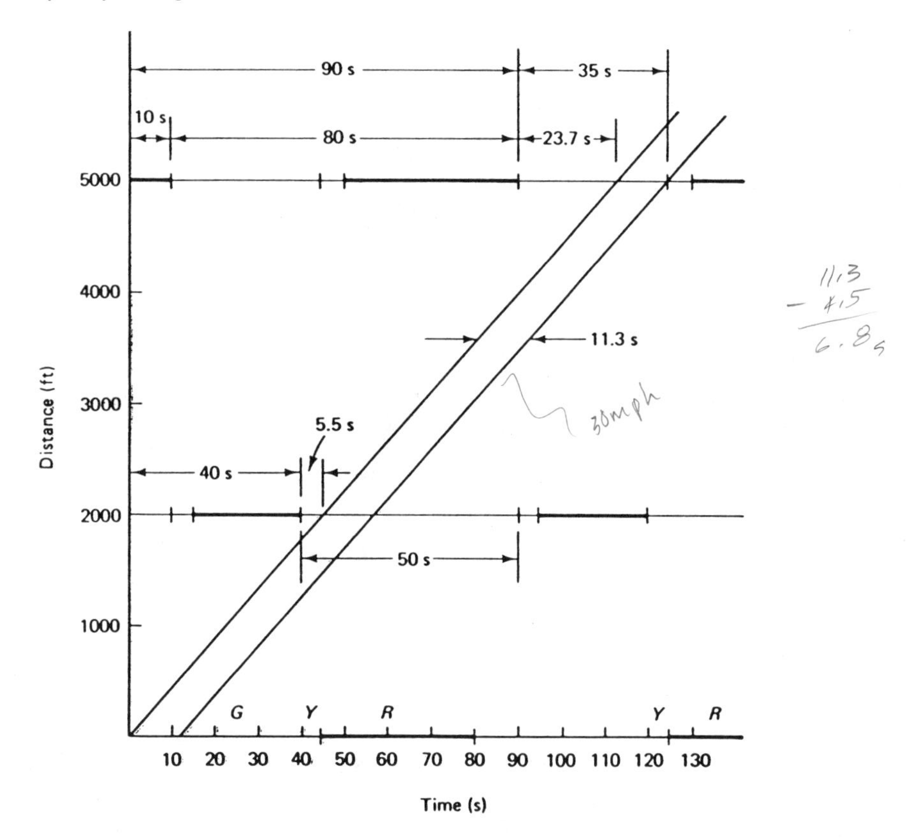

Figure P.5.3

Discussion Often, the width of the through band is taken to include the amber, that is, the last vehicle is allowed to clear an intersection on yellow. In this event, the width of the through band would be reported as 16.3 s. Note that in this example the width of the through band can be increased by increasing the offset of intersection C. As a general rule, allowing a few seconds of green to elapse before the first vehicle in the main platoon reaches a signal is considered good practice because it allows any main- or side-street vehicles caught by the preceding red phase to clear the way before the platoon's arrival.

5.4 CAPACITY OF SIGNALIZED INTERSECTIONS

5.4.1 Background

Under uninterrupted conditions, the definition of flow is simply the number of vehicles that pass a point during a specified time interval. At intersections, a unique point where flow measurements can be taken does not exist. Figure 5.4.1 shows the variety of move-

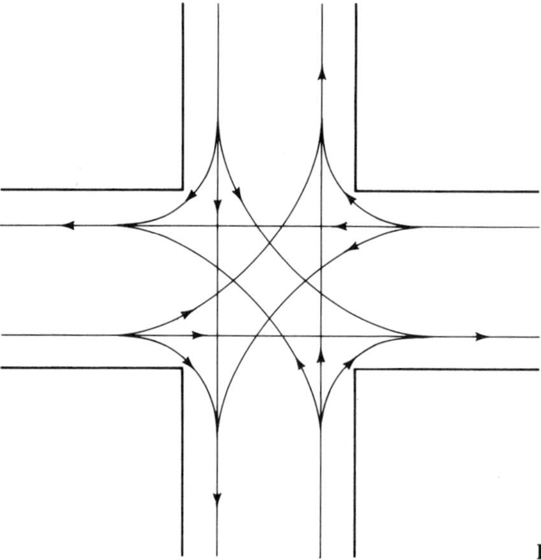

Figure 5.4.1 Intersection movement desires.

ment desires that a typical four-leg intersection is expected to accommodate and the resulting points of conflict between these movements. The ability of a signalized intersection to process the approaching flows is affected by the magnitudes and vehicular composition of these volumes, their movement desires, the geometric design of the intersection, and the characteristics of the signal. The presence of bus stops in the immediate vicinity of the intersection also affects its operating conditions. Several practical methods of signalized intersection analysis are found in the technical literature. Most of these methods are empirical and approximate. Hence, their ability to explain the many subtleties encountered at intersections is, accordingly, limited. Nevertheless, their usefulness for practical analysis cannot be denied.

5.4.2 The 1965 Highway Capacity Manual Method

Until recently, the 1965 *Highway Capacity Manual* method [5.1] enjoyed great popularity. It simplifies the complexity of intersection operations by viewing each approach to the intersection separately. It can be used either to estimate the prevailing level of service given the approach volume and the characteristics of the approach or to estimate the maximum *service volume* (i.e., the maximum volume for a specified level of service) that can be accommodated by the approach. For each approach to the intersection, each of the unique combinations of movements permitted by the various displays of green is examined separately by the most appropriate of four procedures. With some adjustments to ensure consistency, the total service volume for the approach as a whole is determined by summing its parts.

5.4.3 Critical Movement Methods

More recently, a new way of viewing the operation of signalized intersections has emerged. The most notable aspects of this new concept include the following.

First, vehicles that are permitted to proceed simultaneously through the intersection on conflicting paths must be considered together. Thus, *the performance of a particular approach is dependent on the signal and the flow conditions that prevail on other approaches.*

Second, certain movements through the intersection from different approaches occur simultaneously. For example, the left-turning vehicles on the southbound approach of Fig. 5.4.2(b) are required to cross the northbound through volume at the same time that left-turning vehicles from the northbound approach attempt to cross the southbound volume. When such conflicts occur, one of the two movements may be more severe (or critical) than the other. Consequently, *there exists one critical movement for each unique combination of simultaneous green signal indications.* For instance, during the "leading" portion of the green display when the opposing flow is interrupted [Fig. 5.4.2(a)], the left-turning volume constitutes the critical movement, since it is the only one permitted during that time interval. Afterward, one of the conflicting movements would be critical.

Third, when multiple lanes are present, drivers respond to the conditions ahead of them by selecting the most convenient traffic lane [5.5]. Thus *lane utilization is an important determinant of intersection performance.*

Beginning with the work of Capelle and Pinnell [5.6], several researchers have proposed differing *critical movement* methods for the analysis of intersection capacity and level of service. Versions of this method appeared in the Australian, British, and Swedish capacity manuals. In the United States, the Committee on Highway Capacity

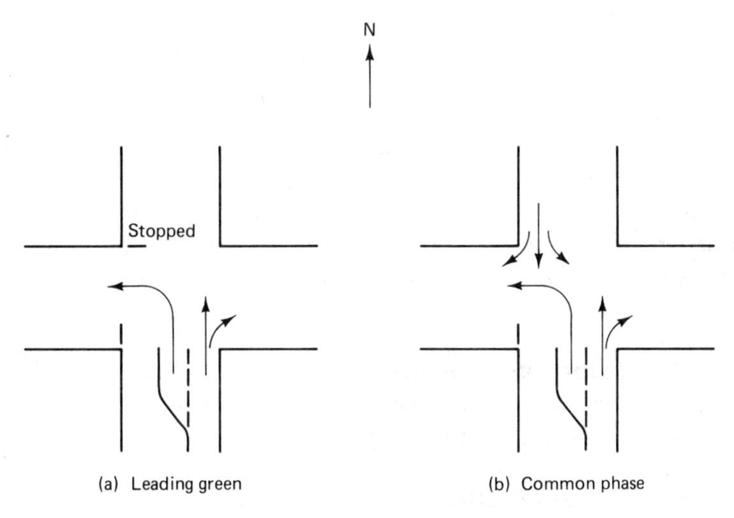

Figure 5.4.2 Leading green—special lane.

and Quality of Service of the Transportation Research Board proposed two procedures of the *critical movement analysis* method [5.7]. Both procedures are based on the same general principle but differ in the degree of detail to which they account for the various factors that affect the intersection's level of service and capacity. The *planning applications* procedure is a quick-analysis method suitable when a rough assessment of the intersection is sufficient, as it assumes "average" or typical conditions. The *operations and design applications* procedure is more appropriate for detailed analysis and final design. Only the planning applications procedure will be covered here. The emphasis of this section is placed on the rationale of the method and not on its subtleties. The 1985 *Highway Capacity Manual* [5.8] has further refined these procedures, but a detailed coverage of these refinements is beyond the scope of this textbook.

5.4.4 Lane Capacity

It was shown in Chapter 4 that under "ideal conditions" (e.g., 12-ft lanes, lateral clearance, and no trucks), the capacity of a single lane of *uninterrupted* highway traffic is about 2000 pc/h. This represents an average headway of 1.8 s. Because of the loss of time incurred due to start-up delays at the beginning of green (see Subsection 5.3.3 and Fig. 5.3.1), the capacity of a single lane under *interrupted* conditions cannot exceed approximately 1800 passenger cars *per hour of green* (pc/hg) and this figure must be further adjusted to account for the effect of various factors, including lane widths other than 12 ft, heavy vehicles, bus operations, conflicting turns, pedestrian flows, parking activity, and peaking characteristics.

5.4.5 The Planning Applications Procedure

The planning applications procedure [5.7] treats the various components of flow in terms of vehicles per hour (rather than passenger car equivalents), assuming an average vehicle mix. Consequently, explicit adjustments for heavy vehicles are not performed. Also, the effect of bus operations in the vicinity of the intersection is ignored. This procedure can be used to assess broadly the level of service that prevails at an existing intersection, to calculate the maximum service volume for a known level of service, to predict the impact of design changes on the level of service, and combinations of the three. Table 5.4.1 summarizes the required adjustment factors, and Fig. 5.4.3 outlines the steps involved in the procedure.

Step 1: Identification of lane geometry A diagram of the entire intersection is prepared, which shows all lanes and the types of movement(s) that are permitted on each lane (e.g., left-only or left-and-through).

Step 2: Identification of demand The left-turning, through, and right-turning volumes that use (or are expected to use) each approach are identified and expressed in

TABLE 5.4.1 LEFT- AND RIGHT-TURN EQUIVALENCE FACTORS

Left	
Opposing through *plus* right flows (veh/h)	Equivalent "through" veh/h
0	1.0
300	2.0
600	4.0
1000+	6.0

Right	
Opposing flow (ped/h)	Equivalent "through" veh/h
0	1.00
100	1.25
600	1.50
1200+	2.00+

SOURCE: Transportation Research Board [5.7]; From Tables 3 & 4, pp. 9–10.

vehicles per hour. The assignment of these volumes to the individual lanes identified in Step 1 is not performed at this stage.

Step 3: Identification of signal phasing The existing or contemplated phases that make up the signal cycle are identified. In this context, a *phase* is a combination of green indications that allows simultaneous movements from one or more approaches. For simplicity, the duration of the amber is included in the duration of a "green" phase. The simplest type of phasing is a two-phase pattern, which alternates the green display between the two streets that form the intersection. Phasing schemes may be classified as *non-overlapping* and *overlapping*. The former accommodate every movement through the intersection during one phase. The latter represent the situation where at least one movement is accommodated by multiple phases. Figure 5.4.4 illustrates this difference.

Step 4: Check of conflicting left-turning vehicles This step is concerned with the question of whether adequate gaps are available in the opposing volume to accommodate left-turning vehicles that do not have a special signal indication. Two vehicles are assumed to clear the intersection on yellow, and the *maximum turning volume* during the green display is controlled by magnitude of the opposing volume V_o and by the duration of green, that is,

$$\max V_T = 1200\left(\frac{G_T}{C}\right) - V_o \text{ veh/h} \tag{5.4.1}$$

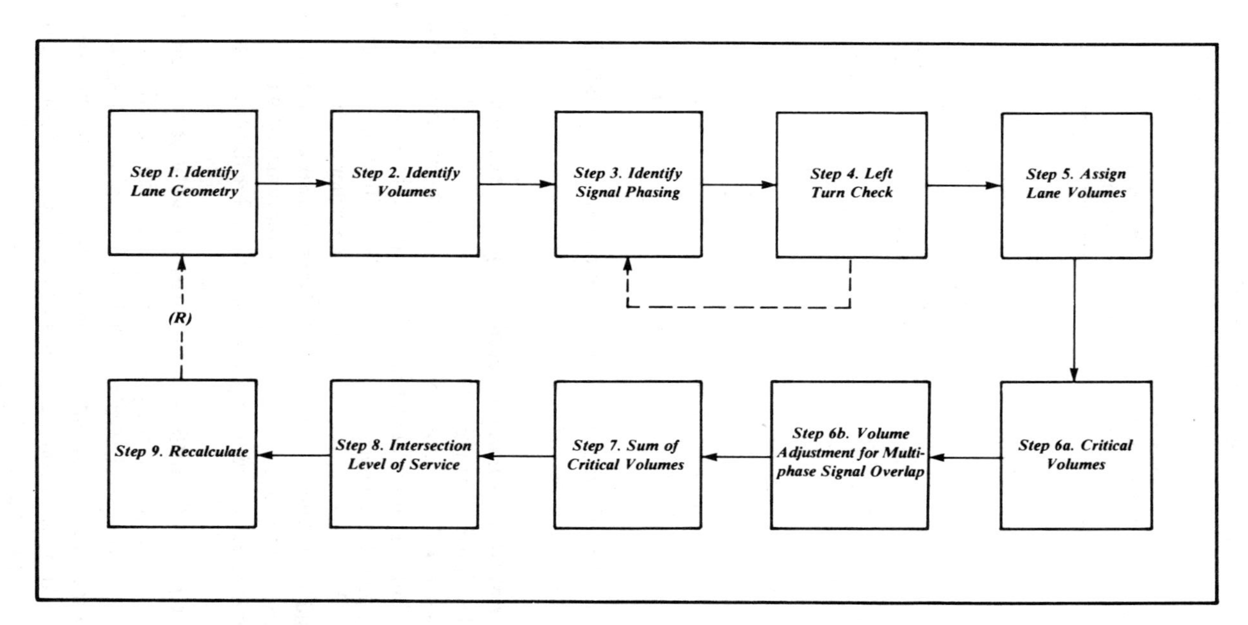

Figure 5.4.3 Critical movement method: planning applications. (*SOURCE*: Transportation Research Board [5.7], Fig. 2, p. 13.)

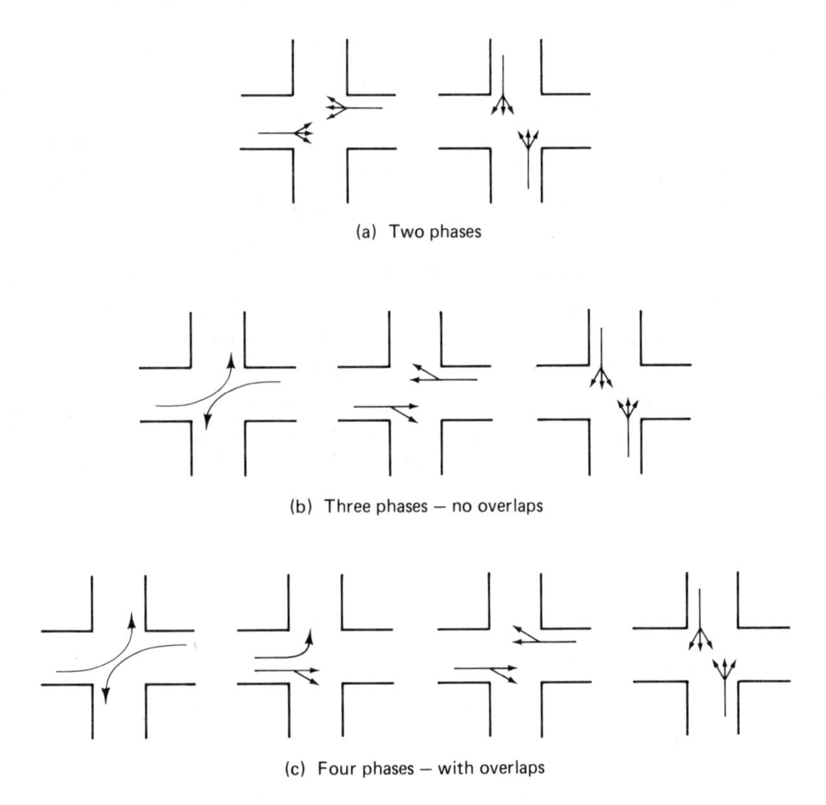

Figure 5.4.4 Examples of signal phasing.

In this equation, G_T is the duration of the green display during which the conflict is permitted and C is the duration of the signal cycle. The ratio of these two values is equal to the fraction of real time during which the conflict occurs. In the limit (i.e., when $G_T = C$ and $V_o = 0$) the maximum turning volume is 1200 veh/h, a value based on empirical findings. With higher opposing volumes and shorter values for G_T, the maximum turning volume that can be accommodated on green is less than 1200 veh/h.

To find the absolute maximum of turning flow that can be processed, the two vehicles per yellow translated to an hourly volume is added to the result of Eq. 5.4.1. Demand volumes that exceed this sum imply poor operating conditions and excessive vehicular delays. The broken feedback line in Fig. 5.4.3 indicates the possibility of returning to the previous step for the purpose of revising the signal pattern in an attempt to alleviate this problem.

Step 5: Assignment of lane volumes This step assigns the approach volumes to the available lanes. When examining an existing intersection, the observed lane utilization can be used. Otherwise, a procedure that estimates the lane choice of drivers is applied. When exclusive turn lanes are present, the turning volume is, naturally, assigned to them. If two turn lanes are provided for the same movement, one is assigned 55% and the other 45% of the turning volume. The volume not using an exclusive turn lane is divided between the lanes that are available to it considering the fact that vehicles going straight through the intersection show a preference to lanes that are not blocked by turning vehicles. The degree to which this phenomenon occurs depends on the number of lanes, the magnitude of the turning volumes, and the magnitude of the opposing volumes against which the turns are made. In the case of left turns, the opposing volume consists of the through *plus* right-turning vehicles that simultaneously proceed into the intersection area from the opposite approach. In the case of right-turning vehicles, the opposing volume most often consists of pedestrians on the cross street. The turning volumes are converted to "equivalent through vehicles per hour" (from Table 5.4.1), and the total approach volume (expressed in equivalent through vehicles per hour) is divided equally among the available lanes. The turning volumes are then converted back to vehicles per hour, and a check is made to ensure that all turning volumes have been assigned to lanes that permit the execution of turns.

Example 5.4

An intersection approach is expected to carry the following hourly volumes:

1000 veh/h going straight through the intersection
200 veh/h turning right
400 veh/h turning left

Three lanes are present: An exclusive left, a middle lane for through vehicles, and a curb lane that is shared by through and right-turning vehicles. Assuming that the vehicles executing right turns are free from pedestrian interference and that the left-turning vehicles face an opposing volume (through plus right) of 400 veh/h, assign the approach volume to three available lanes.

Solution The entire left-turn volume is assigned to the exclusive left lane. Since there is no pedestrian interference, the remaining volume of 1200 veh/h is divided equally between the other two lanes, as shown in the accompanying figure.

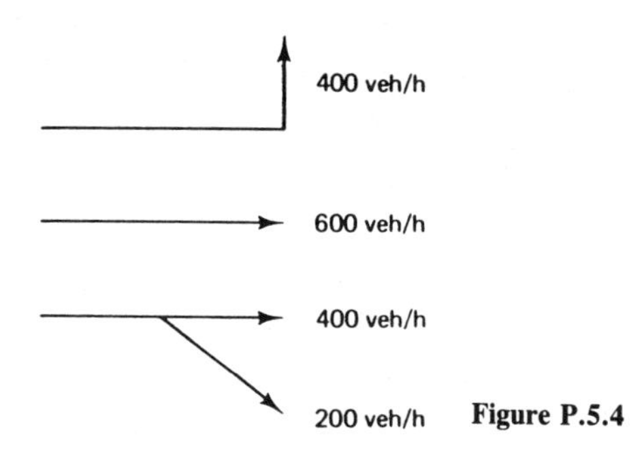

Figure P.5.4

Example 5.5

Repeat the procedure of Example 5.4, assuming that the left lane is not present.

Solution In this case, the center lane will be shared by the left-turning vehicles and a portion of the through volume. The likely distribution by lane is estimated as follows:

1. With an opposing volume of 400 veh/h, a through-vehicle equivalency factor for the left-turning vehicles is obtained by interpolation from Table 5.4.1. This factor is 2.7.
2. The left-turning volume of 400 veh/h is converted to through-vehicle equivalent of (400)(2.7) = 1080.
3. The right-turn equivalency factor is 1.0 because the right-turning vehicles are free of pedestrian interference.
4. The total approach volume, that is, (1080 + 1000 + 200) = 2280 through vehicles per hour, is divided equally between the two lanes, each lane receiving 1140 veh/h.
5. Since the equivalent volume assigned to the center lane (1140) is greater than the left-turning volume (1080 "through" vehicles per hour), the entire left-turning volume has, in effect, been assigned to the center lane.
6. The left-turning volume is converted back to vehicles per hour (i.e., 400 veh/h), and the lane assignment is completed as shown in the accompanying figure.

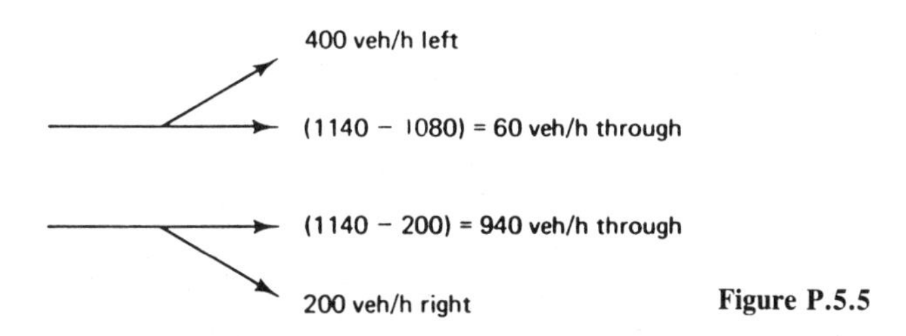

Figure P.5.5

Example 5.6

Repeat Example 5.5 assuming that the left-turning vehicles face an opposing volume of 700 veh/h.

Solution

1. The equivalency factor for left turns is 4.5 (Table 5.4.1, with an opposing volume of 700 veh/h).
2. Expressed in terms of through vehicles, the left-turning volume becomes (4.5)(400) = 1800 through vehicles per hour.
3. The right-turn factor is still 1.00.
4. The total volume, (1800 + 1000 + 200) = 3000 through vehicles per hour, is divided equally between the two lanes, each receiving 1500 veh/h.
5. The 1500 through vehicles per hour assigned to the center lane are less than the total left-turning volume of 1800. Since, in this case, the execution of left turns from the curb lane is not permitted, the preliminary assignment must be revised to place the entire left-turn volume on the center lane.

6. The left-turn volume is converted back to 400 veh/h and the final lane assignment is shown in the accompanying figure.

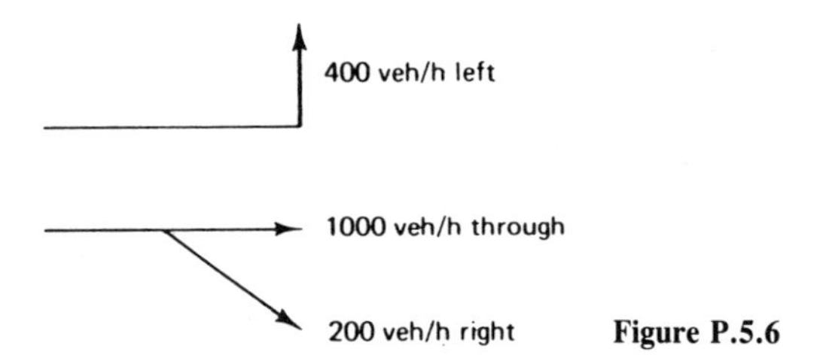

Figure P.5.6

Discussion This example illustrates a situation where, by their choice of lanes, the drivers have, in effect, designated the center lane as an exclusive left-turn lane. This happened because of the excessive lane blockage that is caused by the left-turning vehicles when facing high opposing volumes.

Step 6: Determination of critical volumes for each signal phase For each green signal phase, there is a critical point within the intersection crossed by the highest volume for that phase (i.e., the *critical volume*). The critical point may be on a single path or at the intersection of two paths. Figure 5.4.5 shows a variety of possible critical points, a combination of which would appear during each phase. In Fig. 5.4.5(a), potential critical points on single paths are shown. In (b), points prior to diverging volumes are designated as possible critical points. Finally, (c) shows points where turning vehicles are in conflict with opposing movements. The volume that crosses such points of conflict is given by the sum of the two conflicting volumes. Although not drawn on the figure, the opposing volume includes through plus right-turning vehicles, if applicable. A fundamental assumption of the intersection analysis method described here is that the relative duration of signal phases is proportional to their critical volumes.

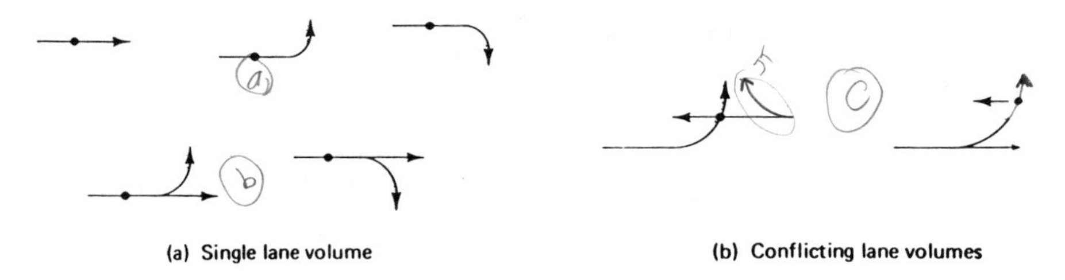

Figure 5.4.5 Examples of possible critical points.

Example 5.7

The movements permitted from the east-west approaches to an intersection during a signal phase are shown in the accompanying figure, along with their lane assignments. Find the critical volume for this phase.

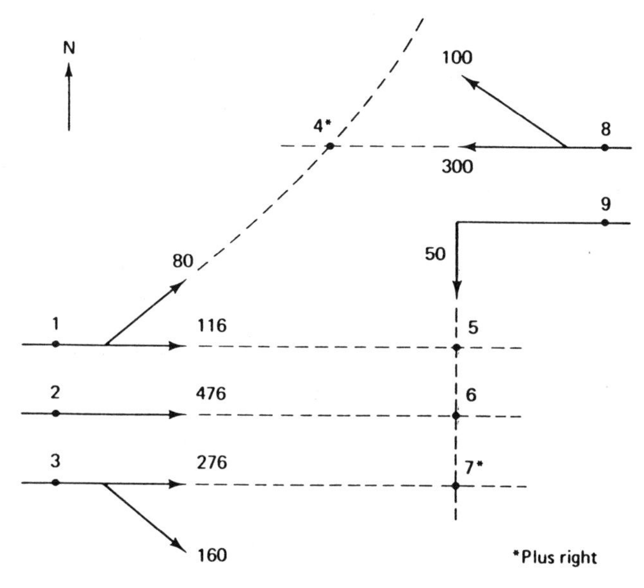

Figure P.5.7

Solution Nine potentially critical points are identified in the figure. The volumes associated with each point are calculated next:

Point		Volume (veh/h)
1	80 + 116	196
2		476
3	276 + 160	436
4	80 + (300 + 100)	480
5	50 + 116	166
6	50 + 476	526
7	50 + (276 + 160)	486
8	300 + 100	400
9		50

The critical volume for this phase is 526 veh/h at point 6. When overlapping occurs as described in Step 4, the procedure becomes a little more complex, as the next example illustrates.

Example 5.8

Consider the north-south approaches to the intersection of Example 5.7 to be as shown in the accompanying figure. Also shown are the *three phases* of the signal cycle that are devoted to these volumes. Compute the critical volume for each of the three phases.

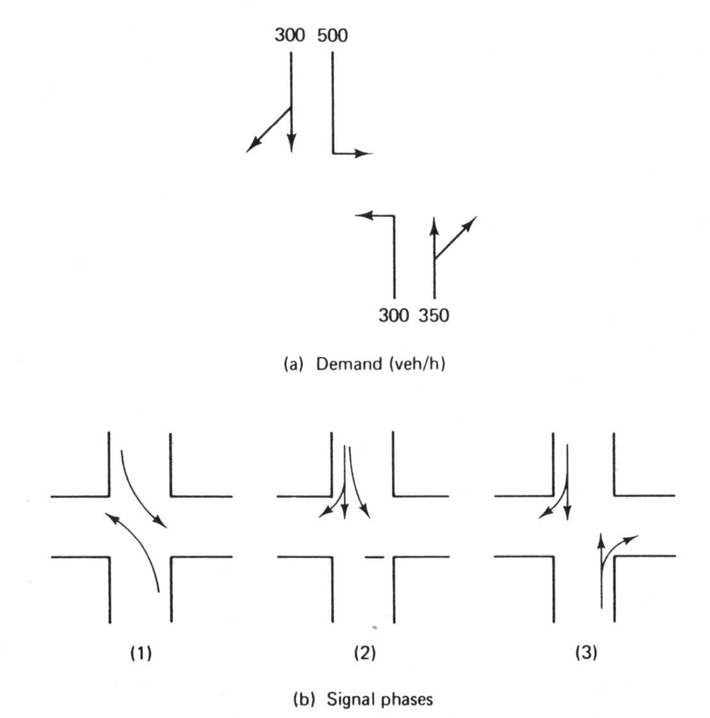

(a) Demand (veh/h)

(b) Signal phases

Figure P.5.8

Solution Overlapping between phase 1 and phase 2 occurs with regard to the left-turning volume on the southbound approach and between phase 2 and phase 3 with regard to the through and right-turning volume on the same approach. A reasonable assumption is that the duration of the phase 1 will be apportioned to accommodate the 300 veh/h in the northbound approach. Thus the critical volume for this phase is 300 veh/h. Of course, 300 veh/h would also be processed from the opposite approach, leaving 200 left-turning vehicles per hour for phase 2 along with 200 through and right vehicles per hour. The critical volume of phase 2 is 200 veh/h. The remaining 400 veh/h in the southbound approach must be accommodated simultaneously with the remaining traffic in the northbound approach, as shown. The critical volume for phase 3 is 400 veh/h.

Discussion This example illustrates how overlapping phasing can be treated. Many other combinations are possible. Some require a good measure of judgment. In typical planning applications, several possible signal phasings would be specified and analyzed to help determine the best one among them.

Example 5.9

For the entire intersection described by the previous two examples taken together, check to see whether the conflicting left turns can be accommodated (i.e., Step 4), assuming that the cycle length C is 90 s.

Solution Designating the signal phase that controls the east-west approaches (Example 5.7) as phase 4, the required check applies to this phase only. With a 90-s cycle, there are 3600/90, or 40, cycles per hour. Allowing two vehicles per cycle to clear the intersection translates to 80 turning vehicles per hour. This is already sufficient for both left-turning volumes of phase 4 without considering the application of Eq. 5.4.1.

Discussion With the known cycle length, the previous check could have been undertaken earlier and the same conclusion would have been reached. However, if the application of Eq. 5.4.1 were necessary, knowledge of the duration (G_T) of that phase would be required. Based on the assumption that the signal cycle is divided among the various phases approximately in proportion to their critical volumes, the duration of the four phases might not have been available until the completion of Step 6. On the basis of the results of examples 5.7 and 5.8, phases 1 through 4 would receive 19, 13, 25, and 33 s per 90-s cycle, respectively.

Step 7: Summation of critical volumes The critical volumes calculated for each phase are summed to arrive at a single measure of the intersection as a whole. In the case of the four-phase intersection of the preceding examples, the *sum of critical volumes* is 300 + 200 + 400 + 526, or 1426, veh/h.

Step 8: Assessment of level of service Table 5.4.2 is used to determine the level of service prevailing at the intersection. The table specifies the ranges of volumes belonging to the various levels of service and for each of three signal patterns, that is, cycles with two, three, and four or more phases. The capacity (i.e., level-of-service E) corresponding to a two-phase signal is 1500 veh/h. As explained earlier, this figure assumes average urban conditions for which the critical movement analysis described in this section has been devised. The capacity of the intersection decreases as more signal

TABLE 5.4.2 INTERSECTION LEVEL OF SERVICE RANGES

	Planning Applications (in veh/h)		
	Maximum sum of critical volumes		
Level of service	Two-phase	Three-phase	Four or more phases
A	900	855	825
B	1050	1000	965
C	1200	1140	1100
D	1350	1275	1225
E	1500	1425	1375
F		Not applicable	

SOURCE: Transportation Research Board [5.7]; Table 6, p. 17.

phases are added, partly due to the fact that more time is lost for more frequent start-up delays. If the sum of critical volumes exceeds the capacity of the intersection, level-of-service F prevails. This is the case with the present example.

Step 9: Modification of design The geometric configuration of the intersection, its signal phasing, or both may be modified. The effect of such modifications on the level of service can then be calculated by returning to Step 1.

5.5 SUMMARY

This chapter addressed the topic of vehicular stream interruptions. The basic elements of transit stations were described, and a model of the capacity of on-line stations was developed. The analysis of urban signalized intersections was considered next. Various signal systems were described, and a method for coordinating a series of equal-cycle pretimed signals that permit the continuous movement of platoons of vehicles was presented. Finally, a practical critical movement method for the analysis of signalized intersection capacity and level of service was presented and illustrated.

5.6 EXERCISES

1. Using the data of Example 5.1, calculate and discuss the station capacity that would result from varying the number of vehicles per train from $N = 2$ to $N = 5$.
2. Computerize the solution procedure for Exercise 1.
3. At time $t = 485$ s after the reference time, a traffic signal is 22 s into its cycle. Assuming that the cycle length is 90 s, calculate the signal's offset.
4. Show graphically that the answers to parts (a) and (b) of Example 5.2 are correct.
5. For the system of intersections of Example 5.3, calculate the width of the through band that would result from changing the offsets at intersections A, B, and C to 10, 60, and 20 s, respectively.
6. Assuming that the street of Exercise 5 is a two-way street, calculate the width of the through band in the other direction.
7. Given a speed of 45 mi/h and the accompanying data, determine whether a balanced signal coordination exists.

Intersection	Green (s)	Amber (s)	Red (s)	Offset (s)	Distance from A (ft)
A	30	5	15	5	—
B	25	5	20	0	660
C		Unsignalized			1430
D	20	5	25	25	1980
E	30	5	15	5	3300

8. Construct a computer program that calculates the through band widths for a series of N intersections given (a) the signal cycles, (b) the signal offsets, (c) the distances between intersections, and (d) the design speed.

9. For the data of example 5.4, recalculate the lane assignments assuming that the right turns are made against 400 pedestrians per hour (ped/h).

10. Redo Example 5.5 assuming that the vehicular flow that opposes the left turns is 300 veh/h and the pedestrian interference to the right turns is caused by 500 ped/h. Compare and discuss the results of the two cases.

11. Estimate the prevailing level of service for the intersection shown in the accompanying figure.

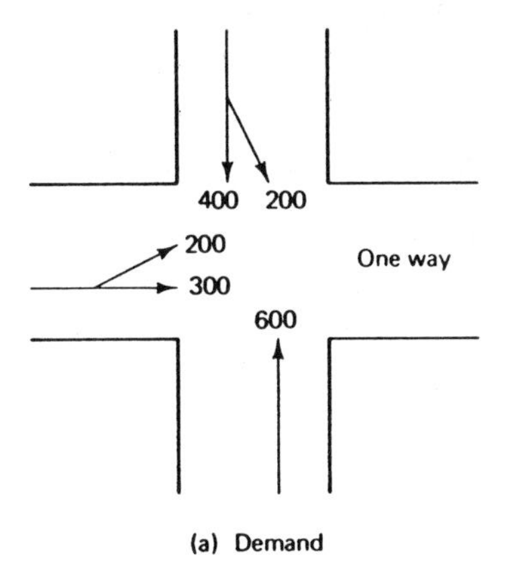

(a) Demand

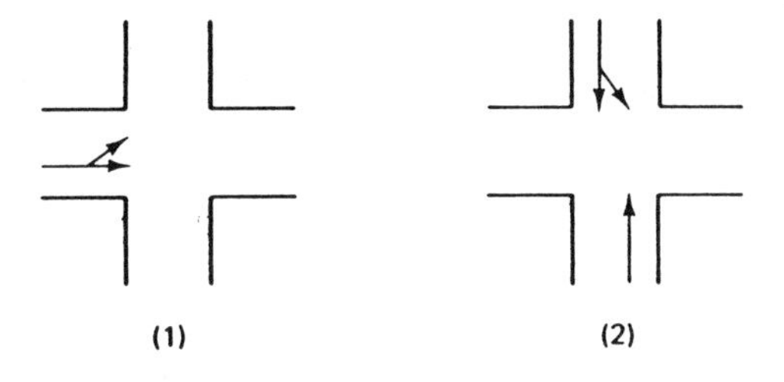

(b) Signal phases

Figure E.5.11

12. Estimate and discuss the effect of changing the signal of Exercise 11 to the three-phase pattern shown in the accompanying figure.

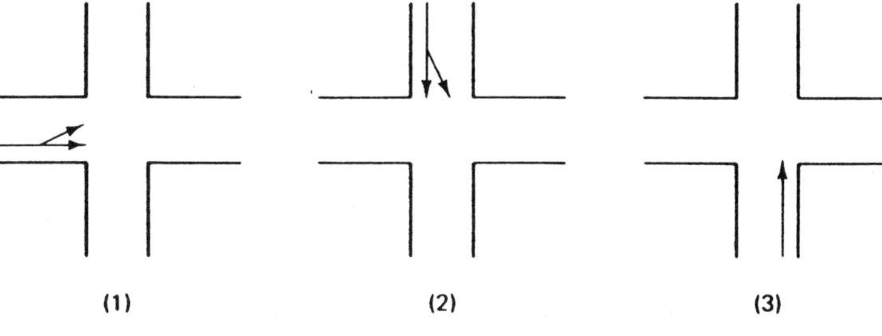

Figure E.5.12

13. All approaches to the intersection shown provide exclusive left-turning lanes. Given the demand shown in the accompanying figure and a simple two-phase signal cycle, calculate the level of service. There is no pedestrian interference.

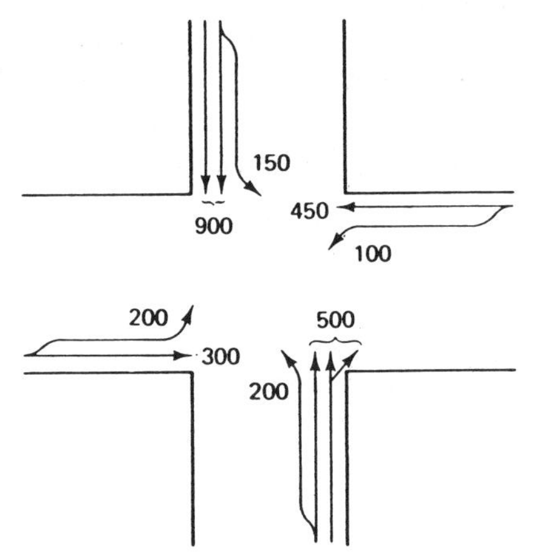

Figure E.5.13

14. Explain how you would apportion an 80-s signal cycle to the two phases of Exercise 13 and check to see if enough gaps exist in the through volumes to accommodate all left turns.

15. Estimate the level of service for the intersection of Grace and Hamada Streets shown in the accompanying figure. Assume that there is no pedestrian interference.

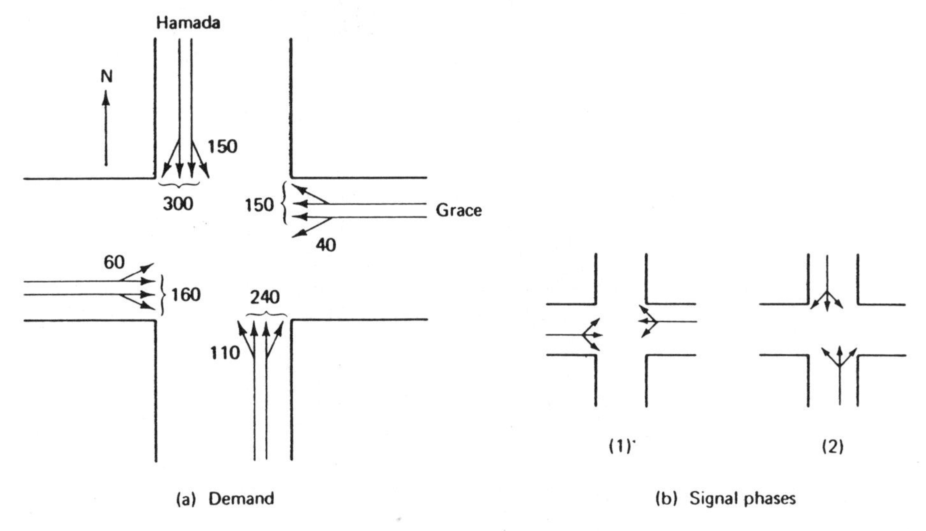

Figure E.5.15

16. Calculate the prevailing level of service at the intersection shown in the accompanying figure.

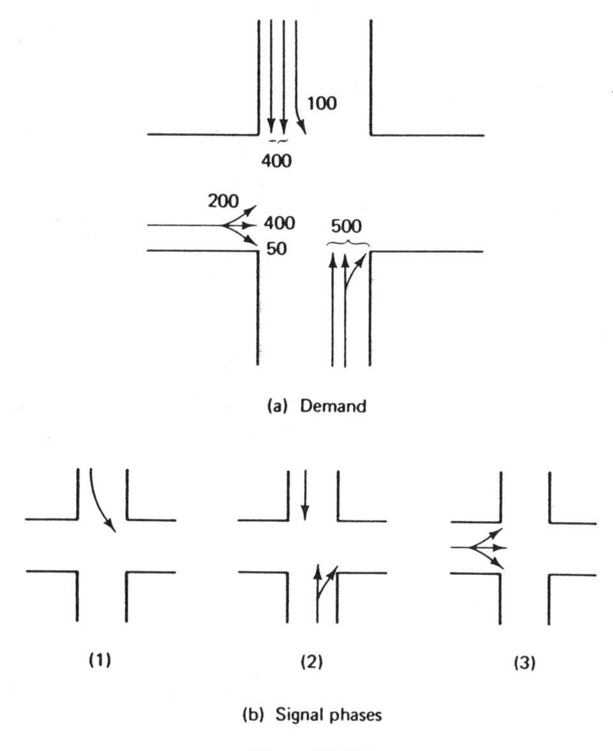

Figure E.5.16

17. Calculate the level of service for the intersection of Exercise 16 assuming a simple two-phase signal cycle, and discuss the implication on the conflict between the left and opposing through volumes.

5.7 REFERENCES

5.1 Highway Research Board, *Highway Capacity Manual,* Special Report 87, National Research Council, Washington, D.C., 1965.

5.2 VUCHIC, VUKAN R., *Urban Public Transportation Systems and Technology,* Prentice-Hall, Inc., Englewood Cliffs, N.J., © 1981, p. 556. Figure 5.2.3 reprinted by permission.

5.3 PIGNATARO, LOUIS J., *Traffic Engineering Theory and Practice,* Prentice-Hall, Inc., Englewood Cliffs, N.J., 1973.

5.4 Institute of Transportation Engineers, *Transportation and Traffic Engineering Handbook,* Prentice-Hall, Inc., Englewood Cliffs, N.J., 1976.

5.5 PAPACOSTAS, C. S., "Influence of Leading Vehicle Turn Signal Use on Following Vehicle Lane Choice at Signalized Intersections," *Transportation Research Record 996,* Transportation Research Board, National Research Council, Washington, D.C., 1984, pp. 37–44.

5.6 Capelle, D. G. and C. Pinnell, "Capacity Study of Signalized Diamond Interchanges," *Highway Research Bulletin 291*, Highway Research Board, National Research Council, Washington, D.C., 1961, pp. 1–25.

5.7 Transportation Research Board, *Interim Materials on Highway Capacity*, Circular 212, National Research Council, Washington, D.C., 1980.

5.8 ———, *Highway Capacity Manual*, Special Report 209, National Research Council, Washington, D.C., 1985.

CHAPTER 6

PROBABILITY, QUEUING, AND SIMULATION MODELS

6.1 INTRODUCTION

When the outcome of a situation or process can be known in advance with absolute certainty, the situation or process is said to be *deterministic*. It may be argued that, in a cause-and-effect universe, the outcome of every situation can be anticipated, assuming that all the factors affecting the situation are clearly understood. Knowing everything about something, however, requires knowing everything about everything else, and this is not a pragmatic claim. Engineering decisions are almost always based on limited information. Hence, all situations entail some degree of uncertainty. When the degree of uncertainty is very low, the situation may be treated as if it were deterministic. Otherwise, some way of incorporating uncertainty is needed. The *theory of probability* is the branch of mathematics that addresses this question. It had its origins in an attempt by Pascal to predict the likely outcome of interrupted gambling games to aid a group of friends in settling their bets and has since been applied to innumerable situations including the study of traffic systems. Queuing (waiting-line) models and computer-simulation models are two examples of *probabilistic models* that may be used to analyze traffic phenomena.

The practical methods of analysis discussed in Chapter 5 are based on knowledge that has been obtained from observing the operation of many facilities, and they approximate the effects of the various factors that influence capacity by the use of empirically derived charts and tables. The percentage of the total approach volume that wishes to execute turning maneuvers, for example, is clearly a major factor affecting the operation of an intersection. However, it is reasonable to expect that not only the percentage, but also the pattern with which the left-turning vehicles arrive at the intersection would affect its operation. For example, turning vehicles arriving one after another during a short interval of time within the hour would result in different conditions than if they were spread out uniformly throughout the hour. Thus, having the knowledge that 20%, for example, of the approach volume consists of left-turning vehicles and that 10% of the approaching vehicles plan to turn right does not specify unequivocably either the sequence in which turning vehicles appear or the movement desire of any one vehicle in the approaching stream; it simply quantifies the likelihood, or probability, with which each vehicle is expected to execute each maneuver. When a more detailed investigation of a system characterized by a high degree of variability is desired, methods that are explicitly based on the theory of probability are often employed.

6.2 ELEMENTS OF PROBABILITY THEORY

6.2.1 Background

The theory of probability is concerned with situations (conventionally referred to as *experiments*) that have many possible *outcomes*. For example, a vehicle approaching an intersection (experiment) may choose one of three possible movements (outcomes): It may go straight through, it may turn right, or it may turn left. Similarly, casting a single die has six possible outcomes: the numbers 1 through 6. Thus, for each experiment there exists a set of possible outcomes collectively known as the *sample, outcome,* or *event space,* usually denoted by the uppercase Greek letter omega (Ω). An *event* is a subset of the sample space. It is *simple* if it consists of a single outcome and *compound* if it contains a combination of single outcomes. For example, when casting a die, "rolling a 2" is a simple event A, whereas "rolling an even number" is a compound event B such that:

$$A = \{2\} \quad \text{and} \quad B = \{2, 4, 6\}$$

The following definitions from set theory are also relevant to the discussion of probability. The *complement* of an event A is denoted by $\overline{A}$ and is defined as the subset of Ω that contains all elements not belonging to A. Thus, the complements of the events A and B are:

$$\overline{A} = \{1, 3, 4, 5, 6\} \quad \text{and} \quad \overline{B} = \{1, 3, 5\}$$

The *empty* (or *null*) *set,* denoted by $\emptyset$, is a set that contains no elements. The *union* of two events A and B, denoted by $A \cup B$, is the set that contains the elements belonging to A or B or both. For example,

$$A \cup B = \{2, 4, 6\} \quad \text{and} \quad A \cup \overline{B} = \{1, 2, 3, 5\}$$

The *intersection* of two events A and B, denoted by $A \cap B$, is the set that contains only the elements that the two events share in common. Thus

$$A \cap B = \{2\} \quad \text{and} \quad \bar{A} \cap B = \{4, 6\}$$

When two events have no elements in common, they are *mutually exclusive*. Clearly, an event and its complement are mutually exclusive. As just defined, pairs of simple events (i.e., single outcomes) are also mutually exclusive.

6.2.2 Definition of Probability

Probability is a measure of the likelihood with which events are expected to occur. Suppose we toss a coin 10 times and record the outcome of each trial as follows:

$$H\ H\ T\ T\ T\ H\ H\ T\ H\ H$$

The observed frequencies of heads (H) and tails (T) were 6 and 4 times, respectively. The *relative frequencies* of the two outcomes can be obtained by dividing the observed frequencies by the total number of trials. In this example,

$$f(H) = 0.6 \quad \text{and} \quad f(T) = 0.4$$

Intuitively, one would expect the two outcomes of tossing a fair coin to occur with equal frequencies. This could be the case when the number of trials is very large. Note that after only one trial, this long-term expectation cannot possibly be satisfied as the relative frequencies would be 1 for one outcome (H in this case) and 0 for the other. The *limiting value* of the relative frequency of an event as the number of trials approaches infinity is defined as the *probability* of occurrence of that event on any one trial. The probability of each outcome may be derived intuitively, or it may be estimated by repeating the experiment a large number of times and computing the relative frequencies of the outcomes. It must be borne in mind that when estimating the probabilities of events by experimentation, the chance always exists that the computed frequencies may deviate significantly from the theoretical probabilities.

It follows from this definition that the probability, $P[A]$, of an event A cannot be negative and cannot exceed 1. Also, the sum of the probabilities of all simple events contained in the sample space of an experiment always equals 1.

Other useful axioms of probability include the following. The probability of the event defined as the union of two events A and B is

$$P[A \cup B] = P[A] + P[B] - P[A \cap B] \tag{6.2.1}$$

The probability of the event defined by the intersection of A and B is subtracted from the sum of the probabilities of the two events to avoid double counting. Since two mutually exclusive events share no elements in common, the probability of the event defined by their union is equal to the sum of the probabilities of the two events. Also,

$$P[\Omega] = 1 \tag{6.2.2}$$

and

$$P[\varnothing] = 0 \tag{6.2.3}$$

Equation 6.2.2 states that the probability of the event defined as the union of all (mutually exclusive) simple events associated with an experiment is equal to 1. Thus, on any trial, *one* of the possible outcomes is certain to occur. Equation 6.2.3 is an alternative way of stating the same concept: It is impossible to obtain none of the single outcomes of an experiment on a given trial. Since the intersection of the two mutually exclusive events E and $\overline{E}$ is equal to the null set, it follows from Eqs. 6.2.1 through 6.2.3 that

$$P[E \cup \overline{E}] = P[\Omega] = P[E] + P[\overline{E}] - P[\varnothing] = 1$$

and

$$P[\overline{E}] = 1 - P[E] \tag{6.2.4}$$

Example 6.1

Consider the experiment of casting a single die. Identify all simple events (outcomes) of the experiment, and calculate the probability of each.

Solution The outcome space for this experiment contains six possible outcomes:

$$\{1, 2, 3, 4, 5, 6\}$$

Assuming that the die is not loaded, the six simple events are equiprobable, each having a probability of occurrence on any trial of $\frac{1}{6}$. Note that all probabilities are nonnegative, and their sum equals unity. Moreover, the probability associated with any outcome not included in the sample space of the experiment (e.g., 9) is 0; that is, such an event is *impossible* given this experiment.

Example 6.2

For the experiment of Example 6.1, define two events A and B as

A: the outcome is odd and B: the outcome is less than 5

Find (a) the probability of each of the two compound events, (b) the probability of their union, and (c) the probability of their intersection.

Solution The two events are defined as

$$A = \{1, 3, 5\} \quad \text{and} \quad B = \{1, 2, 3, 4\}$$

Events A and B contain three and four equiprobable (mutually exclusive) simple events, respectively, each having a probability of $\frac{1}{6}$. Therefore

$$P[A] = \tfrac{1}{6} + \tfrac{1}{6} + \tfrac{1}{6} = \tfrac{3}{6} = \tfrac{1}{2}$$

and

$$P[B] = \tfrac{1}{6} + \tfrac{1}{6} + \tfrac{1}{6} + \tfrac{1}{6} = \tfrac{4}{6} = \tfrac{2}{3}$$

The union of the two events, $\{1, 2, 3, 4, 5\}$, contains five equiprobable events. Hence, $P[A \cup B] = \frac{5}{6}$. Their intersection contains only the elements 1 and 3. So, $P[A \cap B] = \frac{2}{6} = \frac{1}{3}$.

Discussion According to Eq. 6.2.1, the probability of the event defined as the union of A and B is less than the sum of their individual probabilities by an amount that equals the probability of their intersection. Thus

$$P[A \cup B] = P[A] + P[B] - P[A \cap B]$$
$$= \tfrac{3}{6} + \tfrac{4}{6} - \tfrac{2}{6} = \tfrac{5}{6}$$

which is the same result obtained by enumerating the simple events that belong to the union of A and B.

6.2.3 Conditional Probability and Independence

The estimation of the probability of event A is often affected by prior knowledge that event B has occurred because the outcome is restricted to the subset of the sample space B. The *conditional probability* of A given B is:

$$P[A|B] = \frac{P[A \cap B]}{P[B]} \tag{6.2.5}$$

If events A and B are mutually exclusive, their intersection is the null set, which has a probability of 0. Hence, in the case of mutually exclusive events, the probability that A has occurred given that B has taken place is 0. In other words, the occurrence of B excludes the occurrence of A.

When the occurrence of B does not alter the probability associated with A, the two events are known as *independent events*. For independent events:

$$P[A|B] = P[A] \tag{6.2.6a}$$

Substituting Eq. 6.2.6a into Eq. 6.2.5 and solving for the probability of the intersection of A and B,

$$P[A \cap B] = P[A]P[B] \tag{6.2.6b}$$

Thus, for *independent events,* thc probability of joint occurrence is equal to the product of the probabilities of the individual events.

Example 6.3

For the two events defined in Example 6.2, calculate the conditional probability $P[A|B]$.

Solution Substitution of the probabilities obtained in the earlier example into Eq. 6.2.5 yields

$$P[A|B] = \frac{\frac{1}{3}}{\frac{2}{3}} = \frac{1}{2}$$

Discussion The calculated conditional probability for event A is equal to the unconditional probability of the same event. Therefore, the knowledge that event B has occurred does not affect the probability of event A. Hence, the two events are independent.

Example 6.4

If the probability that a vehicle approaching an intersection will turn left is $P[L] = 0.25$ and the probability that it will turn right is $P[R] = 0.15$, calculate the probability that the vehicle will turn right given that it does not turn left.

Solution Event B (i.e., "the vehicle does not turn left") is the complement of event L. According to Eq. 6.2.4, $P[B] = 1 - P[L] = 0.75$. Compound event B contains the simple events of "turning right" (R) and "going through" (T), which are mutually exclusive. Hence, the probability of the intersection of events B and R is simply equal to the probability of R, or 0.15. The probability that the vehicle will turn right given that it does not turn left is:

$$P[R|B] = \frac{P[R \cap B]}{P[B]} = \frac{(0.15)}{(0.75)} = 0.20$$

Discussion Since $P[R|B]$ does not equal $P[R]$, events R and B are not independent. The results just obtained could have been reached by intuitive reasoning. The likelihood that the vehicle will turn right increases when it is known that it will not turn left. The solution, however, applies the formal relationships to illustrate the concept of conditional probability.

6.2.4 Discrete Distributions

A *random variable* is a variable that takes on the values of the outcomes of an experiment. When the number of possible outcomes is finitely or infinitely countable, the random variable is said to be *discrete*. Otherwise, the random variable is *continuous*. Examples of continuous random variables include the time between failures of a machine and the distance from a reference point on a highway where the next accident will occur. In this textbook, random variables are denoted by uppercase letters (e.g., X, Y, or Z) and the particular values that they assume are denoted by lowercase letters (e.g., x, y, z). Thus $X = x$ means the random variable X takes on a particular value x.

A function $p(x) = P[X = x]$, which associates each value of a discrete random variable to its probability, is known as the *probability (mass) function* (pmf), or the *discrete probability distribution*. The histogram of Fig. 6.2.1(a) illustrates graphically the probability function associated with casting a die, and Fig. 6.2.1(b) illustrates the probability function of the vehicle described in Example 6.4. In the case of the former, the values assumed by the random variable are identical to the numerical values of the outcomes of the experiment and can be given that interpretation. In the case of the latter, the numerical values assigned to the random variable are arbitrary and are selected merely for convenience. Since the values of $p(x)$ represent the probabilities of simple events, they must satisfy the following conditions:

$$0 \leq p(x) \leq 1 \quad \text{for all } x \tag{6.2.7a}$$

$$\sum p(x) = 1 \tag{6.2.7b}$$

The probability of the union of several (mutually exclusive) outcomes is equal to the sum of the probabilities of the individual outcomes. The condition of Eq. 6.2.7b simply states

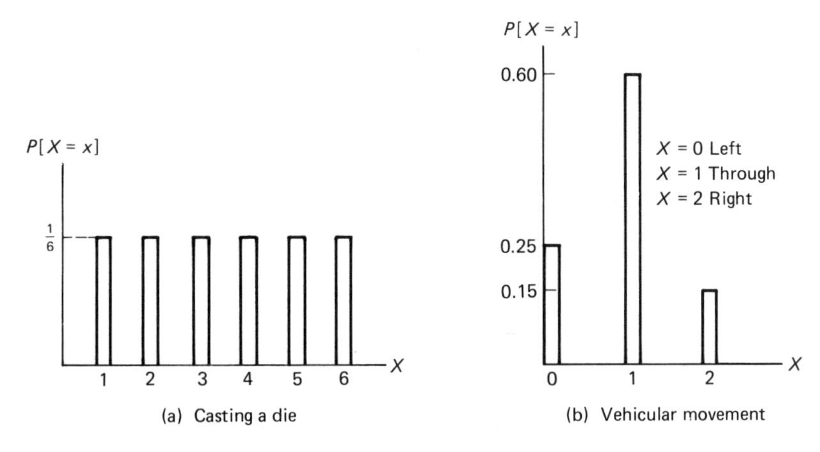

Figure 6.2.1 Discrete probability functions.

that the sum of the probabilities of all single outcomes in the sample space of the experiment is equal to unity. This is merely a restatement of Eq. 6.2.2.

Another useful function of a discrete random variable is its *cumulative distribution function* (cdf), which is defined as:

$$F(x) = P[X \leq x] \tag{6.2.8}$$

In words, the cdf is a function that assumes the values of the probability that a random variable X is less than or equal to a particular value x. Because $p(x)$ is nonnegative, a plot of the cdf against increasing values of x must necessarily be a nondecreasing step function, as illustrated by Fig. 6.2.2. Moreover, the lower and upper limits of this function are 0 and 1, respectively. The upper limit corresponds to the condition described by Eq. 6.2.7b.

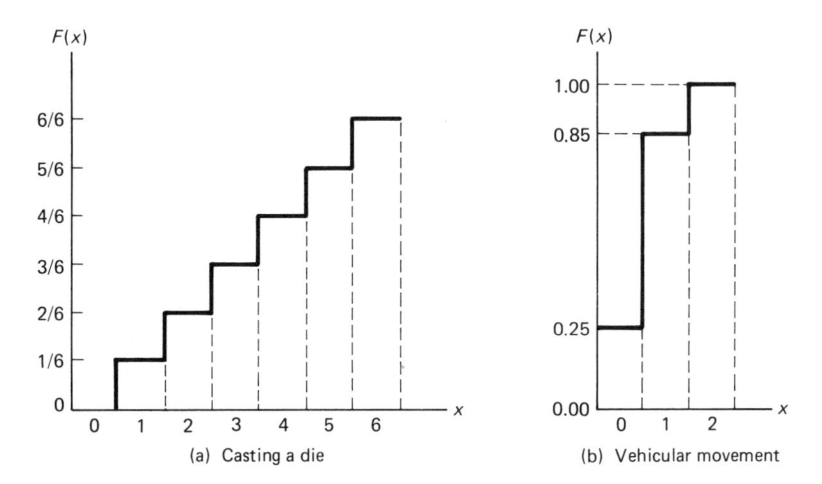

Figure 6.2.2 Discrete cumulative functions.

Two characteristics of a probability function are its *mean* (or *expected value*) and its *variance*. The mean is a measure of the central tendency or the average value of the distribution and the variance is a measure of dispersion or the degree to which the distribution is spread out around the mean.

The mean is usually denoted by the lowercase Greek letter mu (μ) or by $E[X]$, the latter read "expected value." The mean is calculated by:

$$E[X] = \sum_x xp(x) \tag{6.2.9}$$

The variance of a discrete distribution, denoted by σ^2 or by $V[X]$, is defined as the second moment about the mean, or

$$V[X] = \sum_x (x - E[X])^2 \, p(x) \tag{6.2.10}$$

The square root of the variance is known as the *standard deviation* of the distribution, that is,

$$\sigma = S[X] = V[X]^{\frac{1}{2}} \tag{6.2.11}$$

Example 6.5

Calculate the mean, variance, and standard deviation of the discrete distributions of Fig. 6.2.1.

Solution (a) By Eq, 6.2.9, the mean of the distribution shown on Fig. 6.2.1(a) is:

$$E[X] = (1)(\tfrac{1}{6}) + (2)(\tfrac{1}{6}) + \cdots + (6)(\tfrac{1}{6}) = \tfrac{21}{6} = 3.5$$

The variance is given by Eq. 6.2.10:

$$V[X] = (1 - 3.5)^2(\tfrac{1}{6}) + (2 - 3.5)^2(\tfrac{1}{6}) + \cdots + (6 - 3.5)^2(\tfrac{1}{6}) = 2.92$$

The standard deviation is the square root of the variance, or

$$S[X] = 1.71$$

(b) Similarly, for the distribution of Fig. 6.2.1(b),

$$E[X] = (0)(0.20) + (1)(0.60) + (2)(0.15) = 0.9$$

$$V[X] = (0 - 0.9)^2(0.20) + (1 - 0.9)^2(0.60) + (2 - 0.9)^2(0.15) = 0.35$$

$$S[X] = 0.6$$

Discussion The mean of the distribution does not necessarily coincide with one of the outcomes of the experiment. It simply represents the average of a series of trials as the number of trials approaches infinity. In part (a) of this problem, the average represents a value that is meaningful in terms of the magnitudes of the outputs of the experiment. By contrast, the mean value of part (b) depends on the numerical codes selected for the three outcomes. The variance and standard deviation measure the dispersion of each distribution about its mean value.

6.2.5 Some Common Discrete Distributions

Any discrete function that satisfies the conditions of Eqs. 6.2.7 can conceivably be the distribution for some experiment. This subsection presents a number of discrete distributions that are frequently encountered in practice, the characteristics of which are well known. The work of the analyst can be simplified when the problem at hand fits the specifications of one of these common distributions. Formal mathematical derivations for these functions may be found in the technical literature (e.g., [6.1]).

The *uniform distribution* describes experiments that have a finite number of N equiprobable outcomes. The casting of a fair die and the tossing of a fair coin are but two examples of this distribution. In general,

$$p(x) = P[X = x] = \frac{1}{N} \qquad \text{for all } x \text{ in } \Omega \tag{6.2.12}$$

The mean and variance of this distribution can be calculated by Eqs. 6.2.9 and 6.2.10. In the special case when X takes on the values $x = 1, 2, \ldots, N$, the following apply:

$$E[X] = \frac{N + 1}{2} \quad \text{and} \quad V[X] = \frac{N^2 - 1}{12} \tag{6.2.13}$$

The *Bernoulli distribution* applies to experiments that have only two outcomes, often referred to as a "success" S and a "failure" F. Tossing a coin, fair or unfair, is a Bernoulli trial. If, on any trial, the probability of success is p and the probability of failure is q, by Eq. 6.2.7,

$$P[F] = q = 1 - P[S] = 1 - p \tag{6.2.14}$$

In the special case when a success is coded as 1 and a failure as 0, the mean and variance of the Bernoulli distribution become

$$E[X] = 1p + 0q = p \tag{6.2.15a}$$

and

$$V[X] = pq = p(1 - p) \tag{6.2.15b}$$

The *binomial distribution* expresses the probability of x successes in a sequence of n independent Bernoulli trials. The random variable takes on the values $x = 0, 1, 2, \ldots, n$. The binomial probability function is:

$$p(x) = P[X = x] = \frac{n!}{x!(n - x)!} p^x q^{n-x} \tag{6.2.16}$$

The mean and variance of the binomial distribution are

$$E[X] = np \tag{6.2.17a}$$

and

$$V[X] = npq \tag{6.2.17b}$$

The Bernoulli distribution is a particular case of the binomial when $n = 1$.

The *geometric distribution* is also based on a sequence of independent Bernoulli trials. It represents the probability that the first success will occur on the xth trial. This means that A: the first $(x - 1)$ independent trials result in a failure *and* B: the last trial is a success. Considering that events A and B are, by definition, independent, Eq. 6.2.6b yields the following probability that the first success will occur on the xth trial:

$$p(x) = q^{x-1}p \qquad x = 1, 2, \ldots \tag{6.2.18}$$

This is an example of a discrete random variable X that takes on an *infinitely countable* number of values. The mean and variance of the geometric distribution are:

$$E[X] = p^{-1} \tag{6.2.19a}$$

and

$$V[X] = qp^{-2} \tag{6.2.19b}$$

The *negative binomial* (or *Pascal*) *distribution* measures the probability that the kth success will occur on the xth trial of a Bernoulli process. For this to be true, two events must occur, A: there must be $(k - 1)$ successes in the first $(x - 1)$ trials *and* B: the last trial must be a success. The probability of event A is given by the binomial (Eq. 6.2.16) and the probability of event B is p. Since the two events are independent, the probability that the kth success will occur on the xth trial becomes:

$$p(x) = \frac{(x - 1)!}{(k - 1)!(x - k)!} p^k q^{x-k} \qquad \text{for } x = k, k + 1, \ldots \tag{6.2.20}$$

The mean and variance of the negative binomial are

$$E[X] = kp^{-1} \tag{6.2.21a}$$

and

$$V[X] = kqp^{-2} \tag{6.2.21b}$$

The geometric distribution is a special case of the Pascal distribution when $k = 1$.

Finally, a discrete distribution that has found wide application in traffic situations is the *Poisson distribution*. It describes the probability of x occurrences of an event (successes) within a given interval of time (or space) t and applies to experiments that satisfy the following conditions.

1. There exists a small interval dt within which the probability of one occurrence is λdt, whereas the probability of additional occurrences is negligible.

2. The occurrences (or nonoccurrences) of the event in nonoverlapping intervals are mutually *independent*.

The total interval t may be thought to consist of a sequence of small intervals dt, each representing an independent Bernoulli trial with $p = \lambda dt$. In other words, the probability of x successes within the total interval t is given by the binomial. In the limit, that is, when the number of small intervals is very large and the probability of success p is small, the Poisson distribution is obtained:

$$p(x) = \frac{(\lambda t)^x}{x!} e^{-\lambda t} \qquad \text{for } x = 0, 1, \ldots \tag{6.2.22}$$

The mean and variance of the Poisson distribution are:

$$E[X] = V[X] = \lambda t \tag{6.2.23}$$

Example 6.6

The probability that a vehicle will turn left at an intersection is known to be 0.15. Assuming independence, calculate the probabilities of the following events:

(a) The tenth vehicle is not turning left.
(b) Exactly three out of ten vehicles will turn left.
(c) At least three out of ten vehicles will turn left.
(d) No more than three out of ten vehicles will turn left.
(e) The first left-turning vehicle will be the fourth vehicle.
(f) The eighth vehicle will be the third to turn left.

Solution The movement of each vehicle is a Bernoulli trial with $p = 0.15$ and $q = 0.85$.

(a) The probability that the tenth vehicle, and any other vehicle, will not turn left is $q = 0.85$ (Bernoulli distribution).

(b) According to the binomial distribution, the probability that three out of ten vehicles will turn left is

$$p(3) = 0.130$$

(c) The complement of event A: at least three out of ten is event B: zero or one or two out of ten and

$$P[A] = P[X > 2] = 1 - P[B] \qquad \text{for } n = 10$$

But B is the union of three mutually exclusive simple events, the probability of which is given by the binomial. Hence

$$\begin{aligned} P[A] &= 1 - \{p(0) + p(1) + p(2)\} \\ &= 1 - (0.197 + 0.347 + 0.276) = 0.180 \end{aligned}$$

(d) The binomial still applies. The probability of the compound event A: no more than three in ten is

$$P[A] = P[X < 4] = p(0) + p(1) + p(2) + p(3)$$
$$= 0.197 + 0.347 + 0.276 + 0.130 = 0.950$$

(e) This question may be answered either by using the geometric distribution or the negative binomial (Pascal) distribution with $k = 1$. Thus

$$p(4) = (0.85)^3(0.15) = 0.092$$

(f) The Pascal distribution provides the answer to the question of the probability that the kth (i.e., third) left turner is the eighth vehicle, x, is the sequence:

$$p(8) = 0.031 \qquad \text{for } k = 3$$

Discussion The event of which the probability is being sought must be clearly understood. For example, the difference between "exactly three," "at least three," and "no more than three" was illustrated in parts (a), (b), and (c). Also, the appropriate distribution must be selected. It should be remembered that the notation $p(x)$ has a different meaning depending on the particular distribution used. Thus in the case of the binomial, $p(4)$ represents "the probability of four occurrences in n trials," and in the case of the geometric, it represents "the probability that the first occurrence is on the fourth trial."

Example 6.7

It is known that 8% of the drivers in a resort town drive under the influence of alcohol. Assuming independence, calculate the probability of the following events:

(a) No driver in five stopped is under the influence.
(b) Exactly 10 out of 100 stopped are drunk.
(c) Fifty out of 500 are under the influence.

Solution Considering the discovery of a drunken driver to be a "success," each act of stopping a driver is a Bernoulli trial with $p = 0.08$.

(a) The probability of finding no driver to be under the influence of alcohol in five independent Bernoulli trials is the product $q^5 = 0.659$ (see Eq. 6.2.6b). The same result can be obtained by applying the binomial distribution with zero successes in five trials.

(b) In this case, the binomial yields a probability of discovering exactly ten drunken drivers:

$$p(10) = 0.102 \qquad \text{when } n = 100$$

Since p is small and n is large, the Poisson with a mean $np = 8$ (Eq. 6.2.17a) may be applied to approximate the binomial distribution, that is,

$$p(10) = P[X = 10] = 0.099 \qquad \text{when } n = 100$$

(c) Repeating the procedure of part (b), the binomial distribution yields $p(50) = 0.0167$, and the Poisson approximation (with mean 40) results in $p(50) = 0.0177$

Discussion The Poisson approximation to a binomial improves as the number of trials increases. In this particular case, the same conclusion is reached by comparing the mean and variance of the binomial distribution. For part (b) the mean is 8 and the variance is $npq = 7.36$. For part (c), the mean and variance are 40 and 36.8, respectively.

Example 6.8

Cars arrive at a parking garage at a rate of 90 veh/h according to the Poisson distribution. Compute the cumulative distribution for the random variable X that represents "the number of arrivals per minute."

Solution The mean arrival rate is 1.5 veh/min. Hence Eq. 6.2.22 becomes:

$$p(x) = P[X = x] = \frac{(1.5)^x}{x!} e^{-1.5} \qquad x = 0, 1, 2, \ldots$$

The cumulative distribution $F(x) = P[X \leq x]$ is obtained by summing the probabilities of the simple events $0, 1, \ldots, x$. The results are:

x	$p(x) = P[X = x]$	$F(x) = P[X \leq x]$
0	0.223	0.223
1	0.335	0.558
2	0.251	0.809
3	0.126	0.935
4	0.047	0.982
5	0.014	0.996
—	—	—
—	—	—
—	—	—

Discussion Properly, the cumulative distribution approaches 1 as x approaches infinity. According to the Poisson distribution, the random variable X is defined up to this limit. In practical situations, however, X is usually bounded at some lower value. In the situation examined here, for example, the number of cars arriving at the garage within a minute cannot be very large. Thus, at best, the Poisson distribution can serve only as an approximation to this situation. Noting, however, that the calculated probability of more than five arrivals per minute is only 0.004, it is not unreasonable to expect that this approximation would be satisfactory.

6.2.6 Continuous Random Variables

The random variables discussed in the preceding section were allowed to assume a countable number of values. On the other hand, many situations are characterized by an uncountable number of possible outcomes that can be described only by continuous random variables. For example, consider the measurement of the headways between persons as they enter a hall. Conceivably, the headway between any two persons can vary from zero (when they enter simultaneously) to infinity (following the last person *ever* to enter the hall). Assuming that the headways can be measured with absolute precision, the probability of obtaining *exactly* any particular value is zero. In the continuous case, probability is associated with *ranges of the outcome* rather than with single values. The following definitions clarify this statement.

The range over which a continuous random variable is defined (e.g., zero to infinity in the example relating to headways) can be divided into infinitesimal intervals, dx. If the probability that the outcome of an experiment will fall within dx is equal to the area $f(x)\,dx$, then the function $f(x)$ is defined as the *probability density function* (pdf) or the *continuous probability distribution* for that experiment.

Since the probability of the occurrence of any event is nonnegative, a pdf is also nonnegative. Moreover, according to Eq. 6.2.2, the sum of the probabilities of the (mutually exclusive) events defined by each dx over the range of the random variable X must necessarily equal unity. In mathematical terms,

$$f(x) \geqslant 0 \qquad \text{for all } x \tag{6.2.24a}$$

and

$$\int_{-\infty}^{+\infty} f(x)\,dx = 1 \tag{6.2.24b}$$

These conditions correspond to the requirements that must be satisfied by discrete probability distributions expressed by Eqs. 6.2.7. The area under the pdf between points a and b is equal to the probability that the outcome will fall in the interval $\{a, b\}$, or

$$\int_{a}^{b} f(x)\,dx = P[a \leqslant X \leqslant b] \tag{6.2.25}$$

When $a = b$, the area under the curve is zero. Hence, the probability associated with any single value of the random variable is zero.

The mean, the variance, and the standard deviation of a pdf are defined as:

$$E[X] = \int_{-\infty}^{+\infty} xf(x)\,dx \tag{6.2.26}$$

$$V[X] = \int_{-\infty}^{+\infty} (x - E[X])^2 f(x)\,dx \tag{6.2.27}$$

and

$$S[X] = \{V[X]\}^{\frac{1}{2}} \tag{6.2.28}$$

Equation 6.2.26 describes the first moment of the area under the curve about the y-axis. Considering that this area equals unity, the expected value is the x-coordinate of its centroid. Equation 6.2.27 describes the second moment of the area about the centroidal y-axis.

The *cumulative distribution function* (cdf) of a continuous random variable is defined as:

$$P[X \leq x] = \int_{-\infty}^{x} f(x)\,dx \tag{6.2.29}$$

The cdf is a nondecreasing function with a lower limit of 0 and an upper limit of 1. In this respect, it is identical to the cumulative distribution function of a discrete random variable.

6.2.7 Some Common Continuous Distributions

The best-known probability density function is the *normal distribution,* or the "bell-shaped" curve. Because of its mathematical intractability, however, it is not discussed here, even though it is fundamental to the theory of probability.

The *uniform distribution* is defined as:

$$f(x) = \begin{cases} \dfrac{1}{b - a} & \text{for } a \leq x \leq b \\ 0 & \text{otherwise} \end{cases} \tag{6.2.30}$$

In words, it consists of a horizontal line over the range $\{a, b\}$ in such a way that the area under the curve is equal to 1. The mean and variance of the uniform pdf are

$$E[X] = \frac{a + b}{2} \quad \text{and} \quad V[X] = \frac{(b - a)^2}{12} \tag{6.2.31}$$

The (*negative*) *exponential distribution* bears a special relationship to the discrete Poisson distribution. When the occurrence of an event follows the Poisson distribution, the interval between occurrences is distributed according to the negative exponential. For example, if vehicles arrive at an intersection according to the Poisson distribution, the interarrival times (i.e., the headways between successive vehicles) are exponentially distributed. The negative exponential pdf is

$$f(x) = ae^{-ax} \tag{6.2.32}$$

where e is the base of natural logarithms. The mean and variance of the negative exponential are:

$$E[X] = \frac{1}{a} \quad \text{and} \quad V[X] = \frac{1}{a^2} \tag{6.2.33}$$

The mean of this distribution is equal to its standard deviation. Moreover, it is the reciprocal of the mean of the Poisson distribution.

Numerous distributions have been used to describe vehicular headways and other traffic phenomena (e.g., [6.2]). Those just discussed will be sufficient for the purposes of this textbook.

Example 6.9

Given the arrival pattern of Example 6.8, calculate (a) the mean headway, (b) the probability that a headway is less than or equal to 45 s, and (c) the probability of headways longer than 2 min.

Solution

(a) The average, or mean, headway is the reciprocal of the average number of arrivals per unit time. The latter was calculated in Example 6.8 to be 1.5 veh/min. Therefore,

$$E[X] = \frac{1}{a} = \frac{1}{1.5} \text{ min (per vehicle)}$$

(b) This probability is given by the integral of the pdf from 0 to 0.75 min, or the value of the cdf at $x = 0.75$ min. Hence

$$P[X \leq 0.75] = F(0.75) = 1 - e^{-(1.5)(0.75)} = 0.675$$

(c) $P[X > 2] = 1 - P[X \leq 2] = e^{-3} = 0.050$

Example 6.10

Given that the instantaneous location of vehicles along a highway is Poisson distributed and that the average concentration is 100 veh/mi, calculate (a) the probability that 30 vehicles will be found on any quarter of a mile, and (b) the probability that the spacing between any two vehicles is less than or equal to 0.02 mi.

Solution

(a) The average number of vehicles per quarter mile is 25 and the probability that exactly 30 vehicles occupy a quarter mile, according to the Poisson, is

$$p(30) = P[X = 30] = 0.045$$

(b) If the location of the vehicles is Poisson distributed, their spacing is exponentially distributed. With an average spacing of 0.01 mi (i.e., $a = 100$),

$$F(0.02) = P[X \leq 0.02] = 1 - e^{-(100)(0.02)} = 0.865$$

Discussion The relationship between the negative exponential and the Poisson distributions is clearly illustrated by the last two examples. Both are "memoryless". This property implies that the occurrences of events described by the Poisson are mutually independent. Similarly, the intervals between events described by the negative exponential are mutually independent. Specifically, when the negative exponential is used to describe the time interval between successive occurrences, the memoryless property means that occurrences in the future are not influenced by what has happened in the past. In the case of vehicular headways, the negative exponential is most appropriate in the case of low concentration conditions, when the interactions between vehicles are at a minimum and vehicular events occur at random. When used to describe the headways between vehicular arrivals at an intersection, it seems reasonable that the intersection should be isolated, or removed, from other intersections, which—because of the signal control regularity—may impart a definite pattern to the arrivals at the intersection under study.

6.3 QUEUING MODELS

6.3.1 Background

Queuing, or waiting-line, phenomena are everyday occurrences. Examples include vehicles waiting to be served at a gasoline station, passengers or vehicles lined up at a transit terminal, airplanes awaiting clearance for take-off or landing, patients scheduled for use of a hospital's operating room, component parts stockpiled at an assembly plant, computer jobs awaiting execution or printing, vehicles at an intersection, and so forth. Continuous processes may also be described as queuing systems: for example, drinking water in a reservoir "waiting" to be used by households. No matter how complex, queuing systems are characterized by an *arrival pattern*, a *service facility*, and a *queue discipline*. When all three components are constant, the system can be analyzed by deterministic methods. Probabilistic systems, however, are more common.

The arrival pattern describes the way in which the items (or "customers") to be served enter the system. For instance, some examples of the preceding section considered the case of vehicles arriving according to the Poisson distribution, which meant that their interarrival times were exponentially distributed.

The service facility is characterized by the *number and arrangement of servers* and by a *service pattern*. A service facility can be a *single-server* or a *multiserver* facility. Service counters may be arranged in parallel, in series, or in any combination of the two. The service pattern usually measures either the rate at which customers are processed (i.e., vehicles per minute) or the time required to serve individual customers. These characteristics may also be described by appropriate probability functions.

The queue discipline refers to the rules by which the next customer to be served is chosen. Some of the most common rules include the following. A *first-in, first-out* (FIFO) scheme serves customers in the order they arrive: The customer at the front of the waiting line is always selected. Another rule is the *last-in, first-out* (LIFO) rule. For example, program instructions in a computer's stack memory are executed in the reverse order of placement into the stack. The service rule may allow either a *single queue* or *multiple queues*. The customers may be treated equally or they may be treated according to some *priority*. Examples of priority rules include car-pool lanes for use by vehicles carrying a specified minimum number of passengers, express lanes at a supermarket, business-transactions-only counters at a bank, scheduling patients for an operation according to the severity of their maladies, and computer processing of administrative jobs before the jobs submitted by faculty and students. The priority rule may be either *preemptive* or *nonpreemptive*, depending on whether or not a higher-priority customer is permitted to interrupt the processing of a lower-priority customer. For example, emergency vehicles on the roadway have a preemptive priority over other vehicles.

A signalized intersection may be modeled as a multichannel system with complex queue disciplines controlled by the traffic signal. The description of transit stations in Chapter 5 reveals the possibility of analyzing their operations by employing queuing models. Also, platoons of vehicles on the road may be viewed as moving queues. The previous discussion illustrates that queuing systems can range from the very simple to the very complex. Relatively simple systems may be examined by formulating the appropriate mathematical equations and solving them *analytically*. More complex systems become mathematically intractable and are usually solved by *numerical* methods.

The solution to a queuing problem entails the assessment of a system's performance, which, in turn, is described by a set of *measures of performance* (mop's). These may include the number of customers served per unit time, the average delay per customer, the average and maximum length of the waiting lines, the percent of time each service counter is idle, the cost of operating the system, and so forth.

6.3.2 Single-Server FIFO Systems

One of the simplest queuing problems that is amenable to analytical solution is the single-server FIFO system with Poisson arrivals and exponentially distributed customer service times. When in the system, customers are assumed to be patient, that is, they do not leave prematurely. The system is assumed to have an unlimited holding capacity: There is no upper limit on the number of customers that can be in the waiting line. The *state of the system* is described by the random variable X representing the number of customers in the system at any given time, including those that are being served. Any reference book on queuing theory (e.g., [6.3]) may be consulted for a mathematical proof that the steady-state conditions of the above system when the mean arrival rate (λ arrivals per unit time) is less than the mean service rate (μ items served per unit time), X is distributed according to the following function:

$$f(x) = P[X = x] = r^x (1 - r), \qquad x = 0, 1, 2, \ldots \tag{6.3.1}$$

where

$$r = \frac{\lambda}{\mu}$$

The expected value, that is, the average number of customers in the system at any time, is

$$E[X] = \frac{r}{1 - r} \tag{6.3.2}$$

Other useful measures of performance include the following. The average number of customers in the waiting line (*queue length, L_q*) is

$$E[L_q] = \frac{r^2}{1 - r} \tag{6.3.3}$$

The expected time each customer spends in the system and in the queue are calculated, respectively, by dividing the last two equations by λ. Thus

$$E[T] = \frac{1}{\mu - \lambda} \tag{6.3.4}$$

and

$$E[T_q] = \frac{\lambda}{\mu(\mu - \lambda)} \tag{6.3.5}$$

Example 6.11

Bank customers arrive at a single drive-in window at an average rate of 15 veh/hr. On the average, the customers need 3 min each to transact their business. Given that the arrival pattern is described by the Poisson distribution and that the departure time is exponentially distributed, calculate the following:

(a) The percent of time that the bank teller will be idle.
(b) The probability that five customers will be in the system.
(c) The average number of customers in the system.
(d) The average queue length.
(e) The average time each customer spends in the system.

Solution The average arrival rate is 15 customers per hour, the average service rate is 60/3 = 20 customers per hour and $r = 0.75$. Since the service rate of this FIFO system is larger than the arrival rate, the equations just developed apply.

(a) The teller is idle when there are no customers in the system. Hence

$$p(0) = P[X = 0] = (0.75)^0(1 - 0.75) = 0.25$$

or 25% of the time.

(b) The probability that five vehicles will be in the system is given by Eq. 6.3.1:

$$p(5) = (0.75)^5(1 - 0.75) = 0.059$$

or 5.9% of the time.

(c) The average number of customers in the system is:

$$E[X] = \frac{15}{20 - 15} = 3 \text{ customers}$$

(d) By Eq. 6.3.3, the average queue length is

$$E[L_q] = 2.25 \text{ customers}$$

(e) The average time in the system is

$$E[T] = (20 - 15)^{-1} = 0.2 \text{ h, or } 12 \text{ min}$$

Discussion The average number of customers in the queue is not equal to the average number of customers in the system less one because when the system is empty (25% of the time in this example), one customer cannot be meaningfully subtracted from zero customers in the system. As explained in Section 6.2, the average of a discrete distribution need not coincide with an outcome. Thus an average queue length of 2.25 customers is meaningful as a long-term average.

6.3.3 Multiserver FIFO Systems

A more complex queuing system is a FIFO system with N identical service counters in parallel. The average service rate *per counter* is μ and the remaining variables are defined as before. In this case, the distribution of X is as follows.

For $x = 0$:

$$p(0) = \left[\sum_{x=0}^{N-1} \frac{r^x}{x!} + \frac{r^N}{(N - 1)!(N - r)} \right]^{-1} \tag{6.3.6a}$$

For $1 \leq x \leq N$:

$$p(x) = \frac{r^x}{N!} p(0) \tag{6.3.6b}$$

For $x > N$:

$$p(x) = \frac{r^x}{N!\, N^{x-N}} p(0) \tag{6.3.6c}$$

The average number of customers in the system is:

$$E[X] = r + \left[\frac{r^{N+1}}{(N - 1)!(N - r)^2} \right] p(0) \tag{6.3.7}$$

The average queue length is:

$$E[L_q] = \left[\frac{r^{N+1}}{(N - 1)!(N - r)^2} \right] p(0) \tag{6.3.8}$$

The expected time in the system is:

$$E[T] = \frac{E[X]}{\lambda} \tag{6.3.9}$$

Finally, the expected time in the queue is:

$$E[T_q] = \frac{E[L_q]}{\lambda} \tag{6.3.10}$$

Example 6.12

Solve Example 6.11 again, assuming that an identical service counter is added in parallel to the existing one.

Solution The new arrangement is also a FIFO system but one that provides two service counters (i.e., $N = 2$). This means that customers line up in single file and up to two customers can be served simultaneously. The ratio of the arrival to the service rate of a single counter is $r = 0.75$, as before.

(a) The percent of time that *both* tellers are idle is given by Eq. 6.3.6a:

$$p(0) = \left[\left(\frac{0.75^0}{0!} + \frac{0.75^1}{1!}\right) + \frac{0.75^2}{1!(2 - 0.75)}\right]^{-1}$$

$$= 0.455 \text{ or } 45.5\% \text{ of the time}$$

The percent of the time that only one of the two tellers is idle is given by the probability that only one customer is in the system. By Eq. 6.3.6b:

$$p(1) = \frac{0.75}{2!}(0.455) = 0.171, \quad \text{or } 17.1\% \text{ of the time}$$

Thus $45.5 + 17.1 = 62.6\%$ of the time either one or both of the tellers are idle.

(b) The probability that five customers are in the system is given by Eq. 6.3.6c:

$$p(5) = \frac{0.75^5}{2!2^{(5-2)}}(0.455) = 0.007, \quad \text{or } 0.7\% \text{ of the time}$$

(c) Equation 6.3.7 gives the average number of customers in the system:

$$E[X] = 0.75 + \left[\frac{0.75^3}{2!(2 - 0.75)^2}\right](0.455) = 0.811 \text{ customers}$$

(d) According to Eq. 6.3.7 and 6.3.8, the relationship between the average queue length and the average number of customers in the system is:

$$E[L_q] = E[X] - r$$

Hence,

$$E[L_q] = 0.811 - 0.75 = 0.061 \text{ customers}$$

(e) By Eq. 6.3.9, the average time each customer spends in the system is

$$E[T] = \frac{0.811}{15} = 0.054 \text{ h}, \quad \text{or } 3.25 \text{ min}$$

Discussion The new arrangement greatly reduces the queue length from 2.25 to 0.061 customers and the average waiting time from 12 to 3.25 min, but at the expense of having either one or both of the tellers idle 62.6% of the time as compared to 25% of the time for the single-server situation of Example 6.11. Thus there exists a trade-off between the customers' convenience and the cost of running the system. The equations governing the two simple queuing systems just examined clearly show that the mathematical complexity of queuing models increases rapidly. In fact, satisfactory analytical models are unavailable for many problems, especially for those that involve priority scheduling. The next section discusses the elements of digital computer simulation, a numerical technique that can be applied to the investigation and design of complex systems, including queuing systems.

6.4 COMPUTER SIMULATION

6.4.1 Background

The study of complex systems that cannot be sufficiently simplified to be amenable to analytical solution requires alternative methods, the use of simulation models being one possibility. A successful simulation model is an abstraction of a real system that retains the system's essential aspects. The model can be used either to enhance the understanding of how the system works or to investigate the potential effects of proposed modifications to the system. Being an abstraction of a real system, a model cannot be identical to it in all respects. Consequently, a model is employed when direct experimentation with a real system is impossible, too costly, or unsafe. To be useful, any model of a system must realistically represent the system. Although more involved, the steps of model calibration and validation (see Chapter 1) are very important, but a detailed discussion of these topics is beyond the scope of this textbook.

Simulation models can be either deterministic or probabilistic. In addition, simulation models can be either *physical* or *mathematical*. Vehicle crash tests using anthropomorphic dummies are examples of physical models. A model of the Mississippi River system used by the U.S. Corps of Engineers at Vicksburg, Mississippi, is another example. This section is concerned with mathematical models.

6.4.2 Monte Carlo Simulation

Monte Carlo simulation employs an artificial probabilistic experiment (model), the repeated application of which leads to an approximation of the outcome of a system or process. The basic idea of this method is illustrated next.

Consider the now-familiar process of a sequence of independent Bernoulli trials, specifically the tossing of a fair coin. The author repeated a Bernoulli sequence of ten tosses four times and obtained the following results:

1.	*T*	*T*	*T*	*H*	*T*	*H*	*H*	*H*	*H*	*T*
2.	*T*	*H*	*H*	*T*	*H*	*H*	*H*	*H*	*H*	*H*
3.	*T*	*H*	*T*	*T*	*T*	*T*	*H*	*H*	*H*	*H*
4.	*T*	*H*	*H*	*T*	*T*	*T*	*T*	*H*	*T*	*T*

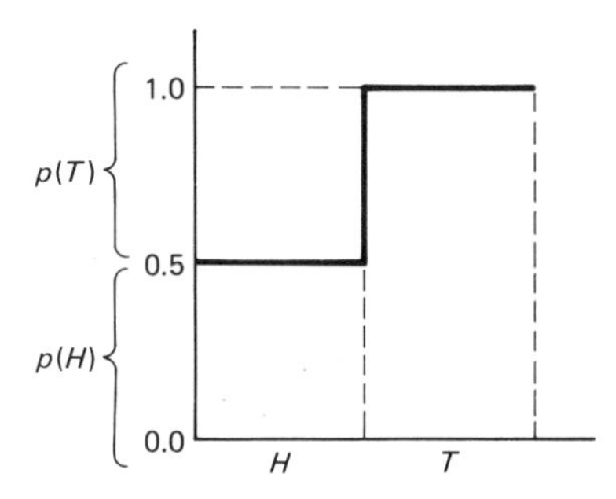

Figure 6.4.1 Generation of discrete outcomes.

Without any knowledge of the underlying process, these four *realizations* of the process may seem to be totally random. Yet it is known in this case that each single outcome listed was the result of a Bernoulli trial with $p = q = 0.5$. In fact, the frequencies of heads and tails in all 40 trials taken together are nearly equal, as would be expected in the long run.

Section 6.2 discussed various distributions that may be used to calculate the probability of compound events, such as the probability of getting x successes in n trials and the probability of obtaining the first success on the xth trial. By contrast, a Monte Carlo model of the previous experiment is intended to produce sequences of outcomes (i.e., realizations) that are consistent with the underlying process, in this case a series of independent Bernoulli trials. If desired, the long-run probabilities of various events can be approximated by analyzing the results of the model for a large number of repetitions. To understand how the technique works, consider the cumulative probability distribution of the coin toss experiment shown in Fig. 6.4.1. The horizontal axis shows the two possible outcomes of each trial, labeled $X = H$ and $X = T$ for head and tail, respectively. The vertical axis represents the cumulative probability $P[X \leq x]$. The difference in the values of the cumulative function for two adjacent outcomes is the probability of the second outcome. Consequently, the range from 0 to 1 on the vertical axis has been divided according to the probabilities of the outcomes of the experiment under discussion. For a sequence of independent and uniformly distributed numbers in the range between 0 and 1, the long-run frequencies with which these *random numbers* would fall within each segment of the vertical axis would be proportional to the probability of the corresponding outcome.

Example 6.13

It is known that 15% of the vehicles approaching an intersection will turn left, 60% will go straight through, and the rest will turn right. Construct the corresponding cumulative distribution and translate the following 10 *random numbers* to outcomes of this process: 0.5954, 0.4501, 0.2590, 0.7081, 0.1405, 0.9740, 0.8676, 0.2729, 0.4474, 0.0166.

Solution On the cumulative distribution for each trial (i.e., approaching vehicle) shown, the ranges on the vertical axis corresponding to left, right, and through movements are {0.00, 0.15}, {0.15, 0.40}, and {0.40, 1.00}, respectively (see the accompanying figure). The first random number (0.5954) falls in the range corresponding to a through movement. Thus the

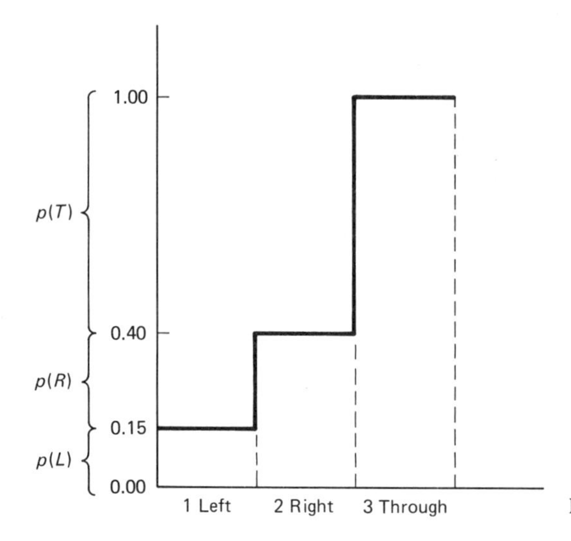

Figure P.6.13

first *simulated* vehicle is going straight ahead. Continuing with the remaining random numbers, the following results are obtained.

Vehicle Number	Movement
1	Through
2	Through
3	Right
4	Through
5	Left
6	Through
7	Through
8	Right
9	Through
10	Left

Discussion The coding scheme selected to represent the three possible outcomes was arbitrary in this case because there exists no natural ordering of the acts of turning left, turning right, and going straight through. Had a different coding scheme been chosen, the generated sequence of approaching vehicles would not have been identical to the one shown in this example. However, both would be consistent with the underlying distribution.

6.4.3 Simulation of Outcomes of a Continuous Random Variable

A similar method can be used to generate a sequence of outcomes for a continuous random variable. Figure 6.4.2 illustrates how a random number in the range of 0.0 to 1.0 can be transformed to a particular outcome x. The transformation entails equating the cumulative distribution to a random number R_N and solving the resulting equation for x. For example, consider the cumulative negative exponential distribution

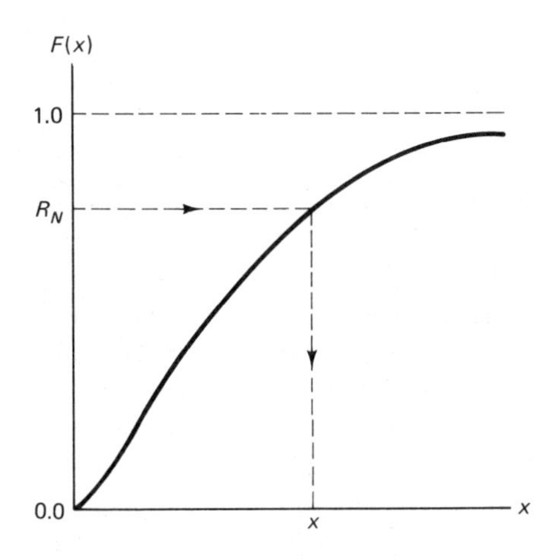

Figure 6.4.2 Generation of continuous random variable outcomes.

$$F(x) = 1 - e^{-ax}$$

Equating $F(x)$ to a random number in the range {0.0, 1.0} and solving for x,

$$x = -\frac{1}{a} \ln(1 - R_N) \tag{6.4.1}$$

Since R_N is a uniformly distributed random number, its complement $(1 - R_N)$ is also a uniformly distributed random number. For this reason it is simpler to use the following equation

$$x = -\frac{1}{a} \ln(R_N) \tag{6.4.2}$$

Example 6.14

Transform the first five of the random numbers given in Example 6.13 to a sequence of vehicular headways, assuming that the average headway is 6.0 s.

Solution In Subsection 6.2.7, the parameter a of the negative exponential was shown to be the reciprocal of its mean value, in this case $a = \frac{1}{6}$. For the purpose of illustration, both Eqs. 6.4.1 and 6.4.2 are applied to this problem as follows:

		Headway (s)	
Vehicle	R_N	(Eq. 6.4.1)	(Eq. 6.4.2)
1	0.5954	5.43	3.11
2	0.4501	3.59	4.79
3	0.2590	1.80	8.11
4	0.7081	7.39	2.07
5	0.1405	0.91	11.78

Discussion These two sequences of headways conform to the same underlying distribution. Hence, they are two realizations of the same process. If needed, more or longer realizations may be produced by using different lists of random numbers.

6.4.4 Generation of Random Numbers

By definition, true random numbers are independent and uniformly distributed. The independence property means that a sequence of random numbers does not follow any systematic pattern. The fact that they are drawn from a uniform distribution implies that any number in the appropriate range is equally likely to be drawn. Theoretically, the uniform distribution of random numbers is continuous. However, in most practical applications, the numbers are limited to the number of significant figures required by the problem at hand. Many sophisticated methods of random-number generation have been devised. For example, the RAND Corporation has published, for use in scientific applications, a sequence of 1 million random digits that were generated by periodically sampling a random electronic noise [6.4].

A simple method for obtaining random digits is the *top hat method:* Ten cards, each bearing one of the ten numbers from 0 to 9, are thoroughly mixed in a receptacle. A card is drawn, its number is recorded, and the card is placed back in the receptacle; the cards are again mixed in preparation for the drawing of the next number. If random numbers within the range from 0 to 1 are desired with, say, five significant figures, the digits drawn from the hat are grouped in ordered sets of five and the decimal point is placed in front of each group.

Although the top hat method can produce a series of as many true random numbers as desired, it is a time-consuming and inefficient method, especially if the random numbers are required at the speed that a computer processes the instructions constituting a simulation program. For this reason, it is necessary to devise rapid generation methods based on carefully developed computer algorithms [6.5–6.8]. It should be noted that the numbers generated in this way are not truly random, since they obey the rules or pattern of the routine used in their generation. For this reason, they are referred to as *pseudorandom* numbers. Nevertheless, the better of the pseudorandom generators are considered to be adequate for most engineering applications.

The *middle-square method* suggested by von Newmann is one of the simplest pseudorandom number generators available. An initial number (the *seed*) is squared and the middle digits of the result are taken to represent the first pseudorandom number, which becomes the seed for the generation of the next number. The sequence of random numbers given in Example 6.13 was generated by this method, using the number 3549 as the seed. Note that the square of the seed is equal to 12595401, of which the middle part constitutes the four digits given as the first random number. A problem with this method is that it eventually tends to degenerate to zeros.

6.4.5 The Simulation Model

The generation of random deviates by the Monte Carlo method is only a part of a larger simulation model. The heart of the model consists of a computer program that imitates the behavior of the system over time. For example, suppose that it is desired to simulate a signalized intersection. The intersection (system) involves (1) certain *entities* (e.g., arriving vehicles, the signal, or the traffic lanes provided), each having several essential *attributes* (e.g., the arrival time and movement desire of a vehicle, the cycle pattern of the signal, the permitted use of lanes); and (2) a set of rules that govern the *interactions* between entities (e.g., left-turning vehicles must use an exclusive lane, or left-turning vehicles must wait for adequate gaps in the opposing traffic). In this example, the headways between vehicular arrivals may be simulated by the method of Example 6.14 for each intersection approach, and the turning desire of each arriving vehicle may be simulated by the method of Example 6.13. The simulation program would then process these arrivals through the intersection according to the rules of interaction and collect data on the *measures of performance* (mop's) that are relevant to the problem at hand, such as vehicular delays or queue lengths. To simulate the passage of time, the model establishes a *simulation clock,* which is advanced periodically as the system changes from one *state* to another. The following two examples illustrate two ways by which the simulation clock may be advanced. The first (*interval-oriented simulation*) updates the clock by a constant time interval, and the second (*event-oriented simulation*) advances the clock to the next event that triggers a change in the system's state.

Example 6.15: Interval-Oriented Simulation

Vehicles arrive at a parking garage at an average rate of 30 veh/h. Assuming that the arrival pattern is described by the Poisson distribution and that the arriving vehicles are served by a single attendant at a *constant* rate of one vehicle per 2.5 min, use the random numbers of Example 6.13 and 6.14 to simulate a sequence of ten 5-minute intervals. Assume that at the start (i.e., clock = 0) the system is empty.

Solution The state of the system may be described as the number of vehicles in the queue awaiting to be served. The clock is advanced by 5-min intervals, and the model generates the number of arrivals during each interval according to the Poisson distribution (i.e., Eq. 6.2.22). A maximum of two vehicles per interval are processed and the (nonnegative) difference between the number of vehicles that arrived and the number of vehicles processed represents the number of vehicles that join the queue at the end of each 5-min interval.

To generate vehicular arrivals, the cumulative Poisson distribution with a mean value of 2.5 vehicles per 5-min period is first calculated as follows:

x	$p(x) = P[X = x]$		$P(x) = P[X \leq x]$
0	0.08		0.08 }$p(0)$
1	0.21		0.29 }$p(1)$
2	0.26		0.55 }$p(2)$
3	0.21		0.76 }$p(3)$
4	0.13		0.89 }$p(4)$
5	0.07		0.96 }$p(5)$
6	0.03	0.99 ≃	1.00 }$p(6)$

An upper limit of six vehicles per period was placed on the distribution as a reasonable approximation, and the ranges in the values of the cumulative distribution corresponding to the seven possible outcomes are noted in the last column of the table.

The simulation entails the generation of the number of vehicular arrivals during each 5-min interval and the processing of up to two vehicles (if present) during the same interval to determine the queue length at the end of the interval. The first random number in the given sequence (i.e., 0.5954; Example 6.13) translates to three arrivals during the first 5-min interval because

$$0.55 \leq 0.5954 \leq 0.76$$

Since two of these three arrivals can be served during the interval, a queue consisting of one vehicle will remain at the end of the interval. The following table summarizes the results obtained for the ten consecutive 5-min intervals:

Interval	Arrivals	Departures	Queue length
1	3	2	1
2	2	2	1
3	1	2	0
4	3	2	1
5	1	2	0
6	6	2	4
7	4	2	6
8	1	2	5
9	2	2	5
10	0	2	3

Discussion This admittedly simple simulation illustrates the interval scanning method of advancing the clock. A total of 23 vehicular arrivals were simulated for the first 50 min. Twenty of these vehicles were served, leaving 3 vehicles in the waiting line at the end of the tenth period. In this particular example, the parking-lot attendant was busy all the time, since there were always vehicles awaiting service. For simplicity, the service time was assumed to be constant. A more realistic model would allow some variability in the number of vehicles that can be served during any 5-min interval. Moreover, the model can be further extended to allow for multiple service channels and service priorities. More complex models necessitate the preparation of a computer program describing the operation of the subject system. Many simulation models have been developed for use in specific contexts including traffic situations (e.g., [6.9, 6.10]). Returning to Example 6.15, it should be noted that a limitation of interval-oriented simulation models is the fact that they are oblivious to the detailed behavior of the system *within* each interval. For example, 3 vehicles were simulated to arrive during the first 5-min interval, but the precise arrival times of these vehicles within the interval are not known. Consequently, certain system characteristics (e.g., the average delay per vehicle) can only be approximated by this model.

Example 6.16: Event-Oriented Simulation

Prepare an event-oriented model of the system described in the previous example and apply this model to simulate the first 11 vehicles that enter the system, assuming that the first vehicle arrives at time zero. The model should be able to calculate the time that each vehicle spends in the waiting line and the percent of time that the attendant is idle. If needed, use the same sequence of random numbers as before.

Solution The time that a vehicle spends in the queue is given by the time interval from the moment it arrives to the moment it begins to be served. The latter coincides with the moment when the servicing of the vehicle ahead has been completed. The arrival time of a vehicle can be computed by adding the headway between the previous arrival and the subject vehicle to the arrival time of the leader. Since the arrival pattern is described by the Poisson distribution, the interarrival times (i.e., headways) are described by the negative exponential (Eq. 6.2.32). They can be generated by applying the procedure of Example 6.14 to transform a sequence of random numbers to a sequence of headways. Since, in this case, the arrival rate is 30 veh/h, the average headway is 2 min.

The first vehicle is assumed to arrive at time zero. It will receive the attention of the attendant immediately. Hence, it will spend no time in the waiting line. Given a constant service time of 2.5 min, the first vehicle will be processed at clock time 0 + 2.5 = 2.5 min and the attendant will be busy during this time. The headway between the first and the second vehicles can be generated by Eq. 6.4.2 using the first random number (0.5954). Thus

$$x = -2.0 \ln(0.5954) = 1.04 \text{ min}$$

The second vehicle will arrive 1.04 min after the first, which arrived at time zero. But the servicing of the first vehicle will not be finished until clock time 2.5 min. Hence, the second vehicle must wait in line until then, for a total of 2.5 − 1.04 = 1.46 min. The following table summarizes the results of the simulation for the first 11 vehicles to enter the system.

Vehicle number	Headway (min)	Arrival time	Service start	Delay (min)	Service finish	Idle time
1	—	0.00	0.00	0.00	2.50	0.00
2	1.04	1.04	2.50	1.46	5.00	0.00
3	1.60	2.64	5.00	2.36	7.50	0.00
4	2.70	5.34	7.50	2.16	10.00	0.00
5	0.69	6.03	10.00	3.97	12.50	0.00
6	3.93	9.96	12.50	2.54	15.00	0.00
7	0.05	10.01	15.00	4.99	17.50	0.00
8	0.28	10.29	17.50	7.21	20.00	0.00
9	2.60	12.89	20.00	7.11	22.50	0.00
10	1.61	14.50	22.50	8.00	25.00	0.00
11	8.20	22.70	25.00	2.30	27.50	0.00

Discussion This simulation model differs from that of the previous example in that it advanced the clock to the next significant occurrence, that is, the arrival time, the start of servicing, or the finish of servicing of each vehicle. The clock began at time zero when the first vehicle arrived. The next event was the arrival of the second vehicle 1.04 min later. This was followed by the finish of the servicing of the first vehicle at clock = 2.50 min. The next event was the arrival of the third vehicle at clock = 2.70 min, and so forth. A total of 11 vehicles were examined after ten iterations of the model. By contrast, the first ten iterations of the alternative model of Example 6.15 covered 23 vehicles. However, that model was not as detailed as the present model. This comparison stresses an important point:

Often, the analyst has a choice between alternative models of the same system. The choice of model involves a balance between the degree of detail required and the available resources.

Consistent with the results of the interval-oriented model of Example 6.15 are the results of the event-oriented model of the present example, which show that the attendant was continuously busy. The average time that each vehicle spent in the waiting line can be computed by dividing the sum of the delays shown in Column 5 of the given table by the total number of vehicles, to obtain 42.10/11 = 3.83 min/veh. A total of 11 vehicles arrived during the 22.70 min of simulated time. This translates to 29.07 veh/h, which is close to the stipulated 30 veh/h. Considering the limited number of vehicles simulated, such close agreement is surprising. Normally, larger deviations between the two values would be tolerated for such a small sample size.

6.5 SUMMARY

This chapter introduced the basic concepts and definitions of the theory of probability. The probability distributions associated with several discrete and continuous random variables were then presented, and the applications of these distributions to traffic phenomena were illustrated by some simple examples. Queuing, or waiting-line, models were presented next, and the analytical solutions to FIFO systems with Poisson arrivals and negative exponential service times were presented. Finally, the basic elements of the powerful numerical technique of computer simulation were presented. These included the generation of random and pseudorandom numbers, the transformation of these numbers to probable outcomes of underlying processes described by cumulative probability distributions, and the use of these realizations to follow the changes in the state of the simulated system to aid in assessing its likely behavior in terms of applicable measures of performance via simulation models.

6.6 EXERCISES

1. The outcome of an experiment is the sum obtained by casting two dice. Enumerate the simple outcomes of the experiment and calculate each probability.
(a) Each simple outcome
(b) An even outcome
(c) An odd outcome greater than 6
(d) An outcome that is either odd or greater than 4
(e) An outcome that is less than 5 but greater than 2

2. For the experiment of Exercise 1, determine whether the following two events are (a) mutually exclusive and (b) independent.
A: the outcome is less than 8
B: the outcome is greater than 5

3. For the experiment of Exercise 1, determine if the following two events are (a) mutually exclusive and (b) independent:

A: {2, 3, 4, 5, 6, 10}
B: {2, 4, 6, 8, 9, 10, 11, 12}

4. Intersection A is located downstream of intersection B. A traffic engineer observed that during the morning peak period, the probability that intersection A is congested is 0.30. There is a 0.50 probability of A being congested given the knowledge that B is congested. On the other hand, the probability of B being congested given the knowledge that A is congested is 0.90. Calculate the probability that (a) B is congested during the peak period and (b) at least one of the two intersections is congested.

5. There are only two traffic-control signals in downtown Kahului, Maui. The *independent* probabilities that each of the signals will malfunction on a given day are 0.05 and 0.04, respectively. System failure is defined by the condition that at least one signal is out. Calculate the probability that the system will fail on any particular day.

6. A study has shown that in cars with a driver and a passenger, the probability that the driver wears a seat belt is 0.35 and the probability that the passenger buckles up is 0.50. If 80% of the passengers of drivers that buckle up do the same, calculate (a) the probability that both the driver *and* the passenger of a car are wearing seat belts and (b) the probability that a particular driver is wearing a seat belt given the knowledge that the passenger is buckled up.

7. The probability that downtown parking garage A is not full is 0.20 and the probability that garage B is full is 0.50. Knowing that at least one of the two garages is full 90% of the time, calculate the probability that a shopper will find parking in garage B given that garage A is full.

8. Prove Bayes' theorem, which states that

$$P[A|B] = \frac{P[B|A]\, P[A]}{P[B]}$$

9. Two alternative highway routes connect a suburb with a downtown area. Define event A: highway 1 is jammed during the peak period, and event B: highway 2 is jammed during the peak period. If $P[A]$ is 0.70, $P[B]$ is 0.60, and $P[B \mid A]$ is 0.50, calculate and interpret $P[A \cap B]$, $P[A \cup B]$, and $P[A \mid B]$.

10. Draw the probability mass function of the experiment described in Exercise 1 and compute its mean and its variance. Also, draw the cumulative distribution.

11. Decide which of the following functions can possibly be discrete probability distributions for the specified sample space.

(a)	X	1	2	3	4	5	6
	$p(x)$	0.2	0.3	0.2	0.2	0.1	0.1
(b)	X	1	2	3	4	5	6
	$p(x)$	0.5	0.4	0.3	0.1	−0.4	0.1
(c)	X	1	2	3	4	5	6
	$p(x)$	0.4	0.2	0.1	0.1	0.1	0.1

12. At a particular intersection approach, 30% of the left-turning vehicles fail to signal their intentions to turn. Assuming independence, calculate each probability.

(a) Three vehicles in a row will fail to signal.

(b) Three vehicles in a row will signal.

(c) The second vehicle will not signal.

(d) The second vehicle to signal will be the fifth vehicle observed.

(e) Two vehicles in five will fail to signal.

(f) The first vehicle to signal will be the fourth vehicle observed.

(g) No more than two vehicles in five will signal.

13. Draw the probability function and the cumulative distribution for the Poisson case described in Example 6.8.

14. Vehicles arrive at an isolated intersection according to the Poisson distribution. Given that the mean arrival rate is 500 veh/h, calculate (a) the probability that zero vehicles will arrive during a 10-s interval and (b) the probability that at least five vehicles will arrive during a 10-s interval.

15. Students arrive at a lecture room at the rate of 15 per minute according to the Poisson distribution. Calculate the probability of (a) *exactly* three arrivals in 20 s, (b) *no more* than three arrivals in 20 s, and (c) *at least* three arrivals in 20 s.

16. The average concentration of vehicles on a highway section is 70 veh/mi. Given that the concentration is distributed according to the Poisson, calculate the probability of finding (a) exactly ten vehicles and (b) five or more vehicles on any particular tenth of a mile.

17. Which of the following continuous functions can serve as probability distributions for the specified range of outcomes?

(a) $f(x) = -1.0 + 0.2x,\ 0 \leqslant x \leqslant 10.0$

(b) $f(x) = x(1.0 - 2.0x),\ 0 \leqslant x \leqslant 0.5$

(c) $f(x) = 24.0x(1.0 - 2.0x),\ 0 \leqslant x \leqslant 0.5$

18. Prove that Eq. 6.2.31 is correct.

19. Airplanes arrive at an airport area at an average rate of six per hour. Assuming that the arrival pattern is Poisson distributed, calculate the probability that the headway between two successive arrivals will be greater than 20 min.

20. The airport control tower (see Exercise 19) processes airplanes in their order of arrival. Assuming that the service time is negative exponential and that the service rate is 10 landings per hour, calculate (a) the average number of airplanes in the system (i.e., being served and stacked), (b) the average number of airplanes awaiting clearance to land, (c) the average time spent in the system, and (d) the average time an airplane is in the queue.

21. A turnpike toll area contains four toll booths arranged in parallel. The arriving vehicles conform to the Poisson distribution, with an average headway of 12 s. Assuming that the average service time is 5 s, that the service time is negative exponential, and that the queue discipline is FIFO, find the average queue length and the expected time in the system if (a) two of the booths are in operation and (b) only one booth is open.

22. Use the random numbers provided in Example 6.13 to simulate, in two different ways, five tosses of two dice (see Exercise 1). Discuss your results.

23. A wheel of fortune is divided into ten equal sectors numbered from 1 to 10. Devise a Monte Carlo simulation of this roulette and produce the result of (a) five spins for which each outcome is a digit from 1 to 10 and (b) ten spins, assuming that the outcome is given by the three events:

$A: x < 3$

$B: 3 \leqslant x \leqslant 7$

$C: x > 7$

24. Extend the simulation model of Example 6.15 to allow for exponentially distributed service time with an *average* of 2.5 min.

25. Expand Example 6.16 to allow for two service channels and a FIFO queue discipline.
26. Extend Example 6.16 to allow for two service lines and a queue discipline stating that the next arrival chooses the shorter of the two lines 80% of the time. When the two queues are equal, the choice of line is made on a 50/50 basis.
27. Construct a simulation model of Exercise 20 incorporating the following modifications: (a) commercial flights constitute 30% of the arrivals and are given priority over general aviation flights, (b) the average service times for commercial and general aviation operations are 8 min and 6 min, respectively, and (c) your model should include as many measures of performance as practicable.
28. Computerize any of Exercises 22 through 27.

6.7 REFERENCES

6.1 BENJAMIN, JACK R., and C. ALLIN CORNELL, *Probability Statistics and Decision for Civil Engineers,* McGraw-Hill, New York, 1970.

6.2 MORSE, PHILIP M., *Queues, Inventory and Maintenance,* John Wiley, New York, 1958.

6.3 GERLOUGH, DANIEL L., AND MATTHEW J. HUBER, *Traffic Flow Theory: A Monograph,* Special Report 165, National Research Council, Transportation Research Board, Washington, D.C., 1975.

6.4 RAND Corporation, *A Million Random Digits with 100,000 Normal Deviates,* Free Press, New York, 1955.

6.5 GALLER, BERNARD A., *The Language of Computers,* McGraw-Hill, New York, 1962.

6.6 GORDON, GEOFFREY, *System Simulation,* 2nd ed., Prentice-Hall, Inc., Englewood Cliffs, N.J., 1978.

6.7 GRAYBEAL, WAYNE, and UDO W. POOCH, *Simulation: Principles and Methods,* Winthrop Publishers, Inc., Cambridge, Mass., 1980.

6.8 JANNSON, BIRGER, *Random Number Generators,* Almqvist and Wiksell, Stockholm, 1966.

6.9 PAPACOSTAS, C. S., "Capacity Characteristics of Downtown Bus Streets," *Transportation Quarterly,* 36, no. 4, (1982): 617–630.

6.10 Transportation Research Board, *The Application of Traffic Simulation Models,* Special Report 194, National Research Council, Washington, D.C., 1981.

CHAPTER 7

TRANSPORTATION PLANNING

7.1 INTRODUCTION

Many treatises and learned essays have been written about the subject of planning and the role of the professional planner in various societal functions. One hears of urban, economic, financial, corporate, industrial, water resource, environmental, and many other kinds of planning. In the field of transportation, professional designations such as highway planner, airport planner, and urban transportation planner, are common. It is thus clear that planning is considered to be an important function in modern society and that, whatever this function is, it has a specific focus—that is, it is concentrated in particular areas, subjects, or systems.

For the purposes of this textbook, planning may be defined as the activity or process that examines the potential of future actions to guide a situation or a system toward a desired direction, for example, toward the attainment of positive goals, the avoidance of problems, or both. Being the conceptual, premeditative process that precedes a decision to act in a certain way, planning is a fundamental characteristic of all human beings. However, as a focused professional discipline, planning is viewed in a wider, yet bounded, context.

The most important aspect of planning is the fact that it is oriented toward the *future:* A planning activity occurs during one time period but is concerned with actions to be taken at various times in the future. However, although planning may increase the likelihood that a recommended action will in fact take place, it does not guarantee that the planned action will inevitably be implemented exactly as conceived and on schedule. Another time element of importance to planning's forward-looking perspective is the lag between the time when the action is to be taken and the time when its effects are felt.

This time lag depends on many factors, including the scope and magnitude of the contemplated action.

It is often said that everything is related to everything else. Therefore, any event or human action affects everything else, ultimately in ways that are beyond the limits of human comprehension. As a matter of practicality, planning is not a search for ultimate answers but only a means to specific ends that is based on the proposition that better conditions would result from premeditative as opposed to impulsive actions. How much premeditation is necessary (i.e., how much planning is good planning) in a particular situation is always an open question: Too little planning is almost like no planning, and too much planning is self-defeating, as it leads to inaction.

By necessity, any particular planning effort has a limited scope and is oriented toward bringing about specific desirable ends. Since desirability cannot be divorced from the value system of human beings, planning is necessarily directed toward the satisfaction of the goals and objectives of particular groups of people. However, within its social context, planning cannot afford to ignore the reactions of other groups; it must, in fact, anticipate these responses as well. In addition, when the group on behalf of which planning is undertaken is heterogeneous, the planning effort must deal with the presence of internal conflicts relating to specific objectives and aspirations. This is especially critical when the government participates in or regulates the planning effort.

The fundamental purpose of transportation is to provide efficient access to various activities that satisfy human needs. Therefore, the general goal of transportation planning is to accommodate this need for mobility. Within specific contexts, however, whose mobility, for what purpose, by what means, at what cost and to whom, and who should do the planning and how are questions that are not amenable to easy answers. Contemporary responses to these questions are largely rooted in history and have been influenced by a confluence of many factors, including *technological innovations, private interests,* and *governmental policies.*

The purpose of this chapter is to illustrate the dynamic nature of transportation planning by briefly tracing this evolutionary process for the case of land transportation. The main objective of the chapter is to bring about an appreciation of the complexity of the transportation-planning methodology, which cannot be said to have reached a historical finality, and to highlight, in broad strokes, its most fundamental elements. More detailed coverage of the colorful history of the United States transportation system and of evolving transportation planning issues may be found in the literature (e.g., [7.1–7.8]).

7.2 HISTORICAL DEVELOPMENT IN THE UNITED STATES

7.2.1 Colonial Era

The migration of European settlers to North America, which led to the establishment of cities, occurred by sea. Thereafter, water transportation using the coastline and natural inland channels was the major form of long-distance transportation. Chartered privately owned ferries offered for-hire service on the rivers. Movement over land utilizing human and animal power was cumbersome and was inhibited by topographic obstacles. Following English practice, the responsibility for planning, building, and maintaining roads rested with local jurisdictions. The use of these primitive roads by travelers was free of charge and their construction and maintenance was accomplished primarily by statute labor, an English practice that required all men over 16 years of age to work on the roads on appointed days.

7.2.2 Turnpikes and Canals

Following the War of Independence, the new nation was underdeveloped, and its immediate transportation needs were primarily related to simple *accessibility* between the cities lying primarily on the eastern seaboard and toward the unexplored lands to the west. The available technology to this end consisted of wagons and coaches for land transportation and boats and barges for movement on rivers and canals. Two major problems that had to be overcome were topography and finance. Because of debts incurred during the war, the states were not in a financial position to accommodate increasing demands to provide the needed facilities. Some states had been obliged a little earlier to adopt the practice, introduced in England a century earlier, of allowing private companies to plan and construct transportation linkages and to charge tolls for their use. This practice ushered in the turnpike and canal eras, during which hundreds of companies were chartered by the states to operate as regulated monopolies. Turnpikes were named for a pike, or pole, that was turned to allow access to the roadway after the payment of the toll. Minimum design standards such as roadway width and maximum gradients were usually included in the charter requirements. The states participated in varying degrees in the construction of these facilities by conferring the right to eminent domain for the taking of land and building materials, by subscribing to company stock, and in some cases by direct subsidies.

At the beginning, the role of the federal government was confined to the building of military roads. Otherwise, a strict interpretation of the U.S. Constitution commanded respect for the sovereignty of the states in matters of local concern including transportation. Indirectly, however, the federal government aided transportation development through land surveys of its territorial holdings, the sale of which was its major source of income. The first national transportation facility inventory was undertaken in 1807 by the secretary of the treasury, Albert Gallatin, who in his report a year later clearly recognized the importance of a good national transportation system to the growth and unity of the nation. Gradually, the federal government took carefully measured steps toward land grants to the states for roads and canals. It also moved toward the allocation of proceeds from land sales to the states to be used for transportation development, among other purposes. A notable exception to the hands-off federal policy was the construction, after bitter debate, of the first national road, the Cumberland Road, through Maryland, Virginia, and Pennsylvania. This road was later extended to Ohio, Indiana, and Illinois. Inadequate congressional appropriations for maintenance and a determination that the federal government was not empowered to charge user tolls led to the transfer of the road to the aforementioned states.

On the technological side, turnpike pavement construction of the heavily traveled routes initially employed the French method of building a heavy stone structural foundation. By 1820, the macadam method (named after the Scottish Engineer McAdam) was preferred. This method relied on the strength of the native soil, over which thin layers of small stones were packed for protection. In the area of water transportation, Fulton's successful, although not original, demonstration of steam power on the Hudson in 1807 enhanced the efficiency of this mode and eliminated the need to pull canal boats by horses, which walked along the shore. The network of individually planned turnpikes and water lines formed the basic long-distance transportation system of the nation until the arrival of the railroads.

7.2.3 Railroads

In their infancy during the early part of the nineteenth century, railroads were expected merely to provide a better roadbed for animal-drawn vehicles. The introduction of the railroad steam engine altered this notion and gave rise to railroad companies essentially as they are now known. Railroad planning and development followed the paradigm of turnpikes and canals but on a grander scale. The states extended charters to railroad companies on a line-by-line basis. When a standard gauge evolved, short lines were consolidated into fewer but larger entities. The superior performance and efficiency of the new technology caused the demise of most private turnpikes and canals.

The federal government contributed to the development of the railroads in the West via land surveys conducted by the U.S. Army Corps of Engineers between 1824 and 1838, by the imposition of tariffs on imported iron in 1832 to support the United States iron industry, and, beginning in 1850, by land grants to the railroads. In return, the recipients of land grants agreed to carry the United States mail and troops. The first transcontinental railroad was completed in 1869 with the driving of the golden spike at Promontory, Utah. The oligopolistic advantage enjoyed by the railroad companies began to be moderated by a series of government regulatory actions, which led to the passage of the 1877 Interstate Commerce Act. With regard to the railroads, this law provided for the regulation of rates and included several anticollusion clauses. The Interstate Commerce Commission (ICC) was established by this act to carry out its provisions.

7.2.4 Rural Highways

Under local control, statute labor laws, and other sources of local support, urban streets were kept in a reasonably adequate condition. Outside the cities, however, the same could be said only for short roadway spurs connecting farms and towns. The importance of good roads was appreciated but the means necessary to plan, finance, construct, and maintain them was lacking. Toward the end of the nineteenth century a good-roads movement swept the country. Newly formed associations of recreational bicyclists who had begun to brave the countryside played a pivotal role in this movement, which was consistent with the later-strengthened United States tradition of organized citizen participation in public planning and decision making.

The states assumed an active role in 1880 by extending aid to the counties and municipalities for the construction of public highways and by establishing highway or public roads commissions empowered with varying degrees of advisory, supervisory, and planning responsibilities. The Commonwealth Highway Plan enacted by the Massachusetts legislature in 1894 was perhaps the first attempt at planning a connected statewide network of public roads.

Two experimental programs, both approved in 1893, marked the formal reentry of the federal government in the planning of rural highways. First, the U.S. Congress approved a mail-delivery experiment on specially designated rural routes beginning in 1896. Later program expansions provided a strong incentive to the states to improve certain roadways in order to qualify for mail-route designation. Second, a temporary Office of Road Inquiry (ORI) was established within the U.S. Department of Agriculture to undertake research in road-building methods and to disseminate its findings to the states. The ORI's 1899 successor, the Office of Public Road Inquiry (OPRI), was merged in 1905 with the Division of Tests of the Bureau of Chemistry that had played an instrumental role in road-building materials research to form the Office of Public Roads (OPR), the precursor of the Bureau of Public Roads (BPR). Much later, in 1966, the BPR was absorbed into the Federal Highway Administration within the then-formed U.S. Department of Transportation.

The early planning-related pioneering work of the ORI included the preparation of a national inventory of macadamized roads, the Good Roads National Map, and the compilation of statistics relating to road usage, including quantified data on trip lengths and user costs for the transportation of farm products. To help meet its charge to disseminate its findings relating to road-building technology, the ORI initiated the construction of short segments of demonstration roads. In the meantime, technological advances were rapidly bringing the motor vehicle (electric, steam, and gasoline-powered) to the forefront of United States transportation. In 1912, a Congressional appropriation was approved, which authorized an experimental determination of the ability of good roads to effect savings to the U.S. Post Office's rural mail delivery. The first full-fledged federal highway aid was extended to the states via the Federal Road Act of 1916, which established a 50-50 construction-cost sharing between he federal government and the states, with the federal contribution to each state determined by a formula. During World War I the federal government seized the railroads and established the Federal Railway Administration to operate them. In addition, it designated a number of military highway routes for use by an increasing number of heavy trucks. This development had three major effects on highway planning after the war. First, it supported the growth of long-distance trucking; second, it renewed the need for improved roadbuilding; and third, it emphasized the need for a physical continuity of the intrastate and interstate highway systems.

The Federal-Aid Highway Act of 1921 required each state to designate up to 7% of their existing highways as part of a national system that would be eligible for federal aid. The BPR established cooperative agreements with some states to aid in the planning and location of this system. In the process, innovative survey methods and studies were developed that had a profound effect on the shaping of transportation planning. These studies included:

> the ownership of motor vehicles; the seasonal, monthly and daily variations in traffic; the origin and destination of cargoes; the size and weight of trucks. . . . In later studies, they examined driver behavior—the average speeds of drivers traveling freely on the highway and their observance of traffic laws, such as those prohibiting passing on hills and curves. In Maine, the researchers discovered a historical relationship between vehicle ownership, population and traffic. By projecting historical trends ahead, they were able to make fair estimates of traffic 5 years in the future [7.1, p. 122].

Highway construction benefited during the Great Depression from federal work-relief programs. In 1934, the Hayden-Cartwright Act permitted the expenditure of up to 1.5% of federal highway funds to be used for "surveys, plans, and engineering investigations of projects for future construction." This led the states, through their highway departments, to undertake massive needs studies by projecting population, traffic volumes, and vehicle ownership trends into the future. The projections were used to identify highway capacity deficiencies, which in turn guided the overall highway planning effort.

The Federal-Aid Highway Act of 1944 set the nation's sights toward a national system of interstate highways and provided for urban extensions of this system. In 1945 the American Association of State Highway Officials (AASHO), a cooperative organization established in 1914 during the good-roads movement, adopted a set of geometric design policies, which became the precursors of the contemporary standards discussed in Chapter 2.

The worldwide political instabilities that followed World War II led to a requirement in the 1948 Federal-Aid Highway Act for a cooperative federal-state study to assess the nation's highway system from the perspective of national defense. This study revealed significant deficiencies in many aspects, including a lack of adequate and uniform geometric designs, and encouraged a stronger federal role in the planning of national highways. About the same time and because of insufficient highway revenues collected from user charges, the states embarked on the construction of high-standard toll highways that mostly followed or paralleled the national interstate system. Most such publicly owned turnpikes opened between 1948 and 1954, when this type of state financing appeared to be the direction of the future. This trend, however, was reversed after the extension of federal funding to the secondary system of highways and the passage of the Federal-Aid Highway Act of 1956. This act and its companion Highway Revenue Act redefined the roles of the federal government and the states in the area of highway planning and had a profound effect on the evolution of a formalized planning process. Among its major provisions were the following:

1. It mandated the construction of the *national system of interstate and defense highways,* the largest single public works undertaking of its kind, in accordance with high and uniform design standards.
2. It established a 90-10% federal-state funding basis for this interstate highway system and provided that the larger federal portion be paid from revenues collected in the form of user taxes and charges that were to be placed in a special *highway trust fund* for this purpose.

3. It required the conduct of supportive planning studies and extended the requirement for the conduct of related *public hearings* in relation to project location, first set forth in 1950, to all federal-aid projects.

7.2.5 Urban Transportation Planning

The extension of federal highway aid to urban areas that began with the 1944 Federal-Aid Act brought about a division of interests between state concerns for interstate highway system continuity on one hand and urban concerns related to local circulation and the growing urban-traffic problem on the other. This fusion of perspectives contributed to the refinement of formalized planning processes and methodologies.

During the preindustrial era, many European cities were laid out according to the conceptual designs of notable city planners. These physical plans reflected a primary concern with the aesthetic qualities of city form and with the dominant location of symbolic structures such as cathedrals and palaces. In this connection, several schools of thought evolved. Early American cities can be traced to these city-planning traditions. Williamsburg (Virginia), Savannah (Georgia), Philadelphia, and L'Enfant's plan of the nation's capitol are notable examples of this trend.

During the late eighteenth and most of the nineteenth centuries, the growth patterns of United States cities were driven by a speculative fever, and city planning, as practiced earlier, disappeared from the scene. Most new cities and towns were built on land hastily subdivided into gridiron street patterns that followed the lines of government surveys. The same spirit permeated the growth of older cities as well; the original city plans were all but ignored, and random development of every available parcel of land ensued. Aided by the technological breakthroughs of the industrial revolution, cities entered a period of rapid expansion by absorbing a massive influx of people from rural areas and from abroad. Industrial and economic forces and the centralizing influence of railroad transportation necessitated the concentration of the population in cities. Among the major technological innovations were the steam engine, which facilitated the growth of the railroads, and the elevator and the frame-construction method, which made the skyscraper possible.

Urban planning reemerged as a professional discipline during the later part of the nineteenth century. This reemergence was aided by four developments that redefined the government's *power of eminent domain* (i.e., the power of taking private rights and property for public purposes) and the *police power* (i.e., the power to regulate the use of private property). Not necessarily in chronological order, the first development affecting modern city planning was related to an increasing involvement of city governments in the alleviation of slum conditions and the urban ills associated with them. New York enacted its first tenement law in 1867 to regulate building structures in an attempt to minimize fire hazards and to enhance the living conditions of the population. The origin of modern *building codes* can be traced here. The second trend was the practice of *districting*, or *zoning*, where the government assumes the power to regulate the use of land,—for example, for commercial, industrial, or residential purposes. Zoning was first applied in Germany in 1884 and spread through Europe before reaching the United States.

The term *zone* originally referred to a concentric ring, or belt, with the central city at its center but was later taken to mean a land area of any shape and location. The first comprehensive zoning code in the United States was enacted by the city of New York in 1916. The third precursor of modern city planning is evident in the *parks movement* advocated by an emerging group of planners and landscape architects, who, praising the virtues of pastoral life, saw public parks as having a beneficial influence on the otherwise drab existence of urban populations. Land for the first major urban park in the United States, New York City's Central Park, was acquired in the 1850s. The fourth major antecedent of modern urban planning was an advocacy for the beautification of *public buildings* within dominating civic squares, the descendents of the cathedral and palace of the earlier planning philosophy. Taking its lessons from European city forms, this movement developed during the closing years of the nineteenth century. The city-beautiful planning movement of the early 1900s was a planning philosophy distilled from these trends, which emphasized the construction of monumental civic centers and urban park systems connected by wide boulevards. It helped legitimize the need for planning and brought into the planning process the civil engineering profession and its road-building and structural-engineering techniques. During this time, the cities began to establish planning commissions composed of influential civic leaders to guide the formulation and implementation of plans, relying on a cadre of consultants to carry out the work. Both practices are extant to this day.

The introduction of streetcar services (see Chapter 1) exerted a decentralizing influence on the urban form by facilitating an outward expansion that reached beyond the city limits in a spokelike pattern. This radial growth left an indelible impression on the way planners thought of cities for decades and directed their attention to the urban region rather than merely the city proper. Public transportation was provided by private companies franchised as public utilities and operated on city-owned streets. Proponents of city planning argued that the award of franchises should be made in an orderly fashion and in accordance with regional city plans.

Consistent with the age of mechanization, a new planning perspective gradually emerged that saw the city as a machine. Although more complex than other mechanical devices, the efficient functioning of its interrelated parts was considered to be amenable to scientific treatment. According to the developing *city practical* (also known as *city efficient* and *city scientific*) planning movement of the 1920s and 1930s, transportation was seen not only as the skeleton of a static city plan but as a force that affects the future shape of the city. As such, it was reasoned, transportation planning should become an integral part of urban planning.

The decentralizing influence of public transit was not confined to residential suburbanization but extended to industrial decentralization as well. Many new towns were built along the principles set forth in Graham R. Taylor's book *Satellite Cities* [7.9], which was influenced by Ebenezer Howard's earlier work on garden cities [7.10]. These principles are reflected in the design of modern suburban communities.

In step with the scientific approach to planning was an increasing reliance on measurement and prediction, for example, the conduct of physical, economic, and demographic inventories, the collection of transportation usage data, and the attempt to discern the relationships between these factors. This kind of planning activity was contemporaneously occurring in relation to intercity highways. Figure 7.2.1 is an early graphical display of transit route usage in the city of Newark, New Jersey [7.8]. The radial pattern of travel demand is clearly evident.

By accelerating residential and industrial decentralization not only along fixed radial routes but also in the spaces between them, the motor vehicle caused another revision of planning practice and also the evolution of a specialized profession, *traffic engineering,* the scope of which was primarily restricted to the orderly expansion of street capacity, parking facilities, and traffic-control strategies to accommodate the quality and safety of ever-increasing automobile flows. Among the major contributions of traffic engineering were advanced traffic and driver-behavior studies and the modeling of land use, popu-

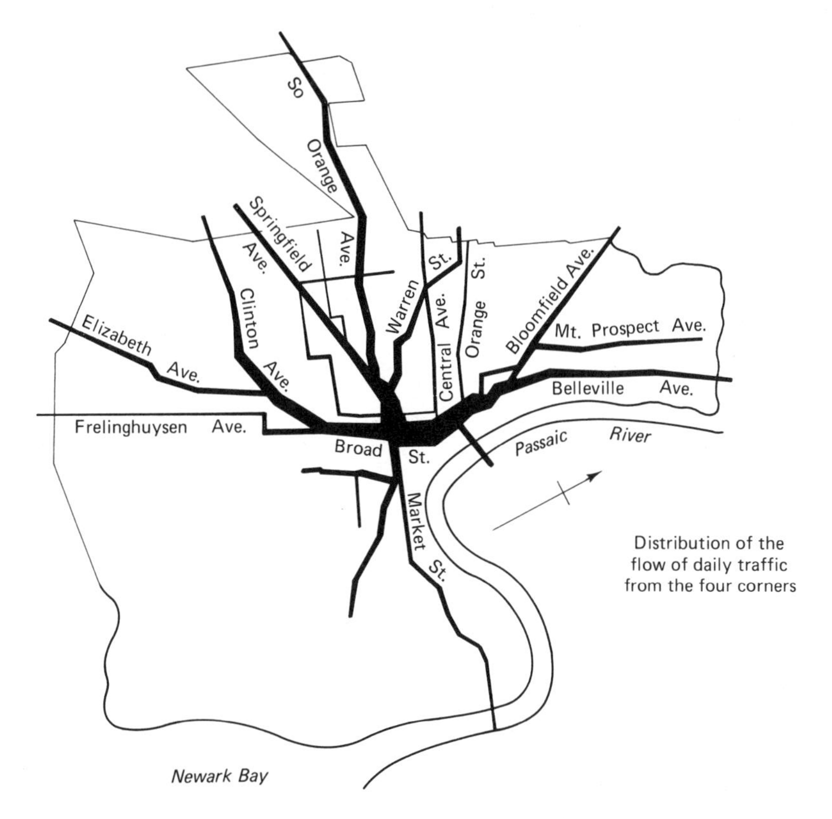

Fundamental data on transit touching conditions past and present, showing routes, traffic density, time and fare zones, etc., will be required. Approximately 200,000 people enter and leave the "Four Corners" in the city of Newark upon the trolley cars each day from 7 A.M. to 7 P.M. The greatest proportion of this travel is north and west, as shown by the width of the bands in the diagram. These illustrate the proportion of travel upon each of the various routes.

Figure 7.2.1 Early transit patronage volume map: Newark c. 1929. (*SOURCE: City Planning* edited by John Nolen. Copyright 1929 by D. Appleton & Co., renewed 1957 by John Nolen, Jr., Gerald Nolen, and Barbara Nolen Strong. A Hawthorn book. Reproduced by permission of E. P. Dutton, a division of New American Library.)

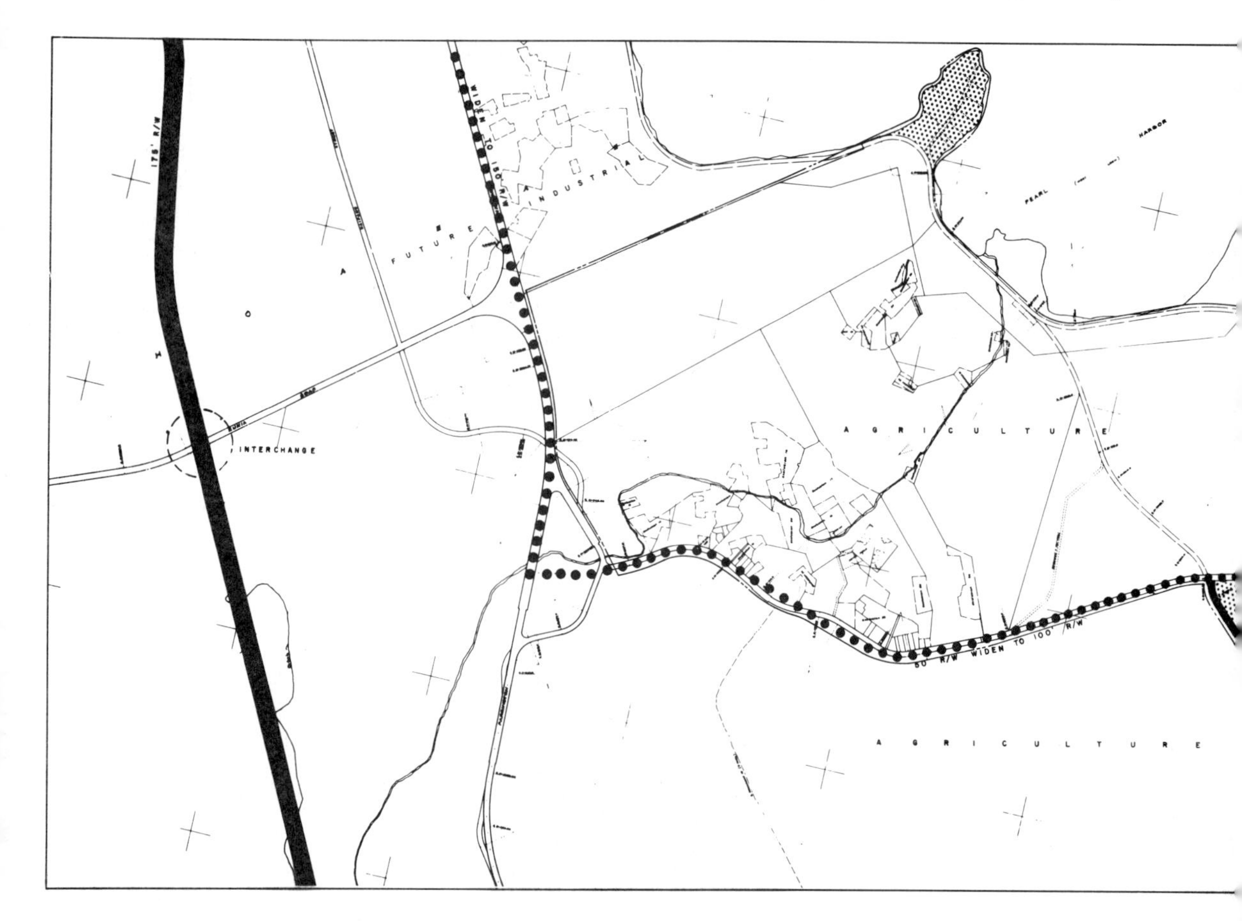

Figure 7.2.2 Portion of a land use map. (*SOURCE*: City and County of Honolulu [7.16].)

lation, and traffic demand relationships. A rudimentary model of land use and traffic was applied in San Juan, Puerto Rico, to plan a freeway system serving a new airport. The invention of the high-speed digital computer made possible the analysis of large quantities of data and the development of more sophisticated planning methods.

By the 1940s, urban planning became an established function of city governments. The *master planning* era of the next two decades emphasized the production of comprehensive regional zoning maps and specifying the planned location of infrastructural systems, including transportation, water supply, and sewage facilities. Figure 7.2.2 shows a portion of the 1950 zoning map of the City of Honolulu, Hawaii [7.16].

The extension of federal aid to the urban portions of the national highway system in 1944 marked the definite entry of the states into the urban-planning scene. This development brought together three overlapping professional perspectives, the interaction of which was fundamental in the evolution of transportation planning: through their highway departments, the states that were predominantly concerned with the connectivity of the intrastate and interstate highway network; the city traffic engineering departments

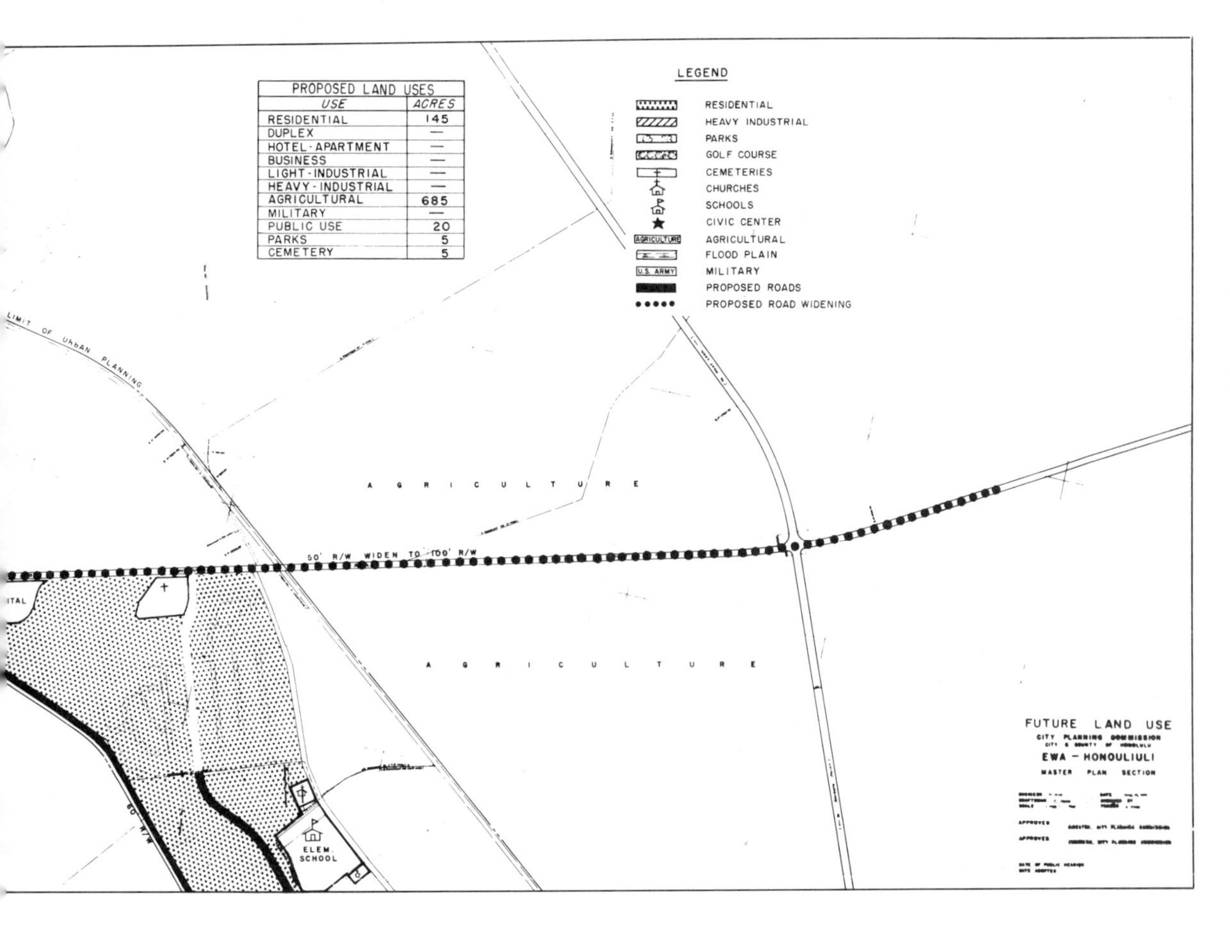

that were primarily concerned with accommodating the efficient and safe operation of the urban street network; and the city (or in some instances, regional) planning departments, which were concerned with regional land use planning, housing, and urban public transportation. Out of this interaction emerged a generally shared, quantitatively based land use–transportation planning methodology.

7.3 DEVELOPMENT OF A FORMAL PLANNING PROCESS

7.3.1 Housing Policies

Direct federal involvement in the area of housing is evident in the Home Loan Bank Act of 1932 and in the National Housing Act of 1934, which established the Federal Housing Administration (FHA). The Housing Act of 1949 set up the Housing and Home Finance

Agency (HHFA) and appropriated funds for the elimination of urban blight through the clearance of slums and the redevelopment of the areas occupied by them. The Housing Act of 1954 shifted the emphasis of this program from leveling and rebuilding to urban renewal, which included the rehabilitation and preservation of existing structures in accordance with a general plan for each locality. Grants for transportation planning, including comprehensive traffic surveys and studies, were provided by the Housing Act of 1961 and administered by the HHFA, which in 1965 became part of the newly formed Department of Housing and Urban Development (HUD). The Demonstration Cities and Metropolitan Development Act of 1966 included additional assistance to urban transit and required the designation by each urbanized area of a regional organization to oversee the orderly development of the program.

7.3.2 The 3C Process

The federal-aid highway program was also gaining a planning perspective that was being adapted to the conditions found in urban areas. The Office of Planning was established within the BPR in 1961, and the Federal-Aid Highway Act of 1962 mandated that after 1965, state eligibility for federal highway aid in major cities would be conditioned on the existence of long-range plans that would

> be based on a *continuing, comprehensive* transportation planning process carried out *co-operatively* by states and local communities . . . [emphasis added]

It also declared that it is

> in the national interest to encourage and promote the development of transportation systems, embracing various modes of transport, in a manner that will serve the states and local communities effectively and efficiently.

This act officially established the requirement for the *3C planning process*.

7.3.3 Social Concerns

Beginning with the movement for racial equality, which led to the passage of the Civil Rights Act of 1964 and other housing and equal opportunity laws, the decade of the 1960s was a decade of social concern. Social activists held the view, sometimes justified and sometimes exaggerated, that the slum clearance and urban highway programs were signs of a "bulldozer mentality" that was insensitive to social needs. These groups learned to organize and lobby at the local, state, and federal levels and to seek judicial relief of their grievances. The provision of public transportation was viewed as one means of addressing the needs of disadvantaged groups.

The Urban Mass Transportation Act of 1964 provided capital assistance for urban public transportation to be administered by HHFA. Federal responsibilities for urban mass transportation remained with HUD until 1968, when the Urban Mass Transportation Administration (UMTA) was established within the Department of Transportation (DOT).

The Federal-Aid Highway Act of 1968 amended the requirements of earlier highway acts relating to the economic effects of highway location to

> economic and social effects for such a location, its impact on the environment, and its consistency with the goals and objectives of . . . urban planning as has been promulgated by the community.

This law allowed the use of federal highway aid for the construction of fringe parking facilities and earmarked funding for traffic engineering measures known as the Traffic Operation Programs to Increase Capacity and Safety (TOPICS). To be eligible for matching funds, fringe parking and TOPICS projects had to be based on the 3C process.

The Urban Mass Transportation Assistance Act of 1970 provided a multiyear commitment for capital (but not operating assistance) for transit projects and encouraged the provision of mass transportation services to the elderly and handicapped, having recognized that

> elderly and handicapped persons have the same right as other persons to utilize mass transportation facilities and services.

7.3.4 National Environmental Legislation

The passage of the landmark National Environmental Policy Act (NEPA) of 1969 consolidated several trends relating to social, economic, environmental impact, and citizen participation in public decisions that were developing in various areas of federal concern including transportation. The act required that proposals for ". . . Federal actions significantly affecting the quality of the human environment" be accompanied by

> a detailed statement by the responsible official on—
>
> (i) the environmental impact of the proposed action,
> (ii) any adverse environmental effects which cannot be avoided should the proposal be implemented,
> (iii) alternatives to the proposed action,
> (iv) the relationship between local short-term uses of man's environment and the maintenance of long-term productivity, and
> (v) any irreversible and irretrievable commitments of resources which would be involved in the proposed action should it be implemented.

Major transportation proposals required the preparation of such an *environmental impact statement* (EIS), the expressed purpose of which was a full and objective disclosure of positive and negative environmental effects in order to aid the decision-making process. Indirect transportation consequences (e.g., traffic congestion and needed capacity) were to be included among the impacts covered by the EIS for nontransportation actions. An important provision of NEPA was the requirement to analyze alternatives to a preferred action including a baseline (or no-build) alternative.

The Clear Air Act of 1970 established national ambient air-quality standards and required the states to develop plans to meet these standards. Motor-vehicle emissions were identified as major contributors to the problem. The Environmental Protection Agency (EPA), which played a central role in subsequent transportation laws, rules, and regulations, was created by this act, which was followed by a series of environmental laws relating to noise, management of coastal and other environmentally sensitive areas, protection of endangered species, water quality, and so on. The 1982 version of the guidelines issued by the Federal Highway Administration (FHWA) relating to the conduct of environmental assessments is included in Appendix A to illustrate the breadth of impacts and transportation alternatives that have been incorporated in the requirements of the 3C planning process.

7.3.5 Toward Planning Coordination

The Intergovernmental Cooperation Act of 1968 recognized a need for a mechanism by which projects seeking federal aid could be reviewed by the various interested and affected agencies. A year later, the Bureau of the Budget issued Circular A-95, which set forth a requirement to designate specific state and metropolitan agencies as clearinghouses to facilitate the project-review process, which was thereafter referred to as the "A-95 review."

A series of highway- and mass-transportation-related laws enacted between 1970 and 1974 extended federal support to mass transit in urban and rural areas and increasingly placed federal aid for both highway and transit projects on essentially identical planning requirements. Both had to be produced by the 3C process; address the same social, economic, and environmental impacts; ensure community participation; and undergo similar agency and public reviews. This and functional overlaps between highways and transit systems using the highways motivated a closer degree of coordination between the FHWA and UMTA program requirements. In 1975, the two agencies issued joint regulations, which required each urban area to designate a single Metropolitan Planning Organization (MPO) with a widely based membership to coordinate the planning activities of the local communities and modal planning agencies within their respective regions. The MPOs were to be certified annually by both FHWA and UMTA to ensure the presence of a satisfactory 3C process. One of the duties of the MPOs was the preparation of an annually updated multimodal transportation plan for the entire metropolitan area consisting of

1. A long-range element addressing a time horizon of the order of 20 years;
2. A transportation systems management element (TSME) containing the region's plan for low-cost operational improvements;
3. A transportation improvement plan (TIP) specifying the region's 5-year priorities drawn from the other two elements and including an annual element (AE), which listed the programs and projects scheduled for the following year.

Like its precursor (i.e., the 1968 TOPICS program), the TSM element addressed the need for short-term, low-cost operational improvements aiming for a better use of existing facilities, but in addition to traffic engineering measures, it included additional options such as car-pooling, the use of taxis and other demand-responsive services, automobile restraints, changes in work schedules, and the like. TSM planning was first required by a 1976 UMTA policy statement as a possible alternative to major transit projects for which the UMTA purse was becoming insufficient. Eventually, the requirement for a separate TSM element in the annual plan was dropped, but by that time a regional TSM option became the de facto baseline alternative against which other proposals were being compared. The attempt to coordinate the FHWA and UMTA programs is also seen in the title of the Surface Transportation Assistance Act of 1978. This act shifted the emphasis of the highway program from construction of new facilities to the renovation of existing highways and authorized additional funding for transit development. Partly because of a financial inability to fund all heavy rail rapid-transit proposals, UMTA issued a policy toward rail transit in 1978, which promulgated its intent to fund such systems on an incremental basis rather than in toto and only when an alternatives analysis has shown them to be superior to all-TSM, light rail, busway, and other options.

Following a 1973 oil embargo by the Organization of Petroleum Producing Countries (OPEC), the Highway Trust Fund also experienced difficulties because of decreasing revenues from gasoline taxes and because of price inflation. Responding to this problem, the U.S. Congress enacted the National Transportation Assistance Act of 1982, which imposed an additional federal tax of 5¢ on each gallon of fuel, of which 4¢ was earmarked for highway purposes and 1¢ for transit assistance.

Toward the latter part of the 1970s, the nation showed signs of a change in mood away from federal intervention in the private sector. The federal government embarked on a trend to deregulate many sectors of the economy and to transfer the responsibility for many programs back to the states.

7.4 PLANNING STUDIES AND METHODS

7.4.1 Background

The preceding section traced the evolution of a formalized transportation planning process, by which transportation plans are produced, revised, and selected for implementation. It also identified the groups of participants in the process and the factors that were deemed relevant to the proper execution of the planning function.

The participating groups include bodies of elected officials, public agencies that have leading and supportive roles in the process, officially appointed citizen advisory commissions and committees, private- and public-transportation system operators, voluntary citizen and professional associations, and interested individuals. These groups and individuals bring into the process differing, often conflicting, and also changing goals and objectives. To complicate matters, not all these groups are particularly interested in a continuous and intensive participation in all aspects of the process; on the contrary, they often feel free to enter or exit the process at will. Moreover, the membership of these groups exhibits a considerable amount of fluidity. It is not unusual, for example, for a member of a voluntary organization to be elected or appointed to public office or for an agency representative to belong to a professional organization and to also reside in the path of a proposed facility.

Institutionalized procedures, such as the requirements for planning documents, interagency reviews, and public hearings and other means of citizen participation have evolved within the larger socio-political system specifically to ensure that the factors considered to be relevant to a particular situation are adequately addressed and in order to facilitate the formation of local consensus in an orderly manner. Transportation engineers participate in various aspects of this complex process. One aspect of engineering involvement that merits further treatment here is the conduct of supportive planning studies that attempt to model and estimate *some* of the many travel, economic, social and environmental factors that have been deemed to be important to transportation planning.

7.4.2 Antecedents to Planning Studies

The first step toward the development of the contemporary transportation-planning methodology may be traced to the conduct of land surveys that supported the layouts of cities and towns and the locations of turnpike, canals, and—later—railroads. The second step was the need to conduct facility inventories, such as the first national inventory of 1807. The third step commenced when the Office of Road Inquiry, toward the end of the nineteenth century, extended data-collection efforts to include information relating to facility use, that is, traffic levels, trip lengths, and user costs. The expanded usage studies that followed the prescription of the Federal-Aid Highway Act of 1921 to plan a connected national network and the transition to studies emphasizing highway planning to meet future needs made possible by the Hayden-Cartwright Act of 1934 established the fundamental elements of transportation planning.

7.4.3 Planning for Future Needs

A major breakthrough of the needs studies of the 1930s and 1940s was the recognition that planning highway network extensions should not be based merely on the static criterion of connectivity but also on continuous efforts to anticipate future demands for travel. Initially, this was accomplished by projecting current traffic measurements into the future by using traffic-growth factors based on discerned relationships between population and economic growth on one hand and traffic levels on the other. For example, based on annual rates of growth in the gross national product (GNP), traffic-growth factors in the range of 3 to 4% were considered to be reasonable. The projected traffic levels could then be checked against the capacity of existing highways to anticipate future capacity deficiencies and, within financial constraints, to plan and schedule capacity improvements accordingly. Figure 7.4.1 illustrates a 1948 statewide traffic-flow map [7.11] that bears a similarity to the urban-transit usage map of Fig. 7.2.1: The widths of

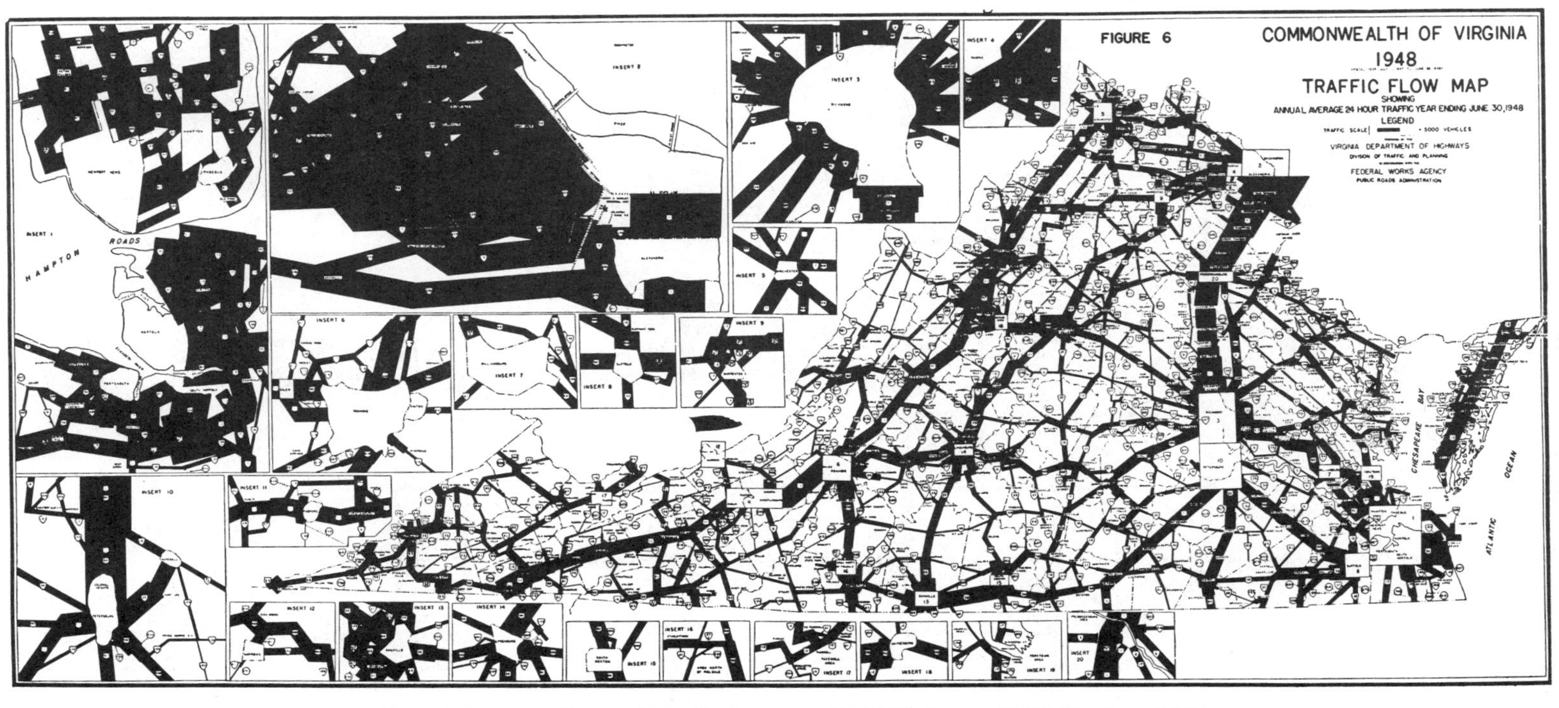

Figure 7.4.1 A 1948 statewide traffic flow map. (*SOURCE*: Stevens [7.11] Fig. 6, p. 455.)

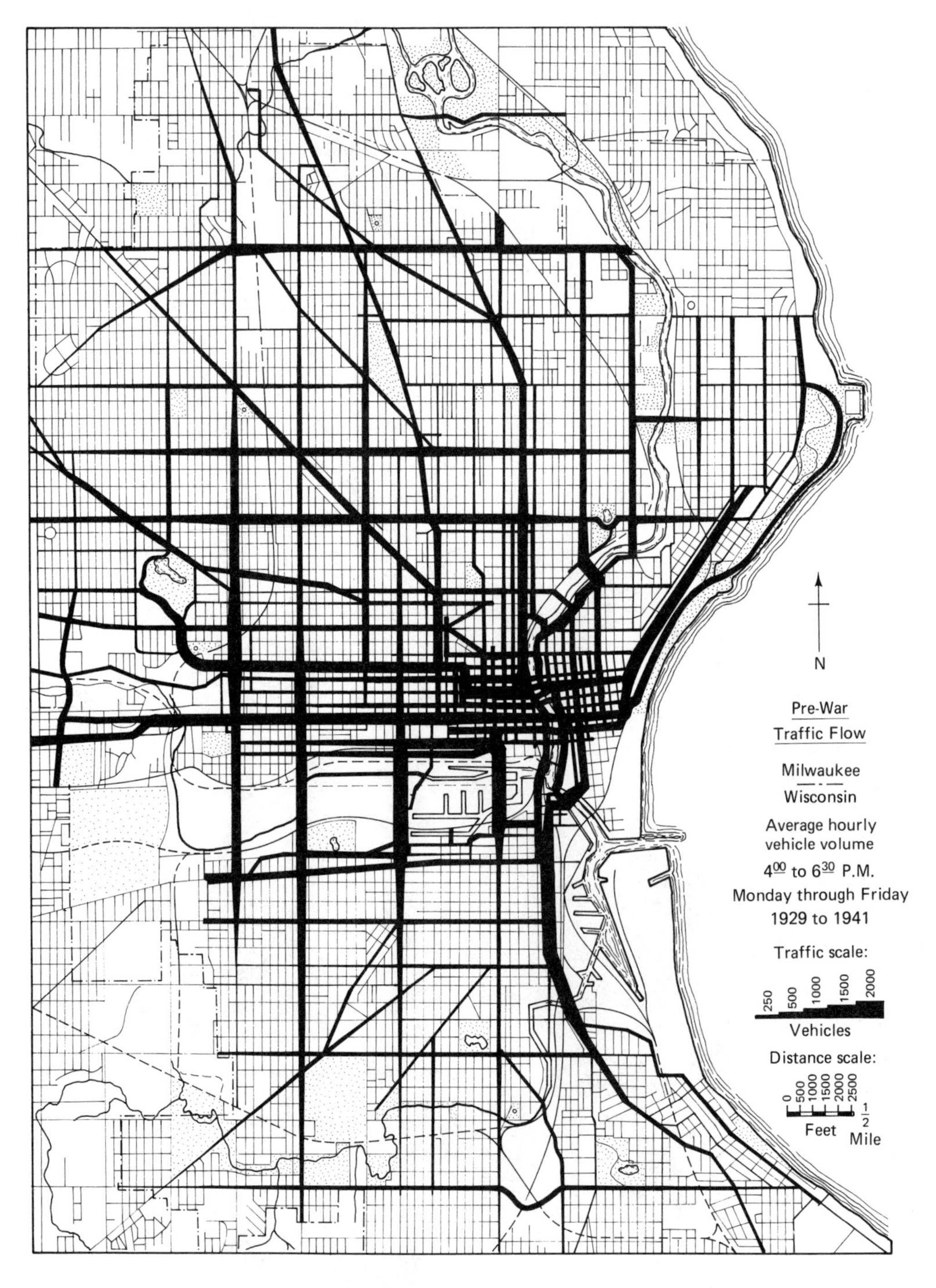

Figure 7.4.2 An early urban traffic flow map. (*SOURCE*: Gamble [7.12], Fig. 9. p. 413.)

the bands shown along the various highway links are proportional to the measured link flows. The inserted heavy flow bands in and around urbanized areas portend the need to pay special attention to these areas.

7.4.4 Large-Scale Urban Travel Surveys

Figure 7.4.2 shows a similar traffic flow map of pre–World War II Milwaukee [7.12] and perhaps the intent of transportation planners to apply the rural travel needs methodology to urban areas. Significant differences in the patterns of urban travel, however,

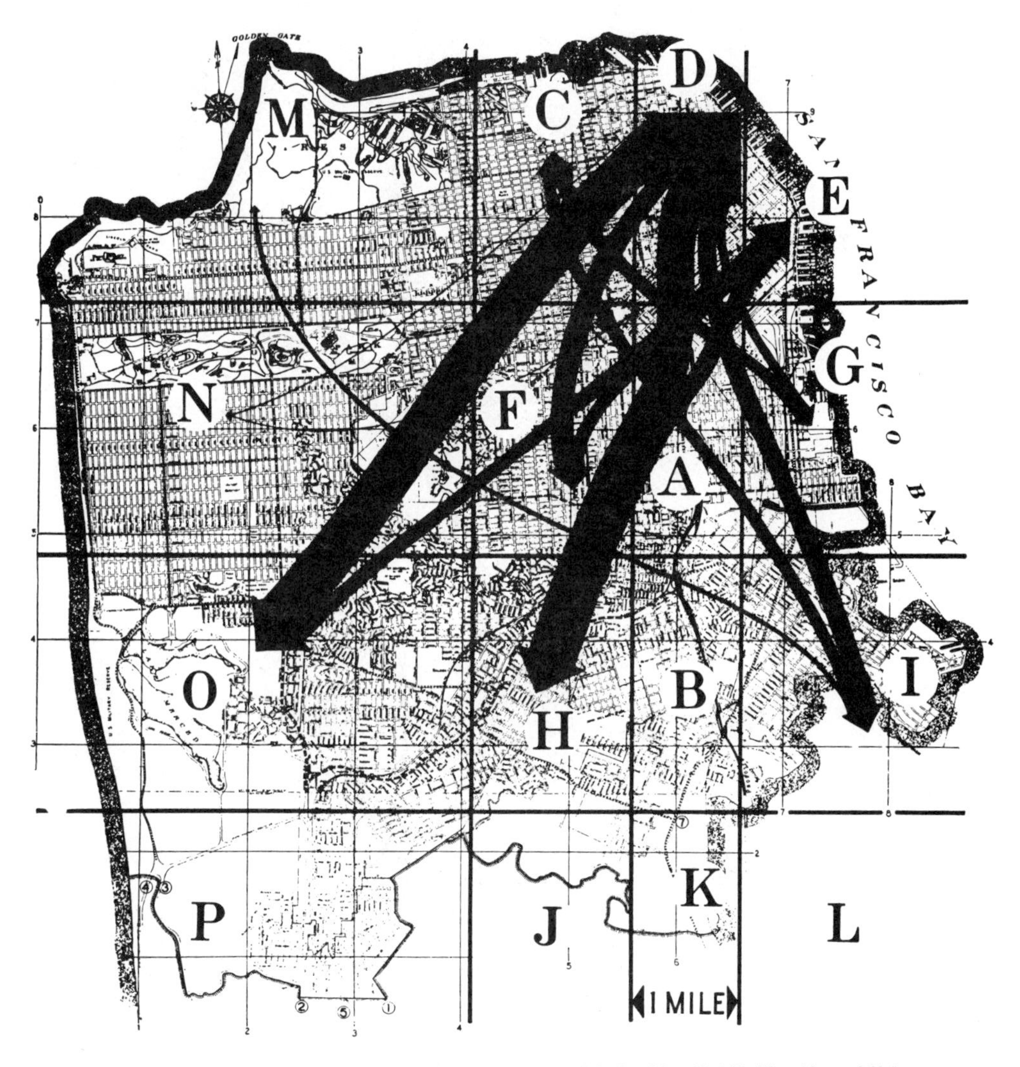

Figure 7.4.3 Desire-line diagram. (*SOURCE*: MacLachlan [7.13], Fig. 13, p. 363.)

necessitated the development of more refined techniques. An important difference was (and still is) the fact that in urban areas, street capacities between various parts of the city involved multiple rather than single routes. If needed, capacity enhancements should consider this combined supply of roadways. Figure 7.4.3 illustrates a *desire line diagram,* which shows the region divided into smaller sectors, or *traffic* (*analysis*) *zones,* and the flows between these zones irrespective of individual roadway links. To obtain this type

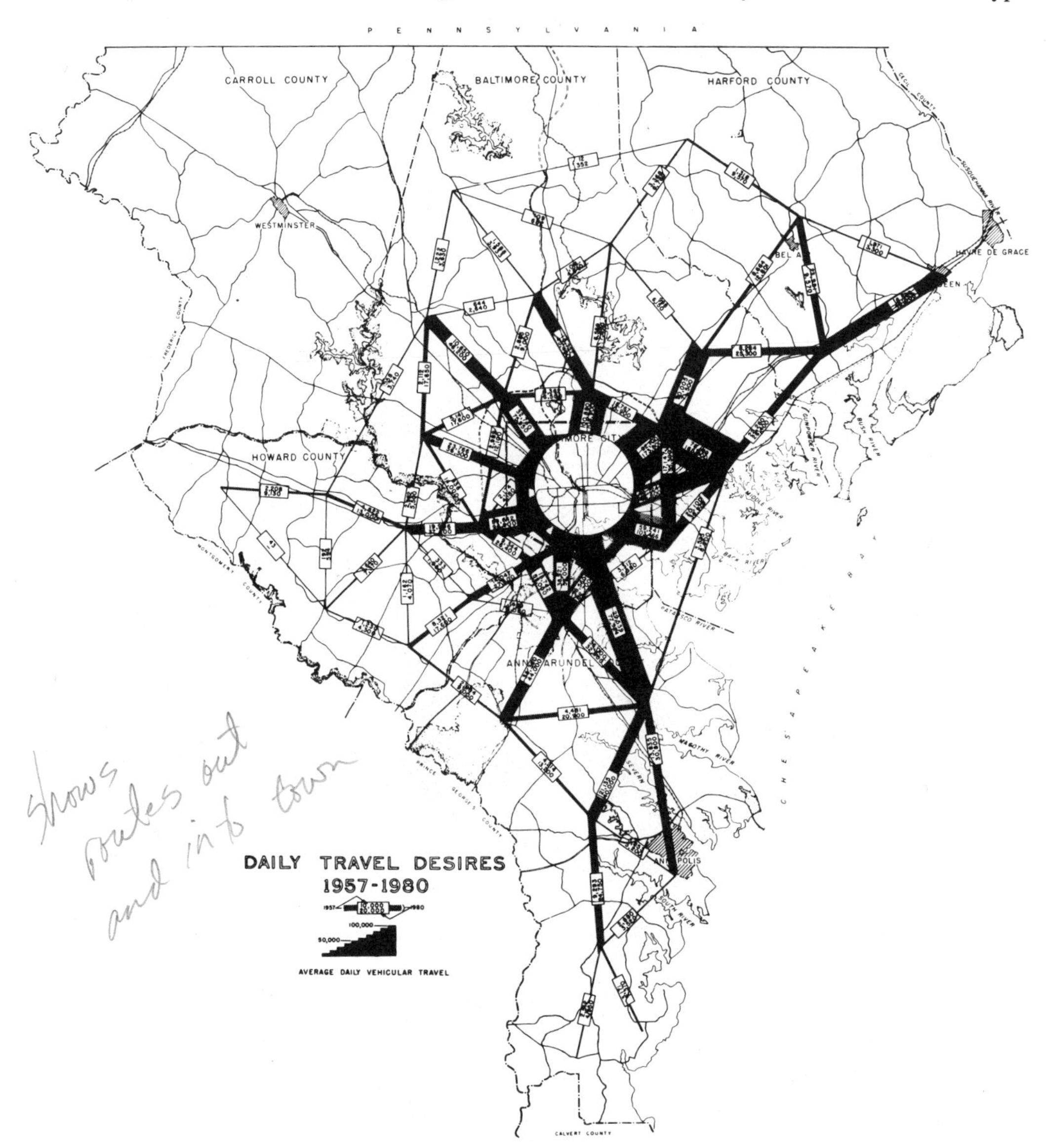

Figure 7.4.4 Observed and projected desire line diagram. (*SOURCE*: Voorhees [7.14], Fig. 1, p. 116.)

of information, new travel-survey and data-reduction methods were developed during the 1940s, including the *origin-and-destination (O-D) surveys* consisting of home interviews, truck interviews, taxi interviews, and parking surveys. The data on travel habits obtained from interviewing a sample consisting of 4 to 5% of the total households in the region and about 20% of the truck and taxi companies were expanded to the overall population by computer-based statistical techniques, and the actual traffic counts crossing selected

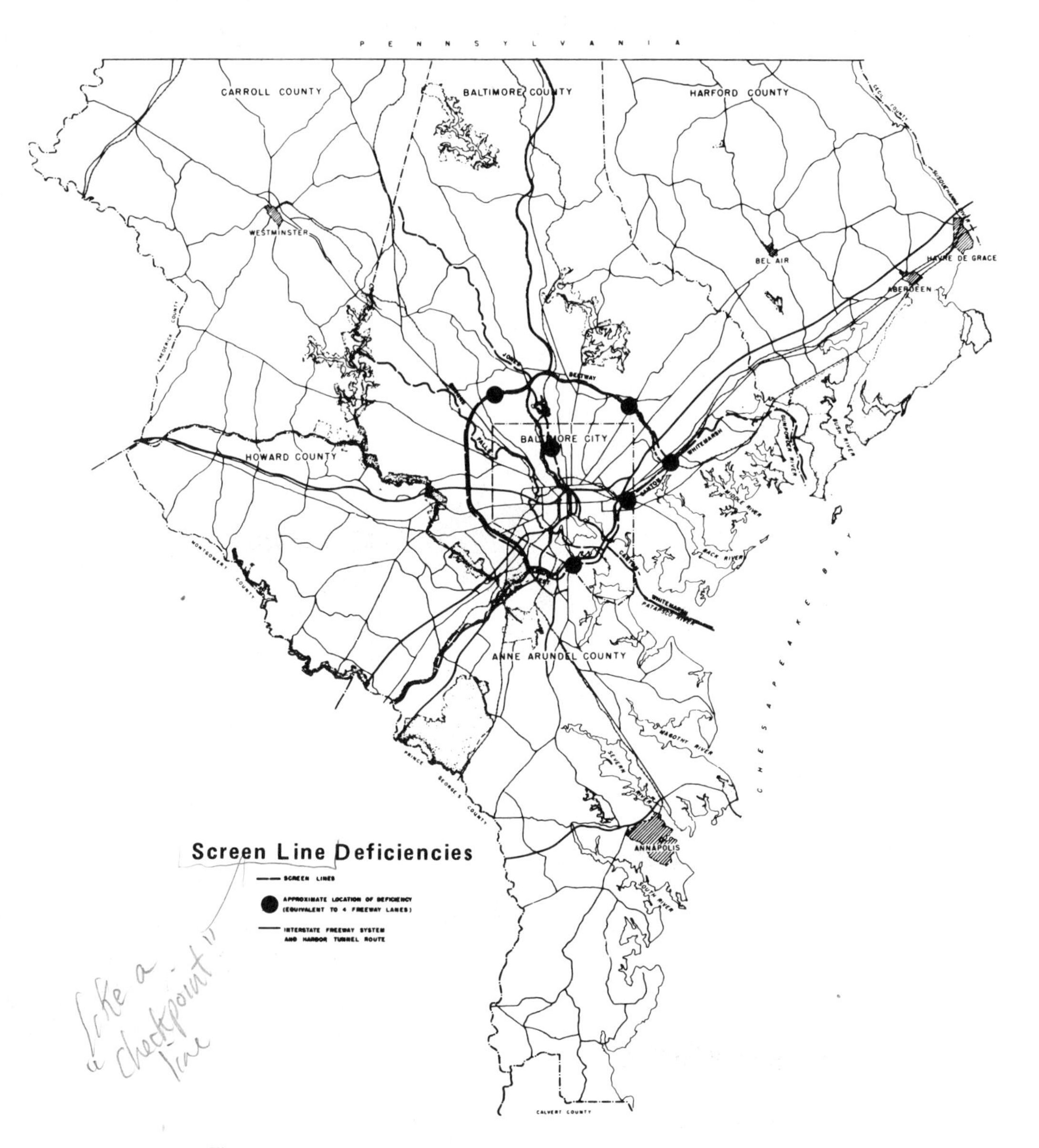

Figure 7.4.5 Screen-line deficiencies. (*SOURCE*: Voorhees [7.14], Fig. 3, p. 119.)

screen lines were used to check the accuracy of the statistical expansion of the sample data [7.13]. The first large-scale travel survey of this type was conducted in Detroit.

Figures 7.4.4 through 7.4.7 illustrate the application of the needs study methodology as applied to the city of Baltimore to project 1957 (*base year*) measurements to 1980 (*target*, or *horizon, year*) freeway needs [7.14]. The desire line diagram of Fig. 7.4.4 superposes the base and target year interzonal flows exclusive of the downtown area, Fig. 7.4.5 identifies the anticipated screen-line capacity deficiencies, Fig. 7.4.6 summarizes the results of a special analysis across a particular screen line, and Fig. 7.4.7 specifies the location of additional freeways selected to rectify the capacity problems disclosed by the planning study.

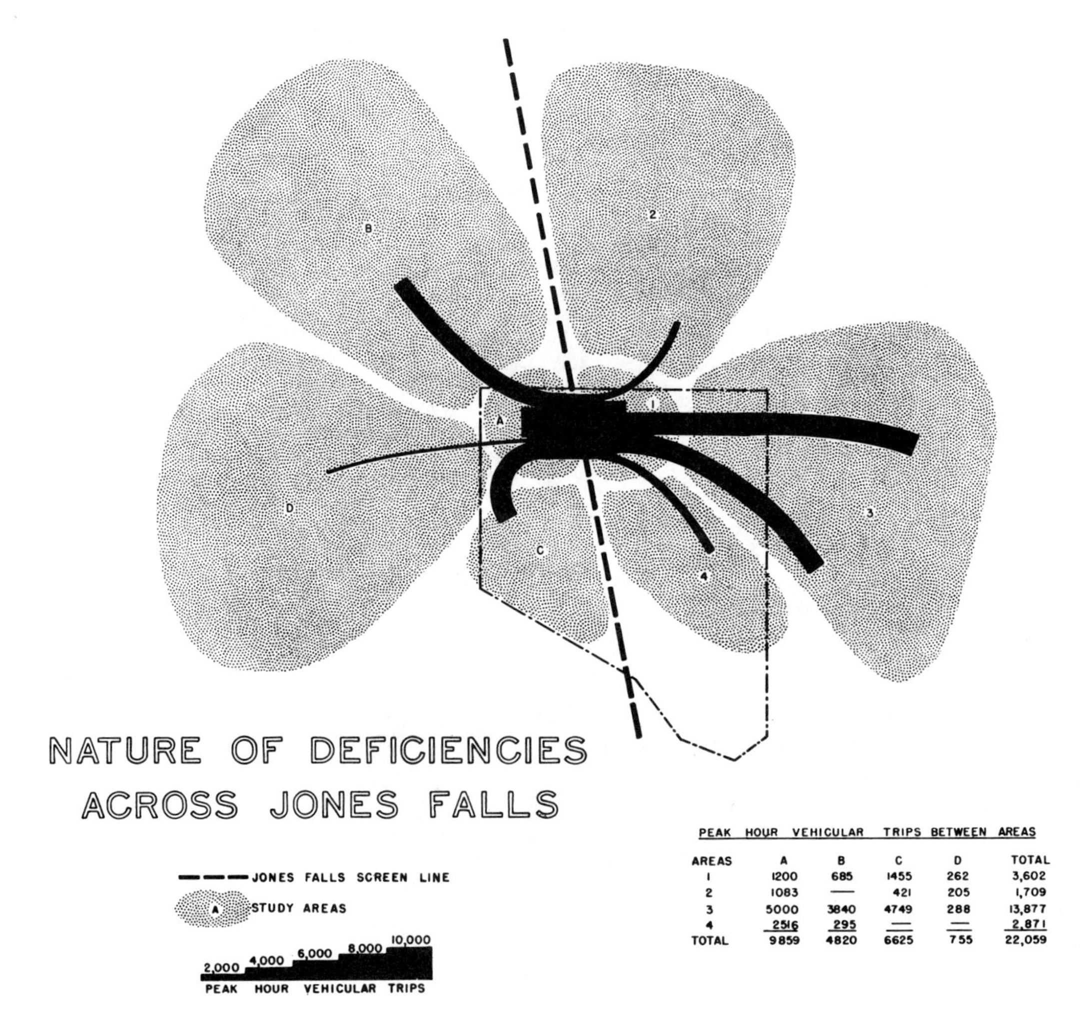

PEAK HOUR VEHICULAR TRIPS BETWEEN AREAS

AREAS	A	B	C	D	TOTAL
1	1200	685	1455	262	3,602
2	1083	—	421	205	1,709
3	5000	3840	4749	288	13,877
4	2516	295	—	—	2,871
TOTAL	9859	4820	6625	755	22,059

Figure 7.4.6 Screen-line special analysis. (*SOURCE*: Voorhees [7.14], Fig. 4, p. 120.)

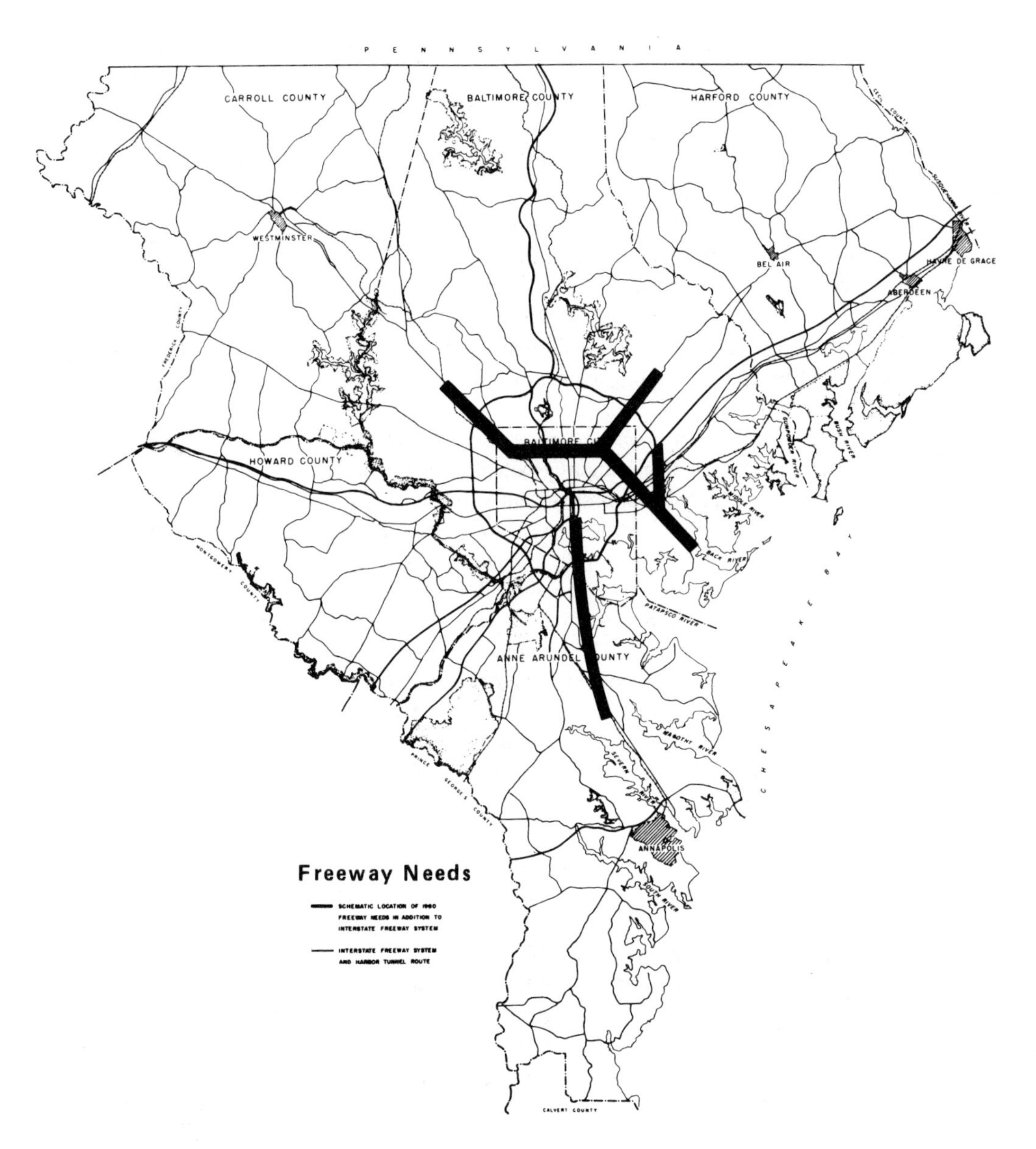

Figure 7.4.7 Identified freeway needs. (*SOURCE*: Voorhees [7.14], Fig. 5, p. 121.)

7.4.5 Travel Demand Forecasts

Initially, the projection of the interzonal *trip distribution* toward the target year was accomplished by applying simple growth factors to the base-year travel desire volumes in a manner that was similar to rural highway practice. Gradually, however, it became evident that the need for added capacity and parking facilities in urban areas was not uniform throughout the region but was dependent on the specific types (e.g., residential, commercial, or industrial) and intensities (residential density, workers per acre, shopping floor space, and the like) of the *land uses* found in each zone. Moreover, the expected regional growth of the population and the economic system was unevenly distributed among the zones owing to differences in the availability and suitablity of developable land for various purposes, urban-planning policies (such as zoning), and accessibility. The first computer-based quantitative *land use* and *socioeconomic projection models* were developed by transportation planners in this connection and were later adopted eagerly by other urban planners.

Mathematical *trip generation models* relating the trip-producing capability of residential areas and the trip-attracting potential of various types of nonresidential land use classes were postulated, calibrated, and validated.

Since the emphasis of these studies was placed on the urban highway system, transit trips had to be subtracted from the projected total interzonal traffic volumes to arrive at an estimate of future highway demands. *Modal split models,* such as the one illustrated by Fig. 7.4.8, were developed to help divide the total flows between the two modes, highway and transit [7.15]. The planning for mass-transit services was generally left to the operators and was considered to be of secondary importance, since transit patronage was experiencing a steady decline.

Of relevance to urban highway design was a prior knowledge of the degree to which arterial street traffic would be attracted to new freeways. Having this knowledge before designing a new facility was important in determining the capacity (e.g., the number of lanes) that it should provide. Models of traffic diversion from arterials to freeways similar in shape to the model choice curve of Fig. 7.4.8 resulted. These route-choice models were later extended to cover large networks and became known as *traffic assignment models*.

Thus trip-generation, trip-distribution, modal choice, and traffic-assignment models evolved, each intended to describe and forecast a different component of travel behavior.

The Chicago Area Transportation Study (CATS) was the first to combine land-use and socioeconomic projection models with these travel demand models to analyze regional long-range transportation alternatives. This urban transportation planning methodology was then applied to other United States metropolitan areas and was also taken to major cities throughout the world by United States consulting firms. In the process, the methodology was further refined and applied to various planning contexts.

Figure 7.4.9 is a simplified flowchart of steps involved in applying the original methodology after the conduct of planning inventories and surveys (e.g., land-use data, economic investigations, and travel surveys) and the postulation and calibration of models forecasting land use and travel demand to fit local conditions.

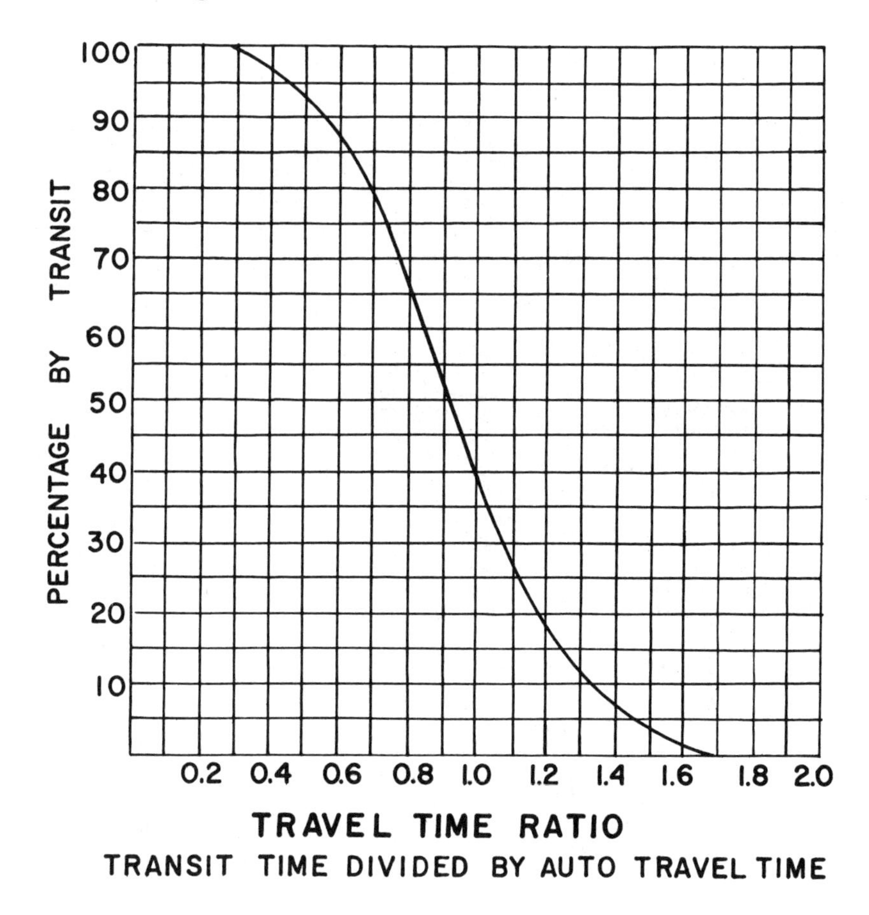

Figure 7.4.8 An early modal split curve. (*SOURCE*: Voorhees [7.15], Fig. 4, p. 112.)

Step 1. Forecasts of the target year the regional population and economic growth for the subject metropolitan area.

Step 2. Allocation of land uses and socioeconomic projections to individual analysis zones in accordance to land availability, local zoning, and related public policies.

Step 3. Specification of alternative transportation plans partly based on the results of Steps 1 and 2.

Step 4. Calculation of the capital and maintenance costs of each alternative plan.

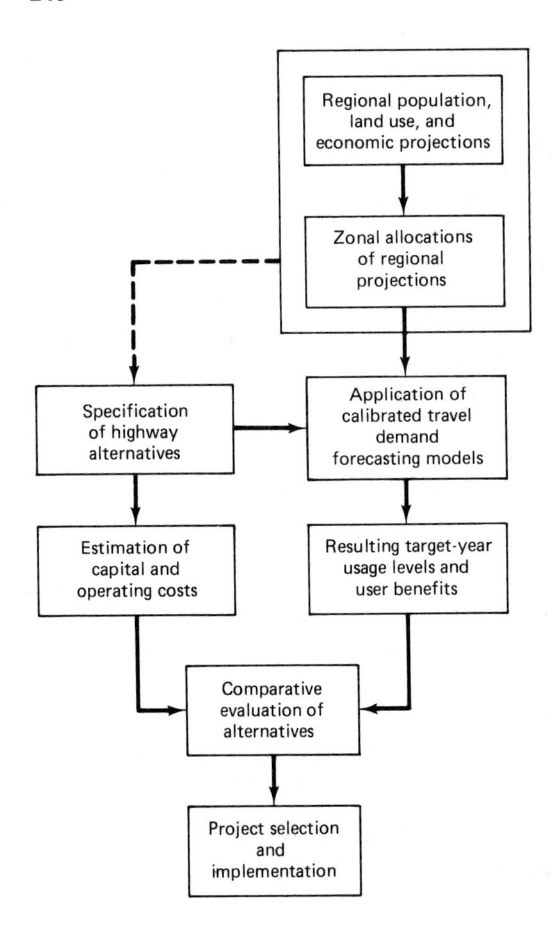

Figure 7.4.9 Simplified version of the original urban transportation planning process.

Step 5. Application of calibrated demand-forecasting models to predict the target year equilibrium flows expected to use each alternative, given the land-use and socioeconomic projections of Step 2 and the characteristics of the transportation alternative (Step 3).

Step 6. Conversion of equilibrium flows to *direct user benefits,* such as savings in travel time and travel cost attributable to the proposed plan.

Step 7. Comparative evaluation and selection of the "best" of the alternatives analyzed based on estimated costs (Step 3) and benefits (Step 6).

This methodology was (and continues to be) refined and expanded to cover additional social, economic, and environmental benefits and costs; to admit a wider range of multimodal transportation alternatives; to be more sensitive to the relationship between land-use and transportation planning; and to admit multiagency and public participation.

7.5 SUMMARY

This chapter defined planning as the forward-looking, organized, and premeditative process that precedes the undertaking of actions intended to guide a particular situation or system in desirable directions but not as a search for the ultimate. The fundamental objective of transportation is to provide the efficient and safe levels of mobility needed to support a wide spectrum of other human needs for a heterogeneous variety of societal groups. Since these needs, goals, and objectives are continuously changing, transportation planning is also an ever-evolving process.

The evolution of contemporary transportation planning in the United States was traced along the historical path of land transportation, paying particular attention to the confluence of three important factors: technological progress, private interests, and changing governmental policy.

The merging and interaction of three disparate planning perspectives (the facility orientation of intercity highway planning, the traffic-operations-oriented traffic engineering approach, and the social consciousness of urban planning) produced the basic elements of the contemporary urban transportation planning process, incorporating technical analyses, widely based citizen participation, and a concern for a large variety of social, economic, and environmental impacts in addition to connectivity and accessibility.

7.6 EXERCISES

1. Obtain an EIS for a major transportation project and write a short report summarizing its major contents.
2. Prepare a synopsis of the transportation impacts covered in an EIS for a nontransportation project such as a residential development, an industrial plant, or a commercial center.
3. Present your own arguments for or against governmental actions to improve the mobility of the elderly and handicapped.
4. What is the major difference between the *needs* studies described in this chapter and the urban transportation-planning methodology illustrated by Fig. 7.4.9?
5. How can the methodology of Fig. 7.4.9 be applied to aid in the planning of a statewide system of airports?
6. Prepare a list of the major ways by which the federal government has been involved in planning land transportation.
7. Review the material included in Appendix A and, in your own words, discuss the potential impacts of building a freeway in a large city.
8. In your own words, describe the major consequences of implementing a high-capacity rapid-transit system in a major urban area.
9. Review an article from the technical literature that addresses the topic of TSM.
10. Discuss the major advantages and disadvantages of privately owned highways.

11. Discuss the major advantages and disadvantages of privately owned urban bus systems.
12. Compile a dossier containing clippings from your local newspaper of transportation-related stories over a 2-week period. Arrange this material in an organized way of your choosing.
13. If a major transportation-related decision is pending in your city or state, identify the major groups involved and briefly describe the thrust of their arguments. Distinguish between qualitatively and quantitatively supported claims.
14. What kinds of transportation impacts do you think the construction of a multistory residential building in a densely populated area would possibly have?
15. Prepare a short report describing the zoning ordinances of your city or town.
16. List the various types of planning-related surveys discussed in this chapter.
17. Make a list of alternative strategies that have the potential of alleviating urban-traffic congestion.
18. Briefly compare the various urban-planning schools of thought described in this chapter. What was the basic view that each held with regard to the role of transportation in the urban milieu?
19. What is the purpose of the Highway Trust Fund?
20. Give several specific examples of the way in which technological development has affected the structure of cities.
21. What do you think was the rationale behind placing provisions for federal aid to urban mass-transit systems in housing laws?
22. What were the objectives of the TOPICS program?
23. How can you adapt the methodology of needs study to the planning of a system of parks and playgrounds within a city?
24. Describe how the methodology discussed in Subsection 7.4.5 of this chapter can be adapted to help plan a regional water supply system.
25. What are the major components of travel demand?

7.7 REFERENCES

7.1 Federal Highway Administration, *America's Highways 1776–1976: A History of the Federal-Aid Program,* U.S. Department of Transportation, U.S. Government Printing Office, Stock No. 050-001-00123-3, Washington, D.C., 1976.

7.2 National Transportation Policy Study Commission, *National Transportation Policies through the Year 2000,* Final Report, U.S. Government Printing Office, June 1979.

7.3 Transportation Research Board, *Urban Transportation Alternatives: Evolution of Federal Policy,* Special Report 177, National Research Council, Washington, D.C., 1977.

7.4 Hoffman, H. W., *Sagas of Old Western Travel and Transport,* Howell-North Books, San Diego, Calif. 1980.

7.5 Gray, G. E., and L. A. Hoel, eds., *Public Transportation: Planning, Operations and Management,* Prentice-Hall, Inc., Englewood Cliffs, N.J., 1979.

7.6 Martin, J., *Mule to MARTA,* vols. I and II, Atlanta Historical Society, Atlanta, Ga., 1977.

7.7 Goodman, W. I., and E. C. Freund, *Principles and Practice of Urban Planning,* International City Managers' Association, Washington, D.C., 1968.

7.8 NOLEN, J., ed., *City Planning,* D. Appleton and Company, New York and London, 1929.

7.9 TAYLOR, G. R., *Satellite Cities: A Study of Industrial Suburbs,* D. Appleton and Company, New York and London, 1915.

7.10 HOWARD, E., *Garden Cities of to-morrow,* first published in 1898 as *Tomorrow: a Peaceful Path to Real Reform,* Faber and Faber Limited, London, 1902.

7.11 STEVENS, J. C., A. W. MANER, and T. E. SHELBURNE, "Pavement Performance Correlated with Soil Areas," Proceedings of 29th Annual Meeting, Highway Research Board, National Research Council, Washington, D.C., 1949, pp. 445–466.

7.12 GAMBLE, R. W., and H. F. ILGNER, "Purpose, Analysis and Application, Origin and Destination Survey, Milwaukee Metropolitan Area," Proceedings of the 26th Annual Meeting, Highway Research Board, National Research Council, Washington, D.C., 1946, pp. 404–421.

7.13 MACLACHLAN, K. A., "The Coordinate Method of O and D Analysis," Proceedings of the 29th Annual Meeting, Highway Research Board, National Research Council, Washington, D. C., 1949, pp. 349–367.

7.14 VOORHEES, A. M., and J. W., BOOTH, "Application of O-D Data in the Baltimore Region," *Highway Research Board, Bulletin 224,* National Research Council, Washington, D.C., 1959, pp. 115–123.

7.15 VOORHEES, A. M., and R. MORRIS, "Estimating and Forecasting Travel for Baltimore by Use of a Mathematical Model," *Highway Research Board, Bulletin 224,* National Research Council, Washington, D.C., 1959, pp. 105–114.

7.16 City and County of Honolulu, *General Plan for Urban and Urbanizing Areas,* Planning Department, August 1960.

CHAPTER 8

SEQUENTIAL DEMAND-FORECASTING MODELS

8.1 INTRODUCTION

Chapter 7 explained that the purpose of the travel forecasting phase of the urban transportation-planning process is to perform a conditional prediction of travel demand in order to estimate the likely transportation consequences of several transportation alternatives (including the do-nothing alternative) that are being considered for implementation. This prediction is also conditional on a predicted target-year land-use pattern. The major components of travel behavior were identified as

1. The decision to travel for a given purpose (trip generation);
2. The choice of destination (trip distribution);
3. The choice of travel mode (modal choice);
4. The choice of route or path (network assignment).

Figure 8.1.1 illustrates that travel-demand models can be chained together in a sequence. In this *sequential-demand-modeling* arrangement, the outputs of each step become inputs to the following step, which also takes relevant inputs from the specification of the alternative plan under study and from the land-use and socioeconomic projection phase. Nonsequential model structures are covered briefly in Chapter 9. Figure 8.1.2 is a more elaborate description of the urban transportation-planning process [8.1]. This figure shows the continuing aspect of the planning process and the need for data collection and model calibration as well. The most frequently used models for each of the four steps of the sequential process are covered in this chapter. For each model, the relevant

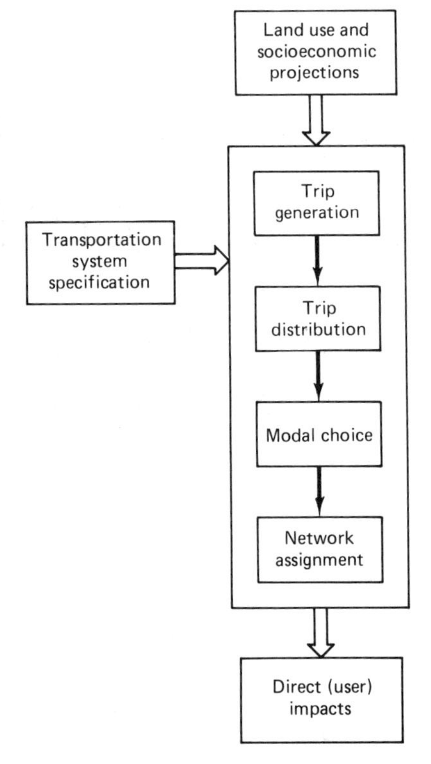

Figure 8.1.1 The sequential forecasting process.

dependent and independent variables are identified, and the method of calibration is described. Additionally, the advantages and disadvantages of each model are discussed. Model selection, of course, should be guided by the rules discussed in Chapter 1 in relation to modeling in general.

8.2 TRIP GENERATION

8.2.1 Background

The objective of a trip-generation model is to forecast the number of person-trips that will begin from or end in each travel analysis zone within the region for a typical day of the target year. Prior to its application, a trip-generation model must be calibrated using observations taken during the base year by means of a variety of travel surveys (see Chapter 7). The total number of person-trips generated constitutes the dependent variable of the model. The independent or explanatory variables include land use and socioeconomic factors that have been shown to bear a relationship with trip making.

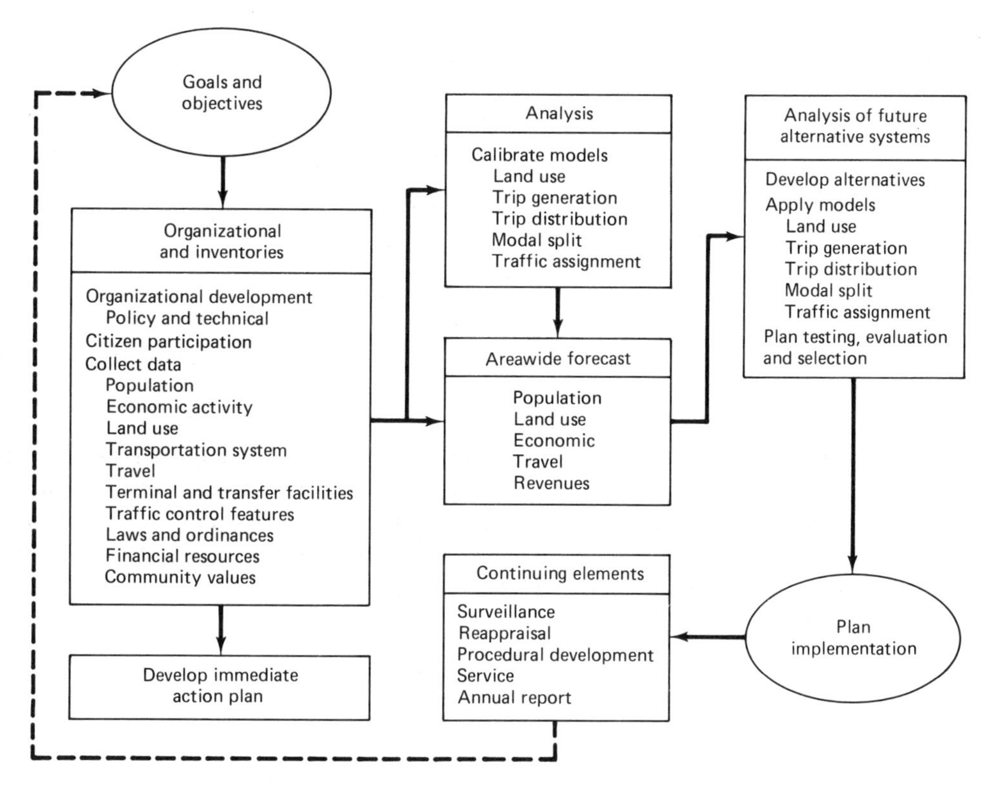

Figure 8.1.2 The continuing urban transportation-planning process. (*SOURCE*: Federal Highway Administration [8.1], Fig. I-1, p. 3.)

When applying a calibrated trip-generation model for predictive purposes, the numerical values of the independent variables must be supplied by the analyst. These values are obtained from the areawide land use and socioeconomic projection phase, which precedes the trip-generation step. As Fig. 8.2.1 illustrates, the output of a trip-generation model consists of the amount of trip making or the *trip ends* Q_I of each zone I within the region.

8.2.2 Trip Purpose

In contemporary transportation planning, the zonal trip making Q_I is estimated separately for each of a number of trip purposes, typically including work trips, school trips, shopping trips, and social or recreational trips. In certain special-context studies, other categories are considered appropriate as well. For example, a study that examined the travel behavior of users of a special service for elderly and handicapped persons in Honolulu, Hawaii, considered travel for medical and rehabilitational purposes to be relevant categories to that analysis [8.2].

The reason separate trip-generation models are usually developed for each trip

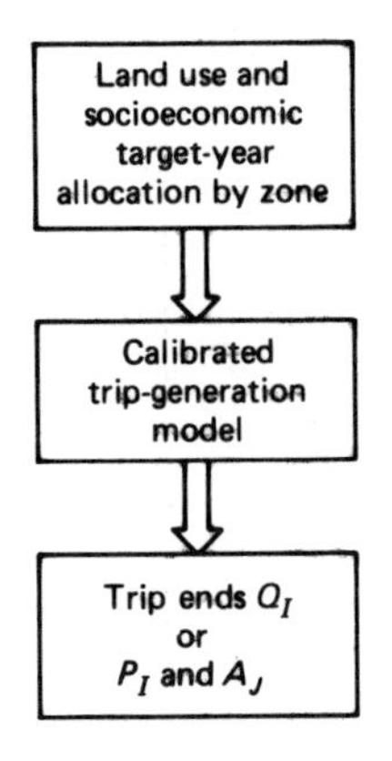

Figure 8.2.1 Trip generation inputs and outputs.

purpose is that the travel behavior of trip makers depends on the trip purpose. For example, work trips are undertaken with daily regularity, mostly during the morning and afternoon period of peak traffic, and overwhelmingly from the same origins to the same destinations. This is also true in the case of school trips. Social and recreational trips, on the other hand, are clearly of a different character. Figure 8.2.2 illustrates that the time-of-day distribution of trips also varies among purposes [8.3].

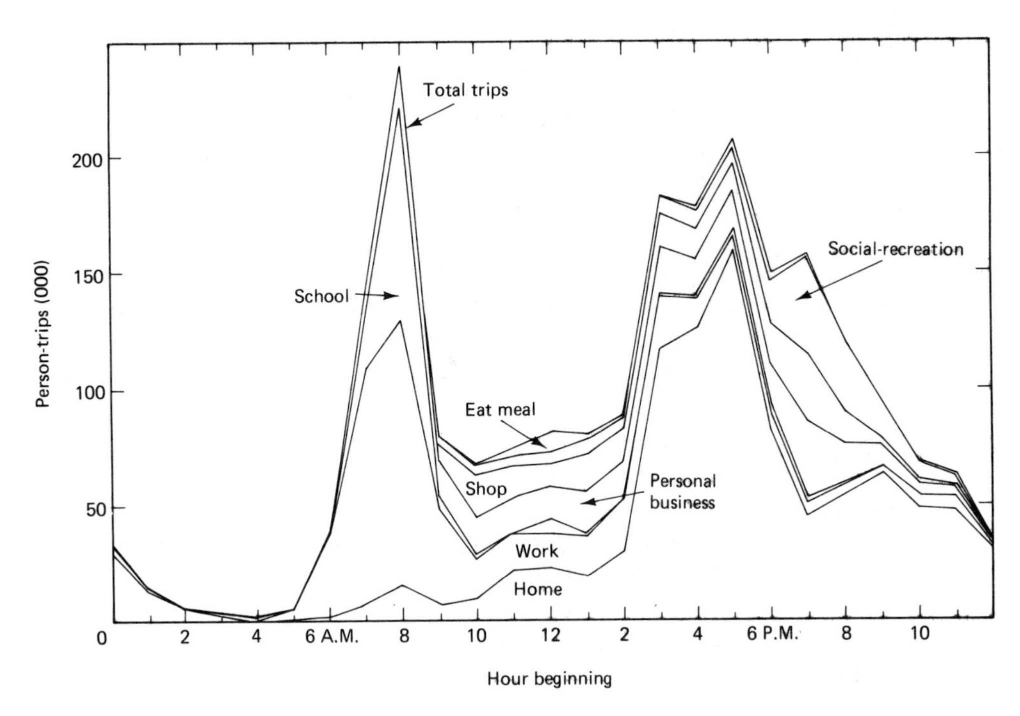

Figure 8.2.2 Hourly distribution of internal person-trips by trip purpose. (*SOURCE*: Keefer [8.3], Fig. 7, p. 16.)

8.2.3 Zonal- versus Household-Based Models

A transportation-planning study cannot possibly trace the travel patterns of every individual residing within a region. As a result, the geographical patterns of trip making are summarized by dividing the region into smaller travel-analysis zones and by associating the estimated trips with these zones. Early models of trip generation considered the zone to be the smallest entity of interest as far as trip making was concerned. Consequently, these models were calibrated on a *zonal basis,* meaning that the overall zonal characteristics were used as independent or explanatory variables. These zonal attributes included variables such as the zonal population, the average zonal income, the average vehicle ownership, and the like. Using zonal averages, however, tends to mask internal (or intrazonal) variability and affects the accuracy of the estimated trip levels. For example, two zones may have the same average income (in the middle income range, for example) but one may be composed of a homogeneous group of households with respect to income, whereas the second may be composed of two heterogeneous groups, one at high and the other at low income. If income is not linearly related to trip generation, a *zone-based* (or *aggregate*) model will not be sensitive to the intrazonal income differences. *Household-based* (or *disaggregate*) models of trip generation are also available.

The rationale of household-based models is that households with similar characteristics tend to have similar travel propensities irrespective of their geographical location within the region. The calibration of household-based models employs a sample of households rather than a sample of zones. These models are known as disaggregate models because they decompose (or disaggregate) each zone into smaller units. However, this disaggregation is not geographical, as households of the various types may be interspersed throughout a zone. Consequently, this decomposition is not necessarily equivalent to delineating smaller zones. In order to arrive at the required estimates of zonal trip generation (thus retaining the spatial characteristics of travel within the region), it is necessary to recombine the contribution of each group of similar households found within the zone into a zonal total. For this reason, the land-use projections that provide the inputs to a trip-generation model must specifically forecast the number of households by type.

8.2.4 Productions and Attractions

The trips that are predicted by a trip-generation model for each zone are often referred to as the trip ends associated with that zone. Trip ends may be classified either as origins and destinations, or as productions and attractions. As used in trip-generation studies, the terms *origin* and *production* on one hand and *destination* and *attraction* on the other are not identical. To understand this difference, consider the two zones I and J of Fig. 8.2.3. Typically, each of these zones will contain residences as well as nonresidential land uses, such as places of business, schools, and commercial establishments. The figure captures this fact by showing a portion of each zone as residential and a portion as nonresidential, even though the two types of activity within each zone may be intermingled. Now consider a single worker whose residence is located in zone I and whose place

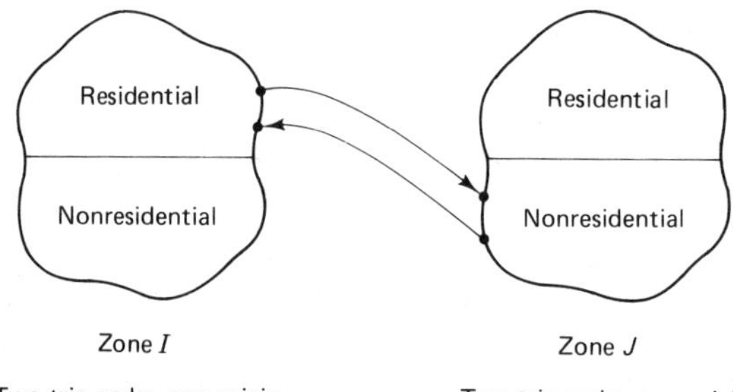

Two trip ends: one origin and one destination, or two productions

Two trip ends: one origin and one destination, or two attractions

Figure 8.2.3 Trip-end definitions.

of employment is in zone J. On a typical workday, this trip-maker will travel from zone I to zone J in the morning and back from zone J to zone I in the evening. In the morning, zone I is the trip-maker's *origin* and zone J is the trip maker's *destination*.

In the evening, zone J becomes the origin and zone I the destination. Thus, origins and destinations are defined in terms of the direction of a given interzonal trip. In this example, each of the two zones experienced two trip ends during the day: one origin and one destination.

The terms *production* and *attraction*, on the other hand, are *not* defined in terms of the directions of trips but in terms of the land use associated with each trip end. A *trip production* is defined as a trip end connected with a residential land use in a zone, and a *trip attraction* is defined as a trip end connected to a nonresidential land use in a zone. On the basis of these definitions, zone I of Fig. 8.2.3 has *produced* two trips, while zone J has *attracted* two trips. This distinction is made because the zonal trip productions can be more easily estimated from the socioeconomic characteristics of the zone's population and the related travel needs of the population for various purposes, whereas the zonal trip attractions depend on the availability and intensity of nonresidential opportunities found within the zone. For example, if a significant portion of the population of a zone consisted of working-age adults, that zone would produce a high number of work trips. On the other hand, if a zone were predominantly nonresidential (a downtown employment zone, for instance), it would be likely to attract many work trips produced by zones that are dispersed throughout the region.

Thus, a typical trip-generation study involves the application of residential trip-production and nonresidential trip-attraction models. The former contain a set of explanatory variables that describe the demographic makeup of the zone's population. The latter rely on a set of explanatory variables that capture the type and intensity of nonresidential activities within the zone. In the general case, each zone I will have a number of productions P_I and a number of attractions A_I.

While the vast majority of the trips occuring within urban areas have a production and an attraction trip end, there are trips for which the definition is not directly applicable, for example, trips that take place between two nonresidential activities, such as a trip from the place of employment to a shopping area. Trips can also be classified as *home-based* or as *non-home-based*. The former category consists of trips that either begin or end at a residence, whereas the latter neither begin nor end at a residence. This leaves a small percentage of trips usually occuring during the noncritical off-peak periods of the day that have both their origins and their destinations in a residence (e.g., a trip to a friend's house). Depending on the prevalence of non-home-based and (to employ an unconventional term) home-to-home trips within the particular region under study and the degree of detail required, special-context studies may be appropriate. The three most common mathematical formulations of trip generation are regression models, trip-rate analysis models, and cross-classification models.

8.2.5 Regression Models

omit

Section 3.5 discussed the underlying theory of least squares regression and classified regression models as linear or nonlinear on one hand and as simple or multiple on the other. All these types of regression models can be employed in connection with trip-generation studies. The selection of the most appropriate form in a particular case is usually based on experience and preliminary investigations into the matter. A frequently used regression model is the linear multiple-regression model, which has the form:

$$Y = a_0 + a_1 X_1 + \cdots + a_r X_r \tag{8.2.1}$$

where Y is the dependent variable, the X's are the relevant independent or explanatory variables, and the a's are the parameters of the model that must be estimated prior to applying the model. In a trip-production multiple-regression model, the dependent variable can estimate either the total trips produced by a zone P_I if it is an aggregate model or the household trip-production rate if it is a household-based model. The independent variables included in a zone-based model are characteristics of the zone as a whole, whereas the independent variables employed by a disaggregate model are household characteristics. The calibration of the former is based on a set of observations for a number of zones, each observation corresponding to a zone; the calibration of a disaggregate model employs a number of base-year observations, each corresponding to an individual household in a sample of households drawn randomly from the region. In the case of multiple-regression models of trip attractiveness, the independent variables consist of nonresidential attributes.

In all cases, each term of the equation can be interpreted as the contribution of the corresponding independent variable to the magnitude of the dependent variable. That is, a unit change in an independent variable is seen to result in a change in the dependent variable, which equals the magnitude of the coefficient of the independent variable. The constant term a_0 captures effects that are not explicitly included in the model.

When calibrating a multiple-regression model, the analyst is faced with the questions of how many and which independent variables to include in the equation. The following rules of thumb provide some guidance in this respect.

Regarding the number of independent variables to be included in a model, practical experience has shown that the law of diminishing returns holds true with respect to accuracy resulting from increasing the number of independent variables. Figure 8.2.4

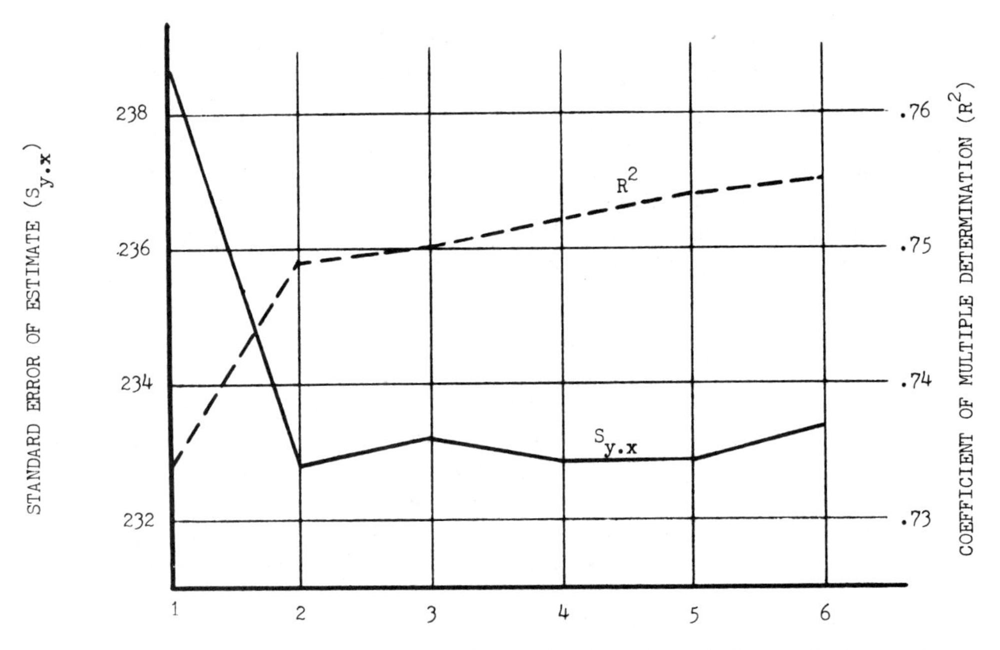

Figure 8.2.4 Graphical representation of the stepwise change in standard error of estimate and coefficient of multiple determination. (*SOURCE*: Federal Highway Administration [8.4], Fig. 13, p. 27.)

illustrates the point by plotting the accuracy obtained by increasingly complex models versus the number of variables employed [8.4]. The figure shows that a point is reached beyond which the extra cost and complexity associated with adding another variable (which includes the need to forecast this variable toward the target year) may not be warranted by the increasingly smaller improvements in accuracy obtained. A maximum of four variables is usually sufficient.

The following four guidelines are helpful in deciding which explanatory variables to include in a model. The selected explanatory variables

1. Must be linearly related to the dependent variable;
2. Must be highly correlated with the independent variable;
3. Must not be highly correlated between themselves;
4. Must lend themselves to relatively easy projection.

The first rule states that the relationship between a selected explanatory variable and the dependent variable must be linear, as required by the mathematical specification of the model. If this is not true, an appropriate transformation of the explanatory variable may be performed as explained in Section 3.5. The second rule states that the explanatory variable must be highly associated with the dependent variable; otherwise it would have no explanatory power. The third rule states that variables that are highly correlated among themselves must not be included in the same equation. If two potential explanatory variables are highly correlated, they essentially measure the same effect or, in other words, they are not independent. If both were to be included in the same equation, double counting would result. Moreover, the resulting equation would not be easy to interpret, as the sensitivity of the dependent variable to a single explanatory variable could not be captured by that variable's coefficient alone. The fourth rule states that the selected explanatory variables must be such that they can be forecast toward the target year with relative ease. The reason that trip-generation models are used in the first place is because it is extremely difficult to project the dependent variable directly. Consequently, the model is calibrated in terms of a set of factors (or independent variables) that explain the dependent variable. Unless these factors are relatively easy to project into the future, the entire effort will prove to be of little value.

By applying these rules, the number of potentially useful alternative specifications of a trip-generation model can be considerably reduced. What remains is to select the best model for this reduced set on the basis of statistical tests for goodness-of-fit and, not to be underestimated, the application of professional judgement to ensure the reasonableness of results [8.1, 8.4].

Example 8.1

The following correlation matrix contains the simple correlation coefficients between pairs of variables that have been computed by Eq. 3.5.15 using base-year data. Discuss the question of which explanatory variables X should be included in a linear multiple-regression model.

	Y	X_1	X_2	X_3	X_4
Y	1.00	0.32	0.92	0.95	0.62
X_1		1.00	0.25	0.19	0.03
X_2			1.00	0.99	0.29
X_3				1.00	0.33
X_4					1.00

Solution Variable X_1 is not highly correlated with the dependent variable Y. Hence, it may be eliminated from further consideration. Although highly correlated with Y, variables X_2 and X_3 are also highly correlated with each other. Therefore they should not appear together in the same equation. Variable X_4 is not highly correlated with either X_1 or X_2. Hence, it can appear in the same equation with either of the two. Based on this discussion, the following alternative linear multiple-regression models may be considered:

1. $Y = a_0 + a_2X_2$
2. $Y = b_0 + b_3X_3$
3. $Y = c_0 + c_4X_4$
4. $Y = d_0 + d_2X_2 + d_4X_4$
5. $Y = e_0 + e_3X_3 + e_4X_4$

Discussion The simple correlation matrix is symmetric, and only the upper or lower half need be specified. The diagonal elements are equal to unity because the correlation between any variable with itself is perfect. The five potential models specified in the solution meet the rules of selection given earlier. Further analysis is required to discover the best among them.

8.2.6 Trip-Rate Analysis

Trip-rate analysis refers to several models that are based on the determination of the average trip production or trip attraction rates associated with the important trip generators within the region. Table 8.2.1, for example, displays the trip-generation rates associated with various land-use categories in downtown Pittsburgh, that were obtained by one of the very first major urban-transportation studies [8.3]. Table 8.2.2, taken from the same source, presents the land-area trip rates in terms of person-trips per acre for several land-use types and locations with respect to the central business district (ring 0). The land-use types include both residential and nonresidential categories, and the location is specified by a series of concentric rings.

The hypothetical trip-attraction rates of Table 8.2.3 are expressed in terms of the number of trips attracted per employee for the case of retail and nonretail land uses and in terms of school trips attracted per student enrolled in each of three types of educational institutions [8.1, 8.5].

TABLE 8.2.1 GOLDEN TRIANGLE FLOOR-SPACE TRIP GENERATION RATES GROUPED BY GENERALIZED LAND-USE CATEGORIES

Land-use category[a]	Square feet (000)	Person trips	Trips per thousand square feet
Residential	2,744	6,574	2.4
Commercial— Retail	6,732	54,833	8.1
Commercial— Services	13,506	70,014	5.2
Commercial— Wholesale	2,599	3,162	1.2
Manufacturing ...	1,392	1,335	1.0
Transportation ...	1,394	5,630	4.0
Public buildings ..	2,977	11,746	3.9
Total[b]	31,344	153,294	...
Average[b]	......	......	4.9

[a]Net floor space as regrouped to match trip end land use categories will not match totals in Table 7.

[b]Includes trips to public open spaces.

SOURCE: Keefer [8.3], Table 9, p. 55.

TABLE 8.2.2 PERSON-TRIPS PER ACRE BY GENERALIZED LAND-USE AND RING

Ring	Resi-dential	Commercial			Manu-facturing	Trans-portation	Public buildings	Public open space	Average	
		Retail	Services	Wholesale					Used land	All land
1	51	340	178	54	141	29	238	2	51	40
2	43	169	103	36	73	10	106	1	30	20
3	37	225	202	46	33	14	150	4	32	22
4	30	268	154	29	29	10	98	2	26	17
5	22	185	146	24	22	5	36	2	17	8
6	18	194	135	19	21	7	19	1	14	5
7	15	152	131	16	14	6	4	1	11	3
Average[a]	24	226	198	31	26	9	46	2	20	9

[a]Includes ring 0.

SOURCE: Keefer [8.3], Table 10, p. 56.

TABLE 8.2.3 EXAMPLE OF PROCEDURE FOR TRIP-ATTRACTION ESTIMATES PERSON-TRIP ATTRACTIONS[a]

Trip purpose	Trips per household	Trips per employee						
			Retail					
		Nonretail	CBD	Shop center	Other	University	High school	Other
Home-based work	—	1.70	1.70	1.70	1.70	—	—	—
Home-based shop	—	—	2.00	9.00	4.00	—	—	—
Home-based school	—	—	—	—	—	0.90	1.60	1.20
Home-based other	0.70	0.60	1.10	4.00	2.30	—	—	—
Nonhome-based[b]	0.30	0.40	1.00	4.60	2.30	—	—	—

[a]Illustration data only—not to be used directly.

[b]Nonhome-based productions and attractions have same rate and are used to allocate to zones and areawide control total developed in the trip production model.

SOURCE: Federal Highway Administration [8.1], Table 10, p. 41.

TABLE 8.2.4 TRAFFIC-GENERATION RATES FOR RESIDENTIAL AREAS

Residential generator	A.M. peak			P.M. peak		
	In	Out	Total	In	Out	Total
Single-family residence subdivision	0.23	0.58	0.81 trips/unit	0.60	0.40	1.00 trips/unit
Multifamily apartments	0.08	0.49	0.57 trips/unit	0.46	0.23	0.69 trips/unit

SOURCE: Institute of Transportation Engineers [8.6], p. 40.

Tables 8.2.4 and 8.2.5 present the trip rates reported by the Institute of Transportation Engineers [8.6] for selected commercial and residential generators. The former are given in terms of trips per 1000 ft^2 of gross floor area (GFA), and the latter are in terms of trips per residential unit. Note that the attraction rates associated with commercial establishments are given for the peak hour of operation for each establishment type and for the traffic peak hour on the adjacent streets. The rates corresponding to residential uses are given directionally for the morning and afternoon peak periods. In the absence of local data, these trip rates can be very useful.

8.2.7 Cross-Classification Models

Cross-classification (or category analysis) models may be thought of as extensions of the simple trip-rate models discussed previously. Although they can be calibrated as area- or zone-based models, in trip-generation studies they are almost exclusively used as disaggregate models. In the residential-generation context, household types are classified according to a set of categories that are highly correlated with trip making. Three to four explanatory variables, each broken into about three discrete levels, are usually sufficient.

The trip rates associated with each type of household are estimated by statistical

TABLE 8.2.5 TRAFFIC GENERATION RATES FOR VARIOUS URBAN COMMERCIAL ACTIVITIES

Commercial generator	Peak hour of operation	P.M. peak street-hour
Drive-in restaurants	257 trips/1,000 ft^2 GFA[a]	108 trips/1,000 ft^2 GFA
Sit-down restaurants	35 trips/1,000 ft^2 GFA	25 trips/1,000 ft^2 GFA
Food stores	14 trips/1,000 ft^2 GFA	12 trips/1,000 ft^2 GFA
Neighborhood shopping centers	15 trips/1,000 ft^2 GFA	14 trips/1,000 ft^2 GFA
Automobile service stations	28 trips/h	23 trips/h
Motels	0.8 trips/unit	0.6 trips/unit
Office buildings	2.3 trips/1,000 ft^2 GFA	2.3 trips/1,000 ft^2 GFA
Hospitals	1.0 trips/bed	0.7 trips/bed

[a]GFA—Gross floor area of building.

SOURCE: Institute of Transportation Engineers [8.6], p. 40.

methods, and these rates are assumed to remain stable over time. Table 8.2.6 presents a cross-classification table that shows the calibrated nonwork home-based trip-production rates for various types of households defined by (1) four levels of household size (i.e., number of persons per household); (2) three levels of car ownership (i.e., vehicles available per household); and (3) three levels of residential density (i.e., dwelling units per acre).

TABLE 8.2.6 EXAMPLE: TOTAL HOME-BASED, NONWORK TRIP RATES

Cross class		Persons/HH[a]			
	Vehicles available/HH area type ↓	1	2,3	4	5+
1 Urban—high density	0	0.57	2.07	4.57	6.95
	1	1.45	3.02	5.52	7.90
	2+	1.82	3.39	5.89	8.27
2 Suburban—medium density	0	0.97	2.54	5.04	7.42
	1	1.92	3.49	5.99	8.37
	2+	2.29	3.86	6.36	8.74
3 Rural—low density	0	0.54	1.94	4.44	6.82
	1	1.32	2.89	5.39	7.77
	2+	1.69	3.26	5.76	8.14

[a]Household

SOURCE: Oahu Metropolitan Planning Organization [8.7], Table 2-7, p. 53.

The documentation of the study that produced this table [8.7] specifies points of demarcation between the levels of density denoted as high (urban), medium (suburban), and low (rural). Each cell of the table contains the calibrated daily trip-production rate per household expressed in terms of person-trips per household per day. Given projections relating to the target-year household composition of a zone, the application of this calibrated model for predictive purposes is straightforward, as the following example illustrates.

Example 8.2: Cross classification

An urban zone contains 200 acres of residential land, 50 acres devoted to commercial uses, and 10 acres of park land. The following table presents the zone's expected household composition at some future (target) year.

Vehicles per household	Persons per household 1	2, 3	4	5
0	100	200	150	20
1	300	500	210	50
2+	150	100	60	0

Using the calibrated cross-classification table of Table 8.2.6, estimate the total nonwork home-based trips that the zone will produce during a typical target-year day. The rates are given as trips per household per day.

Solution The total productions are estimated by summing the contribution of each household type:

$$P_I = \sum_h N_h R_h$$

where N_h and R_h are the number of households of type h and their corresponding production rate. For example, the 300 single-person one-car households contribute (300)(1.45) = 435 nonwork home-based trips per day. Summing over all household types:

$$P_I = 5760 \text{ trips per day}$$

Discussion Only the residential-land-use sector of the zone entered into the solution because trip productions are associated with the residential characteristics of the zone. The commercial and recreational characteristics of the zone would be relevant to the estimation of the attractiveness of the zone for these purposes. In that case, properly calibrated attractiveness models would be required.

8.2.8. The FHWA-Simplified Trip-Production Procedure

Figure 8.2.5 presents a hypothetical example of a residential trip-generation procedure developed by the FHWA [8.1]. This procedure combines several of the concepts discussed in this section. Curve A represents the distribution of households by income and auto

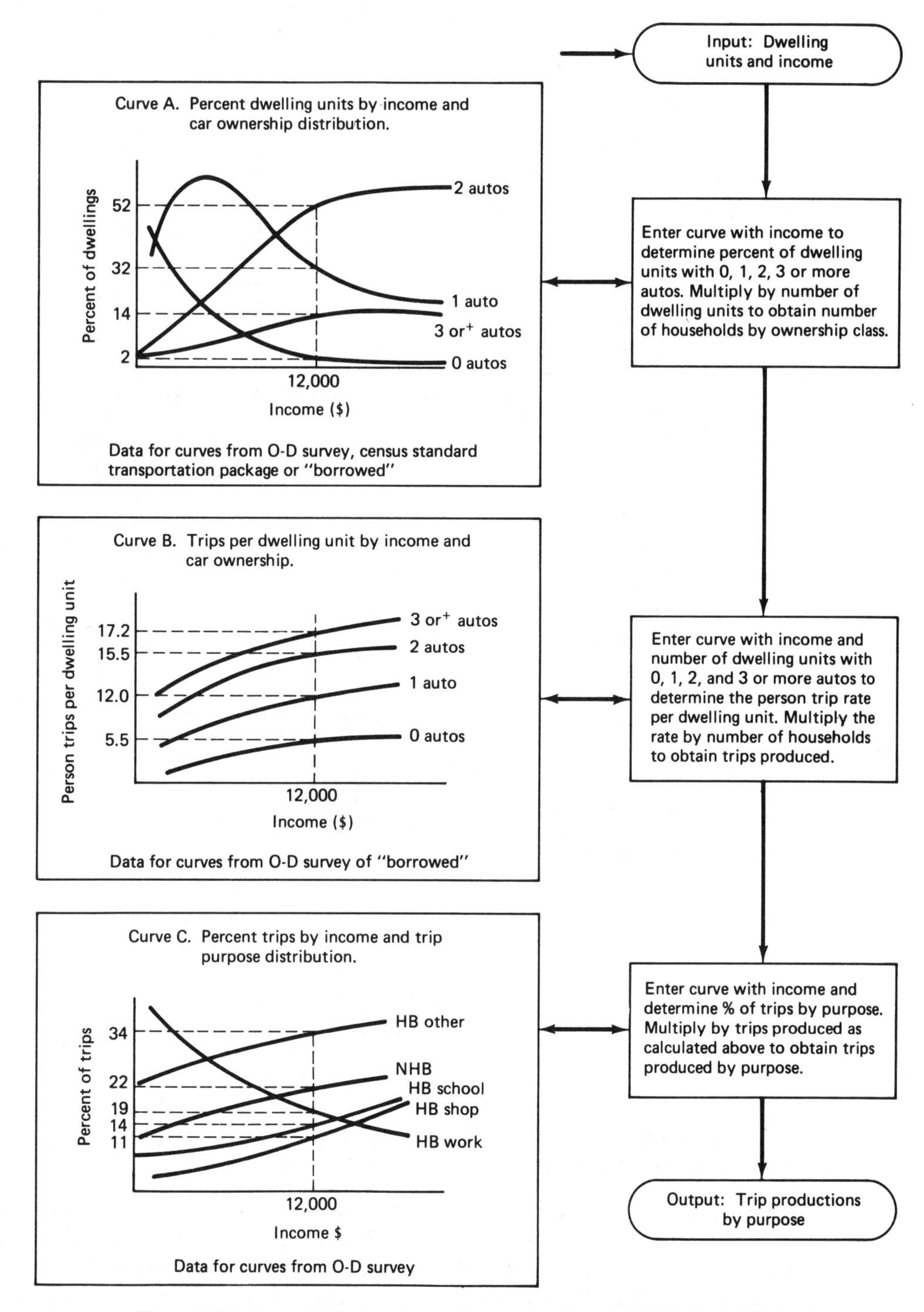

Figure 8.2.5 Example of urban trip-production procedure. (*SOURCE*: Federal Highway Administration [8.1], Fig. 12, p. 45.)

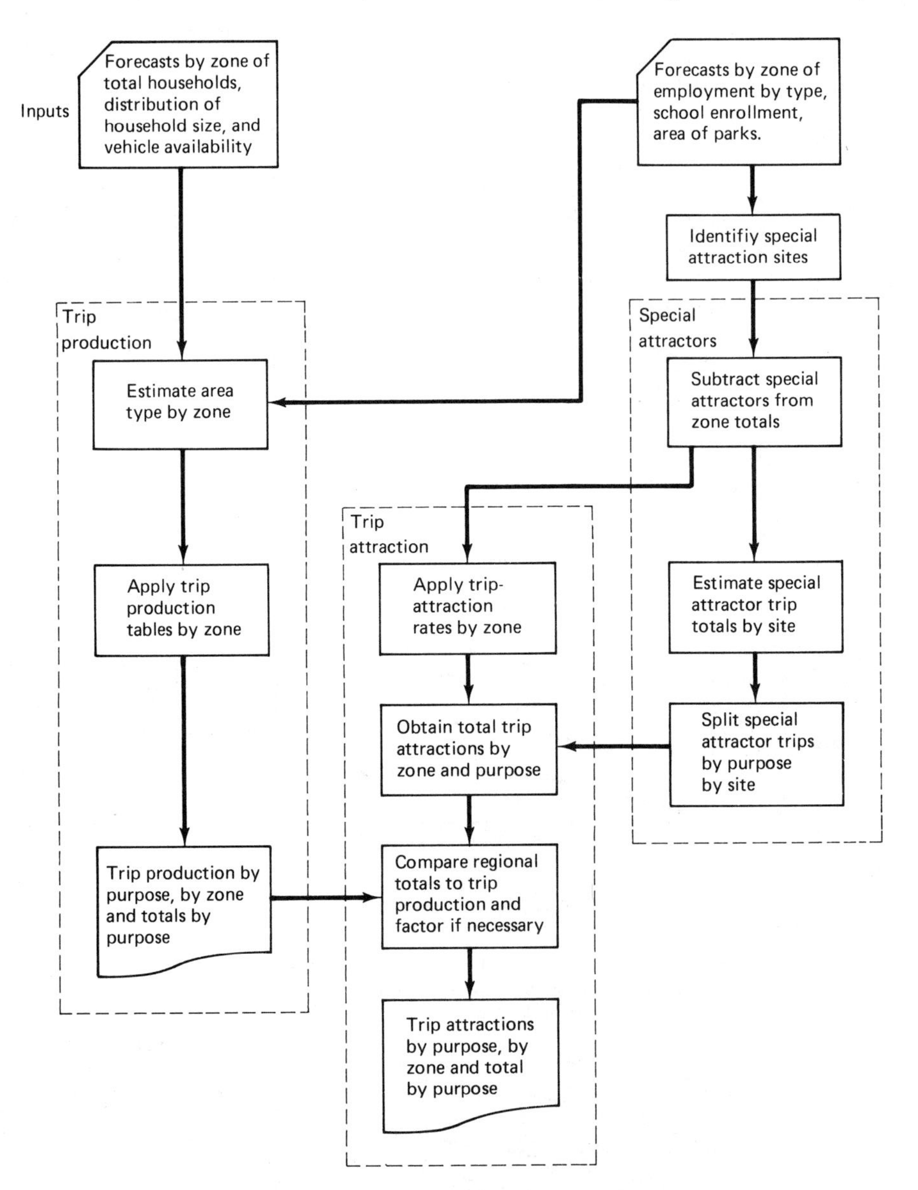

Figure 8.2.6 Application of long-range trip-generation procedure. (*SOURCE*: Oahu Metropolitan Planning Organization [8.7], Fig. 2-1, p. 38.)

ownership. In the example shown, the auto ownership of a group of households with an annual income of $12,000 is distributed as follows: 2% own no autos, 32% own one auto, 52% own two autos, and 14% own three or more autos. Incidentally, depending on the way in which Curve A is calibrated, it may represent a zonal (aggregate) distribution, in which case the income variable would be a zonal average, or it may represent a household-based (disaggregate) distribution, in which case the group of households illustrated may correspond to a subset of all the households in a zone. In the latter case, the percentages obtained can be interpreted as probabilities; for example, the probability that any $12,000 per year household will own two cars is 0.52.

The regression lines of Curve B provide the person-trip rates for household types defined by income and auto ownership, and Curve C divides these trips among several trip purposes. Adherence to the instructions that accompany the figure leads to the target-year estimate of trip productions by purpose.

8.2.9 Summary

The purpose of trip generation is to estimate the target-year trip-ends by travel purpose for each zone within the region. Commonly, these trips are expressed as residential trip productions and nonresidential trip attractions. The most common mathematical forms of trip generation models are multiple-regression equations, trip-rate models, cross-classification models, and their combinations.

Figure 8.2.6 illustrates the trip-generation procedure used to obtain long-range forecasts in a particular urban area [8.7]. This figure shows that two sets of inputs, residential and nonresidential characteristics, were first obtained from zonal socioeconomic and land use projections. The specific variables used are listed among the inputs. Residential projections were used by the trip-production models, which took the form of household-based cross-classification tables to estimate the target-year zonal trip productions by purpose. The nonresidential land-use projections were used primarily in relation to the trip-attraction model, which was of the form of multiple regression. Several special attractors, including airports, major shopping centers, and universities, have been given special treatment because of their unique trip-attraction characteristics. The final outputs were the zonal productions and attractions by trip purpose.

8.3 TRIP DISTRIBUTION

8.3.1 Background

The next step in the sequential forecasting model system is concerned with the estimation of the target-year trip volumes Q_{IJ} that interchange between all pairs of zones I and J, where I is the trip-producing zone and J is the trip-attracting zone of the pair. The rationale of trip distribution is as follows: all trip-attracting zones J in the region are in competition with each other to attract trips produced by each zone I. Everything else being equal, more trips will be attracted by zones that have higher levels of "attractiveness." However, other intervening factors affect the choice of J as well. Consider, for example, the case of two identical shopping centers (i.e., of equal attractiveness) competing for the shopping trips produced by a given zone I. If the distances between zone I and each of the two centers are different, shoppers residing in zone I will show a preference for the closer of the two identical centers. Thus, the intervening difficulty of travel between the producing zone I and each of the competing zones J has a definite effect on the choice of attraction zone. In the shopping center example, distance is cited as a measure of this difficulty of travel, but other measures of this effect may be used, such as travel time or some generalized cost that includes travel time, out-of-pocket cost, and the like. The notation W_{IJ} is used for this generalized cost which is also known as travel *impedance,* or *disutility*. When applying a specific model for predictive purposes, care must be exercised to use the same measure of impedance that was employed to calibrate the model.

Figure 8.3.1 conceptually illustrates that a trip-distribution model estimates the interzonal person-trip volumes Q_{IJ} based on the productions of each zone I, the attractiveness of zone J, and the interzonal impedance W_{IJ}. The production and attraction inputs are obtained from the preceding trip-generation phase, and estimates of the target-year interzonal impedances are obtained from the specification of the alternative transportation plan under investigation.

The most common mathematical formulations of trip distribution include various growth factor models, the gravity model, and a number of *opportunities* models. The following sections discuss the gravity model and one growth factor model (the Fratar model).

8.3.2 The Gravity Model

The gravity model gets its name from the fact that it is conceptually based on Newton's law of gravitation, which states that the force of attraction between two bodies is directly proportional to the product of the masses of the two bodies and inversely proportional to the square of the distance between them, or:

$$F = k\frac{M_1M_2}{r^2} \tag{8.3.1}$$

Variations of this formula have been applied to many situations involving human interaction. For example, the volume of long-distance telephone calls between cities may be modeled in this manner, with the population sizes of the cities replacing the masses

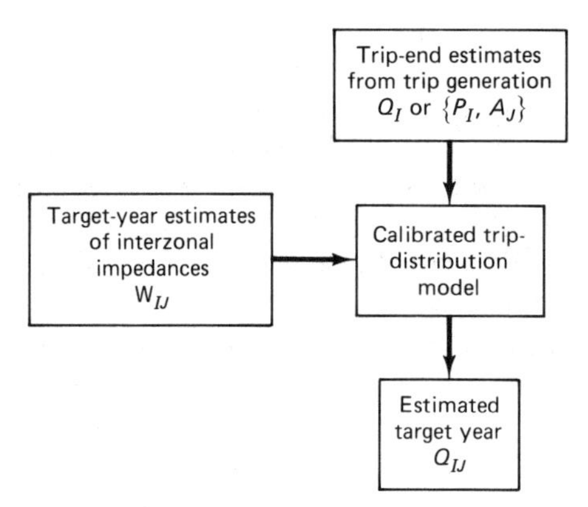

Figure 8.3.1 Trip-distribution inputs and outputs.

of particles and the distance between cities or the cost of telephone calls taking the place of r. The exponent of the impedance term in the denominator, however, need not be exactly equal to 2 but may be replaced by a model parameter c.

The application of this concept to trip distribution takes the form:

$$Q_{IJ} = k \frac{P_I A_J}{W_{IJ}^c} \tag{8.3.2}$$

Equation 8.3.2 states that the interchange volume between a trip-producing zone I and a trip-attracting zone J is directly proportional to the magnitude of the trip productions of zone I and the trip-attractiveness of zone J and is inversely proportional to a function of the impedance W_{IJ} between the two zones.

Using the usual mathematical modeling terminology, the interzonal volume is the dependent variable; the productions, attractions, and impedances are the independent variables; and the constants k and c are the parameters of the model that must be estimated through calibration using base-year data.

The parameter k can be eliminated from Eq. 8.3.2 by applying the *trip-production balance* constraint, which states that the sum over all trip-attracting zones J of the interchange volumes that share I as the trip-producing zone must equal the total productions of zone I, or:

$$P_I = \sum_x Q_{Ix} \tag{8.3.3}$$

Equation 8.3.3 ensures that the model will distribute to the competing zones J exactly as many trips as are produced by zone I.

Substituting Eq. 8.3.2 into Eq. 8.3.3 and taking the terms not involving the index x outside the summation,

$$P_I = kP_I \sum_x \frac{A_x}{W_{Ix}^c} \tag{8.3.4}$$

Solving for k,

$$k = \left[\sum_x \frac{A_x}{W_{Ix}^c} \right]^{-1} \tag{8.3.5}$$

which is the expression for k that ensures that the trip balance Eq. 8.3.3 is satisfied.

Substituting Eq. 8.3.5 into Eq. 8.3.2 leads to the classical form of the gravity model:

$$Q_{IJ} = P_I \left[\frac{A_J/W_{IJ}^c}{\sum_x (A_x/W_{Ix}^c)} \right] \tag{8.3.6}$$

The bracketed term is the proportion of the trips produced by zone I that will be attracted by zone J in competition with all trip-attracting zones x. Note that the numerical value of this fraction would not be affected if all attraction terms were multiplied by a constant. This implies that the attraction terms can measure the relative attractiveness of zones. For example, one employment zone may be said to be twice as attractive as another, for instance, based on the number of employment opportunities available. In this context, the estimated target-year trip attractions of a zone J (denoted by A_J^* to distinguish them from the relative attractiveness term used earlier) may be computed by applying the following *trip-attraction balance* equation to the results of the model:

$$A_J^* = \sum_x Q_{xJ} \tag{8.3.7}$$

The gravity formula is often written alternately as

$$Q_{IJ} = P_I \left(\frac{A_J F_{IJ}}{\sum_x A_x F_{Ix}} \right) \tag{8.3.8}$$

where

$$F_{IJ} = \frac{1}{W_{IJ}^c} \tag{8.3.9}$$

is known as the *travel-time* (or *friction*) *factor*. Note that the calibration constant c is now implicit in the friction factor.

Finally, a set of interzonal *socioeconomic adjustment factors* K_{IJ} are introduced during calibration to incorporate effects that are not captured by the limited number of independent variables included in the model. The resulting gravity formula becomes

$$Q_{IJ} = P_I \frac{A_J F_{IJ} K_{IJ}}{\sum_J A_J F_{IJ} K_{IJ}} = P_I p_{IJ} \tag{8.3.10}$$

where p_{IJ} is the probability that a trip generated by zone I will be attracted by zone J.

Example 8.3: Application of the Gravity Model

The target-year productions and relative attractiveness of the four-zone city have been estimated to be as follows:

Zone	Productions	Attractiveness
1	1500	0
2	0	3
3	2600	2
4	0	5

The calibration of the gravity model for this city estimated the parameter c to be 2.0 and all socioeconomic adjustment factors to be equal to unity. Apply the gravity model to estimate all target interchanges Q_{IJ} and to estimate the total target-year attractions of each zone given that the target-year interzonal impedances W_{IJ} will be as follows.

$I \backslash J$	1	2	3	4
1	5	10	15	20
2	10	5	10	15
3	15	10	5	10
4	20	15	10	5

Solution The gravity model calculations of the interchange volumes are shown in tabular form for the two trip-producing zones ($I = 1$ and $I = 3$).

For $I = 1$, $P_1 = 1500$:

J	A_J	F_{1J}	K_{1J}	$A_J F_{1J} K_{1J}$	p_{1J}	Q_{1J}
1	0	0.0400	1.0	0	0	0
2	3	0.0100	1.0	0.0300	0.584	875
3	2	0.0044	1.0	0.0089	0.173	260
4	5	0.0025	1.0	0.0125	0.243	365
				0.0514	1.000	1500 = P_1

For $I = 3$, $P_3 = 2600$:

J	A_J	F_{3J}	K_{3J}	$A_J F_{3J} K_{3J}$	p_{3J}	Q_{3J}
1	0	0.0044	1.0	0.0	0	0
2	3	0.0100	1.0	0.03	0.188	488
3	2	0.0400	1.0	0.08	0.500	1300
4	5	0.0100	1.0	0.05	0.312	812
				0.16	1.000	2600 = P_3

To find the total target-year trip attractions of the nonresidential zones ($J = 2$, $J = 3$, and $J = 4$), apply the trip-attraction balance (Eq. 8.3.7) to get:

$$A^*_2 = 875 + 488 = 1363$$

$$A^*_3 = 260 + 1300 = 1560$$

$$A^*_4 = 365 + 812 = 1177$$

The solution is summarized by the following *trip table:*

$I \backslash J$	1	2	3	4	
1	0	875	260	365	1500
2	0	0	0	0	0
3	0	488	1300	812	2600
4	0	0	0	0	0
	0	1363	1560	1177	4100

Discussion The trip-generation data indicate that there are three types of zones in this city: Zone 1 is purely residential since it is shown to have productions only, zones 2 and 4 are purely nonresidential because they produce no trips, and zone 3 is a mixed land-use zone because it has both productions and attractions. The impedance matrix represents an estimate of interzonal impedances for the target year. The diagonal elements of this matrix represent intrazonal impedances, that is, the impedances associated with trips that begin *and* end within each zone. It is possible, of course, that trips produced by the mixed-land-use zone 3 to be attracted by the nonresidential sector of the same zone. The sum of each row of the trip table produces the total productions of the corresponding zone I, whereas the sum of each column represents the total attractions of each zone J. Again note that the purely residential zone has no attractions and the purely nonresidential zones have no productions. The mixed zone has both.

Example 8.4: The Generation-Distribution Chain

You are a planning consultant to a trading firm that is considering the construction of a major shopping center in the city of Trinity. At present, the city consists of three residential zones and the central business district (CBD), where all shopping activity is concentrated. Your clients can acquire land for the proposed center at the location shown and are interested in your prediction of the patronage that the center will attract if built to compete with the CBD.

The following data have been made available to you:

1. Daily shopping trip production (*trips per person*):

$X_1 \backslash X_2$	0	1	2	$X_1 \backslash X_2$	0	1	2
≤ 2	0.2	0.3	0.4	≤ 2	0.3	0.4	0.5
3	0.1	0.2	0.3	3	0.2	0.2	0.4
≥ 4	0.1	0.2	0.3	≥ 4	0.2	0.2	0.5
		X_3 = I				X_3 = II	

where

X_1 = household size (persons/household)

X_2 = auto ownership (cars/household)

X_3 = household income level (I or II)

2. Relative shopping attractiveness:

The relative shopping attractiveness of commercial zones has been found to be given by the following multiple regression equation:

$$A = 5\,X_a + 3\,X_b$$

where

X_a = area of shopping floor space provided (acres)

X_b = available parking area (acres)

3. Land-use and socioeconomic projections:

Zone	Residential zones: X_1	X_2	X_3	Number of households Base year	Target year
1	2	0	I	300	500
	2	1	I	300	400
	3	1	I	200	300
	2	2	II	0	50
2	2	1	I	400	500
	2	1	II	300	200
	3	2	I	200	300
	3	0	I	100	400
3	1	1	II	200	200
	2	2	II	300	400
	3	2	II	400	300
	4	2	II	200	400

Commercial zones:

Zone	Base year X_a	Base year X_b	Target year X_a	Target year X_b
4 (CBD)	3.0	2.0	3.0	2.5
5	0.0	0.0	2.0	3.0

4. Gravity model parameters:

(a)

$$\ln F = -\ln W$$

where

$$W = \text{interzonal impedance in minutes}$$

(See the accompanying figure.)

(b) K_{IJ}

$I \backslash J$	4 (CBD)	5 (center)
1	1.0	0.9
2	0.9	1.2
3	1.0	1.0

You are asked to calculate all target-year interchange volumes and the target-year patronage of the two commercial zones.

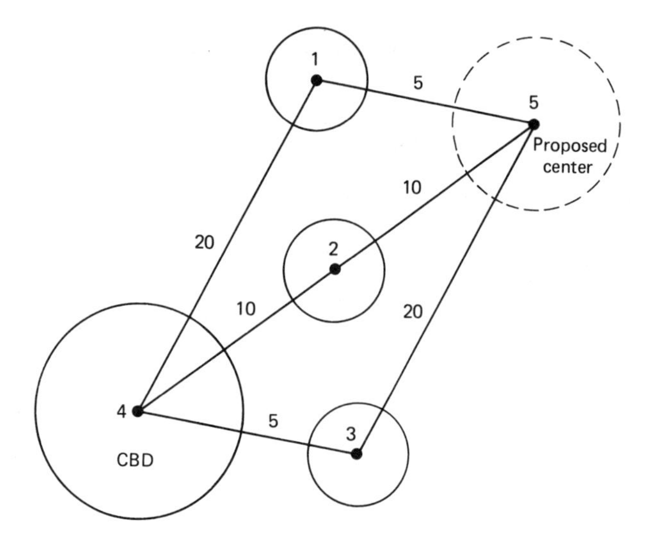

Figure P.8.4

Solution First, apply the calibrated trip-generated models and the available land-use and socioeconomic projections to find the target-year productions and relative attractiveness of the five zones. The shopping-trip-production model is a disaggregated cross-classification model. Considering the units of the calibrated production rate, the contribution of each household type to the total zonal productions is

(number of households)(household size)(trips per person)

Hence, for each of the trip-producing zones:

Zone 1	Zone 2	Zone 3
$500 \times 2 \times 0.2 = 200$	$500 \times 2 \times 0.3 = 300$	$200 \times 1 \times 0.4 = 80$
$400 \times 2 \times 0.3 = 240$	$200 \times 2 \times 0.4 = 160$	$400 \times 2 \times 0.5 = 400$
$300 \times 3 \times 0.2 = 180$	$300 \times 3 \times 0.3 = 270$	$300 \times 3 \times 0.4 = 360$
$50 \times 2 \times 0.5 = \underline{50}$	$400 \times 3 \times 0.1 = \underline{120}$	$400 \times 4 \times 0.5 = \underline{800}$
$P_1 = 670$	$P_2 = 850$	$P_3 = 1640$

The target-year attractiveness of the two competing commercial zones is calculated via the calibrated trip-attractiveness equation and the relevant land-use projections, as follows:

$$A_4 = 5 \times 3 + 3 \times 2.5 = 22.5$$

$$A_5 = 5 \times 2 + 3 \times 3.0 = 19.0$$

The target-year interchange volumes are computed using the gravity model with the given $c = 1$ and the given K_{IJ} factors. Proceeding as in Example 8.3, the following trip table results:

$I \backslash J$	4 (CBD)	5 (center)	P_I
1	166	504	670
2	400	450	850
3	1354	286	1640
A^*_J	1920	1240	

Thus 1240 of the estimated 3160 daily shopping trips (or 39% of the total) will be attracted by the proposed shopping center if built.

Discussion This example illustrates the application of the demand-forecasting models discussed so far and shows how the steps of the sequential forecasting procedure are chained together. The prerequisite selection and calibration of the given models had already been carried out using base-year data. Also, the target-year land-use and socioeconomic projections are given.

The production model is of the cross-classification type, and the production rates are given as trips per person. This is reflected in the calculations where this rate multiplies the total number of persons belonging to each socioeconomic category. The attraction model is a zonal (aggregate) multiple-regression equation using shopping floor space and parking availability as the determinants of attractiveness. The dependent variable is relative attractiveness and not trip attractions.

The gravity model of trip distribution incorporates the effect of interzonal impedance, which is clearly seen in the results. Since the productions and attractions are defined irrespective of direction, the actual patronage of the two centers will be half the attractions just calculated. Note, however, that the same result would be obtained by using half the productions of each zone in the gravity model.

8.3.3 Calibration of the Gravity Model

The calibration of the gravity model in the form of Eq. 8.3.6 involves the determination of the numerical value of the parameter c that fixes the model to the one that reproduces the base-year observations. Equation 8.3.8 is simply another way of expressing Eq. 8.4.6 by substituting Eq. 8.3.9 in the latter. Hence, knowledge of the proper value of c fixes the relationship between the travel-time factor and the interzonal impedance.

Unlike the calibration of a simple linear-regression model where the parameters can be solved for by a relatively easy minimization of the sum of squared deviations (see Section 3.5), the calibration of the gravity formula is accomplished through an iterative procedure: An initial value of c is assumed and Eq. 8.3.6 is applied using the known base-year productions, attractions, and impedances to compute the interzonal volumes Q_{IJ}. These results are then compared with those observed during the base year. If the computed volumes are sufficiently close to the observed volumes, the current value of c is retained as the calibrated value. Otherwise, an adjustment to c is made and the procedure is continued until an acceptable degree of convergence is reached. Most commonly, the friction-factor function F rather than the parameter c is used in the calibration procedure. In that case, Eq. 8.3.8 is employed in the place of Eq. 8.3.6.

The results of calibration are then expressed in terms of the appropriate equation relating the friction factor and the interzonal impedance. Example 8.5 illustrates this procedure and clarifies the role of the socioeconomic adjustment factors K_{IJ} as well [8.5].

The comparison between the computed and the observed values of Q_{IJ} is accomplished by using the *trip-length frequency distribution*. This distribution consists of a plot of the percentages of the regionwide trips versus their interzonal impedance and has the general shape illustrated by Fig. 8.3.2: The frequency of trips eventually decreases with increasing impedance, as should be expected [8.8].

The base-year trip-length frequency distribution may be compared with that resulting from applying the model during each iteration of the calibration procedure until the latter sufficiently conforms to the former. The following example illustrates the major thrust of the gravity-model calibration procedure (Fig. 8.3.3).

Example 8.5: Calibration of the Gravity Model

Consider the five-zone city shown by Fig. 8.3.4(a). Two of the zones are purely residential, and the remaining three are purely nonresidential. The base-year interzonal impedances are specified in terms of travel time in minutes and are shown in parentheses on the arcs joining

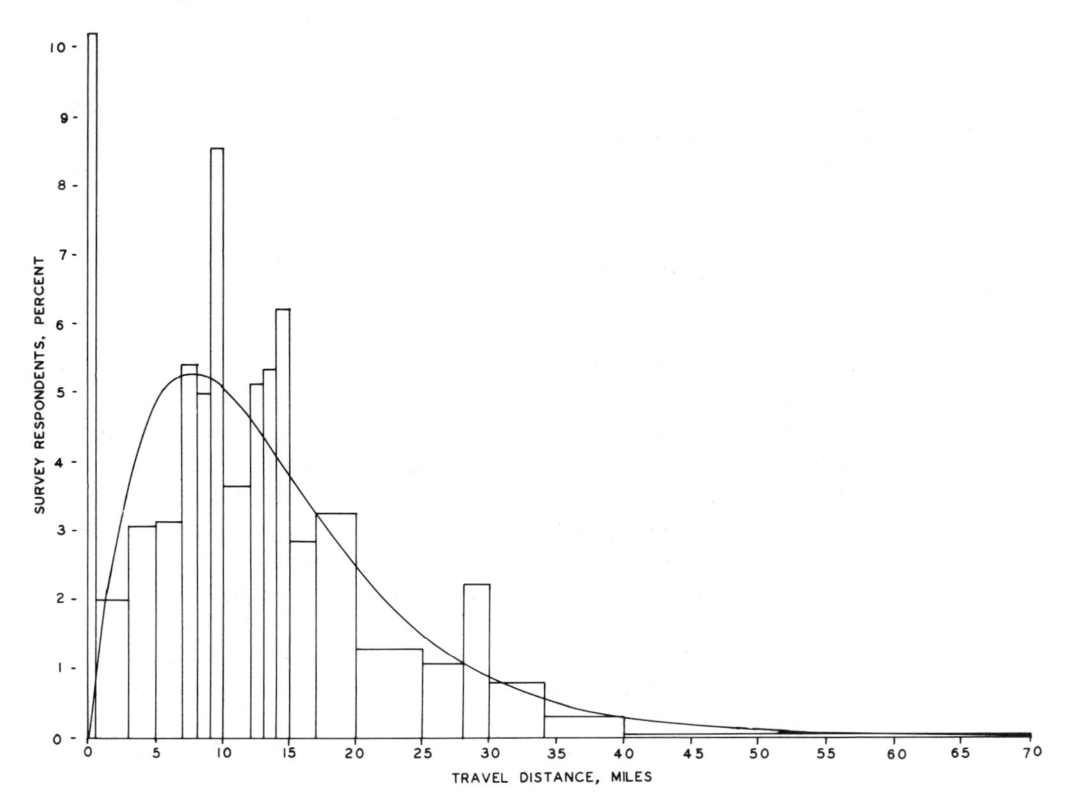

Figure 8.3.2 Frequency distribution in a work-trip survey by reported trip purpose. (*SOURCE*: Bock [8.8], Fig. 14, p. 41.)

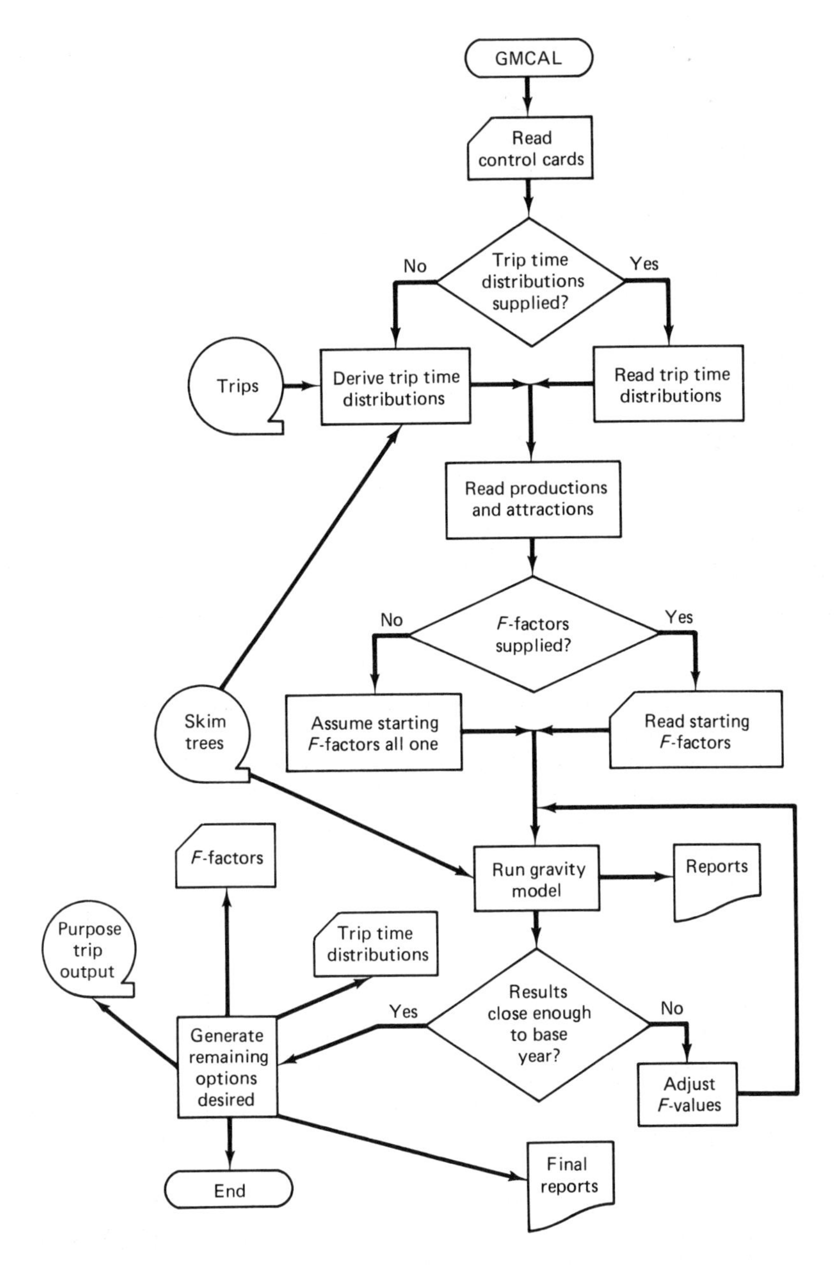

Figure 8.3.3 Gravity model calibration procedure. (*SOURCE*: Federal Highway Administration [8.5], Fig. V-27, p. 133.)

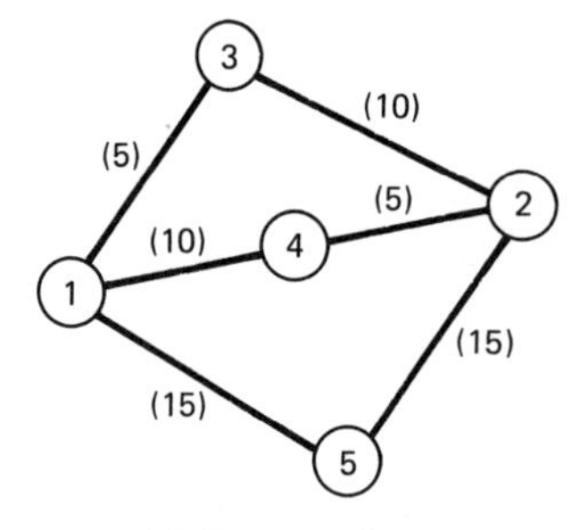

(a) Five-zone city

Zone I	P_I	A_I
1	500	0
2	1000	0
3	0	2
4	0	3
5	0	5

(b) Base-year generation

I \ J	3	4	5
1	300	150	50
2	180	600	220

(c) Base-year distribution

Figure 8.3.4 Base-year data for example 8.5.

pairs of zones. The observed base-year productions, attractiveness, and trip-interchange volumes are inserted in the figure. It is required to find the value of c and the values of K_{IJ} that cause Eq. 8.3.8 to reproduce the observed base-year data.

By taking the natural logarithm of both sides, Eq. 8.3.9 may be rewritten as:

$$\ln F = -c \ln W \tag{8.3.11}$$

In other words, the negative of the parameter c is the slope of a straight line relating the logarithmic transformations of the friction factor and the interzonal impedance.

Frequency computation:

W	ΣQ_{IJ}	f = (2)/sum
5	300 + 600 = 900	0.60
10	150 + 180 = 330	0.22
15	50 + 220 = 270	0.18
	Sum = 1500	1.00

(a) Frequency calculation

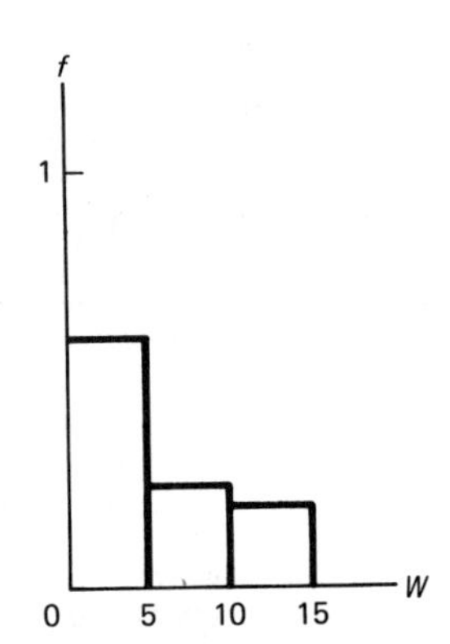

(b) Base-year trip length frequency distribution

Figure 8.3.5 Trip length-frequency distribution.

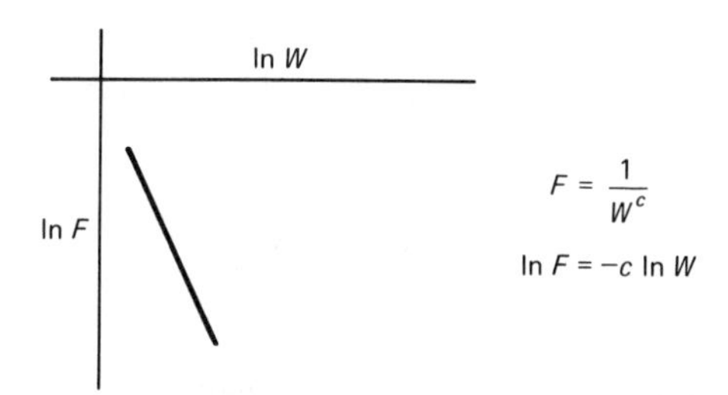

Figure 8.3.6 ln F versus ln W for $c = 2$.

Figure 8.3.5 plots the base-year trip-length frequency distribution using the base-year observations. Impedance is shown in 5-min increments, and the ordinate represents the percent of total trips that travel at the corresponding impedance level.

The calibration procedure begins by assuming an initial estimate for c, say 2.0. This assumption is reflected in the plot of Eq. 8.3.11 shown by Figure 8.3.6, which plots the initially assumed relationship between F and W.

Application of the gravity formula using the assumed value of c leads to the interzonal volume estimates shown in Fig. 8.3.7 along with the *calculated* trip-length frequency distribution superposed on the *observed* trip-length frequency distribution to illustrate the discrepancy between the two. The assumption that $c = 2.0$ is seen to overestimate the percentage of trips at low impedances and to underestimate the percentage at the high impedance

I \ J	3	4	5
1	303	114	83
2	123	741	136

W	ΣQ_{IJ}	f
5	1044	0.70
10	237	0.16
15	219	0.14

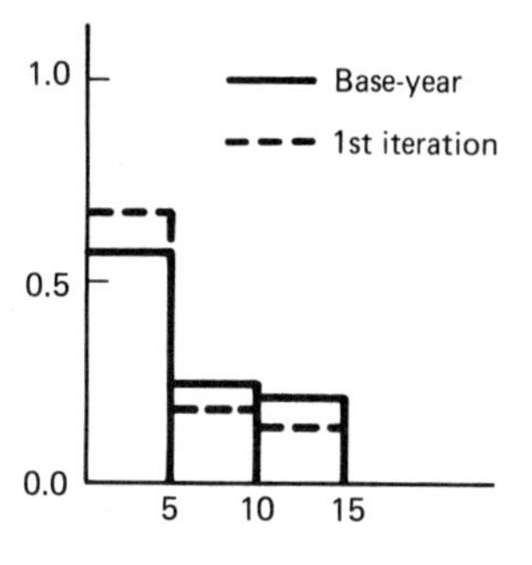

(a) First iteration ($c = 2$)

I \ J	3	4	5
1	251	145	104
2	176	654	170

W	ΣQ_{IJ}	f
5	905	0.60
10	321	0.21
15	274	0.19

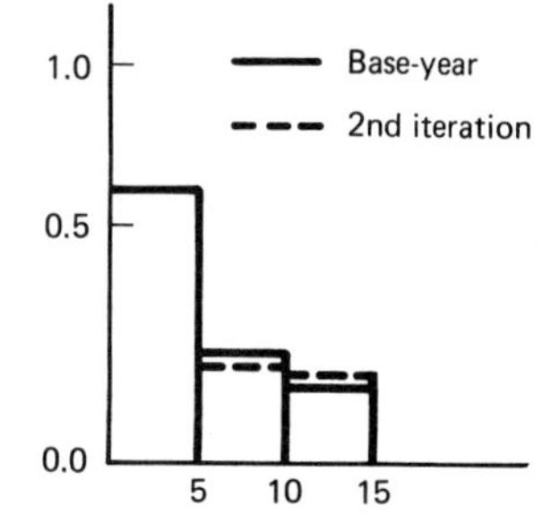

(b) Second iteration (F_{IJ} from Eq. 8.3.12)

Figure 8.3.7 Results of first two iterations.

end. To rectify this situation, the F-factors are adjusted to cause a shift of the calculated distribution toward the observed distribution. A commonly used formula for this adjustment is

$$F^* = F \frac{\text{observed}}{\text{calculated}} \tag{8.3.12}$$

where

F^* = the adjusted friction factor at a given impedance

observed = the corresponding base-year percentage of trips

calculated = the current estimate of the percentage of trips at that impedance level

For example, the assumed friction factor corresponding to an impedance level of 5 min is equal to 5^{-2}, or 0.04. After the first iteration, the adjusted factor becomes

$$F^*_5 = 0.04 \left(\frac{0.6}{0.7}\right) = 0.034$$

The adjusted friction factors obtained in this manner are plotted against the interzonal impedances on Fig. 8.3.8. If a single value of c were desired, simple linear regression could be used to fit the best-fitting straight line through this scatter diagram. However, at this point it becomes clear that the friction factor function need not be linear; it could be allowed to take the form that best describes the scatter diagram. The following general function relating F and W has been suggested by the FHWA [8.5].

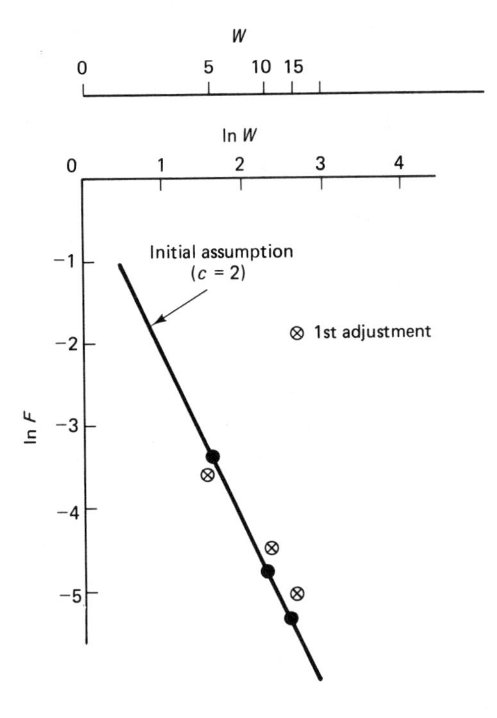

Figure 8.3.8 Friction factor adjustment.

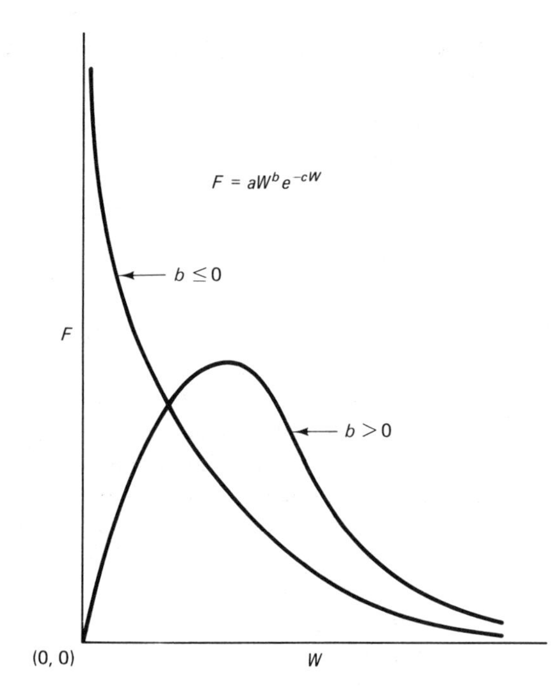

Figure 8.3.9 Shapes assumed by the F-factor. (*SOURCE*: Federal Highway Administration [8.5], Fig. V-26, p. 132.)

$$F = aW^b e^{-cW} \tag{8.3.13}$$

where e is the base of natural logarithms and a, b, and c are calibration constants. Figure 8.3.9 shows the range of shapes that this smoothing function can yield depending on the magnitude of parameter b. The adjusted friction factor function is used in the next iteration and the calibration procedure continues until the computed distribution is sufficiently close to the observed distribution. The friction-factor function used last provides the desired calibration parameters.

Figure 8.3.7 also includes the results of the second iteration of the simple example being described. For simplicity, the new friction factors were applied directly, as computed by Eq. 8.3.12. The new trip-length frequency distribution is now closer to the observed base-year distribution.

Even though the regional trip-length frequency distribution is now close to the observed distribution, certain pronounced discrepancies remain at the interchange level. To adjust for these, the calibration procedure fine tunes the model by introducing a set of *zone-to-zone* socioeconomic adjustment factors

$$K_{IJ} = R_{IJ} \frac{1 - X_I}{1 - X_I R_{IJ}} \tag{8.3.14}$$

where

R_{IJ} = the ratio of observed to calculated Q_{IJ}

X_I = the ratio of the base-year Q_{IJ} to P_I, the total productions of zone I

The following values of K_{IJ} would result if Eq. 8.3.14 were applied at the end of the second iteration of the example problem:

$I \backslash J$	3	4	5
1	1.7	1.0	0.5
2	1.0	0.8	1.4

8.3.4. The Fratar Model

Several naive trend or simple growth-factor models have also been developed for use in special situations. Among these, the Fratar model [8.9] is often used to estimate *external* trips, that is, trips that are either produced and/or are attracted outside the boundaries of the region under study from outlying areas whose character is not explicitly analyzed.

The Fratar model begins with the base-year trip-interchange data as illustrated by Fig. 8.3.10(a). Usually, this model does not distinguish between productions and attractions and considers the interzonal trips irrespective of their direction. Consequently, the values shown represent the total interchange volumes between two zones, and $Q_{IJ} = Q_{JI}$. Since no distinction is made between productions and attractions, the trip generation of each zone is denoted by Q_I; the following trip balance equation provides the necessary relationship between the trip generation of a zone I and the trip interchanges that involve zone I:

$$Q_I = \sum_x Q_{Ix} \tag{8.3.15}$$

The estimate of the target-year trip generation $Q_I(t)$, which precedes the trip-distribution phase, is computed by multiplying the base-year trip generation, $Q_I(b)$, by

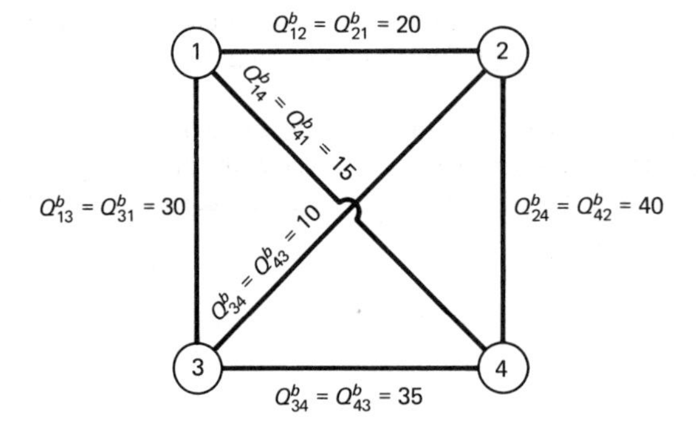

(a) Base-year trip-interchange data

Zone I	G_I
1	2
2	2
3	3
4	1

(b) Estimated growth factors

Figure 8.3.10 Fratar model inputs.

a simple *growth factor,* G_I. This growth factor is based on the anticipated land-use changes that are expected to occur within the zone between the base year and the target year. Thus:

$$Q_I(t) = G_I[Q_I(b)] \tag{8.3.16}$$

Subsequently, the Fratar model estimates the target-year trip distribution $Q_{IJ}(t)$ that satisfies the trip balance (Eq. 8.3.15) for that year. Mathematically, the model consists of successive approximations and a test of convergence in an iterative procedure. During each iteration, the target-year trip-interchange volumes are computed based on the anticipated growth of the two zones at either end of each interchange. The implied *estimated* target-year trip generation of each zone is then computed according to Eq. 8.3.15 and compared to the *expected* target-year trip generation (Eq. 8.3.16). A set of *adjustment factors,* R_I, are then computed by:

$$R_I = \frac{Q_I(t)}{Q_I(\text{current})} \tag{8.3.17}$$

If the adjustment factors are all sufficiently close to unity, the trip-balance constraint is satisfied and the procedure is terminated. Otherwise, the adjustment factors are used along with the current estimate of trip distribution Q_{IJ} (current) to improve the approximation. A comparison of Eq. 8.3.16 and 8.3.17 shows that the adjustment factors that are used in all but the first iteration and the original growth factors that are applied during the first iteration play the same mathematical role. Their interpretation, however, is not the same: The growth factors constitute a prediction of the actual growth of each zone between the base year and the target year, but the subsequent adjustment factors are merely mathematical adjustments that facilitate the convergence of the solution to the predicted zonal-trip generation.

The basic equation employed by the Fratar model to calculate the portion of the target-year generation of zone I that will interchange with zone J is

$$Q_{IJ}(\text{new}) = \frac{[Q_{IJ}(\text{current})]R_J}{\sum\limits_x [Q_{Ix}(\text{current})]R_x} Q_I(t) \tag{8.3.18}$$

This equation is similar to that of the gravity model. The expected trip generation of zone I is distributed among all zones so that a specific zone J receives its share according to a zone-specific term divided by the sum of these terms for all "competing" zones x. When Eq. 8.3.17 is applied to all zones, two estimated values result for each pair of zones: The first represents the portion of the generation of zone I allotted to the interchange due to the influence of zone J (or Q_{IJ}), and the second is the portion of the generation of zone J allotted to the interchange due to the influence of zone I (or Q_{JI}). As the following example shows, these two values are not necessarily equal. Since the Fratar model employs only one interzonal volume estimate $Q_{IJ} = Q_{JI}$, the two values are simply averaged, that is;

$$Q_{IJ}(\text{current}) = Q_{JI}(\text{current}) = \frac{Q_{IJ}(\text{new}) + Q_{JI}(\text{new})}{2} \tag{8.3.19}$$

and these values are used to calculate the new adjustment factors as explained previously.

Example 8.6 Application of the Fratar Model

Consider the base-year trip distribution of the simple four-zone system of Fig. 8.3.10. Assuming that the growth factors for the four zones are as shown, find the target-year trip distribution.

Solution The accompanying trip table summarizes the base-year data. Note that $Q_{IJ} = Q_{JI}$, as required by the Fratar model.

$I \backslash J$	1	2	3	4	$Q_I(b)$	$\times$	G_I	=	$Q_I(t)$
1	0	20	30	15	65		2		130
2	20	0	10	40	70		2		140
3	30	10	0	35	75		3		225
4	15	40	35	0	90		1		90
$Q_J(b)$	65	70	75	90					

Step 1. Use the trip balance Eq. 8.3.15 to compute the base-year trip generation for each of the four zones and multiply this total by the corresponding growth factor to calculate the target-year trip generation of each zone.

The marginal sums of each row or column of the trip table represent the base-year trip generation for the respective zones. The computation of the target-year generation using the row sums is also shown.

Step 2. For the first iteration, equate the adjustment factors to the growth factors and the current interchange flows to the base-year interchange volumes.

Step 3. Apply Eq. 8.3.18 to all pairs of zones I, J to get:

$I \backslash J$	1	2	3	4
1	0	36	81	13
2	51	0	38	51
3	117	39	0	69
4	13	33	44	0

Step 4. Apply Eq. 8.3.19 to arrive at single volume estimates for each interchange:

$I \backslash J$	1	2	3	4	Q_I(current)
1	0	43.5	99.0	13.0	155.5
2	43.5	0	38.5	42.0	124.0
3	99.0	38.5	0	56.5	194.0
4	13.0	42.0	56.5	0	111.5
Q_J(current)	155.5	124.0	194.0	111.5	

Step 5. Apply Eq. 8.3.15 to calculate the target-year trip generation of each zone that is implied in the results of Step 4.

The results of this step are shown in the marginal column and row of the preceding table.

Step 6. Apply Eq. 8.3.17 to compute the adjustment factors:

$$R_1 = \frac{130}{155.5} = 0.84 \qquad R_2 = 1.13 \qquad R_3 = 1.16 \qquad R_4 = 0.81$$

These adjustment factors show that the current solution overestimates the target-year generation of zones 1 and 4 (i.e., the adjustment factors are less than unity) and underestimates it for zones 2 and 3. If a better approximation is desired, the procedure returns to Step 3, using the given adjustment factors and the contents of the trip table of Step 4 as the current interchange volumes.

8.3.5 Limitations of the Fratar Model

The Fratar model suffers from three major drawbacks. First, it breaks down mathematically when a new zone (e.g., a new housing development) is built after the base year, since all base-year interchange volumes involving such a zone would be equal to zero; second, convergence to the target-year generation totals is not always possible; and third, the model is not sensitive to the impedance W_{IJ}, which has been shown to affect significantly the interzonal distribution of trips. For these reasons, the application of the Fratar model is restricted to situations where the more sophisticated models (such as the gravity model) cannot be used.

8.3.6 Summary

The aim of trip distribution is to estimate the target-year interchange volumes between all pairs of zones. The trip productions of each zone I obtained from the earlier trip generation phase are distributed among the trip-attracting zones J. The trip volume that a zone J would attract depends on its relative attractiveness (i.e., the availability of nonresidential activities vis-à-vis all competing zones of attraction) and the relative impedance between the producing zone I and the subject zone J. Estimates of the interzonal impedances are obtained from the specification of the transportation alternative plan under consideration.

The most common formulation of trip distribution is the gravity model, which is conceptually based on Newton's law of gravitation. This section presented the mathematical development of the model, described how it can be calibrated, and illustrated its application. The gravity model can be calibrated separately for each of several trip purposes if the outputs of the antecedent trip generation phase permit it. Also, it may be calibrated for total daily volumes (i.e., person-trips per day) or for smaller time periods of the day (e.g., person-trips per peak period).

A simple growth-factor model, the Fratar model, was described. Although insensitive to interzonal impedance, this model can be useful in special situations where the detailed data required by more sophisticated models are not available.

8.4. MODAL CHOICE

8.4.1 Background

In a typical travel situation, trip-makers can select between several travel modes. These may include driving, riding with someone else, taking the bus, walking, riding a motorcycle and so forth. A *modal choice,* or *modal split,* model is concerned with the trip-maker's behavior regarding the selection of travel mode. The reasons underlying this choice vary between individuals, trip type, and the relative level of service and cost associated with the available modes. If the student were to contemplate the reasons behind his or her choice of travel mode to and from school or work, the student would have a tangible example of what these factors mean. Additionally, it is likely that the student has established a pattern of modal choice that remains relatively constant as long as these conditions remain the same. When significant changes in these conditions occur, trip-makers respond in varying degrees by shifting from one mode to another. For example, a significant increase in the parking fees charged at a destination may induce some people to shift from driving a car to riding a bus.

The characteristics of the trip also have an effect on the choice of mode. It seems more likely, for example, that a person would choose to travel to work or school by a mass-transit system but prefer the private automobile, if available, for social trips. As discussed in relation to trip generation and trip distribution, it is not unusual for a regional transportation study to decompose trip making into trip-purpose categories and to model each component separately. This practice could then be extended to the modal choice phase as well.

In addition to the attributes of the available modes and the trip type, the socioeconomic status of the trip-maker affects the choice of travel mode. Thus, trip-makers may also be classified or disaggregated into finer categories, such as income or age, and separate estimates may be obtained for each of these socioeconomic subgroups. In many transportation planning studies, a particular subgroup (referred to as the *transit-captive* subgroup) has been singled out for special treatment. As this group's name implies, it consists of people who for various reasons do not have ready access to private transportation and, hence, whose mobility is almost exclusively dependent on the public-transit system. Included in this group are many of the elderly, the poor, the very young, and even the second primary individual of one-car households. Because this group is of considerable size, public transportation policy at the federal, state, and local levels has specifically addressed the needs of the members of this group.

Since transit captives do not have access to private transportation, they may be identified on a zonal basis as a percentage of the trip generation. The remaining trip-makers who do have a choice between competing private and public modes are treated by the modal split model, which estimates the percentage of trip-makers who choose to use the public-transportation system (i.e., the *choice riders*). The total ridership of the public transportation system can be obtained by summing the estimated captive and choice riders.

Depending on their positions in the demand-forecasting sequence, modal choice models are classified either as *predistribution* (*trip-end*) models or as *postdistribution* (*trip-interchange*) models (Fig. 8.4.1). As their name implies, the former are applied before the trip distribution step—or, to put it in another way, they operate on the trip ends (i.e., P_I) resulting from the trip-generation step. This practice carries the behavioral implication that trip-makers choose their modes of travel prior to deciding where to go; that is, the choice of attraction-zone J has no effect on their choices of modes. As Table 8.4.1 illustrates [8.10], in these models, the variables that capture the service attributes of the competing modes cannot be specified at the zonal-interchange level; they can only

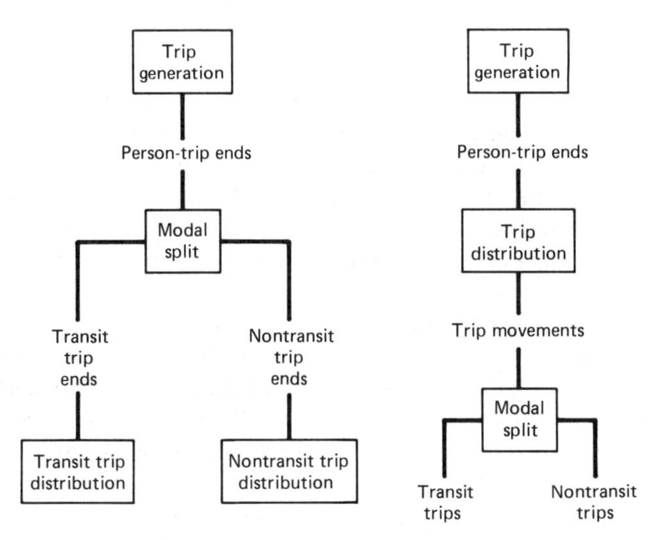

Figure 8.4.1 Location of modal choice with respect to trip generation analysis in the trasportation planning process. (*SOURCE*: Federal Highway Administration [8.1], Fig. 6, p. 30.)

TABLE 8.4.1 VARIABLES USED IN MODAL SPLIT MODELS

Variables	Trip-end models					Trip-interchange models			
	Chicago	Pittsburgh	Erie	Puget Sound	Southeastern Wisconsin	Washington D.C.	Twin Cities	San Juan	Buffalo
Trip characteristics									
Number of trip purposes used	2	3	1	4	7	2	3	2	2
Length of trip									x
Time of day						x			x
Orientation to CBD	x	x							
Trip-maker characteristics									
Auto ownership	x	x		x	x			x	x
Residential density		x		x			x		
Income				x		x	x		
Workers per household									x
Distance to CBD		x							
Employment density							x		
Transportation-system characteristics									
Travel time						x	x	x	x
Travel cost						x		x	
Parking cost						x	x		x
Excess travel time[a]						x			
Accessibility[b]			x	x	x				

[a]Time spent outside the vehicle during a trip: walk, wait, and transfer times for transit trips and parking-delay time for auto trips.

[b]A measure of the level of travel service provided by the transit or highway system to trip ends in the study area.

SOURCE: Fertal [8.10], Table 1, p. 3.

be gross estimates of the regionwide service offered by these modes. This assumption is appropriate for urban areas where public-transportation service is minimal. On the other hand, if the public-transportation system is or is expected to be extensive, it becomes necessary to capture the relative service attributes of the competing modes at the interchange level, since the relative levels of service offered by the competing modes are likely to vary between interchanges. Thus trip-interchange models are applied after trip distribution. In some studies, trip-end and trip-interchange models are used in combination.

To summarize, the mode-choice behavior of trip-makers can be explained by three categories of factors: the characteristics of the available modes; the socioeconomic status of the trip maker; and the characteristics of the trip. These are the categories of independent variables that would be included in mathematical models of modal choice, the dependent variable being the market share or the percent of travelers that are expected to use each of the available modes.

One of the simplest modal split models employs simple *diversion curves,* such as the one illustrated by Fig. 7.4.8. A more elaborate empirical stratified *diversion-type model* and the probability-based *multinomial logit* formulation of modal choice are discussed in this section.

8.4.2 The Stratified Diversion-Curve Model

Figure 8.4.2 illustrates a typical stratified diversion-curve model of modal choice, which superposes the calibration results obtained in Washington, D.C., Philadelphia, and Toronto [8.11] for work trips and two competing modes (i.e., auto and transit). Similar curves were also calibrated for other trip purposes. The independent variables employed by this model include three characteristics of the competing modes—the ratio of transit to auto travel time (TTR), the ratio of transit to auto costs (CR), and the ratio of transit to auto service (L), which is defined as the time spent outside the vehicle—and one characteristic of the trip makers, income category (EC). Each cell of the table corresponds to an income range and a cost-ratio level and contains a family of regression curves relating the travel-time ratio to the percentage of trips choosing transit for each of the four levels of relative service.

The modal characteristics employed by this particular model are given separately for each interchange between a pair of zones. For this reason, this model has come to be known as *the* trip-interchange model even though trip-interchange models of other mathematical forms are possible.

The application of this model is straightforward: The interchange volume obtained from the trip distribution phase is multiplied by the appropriate percentage obtained from Fig. 8.4.2 to arrive at the market shares of the two competing modes of travel.

Example 8.7

The peak-hour target-year work-trip interchange volume between two zones has been estimated to be 2000 person-trips as follows: 200 of these trips are made by captive riders, 600 are made by trip-makers from households of income category EC_3, and the remaining 1200 from economic category EC_5. Apply the Washington, D.C., stratified model of Fig. 8.4.2 to find the market share of the transit system assuming that this model has been calibrated as a disaggregate model based on household-income categories. The following data apply to the interchange under consideration:

$$\text{TTR} = 2.0$$
$$\text{CR} = 0.8$$
$$\text{L} = 4.0$$

Solution For a disaggregate model, the contribution of each economic subgroup to the transit patronage must be computed separately and then summed to arrive at an estimate of the total transit share:

Captives: $200 \times 1.0 = 200$ person-trips
Ec_3 group: $600 \times 0.4 = 240$
EC_5 group: $1200 \times 0.2 = 240$

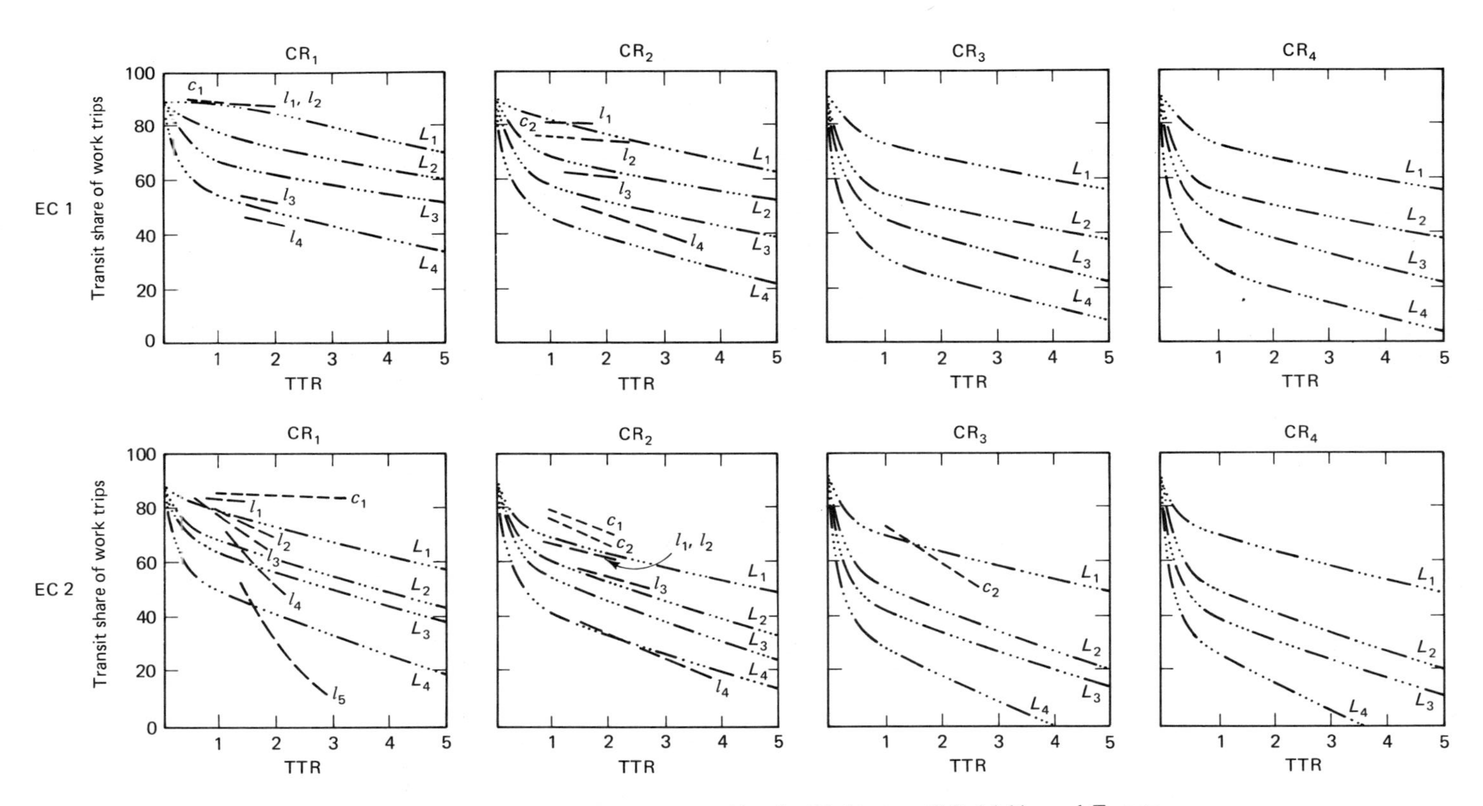

Figure 8.4.2 Work trip modal split relationships for Washington, Philadelphia, and Toronto. (*SOURCE*: Deen [8.11], Fig. 1, pp. 118–19.)

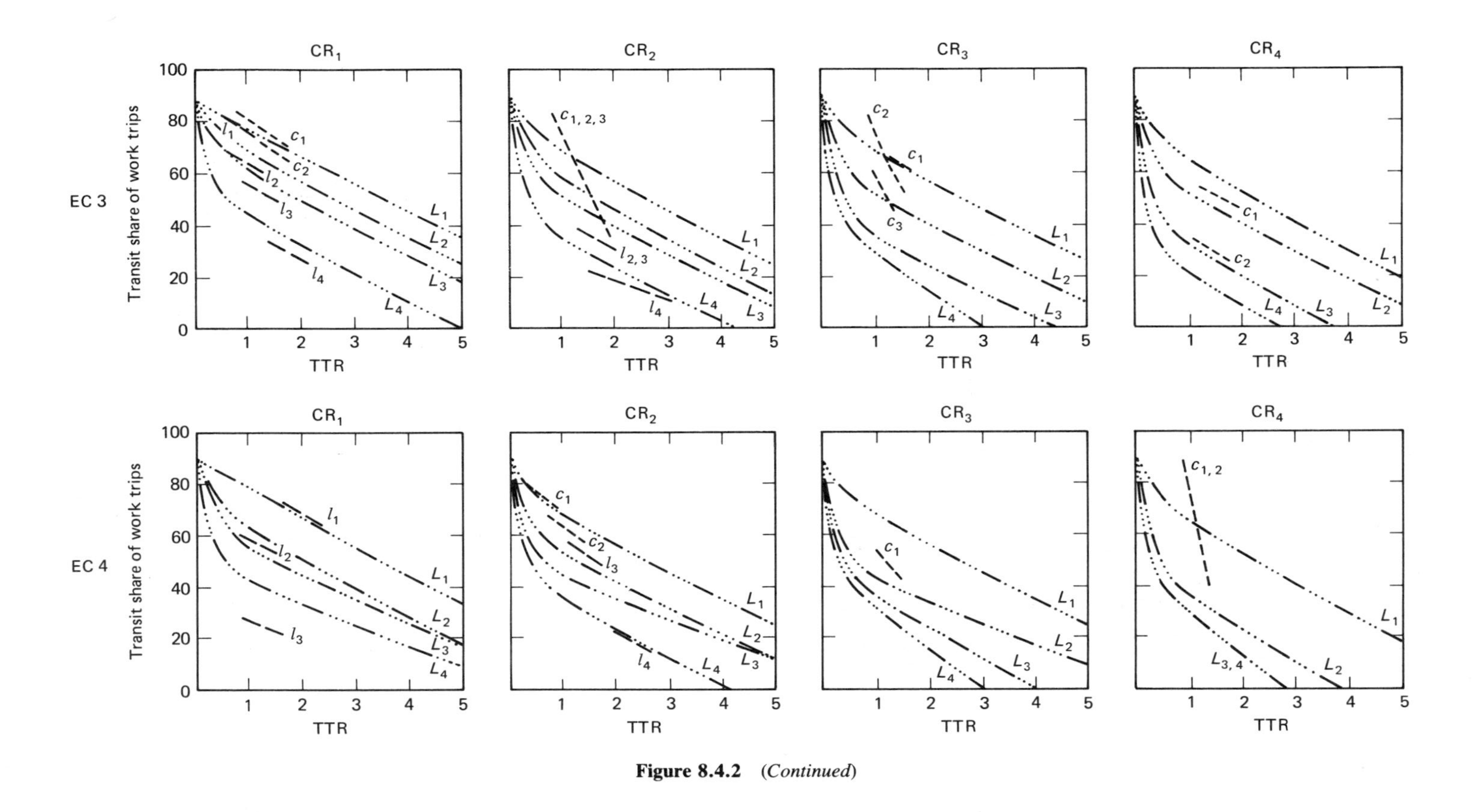

Figure 8.4.2 (Continued)

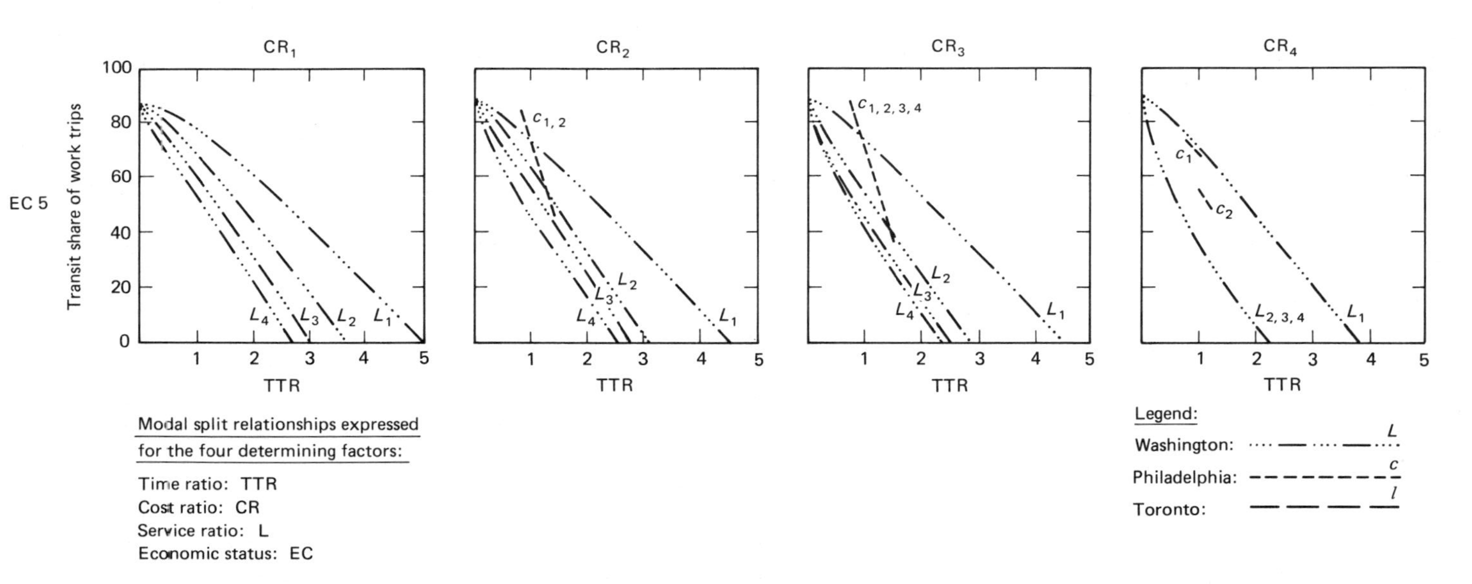

Figure 8.4.2 *(Continued)*

The transit patronage for this interchange is 680 person-trips per peak hour (or about 30% of the total interchange volume).

Discussion This problem assumed that the modal split curves had been calibrated on a disaggregate basis, and the same assumption was retained in the solution. To be able to do this, the trip-generation data were disaggregated into the three market segements. If the modal split curves were calibrated on a zonal basis, two consequences would be observed. First, the curves resulting from a zone-based calibration would not be identical to those resulting from a household-based calibration. Second, assuming that economic status were still the relevant variable, it would represent a zonal-level characteristic (say, the average zonal-income level) and only a single target-year value of this variable would be projected forward. Based on this zonal variable, a single percentage of trips using transit would be obtained and applied to the entire interchange volume rather than the separately calculated contributions to the total by each economic subgroup. It should be noted that, in actuality, the diversion curves of the model had been calibrated on a zonal basis. Hence, their application as disaggregate curves is questionable.

8.4.3 Probabilistic Models

Although simple in concept, the model described previously is awkward to calibrate and use, especially if more than two competing travel modes are to be included. In its full form, which involved a number of trip purposes, the Washington, D.C., model consisted of 160 different curves. More computationally efficient probability-based models of modal choice have been developed including discriminant analysis models, probit analysis models, and the most popular logit analysis models [8.12,8.13]. These models of human choice have been applied to many situations to explain how people select between competing alternatives. Each alternative is described by a utility (or disutility) function, and the probability associated with an individual's choosing of each of the competing alternatives is expressed mathematically in terms of these utilities. Extended to groups of individuals via the theory of probability, these models estimate the proportion of the group that is likely to choose each of the competing alternatives. The development of each model involves two steps: the selection of its mathematical form and the calibration of appropriate utility functions that render the selected model capable of reproducing the available base-year data.

8.4.4 Utility and Disutility Functions

A *utility* function measures the degree of satisfaction that people derive from their choices. A *disutility* function represents the generalized cost (akin to the concept of impedance) that is associated with each choice. The magnitude of either depends on the characteristics (or *attributes*) of each choice and on the characteristics (or socioeconomic status) of the individual making that choice. In the case of modal choice, the characteristics of the trip (e.g., trip purpose) also bear a relationship to the utility associated with choosing a particular mode of travel. In order to specify a utility function, it is necessary to select the relevant variables from this list and to select the particular functional form relating the selected variables. In addition, the analyst or planner is faced with the now-familiar question relating to the level of disaggregation of the modeling effort. Simply stated, this decision relates to whether a calibration will be at the regional, zonal, household or individual level, and also whether the calibration will include different models for other categories, such as trip purpose or time of day. This decision, of course, affects the types of variables that must be included. For example, when separate models are calibrated for each socioeconomic class of trip-makers and for each trip purpose, the utility function contains only variables that are related to the attributes of the competing modes.

The utility (or disutility) function is typically expressed as the linear weighted sum of the independent variables or their transformation, that is,

$$U = a_0 + a_1X_1 + a_2X_2 + \cdots + a_rX_r \tag{8.4.1}$$

where U is the utility derived from a choice defined by the magnitudes of the attributes X that are present in that choice and that are weighted by the model parameters a.

Early attempts to describe the utility associated with travel modes calibrated a *separate* utility function for each mode, as illustrated by the following hypothetical three-mode case:

$$U_1 = 6.2 + 2.4X_1 + 3.5X_2 \tag{8.4.2a}$$

$$U_2 = 3.4 + 3.1X_1 + 2.9X_3 \tag{8.4.2b}$$

$$U_3 = 4.3 + 2.9X_1 + 3.2X_3 \tag{8.4.2c}$$

The three modes in this hypothetical example may be the private auto, a local bus system, an an express bus system, respectively, and the independent variables (or attributes) may represent the cost, level of service, and convenience associated with a mode. This type of formulation is known as a *mode-specific* (and, in the general case, *choice-specific*) model, because the same attributes are assigned different weights for different modes. It is not even necessary to include the same variables in the utility equations of different modes. This, of course, is the same as saying that some attributes are either absent or are given zero weights in certain modes. Although there may be some validity in this hypothesis, it causes a problem when a new mode is introduced. In that case, it would be next to impossible to estimate the utility associated with the new mode because the necessary base-year data required for the calibration of its utility function would be unavailable. This new-product problem has haunted consumer-behavior analysts as well. A way to resolve it was proposed by Lancaster [8.14] as a new approach to consumer theory, where he postulated the idea of a *choice-abstract* (or *attribute-specific*) approach. This theory is based on the hypothesis that when making choices, people perceive goods and services indirectly in terms of their attributes, each of which is weighted identically across choices. Thus, trip-makers perceive two distinct modes offering the same cost, level of service, and convenience as being identical. Continuing with the three-mode example, a *mode-abstract* model of modal choice would use a single equation to measure utility, for example

$$U = 3.1 + 2.8X_1 + 1.2X_2 + 0.9X_3 \tag{8.4.3}$$

Differences in the utilities U associated with each of the competing modes arise because of differences in the magnitudes of the attributes X of these modes. For example, one mode may be faster but costlier than another, and this fact is reflected in their calculated utilities. The attribute-specific approach has a strong conceptual foundation. However, in practical applications, it is not possible to enumerate all the relevant attributes involved in the choice of mode. The first constant term in Eq. 8.4.3 is meant to capture the effect of variables that are not explicitly included in the model. Since it is unlikely that a given set of competing modes will be identical in these excluded attributes, it is reasonable to attempt to capture these unexpressed differences by calibrating for alternative-specific constants but weighting the explicitly identified attributes equally across modes. The calibrated utility function in the case of the three-mode example may then become:

$$U_K = a_K + 2.5X_1 + 1.5X_2 + 0.8X_3 \tag{8.4.4}$$

where U_K is the utility of mode K and a_K is the calibrated mode-specific constant for the same mode. The new-product problem resurfaces but in a milder form, since the selection of a mode-specific constant for a new mode is much more amenable to professional judgement vis-à-vis the mode-specific models, where none of the coefficients are known.

A utility-based modal-choice model estimates the market share of each mode based on the utility associated with it. In a *deterministic* model, it would seem reasonable that all travelers (if they know what is good for them) will select the mode with the highest utility. However, the models being discussed are not deterministic but *probabilistic* (see Chapter 6). In other words, the calculated modal utilities are related to the likelihood that a given mode will be selected or, when dealing with groups of travelers, the proportion or fraction that will select each mode of travel. The relationship between this fraction and the utilities of competing modes has been cast in various forms, the most popular of which is the logit model, which was applied by Stopher [8.15] to the case of two competing modes. It has since been extended to the multimodal case [8.16].

8.4.5 The Multinomial Logit Model

The multinomial logit model calculates the proportion of trips that will select a specific mode K according to the following relationship:

$$p(K) = \frac{e^{U_K}}{\sum_x e^{U_x}} \tag{8.4.5}$$

The general form of this equation resembles the fractional term employed by the gravity model of trip distribution: A term relating to the subject mode K appears as the numerator and the summation of the similar terms corresponding to all competing modes is placed in the denominator. This specification ensures that all trips that have been estimated to occur on a specific interchange are assigned to the available modes, that is, the following trip-balance equation is satisfied:

$$Q_{IJ} = \sum_x Q_{IJx} \tag{8.4.6}$$

Equation 8.4.6. would still be satisfied by writing the proportion attracted by each mode as

$$p(K) = \frac{U_K}{\sum_x U_x} \tag{8.4.7}$$

For reasons that lie beyond the scope of this textbook, the logistic transformation of the utilities (Eq. 8.4.5) is preferred.

Example 8.8: Application of the Logit Model

A calibration study resulted in the following utility equation:

$$U_K = a_K - 0.25X_1 - 0.032X_2 - 0.015X_3 - 0.002X_4$$

where

X_1 = access plus egress time in minutes

X_2 = waiting time in minutes

X_3 = line-haul time in minutes

X_4 = out-of-pocket cost in cents

The trip-distribution forecast for a particular interchange was a target-year volume of $Q_{IJ} = 5000$ person-trips per day. During the target year, trip-makers on this particular interchange will have a choice between the private automobile (A) and a local bus system (B). The target-year service attributes of the two competing modes have been estimated to be:

Attribute	X_1	X_2	X_3	X_4
Automobile	5	0	20	100
Local Bus	10	15	40	50

Assuming that the calibrated mode-specific constants are -0.12 for the automobile mode and -0.56 for the bus mode, apply the logit model to estimate the target-year market share of the two modes and the resulting fare-box revenue of the bus system.

Solution The utility equation yields:

$$U(\text{A}) = -0.745 \quad \text{and} \quad U(\text{B}) = -1.990$$

According to the logit equation (Eq. 8.4.5),

$$p(\text{A}) = 0.78 \quad \text{and} \quad p(\text{B}) = 0.22$$

Therefore the market share of each mode is

$$Q_{IJ}(\text{A}) = (0.78)(5000) = 3900 \text{ trips/day}$$

$$Q_{IJ}(\text{B}) = (0.22)(5000) = 1100 \text{ trips/day}$$

The fare-box revenue estimate is

$$(1100 \text{ trips/day})(\$0.50/\text{trip}) = \$550 \text{ per day}.$$

Discussion The terms of the utility function used in this example are negative. As negative quantities they represent cost (that is, disutility) components. The more negative this quantity, the less attractive the mode. Because of the exponential transformation of the utilities, the market shares are not directly proportional to the magnitudes of utility. Division of the numerator and denominator of Eq. 8.4.5. by $e^{U(\text{A})}$ results in the following form:

$$p(\text{B}) = \frac{e^{U^*}}{1 + e^{U^*}} \quad \text{and} \quad p(\text{A}) = \frac{1}{1 + e^{U^*}} \tag{8.4.8}$$

where U^* is the difference in the utilities of the two modes. This form resembles that advanced by Shopher [8.15]. In the bimodal case, the logistic transformation results a sigmoidal curve, as illustrated by Fig. 8.4.3.

Example 8.9: Introduction of a New Mode

It is desired to examine the effect of introducing a rapid-transit (RT) system in the city of Example 8.8. A related study has projected that the service attributes of the proposed system for the interchange under consideration will be:

$$X_1(\text{RT}) = 10 \qquad X_2(\text{RT}) = 5 \qquad X_3(\text{RT}) = 30 \qquad X_4(\text{RT}) = 75$$

Based on professional experience, the mode-specific constant for the new mode is somewhere between the other two but closer to the bus system, say -0.41. Find the market shares of the three modes that will result from implementing the rapid-transit proposal and the effect on the revenues of the public transportation authority, which operates both the local bus and the rapid-transit systems.

Solution Assuming that the attributes of the existing modes will not be affected by the introduction of the new mode, the utilities of the three alternatives will be:

$$U(\text{A}) = -0.745, \qquad U(\text{B}) = -1.990, \quad \text{and} \quad U(\text{RT}) = -1.420$$

Proceeding as before,

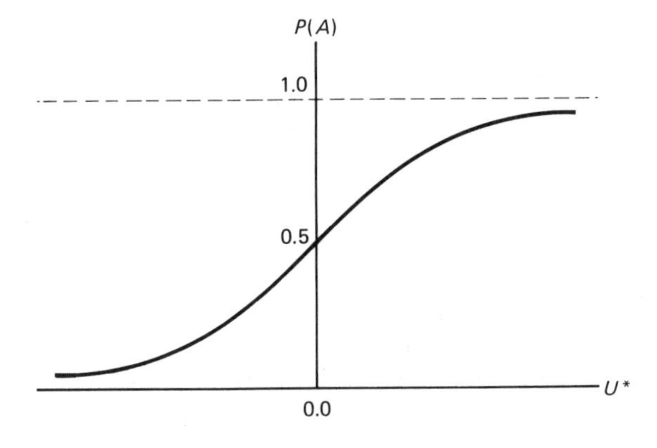

Figure 8.4.3 The binomial logit model.

$$p(\text{A}) = 0.56 \qquad Q_{IJ}(\text{A}) = 2800$$
$$p(\text{B}) = 0.16 \quad \text{and} \quad Q_{IJ}(\text{B}) = 800$$
$$p(\text{RT}) = 0.28 \qquad Q_{IJ}(\text{RT}) = 1400$$

The revenue will be $800 \times 0.5 + 1400 \times 0.75 = \$1450$ per day.

Discussion One of the attractive characteristics of the logit model is the fact that it could be so easily extended to this situation. In this example, the proposed system is seen to attract 28 percent of the interchange volume, or 1400 person-trips, reducing the auto usage by 1100 trips and the local bus patronage by 300 daily trips. In this connection, it is appropriate to mention that the specification of competing modes does not have to be restricted to the generic categories illustrated by this example. Depending on special concerns, finer categories of modes or submodes may be considered for calibration. For example, a study in Honolulu, Hawaii [8.7], which addressed the question of car-pooling, has calibrated mode-specific constants for the following modes:

1. Driving alone
2. Auto with 2 occupants
3. Auto with 3+ occupants
4. Regular bus
5. Express bus

The fare-box revenue on this interchange increased from $550 to $1450 per day. This, however, is not necessarily a sufficient reason to implement the proposed system. This decision must also consider the costs of constructing and operating the system as well as other impacts.

Example 8.10: Sensitivity to Other Policies

A city council is contemplating a proposal to charge a rapid-transit fare of $1.50 rather than $0.75. Determine the effect of this policy on the utilization of the three modes and on the public transportation authority's revenues.

Solution The proposed policy will cause a change in the utility of the rapid-transit system to -1.57 and will affect the patronage of all modes. Proceed as before.

Mode	Proportion	Market share
Auto	0.58	2900
Local bus	0.17	850
Rapid transit	0.25	1250

The revenue will be $850 \times 0.5 + 1250 \times 1.50 = \$2300$ per day.

Discussion This example shows how the response of trip-makers to various public policies and combinations of policies can be examined. The fare increase induced some patrons to shift back to the auto and bus modes. Although the public-transit share decreased, the revenues increased. In other words, the extra fare revenue collected outweighed the losses that resulted from patronage losses. This is not always the case, however (see the discussion of price elasticity in Chapter 9).

8.4.6 Summary

The purpose of a modal choice model is to predict the trip-makers' choice of travel mode. The factors that explain this behavior include:

1. The characteristics of the trip-maker;
2. The characteristics of the trip;
3. The attributes of the available modes of travel.

Trip-end or predistribution models are applied after trip generation and hence can incorporate the attributes of the available modes only on a regionwide level. These models may be applicable to urban areas offering only limited public transportation service. Trip-interchange or postdistribution models are applied after trip distribution and thus operate on estimates of interchange volume. In either case, modal split models may be aggregate or disaggregate, depending on the level at which they are calibrated and applied.

The purely empirical diversion-curve method and the probability-based multinomial logit formulation were presented in this section and the concepts of utility and disutility employed by the latter were explained. The difference between choice-specific and attribute-specific models of consumer behavior was drawn and illustrated.

8.5 NETWORK OR TRIP ASSIGNMENT

8.5.1 Background

The last phase of the sequential transportation-forecasting process is concerned with the trip-maker's choice of path between pairs of zones by travel mode and with the resulting vehicular flows on the multimodal transportation network. This step may be viewed as the equilibration model between the demand for travel (Q_{IJK}) estimated earlier in the process and the supply of transportation in terms of the physical facilities and, in the case of the various possible mass-transit modes, the frequency of service provided. Incidentally, this conceptual framework of economic theory is applicable to earlier steps of the process as well and has been so treated by many authors. Examples 8.8 through 8.10 illustrate how people respond to changes in the availability and price of transportation services. If the price of one mode increases relative to another, its market share will decrease.

Returning to the topic of network assignment, the question of interest is: Given Q_{IJK}, that is, the estimate of interzonal demand by mode, determine the trip-makers' likely choice of paths between all zones I and J along the network of each mode K and

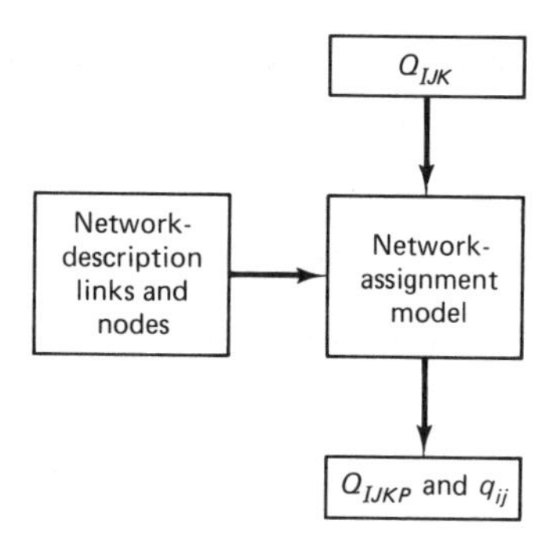

Figure 8.5.1 Network assignment inputs and outputs.

predict the resulting flows q on the individual links that make up the network of that mode (Fig. 8.5.1). The estimates of link utilization can be used to assess the likely level of service and to anticipate potential capacity problems.

The number of available paths between any pair of zones depends on the mode of travel. In the case of private-transportation modes, a driver has a relatively large set of possible paths and path variations and also a good deal of freedom in selecting between them. On the other hand, typical mass-transit modes offer a limited number of path (or route) choices.

Three preliminary questions must be dealt with prior to the performance of network assignment. The first is related to the difference between interzonal person-trips and interzonal vehicle-trips, the second is related to the difference between daily trips (that is, the estimate of the 24-h demand) versus the diurnal distribution of this demand, and the third is concerned with the direction of travel of the trips to be assigned on the transportation network.

8.5.2 Person-trips and Vehicle-trips

The forecasts of the person-trip and vehicle-trip flows that are expected to use the transportation system are both relevant to the assessment of its performance. The estimate of person-trips that desire to use a highway, for example, provides an indication of the passenger throughput that will be accommodated. On the other hand, the level of service (see Chapter 4) that the trip-makers experience when traveling on a highway is related to the *vehicular* flow (e.g., vehicles per hour) that desires to use the highway. For this reason, the estimated interzonal person-trips must be translated into vehicular-trips prior to performing the highway-trip assignment (also known as *traffic assignment*). *Car occupancies* (i.e., persons per car) vary between cities and also between trip types.

Mass-transit (or *transit assignment*) must address another issue as well. In this case, the specification of an alternative system consists not only of the fixed facilities that constitute the modal network but also the scheduling of transit services. This means that the analysis of a particular transit alternative must address the question of whether a proposed fleet size and operating schedule and the related vehicular frequencies (i.e., flows) provide sufficient capacity to meet the anticipated interzonal person-trip demand.

8.5.3 Diurnal Patterns of Demand

In Chapters 4 and 5, the highway flows and intersection-approach volumes that are used to calculate the prevailing level of service were expressed in vehicles per hour. On the other hand, the estimates of interzonal flows that are obtained by the trip generation-distribution modal choice sequence are often based on a 24-h period. As Fig. 8.2.2 illustrates, the demand for transportation exhibits a highly peaked pattern with a sharp peak period in the morning and a generally longer but less pronounced peak period in the evening. It is appropriate, therefore, to investigate the performance of the transportation system under peak-demand conditions, when capacity limitations become most critical. The time variation of demand is most relevant to mass-transit planning because the scheduling of service is typically tailored to the variation of demand over the 24-h period.

The diurnal distribution of demand may be estimated through the use of factors taken from observations during the base year, or it may be explicitly modeled in the preceding steps of the demand-forecasting process. Typically, the morning peak period demand is in the range of 10 to 20% of the total daily demand.

8.5.4 Trip Direction

In the discussion of trip generation, a distinction was drawn between productions and attractions on one hand and origins and destinations on the other. It was also explained why most trip-generation models estimate productions rather than origins. However, it is desirable that the assignment of trips (especially by time of day) retain the direction of these trips. The predominant direction of travel during the morning peak period is toward major activity centers (i.e., CBDs or schools), and the reverse is true during the evening rush hour. The experience and knowledge accumulated through studies of the travel patterns within the region aid in the accomplishment of this task.

8.5.5 Historical Context

The origin of traffic assignment can be traced to the 1950s and early 1960s, when the majority of urban freeways were constructed in United States cities. Typically, highway engineers wanted to know how many drivers would be diverted from arterial streets to a proposed freeway in order to make decisions relating to the geometric design and capacity of proposed urban freeways. The *diversion-curve model* was developed to answer this question. This model employs empirically derived curves to compute the percentage of trips that would use the freeway route between two points on some measure of relative impedance between the freeway route and the fastest arterial route between the two points. Figure 8.5.2 shows that the California diversion curves [8.17] use travel time and travel distance differences between the two alternative paths to estimate the percentage of trips that use the freeway. Figure 8.5.3 illustrates a diversion curve developed by the BPR [8.18], where the ratio of travel times via the two routes serves as the impedance measure.

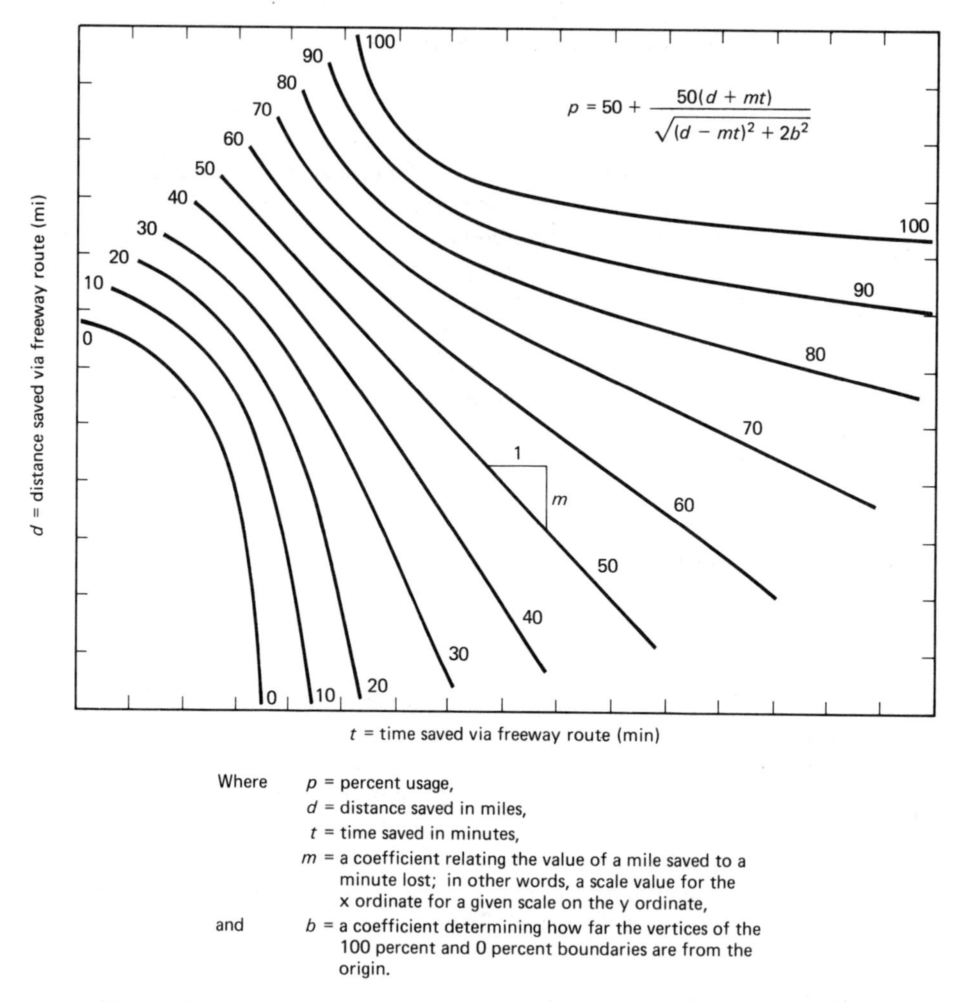

Where
p = percent usage,
d = distance saved in miles,
t = time saved in minutes,
m = a coefficient relating the value of a mile saved to a minute lost; in other words, a scale value for the x ordinate for a given scale on the y ordinate,

and
b = a coefficient determining how far the vertices of the 100 percent and 0 percent boundaries are from the origin.

Figure 8.5.2 California diversion curves. (*SOURCE*: Moskowitz [8.17], Fig. 6, p. 14.)

A shortcoming of the diversion-curve method is the fact that drivers between two points have path options that contain both freeway segments and arterial street segments rather than two distinct all-freeway and all-arterial paths. Moreover, these combinations become computationally complex as the number of zonal pairs and the size of the transportation network increase. Developments in digital computer technology have made it possible to expand the traffic assignment procedure to large networks. A network assignment procedure requires

1. A way of coding the modal network for computer processing;
2. An understanding of the factors affecting the trip-makers' path preferences;
3. A computer algorithm capable of producing the trip-makers' preferred paths.

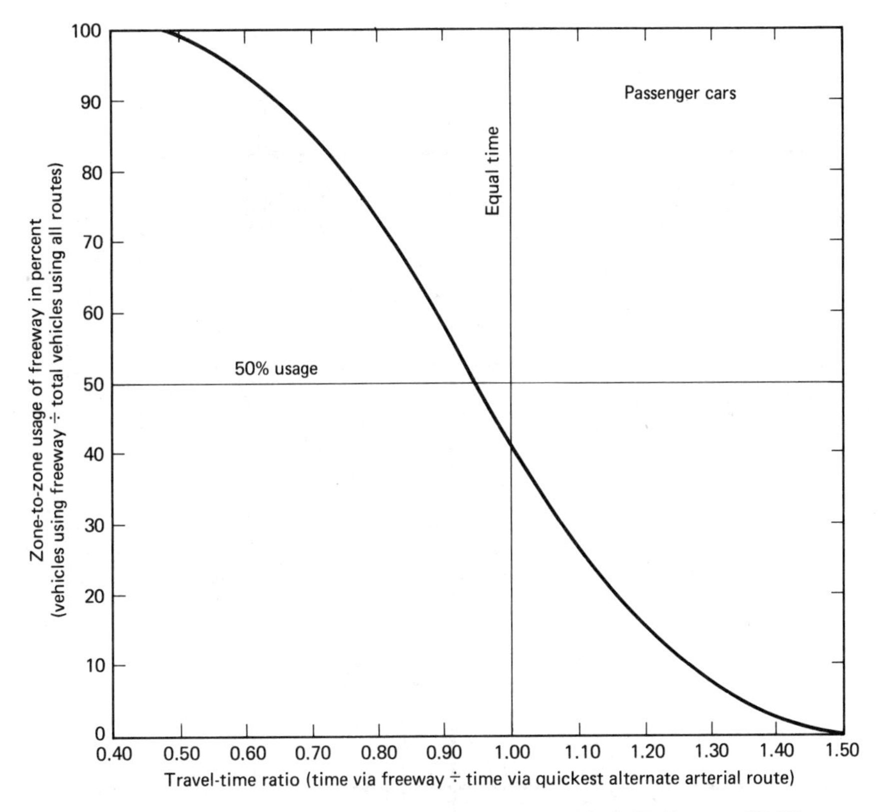

Figure 8.5.3 Bureau of Public Roads diversion curve. (*SOURCE*: Bureau of Public Roads [8.18], Fig. V-9, p. V-13.)

8.5.6 Highway Network Description

Figure 8.5.4 shows a street map of a hypothetical urban highway network consisting of facilities of the various classes discussed in Chapter 2, ranging from local streets to high-type facilities such as freeways and expressways. The figure also shows the boundaries of travel-analysis zones [8.18,8.19].

Figure 8.5.5 contains only those elements of the highway network that would normally be included in the coded traffic assignment network. A comparison of the two figures shows that local and minor streets are not included in the coded network and the remaining fixed facilities (that is, major arterials, expressways, and freeways) are specified by a set of *nodes* (i.e., intersections and interchanges) and *links*. Each node is specified by a numerical code and each link is described by its end nodes. Important characteristics of each link (such as its capacity, free-flow speed or travel time) are also specified. It is often advantageous to select the coding scheme judiciously to reflect other link attributes as well. For example, nodes that lie exclusively on arterial streets may be denoted by one range of numerical codes (say, between 100 and 1000), whereas nodes that lie on

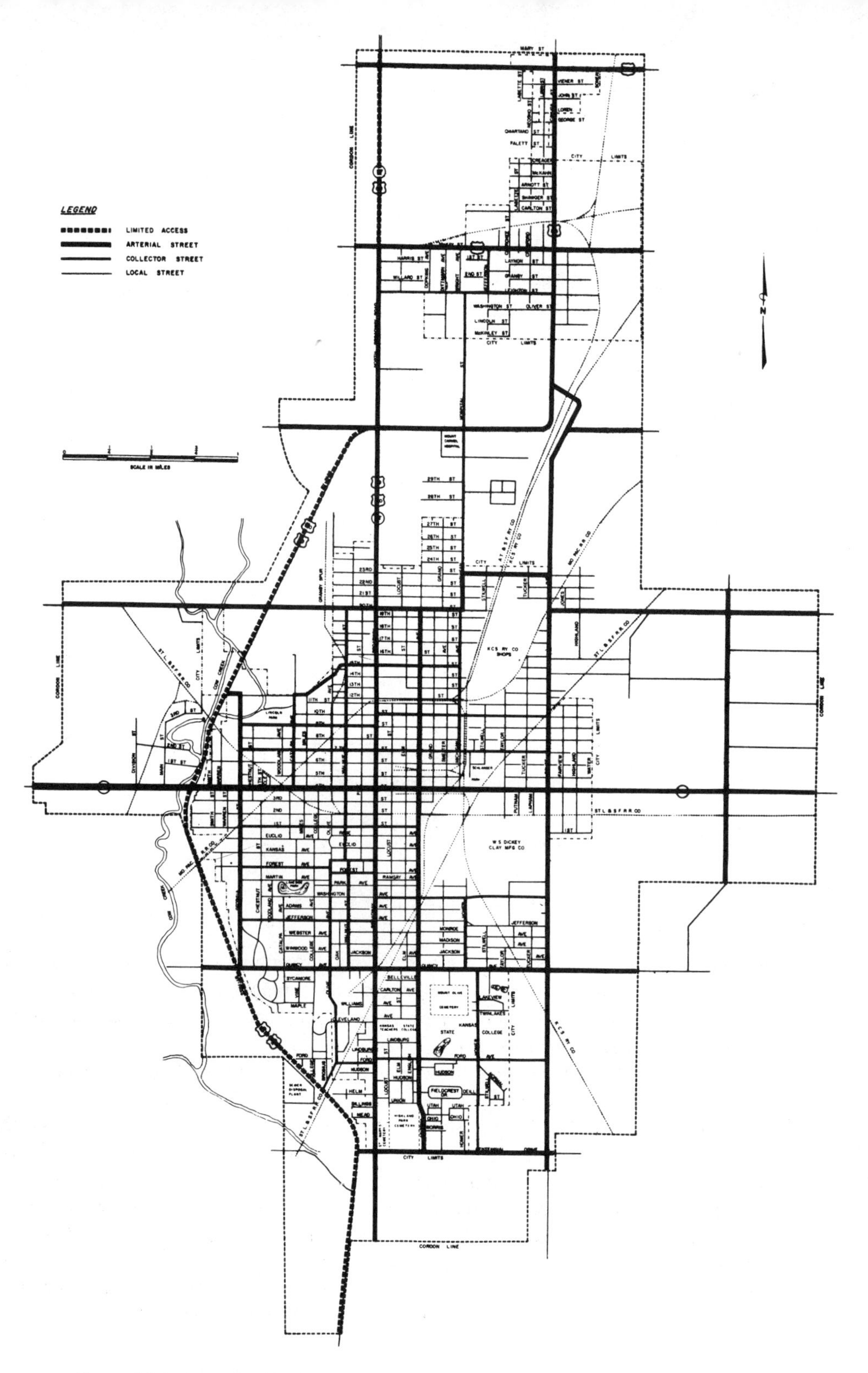

Figure 8.5.4 Street classification and base map. (*SOURCE*: Bureau of Public Roads [8.18], Fig. III-11, p. III-26.)

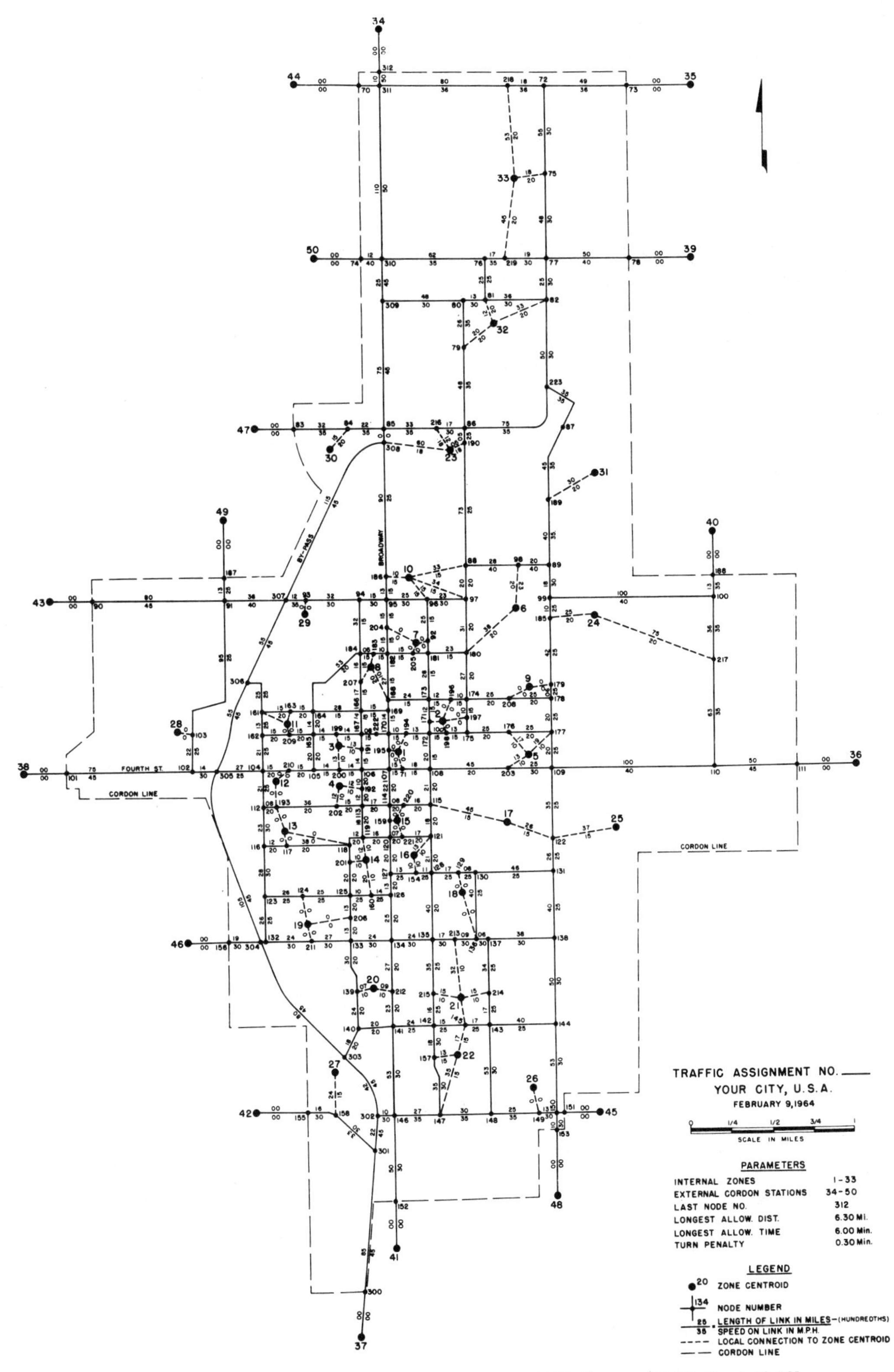

Figure 8.5.5 Sample traffic assignment network map. (*SOURCE*: Bureau of Public Roads [8.18], Fig. III-10, p. III-25.)

higher-type facilities may be coded with numbers in another range (say, greater than 1000). Thus, a link connecting nodes 525 and 666 is clearly a segment of an arterial street, while link 1212-1213 is a segment of freeway. Moreover, links 729-1432 and 1198-888 represent an on-ramp (i.e., connecting an arterial to a freeway) and an off-ramp (i.e., connecting a freeway to an arterial).

Travel-analysis zones are coded as a set of imaginary nodes referred to as *zonal centroids*. To distinguish them from the actual network nodes, they are usually designated by numerical codes at the lower range of positive integers (see the heavy nodes of Fig. 8.5.5). Their geographical location is often taken to coincide with the activity or population centroid of the zones they represent, hence their name. Finally, a set of imaginary links known as *centroidal connectors* (shown by dashes in Fig. 8.5.5) are introduced to connect the zonal centroids to the assignment network. Although not real links, they are typically given link attributes corresponding to the average conditions that trip-makers experience on the noncoded local- and minor-street system.

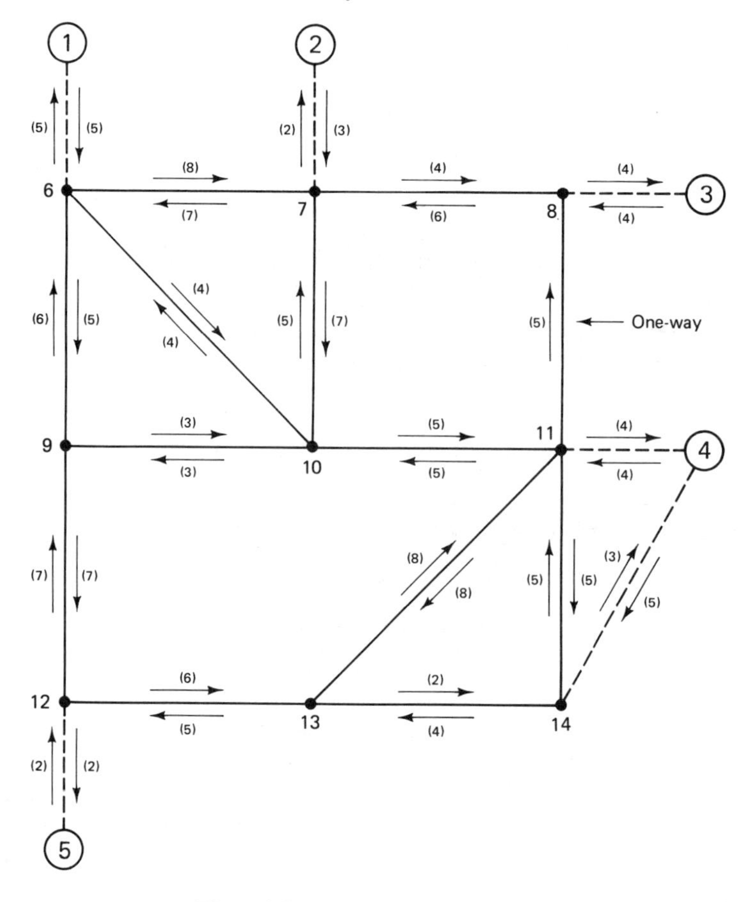

Figure 8.5.6 A hypothetical network.

TABLE 8.5.1 A LINK ARRAY

$i \backslash j$	1	2	3	4	5	6	7	8	9	10	11	12	13	14
1						5								
2							3							
3								4						
4											4			5
5												3		
6	5						8		5	4				
7		2				7		4		7				
8			4				6							
9						6				3		7		
10						4	5		3		5			
11				4				5		5			8	5
12					2				7				6	
13											8	5		2
14				3							5		4	

The simple network of Fig. 8.5.6 consists of 5 zonal centroids (i.e., nodes 1 to 5), 6 centroidal connectors, 9 street intersections (i.e., nodes 6 to 14), and 12 arterial street links. The numerical values in parentheses correspond to the link impedances in the direction shown. This network is described by the *link array* (Table 8.5.1), each cell of which represents a possible direct link between the row and column nodes. A numerical entry in a cell means that there is in fact such a link, the cell value being, say, the link's impedance. The dimensions of the link array may be increased to include other link attributes as well, such as free-flow speed, length, and capacity.

8.5.7 Link Flows and Interzonal Flows

A careful distinction must be made between the terms *interzonal flows* (Q_{IJ}) and *link flows* (q_{ij}). The former refer to the demand for travel between a pair of zones. The latter is the flow that occurs on a specific link (i, j) of the transportation network and is the sum of all interzonal flows that happen to include that particular link on their preferred paths. For the sake of clarity, uppercase letters are employed in this textbook to denote *zones* (I and J) and *interzonal* flow (Q), and lowercase letters are used to denote traffic assignment network *nodes* (i and j) and link flows (q).

8.5.8 Route-Choice Behavior

Trip-makers choose their paths by considering the impedance of the competing paths available to them. A path's impedance is equal to the sum of the impedances of the links that define it. The simplest network-assignment procedure assumes that all travelers between a pair of zones select the *minimum path,* that is, the single path that offers the least impedance. This assignment method is known as an *all-or-nothing* assignment because it allocates the entire interchange volume to one path and no volume to any other path. In reality, there exists considerable evidence that this method is not realistic. For example, the California diversion curves of Fig. 8.5.2 show that even when the freeway route offers savings in travel time and distance, a certain percentage of drivers will still choose to remain on the arterial route. *Multipath* traffic assignment procedures attempt to capture this fact. Traffic assignments of either class may be either *capacity restrained* or *unrestrained.* As explained in a later subsection of this chapter, this depends on whether they take into consideration the effect of vehicular flow on link impedance or not.

8.5.9 Minimum Path Algorithms

Assume that it is required to find the minimum (impedance) path between zones 3 and 5 on the network of Fig. 8.5.6. This task may be accomplished by identifying all possible paths between the two zones, computing their impedances, and choosing the path with the lowest impedance. But even in the case of this extremely simple network, the path-enumeration procedure is time-consuming and inefficient. More efficient minimum-path algorithms have been developed as variations on a theme advanced by Moore [8.20]. Some determine the minimum path between a pair of zones, while others compute the *minimum tree,* which contains all the interzonal minimum paths that emanate from a zone of origin [8.21].

The basic minimum-tree algorithm begins at the node of origin and proceeds outward, successively eliminating links that clearly do not belong on any minimum path emanating from the origin. Figure 8.5.7 illustrates this concept. Suppose that the minimum

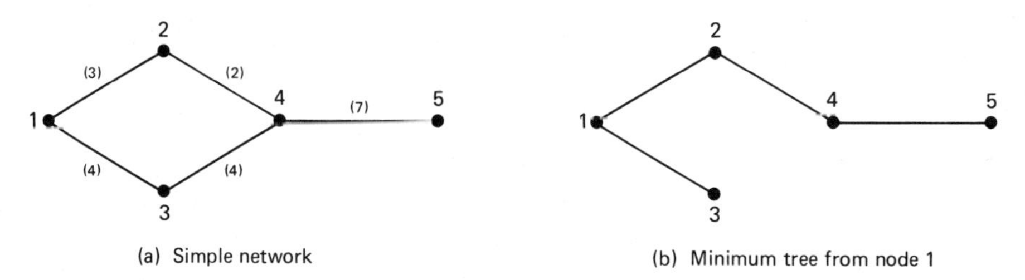

Figure 8.5.7 Link elimination.

TABLE 8.5.2 A SIMPLE TREE-TABLE

Node (j)	Total impedance to node j	Node preceding j
1	0	—
2	3	1
3	4	1
4	5	2
5	12	4

tree emanating from node 1 and terminating in all other nodes of the network is being sought. The minimum path to node 5 passes through node 4. But there are two possible paths to node 4: one via node 2 and the other via node 3. The first takes 5 and the second 8 units of impedance. Therefore, the first is the minimum path to node 4 and to any subsequent node whose path passes through node 4. The last link of the longer path (in this case link 3-4) is eliminated from the minimum tree shown by Fig. 8.5.7(b).

The minimum tree may be described numerically by a *tree table,* as shown by Table 8.5.2. The first column of the tree table contains all network nodes j including the origin. The second column contains the total impedance of the minimum path from the origin to each node j. The last column specifies the node i that immediately precedes node j on the minimum path from the origin to node j. In other words, the pair of nodes (i, j) defines the last link on the minimum path from the origin to node j. Thus, the fourth row of the table says that the minimum path from node 1 to node 4 takes 5 units of impedance and that node 4 is immediately preceded by node 2.

The tree table describes a specific path, say to node 5, as follows: Node 5 is preceded by node 4 (last column of row 5), node 4 is preceded by node 2 (last column of row 4), and node 2 is preceded by node 1 (last column of row 2), which is the origin (last column of row 1). Reversing this order, the path from node 1 to node 5 consists of the following sequence of links: 1-2, 2-4, and 4-5.

8.5.10 A Minimum-Tree-Seeking Procedure

The following procedure produces the tree table that contains every minimum path emanating from the node of origin:

Step 1: Initialize the path impedances of the tree table at zero for the node of origin and a very large number for all other nodes. This large number ensures that the first encountered actual path to a node will be chosen.

Step 2: Enter into a list the links (i, j) that emanate directly from any node i just added to the tree.

Step 3: For each node j included in the list, add the impedance of link (i, j) to the tree table's current total impedance to node i. This quantity represents the total impedance to node j via node i. If this value is smaller than the current tree table entry for node j, replace the current total impedance to j with the new total impedance and enter node i as the node that immediately precedes j. This operation replaces the longer path to node j with the shorter one just discovered. If the new total impedance is greater than the current tree table entry, proceed to the next link in the list.

Step 4: Return to Step 2, unless the list is empty, in which case the tree table contains the solution.

Example 8.11 Minimum-Tree Algorithm

Find the minimum tree emanating from node 1 for the network described by the link array of Table 8.5.1

Solution The graphical solution to this problem is summarized by Fig. 8.5.8. The related calculations are shown by Table 8.5.3 and 8.5.4. Table 8.5.3 shows the changes performed on the tree table as the tree is built outward from the origin (node 1). The second and third columns of the table have been expanded to show these changes as they occur during the procedure. The initial condition (stage I) contains only the node of origin. All links emanating from node 1 are next entered in the list (Table 8.5.4) and are also shown by dashed lines on the graph of the partial tree (Fig. 8.5.8). These links and their link impedances are found in row 1 of the link array (Table 8.5.1). In this case, there is only one entry, link 1-6 with a link impedance of 5 units. The calculations of stage II are shown in Table 8.5.4. The impedance of the new path is computed by adding the impedance of link (1, 6) to the current tree table entry for mode $i = 1$ (i.e., $0 + 5 = 5$). This value is compared to the current tree table entry for node $j = 6$ (i.e., infinity). Since the new path to node 6 is shorter than the current value, the new path is accepted. Stage II of the tree table and the tree diagram reflect this modification. All links emanating from the newly added node (node 6) are placed in the list to be considered at the next stage. They are also shown by dashed lines on the partial tree diagram. At the end of stage III, nodes 7, 9, and 10 are added to the tree, and the links emanating from these nodes (that is, the links found in rows 7, 9, and 10 of the link array) are placed in the list. Note that the stage IV entries to the list contain two alternative paths to node 10: One via node 7 and one via node 9. Of these two, the second is shorter, so the first may be rejected immediately. The path to node 10 via node 9 is also rejected in favor of the current path to 10, which the tree table shows to be via node 6. The procedure continues until stage VI, when all the list entries are rejected, that is, the list is empty. The final tree table emanating from node 1 and the corresponding diagram are shown on Table 8.5.5.

Discussion This example found the minimum tree emanating from node 1 and terminating in all other nodes of the network. It does not contain any other paths. Thus, the sequence of links shown on the tree of Fig. 8.5.8 joining node 3 and node 14 does not represent the minimum path between these nodes. In order to find the minimum tree emanating from node 3, the procedure must be repeated, starting with the appropriate initialization of the tree table.

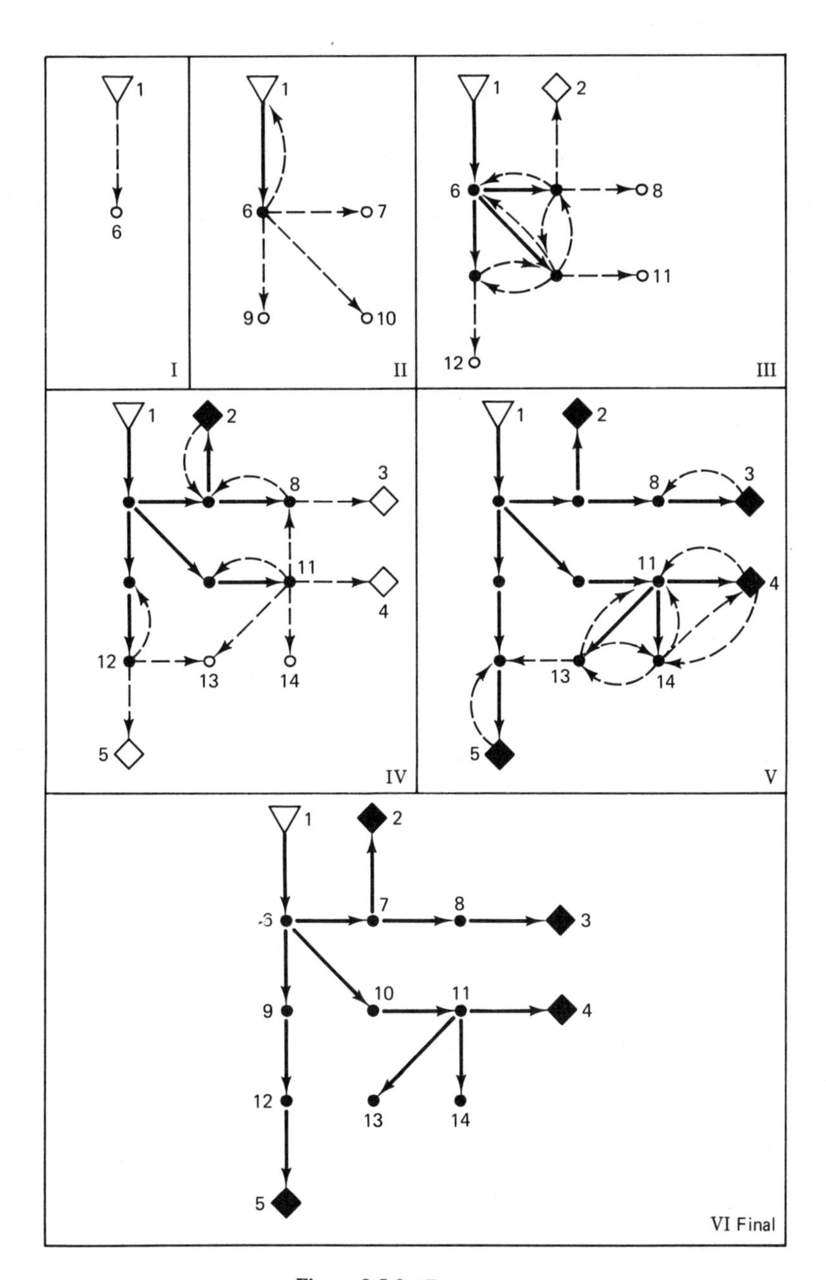

Figure 8.5.8 Tree stages.

TABLE 8.5.3 TREE-TABLE CHANGES AT THE END OF EACH STAGE

Node	Total impedance to node j						Node preceding j					
(j)	I	II	III	IV	V	VI	I	II	III	IV	V	VI
1	0						—					
2	∞			15						7		N
3	∞				21						8	O
4	∞				18						11	
5	∞				19						12	
6	∞	5						1				C
7	∞		13						6			H
8	∞			17						7		A
9	∞		10						6			N
10	∞		9						6			G
11	∞			14						10		E
12	∞			17						9		
13	∞				22						11	
14	∞				19						11	

TABLE 8.5.4 LIST CHANGES AND RELATED CALCULATIONS

Stage N	Links i	j	Compute new path impedance	Compare to tree table stage $N - 1$	Decision
II	1	6	$0 + 5 = 5$	$5 < \infty$	Accept
III	6	7	$5 + 8 = 13$	$13 < \infty$	Accept
		9	$5 + 5 = 10$	$10 < \infty$	Accept
		10	$5 + 4 = 9$	$9 < \infty$	Accept
IV	7	2	$13 + 2 = 15$	$15 < \infty$	Accept
		8	$13 + 4 = 17$	$17 < \infty$	Accept
		10	$13 + 7 = 20$ Reject		Reject
	9	10	$10 + 3 = 13$	$13 > 10$	Reject
		12	$10 + 7 = 17$	$17 < \infty$	Accept
	10	7	$9 + 5 = 14$	$14 < 13$	Reject
		9	$9 + 3 = 12$	$12 > 10$	Reject
		11	$9 + 5 = 14$	$14 < \infty$	Accept
V	8	3	$17 + 4 = 21$	$21 < \infty$	Accept
	11	4	$14 + 4 = 18$	$18 < \infty$	Accept
		8	$14 + 5 = 19$	$19 > 17$	Reject
		13	$14 + 8 = 22$	$22 < \infty$	Accept
		14	$14 + 5 = 19$	$19 < \infty$	Accept
	12	5	$17 + 2 = 19$	$19 < \infty$	Accept
		13	$17 + 6 = 23$ Reject		Reject
VI	All links emanating from nodes 3, 4, 5, 13, and 14 are rejected; the list is now empty and the procedure ends.				

TABLE 8.5.5 FINAL TREE-TABLE

Node (j)	Total impedance to node j	Node preceding j
1	0	—
2	15	7
3	20	8
4	18	11
5	19	12
6	5	1
7	13	6
8	17	7
9	10	6
10	9	6
11	14	10
12	17	9
13	22	11
14	19	11

8.5.11 Free/All-or-Nothing Traffic Assignment

The free/all-or-nothing assignment technique allocates the entire volume interchanging between pairs of zones to the minimum path calculated on the basis of free-flow link impedances. After all interchange volumes are assigned, the flow on a particular link is computed by summing all interzonal flows that happens to include that link on their minimum paths.

Example 8.12

Assign the following interzonal vehicular trips emanating from zone 1 to the network of Example 8.11.

J	2	3	4	5
Q_{1J}	800	500	600	200

Solution The minimum tree emanating from zone 1 is reproduced here. The interzonal flows using each link of the tree are summed to compute the total contribution of the given flows to these links. Thus link 7-2 takes only the total interchange between zones 1 and 2, and link 7-8 takes the flow from zone 1 to zone 3. Link 6-7 takes the sum of the flows from zone 1 to zone 2 and from zone 1 to zone 3, since it belongs to both minimum paths. These links may also be assigned additional flows if they happen to be part of minimum paths that originate from zones other than zone 1.

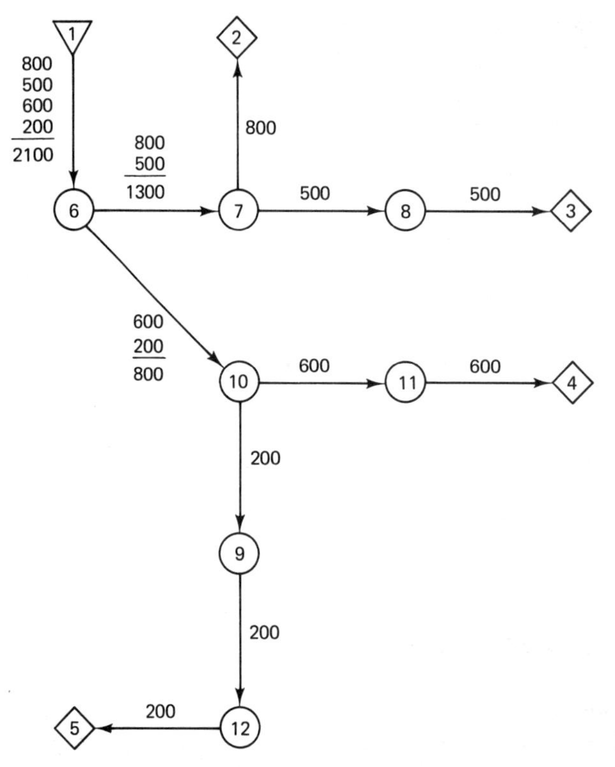

Figure P.8.12

8.5.12 Free/Multipath Traffic Assignment

In essence, a free/all-or-nothing assignment assumes that all trip-makers traveling between a specific pair of zones actually select the same path. In reality, interchange volumes are divided among a number of paths, and algorithms capable of determining several paths between each pair of zones in order of increasing impedance are available. Therefore it is possible to apportion the interchange volume between these paths according to some realistic rule. The diversion-curve method described earlier is a case where the interzonal flows are allocated to two competing paths. Other allocation rules are also possible. For example, Irwin and von Cube [8.22] suggested the following inverse-proportion function to compute the fraction to be assigned to each of a number of interzonal routes:

$$p(r) = \frac{W_{IJr}^{-1}}{\sum_x W_{IJx}^{-1}} \tag{8.5.1}$$

where W_{IJr} is the impedance of route r from I to J. As the following example illustrates, the use of the multinomial logit model (see Section 8.4.5) with disutilities based on path impedances is another possibility.

Example 8.13

A multipath algorithm found the interzonal impedances of the four shorter paths between a pair of zones to be 1.0, 1.5, 2.0, and 3.0 units of disutility. Estimate the percentage of trips to be assigned to each of the four routes according to the multinomial logit model.

Solution Applying Eq. 8.4.5 with the negative of the path disutilities in place of the utility terms,

$$p(1) = 0.47$$

$$p(2) = 0.29$$

$$p(3) = 0.17$$

$$p(4) = 0.07$$

Discussion This example merely illustrates how the multinomial logit model may be applied to the unrestrained multipath assignment problem. Whether this model is adequate for a particular planning study must also be the subject of inquiry. The computational complexity of these models must not escape the student's attention, but computerized algorithms that deal effectively with the repetitive nature of the calculations are available. Of greater complexity are *capacity-restrained* algorithms that incorporate the effect of traffic flow on link impedance.

8.5.13 Capacity-Restrained Traffic Assignment

Chapter 3 showed that as the flow increases toward capacity, the average stream speed decreases from the free-flow speed (u_f) to the speed at maximum flow (u_m). Beyond this point, the internal friction between vehicles in the stream becomes severe, the traffic conditions worsen (i.e., levels of service E and F), and severe shock waves and slow-moving platoons develop.

The implication of this phenomenon on the results of free-traffic assignment presents the following paradox: The interzonal flows are assigned to the minimum paths computed on the basis of free-flow link impedances (usually travel times). But if the link flows were at the levels dictated by the assignment, the link speeds would be lower and the link travel times (i.e., impedances) would be higher than those corresponding to free-flow conditions. As a result, the minimum paths computed *prior* to trip assignment may not be the minimum paths *after* the trips are assigned. Several iterative assignment techniques address the convergence between the link impedances assumed prior to assignment and the link impedances that are implied by the resulting link volumes. These techniques are known as *capacity-restrained* methods or techniques that employ *capacity restraints*.

The relationship between link flow and link impedance is described the the *link-capacity function*. Several such functions are found in the technical literature (e.g., [8.23]). Figure 8.5.9 presents the form developed by the BPR, which is mathematically expressed as:

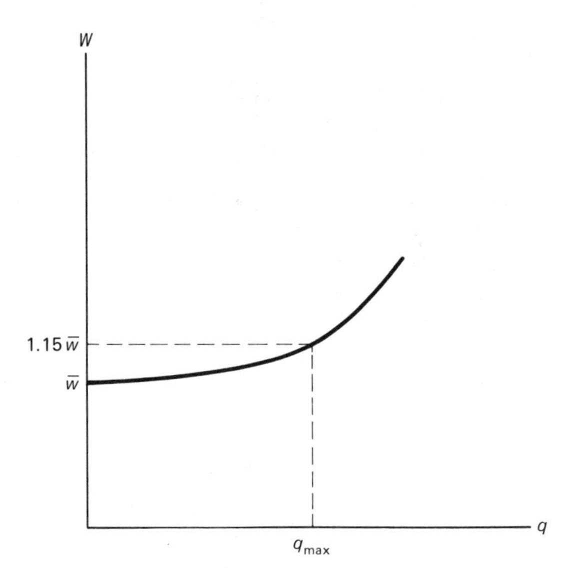

Figure 8.5.9 Bureau of Public Roads link capacity function.

$$w = \bar{w}\left[1 + 0.15\left(\frac{q}{q_{max}}\right)^4\right] \tag{8.5.2}$$

where

w is the impedance of a given link at flow q

$\bar{w}$ is the free-flow impedance of the link

q is the link flow

q_{max} is the link's capacity

This function states that at capacity, the link impedance is 15% higher than the free-flow impedance. If the demand were to exceed the capacity of the link, the resulting shock waves and their dissipation times (see Chapter 3) would cause a rapid deterioration in the link flow conditions.

Capacity-restrained algorithms incorporate link capacity functions in their search for convergence to an equilibrium state. They may be either all-or-nothing or multipath. An example of the former is the algorithm developed by CATS [8.24], where the following assignment procedure is applied: An interchange is chosen at random, the minimum path is determined using the free-flow impedances, and the entire interchange volume (i.e., all-or-nothing) is assigned to this minimum path. The impedances of the links that make up this path are updated according to the assigned flows, and another interchange is randomly chosen for similar treatment. The procedure ends when all interchanges are considered. Although not realistically reproducing particular interchange flows, the incremental updating of link impedances is expected to result in realistic estimates of the equilibrium link flows.

The 1973 edition of the FHWA's traffic-assignment manual [8.19] describes a multipath extension of the CATS method developed by the Control Data Corporation. This method begins with an uncongested network, finds all the minimum paths, and assigns a portion (say, 20%) of each interchange volume to these paths. It then updates the link impedances according to the resulting partial link flows, recomputes the minimum paths, and assigns the next increment of the interchange volumes. The procedure continues until 100% of the interzonal flows are assigned.

The method originally developed by the BPR [8.18] first performs an all-or-nothing assignment based on free-flow link impedances. It then updates all loaded links and repeats the all-or-nothing assignment using the new impedances. After several iterations, paths between pairs of zones are assigned a portion of the interzonal flow in proportion to the number of times that each appeared to be the minimum path. Figure 8.5.10 illustrates the results of this procedure on a small hypothetical network after four iterations [8.25].

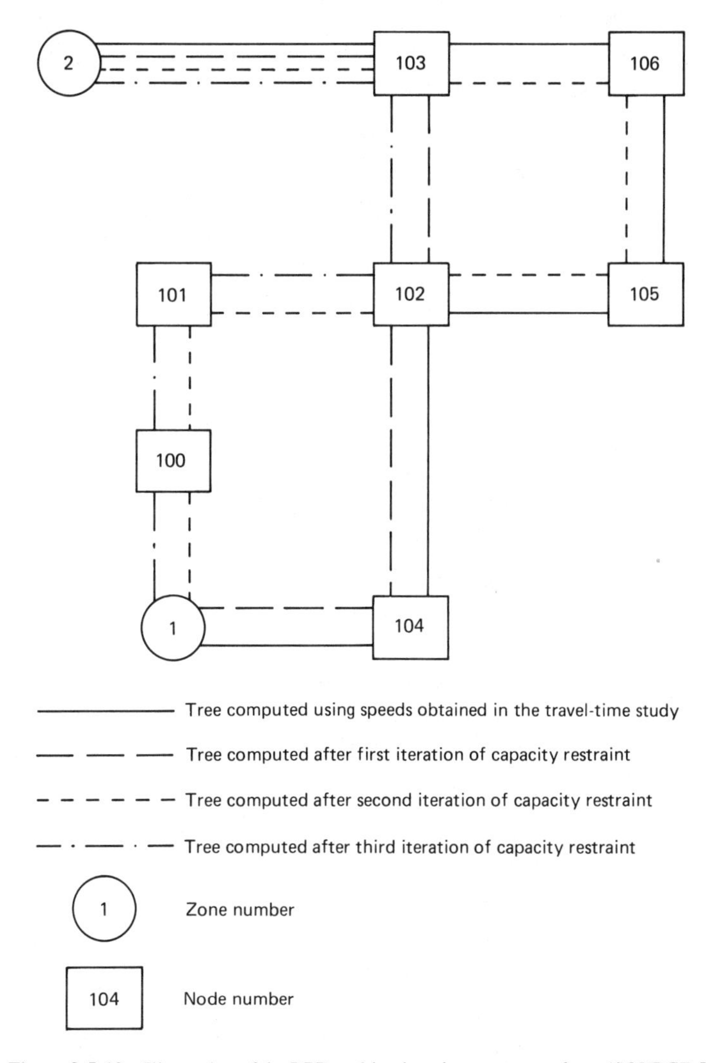

Figure 8.5.10 Illustration of the BPR multipath assignment procedure. (*SOURCE*: Humphrey [8.25], Fig. 1, p. 55.)

The Urban Transportation Planning System (UTPS), a battery of computer programs developed by the FHWA, includes a method that is based on the linear-programming optimization technique [8.26]. Figure 8.5.11 illustrates this method, which begins with a free/all-or-nothing assignment (iteration 0). The simple two-zone diagram shows that 100% of the interzonal flow is assigned to the minimum path. The BPR function (Eq. 8.5.1) is then applied to update the impedances of the loaded links. Iteration 1 repeats the all-or-nothing assignment based on the updated link impedances. At this stage, the linear-programming algorithm is applied to calculate the value of the variable λ, which is used to divide the interzonal volume between the first two paths. The link impedances are updated accordingly, and the procedure continues until λ is close to zero, a sign that an equilibrium stage has been reached.

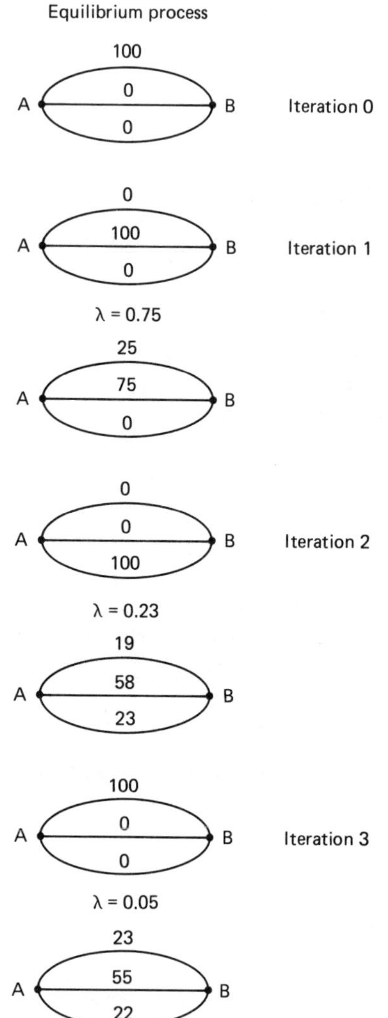

Figure 8.5.11 The UTPS capacity-restrained assignment procedure. (*SOURCE*: Levinsohn [8.26], Fig. III-7, p. III-13.)

Other capacity-restrained assignments have been reported in the literature (e.g., [8.27, 8.28]), including a two-pass Markov model, which allocates traffic to links based on reasonable transition probabilities [8.29].

8.5.14 Transit Assignment

The assignment of interzonal trips to a transit network presents certain complications that are not encountered in traffic assignment. In addition to the transit network of links and nodes, transit operations involve the identification of transit routes and schedules. The temporal pattern and directional orientation of demand coupled with resource limitations (e.g., available fleet size, operating costs) always dictate a service coverage that is not ubiquitous. Overlapping routes, the need to transfer between routes, differences between exclusive right-of-way lines and mixed traffic operations [8.30; 8.31], and variabilities of service in time and space add to the challenges associated with transit assignment. But the methods of transit-network analysis (e.g., [8.32]) are beyond the scope of this introductory textbook.

8.5.15 Summary

Network or trip assignment simulates the way in which trip-makers select their paths between zones. Traffic assignment estimates the expected flows that the links of the highway network are likely to experience to help anticipate potential capacity problems and to plan accordingly. It requires a behavioral hypothesis of route choice, a method of describing the highway network for computer processing, a way of selecting the appropriate interzonal paths, and a way of realistically allocating (i.e., assigning) the interzonal volumes on these paths. Several traffic-assignment models were described in this section, including a simple two-path diversion-curve model. In addition, traffic-assignment models that are more appropriate for the analysis of large networks were described. These models were classified in two ways. First, they were identified either as capacity-restrained or as free-assignment models, depending whether they explicitly account for the effect of congestion or not. Second, they were categorized as either all-or-nothing or multipath models, depending on whether they allocate the interzonal demand on a single or on multiple paths.

In addition to path (or route) allocation, transit assignment must contend with complexities that are not present in traffic assignment. The study of this topic falls outside the scope of this textbook.

8.6 SUMMARY

This chapter presented the fundamental elements of the sequential demand-forecasting process, the purpose of which is to predict how a proposed regional transportation system will be used at some future time. The process is driven by scenaria describing the distribution of future land uses and socioeconomic characteristics between small analysis zones in the region and a description of a regional multimodal transportation system. Consequently, it constitutes a conditional prediction of future demand given these inputs. The process is called *sequential* because it applies a chain of models in sequence to predict the number of trips that each zone will either produce or attract (trip generation), the interchange volumes between pairs of zones (trip distribution), the shares of interzonal volumes that will use each of the available travel modes (modal choice), and the allocation of interzonal trips to the interzonal paths provided by the transportation network (network assignment). The resulting interzonal volumes by mode can be translated to link flows in order to aid in the assessment of the ability of the transportation system to accommodate the demands that will be placed on it.

Given a land-use pattern, several proposed transportation system alternatives (including the do-nothing alternative) are typically examined. The outputs of the demand-forecasting models for each alternative are included among the consequences or impacts (see Chapter 10) that enter the process of system evaluation and selection (see Chapter 11). The demand-forecasting process can also aid in predicting the transportation consequences of land use changes and to provide guidance to related public policies.

Finally, the fact that large-scale transportation-demand forecasting is a monumental enterprise must not escape the attention of the student. The task is facilitated by the availability of computer-software packages that can be used for the calibration and application of the models described in this chapter as well as those covered in the following chapter. The most notable of these computer packages is the UTPS, which was developed and is continually updated by the DOT.

8.7 EXERCISES

1. An origin-destination survey in 10 travel-analysis zones provided the following data relating to zonal residential densities (households/acre) and average daily trip productions per household. Calibrate and plot a model of the form $10^Y = AX^{-B}$

Density X	42	5	25	10	4	15	20	12	14	22
Trip rate Y	1.5	4.0	2.1	2.6	4.8	2.0	2.5	3.3	1.9	2.0

2. A transportation engineer was hired by the city planning department to calibrate a multiple-regression model for trip productions. The department has collected base-year data for the following variables:

$$P_I = \text{trip productions}$$

$$X_1 = \text{zone population}$$

$$X_2 = \text{median income}$$

$$X_3 = \text{median age}$$

$$X_4 = \text{car registrations}$$

$$X_5 = \text{number of dwelling units}$$

A preliminary analysis of the data resulted in the following simple correlation matrix:

	P_I	X_1	X_2	X_3	X_4	X_5
P_I	1.00	0.95	0.83	0.41	0.82	0.85
X_1		1.00	−0.21	0.22	−0.29	0.91
X_2			1.00	0.82	0.89	−0.43
X_4				1.00	−0.19	−0.15
X_5					1.00	−0.22

Specify at least five possible equations that may be tried and give the specific reasons for their selection.

3. A zone in the CBD is projected to contain 1,525,000 ft² of residential space; 3,675,000 ft² of service establishments; and a total retail activity floor area of 2,100,000 ft². Government and other public buildings occupy a total area of 615,000 ft². Using the data obtained in Pittsburgh, calculate the trip generation of this zone.

4. An international hotel chain is planning the construction of a motel/office development in a resort town. The preliminary design includes 2100 rooms, a sit-down restaurant having a total floor space of 2500 ft², and 5000 ft² of office space, which the company is planning to lease to various local firms. Apply the trip rates published by the Institute of Transportation Engineers to estimate the total trip attractions during the afternoon traffic peak hour.

5. A high-rise apartment building containing 350 units is planned for a residential area of a city. Because the area is zoned for low-density residential land uses, the developer has applied for a zoning variance. At the legally required public hearing, several residents of the area have opposed the zoning change, claiming that the proposal will add to the traffic-congestion problem during the peak hours, but they were unable to substantiate their claim. Calculate the likely peak-hour trip generation of the proposed project.

6. Use the cross-classification table (Table 8.2.6) to calculate the total nonwork-home-based productions of each of two zones that are expected to contain the following mixtures of households (HH):

Zone 1: Suburban

Persons/HH \ Veh/HH	0	1	2+
1	50	150	100
2,3	10	500	300
4	100	400	100

Zone 2: Rural

Persons/HH \ Veh/HH	0	1	2+
1	300	50	100
2,3	100	200	100
4	400	300	150

7. A residential zone is expected to have 1500 dwelling units. For a $12,000 average income, calculate (a) the person trips per dwelling unit for units that own 0, 1, 2, and 3+ autos and (b) the total trip generation by trip purpose. Use the income-auto-ownership distribution given in Fig. 8.2.5 and assume that Curve C applies to all subgroups within the zone.

8. Given

1.

Zone	Productions	Attractiveness
1	1000	2
2	0	5
3	2000	1

2. W_{IJ}:

I \ J	1	2	3
1	5	20	10
2	20	5	10
3	10	10	5

K_{IJ}:

I \ J	1	2	3
1	1.1	1.5	0.8
2	0.6	1.2	0.5
3	1.0	1.4	1.3

3. $\ln F = -1.5 \ln W$

Apply the gravity model to calculate all interchange volumes.

9. Complete the following table given that $P_1 = 1000$ trips per day, $c = 2.0$, and all $K_{IJ} = 1.0$.

Zone	A_J	W_{IJ}	F_{IJ}	Q_{IJ}
1	0	—		
2	400	20		
3	300	5		
4	100	5		
5	200	10		

10. Assuming that the relationship between F and W is of the form $F = A\,W^{-c}$, apply the method of least squares to the following data to estimate the parameters A and c.

F	0.03	0.04	0.02	0.03
W	7	5	12	8

11. The final iteration in a calibration of the gravity model yielded the following friction-factor and impedance values:

F	1.0	4.0	0.5	0.3
W	12	4	15	20

(a) Calibrate a relationship of the form $F = aW^{-b}$

(b) Apply your results to the following case:

Two residential zones (1 and 2) are expected to produce 6500 and 3800 person-trips per day, respectively. Two nonresidential zones (3 and 4) are competing for these trips. The planning commission has received a proposal to improve parts of the transportation system, which, if implemented, would affect certain interzonal impedances as shown.

Do-nothing		
$I \backslash J$	3	4
1	10	14
2	8	14

Proposed plan		
$I \backslash J$	3	4
1	10	10
2	8	8

Given the following additional information, calculate the effect of the proposal on the total trips attracted by the nonresidential zones.

$$A_3 = 10, \quad A_4 = 15, \quad \text{and all} \quad K_{IJ} = 1.0$$

12. A base-year trip-generation study obtained the data shown relating to the daily person-trip productions per dwelling unit (Y) and residential density (X dwelling units per acre).

Y	3.5	6.5	4.0	2.2
X	30.0	10.0	50.0	70.0

(a) Calibrate and plot the relationship $Y = (a + bX)^{-1}$

(b) Apply your answers to part (a) to the following situation:

A residential zone I has an area of 500 acres and contains 7500 dwelling units. Two zones (J and L) are competing for the trips produced by I. Given the following information, calculate the trip interchange volumes Q_{IJ} and Q_{IL} if $W_{IJ} = 12$, $W_{IL} = 8$, $\ln F = -1.5 \ln W$, $A_J = 0.5\, A_L$, and all $K_{IJ} = 1.0$.

13. A gravity-model calibration study obtained the following final values for the travel time factors and the interzonal impedances:

F	0.19	0.10	0.07	0.05
W	4	7	9	12

Using F as the dependent variable, calculate the parameter c of Eq. 8.3.9.

14. Given the following data:

I	P	A
1	2000	4
2	0	10
3	0	12

W_{IJ}			
$I \backslash J$	1	2	3
1	5	10	15
2	10	4	10
3	15	10	15

Estimate all interchange volumes assuming that $c = 1.9$ and that all socioeconomic adjustment factors are equal to unity.

15. After calibrating Eq. 8.3.13, the following interzonal information became available. The observed and calculated interzonal flow interchanging between I and J were 2500 and 2100, respectively. The data corresponding to the interchange between zones I and L were 1960 and 2060. Given that the total production of zone I was 12,000 trips, calculate the socioeconomic adjustment factors for the two interchanges.

16. Computerize the application of the gravity model of trip distribution.

17. Perform a second Fratar model iteration using the results of Example 8.6.

18. Computerize the Fratar model, making sure to place an upper limit on the number of iterations in order to avoid infinite looping.

19. Given the utility equation

$$U_K = a_K - 0.003X_1 - 0.04X_2$$

where X_1 is the travel cost in cents and X_2 is the travel time in minutes.

(a) Calculate the market shares of the following travel modes:

Mode K	a_K	X_1	X_2
Automobile	−0.20	120	30
Express bus	−0.40	60	45
Regular bus	−0.60	30	55

(b) Estimate the effect that a 50% increase in the cost of all three modes will have on modal split.

20. Given the utility expression

$$U_K = A_K - 0.05T_a - 0.04T_w - 0.02T_r - 0.01C$$

where T_a is the access time, T_w is the waiting time, T_r is the riding time, and C is the out-of-pocket cost.

(a) Apply the logit model to calculate the shares of the automobile mode ($A_K = -0.005$) and a mass-transit mode ($A_K = -0.05$) if

Mode	T_a	T_w	T_r	C
Auto	5	0	30	100
Transit	10	10	45	50

(b) Estimate the patronage shift that would result from doubling the bus out-of-pocket cost.

21. Computerize the application of the multinomial logit model allowing for N choices and M attributes per choice, where N and M are input variables.

22. The application of a route-building algorithm resulted in the following final tree table:

Node To	Total Time	Node From
1	0	—
2	8	3
3	3	1
4	7	3
5	17	6
6	10	2
7	8	4
8	19	5

Node To	Total Time	Node From
9	13	6
10	14	9
11	17	10
12	18	9
13	18	10
14	25	12
15	23	13
16	22	13

Sketch the minimum tree, and specify the link travel times.

23. Complete the tree table that describes the minimum tree shown in the accompanying figure.

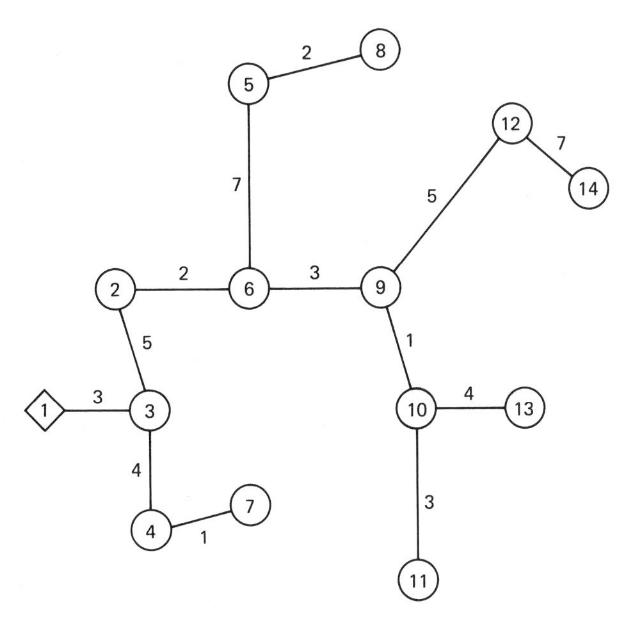

Figure E.8.23

24. Without drawing the entire network described by the accompanying link table, find and sketch the minimum tree emanating from node 1.

i	j	w_{ij}
1	4	2
2	5	4
2	6	3
3	8	5
4	1	2
4	5	6

i	j	w_{ij}
4	8	10
5	2	4
5	4	6
5	6	4
6	2	3
6	5	4
6	7	9
7	6	9
7	8	7
8	3	5
8	4	10
8	7	7

25. Given the link table of Exercise 8.24 (a) find graphically the minimum tree emanating from node 1; (b) using your answer to part (a), calculate Q_{1-2} and Q_{1-3} if $P_1 = 2500$ trips per day, $A_2 = 1.5$, $A_3 = 3.5$, all other P_I and $A_J = 0$, and all $K_{IJ} = 1.0$; and (c) perform an all-or-nothing assignment to allocate the interzonal volumes calculated in part (b) to the links of the network.

26. Write a computer program for the minimum-tree-seeking procedure described in this chapter.

27. Allocate the following peak-hour interchange volumes produced by zone 10 to the network described.

J	11	12	13	14	15	16	17
Q_{IJ}	200	150	190	270	320	110	540

Link Table

i	j	w_{ij}	i	j	w_{ij}
10	14	6	14	13	15
10	15	5	14	15	7
10	16	12	15	10	5
11	14	5	15	11	3
11	15	3	15	14	7
11	17	8	15	16	8
12	14	21	16	10	12
12	16	4	16	12	4
12	17	3	16	13	7
13	14	15	16	15	8
13	16	7	16	17	2
13	17	6	17	11	8
14	10	6	17	12	3
14	11	5	17	13	6
14	12	21	17	16	2

If the capacity of link 10-16 is 1000 veh/hr calculate this link's travel time as implied by your answer.

8.8 REFERENCES

8.1 Federal Highway Administration, *Trip Generation Analysis,* U.S. Department of Transportation, U.S. Government Printing Office, Stock Number 050-001-00101-2, Washington, D.C., 1975.

8.2 PAPACOSTAS, C. S., "Honolulu's Handi-Van: Use and Implications," *Traffic Quarterly,* 34, no. 3 (July 1980): 429–440.

8.3 KEEFER, L. E. (Director), *Pittsburgh Area Transportation Study,* vol I, Study Findings, November 1961.

8.4 Federal Highway Administration *Guidelines for Trip Generation Analysis,* U.S. Department of Transportation, U.S. Government Printing Office, Washington, D.C., June 1967.

8.5 ———, *Computer Programs for Urban Transportation Planning: PLANPAC/BACKPAC General Information,* U.S. Department of Transportation, U.S. Government Printing Office, Stock Number 050-001-00125-0, Washington, D.C., April 1977.

8.6 Illinois Section, Institute of Transportation Engineers, "Trip Generation Study of Selected Commercial and Residential Developments," *Traffic Engineering,* XL, No. 6, 1970.

8.7 Oahu Metropolitan Planning Organization, *Oahu Model Update Study: User's Manual and Training Information,* Honolulu, Hawaii, December 1982.

8.8 BOCK, F. C., *Factors Influencing Modal Trip Assignment,* National Cooperative Highway Research Report 57, Highway Research Board, National Research Council, Washington, D.C., 1968.

8.9 FRATAR, T. J., "Forecasting the Distribution of Interzonal Vehicular Trips by Successive Approximations," Proceedings of the 33rd Annual Meeting, Highway Research Board, National Research Council, Washington, D.C., 1954.

8.10 FERTAL, M. J., et al., *Modal Split: Documentation of Nine Methods for Estimating Transit Usage,* Bureau of Public Roads, U.S. Department of Commerce, U.S. Government Printing Office, Washington, D.C., December 1966.

8.11 DEEN, T. B., W. L. MERTZ, AND N. A. IRWIN, "Application of a Modal Split Model to Travel Estimates for the Washington Area," *Highway Research Record* 38, Highway Research Board, National Research Council, Washington, D.C., 1963, pp. 97–123.

8.12 KANAFANI, A., *Transportation Demand Analysis,* McGraw-Hill, New York, 1983.

8.13 HUTCHINSON, B. G., *Principles of Urban Transport Systems Planning,* McGraw-Hill, New York, 1974.

8.14 LANCASTER, K. J., "A New Approach to Consumer Theory," *Journal of Political Economy,* 64 (1966) 132–157.

8.15 STOPHER, P. R., "A Probability Model of Travel Mode Choice for the Work Journey," *Highway Research Record* 283, Highway Research Board, National Research Council, Washington, D.C., 1969, pp. 57–65.

8.16 RASSAM, P. R., R. H. ELLIS, AND J. C. BENNET, "The *n*-Dimensional Logit Model: Development and Applications," *Highway Research Record* 369, Highway Research Board, National Research Council, Washington, D.C., 1971, pp. 135–147.

8.17 MOSKOWITZ, K., "California Model of Assigning Diverted Traffic to Proposed Freeways," *Highway Research Record* 130, Highway Research Board, National Research Council, Washington, D.C., 1956, pp. 1–26.

8.18 Bureau of Pubic Roads, *Traffic Assignment Manual,* U.S. Department of Commerce, U.S. Government Printing Office, Washington, D.C., June 1964.

8.19 Federal Highway Administration, *Traffic Assignment*, U.S. Department of Transportation, U.S. Government Printing Office, Stock Number 5001-00060, Washington, D.C., August 1973.

8.20 Moore, E. F., "The Shortest Path Through a Maze," Proceedings of the International Symposium on the Theory of Switching, Harvard University, 1957.

8.21 Martin, B. V., *Minimum Path Algorithms for Transportation Planning,* Department of Civil Engineering, Research Report R63-52, Massachussetts Institute of Technology, 1963.

8.22 Irwin, N. A., and H. G. von Cube, "Capacity Restraint in Multi-Travel Mode Assignment Programs," *Highway Research Board, Bulletin* 347, National Research Council, Washington, D.C., 1962, pp. 258–289.

8.23 Huber, M. J., H. B. Boutwell, and D. K. Witheford, "Comparative Analysis of Traffic Assignment Techniques with Actual Highway Use," *National Cooperative Highway Research Report* 58, Highway Research Board, National Research Council, Washington, D.C., 1968.

8.24 Schneider, M., "A Direct Approach to Traffic Assignment," *Highway Research Record* 6, Highway Research Board, National Research Council, Washington, D.C., 1963, pp. 71–75.

8.25 Humphrey, T. F., "A Report on the Accuracy of Traffic Assignment when Using Capacity Restraint," *Highway Research Record* 191, Highway Research Board, National Research Council, Washington, D.C., 1967, pp. 53–75.

8.26 Levinsohn, D., et al. *UTPS Highway Network Development Guide,* Federal Highway Administration, U.S. Department of Transportation, Washington, D.C., January 1983.

8.27 Smock, R., "An Iterative Assignment Approach to Capacity Restraint on Arterial Networks," *Highway Research Board, Bulletin* 347, National Research Council, Washington, D.C., 1962, pp. 60–66.

8.28 Irwin, N. A., N. Dodd, and H. G. von Cube, "Capacity Restraint in Assignment Programs," *Highway Research Board, Bulletin* 297, National Research Council, Washington, D.C., 1961, pp. 109–127.

8.29 Dial, R. A., "A Probabilistic Traffic Assignment Model which Obviates Path Enumeration," *Transportation Research,* 5, no. 2 (1971): 83–222.

8.30 Papacostas, C. S., *Development and Application of the Bimodal Travel Behavior Model,* Masters Thesis, Department of Civil Engineering, Carnegie-Mellon University, 1971.

8.31 Papacostas, C. S., *Pollution and Energy Implications of Bus-Automobile Alternatives,* Ph.D. Dissertation, Department of Civil Engineering, Carnegie-Mellon University, 1974.

8.32 Dial, R. B., G. S. Rutherford, and L. Quillian, *Transit Network Analysis: INET,* Urban Mass Transportation Administration, Report No. UMTA-UPM-20-79-3, U.S. Department of Transportation, Washington, D.C., July 1979.

CHAPTER 9

ALTERNATIVE PLANNING MODELS AND STRUCTURES

9.1 INTRODUCTION

The urban transportation-planning methodology illustrated by Fig. 7.4.9 was originally intended to provide guidance to the selection of a master plan based on the long-term (i.e., 20 years), regional (i.e., urbanized area), and user impacts (travel times and travel costs) of alternative highway proposals. The selected alternative was programmed and implemented in stages, and there was a time lag between the implementation of the various components of the preferred alternative and the occurrence of the estimated long-term impacts on the basis of which the choice of alternative was to be made. The following modeling steps were undertaken for this purpose: First, the long-range future land-use pattern was anticipated by applying specially designed mathematical models; second, potential highway alternatives were specified; and third, the regional travel patterns implied in the projected land-use pattern and the characteristics of each highway alternative were used to forecast the likely user impacts. To accomplish this conditional prediction, the four-step demand-forecasting sequence was applied, as discussed in Chapter 8.

The procedure was adopted worldwide and attained the status of a *de facto* standard methodology. In the United States, this methodology was institutionalized as a principal element of the 3C planning process (see Chapter 7). In its early applications, this quantitative modeling procedure was expected to be capable of producing the information relevant to transportation decisions at the regional and subregional levels. However, during the late 1960s and early 1970s, as more and more urban areas were producing their regional master plans in this manner, certain limitations of the procedure became apparent. Among these were the following:

1. As typically applied, the methodology paid minimal attention to travel modes other than highways and to consequences other than direct user impacts.
2. Because of its large-scale and long-range view, this process was incapable of providing sufficiently detailed information to guide small-scale operational improvements.
3. The method was generally slow to respond to major technological changes, to revised transportation and land-use policies, and to the collective long-term implications of short-range operational and land-use changes.
4. Being driven by a single land use projection, the process was insensitive to the effect of proposed transportation system changes on land-use development.
5. The adequacy of individual travel-demand-forecasting models and the practice of sequentially chaining of these models were questioned.

Initial attempts to modify and expand the original modeling structure to respond to these planning issues led to a general understanding that it is unlikely that a single "super" land-use and transportation model can be devised that is capable of guiding decisions for all places, at all times, and for all levels of aggregation. Consequently, a large variety of models and modeling arrangements have evolved, each intended to produce information that is specifically suited to particular planning situations. As a result, the tasks and responsibilities of transportation planners are no longer restricted to the routine application of a set of standard planning models. One important aspect of contemporary transportation planning is the informed selection of the particular models and modeling structure that are most appropriate to the situation at hand.

This chapter summarizes selected developments related to these questions in order to familiarize the student with the larger context of contemporary transportation planning. Further discussion of these issues can be found in the technical literature [9.1–9.8].

9.2 DEMAND-FORECASTING MODELS

9.2.1 Background

Efforts to improve the modeling of transportation demand have followed two main paths. The first represents a move away from purely empirical models and toward models that are grounded on an improved theoretical understanding of travel behavior. The ultimate test of the appropriateness of these theoretical constructs, however, is not their theoretical eloquence but their ability realistically to describe and predict the real world. The second major thrust of modeling has been toward the discovery of simple models that can facilitate decision-making by providing useful information quickly and inexpensively. Of course, the availability of parsimonious models that are also soundly based on a realistic theory of travel behavior is ideal, but theoretical difficulties and practical constraints prevent the attainment of this ideal.

Chapter 8 surveyed alternative formulations for each of the four components of travel behavior, for example, trip generation, trip distribution, modal choice, and trip assignment. In addition, two alternative calibration approaches (aggregate or disaggregate) and two alternative choice theories (choice-specific and choice-abstract) were discussed. Additional modeling options available to the transportation planner are presented next.

9.2.2 Demand-Model Consistency

Model consistency is an important consideration relating to modeling the demand for transportation. Consider, for example, the difference between free and capacity-restrained traffic-assignment models. As explained in Chapter 8, a free assignment allocates the interzonal flows based on the free-flow interzonal impedances associated with alternative routes between zones. Because the impedances implied by the assigned flows could be significantly different from their assumed values, various capacity-restrained algorithms have been developed to ensure internal consistency between the two sets of interzonal impedances.

The question of consistency between the four steps of the sequential process was also addressed. For instance, it was argued that a conformance must be sought between the interzonal impedances used by the trip-distribution phase and those that result from trip assignment; as a matter of fact, several studies have introduced a feedback link between the two models for this purpose. Figure 9.2.1 illustrates an early attempt made

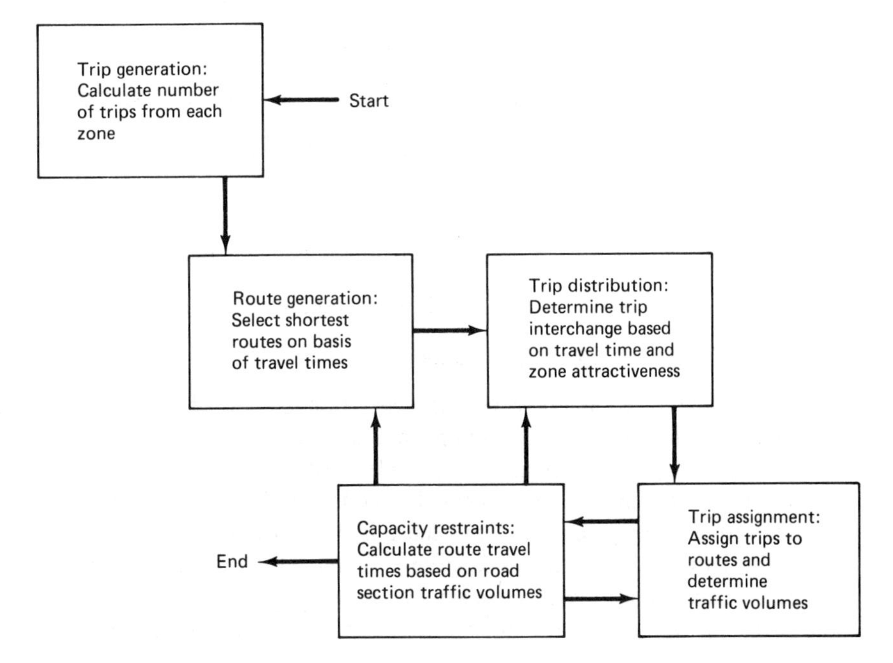

Figure 9.2.1 The Toronto study feedback mechanism. (*SOURCE*: Irwin [9.8], Fig. 1, p. 110.)

by the Toronto Transportation Study [9.9] to introduce feedbacks between trip distribution and traffic assignment. Note that the modal choice step does not appear. Iterating among all four steps in search of overall model consistency is more difficult and resource-intensive than it may seem.

9.2.3 Simultaneous or Direct Demand Formulations

A related travel-demand theory states that an individual makes travel choices simultaneously rather than in a sequence of discrete steps and that a demand model should be calibrated to reflect this behavior. An often-cited example of *simultaneous* models is the Quandt and Baumol [9.10] formulation of intercity travel demand, which, using the notation of this textbook, takes the general form:

$$Q_{IJK} = a_0(P_I)^{a_1} (P_J)^{a_2} (C_{IJ*})^{a_3} \left(\frac{C_{IJK}}{C_{IJ*}}\right)^{a_4} (H_{IJ*})^{a_5} \left(\frac{H_{IJK}}{H_{IJ*}}\right)^{a_6} \left(\frac{D_{IJK}}{D_{IJ*}}\right)^{a_7} (Y_{IJ})^{a_8} \quad (9.2.1)$$

where:

Q_{IJK} = the travel flow between cities I and J via mode K

P_I, P_J = the populations of I and J

C_{IJ*} = the least cost of travel between I and J

C_{IJK} = the cost via mode K

H_{IJ} = the shortest travel time between I and J

H_{IJK} = the travel time via mode K

D_{IJ*} = the departure frequency of the most frequent mode

D_{IJK} = the departure frequency of mode K

Y_{IJ} = the weighted average incomes of I and J

$a_0, \ldots, a_8$ = calibration parameters

This model is a simultaneous trip-generation–trip-distribution–modal choice equation employing land-use variables (populations), socioeconomic characteristics (income levels), and interzonal impedances by mode (costs, travel times, and frequency of service) to estimate the interzonal demands by mode (Q_{IJK}). In keeping with the purpose of the demand-estimating methodology, these interzonal flows would presumably be assigned to the networks of the modes K serving the region to find the equilibrium link flows. The earlier-raised question of consistency between the assumed levels of some of the explanatory variables (travel times, for example) and the levels implied in the results of the assignment phase resurfaces.

In urban situations, the calibration and application of such large models is, to say the least, cumbersome. However, they may be useful for rather coarse estimates at the regional level if the number of zones and the degree of detail in specifying the transportation network are kept to a minimum.

9.2.4 Combined Modeling Strategies

Between the two extremes of sequential model arrangements and large simultaneous models there exist a plethora of options that are partly sequential and partly simultaneous. The following excerpt from a modeling undertaking in Canberra, Australia [9.11], that was intended to be sensitive to the short-term effects of various TSM-type options illustrates this point:

> If all travel choice decisions for all purpose groups were to be modelled, the scope of modelling required would be extensive and consequently very expensive. It is however possible to reduce the scale and range of models by making some *a priori* assumptions as to the travel choice processes exercised by individual travellers or potential travellers. For example it seems reasonable to assume, certainly for the short term, that workplace and schooling location and the frequency of work and school trips are relatively stable and do not vary significantly under the range of practical conditions which are likely to occur. In these particular cases travel mode choice would therefore appear to be the most important travel decision. Using these and similar reasonings for other purpose categories, a listing of the necessary models was prepared. Specifically these models were:
>
> (a) work, mode choice,
> (b) school, mode choice,
> (c) shopping, mode choice,
> (d) shopping, frequency,
> (e) shopping, destination,
> (f) shopping, mode choice/destination,
> (g) social/recreation, mode choice,
> (h) social/recreation, destination, and
> (i) social/recreation, mode choice/destination.
>
> Other purpose groups were reasoned to be either less significant in terms of scale than the above purpose groups or they were to be less responsive to the specific policy measures, which can be manipulated by Canberra transport planners. ([9.11], p. 62)

Models (d) and (e) are trip-generation and trip-distribution models, respectively, calibrated for shopping trips that could be chained in the sequence d-e-c. Model (f) is a simultaneous modal choice and trip distribution model that may be applied after estimating trip generation (i.e., model (d)). Similarly, (g) and (h) are modal choice and trip-distribution models, respectively, and (i) is a simultaneous model of these two choices.

Careful contemplation of the quoted terse statement will reveal the wide variety of modeling choices available to the contemporary transportation planner, the need to tailor specific models and model arrangements to particular levels of planning and policy issues, and the importance of professional judgement in this most important phase of transportation planning.

One common form of simultaneous models of trip distribution and modal choice is the following *share model:*

$$Q_{IJK} = P_I \frac{A_J e^{U_{IJK}}}{\sum_{X,Y} A_X e^{U_{IXY}}} \tag{9.2.2}$$

Note that the inputs to this model are the exogenously estimated zonal trip productions P_I, zonal trip attractiveness A_J, and interzonal modal utilities U_{IJK} (see Chapter 8). The output of this simultaneous logit model consists of interzonal flows by mode. Any change in the values U_{IJK} is permitted to affect both the trip distribution and the modal shares of the interzonal demand at the same time.

9.3 MODELS OF DEMAND ELASTICITY

9.3.1 Background

Many planning situations are concerned with immediate or short-term actions or with relatively small changes to the system that do not warrant an elaborate and detailed analytical treatment. Several simplified methods have been developed for this purpose. For example, consider the situation of a planner who has been hired by a private developer to estimate the traffic impacts of a proposed high-rise residential building as part of an EIS that is a prerequisite to securing the necessary building permits. In this case, a rough estimate of the trip generation based on published trip rates for different types of land uses (e.g., [9.12]) would probably suffice. Simple models are also appropriate to planning studies for rural areas, small- and medium-size urban areas, and certain elements of planning for larger cities [9.13–9.15].

A transportation-demand model that can be used to provide broad predictions of the response of trip-makers to changes in the transportation system is founded in the economic concept of price elasticity of demand.

9.3.2 Definition of Price Elasticity of Demand

In economic theory, the law of demand states that, everything else being constant, the quantity Q of goods or services that consumers demand decreases as their price P increases, and, conversely, when the price is reduced, the quantity demanded rises. Figure 9.3.1 illustrates this law. The parallel to transportation viewed as a service that is subject to market forces is inescapable. For example, a patronage drop should be expected to occur

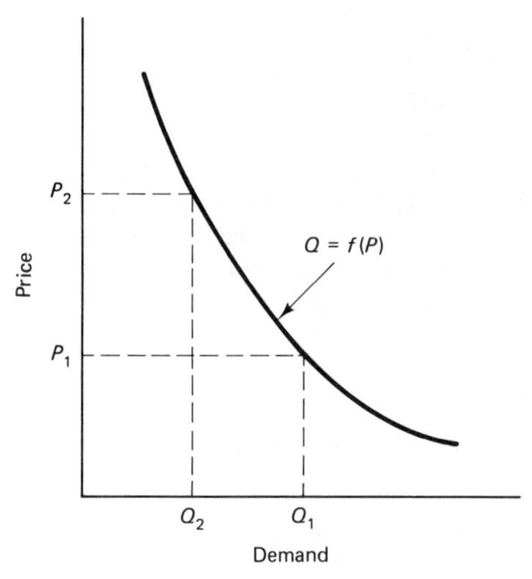

Figure 9.3.1 A hypothetical demand curve.

following an increase in transit fares. Similarly, lowering the downtown parking fees should encourage an increase in automobile use.

The price elasticity of demand, E, is defined as

$$E = \frac{(dQ/Q)}{(dP/P)} = \frac{dQ}{dP}\frac{P}{Q} \tag{9.3.1}$$

In words, it is the ratio of the *relative* change in the quantity demanded to the *relative* change in price.

Example 9.1: Linear-Demand Functions

Given a demand function of the form

$$Q = a - bP \tag{9.3.2}$$

express the price elasticity of demand as a function of price.

Solution Applying Eq. 9.3.1,

$$E = \frac{-Pb}{Q}$$

Substituting Eq. 9.3.2 in this,

$$E = \frac{-Pb}{a - bP}$$

Discussion The negative sign of elasticity reflects the fact that a percentage increase in P will cause a percentage decrease in Q. The solution illustrates that, depending on the demand function, the price elasticity of demand is not constant for all points on the curve. In addition, the value of the price elasticity of demand reflects the implication of a price change on the total revenue (PQ) of the supplier. For example, when $E < -1$, the percent decrease in Q (i.e., the numerator of Eq. 9.3.1) is larger than the percent increase in P (i.e., the denominator of Eq. 9.3.1). In that case, the demand is said to be *elastic* and the total revenue after the price increase decreases because the loss of sales volume outweighs the extra revenue obtained per unit sold. When $E > -1$, the demand is said to be *inelastic* and the total revenue after raising P increases. When $E = -1$, the demand is *unitarily elastic* and the revenue derived from selling less units at a higher price is equal to the total revenue prior to raising the price, for example, more units at a lower price. Thus an upward or downward price change may result in an increase, a decrease, or a constancy of revenue. The value of the price elasticity of demand reflects this fact.

Example 9.2: Product Forms

The demand for a particular transit service has been assessed to be a function of fare F and travel time T as follows:

$$Q = aF^b T^c \tag{9.3.3}$$

Calculate the elasticity of demand with respect to (a) fare and (b) travel time.

Solution The two elasticities can be computed via Eq. 9.3.1 except that partial derivatives should be taken.

The fare elasticity of demand is

$$E_f = \left(\frac{F}{Q}\right) abF^{b-1}T^c$$

Substituting Eq. 9.3.3 in this relationship,

$$E_f = b$$

Similarly, the travel time elasticity of demand is

$$E_t = c$$

Discussion This example illustrates that if the demand function is of the product form (9.3.3), the exponents of the price components represent the elasticity of demand with respect to each component. This is the basic reason why Quandt and Baumol have selected this particular functional form for their simultaneous demand equation (9.2.1). A disadvantage of this form is that it assumes that the elasticities are constant. This may be reasonable for price-level changes near the base-data conditions.

9.3.3 Direct and Cross Elasticities

So far, the discussion of elasticity was confined to the effect of changes in the price of a product on the demand for the *same* product. This type of elasticity is called a *direct* elasticity. On the other hand, a price change in one product often affects the demand for *another* product. Price elasticities reflecting this effect are called *cross* elasticities. Cross effects may be positive or negative depending on whether the two products are complementary or substitutes for each other. An increase in the cost of automobile travel would be expected to cause a decrease in automobile use (direct effect) and an increase in transit patronage (cross effect). Another possible cross effect is a decrease in the demand for automobile tires.

9.3.4 Measurement of Elasticities

The discussion of Example 9.2 implies that one way of obtaining elasticity estimates is to apply Eq. 9.3.1 to calibrated demand models such as those included in Chapter 8 and Eqs. 9.2.1 and 9.2.2. Note that if certain important cost or level-of-service variables are not included in a particular model, their associated effect on demand cannot be derived. It would be distributed among the variables included in the model. Also, if a calibrated model is not readily available, this method of elasticity estimation may be very expensive and time-consuming.

Another method of obtaining estimates of elasticities is by observing the effects of actual price changes in the system under study [9.16, 9.17]. When undertaking this task, special care must be exercised to account properly for demand changes due to factors other than price, such as secular trends attributable to population and demographic changes. When the observed situation involves changes in more than one cost component, it is important to separate the overall demand response to its corresponding individual components. An excellent treatment of these issues may be found in the work reported by Parody and Brand [9.16] relating to a study of the transit system of the city of Jacksonville, Florida.

In that study, various elasticities for several user subgroups were derived and used to predict the transit-demand effects of alternative fare structures. Incidentally, the practice of calibrating demand models specifically for individual market subgroups (known as *market segmentation*) is a matter of increasing concern to planners, especially as it relates to tailoring transportation services to the needs of these groups and, also, as it relates to the investigation of how transportation benefits and costs are distributed among them.

Given an actual price change, say from P_1 to P_2 as shown in Fig. 9.3.1, and an observed demand change from Q_1 to Q_2, the implicit price elasticity of demand (Eq. 9.3.1) may be approximated in several ways:

1. The *shrinkage ratio,* defined as

$$E_{\text{shr}} = \frac{(Q_2 - Q_1)/Q_1}{(P_2 - P_1)/P_1} \tag{9.3.4}$$

2. The midpoint (or linear) *arc elasticity,* computed as

$$E_{\text{arc}} = \frac{(Q_2 - Q_1)/(Q_1 + Q_2)}{(P_2 - P_1)/(P_1 + P_2)} \tag{9.3.5}$$

3. The *log-arc elasticity,* calculated as

$$E_{\text{log-arc}} = \frac{\log Q_2 - \log Q_1}{\log P_2 - \log P_1} \tag{9.3.6}$$

These three measures of elasticity yield approximately equal values for relatively small price changes. For larger differences, the shrinkage ratio begins to deviate significantly from the other two.

Example 9.3: Application of Elasticities

Given that the log-arc elasticity of demand is -0.28, calculate the effect of an increase in transit fares from 50¢ to 80¢ given that the patronage prior to the price increase is 20,000 riders per day.

Solution Equation 9.3.6 yields

$$-0.28 = \frac{\log Q_2 - \log 20{,}000}{\log 80 - \log 50}$$

Solving for Q_2,

$$Q_2 = 17{,}534 \text{ riders per day}$$

Discussion Since the given direct elasticity was of the log-arc form, Eq. 9.3.6 was applied. To illustrate the differences between the three measures of elasticity, the shrinkage ratio and the arc elasticity implied in the above results may be computed. Equation 9.3.4 with $Q_2 = 17{,}534$ yields $E_{\text{shr}} = -0.21$, and Eq. 9.3.5 gives $E_{\text{arc}} = -0.29$. As stated previously, the shrinkage ratio tends to deviate from the other two measures.

Example 9.4: Multiple Price Changes

The shares of the automobile and a transit mode along a corridor are 4,500 and 1,000 persons per peak period, respectively. The prevailing out-of-pocket costs and travel times associated with the two modes are as follows:

	Time (min)	Cost ($)
Auto	35	2.00
Transit	50	1.00

The shrinkage ratios with respect to transit prices have been estimated to be:

	Time (min)	Cost ($)
Auto	0.05	0.04
Transit	−0.52	−0.30

In other words, the direct elasticity of transit demand with respect to transit travel time is −0.52, the cross elasticity of auto demand with respect to transit cost is 0.04, and so forth. The shrinkage ratios with respect to auto prices are:

	Time (min)	Cost ($)
Auto	−0.58	−0.20
Transit	0.12	0.03

The city department of transportation services is contemplating the opening of an exclusive bus lane that would save an average of 10 min per trip. At the same time, the city council is holding public hearings on a proposal to raise downtown parking rates and thus cause an increase in automobile travel costs to $2.60. Estimate the likely effects on peak-hour travel demand of both actions combined.

Solution The direct effect of reducing the transit travel time on transit patronage may be predicted by Eq. 9.3.4, which may be rewritten as

$$Q_2 - Q_1 = \frac{E_{\text{shr}} Q_1 (T_2 - T_1)}{T_1}$$

$$= \frac{(-0.52)(1000)(40 - 50)}{50}$$

$$= 104$$

Thus the transit patronage would increase by 104 peak-hour trips, or by 10.4% in relation to the initial demand of 1000, as a result of a 20% decrease in travel time. Because of the way in which shrinkage ratios are defined, the same answer could have been obtained by proportioning the given shrinkage ratio. Specifically, this ratio states that a 1% increase (decrease) in travel time would result in a 0.52% decrease (increase) in transit patronage. Since the contemplated decrease in travel time is 20%, the percentage of increase in patronage would be $20 \times 0.52 = 10.4\%$ of the original demand, or $1000 \times 0.104 = 104$ trips.

The remaining likely direct and cross effects are summarized next:

Action	Demand changes Automobile	Transit system
20% transit-time reduction	−45	+104
30% auto-cost increase	−270	+9
Combined Effects	−315	+113

Discussion In combination, the two actions would result in a decrease of 315 auto person-trips per peak and an increase in transit patronage of 113. The available information precludes any definite answers to the question of what would happen to the net loss of 202 peak-hour person-trips, for example, whether they would shift to another time period, whether they would be given up, or whether they would shift to another mode not included in the analysis.

The question of internal consistency discussed in Subsection 9.2.2 merits consideration: The predicted decrease in auto trips may, in fact, cause a reduction in auto travel times, whereas the added transit patronage may induce the scheduling of additional departures, thus decreasing the average waiting times and, consequently, travel times. These changes may have further direct and cross effects on the peak hour demand before a new equilibrium is reached.

9.4 OTHER PLANNING ISSUES

9.4.1 Background

The introduction to this chapter identified several weaknesses of the long-term transportation master-planning procedure as typically applied during the 1960s and early 1970s. Among these issues were the problem of joint transportation and land-use planning, the treatment of uncertainty about future policy changes, and the problem of coordinating long-range and on-going planning. This section addresses these issues in very general terms.

9.4.2 Transportation and Land Use

That there exists an intimate relationship between transportation and land development has been understood for centuries [9.18, 9.19]. An understanding of this interaction is also evident in the principles of the city practical approach described in Chapter 7. In that case, the city form preferred by certain planners was closely related to the transportation technology of the day: radially expanding urban development along heavily traveled fixed-route streetcar and heavy rail lines. The subsequent proliferation of the ubiquitous automobile all but eliminated the search for ideal city forms and facilitated a wider range of urban structure possibilities. Gradually, the prescriptive nature of early master planning gave way to an adaptive approach that aimed instead at providing guidance for an orderly development of the region. To this day, zoning maps accompanied by zoning ordinances and other land-use policies remain the major tools of this approach. The zoning map specifies the type (e.g., residential, manufacturing, mixed, open space) and intensity (e.g., high-rise, low-density) of the land uses permitted at designated locations within the region. However, if developed to the limits permitted by the zoning map, the population and land-based activities in the region would far exceed the growth that is typically anticipated within normal planning horizons. The land-use policy expresses the community's principles and procedures that are intended to guide land development in desirable directions. Among these rules are provisions for the issuance of *zoning variances* (special permission to private or public-sector developers to deviate from the specifications of the current zoning map). In addition to zoning-map revisions, major changes in land-development policies take place in response to changing economic, social, and political conditions.

Since the basis of long-term regional-transportation prediction models is the future land-use pattern and since the zoning map provides room for a variety of future patterns, there exists a need to forecast the most likely pattern subject to zoning constraints and current land-use policy. This is precisely the purpose of the land-use prediction phase shown in Fig. 7.4.9. However, the accumulated effect of zoning variances, the sequence in which major projects are implemented, and possible revisions of the underlying land-use policies introduce a significant degree of uncertainty to a single land-use forecast. Moreover, if implemented, major recommended modifications in the regional transportation system that are partly based on these forecasts would have an effect on the future land use by making certain areas within the region more accessible than others. This gives rise to the problem of model consistency (see Subsection 9.2.2) on the grand scale: The predicted transportation demand may not be consistent with the assumptions of the land-use projection. Conceptually, the modeling of this dynamic effect may be rectified by introducing a feedback link between the output of the travel-forecasting procedure and the land-use prediction phase to facilitate an iterative equilibrium solution. If such an approach were to be taken, the transportation forecasting models used would most probably need to be simplified, at least for the larger urban areas. Specifically, the number of traffic-analysis zones would have to be kept at a minimum, whereas the transportation network would be specified at an aggregate (e.g., corridor) level rather than at the individual-facility link level. Planning analysis at a relatively high level of aggregation is known as *sketch,* or *strategic,* planning.

An alternative to the closed-form equilibrium-solution method just described is an approach that examines several alternative land-use scenaria in connection with the alternative transportation options. In this manner, the analysis of combined transportation and land-use alternatives may provide some guidance for joint planning. Although not attempting to predict a single future pattern, this approach can address a larger set of alternatives, including land-use and transportation combinations that appear to be consistent with each other. For example, a fixed-guideway rapid-transit system may be examined in relation to a potential land-use policy that guides land development along the transit corridor and especially in the vicinity of transit stations [9.20]. Sketch planning models would seem more appropriate for this type of analysis as well.

9.4.3 Project, System, and Operational Planning

Long-term regional strategic planning may disclose a need to enhance the capacity of a certain travel corridor either in general terms or specifically in terms of highways or transit. In either case, it would normally not be able to supply sufficiently detailed information for *project-level* planning. Depending on the way in which the problem is expressed and its specificity regarding the admissible range of alternative options, a series of increasingly detailed planning studies leading to the stage of final design would normally be undertaken. The following quotation from a request for consultation services issued by the Honolulu Department of Transportation Services (DTS) in July 1985 illustrates this point.

> CONCEPTUAL ENGINEERING FOR HONOLULU RAPID TRANSIT. To reactivate specific planning and engineering elements of the Honolulu Area Rapid Transit Study. Develop architectural, engineering, and operating system design criteria. Develop elements of definitive engineering, architectural and operating system plans, and geotechnical investigations as necessary. Develop elements of supplemental EIS as necessary to handle major alignment and/or station shifts from current approved HART EIS. Develop materials for the conduct of public information and citizen involvement programs to keep people apprised on program development and to obtain inputs to aid system design. Perform new ridership estimates based on land use changes based on the approved Development Plans and the OMPO Long-Range Program. [9.21], p. D-10

OMPO is the metropolitan planning organization (see Chapter 7) that has been designated as the 3C process-coordinating agency for the island of Oahu, where the city of Honolulu is located. Close study of this terse statement can help the reader appreciate the issues discussed in this and earlier chapters of the textbook.

In addition to multimodal regional sketch planning and planning for new capital-intensive projects, there exists a variety of on-going planning studies at various geographical scales and time horizons for the modal components of the regional system. To illustrate this point, consider the following requests for consulting services issued by the Honolulu DTS at the same time as the one quoted earlier.

> COMPREHENSIVE ISLAND-WIDE TRANSIT SYSTEM STUDY. Develop short-, intermediate-, and long-range bus transit plans including improvements for bus fleet, maintenance facilities, and transit operations. Other tasks include on-board bus survey, evaluation of existing system, transit financing feasibility of use of small shuttle bus concept and contract supplemental bus service.

With regard to traffic operations.

> OAHU VEHICLE COUNTS AND TRAVEL DATA. Collect and process current traffic data in order to permit evaluation of both the effectiveness of short-term improvements and the accuracy of travel forecasts on both State and County facilities.

The three planning studies just described would be undertaken more or less at the same time by different consultants under the coordination of the DTS, which is one of the many agencies participating in the 3C planning process. Moreover, other such land-use and transportation-related issues that were being addressed at that time in Honolulu included a major freeway project that was in litigation in the federal court system, a major deep-draft harbor, the expansion of the Honolulu International Airport, the selection of a site for a general aviation airport, and several proposals for major industrial centers and residential developments, some of which involved applications for zoning variances. The sequence in which some of these projects would be implemented might require revisions of the regional long-range plan to incorporate committed, programmed, and implemented projects. The last sentence of the quotation relating to planning for the

Honolulu rapid-transit system illustrates that uncommitted projects may subsequently have to be restudied.

9.4.4 Planning at the Statewide and National Levels

The examples given in the preceding subsection were drawn from the urban context. Planning for single-mode and multimodal transportation systems in larger areas (i.e., statewide and national) are also undertaken by various planning entities. As an illustration, consider the following quotation from the National Airport System study conducted by the Federal Aviation Administration (FAA) [9.22].

> The 1978 National Airport System Plan (NASP) provides, in accordance with Section 12 of the Airport and Airway Development Act of 1970, as amended, a compilation of development needs for the Nation's civil airports in the decade ahead. The NASP, although published periodically, represents a continuous planning process and is constantly being updated. It is a traditional "needs" study and, as such, does not consider alternative levels of service related to different investment commitments. The generation of such assessments will require the development of performance measures and an appropriate data base . . . .
>
> Aviation as well as other forms of transportation must compete for limited resources at the state and local levels and must be reconciled with other, sometimes conflicting, priorities such as environmental and energy considerations. [9.22], p. iii

The need for strategic, project-level, and operational planning is expressed in this context as well.

9.4.5 The Problem-Solving Process

None of the planning studies just mentioned is expected to provide all the answers relating to the national, state, or local transportation systems. Each has a specific purpose and a constrained scope. It is appropriate that each study be systematically structured to identify clearly its purpose, scope, approach, and limitations. The *problem-solving process* consists of several activities that can aid in this effort. Stated in general terms these activities include the following:

1. A clear statement of the problem, the specification of the problem's scope, and the delineation of its constraints.
2. Formulation of specific study goals, objectives, and measures of performance.
3. Identification of admissible potential alternative solutions to the problem.
4. Selection of the method of analysis and identification of data needs.
5. Data collection and model calibration.
6. Analysis of alternative proposals.

7. Selection of best alternative.
8. Programming and implementation.
9. Monitoring of the implemented alternative and the system of which it is a part.

These items are not intended to specify a rigid sequence of steps but only a set of interrelated study components. The completeness and appropriateness of a particular study can be enhanced by explicitly addressing these questions at appropriate points.

9.5 SUMMARY

This chapter surveyed several demand-forecasting models and model structures not covered in Chapter 8. These included models of demand elasticity, simultaneous or direct-demand models, and various combinations of sequential and simultaneous models. It also provided a cursory commentary on several contemporary planning issues, including joint land-use and transportation planning, planning for different levels of detail and time horizons, and the coordination between long-term regional plans with on-going project, system, and operational planning. The elements of the problem-solving process that can aid in the proper conduct of planning studies were also identified.

9.6 EXERCISES

1. Identify the characteristics of the following three transportation-demand models and indicate their role in the demand-forecasting process.

$$Q_{IJ} = aP_I A_J W^b{}_{IJ}$$

$$Q_{IJ} = aY^b{}_I X^c{}_I\, W^d{}_{IJ}$$

$$Q_{IJK} = aX^b{}_I Y^c{}_I\, Z^d{}_J\, W^e{}_{IJK}$$

where

P_I = productions of zone I

A_J = attractions of zone J

W_{IJ} = travel impedance from I to J

Y_I = average income in zone I

X_I = population of zone I

Z_J = total employment in zone J

W_{IJK} = impedance from I to J via mode K

2. Specify and discuss the forecasting model structures that are possible given the models calibrated for Canberra, Australia (see Subsection 9.2.4).
3. Calculate and interpret the income elasticity of demand in model 2 of Exercise 1 assuming that a, b, c, d, and e are constants.
4. An increase of transit fares from 40 to 60¢ has resulted in a decrease in transit patronage from 500,000 to 450,000 trips per day. Calculate the shrinkage ratio, the linear-arc elasticity, and the log-arc elasticity.
5. An increase in gasoline prices from \$1.00 to \$1.30 per gallon resulted in a decrease of automobile use from 1,000,000 to 960,000 trips. Estimate the likely impact of an increase in gasoline prices from \$1.30 to \$1.50. Solve this problem using the three alternative measures of elasticity.
6. A special service for the elderly and handicapped currently serves 2500 persons per day. Given that the current fare is 50¢ and that the linear-arc fare elasticity of demand is -0.45, calculate (a) the loss of patronage that would result from doubling the fare, (b) the effect on fare-box revenues, (c) the implied shrinkage ratio, and (d) the implied log-arc elasticity.
7. A 20% increase in automobile costs has been observed to cause a 5% increase in transit patronage relative to the patronage prior to the increase and a 10% decrease in auto usage. Calculate the implied direct and cross elasticities of demand as measured by E_{sh}, E_{arc}, and $E_{\text{log-arc}}$.
8. A zonal interchange is served by a local bus route and an express bus route. The current travel times and fares associated with the two types of service are

	Travel time (min)	Fare (\$)
Local	50	0.50
Express	30	1.00

Given the following linear-arc elasticities of demand and that the current transit patronage of 4000 trips per peak period is split 40-60 between the express and local bus services, calculate the effect of raising the express bus fare to \$1.50.

	Local		Express	
	Time	Fare	Time	Fare
Local	-0.02	-0.03	$+0.01$	$+0.02$
Express	$+0.09$	$+0.62$	-0.08	-0.15

9. For the system of Exercise 8, estimate the effect of expanding the number of express buses and thus reducing the express bus travel time to 25 min.
10. Examine the effect that a 10-min reduction in the travel time offered by the local bus service would have on the total peak-hour transit usage between the two zones described in Exercise 8.
11. Assuming that the elasticities given in Exercise 9 are shrinkage ratios, estimate the combined effect of raising express bus fares to \$1.30 *and* lowering the local bus fare to \$0.40.

12. Repeat Exercise 8 assuming that the given elasticities are log-arc elasticities.
13. Repeat Exercise 8 assuming that the given elasticities are shrinkage ratios.
14. You have been assigned the task of developing materials for the conduct of public-information and citizen-involvement programs as specified in the request for consulting services quoted in Subsection 9.4.3. Research the topic and write a report not to exceed 10 typewritten pages.
15. Using the resources of your school's library, write a report that describes a particular study of a major transportation project or program. Your report must address the components of the problem solving process that are listed in Subsection 9.4.5.

9.7 REFERENCES

9.1 Transportation Research Board, *Urban Transportation Planning in the 1980s,* Special Report 196, National Research Council, Washington, D.C., 1982.

9.2 ———, *Transportation and Land Use Development,* Special Report 183, National Research Council, Washington, D.C., 1978.

9.3 ———, *Transportation Systems Management in 1980: State of the Art and Future Directions,* Special Report 190, National Research Council, Washington, D.C., 1980.

9.4 ———, *Travel Analysis Methods for the 1980s,* Special Report 201, National Research Council, Washington, D.C., 1983.

9.5 Highway Research Board, *Urban Travel Demand Forecasting,* Special Report 143, National Research Council, Washington, D.C., 1972.

9.6 Bellomo, S. J., et al., "*Evaluating Options in Statewide Transportation Planning/Programming: Techniques and Applications,* National Cooperative Highway Research Program Report 199, Transportation Research Board, National Research Council, Washington, D.C., March 1979.

9.7 Allaman, P. M., T. J. Tardiff, and F. C. Dunbar, *New Approaches to Understanding Travel Behavior,* National Cooperative Highway Research Program Report 250, Transportation Research Board, National Research Council, Washington, D.C., September 1982.

9.8 Irwin, N. A., N. Dodd, and H. G. van Cube, "Capacity Restraint in Assignment Programs," *Highway Research Board, Bulletin* 297, National Research Council, Washington, D.C., 1961, pp. 109–127.

9.9 Hamburg, J. R., G. T. Lathrop, and E. J. Kaiser, *Forecasting Inputs to Transportation Planning,* National Cooperative Highway Research Program Report 266, Transportation Research Board, National Research Council, Washington, D.C., December 1983.

9.10 Quandt, R. E., and W. J. Baumol, "The Demand for Abstract Modes—Theory and Measurement," *Journal of Regional Science,* 6, no. 2 (1966): 13–26.

9.11 Wigan, M. R., ed., *New Techniques for Transport Systems Analysis,* Austrialian Road Research Board and Bureau of Transport Economics, Special Report 10, 1977.

9.12 Institute of Transportation Engineers, *Transportation and Traffic Engineering Handbook,* Prentice-Hall, Inc., Englewood Cliffs, N.J. 1976.

9.13 Sosslau, A. B., et al., *Travel Estimation Procedures for Quick Response to Urban Policy Issues,* National Cooperative Highway Research Program Report 186, Transportation Research Board, National Research Council, Washington, D.C., 1978.

9.14 Transportation Research Board, *Transportation Planning for Small and Medium-Sized Communities,* Special Report 187, Washington, D.C., 1980.

9.15 ———, *State Transportation Issues and Actions,* Special Report 189, Washington, D.C., 1980.

9.16 Parody, T. E., and D. Brand, "Forecasting Demand and Revenue for Transit prepaid Pass and Fare Alternatives," *Transportation Research Record* 719, Transportation Research Board, 1979, pp. 35–41.

9.17 Federal Highway Administration, *Traveler Response to Transportation System Changes,* 2nd ed., U.S. Department of Transportation, Washington, D.C., July 1981.

9.18 Hall, P., ed., *Von Thunen's Isolated State,* C.M. Pergammon Press, Oxford, 1966.

9.19 Losch, A., "The Nature of Economic Regions," *Southern Economic Journal, 5 (1938): 71–78.*

9.20 U.S Subcommittee on the City, *New Urban Rail Transit: How Can its Development and Growth-Shaping Potential Be Realized,* Committee on Banking, Finance and Urban Affairs, U.S. House of Representatives, 96th Congress, First Session, U.S. Government Printing Office, Washington, D.C., 1980.

9.21 *Honolulu Star-Bulletin,* July 30, 1985.

9.22 Federal Aviation Administration, *National Airport System Plan 1978–1987,* U.S. Department of Transportation, U.S. Printing Office, Washington, D.C., 1977.

CHAPTER 10

AIR QUALITY, NOISE, AND ENERGY IMPACTS

10.1 INTRODUCTION

The main objective of the travel-demand-forecasting models examined in Chapters 8 and 9 is to estimate the impacts of transportation systems that are directly related to travel. These impacts include the amount of trip making, the geographical distribution and orientation of trips, the utilization of the available and proposed modes of travel, and the consequences of these travel choices on the loading of the transportation network in terms of link flows, and in terms of the impedances (e.g., travel times) experienced by the users of the system.

Up to the 1960s, transportation decisions in the public sector were generally based on the assessment of the capital and operating costs of transportation facilities vis-à-vis the expected direct improvements in the levels of service and travel times experienced by the user. The explicit consideration of indirect and nonuser impacts was generally confined to practical cost-related items such as the appropriate or just compensation of individuals and businesses for right-of-way acquisition and relocation.

As Chapter 7 described, the civil rights and the environmental movements of the 1960s contributed to the evolution of an altered perspective. Civil rights concerns affected the understanding of the role of transportation by addressing issues relating to the rights to mobility and accessibility to employment and other opportunities on the part of various societal subgroups. The environmental movement resulted in an increasing awareness about many indirect socioeconomic and environmental effects of transportation decisions (see Appendix A).

This chapter addresses three of the many transportation-related impacts that have become an integral part of contemporary transportation planning and decision-making. These are air quality, noise generation, and energy consumption. For each of these impacts, a brief historical note is presented, several mitigation strategies are described, and practical models for estimating the impact are illustrated.

10.2 AIR POLLUTION

10.2.1 Background

The release of air pollutants in the atmosphere is a concomitant result of human activities. In some instances, naturally produced air pollutants outweigh man-made pollution, but the latter tends to be concentrated in urbanized areas where people live and work. The problem of air pollution is not new. In early fourteenth-century London, the smoke and odor consequences of coal burning became such a public nuisance that several commissions were appointed to combat them. In his book on the subject of air pollution, Perkins [10.1] quotes the following declaration by King Edward I:

> Be it known to all within the sound of my voice, whosoever shall be found guilty of burning coal shall suffer the loss of his head.

More recently, connections between air pollution and respiratory disease have been demonstrated and detrimental environmental effects on the global scale have been discerned. Several localized pollution episodes have resulted in documented deaths and have highlighted the severity of the problem. A December 1948 episode in Donora, Pennsylvania, and a December 1956 episode in London are most notable.

The first major law enacted by the U.S. Congress in relation to air pollution was the 1955 Air Pollution Act, which provided federal support for research into the subject. The Clean Air Act of 1963 recognized the contribution of "urbanization, industrial development, and increasing use of motor vehicles" to the problem and encouraged automobile manufacturers to address it. Two years later, the 1965 Motor Vehicle Air Pollution Control Act provided for the establishment of vehicle-emission standards and opened the way to a series of amendments that led to the Air Quality Act of 1970, which provided for national ambient air-quality standards, for a reduction of vehicle emissions of several pollutants by 90% of their 1970 levels, and for state implementation plans to conform to these provisions. The 1970 Federal-Aid Highway Act explicitly required that highway planning must be consistent with implementation plans to attain and maintain established regional ambient air quality standards. Table 10.2.1 presents the national ambient standards for several air pollutants as issued by the EPA in 1971 [10.2]. This requirement resulted in an accelerated level of activity regarding the monitoring and modeling the air-quality impacts of transportation systems and in the integration of air-quality considerations into the transportation-planning process. The subsequent legislative history of the issue has been, to say the least, tumultuous. Nevertheless, the problem has come to the

TABLE 10.2.1 1971 NATIONAL AMBIENT AIR-QUALITY STANDARDS

Pollutant	Type of standard	Averaging time	Frequency parameter	Concentration mg/m^3	ppm
Carbon monoxide	Primary[a] and Secondary[b]	1 h	Annual maximum[c]	40,000	35
		8h	Annual maximum	10,000	9
Hydrocarbons (nomethane)	Primary and Secondary	3 h (6–9 A.M.)	Annual maximum	160[d]	0.24[d]
Nitrogen dioxide	Primary and Secondary	1 year	Arithmetic mean	100	0.05
Photo-chemical oxidants	Primary and Secondary	1 year	Annual maximum	160	0.08
Particulate matter	Primary	24 h	Annual maximum	260	—
		24 h	Annual geometric mean	75	—
	Secondary	24 h	Annual maximum	150	—
		24 h	Annual geometric mean	60[e]	
Sulfur dioxide	Primary	24 h	Annual maximum	365	0.14
		1 h	Arithmetic mean	80	0.03
	Secondary	3 h	Annual maximum	1,300	0.5
		24 h	Annual maximum	260[f]	0.1[f]
		1 h	Arithmetic mean	60	0.02

[a]Primary standards are those required to protect public health.

[b]Secondary standards are those required to protect public welfare.

[c]Not to be exceeded more than once per year.

[d]As a guide in devising implementation plans for achieving oxidant standards.

[e]As a guide to be used in assessing implementation plans for achieving the annual maximum 24-h standard.

[f]As a guide to be used in assessing implementation plans for achieving the annual arithmetic mean standard.

SOURCE: Environmental Protection Agency [10.2].

forefront and has claimed a special place in the planning, design, and implementation of transportation projects.

10.2.2 Problem Dimensions

The combustion of transportation fuels releases several contaminants into the atmosphere, including carbon monoxide, hydrocarbons, oxides of nitrogen, and lead and other particulate matter. Hydrocarbons, of which more than 200 have been detected in exhaust emissions, are the result of the incomplete combustion of fuel. Particulates are minute solid or liquid particles that are suspended in the atmosphere; they include aerosols, smoke, and dust particles. Photochemical smog is the result of complex chemical reactions of oxides of nitrogen and hydrocarbons in the presence of sunlight.

Once emitted into the atmosphere, air pollutants undergo mixing or diffusion, the degree of which depends on topographic, climatic, and meteorological conditions. These include wind speed and direction and atmospheric stability.

The assessment of the air-pollution effects of transportation may be undertaken at three levels: microscale analysis in the immediate vicinity of a transportation facility such as a highway, mesoscale analysis in areas that are somewhat removed from the facility, which includes the contribution of other mobile and stationary sources of pollution, and macroscale analysis, extending from the regional to the global levels. Available air-pollution estimation models range from simple models that provide rough estimates of emission levels to very complex numerical models that trace the diffusion of pollutants in space and time and also simulate the chemical processes that follow.

10.2.3 Emission Levels

Vehicular emissions of air pollutants are usually measured in grams per vehicle-mile of travel and are related to several factors, including vehicle type and age, ambient temperature, and altitude. The operating cycle, which consists of starts and stops, speed changes, and idling time, is also an important factor. A disproportionate fraction of carbon monoxide and hydrocarbons are emitted during cold starts of the engine. The EPA periodically issues reports relating to emission factors for various types of vehicles [10.3].

The general relationships between speed and emissions are illustrated by Fig. 10.2.1. Carbon monoxide emissions generally decrease with speed, partly due to the air-to-fuel ratio supplied to the engine at different speeds. Up to about 30 to 40 mi/h, a similar relationship occurs in the case of hydrocarbons, but a mild increase in emissions is seen thereafter. The emission of nitrogen oxides exhibits a different pattern—that is, it generally increases with speed.

A number of emission models utilizing these factors have been developed and many traffic-simulation models (e.g., [10.4]) have been supplemented by emission-estimating subroutines. The EPA has developed [10.5] a computer program that estimates the emissions that result from various combinations of traffic flows, vehicle mixes, and other factors. A simplified model for carbon monoxide based on the EPA program has been proposed by Raus [10.6]. This model uses several nomographs that are based on a typical 1980 vehicle mix for various altitudes and ambient temperatures. The family of curves corresponding to altitudes up to 4000 ft above sea level is shown in Fig. 10.2.2.

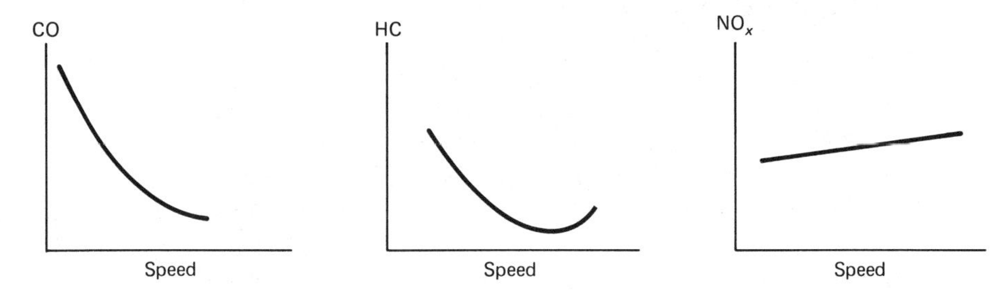

Figure 10.2.1 General relationship between speed and emissions.

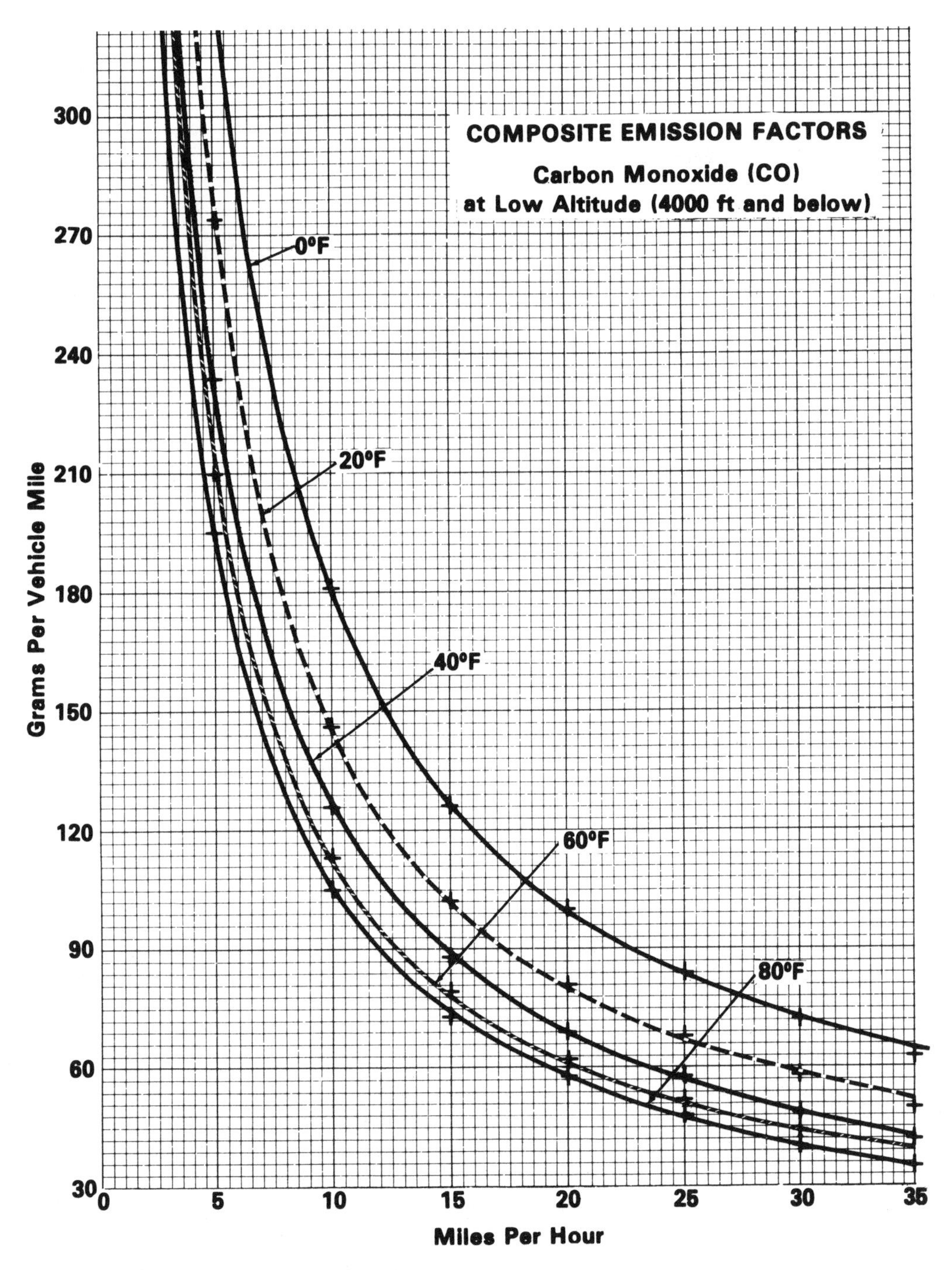

Figure 10.2.2 Carbon monoxide emission factors—1980 vehicle mix. (*SOURCE*: Raus [10.6], Fig. 9, p. 25.)

Example 10.1

According to a traffic forecast, a proposed 4-mi highway is expected to carry 3500 veh/h during the 2-h peak period of the day at an average travel time of 16 min. Apply the Raus model to estimate the total peak-hour emissions of carbon monoxide on the highway for the typical autumn day (60°F).

Solution The total number of vehicle-miles traveled during the typical peak period is:

$$(3500 \text{ veh/h})(2 \text{ h/peak})(4 \text{ mi}) = 28{,}000 \text{ veh-mi/peak period}$$

The estimated average speed is 15 mi/h and, according to Fig. 10.2.2, the emission rate corresponding to this speed is 78 g/veh-mi. As a result, the total emissions of carbon monoxide are estimated to be 2,184,000 g, or 4,811 lb, per peak period.

10.2.4 Air-Pollution Dispersion

While the emission level is an important measure of the air-pollution impact of various sources, it is the concentration of pollutants in the atmosphere that defines the levels and times of exposure. Following the emission of pollutants, dispersion and chemical oxidation take place in the atmosphere. The dispersion of a pollutant is affected by the strength of the source and by topographic and meteorological conditions. The topography of the terrain in the vicinity of the source of pollution affects, among other items, the wind profile near the ground and the generation of turbulance in the form of eddies. Special conditions related to highway facilities also affect the dispersal of highway-generated pollution. For example, the EPA HIWAY model [10.7] analyzes at-grade and depressed highways differently to estimate the concentrations of nonreactive pollutants from highway traffic at various downwind locations. Also, air pollutants released on roadways passing through densely developed urban areas tend to be trapped in the street canyons that are formed by rows of buildings at both ends of the roadway.

One of the most important meteorological conditions that affect the mixing of pollutants is the temperature lapse rate, which is defined as the rate of change of temperature with altitude. This rate is usually referenced to the *adiabatic lapse rate* of −5.4°F per 1000 ft, which corresponds to an atmosphere that is characterized by neutral stability, that is, a situation where air particles tend to maintain their positions. When the temperature drops at a faster rate than the adiabatic (i.e., at a *superadiabatic lapse rate*), the atmosphere is unstable, and vigorous mixing takes place. On the other side of the adiabatic lapse rate, *subadiabatic lapse rates* tend to inhibit mixing. Due to various meteorological combinations, sometimes certain layers in the atmosphere experience an increase of temperature with altitude. This is known as a *temperature inversion* and is critical especially when it occurs in a layer close to the ground because pollutants are trapped within this layer. The *mixing height* is the height of the atmospheric layer within which mixing occurs. This height varies from locality to locality and also exhibits daily and seasonal variation. The degree of mixing is a function of the atmospheric stability of this layer. Typically, the atmosphere near the earth's surface becomes unstable in the morning, allowing for energetic mixing within the mixing layer, which attains its maximum height in the afternoon [10.7].

One of the simplest mathematical models of air pollution diffusion is the box model, which is described below in the next subsection. More sophisticated models employing numerical integration of complex Gaussian equations [10.8] and the modeling of chemical processes [10.9] usually require the use of computer algorithms.

10.2.5 The Box Model

The *box model* may be used to approximate the concentration of air pollution within an atmospheric volume defined by a rectangular area and extending to the altitude of the mixing height H, as shown by Fig. 10.2.3. Pollutants emitted into the box at a constant rate E in pollutant weight per unit time are assumed to be mixed instantaneously with the air volume of the box. Clean air is assumed to enter the box at a speed U, and air containing the same concentration as the interior of the box is assumed to exit from the opposite side. The concentration $C(t)$ at any time t inside the box is expressed in pollutant weight per unit volume. Based on these assumptions, the following balance equation applies:

$$E - FC = V\left(\frac{dC}{dt}\right) \tag{10.2.1}$$

where:

$$F = ULH = \text{air flow (volume per unit time)}$$

$$V = L^2H = \text{box volume}$$

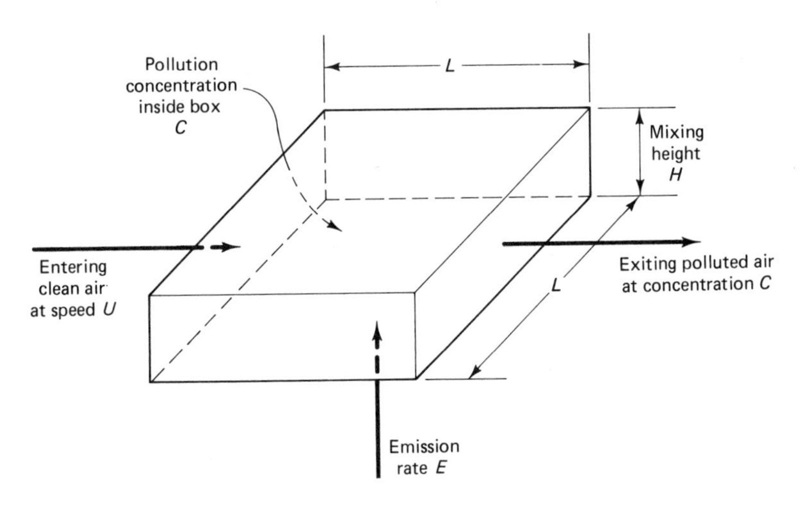

Figure 10.2.3 The box model.

Equation 10.2.1 expresses the rate of change of pollution inside the box as the difference between the amount of pollution entering the box (E) and the amount of pollution exiting the box (FC).

Example 10.2

Solve Eq. 10.2.1 for concentration as a function of time assuming that the air within the box is initially clean (i.e., $C_0 = 0$) and that U, E, and H are constant.

Solution Rewritten as

$$\frac{dC}{dt} + \frac{F}{V}C = \frac{E}{V} \tag{10.2.2}$$

Equation 10.2.2 is a first-order linear differential equation of the form:

$$\frac{dy}{dx} + p(x)y = g(x) \tag{10.2.3}$$

which can be solved by multiplying both sides by the integrating factor

$$f(x) = e^{\int p(x)\,dx} \tag{10.2.4}$$

thus rendering the left-hand side into the exact differential of the product $yf(x)$. In this case, the integrating factor is

$$f(t) = e^{(F/V)t} \tag{10.2.5}$$

Hence,

$$\frac{d}{dt}(C\,e^{(F/V)t}) = \frac{E}{V}e^{(F/V)t}$$

Integrating with respect to t,

$$C\,e^{(F/V)t} = \frac{VE}{FV}\,e^{(F/V)t} + K$$

or

$$C = \frac{E}{F} + Ke^{-(F/V)t} \tag{10.2.6}$$

where K is the constant of integration, which can be evaluated at the initial condition $C(0) = 0$ to be

$$K = -\frac{E}{F}$$

As a result, the solution to Eq. 10.2.1 becomes

$$C = \frac{E}{F}(1 - e^{-(F/V)t}) \tag{10.2.7}$$

which is plotted in Fig. 10.2.4. Thus, under the simplifying assumptions of this model, the pollution concentration of the interior of the box tends toward a steady-state level of E/F.

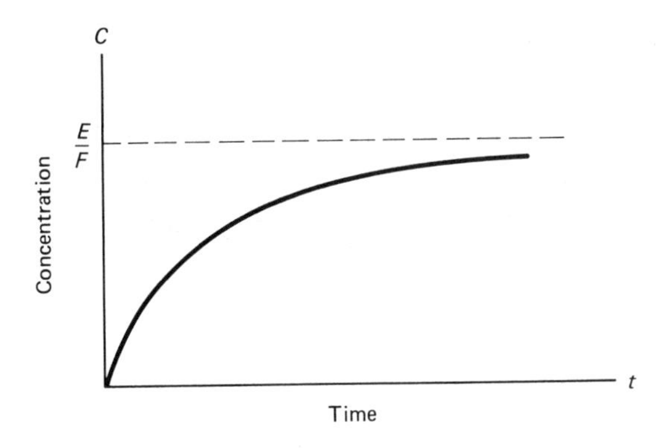

Figure 10.2.4 Pollutant concentration as a function of time.

10.3 NOISE GENERATION

10.3.1 Background

Sound is acoustical energy released into the atmosphere by vibrating or moving bodies. Therefore sound is amenable to objective scientific measurement and investigation. On the other hand, noise is undesirable or unwanted sound and as such it is cloaked with a certain degree of subjectivity. Extended exposure to excessive sound has been shown to produce physical and psychological damage. Because of its annoyance and disturbance implications, noise adds to mental stress and hence affects the general well-being of those that are exposed to it. Undoubtedly, noise has always been a major source of friction between individuals.

Transportation operations are major contributors to noise in the modern urban environment. Noise is generated by the engine and exhaust systems of vehicles, by aerodynamic friction, and by the interaction between the vehicle and its support system (e.g., tire-pavement and rail wheel-rail interactions). Because noise diminishes with distances from the source, the most serious transportation-related noise problems are confined to transportation corridors (e.g., highway and railway corridors and aircraft flight paths) and at major transportation hubs (e.g., airports and transit terminals).

Seiff [10.10] reports that in 1970 the Bureau of Motor Carrier Safety issued rules relating to noise levels in the interior of commercial vehicles based in the belief that the safety of these operations would be compromised by the resulting driver fatigue and hearing problems. About the same time, various states and local communities began to establish community noise regulations, including motor-vehicle noise standards. The passage of the Noise Control Act of 1972 at the federal level, marked the recognition of the problem as a major detriment to urban living of nationwide proportions. Pursuant to the provisions of this act, the FHWA issued the 1973 Policy and Procedure Memorandum [10.11], which promulgated noise standards for various types of land use and stated that the FHWA:

. . . encourages the application of the noise standards at the earliest appropriate stage in the project development process.

Table 10.3.1 presents the noise standards issued by the FHWA in 1973 for several categories of land use. Thus concern about the noise impacts of transportation vehicles and facilities officially entered the calculus of transportation design, planning, and implementation.

TABLE 10.3.1 FHWA NOISE STANDARDS

(a) Design noise level/land-use relationships

Land-use category	Design noise level-L_{10}	Description of land-use category
A	60 dBA (Exterior)	Tracts of land in which serenity and quiet are of extraordinary significance and serve an important public need, and where the preservation of those qualitites is essential if the area is to continue to serve its intended purpose. Such areas could include amphitheaters, particular parks or portions of parks, or open spaces which are dedicated or recognized by appropriate local officials for activities requiring special qualities of serenity and quiet.
B	70 dBA (Exterior)	Residences, motels, hotels, public meeting rooms, schools, churches, libraries, hospitals, picnic areas, recreation areas, playgrounds, active sports areas, and parks.
C	75 dBA (Exterior)	Developed lands, properties or activities not included in categories A and B.
D	—	For requirements on undeveloped lands see paragraphs 5a(5) and (6), this PPM.
E[a]	55 dBA (Interior)	Residences, motels, hotels, public meeting rooms, schools, churches, libraries, hospitals and auditoriums.

[a]See Part b.

(b) Noise-reduction factors

Building type	Window condition	Noise reduction due to exterior of the structure	Corresponding highest exterior noise level that would achieve an interior design noise level of 55 dBA
All	Open	10 dB	65 dBA
Light frame	Ordinary sash		
	closed	20	75
	with storm windows	25	80
Masonry	Single glazed	25	80
Masonry	Double glazed	35	90

SOURCE: Federal Highway Administration [10.11] pp. B-1 and B-4.

10.3.2 Noise Measurement

The quantity of energy or the intensity of a single sound is usually measured on a relative logarithmic scale that employes a unit called a *bel* or in terms of its subdivision, the *decibel*. A bel represents a 10-fold increase in energy and is measured in relation to a reference intensity I_0, which is usually taken at the threshold of human hearing. The intensity I of a sound corresponding to L bels is:

$$I = 10^L I_0 \tag{10.3.1}$$

Solving for L,

$$L = \log_{10}\left(\frac{I}{I_0}\right) \text{ B} \tag{10.3.2}$$

At the threshold of hearing, $I = I_0$ and the noise level L is equal to zero. When L is about 14, the sound becomes painful to the human ear.

For finer scaling, the bel is divided into 10 dB, and Eq. 10.3.2 becomes:

$$L = 10 \log_{10}\left(\frac{I}{I_0}\right) \text{ dB} \tag{10.3.3}$$

An alternative formulation of Eq. 10.3.2 is based on the fact that the sound energy is proportional to the square of the frequency f of the sound, that is,

$$I = af^2 \tag{10.3.4}$$

where a is a proportionality factor. Substitution of this equation in Eq. 10.3.2 yields

$$L = 20 \log_{10}\left(\frac{f}{f_0}\right) \text{ dB} \tag{10.3.5}$$

where f is the frequency of the sound being measured and f_0 is the reference frequency at the threshold of hearing.

Equations 10.3.1 through 10.3.5 apply to sounds that consist of a single frequency. However, typical environmental noises consist of combinations of frequencies of which only those in the approximate range from 500 to 10,000 Hz are detectable by humans. A single noise-level scale in decibels that combines the effect of multifrequency noises in a manner that simulates the sensitivity and response of humans discriminates or weighs against frequencies that lie outside this range. The most common weighting scheme is referred to as the *A-weighted scale* and gives measurements that are measured in A-weighted decibels, or dBA. Figure 10.3.1 presents the A-weighted decibel levels of several common environmental sounds that lie between the threshold of hearing (i.e., dBA = 0) and the level of physiological pain [10.12].

Sound levels and human response		
Common sounds	Noise level (dB)	Effect
Carrier deck jet operation Air raid siren	140	Painfully loud
	130	
Jet takeoff (200 ft) Thunderclap Discotheque Auto horn (3 ft)	120	Maximum vocal effort
Pile drivers	110	
Garbage truck	100	
Heavy truck (50 ft) City traffic	90	Very annoying Hearing damage (8 hrs)
Alarm clock (2 ft) Hair dryer	80	Annoying
Noisy restaurant Freeway traffic Man's voice (3 ft)	70	Telephone use difficult
Air conditioning unit (20 ft)	60	Intrusive
Light auto traffic (100 ft)	50	Quiet
Living room Bedroom Quiet office	40	
Library Soft whisper (15 ft)	30	Very quiet
Broadcasting studio	20	
	10	Just audible
	0	Hearing begins

Figure 10.3.1 Sound levels and human response. (*SOURCE*: Environmental Protection Agency [10.12].)

10.3.3 Noise Propagation and Mitigation Strategies

Once generated at a source, unshielded noise spreads out spherically as it travels through the air away from the source. Consequently, the intensity of the sound diminishes with distance from the source. In addition to these losses in intensity due to spreading, absorption losses also take place as the sound energy is transferred between air particles.

When the sound waves encounter natural and manufactured solid objects, they undergo bending or diffraction and reflection, the degree of which depends on the characteristics of the object. Trees and other vegetation, for example, tend to reflect the sound waves in a diffused pattern and are considered to be good interceptors of noise.

The major thrust of noise-control strategies is to minimize the noise levels to which the population is exposed. Figure 10.3.2 summarizes the overall problem of community noise and amelioration strategies as described by Borthwick [10.13]. Part (a) enumerates the various sources of community noise that have been identified in 1974 by the noise-control section of the Florida Department of Pollution Control. Part (b) specifies three categories of transportation noise-control strategies: source controls, noise-path controls, and receiver-side controls. Part (c) lists a variety of potential source controls, including vehicle-control devices, vehicle-maintenance practices, traffic controls, and highway-design controls. Part (d) shows that noise-path controls include the erection of appropriately designed noise barriers that reflect and diffuse noise and the provision of buffer zones between the transportation facility and the population to provide a distance over which noise can be attenuated. Finally, part (e) lists a series of noise-control strategies at the receptor site, including public-awareness programs and building-design practices.

10.3.4 Noise Measures

Figure 10.3.3 shows that the noise levels generated by transportation facilities show a good amount of variability with respect to time. It is, therefore, necessary to establish meaningful statistical noise measures that describe the magnitude of the problem while capturing this variability. Commonly used statistical measures include the following:

1. L_p denotes the noise level at a receptor site that is exceeded p percent of the time. Commonly used levels of this measure include the noise level that is exceeded 10, 50, and 90% of the time. L_{10} is a peak noise level used by most highway departments in the United States and endorsed by the FHWA. Noise level L_{90} is a background level that is exceeded most of the time.
2. The equivalent noise level denoted by L_{eq} is defined as

$$L_{eq} = 10 \log_{10} \left(\frac{1}{T} \int_0^T \frac{f^2}{f_0^2} \, dt \right) \tag{10.3.6}$$

where T is the period of time over which the measurement is made. The equivalent noise level may be approximated by a series of N discrete measurements as follows:

$$L_{eq} = 10 \log_{10} \left(\frac{1}{N} \sum_i 10^{(L_i/10)} \right) \tag{10.3.7}$$

where L_i is the average noise level during interval i.

Other noise-impact measures for the assessment of transportation noise have been proposed. Some of these combine the above measures in various ways that attempt to

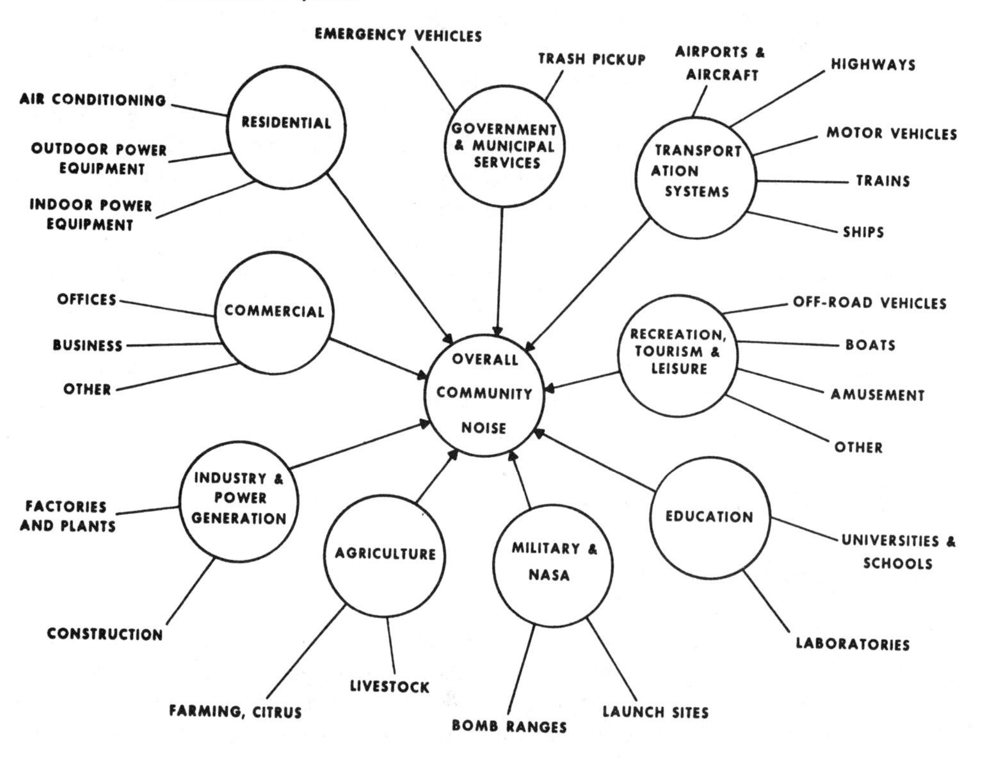

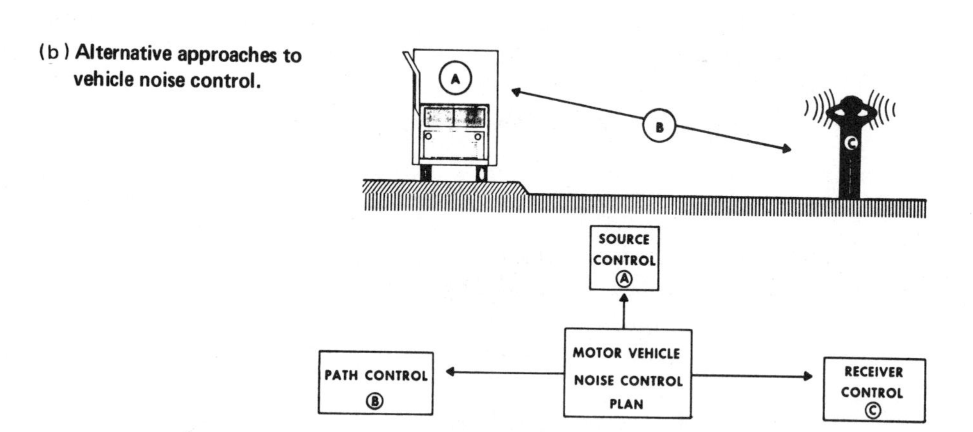

Figure 10.3.2 Florida noise control program elements. (*SOURCE*: Borthwick [10.13], Figs. 2–6, pp. 87 and 89.)

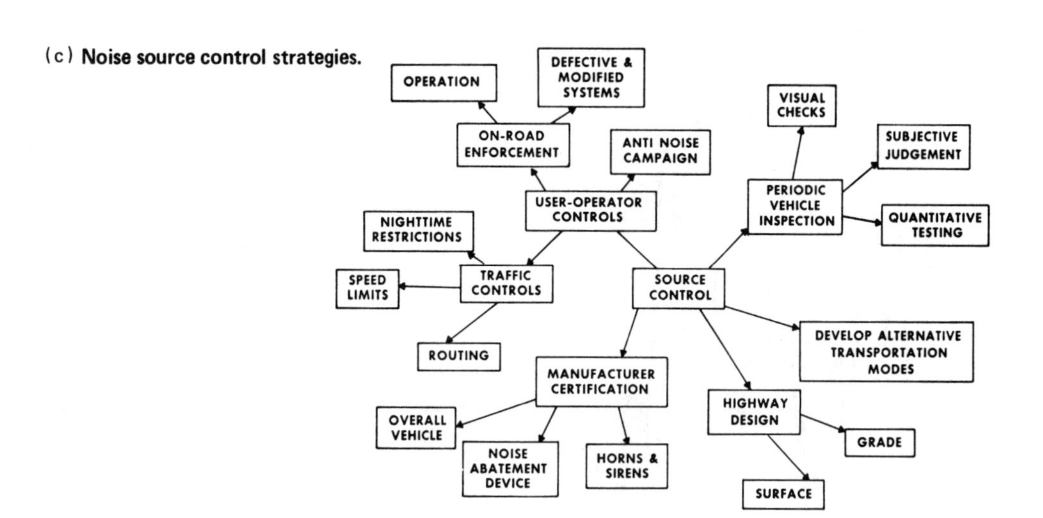

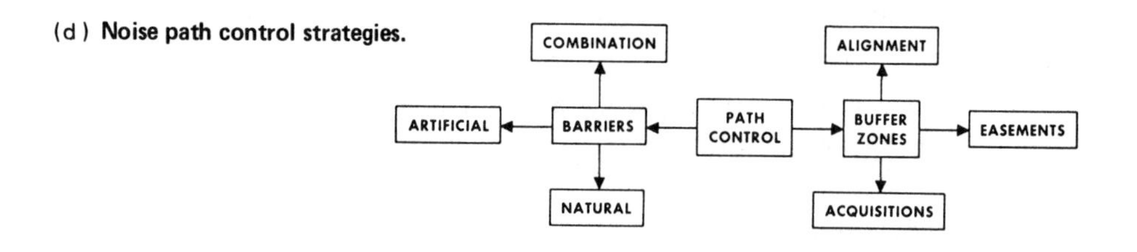

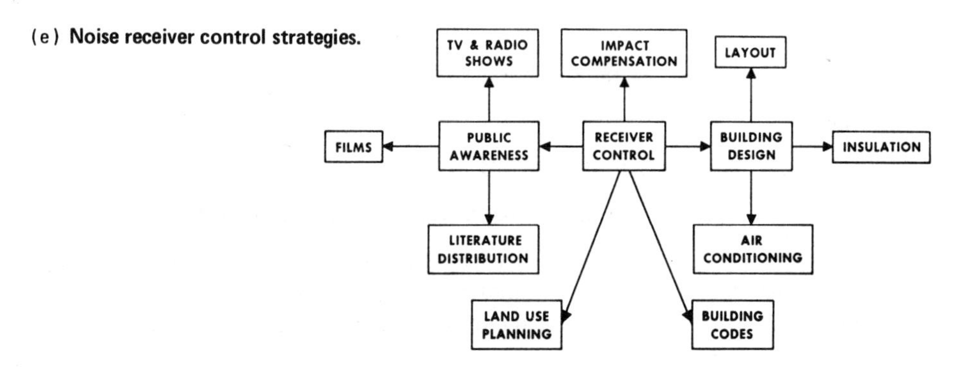

Figure 10.3.2 *(Continued)*

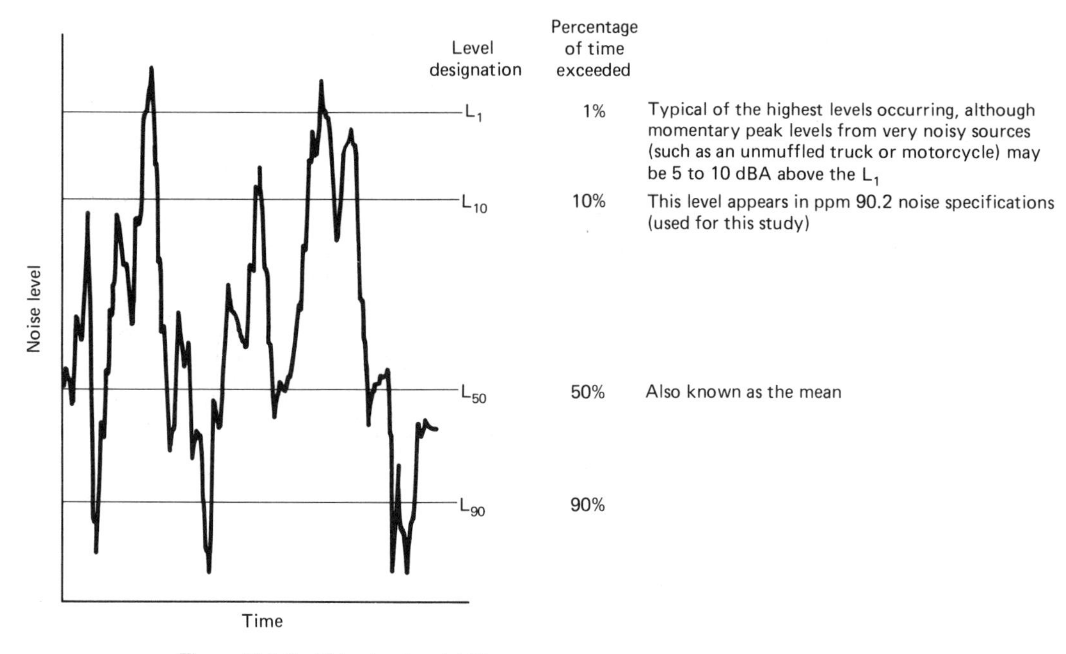

Figure 10.3.3 Noise level variability. (*SOURCE*: U.S. Department of Transportation [10.14].)

capture the annoyance caused by the noise. Hall and Allen [10.15] summarize several of these alternative measures.

10.3.5 Mathematical Models of Transportation Noise

Wesler [10.16] traces the first mathematical formulation of traffic noise to the following empirical equation presented in the 1952 Wright Air Development Center Handbook of Acoustic Noise Control [10.17]:

$$L_{50} = 68 + 8.5 \log V - 20 \log D \text{ dB} \tag{10.3.8}$$

where

V = traffic volume in veh/h

D = distance from a traffic line to the observer in ft

Since then, many researchers have attempted to calibrate highway-related noise models for various traffic conditions. The state of the art has recently been greatly enhanced, and various manual and computer-based models are available for the analysis of noise impacts and for the design of noise-amelioration devices such as noise barriers. The FHWA, for example, has published several models, which have been subsequently enhanced and refined [10.18]. These models include several manual and computerized solution procedures. Figure 10.3.4 is a nomograph that can be used to estimate the unshielded noise level (i.e., in the absence of noise barriers) at some distance from a highway. Inputs to this model are the volumes and speeds of automobiles, medium trucks, and heavy trucks using the highway, and the output consists of an estimate of L_{10} at a given distance away. The noise level caused by each component is calculated by the procedure described next and added logarithmically to arrive at the total highway noise level. The medium-truck volume is converted to automobile equivalents by a factor of 10. If the speeds of medium trucks and automobiles are equal, the two can be combined into one group. Heavy trucks are always analyzed separately. Automobiles and medium trucks differ from heavy trucks in that the major part of the noise emitted by the former is at the pavement level, due to the interaction between the tires and the pavement. Heavy-truck noise, on the other hand, is emitted from exhaust systems, which are located about 8 ft above the pavement level. This difference is denoted on the noise nomograph but is

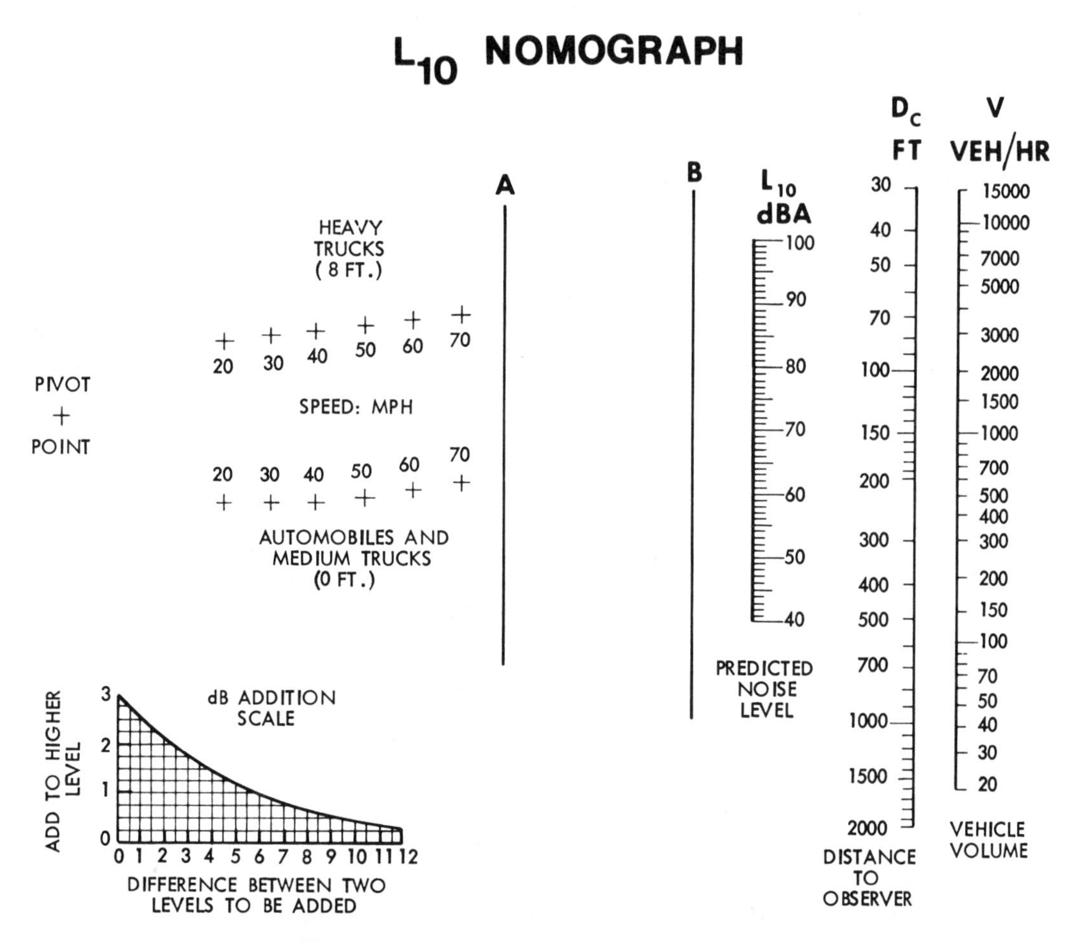

Figure 10.3.4 L_{10} nomograph. (*SOURCE*: Kugler [10.18], p. 185.)

more important to the design and analysis of barriers than to the simplified estimation of unshielded noise addressed here. To estimate the noise level produced by highway traffic, the first three steps of the following procedure are applied to each vehicular volume component and the results are combined, as explained in step four.

Step 1: A straight line joining the pivot point at the extreme left-hand side of the nomograph to the point corresponding to the mean speed is extended until it intersects line A. Note that two sets of speed-related points are included: one for automobiles and medium trucks and the other for heavy trucks.

Step 2: A second straight line is drawn from the above point of intersection to the traffic volume V on the scale located at the extreme right-hand side of the chart. The point of intersection of the second line and line B is noted.

Step 3: A third line is drawn from the point of intersection on line B to the distance D_c for which the noise level is calculated. The intersection of the third line and the L_{10} scale next to line B represents the required L_{10} estimate. The distance to the observer D_c may be either taken approximately from the middle of the highway or, if desired, from the middle of individual lanes. In the latter case, the volume and speed inputs must be known by lane.

Step 4: The calculated L_{10} levels for the various highway flow components are combined. Because of the logarithmic nature of the dBA scale, the L_{10} levels cannot be added arithematically. Instead, if two sounds are to be added, an incremental amount, depending on the difference in the two noise levels, is added to the higher of the two. The insert located at the lower left-hand side of the chart gives the magnitude of the incremental amount. Thus, two sounds of equal intensity (i.e., zero difference) combine into a level that is only 3 dBA higher. The proof of this fact is given in Example 10.3.

Example 10.3

Prove that two sounds of equal intensity produce a decibel level that is only 3 dBA higher.

Solution The energy contained in the two sounds combined is equal to two times the sound energy I of either of the two alone. By Eq. 10.3.3, the combined level L is:

$$L = 10 \log_{10}\left(\frac{2I}{I_0}\right)$$

$$= 10 \log_{10}\left(\frac{I}{I_0}\right) + 10 \log_{10}2$$

$$= 10 \log_{10}\left(\frac{I}{I_0}\right) + 3$$

Discussion The first term on the right side is the decibel level corresponding to the sound intensity I to which 3 dB are added when the two sounds are combined. In conjunction with the sound-addition insert to Fig. 10.3.3, when more than two noise sources are to be added, their magnitudes are first listed in decreasing order. The increment contributed by lowest level to the next lowest is read from the graph and added to the latter. The result is then combined with the next list entry, and the procedure continues until all components have been included.

Example 10.4

A straight at-grade highway accommodates 3600 passenger cars and 40 medium trucks per hour. The average speed of the two vehicle types is the same and equals 40 mi/h. Plot the relationship between the noise level, L_{10}, and distance from the highway.

Solution The procedure relating to Fig. 10.3.3 is applied, using a combined volume of

$$3600 + 40 \times 10 = 4000 \text{ automobile equivalents per hour}$$

and the results obtained in relation to various distances D_c are plotted in the accompanying figure. The figure illustrates the attenuation of noise over distance from about 78 dBA at a distance of 30 ft to about 51 dBA at a distance of 1500 ft.

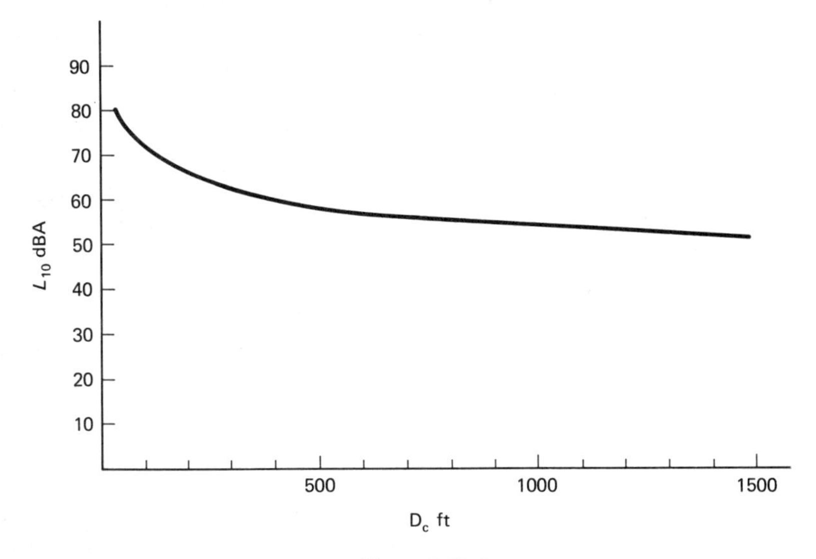

Figure P.10.4

10.4 ENERGY CONSUMPTION

10.4.1 Background

The enormous strides in industrial and economic growth that occurred in the United States during the twentieth century have been closely related to an ample supply of inexpensive energy, particularly energy derived from fossil fuels. Around 1970, the population of the

United States constituted about 6% of the world's population but used approximately 30% of the global petroleum consumption. A little more than half of the petroleum used in this country is expended for transportation-related purposes, and of this amount the private automobile accounts for close to two-thirds, or about one-third of the total petroleum consumed in the United States. The potential impact that energy shortages can have was experienced during World War II, when strict rationing and allocation of energy and other resources had to be imposed. After the war, energy consumption resumed its upward spiral and the problem came to the forefront in 1973 when the Organization of Petroleum Exporting Countries (OPEC) imposed an oil embargo and subsequently raised the price of crude oil. The economic effects of this action reverberated around the globe.

10.4.2 National Response to the Emergency

The immediate response of the nation to the 1973–74 energy embargo was to first deal with the emergency situation at hand. Among the earliest actions of the U.S. Congress was the passage of the 1973 Emergency Petroleum Allocation Act, which empowered the executive branch to establish an allocation plan for various sectors of the economy and geographical regions. Related actions included extensions of the Daylight Savings Time, the establishment of a national highway speed limit of 55 mi/h, which became effective in 1974, and the creation of a Federal Energy Office to deal with the problem. The 1975 Energy Policy and Conservation Act provided for the development of a national energy contingency plan, which was issued by the Federal Energy Administration in 1976. The same act mandated a schedule for improving the fuel economy of new automobiles sold in the United States. At that time energy-related responsibilities were scattered among several federal agencies and programs. Persuant to Executive Order 12009, the U.S. Congress established in 1977 the Department of Energy (DOE). This new federal department combined the Energy Research and Development Administration (ERDA) and the Atomic Energy Commission (AEC) and was charged with the lead role in coordinating the national response to the problem of energy and to seek short-, medium-, and long-term solutions under a multifaceted program, which came to be known as "Project Independence" [10.19].

A second fuel shortfall occurred in 1979 and caused significant disruptions despite the implementation in the meantime of various gasoline rationing schemes. In the same year, the U.S. Congress passed the 1979 Emergency Energy Conservation Act, which directed the executive branch to establish energy conservation targets for the federal government and the states and required the states to submit their plans, including a transportation element, within 45 days of the issuance of the targets. In 1980, the newly elected administration ushered in a different perspective toward the problem by shifting the emphasis from central management to a reliance on a free-market approach. Proposals directed toward the abolishment of the DOE were sent forth and, in 1981, Executive Order 12287 was issued, which eliminated the then-existing allocation and price controls on crude oil and petroleum products. Both approaches to the problem of energy have their strong proponents, and the nation's response to the problem continued to be the subject of national debate.

10.4.3 Transportation-User Reactions

The 1973–74 oil embargo found the nation's transportation system ill prepared, and long queues at gasoline stations became commonplace. According to subsequent reviews of the major events that occurred during the period of low fuel supplies, the general reaction of highway users was to curtail automobile usage by about 20%, mainly by reducing recreational and nonessential trips [10.20]. Localized differences not withstanding, modal shifts to transit on a national scale were minimal during the emergency. This has been attributed to a lack of adequate transit capacity and to uncertainties about the expected duration of the emergency situation. However, a trend toward the use of more efficient motor vehicles and other transportation equipment became evident. In this connection, the 1975 Energy Policy and Conservation Act prescribed a time schedule for fuel economy improvements and required the sales-weighted average fuel economy of each domestic manufacturer to adhere to this schedule.

Other transportation-intensive sectors of the economy responded similarly to the fact that an increasing share of their operating costs were attributed to fuel costs. For example, Johnson and Saricks [10.21] report that most intercity freight carriers began to convert to more fuel-efficient equipment and devices through replacement and retrofit programs and to modify their maintenance and scheduling practices. Similarly, Horn [10.22] reports that the airline industry also moved toward the purchase of fuel-efficient aircraft, implemented new operational and maintenance practices, and reduced cruise speeds. In 1974, the airlines dropped a few thousand daily flights in order to increase passenger-load factors and thus minimize their consumption of fuel. Highway- and transit-operating agencies also took measures to improve their own consumption rates. Among the actions taken by highway agencies was a conversion to fuel-efficient highway-lighting systems.

10.4.4 Energy-Related Transportation Actions

The predominant view of the energy problem among transportation-planning agencies at the local, state, and federal levels was driven by the possibility of petroleum-supply interruptions, and the secret to the solution of the energy problem was understood to lie in emergency preparedness and in conservation. This view is reflected in the requirement of the 1979 Emergency Energy Conservation Act of Transportation Energy Contingency Plans [10.23, 10.24] and in proposed rules issued by the DOT in 1980, which required that energy conservation be considered in transportation-planning programs receiving federal support. Possible energy-conservation strategies may be classified into those that are aimed to cause

1. Technological innovations;
2. Improvements in traffic flow;
3. Reductions in the total vehicle miles of travel (VMT).

Technological innovations include improvements in the fuel efficiency of in-use technology. By converting to more fuel-efficient vehicles, highway users were able to sustain their trip-making levels while expending less, although more-expensive, fuel. An interesting side effect of this development has been its impact on the revenues of agencies responsible for the construction, operation, and maintenance of highway facilities, because the source of funding for these activities had been primarily in the form of user charges, mainly gasoline taxes levied on a per gallon basis. Another development in relation to technological innovation was an accelerated level of often federally sponsored research and development in the areas of new engines and toward the utilization of alternate transportation fuels. Examples of new engine types include various external combustion engines such as the Stirling and the Rankine engines, continuous-combustion turbine devices, and various configurations of electric and hybrid electric vehicles. Fuels that have been proposed as replacements for conventionally derived petroleum products in existing and new engine designs include gasoline and distillates (diesel fuel), which can be derived from coal and shalc, alcohol fuels such as methanol and fuel blends, hydrogen, and electricity, which can be derived from various sources.

Highway level of service and the search for traffic-flow improvements have always been matters of direct concern to transportation engineers. In addition, the effect of highway design and maintenance (e.g., grades, curvature, and pavement condition) on fuel-consumption rates had traditionally been included in the calculation of motor-vehicle operating costs [10.25]. It was, therefore, natural that the inclusion of fuel-consumption considerations in the evaluation of highway designs and congestion-reducing schemes would be given new emphasis in view of the evolution of the global energy situation. A sampling of related investigations includes the use of freeway shoulders as low-cost traffic lanes to improve traffic flow, allowing right turns on red to reduce idling times, providing left turn lanes at signalized and unsignalized intersections, improving arterial access, and implementing signal systems. The energy effects of other strategies such as the spreading of the peak-period demand for highway travel through the implementation of staggered work schedules and other transportation system management (TSM) actions have also been addressed.

Strategies aimed at reducing the vehicle-miles traveled represent a departure from the other two categories of actions in that they require significant changes in the public's travel habits. Ways to reduce the VMT range from policies that encourage high vehicle occupancies to urban-planning processes that emphasize the joint development of transportation and land-use to minimize the need for travel without adversely affecting the accessibility of the population to activities.

10.4.5 Vehicle-Propulsion Energy

The propulsion energy expended by individual vehicles is typically reported either in terms of *energy economy rates* (i.e., distance traveled per unit energy) or in terms of its reciprocal, that is, the *energy consumption rate*. The energy measure is usually specified either in terms of the amount of a particular fuel or, when applicable, in terms of electrical energy. Thus the energy economy of passenger cars is specified as gallons of gasoline per vehicle mile and for electrically propelled transit vehicles, as kilowatt-hours per vehicle mile. In order to be able to compare the energy efficiency of vehicles using different types of fuel, several analysts resort to the conversion of energy requirements to a common unit such as the British thermal unit (Btu) or the joule. Comparisons based on such conversions, of course, are not sensitive to the particular source of the energy used (i.e., crude oil, coal, or nuclear energy), which have certain important policy implications.

A considerable body of research exists relative to the propulsion efficiency of highway vehicles and the factors that influence it. Among these factors are vehicular characteristics (e.g., vehicle type, weight, age, and engine displacement), highway geometrics and condition (e.g., grades, curvature, and pavement maintenance), and traffic-flow conditions (i.e., free-flow to jammed). Figure 10.4.1 illustrates the general shape of the relationship between sustained uniform speed and fuel consumption for highway vehicles. This figure shows that the minimum fuel-consumption rate corresponds to a uniform speed of about 35 mi/h, depending on vehicle type and the other factors just mentioned. Fuel-consumption curves similar to Fig. 10.4.1 are available in the technical literature for different types of vehicles, including passenger cars, light and heavy trucks, buses, and composite vehicles reflecting various vehicle combinations [10.26].

Regarding the propulsion efficiency of nonhighway transit vehicles and systems, it suffices to state that a great variability is found, depending on the type of system, its propulsion technology, and geometric characteristics, including station spacing and gradients.

To calculate the propulsion-energy requirements for a transportation network, estimates of the vehicle mixes and traffic-flow conditions are required, which, in a planning context, may be provided by transportation demand-forecasting model systems such as those described in Chapters 8 and 9 [10.27]. Observed before-and-after traffic-flow conditions may also be used to assess the energy effects of various short-term policies. Vehicular volumes can then be translated to fuel consumption by the use of appropriately calibrated fuel relationships.

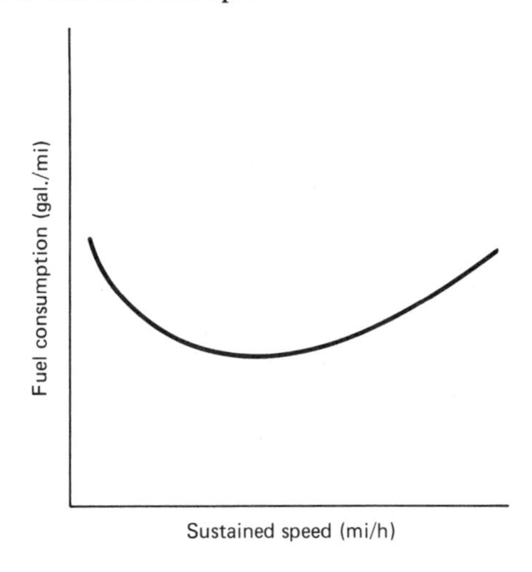

Figure 10.4.1 General relationship between sustained speed and fuel consumption.

In the case of travel on urban arterials, the traffic-flow characteristics involve interruptions by the control system and flow variations due to factors that are internal to traffic streams. The General Motors Research Laboratory [10.28] has calibrated a model relating consumption to travel time for various types of vehicles and vehicle mixes in urban arterial driving conditions. The following linear relationship was found to apply for average arterial system speeds of up to 35 mi/h.

$$f = k_1 + k_2 t \tag{10.4.1}$$

where

f = fuel-consumption rate (e.g., gallons per mile)

t = travel time (e.g., hours per mile)

k_1 = calibration constant (gallons per vehicle-mile)

k_2 = calibration constant (gallons per hr)

Equation 10.4.1 may be rewritten in terms of average speed as

$$f = k_1 + \frac{k_2}{u}, \qquad u < 35 \text{ mi/h} \tag{10.4.2}$$

which has a shape similar to Fig. 10.4.1 but is actually calibrated for the average speed over an urban-trip cycle rather than for sustained uniform speeds.

To calculate the fuel consumption F for a single vehicular trip in urban traffic, Eq. 10.4.1 is multiplied by the length of the trip D to yield

$$F = k_1 D + k_2 T \tag{10.4.3}$$

where T is the travel time for the entire trip.

Figure 10.4.2 represents General Motors' (GM) calibrated relationship for a typical passenger car mix consisting of 1973 to 1976 car models [10.6] with calibration constants $k_1 = 0.0362$ gal./veh-mi and $k_2 = 0.746$ gal./h. A similar relationship relating to diesel engine tractor-trailers with gross vehicle weights (GVW) of 33,000 lbs and over is illustrated by Fig. 10.4.3. Finally, Fig. 10.4.4 shows the fuel-consumption rates of city buses in reference to the number of stops per mile rather than to the average trip speed. The number of stops per mile used to enter the graph includes scheduled stops, stops that are caused by the traffic-flow conditions, and interruptions due to the control system.

Example 10.5

During the typical 1976 peak period, 4000 passenger cars traveled from a suburb to the CBD along a 6-mile arterial route at an average speed of 18 mi/h. One of the lanes on the route was subsequently reserved for carpools. This action resulted in a mild reduction in the peak period vehicle trips. A postimplementation count showed that the special lane was used by 1000 vehicles (which included previous and new car-poolers) at an improved speed of 24 mi/h. However, 2800 vehicles used the regular lanes, and this caused a speed reduction to

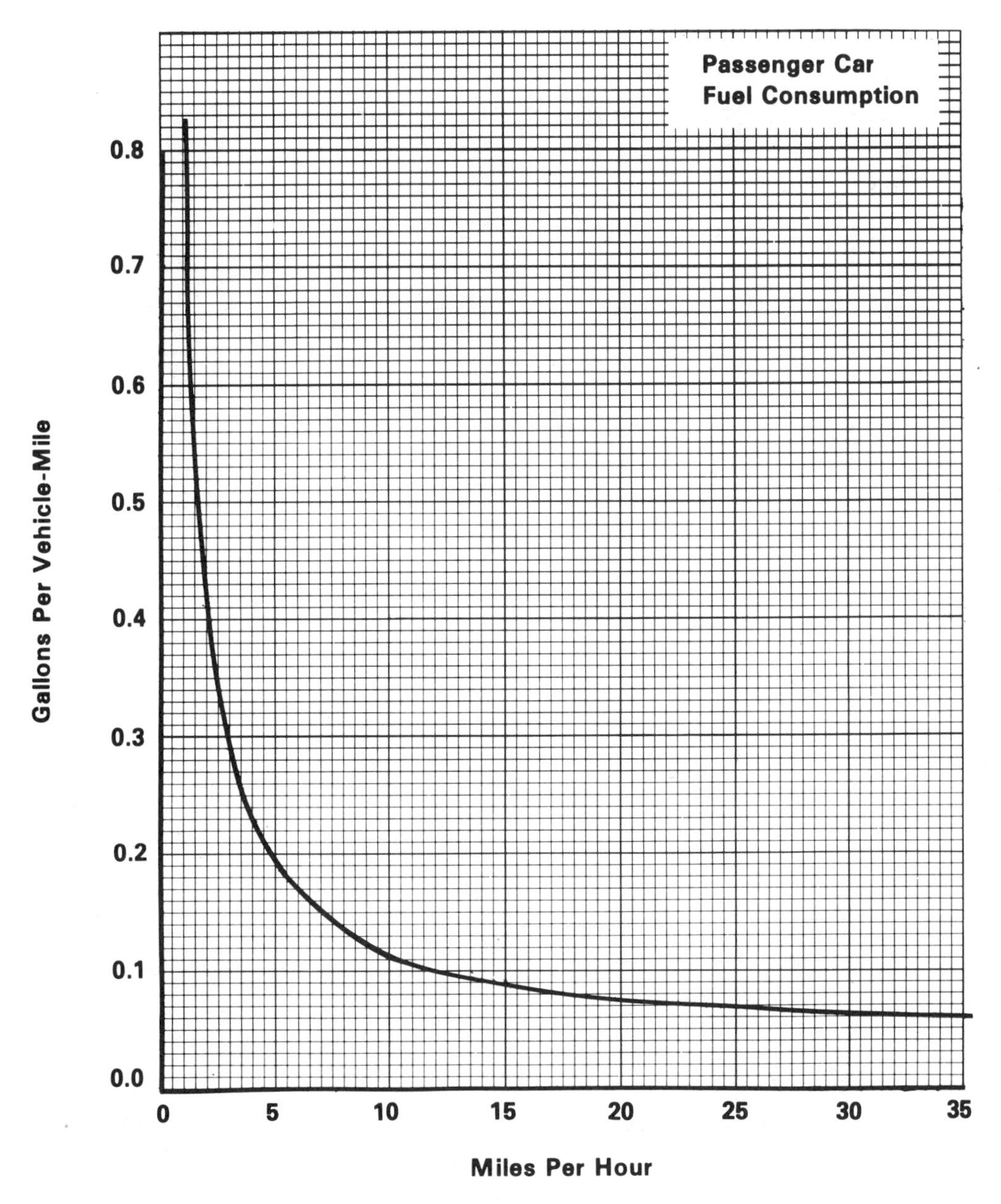

Figure 10.4.2 Passenger-car fuel consumption. (*SOURCE*: Raus [10.6], Fig. 1, p. 8.)

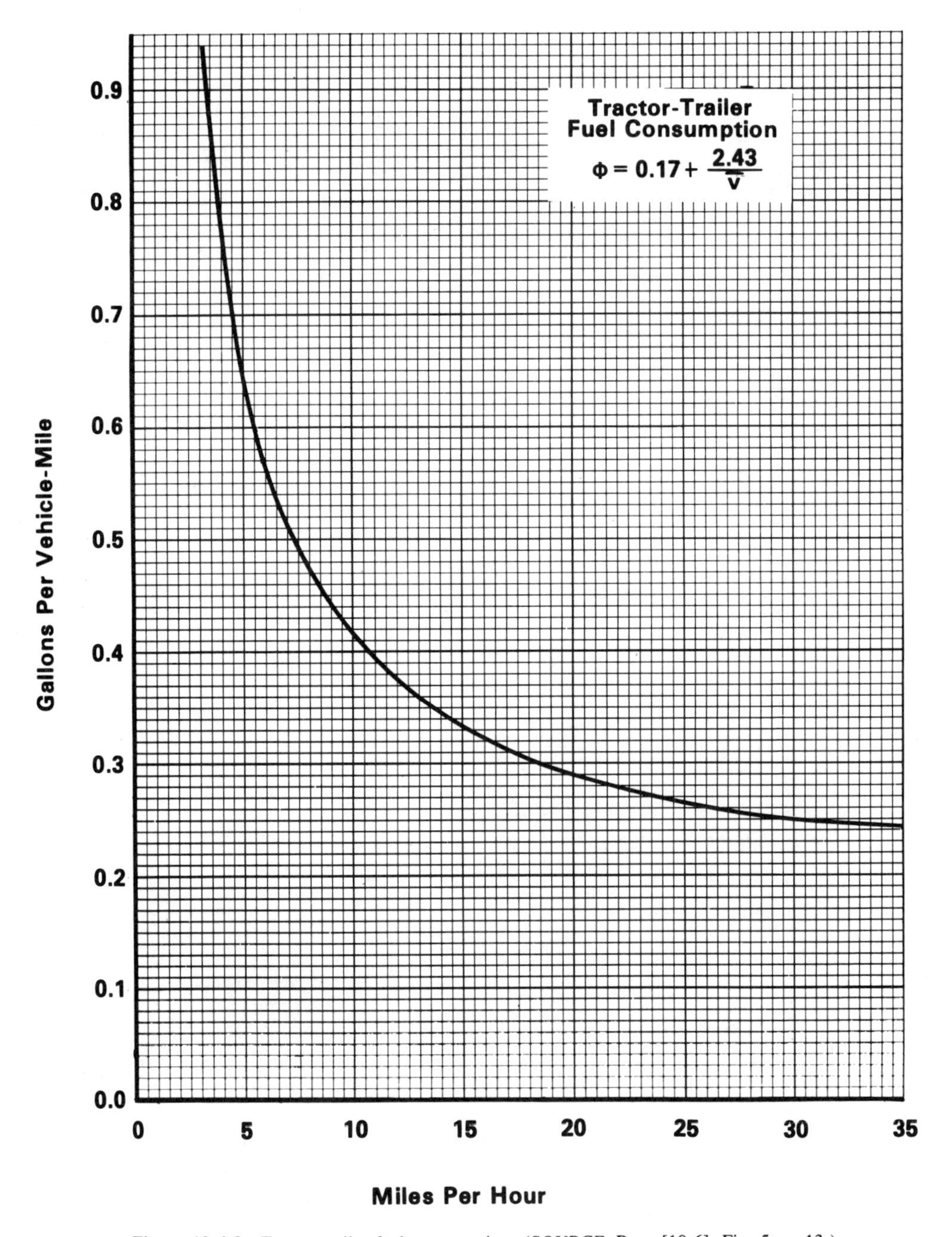

Figure 10.4.3 Tractor-trailer fuel consumption. (*SOURCE*: Raus [10.6], Fig. 5, p. 13.)

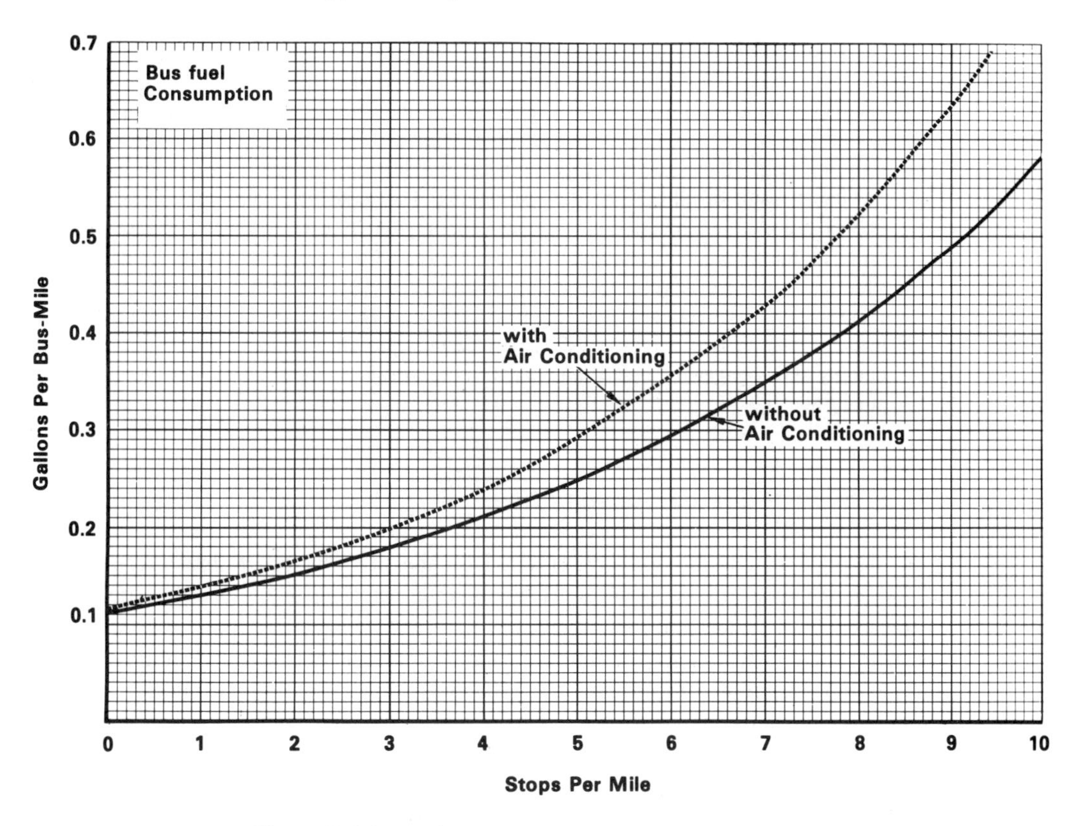

Figure 10.4.4 Bus fuel consumption. (*SOURCE*: Raus [10.6], Fig. 7, p. 15.)

12 mi/h for this component. Calculate the fuel consumed during the peak period (a) prior to and (b) subsequent to the opening of the car-pool lane.

Solution

(a) Prior to the project, the fuel consumption of the average vehicle over the 6-mile route was, according to Eq. 10.4.3 and the GM calibration constants,

$$F = (0.0362)(6) + \frac{0.746}{3} = 0.466 \text{ gal./veh}$$

A total of 4000 vehicles traversed the route during the peak period. Hence, the total fuel consumption was

$$(4000)(0.466) = 1864 \text{ gal. per peak period.}$$

(b) Following the opening of the car-pool lane, the flow was segregated into regular lane traffic, and car-pool lane traffic. Applying Eq. 10.4.3 twice and summing the results, the total consumption became

$$(2800)(0.590) + (1000)(0.0404) = 2066 \text{ gal./peak}$$

Discussion The peak-period propulsive fuel consumption on an arterial route was calculated for two operational strategies. In this particular case, the fuel consumption following the opening of a car-pool lane increased even though the vehicle-miles traveled during the peak actually decreased from 24,000 (i.e., 4000 veh × 6 mi) to 22,800. This was due to the resulting traffic-flow conditions given in the problem and should not be considered as the inevitable result of all car-pool lane situations. The route fuel consumption for each case may be reported in terms of the aggregate economy rate (AER) by dividing the total vehicle-miles by the total fuel consumption. Thus, the AER for the pre- and the post-car-pool lane situations was, respectively, 12.9 and 11.0 veh-mil/gal. The conclusion reached by comparing these two rates is identical to that drawn on the basis of the fuel consumption alone. However, neither of these two vehicle-mile-based measures provides definite information about the number of passenger-miles accommodated by the two alternatives, which may be an important policy question.

10.4.6 Indirect Energy Consumption

The foregoing discussion has concentrated on the propulsive, or direct, energy consumption of transportation systems. A complete accounting of the energy requirements of transportation systems, on the other hand, also includes indirect energy expenditures, consisting of construction, maintenance, and operational energy expenditures. Several analysts have attempted to estimate the total (i.e., direct *and* indirect) energy needs of various modes and systems. It suffices to state that these estimates depend on the components of indirect energy that each analyst chose for inclusion in the calculation. Any attempt to trace the full energy implications of transportation systems is ultimately difficult, as it may include the energy expended for the extraction, refinement, conversion, and transportation of energy resources and fuels and even items such as the energy imbedded in the manufacture of the vehicles. Consequently, a detailed review of total transportation energy studies and their energy policy and economic implications is beyond the scope of this textbook.

10.5 SUMMARY

This chapter discussed the air quality, noise, and energy impacts of transportation, described and illustrated several models that can be used to estimate these impacts, and presented strategies that have the potential of addressing these issues.

The major contribution of transportation to air pollution is in the form of carbon monoxide, hydrocarbons, nitrogen oxides, lead and other particulate matter, and photochemical smog. The degree of this contribution depends on emission levels, which are related to vehicle technology, traffic-flow levels, and traffic characteristics, and on the subsequent processes of mixing, diffusion, and chemical oxidation. A method developed by Raus of the FHWA for calculating the emission rates on highway facilities and a simple mathematical pollutant diffusion model (the box model) were described.

Noise was defined as undesirable or unwanted sound and was related to physical and mental health problems. It is typically measured in terms of A-weighted decibel levels on a logarithmic scale that simulates human responses. The intensity of noise decreases with distance from the source because of spreading and absorption energy losses and is also intercepted and reflected by solid objects. These attributes of noise suggest mitigation strategies that include the placement of noise barriers and buffer zones between the source and the receiver in addition to vehicle related and other actions. The simplest of several noise-estimation models was included. This model applies to long, straight segments of highways in the absence of noise barriers.

A significant portion of the national consumption of energy, particularly petroleum-based, is expended for transportation purposes. A recognition of the ultimate depletion of crude oil and international developments involving oil producing countries have brought this issue into sharp focus. The problem elicited differing reactions from several perspectives, including the users of transportation fuels, the highway- and transit-operating agencies, the transportation-planning organizations, and the regional and national energy policy analysts. A method for estimating the propulsive energy requirements of transportation systems was included.

Suggested actions that have important implications with respect to all three impacts covered in this chapter were classified into those that aim at the technological performance of vehicles, those that are concerned with geometric design and traffic flow operations, those that encourage significant changes in travel behavior, particularly modal choice, and those that propose alternative urban structural forms.

10.6 EXERCISES

1. The one-directional speed-concentration relationship for a 10-mi-long segment of a two-lane rural highway is

$$u = 45.0 - 0.3k$$

Apply the Raus model to estimate the total emissions of carbon monoxide assuming that the highway operates at capacity for an entire hour. The ambient temperature at the low altitude highway is 40°F.

2. A proposed increase of parking fees in a downtown area is expected to cause a reduction in the one-directional peak hour flow of a radial six-lane highway from 5100 veh/h to 4200 veh/h. Given that the flow-concentration relationship for each highway lane is

$$q = 42.0k - 0.25k^2 \text{ mi/h per lane,}$$

estimate the effect that the parking policy would have on the emission of carbon monoxide during the peak hour. Assume that the flow is distributed equally among the three lanes of traffic, the ambient temperature is 0°F, and the highway was originally operating at level of service F.

3. The pollutant emission rate E has been estimated to change with respect to time as

$$E = Ae^{-Bt}$$

where A and B are constants. Assuming a constant air flow F and a box volume V, apply the box model to express the pollutant concentration as a function of time. The initial concentration in the box at time $t = 0$ is K.

4. Repeat Exercise 3 assuming that the emission rate is give by

$$E = A\,(1 - e^{-Bt})$$

5. The air-pollution emission rate E in a parking lot may be approximated by the following step function:

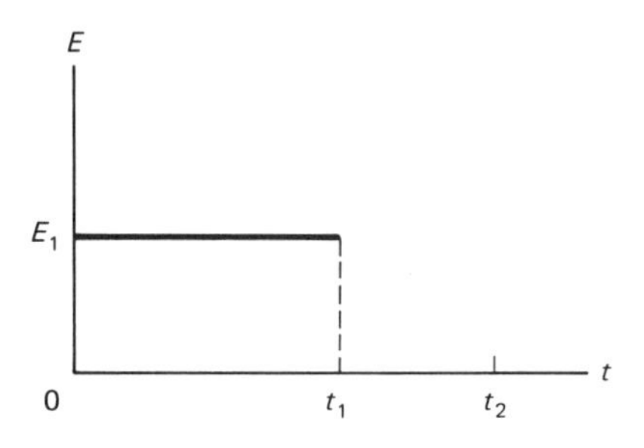

Figure E.10.5

Assuming a constant air flow F and zero initial pollutant concentration, plot the C as a function of time.

6. At a given location, the measured noise level during 15 consecutive time intervals was

80, 75, 76, 75, 71, 72, 72, 73, 74, 76, 75, 72, 74, 73, 72

dB. Use this limited set of data to (a) approximate the cumulative distribution of noise level, (b) estimate the L_{10}, L_{50}, and L_{90} levels, and (c) calculate the L_{eq} noise level.

7. Bicyclists A and B rode along the bikeways shown at 15 and 20 mi/h, respectively. Bicyclist A encountered 180 vehicles during his 1.2-mile ride against traffic, and bicyclist B was overtaken by 30 more vehicles than she overtook during her 1.2-mi ride with traffic. (See accompanying figure.) Assuming that the traffic stream consisted of passenger cars only, calculate the L_{10} noise level to which each of the bicyclists was exposed.

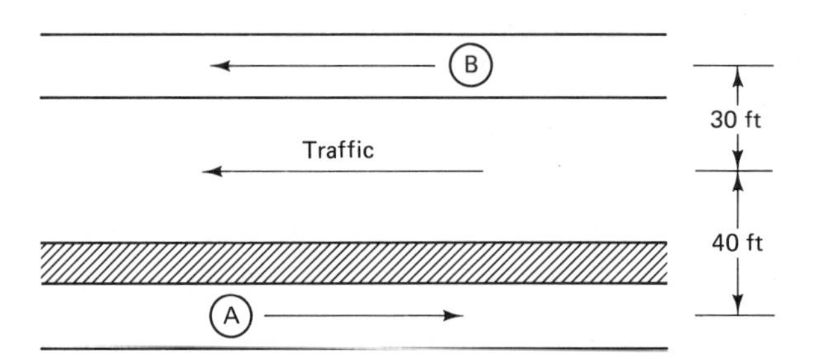

Figure E.10.7

8. The traffic flows on each of the two lanes of a highway are shown in the accompanying figure. Calculate the L_{10} noise level at point P.

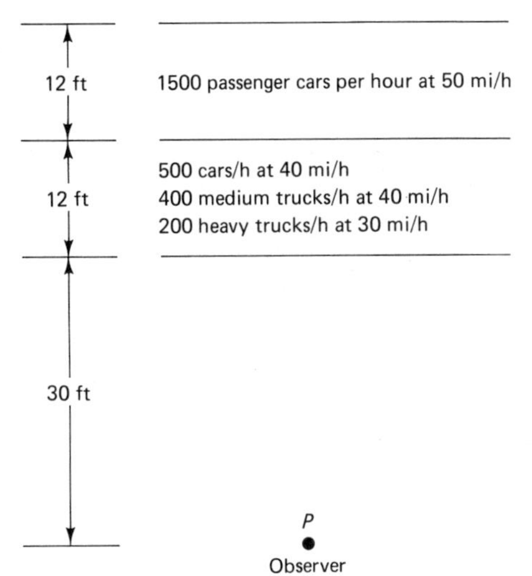

Figure E.10.8

9. Apply Eq. 10.3.2 to calculate the combined effect of the following four decibel levels:

$$71, \quad 77, \quad 72, \quad \text{and} \quad 73$$

10. Combine the four noise levels given in Exercise 9 by means of the insert to Fig. 10.3.4

11. The combined noise level from two sources is 68.5 dBA. The noisier of the two sources produces a noise level of 68.0 dBA. Estimate mathematically the level produced by the other source.

12. The flow on a highway consists of 100 heavy trucks per hour traveling at 50 mi/h, 30 medium trucks per hour traveling at 40 mi/h, and 600 passenger cars per hour traveling at 50 mi/h. Assuming a highway width of 50 ft, specify the width of a buffer zone that ensures that the noise level in an adjacent park will not exceed the 1973 FHWA standard.

13. How close to the highway of Exercise 12 can a single-glazed masonry school building be located and still meet the FHWA noise standard?

14. The flow-concentration relationship for a roadway is

$$q = 60.0k - 4.0k^{1.5} \text{ veh/h}$$

Using the GM model, derive and plot the fuel consumption rate f as a function of traffic stream concentration (veh/mi). Assume that the traffic stream consists of passenger cars only.

15. Find the fuel consumption rate corresponding to $q_{\max}$ for the roadway of Exercise 14.

16. A bus line operates in mixed traffic and carries 4000 passengers per peak hour at an average speed of 10 mi/h. Typically each bus makes 2 scheduled stops per mile and is interrupted by the traffic control system and by other vehicles 6 times per mile. Given an average occupancy of 50 persons per bus and a 5-mi trip, calculate the number of buses needed to serve the passenger demand and the total amount of fuel consumed during a typical peak hour.

17. Calculate the effect on the fleet size and the fuel consumption of the bus system of Exercise 16 assuming that an exclusive bus lane were to be implemented. The resulting conditions include a reduction of nonscheduled stops from six to two, and an average speed of 15 mi/h.

10.7 REFERENCES

10.1 PERKINS, H. C., *Air Pollution,* McGraw-Hill, New York, 1974.

10.2 Environmental Protection Agency, *Federal Register,* 36, no. 84 (Friday, April 30, 1971).

10.3 ———, *Compilation of Air Pollution Emission Factors,* Office of Air Quality Planning and Standards, Publication AP-42, Research Triangle Park, N.C., various annual revisions.

10.4 LEE, C. E., AND LEE, F.-P., "Simulation of Traffic Performance, Vehicle Emissions, and Fuel Consumption at Intersections: the TEXAS-II Model," *Transportation Research Record* 971, Transportation Research Board, National Research Council, Washington, DC, 1984, pp. 133–140.

10.5 Environmental Protection Agency, *User's Guide to MOBILE I: Mobile Source Emissions Model,* Office of Air, Noise, and Radiation, Washington, D.C., 1978.

10.6 RAUS, J., *A Method for Estimating Fuel Consumption and Vehicle Emissions on Urban Arterials and Networks,* Office of Research and Development, Federal Highway Administration, Report Number FHWA-TS-81-210, Washington, D.C., 1981.

10.7 ZIMMERMAN, J. R., AND R. S. THOMPSON, *User's Guide for HIWAY, A Highway Air Pollution Model,* Office of Research and Development, U.S. Environmental Protection Agency, Research Triangle Park, N.C., 1975.

10.8 TURNER, B. D., *Workbook on Atmospheric Dispersion Estimates,* U.S. Environmental Protection Agency, Research Triangle Park, N.C., 1970.

10.9 DEMERJIAN, K. L., "Oxidant Modeling Status," *Transportation Research Record* 670, Transportation Research Board, National Research Council, Washington, D.C., 1978, pp. 1–6.

10.10 SEIFF, H. E., "Enforcement of Control of Interstate Motor Carrier Noise: A Federal Perspective," *Motor Vehicle Noise Control,* Transportation Research Board, Special Report 152, National Research Council, Washington, D.C., 1975, pp. 66–72.

10.11 Federal Highway Administration, *Noise Standards and Procedures,* Policy and Procedure Memorandum, Transmittal 279, 90-2, Washington, D.C., February 8, 1973.

10.12 Environmental Protection Agency, *Noise and its Measurement,* Office of Public Affairs, February, 1977.

10.13 BORTHWICK, J. O., "A Status Report on the Florida Motor Vehicle Noise Control Plan," *Motor Vehicle Noise Control,* Transportation Research Board, Special Report 152, National Research Council, Washington, D.C., 1975, pp. 85–93.

10.14 U.S. Department of Transportation, *Organization and Content of Environmental Assessment Materials,* Notebook 5, U.S. Government Printing Office, Stock No. 050-000-00109-1, Washington, D.C., 1975.

10.15 HALL, F. L. AND B. L. ALLEN, "Toward a Community Impact Measure for Assessment of Transportation Noise," *Transportation Research Record* 580, Transportation Research Board, National Research Council, Washington, D.C., 1976, pp. 22–35.

10.16 WESLER, J. E., "Introduction and History of Highway Noise Prediction Methods," *Transportation Research Circular* 174, Transportation Research Board, National Research Council, Washington, D.C., 1975, pp. 9–13.

10.17 Wright Air Development Center, *Handbook of Acoustic Noise Control,* WADC Technical Report 52-204, 1952.

10.18 KUGLER, B. A., D. E. COMMINS, AND W. J. GALLOWAY, *Highway Noise: A Design Guide for Prediction and Control,* National Cooperative Highway Research Program, Report 174, Transportation Research Board, National Research Council, Washington, D.C., 1976.

10.19 U.S. Federal Energy Administration, *Project Independence Report,* U.S. Government Printing Office. Number 4118-000019, November 1974.

10.20 CHESLOW, M. D., "Potential Use of Carpooling During Periods of Energy Shortages," *Considerations in Transportation Energy Contingency Planning,* Special Report 191, Transportation Research Board, National Research Council, Washington, D.C., 1980, pp. 38–43.

10.21 JOHNSON, L. R., AND C. L. SARICKS, "An Evaluation of Options for Freight Carriers During a Fuel Crisis," *Transportation Research Record* 935, National Research Council, Washington, D.C., 1983, pp. 5–11.

10.22 HORN, K. W. "Energy and the Airline Industry," *Considerations in Transportation Energy Contingency Planning,* Special Report 191, Transportation Research Board, National Research Council, Washington, D.C., 1980, pp. 69–70.

10.23 Transportation Research Board, *Considerations in Transportation Energy Contingency Planning,* Special Report 191, National Research Council, Washington, D.C., 1980.

10.24 ———, Proceedings of the Conference on Energy Contingency Planning in Urban Areas, Special Report 203, National Research Council, Washington, D.C., 1983.

10.25 CURRY, D. A., AND D. G. ANDERSON, *Procedures for Estimating Highway User Costs, Air Pollution, and Noise Effects,* National Cooperative Highway Research Program, Report 133, Transportation Research Board, National Research Council, Washington, D.C., 1972.

10.26 CLAFFEY, P. J., *Running Costs of Motor Vehicles as Affected by Road Design and Traffic,* National Cooperative Highway Research Program, Report 111, Transportation Research Board, National Research Council, Washington, D.C., 1971.

10.27 PAPACOSTAS, C. S., *Pollution and Energy Implications of Urban Bus-Automobile Alternatives,* Ph.D. Dissertation, Carnegie-Mellon University, 1974.

10.28 CHANG, M. F., et al., *The Influence of Vehicle Characteristics, Driver Behavior, and Ambient Temperature on Gasoline Consumption in Urban Areas,* General Motors Corporation, Warren, Michigan, 1976.

CHAPTER 11

EVALUATION AND CHOICE

11.1 INTRODUCTION

Even when presented a single proposal, decision-makers have a choice between it and doing nothing. Therefore every decision involves at least two options. *Evaluation* facilitates decision-making by appraising the merits (*positive impacts*) and demerits (*negative impacts*) of alternative options in terms of either a single or multiple decision criteria. Determining which impacts are relevant to a particular decision and specifying the appropriate decision criteria are related to the value system within which the choice is to be made. In the case of transportation decisions in the public sector, the operating value system is not that of any single individual or subgroup but that of the community as a whole. Chapters 1 and 7 recognized the existence of conflicting value systems within society. Consequently, transportation decision-making also entails the resolution of conflicts.

Two types of evaluation studies are commonly undertaken: preimplementation studies, which facilitate the choice of the best course of action from among several alternative proposals, and postimplementation studies, which assess the performance of already implemented actions. Postimplementation studies are important for two reasons. First, they help to discover whether or not the implemented alternative performs well, and second, they help to determine whether or not it continues to perform properly over time. This is especially important in the case of transportation systems, which are subject to changing conditions and also to evolving goals and objectives. Continuous monitoring and periodic performance evaluation can help identify emerging problems and also provide guidance to the design of possible improvements. Chapter 9 has shown that problem definition is the first step of the decision-making process, which eventually leads to the comparative evaluation of alternative improvement strategies prior to implementation and the selection of the best option among them.

To be selected for implementation, an alternative must be both feasible *and* superior to all other alternatives. The prerequisites to the admission of an alternative to the list of acceptable options include the conditions of technological feasibility, economic efficiency and cost-effectiveness, and availability of the needed resources.

This chapter presents the fundamental elements of efficiency and effectiveness evaluation techniques, along with a brief description of their conceptual foundations and their major strengths and weaknesses.

11.2 FEASIBILITY AND IMPACT ENUMERATION

11.2.1 Measures of Feasibility

Technological feasibility refers to the ability of a system to function according to the laws of nature and not to its desirability: A perpetual-motion machine may be highly desirable but technologically impossible. Engineers and other technologists are qualified to deal with questions relating to technology. Research and development are on-going activities that occasionally lead to technological breakthroughs. The vast majority of practical applications, however, involve the use of existing technology. Even then, innovative and creative ways of combining off-the-shelf technology are common. Consequently, the question of technological feasibility is an aspect of evaluation that cannot be ignored.

Efficiency is defined as the ratio of the quantity produced (*output*) to the resources required for its production (*input*). *Physical* or *machine efficiency* is the ratio of the energy delivered by a machine or a process to the energy supplied to it. Although expressed in the same unit of measurement, the input and the output energy differ in form, for example, energy in the form of electricity vis-à-vis energy in the form of work done by the system. Machine efficiency is always less than unity because of the unavoidable energy losses that are incurred in the process. This waste can be justified only when the usefulness, or utility, of the output exceeds that of the input. When both the numerator and the denominator are converted to the same measure of economic value, their ratio is referred to as the *economic efficiency* of the machine, which must be greater than unity if the machine is to be economically feasible. The idea of economic efficiency has been extended to the evaluation of systems to contrast the economic value of the advantages (or benefits) that are derived from the system to its disadvantages (or costs).

Effectiveness is defined as the degree to which an action accomplishes its stated objectives. It differs from efficiency in that it need not have to explicitly express all impacts in the same scale of measurement. For example, the effectiveness of a regional transportation system for elderly and handicapped persons may be expressed as the proportion of eligible users that live within the service area of the system or as the total number of persons served, whereas its operating costs may be expressed in terms of dollars. *Cost-effectiveness* evaluation is the attempt to determine the efficacy of alternatives by comparing their cost to their effectiveness. Of course, if an objective method for collapsing all impacts to the same dimension were available, efficiency and effectiveness would lead to identical results, but no such method exists. Consequently, both evaluative methods are used, sometimes separately and sometimes in combination [11.1, 11.2].

An alternative may be technologically feasible, economically efficient, and cost-effective and yet not be a prudent choice for implementation because of the unavailability of the financial and other resources that are needed for its implementation. Problems of affordability or resource availability are not uncommon. Consider, for example, the case of financial resources. Usually, there exists a lag between the time when financial resources are expended and the time when the returns of the investment are realized. Lack of access to financial resources during this critical time lag would render the investment infeasible. Another common problem of financial affordability that is especially true in the case of public projects is related to the fact that the benefits derived by a public investment do not usually return in the form of money to the agency that expends the financial costs for the project. Unless the agency is in a position to afford these expenditures, it would not be able to produce the benefits for whomever they would otherwise accrue.

11.2.2 Impact Trade-Offs

Determining the feasibility of each alternative is only half of the evaluation process. The other half involves the comparison of all proposals (including the do-nothing alternative) in order to select the best one among them. Based on the assignment of relative weights to the impacts of each alternative, this step involves *impact trade-offs*. Consider, for example, a choice between two transportation alternatives requiring equal and available financial expenditures. Further, assume that one of the two would provide a higher level of mobility than the other but would also discharge higher quantities of atmospheric pollutants. This statement implies that three impacts have been identified as relevant to the choice, that appropriate measures of performance have been established to express them, and that the likely levels of these impacts have been predicted for each alternative, perhaps using the methods of Chapter 8 through 10. When comparing the two alternatives, a trade-off between mobility on one hand and environmental quality on the other becomes apparent. In the final analysis, the evaluation method used to aid this decision must incorporate the assignment of relative weights to the impacts.

11.2.3 Generalized Impact Matrices

The foregoing example of evaluation raises a problem that is inherent in situations where the decision-makers are faced with multiple decision criteria. On the side of costs, the direct cost of operating the system and a *negative externality* (i.e., the unintended undesirable impact of air pollution) were identified. Direct benefits (e.g., mobility) and potential *positive externalities* are typically included in the evaluative calculus. All recognizable impacts, whether intended or concomitant, can be classed into positive impacts (i.e., advantages or benefits) and negative impacts (i.e., disadvantages or costs) and the results of the impact estimation process that precedes the evaluation phase (see Chapter 8, 9 and 10) may be summarized in an *impact matrix,* as illustrated by Fig. 11.2.1.

This array lists the estimated impacts associated with each alternative expressed in terms of the applicable measures of performance, which differ with regard to their units of measurement. Moreover, some are expressed in terms of quantitative measures (i.e., carbon monoxide concentration), and others are qualitative.

Table 11.2.1 lists the impacts that were considered in the EIS for a proposed Honolulu Area Rapid Transit (HART) System [11.3]. The first column summarizes the goals and objectives set forth in the regional general plan for the island of Oahu, where the city of Honolulu is located. The second column presents the specific goals identified by an earlier Oahu transportation study. Following are the objectives established by two previous Preliminary Engineering Evaluation Program studies of transit alternatives (PEEP I and II). The fourth column lists the criteria that were selected to measure the performance of alternative systems. Also noted is the potential applicability of these criteria to three characteristics of alternative proposals, that is, route location, transit system type, and system length. The rapid transit alternatives are augmented by feeder bus services.

Table 11.2.2 summarizes the analytical results obtained by applying the sequential transportation demand-forecasting process described in Chapter 8. This table includes only direct impacts.

Table 11.2.3 is the generalized impact matrix developed in connection with the HART EIS. It includes the direct and indirect impacts of each alternative either in quantitative terms or qualitatively.

Impact category	$ costs		Mobility		Environmental quality			Social
Measures of performance	Capital	O & M	Travel time	Travel cost	Air	Noise	. . .	. . .
Do nothing								
Alternative A								
Alternative B								
⋮								

Figure 11.2.1 A generalized impact matrix.

TABLE 11.2.1 EXAMPLE OF GOALS, OBJECTIVES, AND CRITERIA

Transportation goals Oahu general plan	Transportation goals Oahu transportation study	Transit development objectives PEEP I and II	Transit development criteria for alternatives analysis	Applicable criteria for specific alternative analysis		
				Route location	System type	System length
1. Provide transportation facilities to enable travel from any point in the region to any other point within reasonable travel time by one or more modes	1. [a]Provide transportation facilities for ease of movement throughout Oahu; and provide a variety of modes of travel which will best serve the different requirements of the community	1. *Improve accessibility* by service and interconnecting existing and future urbanized areas of Oahu	a. Availability & coverage	—	√	√
			b. Average trip time	√	√	√
			c. Service reliability	—	√	√
			d. Rider convenience	√	√	√
			e. Rider comfort	√	√	√
2. A transportation system which will provide the greatest efficiency and service to the community with the least overall expenditure of resources	2. Provide a balanced transportation system which will result in optimum service with the least public expenditure	2. [a]*Provide a balanced transportation system* of transit and highways	a. System patronage	√	√	√
			b. System capacity	√	√	√
		3. [a]*Minimize expenditure of resources* and disruption to community	a. Consumption of land	—	√	√
			b. Displacement of residents	√	√	√
			c. Displacement of businesses	√	√	√
			d. Reduction of comm. amenities	√	√	√
			e. Disruption to future dvlpmt.	√	√	√
			f. Disruption to local circulation	√	√	√
			g. Disruption—constr. activity	—	√	√
			h. Savings in energy	—	√	√
			i. Technical risk	—	√	√

(*continued*)

TABLE 11.2.1 *(Continued)*

Transportation goals Oahu general plan	Transportation goals Oahu transportation study	Transit development objectives PEEP I and II	Transit development criteria for alternatives analysis	Applicable criteria for specific alternative analysis		
				Route location	System type	System length
3. A transportation system to be designed as an integral part of and complementary to land use policies	3. Integration of the transportation system with land use	4. *Support land use* and development policies	a. Support regional development b. Support comm. development	√ √	√ √	√ √
4. [a]Preserve and maintain significant historic sites, scenery and natural assets of Oahu	4. Preserve Oahu's beauty and amenities	5. *Preserve environment*	a. Reduction air pollution b. Noise level c. Visual intrusion d. Vistas e. Historic sites	√ √ √ √ √	√ √ √ √ √	√ √ √ √ √
5. Safety	5. Safety	6. *Safety*	a. Reduce accident exposure b. Security	— —	√ √	√ √
6. [b]Provide a transportation system which will provide the greatest efficiency and service to the community with the least overall cost	6. [b]Provide a balanced transportation system which will result in optimum service at the least cost to the public	7. *Provide the most economical system* which best meets all other objectives	a. Total annual cost b. Cost per trip c. Benefit-cost ratio	√ — —	√ √ √	√ √ —
[a]Stated as one of the general goals [b]Stated separately from 2 to differentiate between expenditure of resources and least cost	[a]Combines Goals 1 & 3 of OTS [b]Stated separately from 2 to differentiate between expenditure of resources and least cost	[a]Goal 2 stated as two separate objectives				

SOURCE: Urban Mass Transportation Administration [11.3], Table III-8, p. III-29.

TABLE 11.2.2 EXAMPLE SUMMARY OF ANALYTICAL RESULTS

System	Travel characteristics						Operating characteristics				Cost[a]	
	Total Daily Transit Trips	Mode Split (Total) %	Daily Trips on Gwy.	% Pk. Hr. Work Trips By Transit	Avg. Trip Length (Mi.)	Avg. Trip Time (Min.)	Vehicles required (with spares)		Vehicle Miles Operated Daily		Total Capital Cost ($1,000)	Annual Operating Cost ($1,000)
							Gwy.	Feeder	Gwy.	Feeder		
7-mi busway	456,250	13.8	288,200	42.4	7.31	36.3	179	752	30,308	121,408	414,411	49,510
LRT 28 mi	474,520	14.4	358,750	44.6	7.22	32.4	410	443	79,515	71,645	712,289	47,660
23 mi	474,520	14.4	353,700	44.6	7.21	32.3	325	477	75,530	75,910	646,537	46,320
14 mi	473,300	14.3	306,900	44.2	7.26	33.7	198	580	45,840	94,260	529,321	44,310
7 mi	459,300	13.9	277,300	42.8	7.19	35.2	109	774	23,580	124,605	406,808	50,170
Fixed guideway 23 mi	490,000	14.8	332,600	46.0	7.50	31.6	421	493	111,495	78,390	647,900	46,940
14 mi	473,300	14.3	306,900	44.2	7.26	33.7	264	580	64,225	94,260	517,318	43,890
7 mi	459,300	13.9	277,300	42.8	7.19	35.2	161	774	34,335	124,605	398,676	50,070

[a] All costs shown are in 1975 dollars.

SOURCE: Urban Mass Transportation Administration [11.3], Table III-7, p. 328.

TABLE 11.2.3 EXAMPLE OF COMPARISON MATRIX FOR ALTERNATIVE SYSTEMS

	Short 7-mi length			Medium 14-mi length		Long 23- and 28-mi lengths		
	Busway	LRT	Fixed guideway	LRT	Fixed guide.	23-mi LRT	28-mi LRT	23-mi F.G.
Objective 1								
a. Availability & coverage	Same	Same	Same	Same	Same	Same	Same	Same
b. Avg. trip time (min.)	36.3	35.2	35.2	33.7	33.7	32.3	32.4	31.6
c. Service reliability	(2)[a]	(1)	(1)	Same	Same	(2)	(2)	(1)
d. Rider convenience	(1)	(2)	(2)	Same	Same	(2)	(1)	(2)
e. Rider comfort	(2)	(1)	(1)	Same	Same	Same	Same	Same
Objective 2								
a. System patronage (million)	137.8	138.7	138.7	142.9	142.9	143.3	143.3	148.0
b. System capacity	*[b]	Same	Same	Same	Same	Same	Same	Same
Objective 3								
a. Consumption of land (acres)	42	21	20	23	22	36	36	32
b. Displacement of residents (units)	233	152	148	166	162	179	179	167
c. Displacement of businesses (units)	257	168	164	187	183	194	194	184
d. Reduction of community amenities	Same	Same	Same	Same	Same	Same	Same	Same
e. Disruption to future dvlpmt.	Same	Same	Same	Same	Same	Same	Same	Same
f. Disruption to local circulation	Same	Same	Same	Same	Same	(2)	(3)	(1)
g. Disruption from constr. activities	Same	Same	Same	Same	Same	(1)	(2)	(1)

h. Savings in energy (million gal/yr.)	10.0		8.5		8.9		8.5		9.4		5.0		4.8		8.5	
i. Technical risk	(3)		(1)		(2)		(1)		(2)		(1)		(1)		(2)	
Objective 4																
a. Support regional dvlpmt.	Same		Same		Same		Same		Same		Same		Same		Same	
b. Support comm. dvlpmt.	Same		Same		Same		Same		Same		Same		Same		Same	
Objective 5																
a. Reduction Air pollution (tons/yr.)	2,970		3,240		3,260		4,110		4,150		4,120		4,140		4,930	
b. Noise level (dBA)	86–88		77–81		77		77–81		77		77–81		77–81		77	
c. Visual intrusion	(3)		(2)		(1)		(2)		(1)		(2)		(2)		(1)	
d. Vistas	(2)		(3)		(1)		(2)		(1)		(1)		(1)		(2)	
e. Historic sites	Same		Same		Same		Same		Same		Same		Same		Same	
Objective 6																
a. Reduce accident exposure	Same		Same		Same		Same		Same		(2)		(2)		(1)	
b. Security	Same		Same		Same		Same		Same		Same		Same		Same	
Objective 7[c] *Interest Rates*	4%	10%	4%	10%	4%	10%	4%	10%	4%	10%	4%	10%	4%	10%	4%	10%
a. Total annual cost ($ million)	77.43	96.90	76.98	96.17	76.41	95.21	77.38	102.60	76.26	101.01	85.73	116.66	90.73	124.84	86.51	117.48
b. Cost per trip	56.2¢	70.3¢	55.5¢	69.3¢	55.1¢	68.6¢	54.1¢	71.8¢	53.4¢	70.7¢	59.8¢	81.4¢	63.3¢	87.1¢	58.5¢	78.4¢
c. Benefit-cost ratio	2.24	1.50	2.28	1.55	2.31	1.58	2.40	1.47	2.47	1.51	2.06	1.24	1.87	1.13	2.19	1.32

[a]Numbers in parenthesis (1) show ranking of alternatives based on how well they met the objective

[b]Practical capacity for busways are unknown and assumed to be less than for guided systems

[c]All costs shown are in 1975 dollars.

SOURCE: Urban Mass Transportation Administration [11.3], Table II-9, p. III-35.

11.3 ENGINEERING ECONOMIC ANALYSIS

11.3.1 Background

Traditional engineering economic analysis is based on the principle that the quantified impacts of alternatives should and can be converted to their monetary equivalents and treated just as if they were money. With this conversion, the calculation of economic efficiency and the comparison of alternatives on the basis of their costs and benefits can be conducted. The basic unit of measurement employed (i.e., money) has certain attributes that must be retained in the calculation of benefits and costs. A fundamental characteristic of money is its time value. Simply stated, this says that "a dollar today is not the same as a dollar tomorrow." To illustrate this point, consider the situation where an amount of \$100 is deposited in a bank at an interest rate of 10%. One year from the day of deposit, \$110 may be withdrawn from the bank. In this case, \$100 today is equivalent to \$110 dollars a year from today. The *interest* or *discount* rate affects this equivalency.

11.3.2 Project Evaluation

Based on the axiom that the consequences that are relevant to the impending decision can be equated with money, each alternative may be considered to consist of two cash flows: a cash flow of benefits and a cash flow of costs, both shown as money equivalents at the times when they are expected to occur (Fig. 11.3.1). A proposed alternative is considered to be economically feasible when the benefits to be derived from it exceed its costs. This comparison between benefits and costs is legitimate only when the two cash flows are placed on the same time basis. Given an appropriate interest rate, the *present worth of benefits* (PWB) and the *present worth of costs* (PWC), or their equal series cash-flow equivalents, may be calculated. Appendix B develops the appropriate formulas that can be used for this task, which the student may wish to review before continuing with the rest of this chapter.

The *net present worth* (NPW) of an alternative is defined as the present worth of its benefits minus the present worth of its costs. Hence, a positive NPW implies economic feasibility. Another way of contrasting benefits and costs is the use of the *benefit-cost*

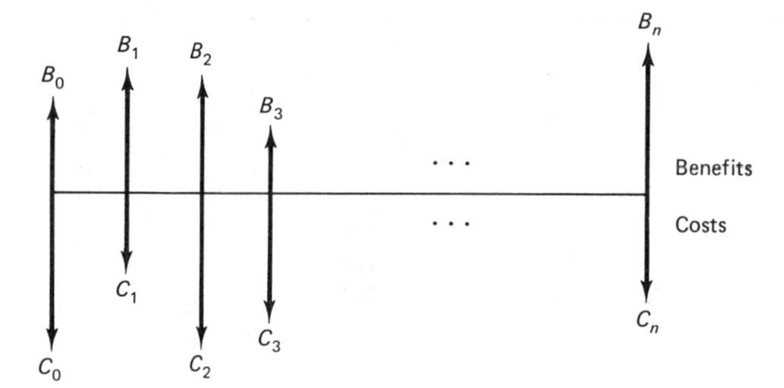

Figure 11.3.1 Streams of benefits and costs.

(B/C) *ratio,* in which case the economic feasibility criterion requires a B/C ratio that is greater than unity. A third method of assessing the economic feasibility of an alternative is one that calculates the *internal rate of return* (IRR), which is defined as the interest rate that just equates benefits and costs, that is, the rate at which the NPW equals zero and the B/C ratio equals unity. This rate is then compared with a predetermined *minimum attractive rate of return* (MARR) reflecting managerial policy and profit expectations to assess whether the project is attractive or not.

11.3.3 Independent and Mutually Exclusive Alternatives

Before discussing the mechanics of economic evaluation of alternatives, it is appropriate to explain several principles that are explicitly or implicitly encompassed by the final choice.

First, the set of alternatives being considered should include the do-nothing, or baseline, alternative. Second, pairs of alternatives can be either *independent* or *mutually exclusive*. Two alternatives are *independent* when the selection of one does not necessarily prohibit the selection of the other. For example, a state department of transportation may be contemplating the provision of subsidies to the bus systems of two different cities. Assuming that the necessary resources are available to the department, a decision to subsidize one city does not necessarily eliminate a favorable outcome for the other. By contrast, a pair of alternatives are said to be *mutually exclusive* if the choice of one renders the other impossible. A metropolitan transit authority engaged in the comparative evaluation of two technologically incompatible transit systems on a single alignment is faced with mutually exclusive alternatives. Third, the do-nothing alternative and each of the do-something alternatives are mutually exclusive. Fourth, the list of options under consideration includes all possible combinations of independent alternatives. For example, when two independent projects are being considered, the list of available options contains four entries: the do-nothing alternative, each of the two projects alone, and the two in combination. When viewed in this manner, the four options are actually mutually exclusive, as it is not possible to implement one project alone and both projects together at the same time. The problem of economic evaluation and project selection becomes one of discovering the alternative combination of feasible projects that maximizes the benefits to be derived from the expenditure of available resources.

Example 11.1

A regional planning organization is considering the following proposals: two mutually exclusive alignments for a highway in County A (Projects A1 and A2), two mutually exclusive alignments for a highway in County B (projects B1 and B2), and a special transportation system for handicapped persons in City C. What is the number of available options?

Solution Considering that with regard to the first and second highways, three possibilities exist (that is, not building, selecting alternative 1, and selecting alternative 2) and that two choices are possible with regard to alternative C, the total number of proper combinations

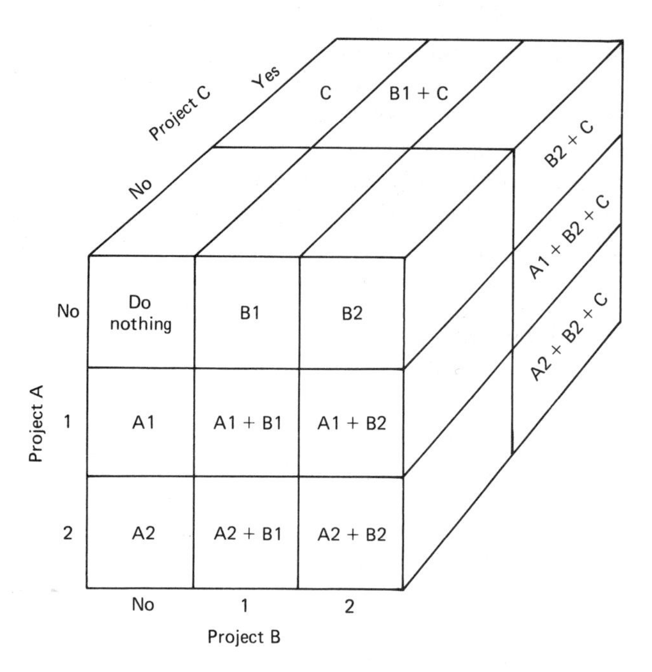

Figure 11.3.2 Alternative combinations of options.

is 3 × 3 × 2 = 18, as illustrated by Fig. 11.3.2. If any one of the projects is infeasible, the total number of options is reduced accordingly. If, for example, alternative A1 were judged to be infeasible, the total number of options would become 3 × 2 × 2 = 12. Similarly, if project C were found to be infeasible, the remaining options would number 3 × 3 × 1 = 9.

11.3.4 Evaluation of Mutually Exclusive Alternatives

Consider two mutually exclusive do-something alternatives with the following discounted benefits and costs expressed in millions of dollars.

Alternative	PWB	PWC	NPW	B/C
A	1.89	1.2	0.6	1.50
B	2.9	2.2	0.7	1.32

According to the NPW criterion, alternative B is superior to alternative A, but, according to the B/C criterion, alternative A is better than alternative B. This inconsistency between the two methods can be rectified by augmenting the B/C evaluation with an *incremental analysis*. To understand the rationale of incremental analysis, consider the simplified situation where the total $2.2 million is in hand and no other investment option is possible; that is, the available amount of money could either be expended in one of the two projects or placed in a safe deposit box, where it would earn no interest. Under these assumptions, the *overall* investment strategies associated with each of the two alternatives are (1) to invest $1.2 of the $2.2 million in the less costly alternative A, which will return $1.8 million in benefits, and place the remaining $1.0 million in the safe deposit box, which will return no additional benefits, and (2) to invest the entire $2.2 million in the more costly alternative, which will derive total benefits of $2.9 million. The present worth of the benefits resulting from the first strategy would equal to $1.8 million plus $1.0 million, or $2.8 million, as compared to the $2.9 million associated with the more costly alternative. Hence, investing in the second option is the more prudent choice. Another way of stating the above is that the *incremental benefits* ($2.9 − $1.8 = $1.1 million) derived from the costlier alternative outweigh the *incremental costs* ($2.2 − $1.2 = $1.0 million) it entails, or that the *incremental B/C* ratio between the two options is greater than unity. Thus when both alternatives are feasible in themselves, the incremental B/C ratio and the NPW criteria lead to identical conclusions. The incremental ratio analysis of feasible options is conducted as follows: The feasible alternatives are listed according to increasing cost, with the least costly alternative at the top of the list. If the incremental ratio between the first two entries is greater than unity, the more costly alternative is selected; otherwise the less costly alternative is retained. The chosen alternative is then compared with the next list entry and the procedure continues until all alternatives have been considered and all but the best alternative have been eliminated.

Example 11.2

The benefits and costs associated with the following five mutually exclusive alternatives have been discounted to their present worth and the alternatives have been listed according to increasing cost. Apply the B/C ratio method to select the best option.

Alternative	PWC	PWB	B/C
A	100	150	1.50
B	150	190	1.27
C	200	270	1.35
D	300	290	0.97
E	320	350	1.09

After forming the B/C ratio, alternative D is found to be infeasible and therefore is dropped from further consideration. The incremental B/C between A and B is (190 − 150)/(150 − 100) = 0.8, and the costlier alternative B is dropped. The incremental ratio between A and the next feasible alternative in the list (i.e., C) is equal to (270 − 150)/(200 − 100) = 1.2 and C is favored over A. Finally, the comparison between C and E yields an incremental ratio of 0.67. Since this is less than unity, the less costly alternative C is retained as the best option.

Discussion Alternative C has been selected even though alternative A has a larger individual B/C ratio. It can easily be shown that the NPW criterion leads to the selection of the same alternative. The incremental ratio analysis must be preceded by an individual ratio analysis to eliminate all infeasible alternatives. If the incremental ratio analysis were to be applied directly to a list that happened to contain only infeasible alternatives, it would result in the selection of the least infeasible without any indication that the selected option is, in fact, infeasible. Serious problems related to this point arise in situations where, for practical reasons, the benefits and costs of do-something alternatives are calculated relative to the do-nothing alternative. For example, travel time or fuel savings are often considered to be benefits associated with proposed highways as compared to the do-nothing alternative. In that case, the B/C analysis is an incremental analysis from the start. To illustrate this point consider the following simple example: The benefits and costs associated with an existing highway (do-nothing) and a proposed highway are:

Alternative	PWB	PWC
Existing	1.2	1.8
Proposed	1.9	2.4

Clearly, neither of the two is feasible. However, if the benefits and costs of the proposed highway were to be reported only in relation to the do-nothing alternative, the proposed project would have an appearance of feasibility and an incremental B/C ratio of 1.17. Moreover, the NPW of the relative benefits and costs would also be misleading. To avoid problems of this nature, ways of measuring benefits and costs in absolute rather than relative terms have been proposed. One such method is based on the *theory of consumer surplus* [11.4] but, although conceptually attractive, these attempts are not without practical difficulties.

11.3.5 Identification and Valuation of Benefits and Costs

The conduct of economic evaluation procedures for the selection of the best alternative requires the conversion or valuation of quantified impacts to monetary terms. Impact valuation presents varying degrees of difficulty. Some impacts, such as construction and maintenance costs, are already expressed in monetary terms. The rest must be translated into monetary equivalents. As an illustration, Fig. 11.3.3 presents a family of curves suggested by a 1977 AASHTO Manual [11.5] for the conversion of travel time savings to dollars. These curves are based on extensive economic explorations into the matter and—unlike earlier versions, which assumed a linear relationship between time saved and dollar value irrespective of trip purpose—the 1977 version provides for a nonlinear relationship and for a sensitivity to trip purpose. A linear relationship at, say, $1.50 or $2.80 per hour saved would be highly inappropriatc if millions of daily trips, each saving a few minutes, were to be simply added together. According to Fig. 11.3.3, such small time savings are insignificant individually and, hence, collectively. Other impacts of transportation projects (e.g., effect of rural lifestyles or aesthetics) are much more difficult to quantify, let alone express in dollar equivalents. However, in order to be included in a B/C economic evaluation, they must be quantified and valuated.

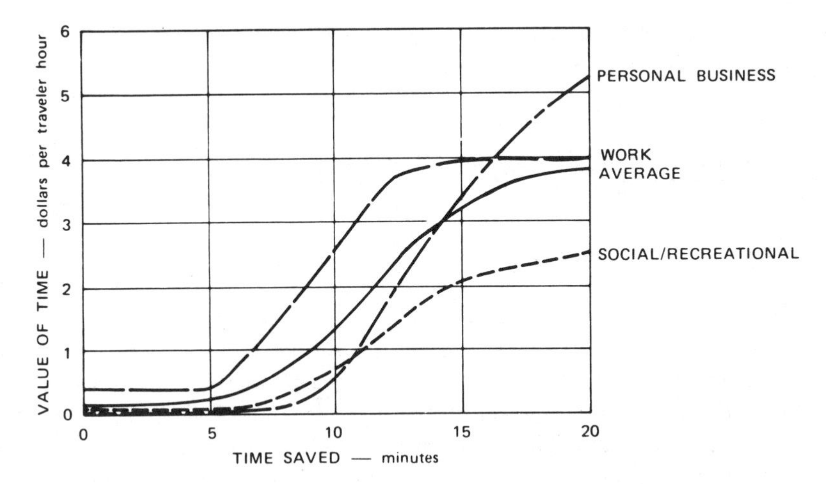

Figure 11.3.3 Value of time saved by trip purpose. (*SOURCE*: American Association of State Highway and Transportation Officials [11.5], Fig. 2, p. 16.)

11.3.6 Limitations of Economic Evaluation

The foregoing commentary brings to light the fact that economic efficiency analysis is not as objective as it may seem at first glance. Its strongest advantage is that it provides a useful quantitative but partial picture of the subject matter. Its major limitations may be classed into problems of impact enumeration, valuation, and distribution. The selection of an appropriate interest rate and the treatment of price inflation and deflation are also problematic.

The question of *impact enumeration* refers to the fact that not all impacts considered to be important can be included in the analysis. Even though no evaluation technique can possibly include all ramifications of major transportation projects, economic efficiency analysis further restricts the admissible set.

The problem of *impact distribution* refers to the fact that the benefits and costs are distributed unevenly between individuals and groups. For example, some persons may have to relocate their residences or businesses to permit the construction of a highway that could result in travel time and fuel savings for another group, the users of the new highway. Similarly, it may be argued that subsidizing a public-transportation system entails the taking of tax dollars from everyone in order to enhance the mobility of the few that ride the system. In this connection, the first piece of federal legislation to require a B/C analysis for public projects explicitly stated that public projects are justified:

> . . . if the benefits *to whomsoever they may accrue* are in excess of the estimated costs. ([11.6], emphasis added)

Of course, counterarguments are possible in both examples just cited, but this is not the proper place to address them. It is clear, however, that *those who perceive that they will be adversely affected by a proposed project are not obliged to acquiesce on the grounds that the calculated overall B/C ratio is greater than unity.*

11.4 EFFECTIVENESS ANALYSIS

11.4.1 Background

The preceding discussion has pointed out that, even when they can be quantified in terms of specific measures of performance, the various impacts associated with proposed alternatives are often difficult to express in monetary terms. *Effectiveness,* which has been defined as the degree to which the performance of an alternative attains its stated objectives, seeks to rectify this problem by explicitly accounting for such impacts and for providing a framework within which these impacts can be clearly defined and traded off via the choice of alternative. The effectiveness approach to evaluation and decision-making is founded on the axiom that more-informed and, hence, better decisions would result if the decision-makers were presented with the maximum amount of available information about the subject. Within this framework, the basic role of the analyst becomes more concerned with facilitating the decision-making process by devising well-organized ways to summarize and transmit to the decision makers the data required for the decision and less with applying a specific technique that presumes to determine unambiguously the "best" alternative. At the same time, the role of the decision makers becomes more demanding as they are given the added responsibility of ultimately assigning relative values to the merits and demerits of the alternatives being considered. The vast technical literature on specific techniques that may be used to measure effectiveness (ranging from purely subjective to highly quantitative) as well as the decision-making processes and the institutional structures for which these techniques are best suited spans several disciplines. Only the basic elements of effectiveness analysis are discussed here.

11.4.2 Cost-Effectiveness

The application of economic efficiency methods to public projects had its origins in the civilian sector and the provision flood protection. Cost-effectiveness, on the other hand, was first applied in connection with the evaluation of military systems. In its strictest sense, it was an extension of the principles of economic efficiency, as it was concerned with maximizing the returns (in terms of effectiveness) of public expenditures described in terms of the monetary costs associated with the life cycles of proposed systems. The following simple example illustrates the essence of the method.

Suppose that the administrative team of a university (i.e., the decision-making body) is faced with the task of selecting a new computer system for the college of engineering. Because the system is to be used primarily for undergraduate instruction, it has been agreed that it should maximize the number of users it can accommodate si-

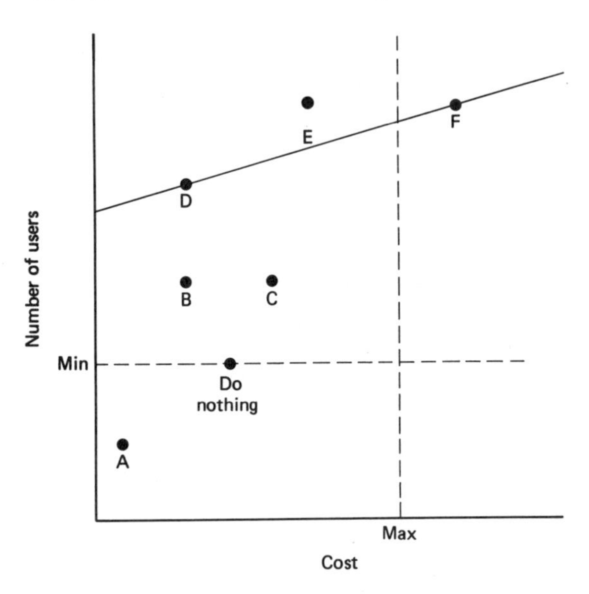

Figure 11.4.1 Example of cost versus effectiveness.

multaneously and that this number must be at least equal to that supported by the existing system. On the other hand, the administration has established a maximum cost constraint as well. Several computer manufacturers responded to a request for bids with the six mutually exclusive proposals shown in Fig. 11.4.1. In accordance with the agreed-upon rules, alternative A would be dropped because it fails to meet the minimum effectiveness level and alternative F would be eliminated as its costs exceed the maximum available resources. Furthermore, alternatives B and C and the do-nothing alternative would also be eliminated, as they cost at least as much but offer no better level of effectiveness than alternative D. The final choice would rest between alternatives D and E and would involve a trade-off between dollars and the number of potential users. This choice is an incremental consideration, but, unlike the incremental analysis applied to the B/C ratio, the relative worth of the two impacts being traded off would be implicit in the final choice. The choice of alternative E would imply that the extra benefits are *at least* equivalent to the extra costs required. Conversely, the selection of alternative D would carry the implication that the worth of the incremental effectiveness associated with alternative E is less than the worth of the incremental dollar costs it would entail.

The problem of selecting the best computer system would be further complicated if the system's effectiveness were multidimensional—for example, if the availability of engineering software (however measured) were also considered to be important. Thus, as the dimensions of effectiveness increases, so does the complexity of determining the relative worth of the alternatives (i.e., evaluating them). Consequently, an individual decision maker soon becomes overwhelmed with vast amounts of often-conflicting information. The matter becomes worse as the number of individuals constituting the decision-making group increases. Hence, a need arises to organize the available information and to establish procedures that aid the attainment of consensus.

Several ways by which the relative assessment of alternatives may be accomplished are as follows:

1. The decision makers select the best based on their unexpressed subjective judgments.
2. Aided by the analyst, decision makers *rank* alternative options in an ordinal sense (that is, A is better than B) and make selection by one of several *rank-ordering* procedures.
3. Aided by the analyst and other sources, the decision makers assign a score (usually based on the relative weights of impacts) to each alternative and select the one with the highest score.

11.4.3 Rank-Ordering Techniques

One rank-ordering technique with obvious application to the topic is one that Sage [11.7] treats with mathematical formalism and which has been applied in several variations by others. In simplified form, the method works as follows.

The decision maker, faced with n alternatives, is asked to compare them in pairs according to a contextual relationship, such as "alternative i is superior to alternative j." After the decision maker has completed the consideration of all pairs, the following rules are examined to ensure consistency. First, an alternative cannot be superior to itself. Second, if i is superior to j, then j cannot be superior to i. Third, if i is superior to j and j is superior to k, then i is superior to k. If the decision maker violates any of these rules, an inconsistency is detected that should be resolved.

Example 11.3

Considering four options, a decision maker has completed the following array by placing a 1 in cell (i, j) if the answer to the question "option i is superior to option j" was affirmative and a 0 otherwise. Check for any inconsistencies in the decision-maker's logic, and, if none are found, identify the rank-order of the four options.

$i \backslash j$	A	B	C	D
A	0	0	1	1
B	1	0	0	1
C	1	1	0	1
D	0	0	0	0

Solution The diagonal elements are all 0, as expected. However, A has been designated to be superior to C at the same time that C was considered to be superior to A. Moreover, a circularity exists between A, B, and C: B was considered to be superior to A, C superior to A, and B superior to C. Therefore a defect in the assessment is revealed. The same conclusion may be reached by drawing the directed graph that follows, where each arrow is directed from the inferior to the superior option.

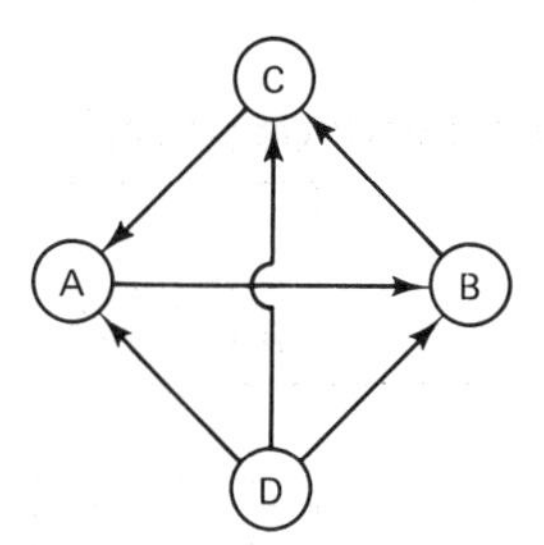

Figure P.11.3

Example 11.4

Assume that the inconsistency of Example 11.3 was pointed out to the decision maker and that, after considerable thought, the decision maker revised the original assessment by rating option A inferior to option C. Revise the solution of Example 11.3.

Solution The revised directed graph is shown in the accompanying figure. Furthermore, by eliminating redundant arrows (e.g., from D to C), a clear rank-order emerges.

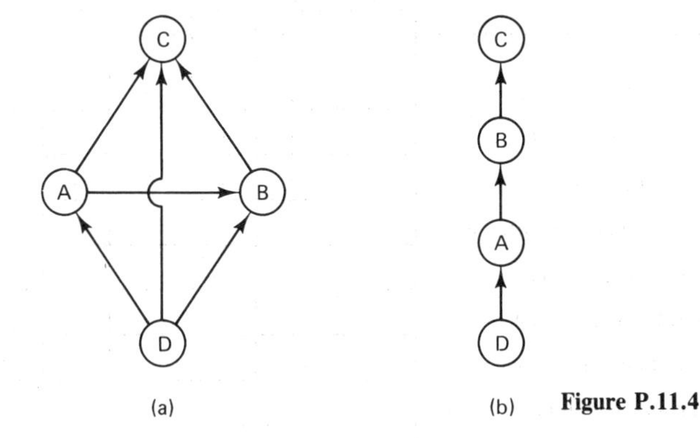

Figure P.11.4

Discussion This method produces a consistent ranking of the options based on the subjective judgment of the decision makers that can provide guidance to the discovery of inconsistencies that need to be clarified and resolved. When the decision-making body consists of many individuals, an overall compromise must be made. One way of accomplishing this is the method by which the "number 1 college football team" is selected in the United States: a panel of experts (i.e., football coaches and sports reporters) are asked to rank the top teams and the team that receives the most first-place votes is ranked as being the best. Alternatively, each first-place, second-place, and so on, etc. vote is weighted and combined to derive an overall score.

Table 11.4.1 illustrates the application of the ranking techniques to eight alternatives considered in the 1979 Honolulu study, which is described in subsection 11.2.3. Note that the number of firsts, seconds, and thirds have been tabulated as well. Table 11.4.2 is a similar summary of rankings for the baseline alternative, an alternative consisting of a combination of TSM strategies and a 14-mile-long fixed-guideway rapid-transit alternative.

Table 11.4.3 presents some details relating to the basis on which several of the rankings of Table 11.4.2 were derived.

TABLE 11.4.1 SUMMARY OF RANKINGS FOR EIGHT ALTERNATIVES

	Bus.	7 mi LRT	7 mi FG	14 mi LRT	14 mi FG	23 mi LRT	28 mi LRT	23 mi FG
Objective 1								
a. Availability & coverage	—	—	—	—	—	—	—	—
b. Avg. trip time (min.)	2	1	1	—	—	2	3	1
c. Service reliability	2	1	1	—	—	2	2	1
d. Rider convenience (transfers per trip)	1	2	2	—	—	2	1	2
e. Rider comfort	2	1	1	—	—	—	—	—
Objective 2								
a. System patronage	2	1	1	—	—	2	2	1
b. System capacity	2	1	1	—	—	—	—	—
Objective 3								
a. Consumption of land (acres)	3	2	1	2	1	2	2	1
b. Displacement of residents (units)	3	2	1	2	1	2	2	1
c. Displacement of businesses (units)	3	2	1	2	1	2	2	1
d. Reduction of community amenities	—	—	—	—	—	—	—	—
e. Disruption to future dvlpmt.	—	—	—	—	—	—	—	—
f. Disruption to local circulation	—	—	—	—	—	2	3	1
g. Disruption from constr. activities	—	—	—	—	—	1	2	1
h. Savings in energy (million gal/year)	1	3	2	2	1	2	3	1
i. Technical risk	3	1	2	1	2	1	1	2
Objective 4								
a. Support regional dvlpmt.	—	—	—	—	—	—	—	—
b. Support comm. dvlpmt.	—	—	—	—	—	—	—	—
Objective 5								
a. Reduction Air pollution (tons/year)	3	2	1	2	1	3	2	1
b. Noise level (dBA)	3	2	1	2	1	2	2	1
c. Visual intrusion	3	2	1	2	1	2	2	1
d. Vistas	2	3	1	2	1	1	1	2
e. Historic sites	—	—	—	—	—	—	—	—

(*continued*)

TABLE 11.4.1 *(Continued)*

	Bus.	7 mi LRT	7 mi FG	14 mi LRT	14 mi FG	23 mi LRT	28 mi LRT	23 mi FG
Objective 6								
a. Reduce accident exposure	—	—	—	—	—	2	2	1
b. Security	—	—	—	—	—	—	—	—
Objective 7								
a. Total annual cost	3	2	1	2	1	1	3	2
b. Cost per trip	3	2	1	2	1	2	3	1
c. B/C ratio	3	2	1	2	1	2	3	1
No. of firsts	2	6	15	1	11	4	3	15
No. of seconds	6	10	3	11	1	14	10	4
No. of thirds	10	2	0	0	0	1	6	0

SOURCE: Urban Mass Transportation Administration [11.3], Table III-10, p. III-36.

TABLE 11.4.2 SUMMARY OF RANKINGS—BASELINE, TSM, AND FIXED GUIDEWAY

	Approach A		
Evaluation factors	Baseline	TSM	14-mi fixed gwy.
Objective 1			
a. Availability & coverage	2	1	1
b. Avg. trip time	3	2	1
c. Service reliability	3	2	1
d. Rider convenience	2	2	1
e. Rider comfort	2	2	1
Objective 2			
a. System patronage	3	2	1
b. System capacity	3	2	1

(continued)

TABLE 11.4.2 *(Continued)*

Evaluation factors	Approach A Baseline	TSM	14-mi fixed gwy.
Objective 3			
a. Consumption of land	1	2	3
b. Displacement of residents	1	1	2
c. Displacement of businesses	1	2	3
d. Reduction of community amenities	1	1	2
e. Disruption of future development	1	1	2
f. Disruption of local circulation	3	2	1
g. Disruption from constr. activities	1	1	2
h. Savings in energy	3	2	1
i. Technical risk	1	1	2
Objective 4			
a. Support regional development	2	2	1
b. Support comm. development	2	2	1
Objective 5			
a. Reduction Air pollution	3	2	1
b. Noise level	2	2	1
c. Visual intrusion	1	1	2
d. Vistas	1	1	2
e. Historic sites	1	1	2
Objective 6			
a. Reduce accident exposure	3	2	1
b. Security	2	2	1
Objective 7			
a. Total annual cost	1	2	3
b. Total annual cost per trip	1	2	3
c. Benefit-cost ratio	—	2	1
No. of firsts	12	9	16
No. of seconds	7	19	8
No. of thirds	8	0	4

SOURCE: Urban Mass Transportation Administration [11.3], Table III-12, p. III-42.

TABLE 11.4.3 COMPARATIVE EVALUATION MATRIX—BASELINE, TSM, AND FIXED GUIDEWAY

Evaluation factors	Approach A		
	Baseline	TSM	14-mi fixed gwy.
Objective 1			
a. Availability & coverage[a]	(2)	(1)	(1)
b. Avg. trip time (min.)	40.7	40.1	33.7
c. Service reliability[a]	(3)	(2)	(1)
d. Rider convenience[a]	(2)	(2)	(1)
e. Rider comfort*	(2)	(2)	(1)
Objective 2			
a. System patronage-1985 (million/year)	64.7	83.6	102.4
b. System capacity[a]	(3)	(2)	(1)
Objective 3			
a. Consumption of land (acres)	—	3	22
b. Displacement of residents (units)	—	—	162
c. Displacement of businesses (units)[a]	—	2	183
d. Reduction of community amenities[a]	(1)	(1)	(2)
e. Disruption of future development[a]	(1)	(1)	(2)
f. Disruption of local circulation[a]	(3)	(2)	(1)
g. Disruption from constr. activities[a]	(1)	(1)	(2)
h. Savings in energy (million gal/year)	—	0.9	4.5
i. Technical risk[a]	(1)	(1)	(2)
Objective 4			
a. Support regional development[a]	(2)	(2)	(1)
b. Support comm. development[a]	(2)	(2)	(1)
Objective 5			
a. Reduction Air pollution (tons/year)	—	220	2260
b. Noise level (dBA)	86–88	86–88	77
c. Visual intrusion[a]	(1)	(1)	(2)
d. Vistas[a]	(1)	(1)	(2)
e. Historic sites[a]	(1)	(1)	(2)

(*continued*)

TABLE 11.4.3 *(Continued)*

Evaluation factors	Approach A		
	Baseline	TSM	14-mi fixed gwy.
Objective 6			
a. Reduce accident exposure[a]	(3)	(2)	(1)
b. Security[a]	(2)	(2)	(1)
Objective 7			
a. Total annual cost[b]-1985 ($ million)	32.9	45.0	66.2
b. Total annual cost per trip ($)	0.508	0.538	0.647
c. B/C ratio[c]	—	1.12	1.13

[a]For comparative measures, alternatives are ranked in the order of how well they met the objective.

[b]All costs based on constant 1975 dollars and interest rate of 7%.

[c]Based on constant 1975 dollars.

SOURCE: Urban Mass Transportation Administration [11.3], Table III-11, p. III-41.

11.4.4 Scoring Techniques

The objective of *scoring techniques* is the assignment of meaningful grades to the alternatives in a manner that reflects the degree to which they differ from each other. Numerous scoring techniques and procedures are reported in the technical literature. The following discussion is an amalgamation of these methods, emphasizing their rationale rather than an in-depth examination of any one in particular.

Figure 11.4.2 is an expanded version of the generalized impact matrix of Figure 11.4.1 as it relates to one of the alternatives being evaluated. The impacts that are considered to be relevant to the evaluation are listed in the first row of Figure 11.4.2. Related *impacts* are combined into a smaller number of evaluation *criteria,* which are themselves combined to yield the alternative's *overall score*. Conceptually, the combination of a set of impacts into a criterion is identical to the derivation of the overall score from a set of quantified criteria. Furthermore, the evaluation of very complex systems may require more than the three levels of aggregation illustrated. At the other extreme, the simplest case involves a scoring scheme that is based on a single criterion, which is identical to a single impact. A slightly more complex case entails a single criterion that is composed of several impacts. The composite grade of any criterion involves the following steps:

1. The impacts that constitute the criterion are identified and quantified, usually on different scales of measurement.
2. The quantified impacts are placed on the same scale of measurement.
3. The scaled impacts are assigned relative weights and combined.

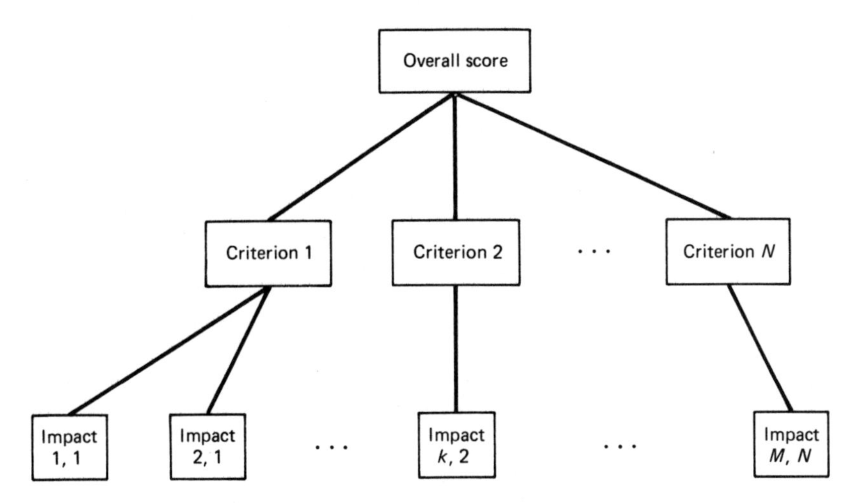

Figure 11.4.2 Impacts, criteria, and overall score.

For instance, the NPW which incorporates the net effect of many impacts, may serve as one of several evaluation criteria. As explained in Section 11.3, the NPW of an alternative is derived by first predicting the likely impacts of the alternative (Step 1), translating the disparately quantified impacts to dollar equivalents (Step 2), and weighting them equally as if they were, in fact, dollars (Step 3). The general scoring methods discussed here allow for (1) the use of a common scale other than a monetary scale, and (2) the assignment of unequal weights to the impacts. This is the essential difference between measures of economic efficiency on one hand and measures of effectiveness on the other.

Example 11.5

An elected official wishes to evaluate three transportation proposals on the basis of three criteria: economic worth, aesthetic quality, and electorate reaction. The economic worth of the alternatives is measured by their NPW, which has been calculated by a consulting firm according to accepted practice. The aesthetic attributes of the alternatives have been assessed by a survey conducted by a marketing-research company and is measured by the percent of respondents that are pleased with each alternative. The probable electorate reaction has been reported by the official's staff, who maintain contacts with the voters in the official's district. The following table summarizes the available information.

Alternative	NPW (millions of dollars)	Aesthetics (%)	Electorate
A	6	70	Neutral
B	13	40	Favorable
C	14	90	Unfavorable

Three possible scoring ways are presented.

1. *Combined rankings*. The alternatives may first be ranked according to each criterion from worst (lowest ranking) to best (highest ranking), and a composite score may be derived by summing the rankings of each alternative. Thus

$$S_i = \sum_j R_{ij} \tag{11.4.1}$$

where S_i is the score of alternative i and R_{ij} is the rank of alternative i with respect to criterion j.

For the current example, the scores of the three alternatives become:

Alternative	NPW	Aesthetics	Electorate	Score
A	1	2	2	5
B	2	1	3	6
C	3	3	1	7

This method applies equal weights to the criteria. Moreover, it is oblivious to the degree to which the alternatives differ from each other with respect to each criterion.

2. *Weighted rankings*. The criteria may be assigned relative weights, which will affect the contribution of each criterion to the overall scores:

$$S_i = \sum_j w_j R_{ij} \tag{11.4.2}$$

where w_j is the relative weight of criterion j.
Assuming that the official considers satisfying the electorate to be four times as important as aesthetics and twice as important as economic worth, that is,

$$w(\text{NPW}) = 2 \qquad w(\text{aesthetics}) = 1 \qquad w(\text{elect.}) = 4$$

the scores of the three alternatives become:

Alternative	Score
A	$2 \times 1 + 1 \times 2 + 4 \times 2 = 12$
B	$2 \times 2 + 1 \times 1 + 4 \times 3 = 18$
C	$2 \times 3 + 1 \times 3 + 4 \times 1 = 13$

The weights assigned to each criterion are reflected in the overall score of the alternatives. However, the problem of scaling the magnitudes associated with the alternatives with respect to each criterion still remains unsolved. Thus, the differences in NPW between alternatives A versus B on one hand and B versus C on the other are not captured by this method.

3. *Scaled criteria*. The three criteria used in this example are measured on different scales: The NPW is a quantitative measure that is unbounded at either end. The scale that has been selected to measure aesthetic quality ranges from 0 to 100. Finally, electoral reaction has been reported on an ordinal scale. If the three criteria are to be

combined into a single score, they must be placed on a common scale. For the sake of illustration, consider a common ordinal scale ranging from 0 to 100. The criterion relating to aesthetics is already measured on this scale. The NPW of each alternative may be mapped onto the common scale by assigning a grade, say 90, to alternative C and proportioning accordingly the grades of the other two. With respect to the third criterion, a neutral reaction may be used as an anchor midway on the scale.

Alternative	NPW	Aesthetics	Electorate	Score I	Score II
A	40	70	50	160	350
B	85	40	80	205	580
C	90	90	40	200	450

Two scores are shown in this table. Score I was derived using a function similar to Eq. 11.4.1 with the criteria levels associated with each alternative replacing the raw rankings. Score II is based on a weighting scheme, as in Eq. 11.4.2.

Discussion This example illustrates the mechanics of only four out of a very large number of possible scoring techniques. Theoretically inclined individuals may even be tempted to apply one or more of the scoring techniques described here to combine the various scores derived above into a super score, but such a process has no bound. The potential for an infinite number of scoring variations, each leading to a different decision, may give to the process the appearance of capriciousness or arbitrariness. But no evaluation technique can be an end in itself. Thus, the usefulness of any technique lies in its ability to help organize the decision-making process in an explicit and systematic way and not in its ability automatically to yield an unequivocable result. This presupposes a predisposition on the part of the decision maker to participate actively in all stages of the process, including the identification of impacts and criteria, their scaling and weighing, and, ultimately, the final decision. As to the choice of technique, it is largely situational, and it depends on the quantity and quality of the available information.

11.4.5 Group Consensus

Perhaps the major source of difficulty associated with effectiveness analysis is the dependence on the subjective judgment of the decision maker. This dependence is often moderated by the reliance on decision-making bodies that consist of many individuals. But precisely because of the differences that exist between individuals, group decision-making requires the attainment of group consensus. Traditional means for reaching consensus include group discussion, debate, argumentation, and brainstorming. The advantages of these methods include the exposure of the group to differing points of view. A major drawback is that certain individuals tend to dominate the process because of rank, strength of conviction, or persuasive ability. Several methods that attempt to eliminate this difficulty have been devised. Theoretically, the group's consensus may be revealed by statistically summarizing the responses of the members of a panel to the questions required by the ranking and scoring techniques discussed above. The *delphi method,* originally proposed by the Rand Corporation [11.8], encompasses several procedures that attempt to facilitate collective decisions via a series of questionnaires administered to all members of a panel and accompanied by summaries of the panel's earlier responses. The final decision is enhanced by anonymity, by equal treatments of all points of view, and by the fact that the participants are free to revise their positions.

11.5 SUMMARY

This chapter introduced the concepts of project evaluation and described the elements of some commonly used methods that can aid the evaluation of alternative courses of action and can facilitate the selection of an alternative for implementation. The complex nature of transportation-related decisions was conveyed only by implication because a detailed examination of the political, legislative, and judicial reverberations of transportation decisions is beyond the scope of this introductory textbook.

Evaluation methods were classified into economic efficiency methods and effectiveness methods. The former require that the quantified impacts that are relevant to evaluation be translated into money equivalents and be treated as such. The traditional economic efficiency evaluation measures of net present worth and B/C analysis were then described and illustrated. Finally, the case was made for expanding the evaluation framework to incorporate impacts that are either impossible or difficult to quantify in terms of dollars. Within this expanded framework various measures of effectiveness as well as measures of economic efficiency can serve as evaluative criteria for the ranking and scoring of alternatives.

11.6 EXERCISES

1. Drawing on the store of knowledge you have amassed so far, discuss the contents of Table 11.2.1.
2. Discuss several possible ways by which each of the travel, operating characteristics, and costs listed in Table 11.2.2 could have been estimated. Be as specific as you can.
3. Referring to Table 11.2.2, explain why the projected total daily transit patronage is different for each transportation alternative studied. Which part of the sequential travel-demand forecasting methodology do you think produced these results? Explain specifically the most likely model variables that capture this effect.
4. In reference to Table 11.2.2, why do you think the estimated daily trips on the 7-mi fixed guideway alternative are the same as those corresponding to the 7-mi LRT?
5. Perform an incremental B/C analysis of the alternatives listed in Table 11.2.3, assuming an interest rate of 4%. Why is the interest rate important in the B/C ratio method of evaluation?
6. Repeat Exercise 5 assuming an interest rate of 10%.
7. With reference to objective 7 of Table 11.4.2, why wasn't the B/C ratio of the baseline alternative reported? What implication can this fact have on the feasibility of the other two alternatives?

8. Perform an incremental analysis of the three alternatives listed in Table 11.4.3 and discuss your results.

9. Determine the preferred alternative of a decision maker who has completed the following array on the basis of the contextual relationship alternative i is better than alternative j.

$i \setminus j$	A	B	C	D
A	0	0	0	0
B	1	0	0	1
C	1	1	0	1
D	0	0	0	0

10. Using the data given in Table 11.4.2, (a) calculate the simple combined rankings score of each of the three alternatives with respect to each of the seven objectives; (b) rank the alternatives for each objective according to the scores derived in part a; (c) apply the simple combined rankings technique to the results of part b; (d) use the following weights to calculated the weighted-ranking scores derived in part (b).

i	1	2	3	4	5	6	7
w_i	2	4	1	4	5	2	7

Explain any assumptions you felt were necessary to complete this exercise and explain why a universally applicable effectiveness analysis method is not possible.

11. Three alternative plans (A, B, and C) have been ranked with respect to four criteria (I to IV) as follows:

	I	II	III	IV
A	2	1	3	2
B	1	2	2	1
C	3	3	1	3

where 1 means best. Apply the single combined-rankings technique to derive an overall score for each alternative.

12. Given the following weights for the four criteria of exercise 11, compute the weighted-rankings scores for the three alternatives.

i	I	II	III	IV
w	2	4	1	2

13. Discuss the steps you would follow in order to apply the B/C ratio method to evaluate alternative highway-safety proposals consisting of all possible combinations of 12 accident-reducing actions such as signalization, curve widening, street lighting, and so on.

14. From the government documents section of your school's library, obtain a planning study for a major transportation action and report on the evaluation method employed.

15. Discuss the possible differences in the perspectives of an environmentalist, a construction firm president, and a federal judge regarding a proposal to build a multilane highway through a conservation district. Use Appendix A as a guide to your answer.

11.7 REFERENCES

11.1 THOMAS, E. N., AND J. L. SCHOFER, *Strategies for the Evaluation of Alternative Transportation Plans,* National Cooperative Highway Research Program Report 96, Highway Research Board, National Research Council, Washington, D.C., 1970.

11.2 MANHEIM, M. L., et al., *Transportation Decision-Making: A Guide to Social and Environmental Considerations,* National Cooperative Highway Research Program Report 156, Transportation Research Board, National Research Council, Washington, D.C., 1975.

11.3 Urban Mass Transportation Administration, *Draft Environmental Impact Statement: Honolulu Area Rapid Transit Project,* UMTA Project Report No. HI-03-0005, U.S. Department of Transportation, Washington, D.C., July 1979.

11.4 WOHL, M., *Transportation Investment Planning: An Introduction for Engineers and Planners,* Lexington Books, D.C. Heath And Company, 1972.

11.5 American Association of State Highway and Transportation Officials, *A Manual on User Benefit Analysis of Highway and Bus-Transit Improvements 1977,* Washington, D.C., copyright 1978. Used by permission.

11.6 *United States Code,* p. 2964, U.S. Government Printing Office, Washington, D.C., 1940.

11.7 SAGE, A. P., *Methodology for Large-Scale Systems,* McGraw-Hill, New York, 1977.

11.8 DALKEY, N., AND O. HELMER, "An Experimental Application of the Delphi Method to the Use of Experts," *Management Science,* 9, 3 (April 1963): 458–467.

APPENDIX A

1982 GUIDELINES FOR THE PREPARATION OF ENVIRONMENTAL DOCUMENTS

FEDERAL HIGHWAY ADMINISTRATION
U.S. DEPARTMENT OF TRANSPORTATION

GUIDANCE MATERIAL FOR THE PREPARATION OF ENVIRONMENTAL DOCUMENTS

Background

The purpose of this material is to provide guidance to FHWA field offices and project applicants on National Environmental Policy Act (NEPA) actions and to provide the public with a further explanation of FHWA internal operating procedures in the development of the reports and documentation required by NEPA. This material also provides the guidance required by 23 U.S.C. 109(h) to assure the full consideration of possible adverse economic, social, and environmental effects of proposed FHWA projects. While the material was developed primarily to provide guidance in the development of environmental impact statements (EIS's), it is also applicable, to the extent appropriate, for environmental assessments and other environmental studies deemed necessary prior to the advancement of a project with a categorical exclusion determination or a finding of no significant impact. This material is not regulatory, but has been developed to provide uniform and consistent guidance for the development of environmental documents. Each project will need to be carefully evaluated and the appropriate environmental document developed based on each individual situation.

The FHWA fully subscribes to the Council on Environmental Quality (CEQ) philosophy that the goal of the NEPA process is better decisions and not more documentation.

*FHWA Technical Advisory T 6640.8, February 24, 1982.

As noted in the CEQ regulations, EIS's should normally be less than 150 pages for most projects and not more than 300 pages for the most complex projects.

The FHWA considers the early coordination process to be a valuable tool to assist in identifying and focusing on the significant environmental issues. On April 30, 1981, the CEQ issued a memorandum entitled "Scoping Guidance" which discusses various techniques that will ensure participation in the scoping process. The CEQ also issued, on March 6, 1981, a memorandum entitled "Questions and Answers about the NEPA Regulations." Both of the documents are nonregulatory; however, they do provide CEQ views on various issues and are available from the FHWA Office of Environmental Policy (HEV-10).

1. ENVIRONMENTAL ASSESSMENT (EA)

Title 23, Code of Federal Regulations, Part 771, Environmental Impact and Related Procedures, describes those circumstances where the preparation of an EA is appropriate. The CEQ regulations require that an EA is to include the information listed in 40 CFR Part 1508.9. The following format, which assures this coverage, is suggested:

a. *Cover Sheet*. There is no *required* format for the EA. However, it is recommended the EIS cover sheet format, as shown on page 410, be followed *where appropriate*. Since the EA is not formally circulated, there is no need to include the "comments due" paragraph listed on page 411.

b. *Description of the Proposed Action*. Describe the locations, length, termini, proposed improvements, etc.

c. *Need*. Identify and describe the problem which the proposed action is designed to correct. Any of the items discussed under the "Need" section in Section 3 (EIS—Format and Content) may be appropriate.

d. *Alternatives Considered.* Discuss all reasonable alternatives to the proposed action which were considered. The EA may either discuss (1) the preferred alternative and the alternatives considered or (2) if the applicant has not identified a preferred alternative, the alternatives under consideration.
e. *Impacts.* Discuss the social, economic and environmental impacts of the alternatives considered and describe why these impacts are considered not significant.
f. *Comments and Coordination.* Describe coordination efforts and comments received from government agencies and the public. If the EA includes a Section 4(f) evaluation, the EA and the Section 4(f) evaluation may be circulated to the appropriate agencies for Section 4(f) coordination, or the Section 4(f) evaluation may be supplemented by any additional information necessary to properly explain the project and circulated as a separate document.
g. *Appendices (if any).* Include only analytical information that substantiates an analysis which is important to the document. Other information should be incorporated by reference only.

2. FINDING OF NO SIGNIFICANT IMPACT (FONSI)

771.121 of 23 CFR 771, entitled Environmental Impact and Related Procedures, describes the approval process for a FONSI. Section 1508.13 of the CEQ regulations describes the content of a FONSI. The EA should be modified to reflect all applicable significant environmental comments received as a result of the public hearings or other significant environmental comments received as a result of the public and clearinghouse notification process. The EA, revised as appropriate, including appropriate responses to any comments received, is then submitted to the FHWA Division Administrator along with the applicant's recommendation. The basis for the applicant's recommendation should be documented in the EA. After review of the EA and any other appropriate information, the FHWA Division Administrator may determine that the proposed action has no significant impacts. This is documented by attaching to the EA a separate statement (example follows) which clearly sets forth the FHWA analysis of the EA along with any other supporting documentation that has resulted in a FONSI. As appropriate, the FHWA Division Administrator may choose to expand on the discussion in the sample FONSI to identify the basis for the decision. The EA/FONSI should document compliance with the requirements of all applicable environmental laws, Executive Orders, and other related requirements. If full compliance is not possible by the time the FONSI is prepared, it should reflect consultation with the appropriate agencies and provide reasonable assurance that the requirements will be met.

FEDERAL HIGHWAY ADMINISTRATION
FINDING OF NO SIGNIFICANT IMPACT
FOR
(Title of Proposed Action)

The FHWA has determined that this project will not have any significant impact on the human environment. This finding of no significant impact is based on the attached environmental assessment (reference other environmental documents as appropriate) which has been independently evaluated by the FHWA and determined to adequately and accurately discuss the environmental issues and impacts of the proposed project. It provides sufficient evidence and analysis for determining that an environmental impact statement is not required. The FHWA takes full responsibility for the accuracy, scope, and content of the attached environmental assessment.

__________ ______________________________ __________

Date Responsible Official Title

3. EIS—FORMAT AND CONTENT

Each EIS should have a cover sheet containing:

(EIS number)

(Route, Termini, City or County, and State)
Draft (Final)
Environmental Impact Statement
Submitted Pursuant to 42 U.S.C. 4332 (2) (c) (and
where applicable, 49 U.S.C. 1653(f)) by the
U.S. Department of Transportation
Federal Highway Administration
and
State highway agency (HA)
and
(As applicable, local highway agency (HA)

Cooperating Agencies
List Here

_______________ ____

Date of Approval For FHWA Title

The following persons may be contacted for additional information concerning this document:

(Name, address, and telephone number of FHWA division office contact)

(Name address, and telephone number of HA contact)

A one-paragraph abstract of the statement.

Comments on this draft EIS are due by (*date*) and should be sent to (*name and address*).

The top left-hand corner of the cover sheet of all draft and final EIS's contains a number parallel to that in the following example:

FHWA-AZ-EIS-81-01-D(F)(S)

FHWA—name of Federal agency
AZ—name of State (cannot exceed four characters)
EIS—environmental impact statement
81—year draft statement was prepared
01—sequential number of draft statement for each calendar year
D—designates the statement as the draft statement
F—designates the statement as the final statement
S—designates supplemental statement

The EIS's should be printed on $8\frac{1}{2} \times 11$-inch paper with all graphics folded for insertion to that size. The wider sheets should open to the right with the title or identification on the right. The use of a standard size will facilitate administrative recordkeeping.

Summary

The summary should include:

a. A brief description of the proposed FHWA action indicating route, termini, type of improvement, number of lanes, length, county, city, State, etc., as appropriate.
b. A description of any significant actions proposed by other government agencies in the same geographic area as the proposed FHWA action.
c. A summary of major alternatives considered. (The final EIS should identify the preferred alternative.)
d. A summary of *significant* environmental impacts, both beneficial and adverse.
e. Any areas of controversy (including issues raised by both agencies and the public).
f. Any significant unresolved issues.
g. A list of other Federal actions required because of this proposed action (i.e., permit approvals etc.).

Table of Contents

a. Cover sheet.
b. Summary.
c. Table of Contents.
d. Purpose of and Need for Action.
e. Alternatives Including Proposed Action.
f. Affected Environment.
g. Environmental Consequences.
h. List of Preparers.
i. List of Agencies, Organizations, and Persons to Whom Copies of the Statement are Sent.
j. Comments and Coordination.
k. Index.
l. Appendices (if any).

Purpose of and Need for Action

Identify and describe the transportation problem(s) which the proposed action is designed to address. This section should clearly demonstrate that a "need" exists and must define the "need" in terms understandable to the general public. This discussion will form the basis for the "no action" discussion in the "Alternatives" section. The following is a list of items which may assist in the explanation of the need for the proposed action. It is by no means all-inclusive or applicable in every situation and is intended only as a guide.

a. System Linkage—Is the proposed project a "connecting link"? How does it fit in the system? Is it an "essential gap" in the Interstate System?
b. Capacity—is the capacity of the present facility inadequate for the present traffic? Projected traffic? What capacity is needed? What is the level of service?
c. Transportation Demand—Including relationship to any statewide plan or adopted urban transportation plan.
d. Federal, State, or local governmental authority (legislation) directing the action.
e. Social Demands or Economic Development—New employment, schools, land use plans, recreation, etc. What projected economic development/land use changes indicate the need to improve or add to the highway capacity?
f. Modal Interrelationships—How will the proposed facility interface with and serve to complement airports, rail and port facilities, mass transit services, etc.
g. Is the proposed project necessary to correct an existing or potential safety hazard? Is the existing accident rate excessively high? Why? How will the proposed facility improve it?

Alternatives Including Proposed Action

The "Alternatives" section of the draft EIS should begin with a concise discussion of how the "reasonable alternatives" were selected for detailed study. It should also describe those "other alternatives" that were eliminated early in project development and the basis for their elimination. The alternatives to be considered in this section will normally include the following:

a. The "no-action" alternative, which would include those usual short-term minor reconstruction types of activities (safety improvements, etc.) that are a part of an ongoing plan for continuing operation of the existing roadway system in the project area.
b. A Transportation System Management (TSM) alternative which would include those types of activities designed to maximize the utilization and energy efficiency of the present system. Possible subject areas to include in this alternative are options such as fringe parking, ridesharing, high-occupancy vehicle (HOV) lanes on existing roadways, and traffic signal timing optimization. This limited construction alternative should be given appropriate consideration when major urbanized area construction activities are proposed. On major new urbanized area highway projects, the option of including and/or designating HOV lanes should be a consideration. Consideration of this alternative may be accomplished by reference to the regional transportation plan, when that plan considers this option. In the case of regional transportation plans which do not reflect consideration of this option, it may be necessary to evaluate the feasibility of this alternative. The effects that reducing the scale of a link in the regional transportation plan will have on the remainder of the system will need to be discussed during the evaluation of this alternative. While this discussion relates primarily to major projects in urbanized areas, the concept of achieving maximum utilization of existing facilities is equally important in rural areas. Before major projects on new location are proposed, it is important to demonstrate that reconstruction and rehabilitation of the existing system will not adequately correct the identified deficiencies. Appendix A of 23 CFR 450 provides additional discussion on the goals and scope of the TSM concept.
c. All other proposed "construction" alternatives discussions should include, where relevant, those reasonable and feasible alternatives (i.e., transit options) which may not be within the existing funding authority of FHWA. Some urban projects may be multimodal, thus requiring close coordination with the Urban Mass Transportation Administration (UMTA). In these situations, UMTA should be consulted early in the project development process. Depending on the extent of UMTA involvement and the possible use of UMTA funds for portions of the proposal, the need to request UMTA to be either a "lead agency" or a "cooperating agency" should be considered at the earliest stages of project development. Where applicable,

cost-effectiveness studies that have been performed should be summarized in the EIS.

The discussion of alternatives in this section can be best accomplished by a brief written description of each alternative, supplemented with maps and other appropriate visual aids such as photographs, drawings, or sketches which would assist the reader in better understanding the various alternatives, impacts, and mitigation measures. In some situations, design level details may be appropriate to evaluate impacts. However, final design details are not normally available at this stage in project development. The material should provide a clear understanding of each alternative's termini, location, costs, and major design features (number of lanes, right-of-way requirements, median width, etc.) which will contribute to a reader's better understanding of each alternative's effects on its surroundings or the community.

Generally, each alternative should be developed to a comparable level of detail in the draft EIS. Normally, the draft EIS should state that all alternatives are under consideration and that a decision will be made only after the public hearing transcript and comments on the draft EIS have been evaluated. However, in those situations where the HA has identified a "preferred" alternative based on its early coordination and environmental studies, the HA may so indicate in the draft EIS. However, the EIS should include a comment to the effect that the final selection will not be made until the results of the EIS circulation and the public involvement process have been fully evaluated. The final EIS must identify the preferred alternative and discuss the basis for the selection.

Affected Environment

This section should provide a *concise* description of the existing social, economic, and environmental setting for the area affected by all of the alternative proposals. The description should be a single general description for the area rather than a separate one for each alternative. All environmentally sensitive locations or features should be identified. However, it may be desirable to exclude from environmental documents certain specific location data on archeological sites to prevent vandalism.

To reduce paperwork and eliminate the presentation of extraneous background material, the discussion should focus on significant issues and values. Prudent use of photographs, illustrations, and other graphics within the text can be effective in giving the reviewer an understanding of the area. The statement should describe other related Federal activities in the area, their interrelationships, and any significant cumulative environmental impacts.

Data and analyses in the statement should be in proportion to the significance of the impacts which will be discussed later in the document. Less important material should be summarized or referenced. This section should also describe the scope and status of the planning process for the area. The inclusion of a map of any adopted land use and transportation plan for the area would be helpful in relating the proposed project to the areawide planning process.

Environmental Consequences

This section will discuss the probable social, economic, and environmental effects of the alternatives and the measures to mitigate adverse impacts.

There are several ways of preparing this section. Normally, it is preferable to discuss the impacts and mitigation measures separately for each of the alternatives. However, in some cases (such as where there are few alternatives), it may be advantageous to present this section with the impacts as the headings. Where possible, a subsection should be included which would discuss the general impacts and mitigation measures that are the same regardless of the alternative selected. This would reduce or eliminate repetition under each of the alternative discussions.

When the final EIS is prepared, the impacts and mitigation measures associated with the selected alternative may need to be discussed in more detail than in the draft EIS. In discussing the impacts, both beneficial and adverse, the following should be included in both the draft and final EIS.

a. A summary of studies undertaken and major assumptions made, with enough data or cross referencing to determine the validity of the methodology.
b. Sufficient information to establish the reasonableness of the conclusions concerning impacts.
c. A discussion of mitigation measures. Prior to completion of the final EIS, these measures normally should be investigated in appropriate detail so that a commitment can be included in the final EIS.

Charts, tables, maps, and other graphics illustrating comparisons between the alternatives (i.e., costs, residential displacements, noise impacts, etc.) are useful as a presentation technique.

In addition to normal FHWA program monitoring of design and construction activities, special instances may arise when a formal program for monitoring impacts or mitigation measures will be appropriate. In these instances, the final EIS should describe the monitoring program.

Listed below are examples of the potentially significant impacts of highway projects. These factors should be discussed *to the extent applicable* for each alternative. This list is by no means all-inclusive and on specific projects there may be other significant impacts that require study.

Social and Economic Impacts

The statement should discuss:

a. Changes in the neighborhoods or community cohesion for various groups as a result of the proposed action. These changes may be beneficial or adverse, and may include splitting neighborhoods, isolating a portion of an ethnic group, new development, changed property values, or separation of residences from community facilities, etc.

b. Changes in travel patterns and accessibility (e.g., vehicular, commuter, bicycle, or pedestrian). If any cross streets are terminated, the EIS should reflect the views of the involved city or county on such street closings.

c. Impacts on school districts, recreation areas, churches, businesses, police and fire protection, etc.

d. The impacts of alternatives on highway and traffic safety as well as on overall public safety.

e. Regional economic impacts, such as the effects of the project on development, tax revenues and public expenditures, employment opportunities, accessibility and retail sales. Any significant impacts on the economic viability of affected municipalities should also be discussed together with a summary of any efforts taken and agreements reached for using the transportation investment to support both public and private development plans. To the extent possible, this discussion should rely upon reviews by affected State, county, and city officials and upon studies performed under 23 U.S.C. 134.

f. For projects that might lead to or support large commercial development, the EIS should provide information on any significant effects the pending action would have on established business districts, and any opportunities for mitigation by the public and/or private sectors.

g. The general social groups specially benefitted or harmed by the proposed action should be identified. Particular effects of a proposal on the elderly, handicapped, nondrivers, transit-dependent, or minorities should be described to the extent these can be reasonably predicted. For example, where minority impacts may be a significant concern, EIS's should contain, when applicable, the following information, broken down by race, color, and national origin: the population in the study area, the number of displaced residents, the type and number of displaced businesses, and the type and number of displaced employees. Secondary sources of information such as census data reports can be utilized for obtaining this type of background information. Changes in minority employment opportunities, the relationship of the proposed action to other Federal actions which may serve or affect the minority population, and proposed mitigation measures to reduce or avoid impacts on minority populations should also be discussed.

Relocation Impacts

The relocation information necessary for the draft EIS may be included in the draft statement, either in the form of a complete conceptual stage relocation plan, or summarized in sufficient detail to adequately explain the relocation situation along with a resolution of anticipated or known problems. When the relocation information is summarized, the conceptual stage relocation plan should be referenced in the draft EIS.

A discussion of the information listed below is to be included in the draft EIS *to the extent appropriate* for the project.

a. An estimate of households to be displaced, including the family characteristics (e.g., minorities, handicapped, income levels, the elderly, large families, length of occupancy, and owner/tenant status). Where the project is not complex from a relocation viewpoint and the impact on the community is slight, this information may be obtained by visual inspection and from available secondary sources. On complex relocation projects where the relocation will have a major impact on the community, a survey of affected occupants may be needed. This survey may be accomplished by a sampling process.
b. A discussion of available housing in the area and the ability to provide suitable relocation housing for each type of family to be displaced within the financial capabilities of the relocatees.
c. A description of any special advisory services that will be necessary for unique relocation problems.
d. A discussion of the actions proposed to remedy insufficient relocation housing, including a commitment to housing of last resort, if necessary.
e. An estimate of the number, type, and size of businesses to be displaced. The approximate number of employees for each business should be included along with the general impact on the business dislocation(s) on the economy of the community.
f. A discussion of the results of early consultation with the local government(s) and any early consultation with businesses potentially subject to displacement, including any discussions of potential sources of funding, financing, planning for incentive packaging (e.g., tax abatement, flexible zoning, and building requirements), and advisory assistance which has been or will be furnished along with other appropriate information.
g. Impact on the neighborhood and housing community services where relocation is likely to take place. If there will be extensive residential and/or business displacement, the affected community may want to investigate other sources of funding from local and State entities as well as HUD, the Economic Development Administration, and other Federal agencies, to assist in revitalization of the community.
h. The results of discussions with local officials, social agencies, and such groups as the elderly, handicapped, nondriver, transit-dependent, and minorities regarding the relocation impacts.
i. A statement that the housing resources are available to all relocatees without discrimination.

The effects on each group should be described to the extent reasonably predictable. The analysis should discuss how the relocation caused by the proposed project will facilitate or inhibit access to jobs, educational facilities, religious institutions, health and welfare services, recreational facilities, social and cultural facilities, pedestrian facilities, shopping facilities, and public transit services.

Air Quality Impacts

The EIS should contain a brief discussion of air quality effects or a summary of the carbon monoxide (CO) analysis if such an analysis is performed. The following provides additional guidance:

a. A microscale CO analysis to determine air quality impacts is probably unnecessary where such impacts are judged to be minimal or insignificant.
   The judgment on the degree of CO impacts may be based on: (1) previous analyses for similar projects, (2) previous general analyses for various classes of projects, or (3) simplified graphical or "table look-up" analyses.
b. If the impacts of CO are judged to be minimal or insignificant, a brief statement to this effect is sufficient. The basis for the statement should be given in the EIS.
c. If the project CO contribution plus the background level are known to be well below the 1- and 8-hour National Ambient Air Quality Standard or other applicable standard, then the air quality CO impact is judged to be insignificant.
d. For those projects where a CO microscale analysis is performed, then the total CO concentration (project contribution, plus estimated background) at identified reasonable receptor sites for all alternatives should be reported and compared with applicable State and national standards.
e. If a CO analysis is performed, a brief summary of the methodologies and assumptions used should be given in the EIS.
f. In addition to the CO impact assessment, one of the two following statements should be included in the EIS:
   (1) This project is in an area where the State implementation plan does not contain any transportation control measures. Therefore, the conformity procedures of 23 CFR 770 do not apply to this project.
   (2) This project is in an air quality nonattainment (or attainment) area which has transportation control measures in the State implementation plan (SIP) which was (conditionally) approved by the Environmental Protection Agency on (date). The FHWA has determined that both the transportation plan and the transportation improvement program conform to the SIP. The Federal Highway Administration has determined that this project is included in the transportation improvement program for the (indicate 3C planning area). Therefore, pursuant to 23 CFR 770, this project conforms to the SIP.

Noise Impacts

The EIS should contain a summary of the noise analysis including the following:

a. A brief description of noise sensitive areas, including information on the numbers and types of activities which may be affected. If the project has significant noise impacts, noise contours of the proposed action and alternatives may be appropriate to assist in understanding those impacts.

b. The extent of the impact (in decibels). This should include a comparison of the predicted noise levels with both the FHWA design noise levels and the existing noise levels.
c. Noise-abatement measures which have been considered and those measures that would likely be incorporated into the proposed project.
d. Noise problems for which no prudent solution is reasonably available and the reasons why.

Energy

Draft and final EIS's should discuss in *general terms* the energy requirements and conservation potential of various alternatives under consideration. This general discussion might recognize that the energy requirements of various construction alternatives are similar and are generally greater than the energy requirements of the no-build alternative. Additionally, the discussion could point out that the post-construction, operational energy requirements of the facility should be less with the build alternative as opposed to the no-build alternative. In such a situation, one might then conclude that the savings in operational energy requirements would more than offset construction energy requirements and thus, in the long term, result in a net saving in energy usage. For most projects, a detailed energy analysis including computations of BTU requirements, etc., is not needed, but the discussion should be reasonable and supportable.

For major projects with potentially significant energy impacts (an example would be the Westway project in New York City), both the draft and final EIS should discuss any *significant* direct and/or indirect energy impacts of the proposed action. Direct energy impacts refer to the energy consumed by vehicles using the facility. Indirect impacts include construction energy and such items as the effects of any changes in automobile usage. The action's relationship and consistency with any State and/or regional energy plan should also be indicated.

The final EIS should identify any energy conservation measures that will be implemented as a part of the recommended alternative. Measures to conserve energy include the use of high-occupancy vehicle incentives, measures to improve traffic flow, and also pedestrian and bicycle facilities.

Wild and Scenic Rivers

If the proposed action could have an adverse effect on a river on the National Wild and Scenic Rivers System or a river listed in the Nationwide Inventory of rivers with potential for inclusion in the National Wild and Scenic Rivers System, there should be early coordination with the National Park Service (NPS) or the Department of Agriculture (USDA). The EIS should identify any potential significant adverse effects on the natural, cultural, and recreational values of the inventory river. Adverse effects include alteration of the free-flowing nature of the river, alteration of the setting, or deterioration of water quality. If it is determined that the proposed action could foreclose options to designate the river under the act, the EIS should reflect consultation with the NPS or USDA on avoiding or mitigating the impacts. The final EIS should indicate measures which will be included in the action to avoid or mitigate impacts. The October 3, 1980, memorandum from the Office of Environmental Policy provides additional information on this subject area.

Floodplain Impacts

The draft EIS should contain a summary of the "Location Hydraulic Studies" required by FHPM 6-7-3-2, Location and Hydraulic Design of Encroachments on Floodplains. Exhibits defining the floodplains or regulatory floodway, as appropriate, should be provided whenever possible. When there is no practicable alternative to an action which includes a significant encroachment, the final EIS should contain the finding required by FHPM 6-7-3-2, paragraph 8, in a separate subsection titled "Only Practicable Alternative Finding." When there is a regulatory floodway affected by the proposed action, the final EIS should contain a discussion of the consistency of the project with the regulatory floodway.

Coastal Zone Impacts

Where the proposed action is within, or may affect land or water uses within, the area covered by a State Coastal Zone Management Program (CZMP) approved by the Department of Commerce, the environmental document should briefly describe the CZMP plan, identify the potential impacts, and include evidence of coordination with the State Coastal Zone Management agency or appropriate local agency. For FHWA assisted activities, the EIS should include the State Coastal Zone Management agency's determination as to whether the project is consistent with the State CZMP plan. For direct Federal actions, the EIS should include the lead agency's consistency determination. If it is determined that the proposed action is inconsistent with the State's approved CZMP, FHWA will not approve the action except upon a finding by the Secretary of Commerce that the proposed action is consistent with the purposes or objectives of the Coastal Zone Management Act or is necessary in the interest of national security. The final environmental document for the proposed action will document all findings.

Wetlands Impacts

a. All draft EIS's for projects involving new construction in wetlands should include sufficient information to: (1) identify the type of wetlands involved, (2) describe the impacts to the wetlands, (3) evaluate alternatives which would avoid these wetlands, and (4) identify practicable measures to minimize harm to the wetlands. Exhibits showing the wetlands in relation to the alternatives, including the alternatives to avoid construction in the wetlands, should be provided.

b. Executive Order 11990, Protection of Wetlands, requires Federal agencies ". . . to avoid to the extent possible the long and short term adverse impacts associated with the destruction or modification of wetlands and to avoid direct or indirect support of new construction in wetlands wherever there is a practicable alternative. . . ." In evaluating the impact of the proposed project on wetlands, the following two questions should be addressed: (1) what is the importance of the impacted wetlands! and (2) what is the significance of this impact on the wetlands? Merely listing the number of acres taken by the various alternatives of a highway proposal does not provide sufficient information upon which to determine the degree of impact on the wetland's ecosystem. The wetlands analysis should be sufficiently detailed to allow a meaningful discussion of these two questions.

c. In evaluating the importance of the impacted wetlands, the analysis should consider such factors as: (1) the primary functions of the wetlands (e.g., flood control, wildlife habitat, erosion control, etc.), (2) the relative importance of these functions to the total wetlands resource of the area, and (3) other factors such as uniqueness that may contribute to the wetlands importance.

d. In determining the significance of the highway impact, the analysis should focus on how the project affects the stability and quality of the wetlands. This analysis should consider the short- and long-term effects on the wetlands and the significance of any loss such as: (1) flood control capacity, (2) erosion control potential, (3) water pollution abatement capacity, and (4) wildlife habitat value. Knowing the importance of the wetlands involved and the significance of the impact, the SHA and FHWA will be in a better position to determine what mitigation efforts are necessary to minimize harm to these wetlands.

e. For purposes of analyzing alternatives and the wetlands finding, "located in wetlands" means that the proposed right-of-way or easement limits of the highway are located wholly or partially in wetlands or that the highway is located in the vicinity of the wetlands and there is evidence that the new construction will directly cause long-term damage or destruction of the wetlands.

f. Mitigation measures which should be considered include enhancement of existing wetlands, creation of new wetlands, and erosion control. It should be noted that any mitigation measure should be related to the actual adverse impact caused by the project and that acquisition of privately owned wetlands for purposes of protection should only be considered as a last resort.

g. When there is no practicable alternative to an action which involves new construction located in wetlands, the final EIS should contain the finding required by Executive Order 11990 and by DOT Order 5660.1A, entitled Preservation of the Nation's Wetlands, August 24, 1978, in a separate section or exhibit titled "Wetlands Finding." Approval of the final EIS containing this finding will document compliance with the requirements of Executive Order 11990. The finding should contain in summary form and with reference to the detailed discussions contained elsewhere in the final EIS:

(1) a reference to executive Order 11990;

(2) a discussion of the basis for the determination that there are no practicable alternatives to the proposed action;

(3) a discussion of the basis for the determination that the proposed action includes all practicable measures to minimize harm to wetlands; and

(4) a concluding statement as follows: "Based upon the above considerations, it is determined that there is no practicable alternative to the proposed new construction in wetlands and that the proposed action includes all practicable measures to minimize harm to wetlands which may result from such use."

h. A formal wetlands finding is required for all projects processed with EIS's or FONSI's that involve new construction in wetlands. In the case of a project processed as a categorical exclusion, the division office's administrative record should document evaluations of alternatives and measures to minimize harm for these actions.

Land Use Impacts

This discussion should begin with a description of current development trends and the State and/or local government plans and policies with regard to land use and growth in the area. These plans and policies will be reflected in the area's comprehensive development plan, including land use, transportation, public facilities, housing, community services, and other areas.

The land use impact analysis should assess the consistency of the alternatives with the comprehensive development plans adopted for the area. The secondary social, economic, and environmental impacts of *significant* induced development should be presented.

The EIS should note any proposed alternatives which will stimulate low density, energy intensive development in outlying areas and will have a significant adverse effect on existing communities. Throughout this discussion, the distinction between planned and unplanned growth should be clearly identified.

Joint Development

When applicable, the EIS should discuss how the implementation of joint development projects will preserve or enhance the community's social, economic, environmental, and visual values. This discussion should be included as part of the land use impact presentation.

Historic and Archeological Preservation

The draft EIS should contain a discussion demonstrating that a survey meeting the requirements of 36 CFR Part 800.4 has been performed for each alternative under consideration. The discussion should begin by describing the resources and summarizing the impacts that each alternative will have on these resources that might meet the criteria for inclusion on the National Register of Historic Places. There should be a record of coordination with the State Historic Preservation officer concerning the significance of the identified resources, the likelihood of eligibility for the National Register, and an evaluation of the effect of the project on the resources.

The draft EIS can serve as a preliminary case report for Section 106 requirements if the document indicates this and it contains the necessary information (36 CFR 800.13). The transmittal memorandum to the Advisory Council on Historic Preservation should specifically request consultation.

The final EIS should demonstrate that all the requirements of 36 CFR Part 800 have been met. If the selected alternative has an effect on a resource that is on or eligible for inclusion on the National Register, the final EIS should contain (a) a determination of no adverse effect concurred in by the Executive Director of the Advisory Council on Historic Preservation or (b) an executed memorandum of agreement or (c) in the case of a unique situation where FHWA is unable to conclude the memorandum of agreement (MOA), a copy of comments transmitted from the Advisory Council to the Secretary of Transportation. When necessary, the discussion should indicate that archeological recovery will be performed. The proposed use of land from a site on or eligible for inclusion on the National Register will normally require a determination pursuant to Section 4(f) of the DOT Act. The treatment of archeological sites is discussed in 23 CFR 771.135(f). Additional details regarding the type of information needed at the draft EIS and final EIS stages are contained in the May 14, 1980, memorandum from the Office of Environmental Policy to all regional offices.

Water Quality Impacts

This discussion should include summaries of analyses and consultations with the State and/or local agency responsible for water quality. Coordination with the Environmental Protection Agency (EPA) under the Federal Clean Water Act may provide assistance in this area. The EIS should discuss any locations where roadway runoff may have a significant affect on downstream water uses, including existing wells. A 1981 FHWA research report entitled "Constituents of Highway Runoff" contains procedures for estimating pollutant loading from highway runoff.

Section 1424(e) of the Safe Drinking Water Act requires that proposed actions which may impact those areas that have been designated as principal or sole-source aquifers be coordinated with EPA. The EPA will furnish information on whether any of the alternatives affect the aquifer. If none of the alternatives affect the aquifer, the requirements of the Safe Drinking Water Act are satisfied. If an alternative is selected which affects the aquifer, a design must be developed to assure, to the satisfaction of EPA, that it will not contaminate the aquifer.

If a rest area is involved, a Section 402 permit is required for point source discharge. Any potential Section 402 permits should be identified in the EIS. Also, for both the Section 402 and Section 404 permits, a water quality certification from the State agency responsible for water quality is necessary.

The MOA with the Corps of Engineers allows for application for permit as soon as the preferred alternative is identified (i.e., final EIS stage). Use of the procedures in the MOA is encouraged to minimize possible delays in the processing of Section 404 permits later in project development. The final EIS should indicate the general location of the fill or dredged activity, approximate quantities of fill or dredged material, general construction grades, and proposed mitigation measures, and should include evidence of coordination with the Corps.

Threatened or Endangered Species

The HA shall request from the Departments of the Interior (DOI) and/or Commerce (DOC) information on whether any species listed or proposed as endangered or threatened may be present in the area of the proposed construction project. If those Departments advise that there are no such species in the area, the requirements of the Endangered Species Act have been met. If those Departments advise that such a species may be present, the FHWA/HA shall undertake a biological assessment to identify any threatened or endangered species which are likely to be affected by the proposed action. This biological assessment should include:

a. An onsite inspection of the area affected by the proposed project.
b. Interviews with recognized experts on the species at issue.
c. A literature review to determine the species distribution, habitat needs, and other biological requirements.
d. An analysis of possible impacts to the species.
e. An analysis of measures to minimize impacts. This biological assessment should be forwarded to DOI/DOC for a biological opinion. The Fish and Wildlife Service (F&WS) is responsible for the protection of terrestrial and fresh-water species and the National Marine Fisheries Service (NMFS) is responsible for the protection of marine species.

Upon completing their review of the biological assessment, the F&WS/NMFS may request additional information and/or a meeting to discuss the project or issue a biological opinion stating that the project: (a) is not likely to jeopardize, or (b) will promote the conservation of or (c) is likely to jeopardize the threatened or endangered species. In selecting a preferred alternative, jeopardy to an endangered or threatened species must be avoided. If either a finding of (a) or (b) is given, the requirements of the Endangered Species act are met. If a detrimental finding is presented, the proposed action may be modified so that the species is no longer jeopardized. In unique circumstances, an exemption may be requested. If an exemption is denied, the action must be halted or modified. The final EIS should document the results of the coordination of the biological assessment with the appropriate agencies.

Prime and Unique Agricultural Lands

Information on prime and unique agricultural lands should be solicited through early consultation with the Department of Agriculture (USDA), and the EIS should identify the direct and indirect impacts of the proposed action on these lands, including:

a. An estimate of the number of acres that might be directly affected by right-of-way acquisition.
b. Areas where agricultural operations might be disrupted.
c. Potential indirect effects such as those related to project-induced changes in land use.

The EIS should contain a map showing the location of prime and unique agricultural lands in relation to the project alternatives, summarize the results of consultations with the USDA, and include copies of correspondence with USDA regarding the project. Specific actions to avoid or, if that is not possible, to reduce direct and indirect effects on these lands should be identified.

Construction Impacts

The EIS should discuss significant impacts (particularly air, noise, water, detours, safety, visual, etc.) associated with construction of each of the alternatives. Also, where applicable, the impacts of disposal and borrow areas should be discussed along with any proposed measures to minimize these impacts.

Considerations Relating to Pedestrians and Bicyclists

Section 682 of the National Energy Policy Act of 1978 recognizes that bicycles are an efficient means of transportation, represent a viable commuting alternative to many people, and deserve consideration in a comprehensive national energy plan. The FHWA recognizes that bicyclists are legitimate highway users and that FHWA has a responsibility to provide for their transportation needs. Section 109(n) of 23 U.S.C. provides that "the Secretary shall not approve any project under this title that will result in the severance or destruction of an existing major route for nonmotorized transportation traffic and light motorcycles, unless such project provides a reasonable alternate route or such a route exists. The FHWA policy regarding Bicycle Program Activities is further defined in an August 20,

1981, memorandum from Administrator Barnhart to all regional administrators. Where appropriate, the EIS should consider pedestrian and bicycle use as an integral feature of the project and include a discussion of the relationship of the proposed project to local plans for bicycles and pedestrian facilities and evidence that the project is consistent with 23 U.S.C. 109(n).

Stream Modification and Wildlife Impacts

Title 16 U.S.C. 662(a) requires consultation with the Fish and Wildlife Service and the appropriate State agency regarding any Federal action which involves impoundment (surface area of 10 acres or more), diversion, channel deepening, or other modification of a stream or body of water. Exhibits should be used to identify stream modifications. The use of the stream or body of water for recreation or other purposes should be identified. It should also discuss any significant impacts on fish and wildlife resources, including direct impact to fish and wildlife, loss or modification of habitat, and degradation of water quality.

Visual Impacts

This discussion should include an assessment of the visual impacts of the proposed action, including the "view from the road" and the "view of the road." Where relevant, the EIS should document the consideration given to design quality, art, and architecture in the project planning. These values may be particularly important for facilities located in sensitive urban settings. Where relevant, the draft EIS should be circulated to officially designated State and local arts councils and, as appropriate, other organizations with an interest in design, art, and architecture.

List of Preparers

This section will include lists of:

a. State (and local agency) personnel, including consultants, who were primarily responsible for preparing the EIS or performing environmental studies, and their qualifications, including educational background or experience.
b. The FHWA personnel primarily responsible for preparation or review of the EIS, and their qualifications.
c. The areas of EIS responsibility for each preparer.

List of Agencies, Organizations, and Persons to Whom Copies of the Statement are Sent

List all entities from which comments are being requested (draft EIS) and identify those that submitted comments (final EIS).

Comments and Coordination

a. The draft EIS should summarize the early coordination process, including scoping, meetings with community groups and individuals, and the key issues and pertinent information received from the public and government agencies through these efforts.
b. The final EIS should include a copy of all substantive comments received (or summaries thereof, where the response has been exceptionally voluminous), along with a response to each substantive comment. When the EIS is revised as a result of the comments received, a copy of the comments should contain marginal references indicating where revisions were made, or the discussion of the comments should contain such references. The FHWA comment(s) on the draft EIS should not be included in the final EIS. However, the document should include adequate information for the FHWA reviewer to ascertain the disposition of the comment(s). Formal comments by the Department of Transportation should be included in the final EIS along with an appropriate response to each comment.
c. The final EIS should document compliance with requirements of all applicable environmental laws, Executive Orders, and other related requirements. To the extent possible, all environmental issues should be resolved prior to the submission of the final EIS. Where this is not possible, the final EIS should clearly identify any remaining unresolved issues, the change taken to resolve the issues, and the positions of the respective parties.
d. The final EIS should contain a summary and disposition of substantive comments on social, economic, and environmental issues made at any public hearing or other public involvement activity or which were otherwise considered.

Index

The index should include major subjects and areas of significant impacts so that a reviewer need not read the entire EIS to obtain information on a specific subject or impact.

23 CFR 771 requires compliance to the extent possible with other applicable environmental laws, Executive Orders, and other related requirements. This includes the certifications and reports required by 23 U.S.C. 128 relating to public hearings, considerations of social, economic, and environmental (SEE) effects and consistency of the project with urban planning goals promulgated by the community. The certifications normally are made at the time the final EIS or FONSI is submitted to the FHWA Division Administrator. The report of SEE effects required by 23 U.S.C. 128 will normally be satisfied by the final EIS, FONSI, or identification of the project as a categorical exclusion.

Appendices

Material prepared as appendices to the EIS should:

a. consist of material prepared in connection with the EIS (is distinct from material which is not so prepared and which is incorporated by reference);

b. consist of material which substantiates an analysis which is fundamental to the EIS;
c. be analytic and relevant to the decision to be made; and
d. be circulated with the EIS or be readily available on request. Other reports and studies referred to in the EIS should be readily available for review or for copying at a convenient location.

Alternate Process for Final EIS's

Paragraph 1503.4 of the CEQ regulation (40 CFR 1500, et seq.) provides the opportunity for expediting final EIS preparation in those instances when, after receipt of comments resulting from circulation of the draft EIS, it is apparent that the changes in the proposal or in the EIS in response to the comments received are minor and that:

a. all reasonable alternatives were studied and discussed in the draft EIS, and
b. the analyses in the draft EIS adequately identified and quantified the environmental impacts of all reasonable alternatives.

When these two points can be established, the final EIS can consist of the draft EIS and an attachment containing the following:

a. Errata sheets making corrections to the draft EIS, if applicable.
b. A section identifying the preferred alternative and a discussion of the reasons it was selected. The following should also be included in this section, if applicable:
   (1) final Section 4(f) evaluations containing the information described in Section 6 of these guidelines,
   (2) wetlands finding(s),
   (3) floodplain finding(s), and
   (4) a list of commitments for mitigation measures for the preferred alternative.
c. Copies (or summaries) of comments received from circulation of the draft EIS and public hearing and responses thereto.

4. DISTRIBUTION OF EIS'S AND SECTION 4(f) EVALUATIONS

Environmental Impact Statements

a. Copies of all draft EIS's should be circulated for comments to all public officials, private interest groups, and members of the public having or expressing an interest in the proposed action or the draft EIS, and to all Government agencies expected to have jurisdiction, responsibility, interest, or expertise in the proposed action. Internal FHWA distribution of draft and final EIS's is subject to change and is noted in memorandums to the Regional Administrators as requirements change. The FHWA transmittal letter to the Washington Headquarters should include a recommendation regarding the need for the prior concurrence of the Washington Headquarters in accordance with 23 CFR 771(e).

b. Copies of all approved final EIS's should be distributed to all cooperating agencies, to all Federal, State, and local agencies and private organizations, and members of the public who commented substantively on the draft EIS. A copy of all approved delegated EIS's should be forwarded to the FHWA Washington Headquarters (HEV-10) for recordkeeping purposes.

   Copies of all draft and final EIS's in the categories listed in 23 CFR 771(e) should be provided to the Regional Representative of the Secretary of Transportation at the same time as they are forwarded to the FHWA Washington Headquarters.

c. Copies of all EIS's should normally be distributed as follows, unless the agency has indicated to the FHWA offices the need for a different number of copies:
   (1) The EPA Headquarters: five copies of the draft EIS and five copies of the final EIS (this is the "filing requirement" in Section 1506.9 of the CEQ regulation; the correct address is listed therein).
   (2) The appropriate EPA regional office responsible for EPA's review pursuant to Section 309 of the Clean Air Act: five copies of the draft EIS and five copies of the final EIS.
   (3) The DOI Headquarters:
      (a) All States in FHWA Regions 1, 3, 4, and 5, plus Hawaii, Guam, American Samoa, Arkansas, Iowa, Louisiana, Missouri, and Puerto Rico: 12 copies of the draft EIS and 7 copies of the final EIS.
      (b) Kansas, Nebraska, North Dakota, Oklahoma, South Dakota, and Texas: 13 copies of the draft EIS and 8 copies of the final EIS.
      (c) New Mexico and all States in FHWA Regions 8, 9, and 10, except Hawaii, North Dakota, and South Dakota: 14 copies of the draft EIS and 9 copies of the final EIS.

Section 4(f) Evaluation

If the Section 4(f) evaluation is included in an EIS, DOI Headquarters should receive the same number of copies listed above for EIS's for consultation in accordance with the requirements of 23 U.S.C. 138. If the Section 4(f) evaluation is processed as a separate document or as part of an EA, the DOI should receive seven copies of the draft Section 4(f) evaluation for coordination and seven copies of the final Section 4(f) statement for information.

In addition, draft Section 4(f) evaluations, whether in a draft EIS, an EA, or a separate document, are required to be coordinated where appropriate with HUD and USDA.

5. RECORD OF DECISION—FORMAT AND CONTENT

The record of decision (ROD) must set forth the reasons for the project decision, based on the material contained in the environmental documents. While cross referencing and incorporation by reference of other documents is appropriate, the ROD should explain the basis for the project decision as completely as possible.

a. *Decision*. Identify the selected alternative. Reference to the final EIS may be used to reduce detail and repetition.

b. *Alternatives Considered*. This information can be most clearly organized by briefly describing each alternative (with reference to the final EIS, as above), then explaining and discussing the balancing of values underlying the decision. This discussion must identify the alternative or alternatives which were considered preferable from a strictly environmental point of view. If the selected alternative is other than the environmentally preferable alternative, the ROD should clearly state the reasons for that decision. In addition, if use of Section 4(f) land is involved, the required Section 4(f) approval should be summarized.

   For each individual decision (final EIS), the values (economic, environmental, safety, traffic service, community planning, etc.) which are significant factors in the decision-making process may be different and may be given different levels of relative importance. Accordingly, it is essential that this discussion clearly identifies each significant value and the reasons some values were considered more important than others. While any decision represents a balancing of the values, the ROD should reflect the manner in which these values were considered in arriving at the decision.

   It is also essential that legislation requirements in 23 U.S.C. be given appropriate weight in this decisionmaking process. The mission of FHWA is to implement the Federal-aid highway program to provide safe and efficient transportation. While this mission must be accomplished within the context of all other Federal requirements, the beneficial impacts of transportation improvements must be given proper consideration and documentation in this ROD.

c. *Measures to Minimize Harm*. Describe all measures to minimize environmental harm which have been adopted for the proposed action. State whether all practicable measures to minimize environmental harm have been incorporated into the decision and, if not, why.

d. *Monitoring or Enforcement Program*. Describe any monitoring or enforcement program which has been adopted for specific mitigation measures, as outlined in the final EIS.

6. SECTION 4(f) EVALUATIONS—FORMAT AND CONTENT

Draft Evaluation—Format

a. Describe proposed action (if separate document).
b. Describe Section 4(f) resource.
c. Impacts on resource (by alternative).
d. Avoidance alternatives and their impacts.
e. Measures to minimize harm.
f. Coordination with appropriate agencies.
g. Concluding statement (final document only).

In the case of a complex Section 4(f) involvement, it is desirable to include the analysis in a separate section of the draft EIS, EA, or for projects processed as categorical exclusions, in a separate document. A Section 4(f) evaluation should be prepared for each location within the project where the use of Section 4(f) land is being considered.

Draft Evaluation—Content

The following information should be included in the Section 4(f) evaluation, as appropriate:

a. A brief description of the project and the need for the project (when the Section 4(f) evaluation is circulated separately).
b. A detailed map or drawing of sufficient scale to identify essential elements of the highway/Section 4(f) land involvement.
c. Size (acres or square feet) and location (maps or other exhibits such as photographs, sketches, etc.) of involvement.
d. Type of property (recreation, historic, etc.).
e. Available activities at the property (fishing, swimming, golfing, etc.).
f. Description and location of all existing and planned facilities (ball diamonds, tennis courts, etc.).
g. Usage (approximate number of users/visitors, etc.).
h. Relationship to other similarly used lands in the vicinity.
i. Access (pedestrian and vehicular).
j. Ownership (city, county, State, etc.).
k. Applicable clauses affecting the title, such as covenants, restrictions, or conditions, including forfeiture.
l. Unusual characteristics of the Section 4(f) land (flooding problems, terrain conditions, or other features that either reduce or enhance the value of portions of the area).

m. The location (using maps or other exhibits such as photographs or sketches) and the amount of land (acres or square feet) to be used by the proposed project including permanent and temporary easements.
n. The probable increase or decrease in environmental impacts (noise, air pollution, visual, etc.) of the alternative locations and designs considered on the Section 4(f) land users.
o. A description of all reasonable and practicable measures which are available to minimize the impacts of the proposed action on the Section 4(f) property. Discussions of alternatives in the draft EIS or EA may be referenced rather than repeated.
p. Sufficient information to evaluate all alternatives which would avoid the Section 4(f) property. Discussions of alternatives in the draft EIS or EA may be referenced rather than repeated. However, this section should include discussions of design alternatives (to avoid Section 4(f) use) in the immediate area of the Section 4(f) property.
q. The determination that there are no feasible and prudent alternatives is not normally addressed at the draft EIS, EA, or preliminary document stage until the results of the formal coordination have been completed.
r. The results of preliminary coordination with the public official having jurisdiction over the Section 4(f) property and with regional (or local) offices of DOI and, as appropriate, the regional (or local) office of USDA and HUD.

Section 4(f) Discussion in Final Document

When the selected alternative involves the use of Section 4(f) land, a Section 4(f) evaluation may be included as a separate section in the final EIS or FONSI or for projects processed as categorical exclusions, in a separate final Section 4(f) evaluation. The final evaluation should contain:

a. All information required above for a draft evaluation.
b. A discussion of the basis for the determination that there are no feasible and prudent alternatives to the use of the Section 4(f) land. The supporting information must demonstrate that there are unique problems or unusual factors involved in the use of alternatives and that the cost, environmental impact, or community disruption resulting from such alternatives reaches extraordinary magnitudes.
c. A discussion of the basis for the determination that the proposed action includes all possible planning to minimize harm to the Section 4(f) property.
d. A summary of the appropriate formal coordination with the Headquarters Offices of DOI, and as appropriate, the Headquarters Offices of USDA and HUD.
e. Copies of all formal coordination comments received and an analysis and response to any questions raised.

f. Concluding statement as follows: "Based upon the above considerations, it is determined that there is no feasible and prudent alternative to the use of land from the (Section 4(f) property) and that the proposed action includes all possible planning to minimize harm to the (Section 4(f) property) resulting from such use."

A Section 4(f) approval is the written administrative record which documents the approval required by 23 U.S.C. 138. The Section 4(f) approval will be incorporated into either the final EIS or the ROD. When the Section 4(f) approval is contained in the ROD, the information noted in items (a) through (e) above may be incorporated by reference to the EIS. For a project processed as a categorical exclusion, any required Section 4(f) approval will normally be prepared as a *separate* document.

7. PREDECISION REFERRALS TO CEQ

a. Any FHWA office receiving a notice of intent of referral from another agency should provide a copy of that intent of referral to the FHWA Washington Headquarters, Office of Environmental Policy (HEV-10), and the involved Regional Office, Division Office, and HA. This notice of intent of referral would generally be received as part of an agency's comments on the draft EIS. The exception would be when an agency indicates that the draft EIS did not contain adequate information to permit an assessment of the proposal's environmental acceptability. Every reasonable effort should be made to reach agreement with the agency prior to filing of the final EIS. If agreement cannot be reached, the final EIS should document the attempts to resolve the issues and summarize the remaining differences. Prior concurrence of the Washington Headquarters is necessary in the case of Government opposition on environmental grounds.
b. The response to the notice of referral will be prepared by the Washington Headquarters with input from the Regional, Division, and State offices. The FHWA Washington Headquarters will obtain the concurrence of the Department of Transportation prior to the response to CEQ.
c. Upon reviewing the draft EIS from another Federal Agency, if the FHWA Regional or Division Office believes a referral will be necessary, it should so advise HEV-1. The Office of Environmental Policy (HEV-1) will review the proposed referral and, if appropriate, will advise the Departmental Office of Environment and Safety (P-20), which will coordinate DOT comments on the draft EIS, including the notice of intended referral. Every reasonable effort should be made to resolve the issues after providing notice of intent to refer and prior to the lead agency's filing of the final EIS with EPA. In the event that the issues have not been resolved, the appropriate field office should prepare a referral to CEQ to be submitted through HEV to P-20 for a determination as to whether a referral to CEQ is appropriate.

8. OTHER AGENCY STATEMENTS

a. The FHWA review of statements prepared by other agencies will consider the environmental impact of the proposal on areas within FHWA's functional area of responsibility or special expertise.

b. Agencies requesting comments on highway impacts usually forward the draft EIS to the FHWA Washington Headquarters for comment. The FHWA Washington Headquarters will normally distribute these EIS's to the appropriate regional office and will indicate where the comments should be sent. The regional office may elect to forward the draft statement to the division office for response.

c. When a field office has received a draft EIS directly from another agency, it may comment directly to that agency if the proposal does not fall within the types indicated in item (d) of this section. If more than one DOT Administration is commenting at the regional level, the comments should be coordinated by the DOT Regional Representative to the Secretary or designee. Copies of the FHWA comments should be distributed as follows:

    (1) Requesting agency—original and one copy.

    (2) P-20—one copy.

    (3) DOT Secretarial Representative—one copy.

    (4) HEV-10—one copy.

d. The following types of actions contained in the draft EIS require FHWA Washington Headquarters review and such EIS's should be forwarded to the Associate Administrator for Right-of-Way and Environment (HRE-01), along with regional comments, for processing:

    (1) actions with national implications, and

    (2) legislation or regulations having national impacts or national program proposals.

9. PROPOSALS FOR LEGISLATION OR REGULATIONS

Proposals for regulations and legislation will be evaluated by the initiating Washington Headquarters office for compliance with the appropriate NEPA requirements. The proposal may require the development of an EA and FONSI, or an EIS which will be the responsibility of the initiating office in consultation with HEV-10. When a draft EIS for proposed legislation is appropriate, it will be submitted to OST for transmittal to the Office of Management and Budget for circulation in the normal legislative clearance process. Any comments received on the EIS will be transmitted to Congress. Except as provided in 40 CFR Part 1506(b)(2) there need not be a final EIS.

APPENDIX B

ELEMENTS OF ENGINEERING ECONOMY

B.1 MONEY AND ITS TIME VALUE

Money's *raison d'être* is its acceptability as a medium of exchange. It can be used in exchange for goods and services much more efficiently than the direct trading of goods and services (i.e., barter). Because money can be used for the purchase of many items, it can serve as a standard of value for them, at least in a relative sense. Because it can retain the ability to be exchanged for other commodities at various times, money is also a store of value.

In one view, the term *value* of a commodity is synonymous with the number of monetary units (or the *price*) that it commands. Others use the term value to refer to the degree to which a particular good or service satisfies the needs of individuals and employ the term *utility* to clarify this difference. The fact is that such a difference between price and utility exists and that the term value is often used for both. The context in which it is used usually clarifies the connotation intended.

Often the *value of money* is defined as the reciprocal of the prices of the goods and services for which it can be exchanged. Thus if for various reasons the number of monetary units (e.g., dollars or yen) required to obtain a given item were to increase, the situation could be described either as an increase in the price of that item or, conversely, a decrease in the value of the monetary unit. A major difficulty associated with this definition for the value of money lies in the fact that the prices of the myriad of goods and services that are daily exchanged in markets do not all behave in the same way. The prices of some may be on the decrease, whereas the prices of others are either stable or increasing. These price changes are caused by many conditions, including changes in the quantities demanded, technological breakthroughs that result in more efficient or less costly production methods, and changes in the availability of resources (or factors of production) through depletion, new discoveries, or even catastrophic events such as wars. To complicate matters, the supply of money in the form of currency and credit also affects prices. Even though the prices of individual goods and services vary differentially, the general behavior of prices may, nevertheless, be described by several indicators. The most well known of these indicators is the *consumer price index* (CPI), which is compiled by the U.S. Bureau of Labor Statistics to capture the price changes of a combination of goods that the typical family considers essential. When the general price level is on an upswing, the economy is said to experience price *inflation*. When prices are falling the economy is in a *deflationary period*. The value of money as defined in this way decreases with price inflation and increases with price deflation.

People and firms exchange goods and services in order to maximize the satisfaction (i.e., utility) they derive from them. For example, firms give up money (and, indirectly, other goods and services) to purchase the services of employees and needed factors of production for the purpose of deriving profits from the sale of the goods and services they produce. Exchange is possible because the utility that individuals and other economic entities attach to the items being exchanged is not identical. Both parties to the exchange give up something they consider less desirable for something they consider more desirable. Since, as a store of value, money stands for the opportunities it represents to consumers and producers, it is imbued with the characteristics shared by all commodities, including the ability to satisfy human wants—that is, utility. As a major factor of production, it carries the ability to earn profits, and this earning power of money is reflected in the *time value of money*. Simply stated, a dollar in hand at present is not the same as a dollar in hand at some future date, because in the future, the present dollar would be incremented by the return it would earn in the meantime. Economic entities are willing to borrow and lend money at a premium because of the various profit-making opportunities they are able to pursue. Typically, the lender is satisfied with the "rental" to be received from a borrower for the use of the lender's money, whereas the borrower is looking for an opportunity to put the borrowed money to some use that would gain for the borrower a satisfactory profit above the cost of "renting" the money.

B.2 INTEREST AND DISCOUNT

The premium paid or received for the use of money is known as *interest*. The rate at which interest accumulates (i.e., the *interest rate*) is quoted as the percentage gained over a specified time period, known as the *interest period*. Thus the interest rate relates a sum of money presently in hand to its equivalent sum at some future date. The rate that relates a sum of money at some future date to its equivalent at present is known as the *discount rate*.

The value of money is affected by price instabilities. Consequently, the interest rate that lenders seek and borrowers are willing to pay is affected by (1) their expectations relating to potential movements of the price level (i.e., the *purchasing power* of money) and (2) their desired return or profit (i.e., the *earning power* of money). Assuming constant dollars (i.e., ignoring inflation) facilitates the understanding of the basic concepts covered by this section. Incidentally, the term *current dollar* refers to the reciprocal of the general price level at any given time, and, therefore, includes the effect of inflation.

Example B.1

A business firm borrows \$10,000 and agrees to pay back \$10,200 at the end of one month. Calculate the interest rate involved in the transaction.

Solution The total interest paid at the end of the month is \$2000. The interest period is 1 month and the interest rate is:

$$\frac{\$200}{\$10{,}000} = 0.02 \text{ or } 2\% \textit{ per month}$$

Discussion The interest rate translates a present sum to a future sum. The terms *present* and *future* are defined in relation to each other and not to specific calendar times. In other words, the previous calculation would be the same as long as the two times are separated by one month. The discount involved in this transaction is also \$200. It relates the future sum (\$10,200) to its present equivalent (\$10,000). By definition, the discount rate is 2% per month, that is, the difference between the future and present sums divided by the *present sum* (see Example B.2).

Example B.2

An investor purchases a zero coupon bond for \$867.98. The bond has a face value of \$1000 and matures in 1 year. This means that the bond can be cashed after 1 year for \$1000. Calculate the discount rate involved in the transaction.

Solution The future sum (\$1000) was discounted by \$132.02. The discount rate was 132.02/867.98 = 0.1521, or 15.21% per year.

Discussion The same transaction may be viewed as follows: The investor's principal of \$867.98 earned an interest of \$132.02 in 1 year at an interest rate of 15.21% per year.

B.3 SIMPLE AND COMPOUND INTEREST

In the preceding two examples, the time over which the interest was earned (i.e., 1 month and 1 year, respectively) coincided with the interest period for which the interest and the discount rates were either calculated or quoted. This need not always be the case. The interval of time between the present and the future can be longer than a single interest period, in which case the present sum continues to earn interest at the quoted rate. *Simple interest* refers to the case where the a percentage of the *original* sum of money is added at the end of each interest period. In the case of *compound interest,* both the original sum (principal) and the interest earned are allowed to earn interest during subsequent periods. The difference between the two is illustrated next.

Example B.3

A person who has a sum of $10,000 to invest is faced with the options of (a) earning simple interest at an annual rate of 9% per year or (b) earning compound interest at an annual rate of 8% per year. In both cases, the principal and interest are to be withdrawn at the end of a 5-year period. Compare the two investment options.

Solution

The consequences of each of the two options are tabulated as follows.

Year	Principal and interest at the start of the year	Interest added at the end of the year	Principal and interest at the end of the year
	Option (a): Simple interest at 9% per year		
1	$10,000.00	$ 900.00	$10,900.00
2	10,900.00	900.00	11,800.00
3	11,800.00	900.00	12,700.00
4	12,700.00	900.00	13,600.00
5	13,600.00	900.00	14,500.00
	Option (b): Compound interest at 8% per year		
1	$10,000.00	$ 800.00	$10,800.00
2	10,800.00	864.00	11,664.00
3	11,664.00	933.12	12,597.12
4	12,597.12	1007.77	13,604.89
5	13,604.89	1088.39	14,693.28

Discussion From the borrower's perspective, the annual 9% simple interest rate is superior to the 8% annually compounded rate up to the end of the third year. Beyond that, the latter becomes the better option. From the lender's point of view, the reverse is true. Thus, both the magnitude of the interest rate and the number of interest periods affect the relative consequences of the two types of interest. The future worth F of a present sum P can be calculated by

$$F = P(1 + in) \tag{B.3.1}$$

for the case of simple interest and by

$$F = P(1 + i)^n \tag{B.3.2}$$

for the case of compound interest, where

i = the interest rate (percent per period divided by 100)

n = the number of interest periods separating P and F

The term multiplying the single sum P in Eq. B.3.2 is one of several useful factors and is known as the *single-sum* (or single-payment) *compound-amount factor* for an interest rate i per period and n periods separating P and F (CAF′, i, n). Solving Eq. B.3.2 for P,

$$P = F \frac{1}{(1 + i)^n} \tag{B.3.3}$$

and the factor that discounts a future sum F to a present sum P is known as the *single-sum present-worth factor* (PWF′, i, n).

Example B.4

A sum of \$100,000 is invested at an annually compounded interest rate of 8% per year. Calculate its equivalent at the end of 20 years.

Solution For P = \$100,000, i = 0.08, and n = 20, Eq. B.3.2 yields

$$F = \$100{,}000\ (1 + 0.08)^{20}$$

$$F = \$100{,}000\ (4.66096) = \$466{,}096$$

The single-sum compound-amount factor is 4.66096.

B.4 NOMINAL AND EFFECTIVE INTEREST RATES

Frequently, interest rates are specified on the basis of a period (usually a year) when compounding occurs more frequently than the specified period. By convention, the magnitude of the quoted *nominal interest rate* is equal to the product of the interest rate per interest period times the number of interest periods in the specified period. For example a nominal annual rate of 12% compounded semiannually means that the interest rate is 6% per 6-month interest period. Similarly, a nominal interest rate of 12% compounded monthly implies an interest rate of 1% per month. The following example shows that the *effective interest rate* is larger than the nominal interest rate because the interest earned at the end of each interest period is subsequently allowed to earn interest as well.

Example B.5

Compute the equivalent of \$1,000,000 at the end of 5 years if the annual interest rate is (a) 8% per year compounded quarterly and (b) 8% per year compounded semiannually. For each case, calculate the effective *annual* interest rate.

Solution For part (a), the effective quarterly rate is 2% per quarter. A 5-year period contains 20 quarters. Therefore substituting i = 0.02 and n = 20 in Eq. B.3.2 results in

$$F = \$1{,}000{,}000\ (1 + 0.02)^{20} = \$1{,}485{,}947$$

To find the effective annual rate, consider compound-amount factor for 1 year expressed in terms of the annual effective rate i and the annual nominal rate r compounded m times a year. The two must yield the same relationship between P and F 1 year apart. Therefore

$$(1 + i) = \left(1 + \frac{r}{m}\right)^m$$

Consequently, the effective annual rate i is:

$$i = \left(1 + \frac{r}{m}\right)^m - 1 \tag{B.4.1}$$

Therefore the effective annual rate for part (a) of this example is

$$i = (1 + 0.02)^4 - 1 = 0.082432, \quad \text{or} \quad 8.2432\% \text{ per year}$$

To illustrate its use, Eq. B.4.1 is applied to the solution of part (b) of this example. With $m = 2$ interest periods per year, the effective annual rate is

$$i = (1 + 0.04)^2 - 1 = 0.0816, \quad \text{or} \quad 8.16\% \text{ per year}$$

Using this effective annual rate, at the end of 5 years, the initial $P = \$1{,}000{,}000$ becomes

$$F = \$1{,}000{,}000(1 + 0.0816)^5 = \$1{,}480{,}244$$

The same result would have been obtained by using an effective semiannual interest rate of 4% per 6-month period and 10 interest periods (i.e., 5 years times two 6-month periods in a year).

B.5 DISCRETE AND CONTINUOUS COMPOUNDING

In the foregoing examples, compounding was considered to occur with finite interest periods such as a year, 6-months, a quarter of a year, a month and so forth. This is called *discrete compounding,* since the interest is paid at the end of each dicrete interest period. *Continuous compounding* represents the limiting case when the interest period approaches zero. Given a nominal interest rate r under continuous compounding, the effective interest rate would the limit of i in Eq. B.4.1 as the number of interest periods m approaches infinity. In that case, the *effective interest rate for continuous compounding* is equal to $(e^r - 1)$, where e is the base of natural logarithms.

According to Eq. B.3.2, when interest is compounded continuously at a nominal interest rate r per specified period, the relationship between single sums separated by n periods is:

$$F = Pe^{rn} \tag{B.5.1}$$

$$P = Fe^{-rn} \tag{B.5.2}$$

The multiplier of P in Eq. B.5.1 is known as the *single-sum compound amount factor* (CAF', r, n) and the multiplier of F in Eq. B.5.2 is called the *single-sum present-worth factor* (PWF', r, n), both with continuous compounding. The subscript r refers to the *nominal* interest rate per period.

Example B.6

Solve Example B.5 for the case of continuous compounding.

Solution The nominal annual rate is still 8%. Hence, for a 5-year period between P and F,

$$F = Pe^{(0.08)(5)} = \$1{,}491{,}825$$

The effective annual interest rate is approximately equal to 8.33% per year.

Discussion For the same nominal interest rate, the magnitude of F increases as the number of compounding interest periods m increases. The maximum occurs when m approaches infinity, that is, when the interest is compounded continuously.

B.6 CASH FLOWS

Up to this point, the discussion of money equivalencies was restricted to the case of two single sums (or payments) separated by a time interval. The general case of a *cash flow* such as the one illustrated by Fig. B.6.1 is frequently encountered, and the equivalent single sum E_k of the cash flow at at a time k may be desired. This task can be accomplished by summing the equivalent sums at time k of each single payment in the cash flow using the appropriate single-sum present-worth or compound-amount factors as follows:

$$E_k = \sum_{j=0}^{k} S_j\,(\text{CAF}'*, k - j) + \sum_{j=k+1}^{n} S_j\,(\text{PWF}'*, j - k) \tag{B.6.1}$$

The first subscript of the factors, which is designated by the asterisk, is either the effective interest rate per period, i, for discrete compounding or the nominal interest rate, r, per period for continuous compounding. Note that the single payment S_k has been included as the last term of the first summation but the fact that, when $j = k$, $(k - j) = 0$ leaves that single payment intact. The terms S_j can be positive, zero, or negative. When they are specified by difference between receipts and payments at each time j, the cash flow is referred to as the *net cash flow*.

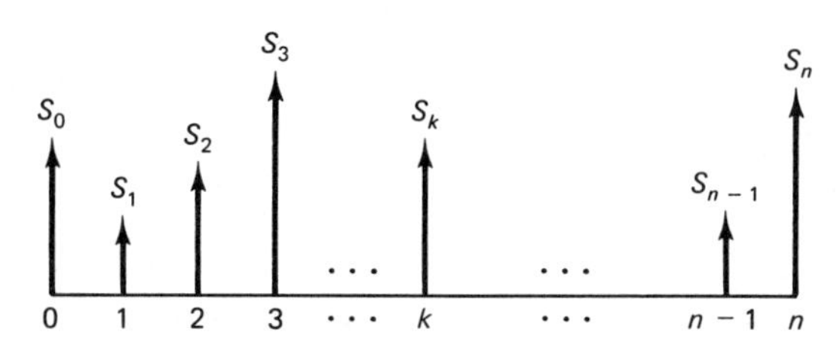

Figure B.6.1 A cash flow.

Example B.7

Given the following cash flow, calculate its equivalent single sum at (a) the end of the sixth period, (b) the end of the fourth period, and (c) time zero. Assume discrete compounding at 10% per period.

Solution This problem entails the application of Eq. B.6.1. The solution to part (a) is tabulated next. It involves only the first summation shown in the equation because $k = n$.

j	0	1	2	3	4	5	6
S_j	100.00	200.00	50.00	0.00	150.00	50.00	200.00
$(k - j)$	6	5	4	3	2	1	0
$S_j(\text{CAF}')$	177.16	322.10	73.21	0.00	181.50	55.00	200.00
						Sum =	1,008.97

The solution to part (b) may be obtained by applying Eq. B.6.1 with $k = 4$. However, since the single sum obtained in part (a) is equivalent to the original cash flow, all that is needed is to find its equivalent at the end of the fourth period, or two periods earlier than the sixth. The single-sum present-worth factor for discrete compounding with an interest rate $i = 0.10$ and $n = 2$ yields:

$$E_4 = (1008.96)(0.82645) = 833.86$$

Similarly, the equivalent single payment at time zero can be computed by Eq. 11.2.5 with $k = 0$. Alternatively, it can be calculated by discounting E_6 to its equivalent six periods earlier, or by discounting E_4 to its equivalent four periods earlier. Either one of the last two methods is simpler than the direct application of the long equation. Hence

$$E_0 = (1008.96)(0.56447) = 569.54$$

or

$$E_0 = (833.86)(0.68301) = 569.54$$

Discussion This example illustrates the fact that individual components of a cash flow can be treated separately and the final result obtained by superposition. Care must be exercised to move the individual components to the desired point in time using (1) the appropriate time separation by noting that the terms *present* and *future* refer to a *relative* time difference, and (2) the correct present worth and compound-amount factors. Equation B.6.1 automatically takes care of these requirements. It also accounts properly for the situation where no payment exists at the end of one or more periods (e.g., the third period in this problem), since the corresponding term in the summation reduces to zero. The same equation may be used for discrete cash flows under continuous compounding. In that event, the present worth and compound-amount factors corresponding to continuous compounding must be used.

B.7 EQUAL SERIES OF PAYMENTS

A special cash flow profile is a series of n equal payments as shown by Fig. B.7.1(a). The first and last payments occur *at the end* of the first and last periods, respectively.

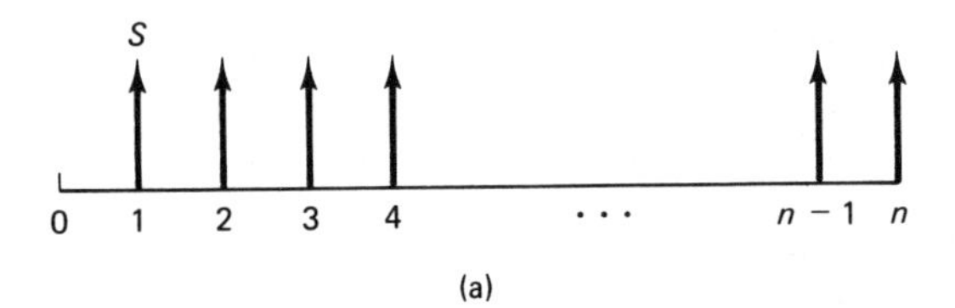

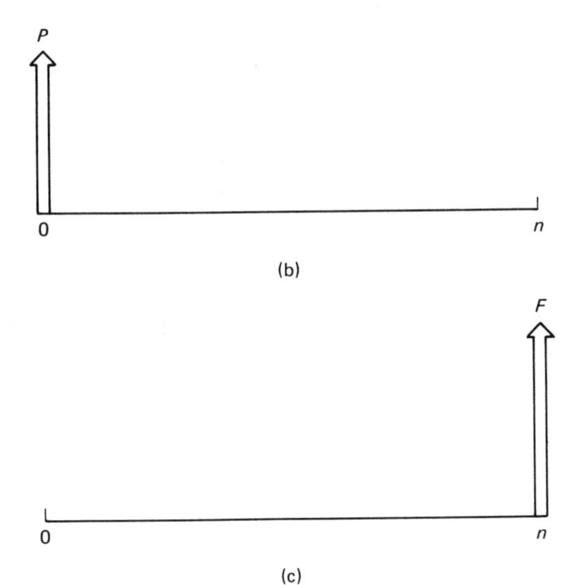

Figure B.7.1 Equal series, present and future single-payment equivalents.

The single-sum equivalent of the entire series either at time zero (i.e., the beginning of the first period; see Fig. B.7.1(b)) or at the end of the last period may be desired (Fig. B.7.1(c)). Conversely, a single sum at the beginning of the first period or at the end of the last period may be converted to their equivalent series of equal payments (Fig. B.7.1(a)). Rather that having to apply Eq. B.6.1 each time such a conversion is needed, four *equal-payment factors* have been developed. These are summarized in Table B.7.1 along with the two single-sum factors discussed earlier. Note that the acronyms for the single-sum factors have primes attached to distinguish them from the equal-payment factors of the same name.

As a mathematical illustration, the formulas for the equal-payment compound amount and sinking factors under discrete compounding are derived as follows:

Applying Eq. B.6.1 to the series of equal payments of Fig. B.7.1(a) with $h = 0$, $k = n$, $S_0 = 0$, and all other $S_j = S$,

$$F = S\,[(1 + i)^{n-1} + \cdots + (1 + i)^2 + (1 + i) + 1]$$

Multiplying this equation by $(1 + i)$ and subtracting it from the result,

$$F\,(1 + i) - F = S[(1 + i)^n - 1]$$

TABLE B.7.1 DISCRETE COMPOUNDING FACTORS

Factor	Notation	Formula	Given	Find
1. Single sum factors				
a. Compound amount factor	(CAF′,i,n)	$(1 + i)^n$	P	F
b. Present worth factor	(PWF′,i,n)	$\frac{1}{(1 + i)^n}$	F	P
2. Equal series factors				
a. Compound amount factor	(CAF,i,n)	$\frac{(1 + i)^n - 1}{i}$	S	F
b. Sinking fund factor	(SFF,i,n)	$\frac{i}{(1 + i)^n - 1}$	F	S
c. Present worth factor	(PWF,i,n)	$\frac{(1 + i)^n - 1}{i(1 + i)^n}$	S	P
d. Capital recovery factor	(CRF,i,n)	$\frac{i(1 + i)^n}{(1 + i)^n - 1}$	P	S

P = "present" single sum
F = "future" single sum
S = single sum in a series
n = number of periods

Solving for F,

$$F = S\left[\frac{(1 + i)^n - 1}{i}\right] \tag{B.7.1}$$

The bracketed term is the *equal-series compound-amount factor for discrete compounding* (CAF, i, n). Solving Eq. B.7.1 for S, the corresponding *sinking-fund factor* (SFF, i, n) that converts a single sum F to an equal-payment series is seen to be the reciprocal of the (CAF, i, n). The rest of the equal-payment factors for discrete compounding as well as those corresponding to continuous compounding (see Table B.7.1) can be derived in a similar manner. Also, useful relationships between the six factors for each compounding method may be reasoned out. For example, to find S given P, the latter is multiplied by the CRF. If P were to be multiplied by CAF′ to find F and if this result were to be multiplied by SFF, the same equivalent equal-payment series would result. Therefore,

$$\text{CRF} = (\text{CAF}')(\text{SFF}) \tag{B.7.2}$$

In fact, all six factors can be expressed in terms of one single-sum and one of the equal-payment factors. Moreover, the continuous-compounding factors can be derived by substituting the effective rate per period $i = e^r - 1$ into the discrete compounding factors.

Example B.8

An automobile salesperson has offered the following terms to a customer who is interested in purchasing a $10,000 car: No down payment and 48 equal monthly payments, the first to be paid at the end of the first month after the purchase. Calculate the monthly payments and the the equivalent single sum at the end of the 48-month period if the interest rate were 12% per year compounded monthly.

Solution The effective interest rate per month is 1%, $i = 0.01$, and $n = 48$. Hence, the monthly payment S is:

$$S = P(\text{CRF}, i, 48) = \$(10{,}000)(0.026338) = \$263.34 \text{ per month}$$

To find the equivalent single sum after 48 months, this equal-payment series can be converted using the CAF:

$$F = S\,(\text{CAF}, i, 48) = (263.38)(61.22258) = \$16{,}122.26$$

or the original single sum can be converted using the single-sum compound-amount factor:

$$F = P(\text{CAF}', i, 48) = (10{,}000)(1.612226) = \$16{,}122.26$$

Moreover, the same result can be obtained by first determining the effective annual interest rate via Eq. B.4.1 to be equal to 0.126825 and then applying the discretely compounded single-sum compound amount factor with this rate and 2 periods (i.e., 48 months = 2 years).

Discussion In addition to the use of equal-payment factors, this example reviews several important principles. First, the interest period was matched with the payment period by converting the given monthly compounded annual nominal rate of 12% to a monthly effective rate of 1%. Second, three possible alternative methods of obtaining the single future sum were illustrated. The first two imply the following relationship between factors:

$$(\text{CRF})(\text{CAF}) = (\text{CAF}')$$

The third method by which F was obtained shows that the effective annual interest rate is larger than the quoted nominal annual rate (i.e., 12.6825% versus 12.00%).

B.8 SUPERPOSITION OF CASH FLOWS

A cash flow may be described as the superposition of its individual single payment components. The same principle of superposition applies to the case of complex cash flows that can be decomposed into several simpler cash flows. In each case, several alternative ways of decomposing and superposing the cash flow's parts are possible. It is advisable to contemplate these alternatives in order to discern the simplest way of solving the problem prior to undertaking any calculations. This principle is illustrated by the following example.

Example B.9

Find the *present worth* (i.e., the equivalent single sum at time zero) of the cash flow shown in the accompanying figure. The effective interest rate is 8% per period.

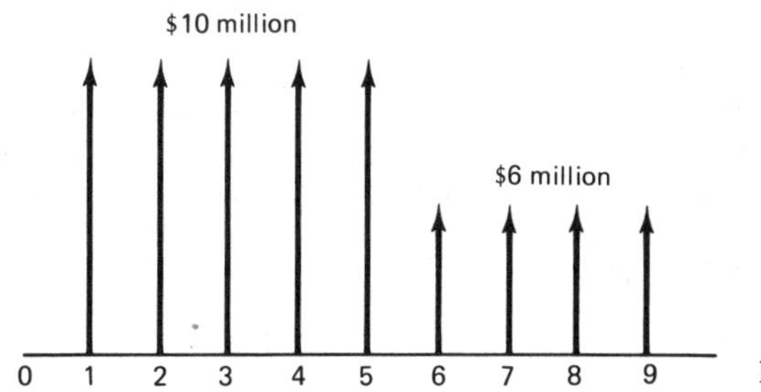

Figure P.B.9

Solution The series shown may be decomposed into simpler series in several ways. Three possibilities are:

(a) A series of nine \$6 million payments plus a series of five \$4 million payments, both series beginning at the end of the first period.
(b) A series of five \$10 million payments beginning at the end of the first period plus a series of four \$6 million payments beginning at the end of the fifth period.
(c) A series of nine \$10 million payments beginning at the end of the first period minus a series of four \$4 million payments beginning at the end of the fifth period.

In this particular case, the first method of decomposition seems to be the simpler of the three. However, for the purpose of illustration, several solutions are attempted.

Using the first method of decomposition, the present worth of the original series is equal to:

$$P = 6(\text{PWF}, i, 9) + 4(\text{PWF}, i, 5)$$
$$= 6(6.24689) + 4(3.99271) = \$53.45 \text{ million}$$

Using the second method of decomposition, the following two solutions are equivalent:

$$\text{(a) } P = 10(\text{PWF}, i, 5) + 6(\text{PWF}, i, 4)(\text{PWF}', i, 5)$$
$$= 10(3.99271) + 6(3.31213)(0.68058) = \$53.45 \text{ million}$$

$$\text{or (b) } P = 10(\text{PWF}, i, 5) + 6(\text{CAF}, i, 4)(\text{PWF}', i, 9)$$
$$= 10(3.99271) + 6(4.50611)(0.50025) = \$53.45 \text{ million}$$

Using the third method of decomposition, the following two solutions are also equivalent:

$$\text{(a) } P = 10(\text{PWF}, i, 9) - 4(\text{PWF}, i, 4)(\text{PWF}', i, 5)$$
$$= 10(6.24689) - 4(3.31213)(0.68058) = \$53.45 \text{ million}$$

$$\text{or (b) } P = 10(\text{PWF}, i, 9) - 4(\text{CAF}, i, 4)(\text{PWF}', i, 9)$$
$$= 10(6.24689) - 4(4.50611)(0.50025) = \$53.45 \text{ million}$$

B.9 EXERCISES

1. A school transportation company has purchased a new bus on the following terms: \$20,000 down and a monthly payment of \$2704 for 5 years at a nominal annual interest rate of 9%. What was the cash price?
2. Find the equivalent of the cash price of the bus described in Exercise 1 at the end of the 5-year period.
3. Using an annual interest rate $i = 8\%$, find the present worth of the cash flows given in the accompanying figure.

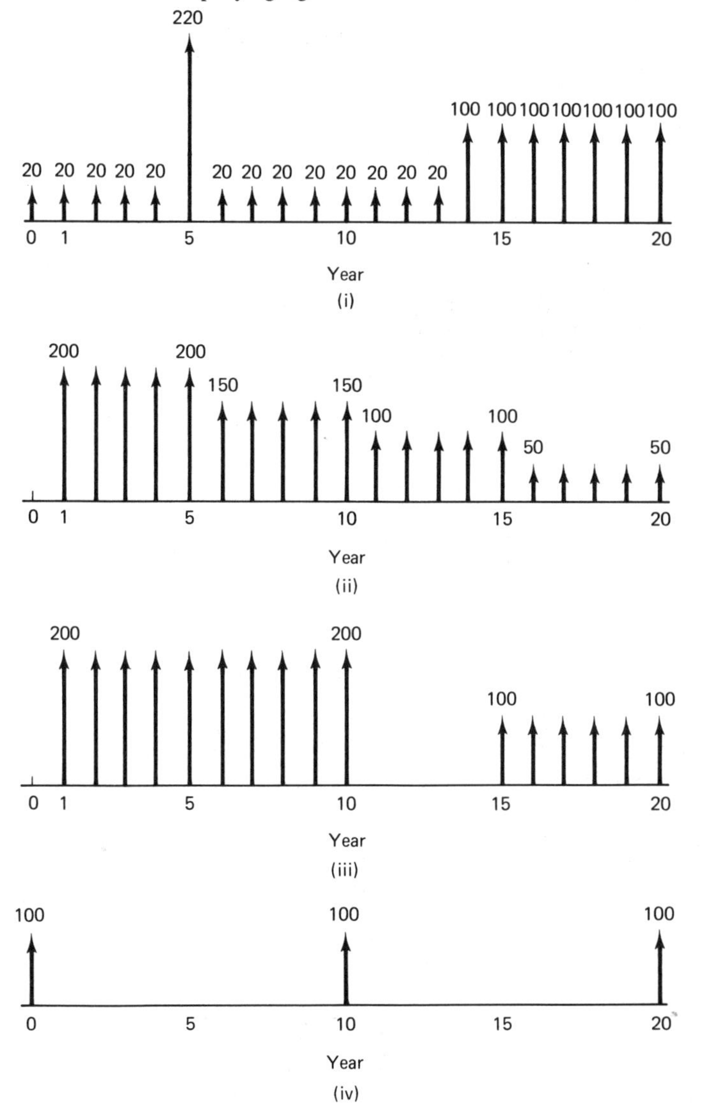

Figure E.B.3

4. Find the worth of the cash flows of Exercise 3 at the end of the tenth year.
5. Referring to the cash flow shown, which of the following equations are true?

$$P = 20 + [4(\text{CAF}, i, 5) + 4(\text{PWF}, i, 10)]\,(\text{PWF}, i, 5)$$

$$P = 20 + 8(\text{PWF}, i, 15) - 4(\text{PWF}, i, 5)$$

$$P = 20 + [4(\text{CAF}, i, 15) + 4(\text{CAF}, i, 10)](\text{SFF}, i, 15)$$

$$P = 8(\text{CAF}', i, 15) + 4(\text{PWF}, i, 15)(\text{CAF}', i, 15) + 4(\text{CAF}, i, 10)$$

$$P = 20 + 4(\text{PWF}, i, 15) + 4(\text{CAF}, i, 10)(\text{PWF}', i, 15)$$

$$P = [20(\text{CAF}', i, 15) + 4\,(\text{CAF}, i, 15) + 4\,(\text{CAF}, i, 10)]\,(\text{PWF}', i, 15)$$

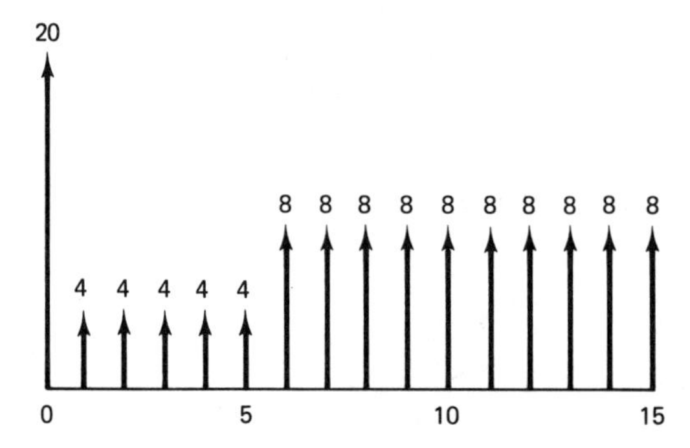

Figure E.B.5

INDEX

The index covers all chapters and appendices. Page numbers in parentheses indicate entries to be found among the references at the end of each chapter; page numbers followed by the letter "T" refer to tables; and those followed by the letter "F" indicate figures. Names appearing in credit lines are also included.